'A landmark study on one of the most pressing problems facing society, balancing economic growth and ecological protection to achieve a sustainable future.'

Simon Levin, Moffett Professor of Biology, Department of Ecology and Evolution Behavior, Princeton University, USA

'TEEB brings a rigorous economic focus to bear on the problems of ecosystem degradation and biodiversity loss, and on their impacts on human welfare. TEEB is a very timely and useful study not only of the economic and social dimensions of the problem, but also of a set of practical solutions which deserve the attention of policy-makers around the world.'

Nicholas Stern, I.G. Patel Professor of Economics and Government at the London School of Economics and Chairman of the Grantham Research Institute on Climate Change and the Environment

'The [TEEB] project should show us all how expensive the global destruction of the natural world has become and, it is hoped, persuade us to slow down.'

The Guardian

'Biodiversity is the living fabric of this planet — the quantum and the variability of all its ecosystems, species, and genes. And yet, modern economies remain largely blind to the huge value of the abundance and diversity of this web of life, and the crucial and valuable roles it plays in human health, nutrition, habitation and indeed in the health and functioning of our economies. Humanity has instead fabricated the illusion that somehow we can get by without biodiversity, or that it is somehow peripheral to our contemporary world. The truth is we need it more than ever on a planet of six billion heading to over nine billion people by 2050. This volume of "TEEB" explores the challenges involved in addressing the economic invisibility of biodiversity, and organises the science and economics in a way decision makers would find it hard to ignore.'

Achim Steiner, Executive Director, United Nations Environment Programme

The Economics of Ecosystems and Biodiversity
Ecological and Economic Foundations

Human well-being relies critically on ecosystem services provided by nature. Examples include water and air quality regulation, nutrient cycling and decomposition, plant pollination and flood control, all of which are dependent on biodiversity. They are predominantly public goods with limited or no markets and do not command any price in the conventional economic system, so their loss is often not detected and continues unaddressed and unabated. This in turn not only impacts human well-being, but also seriously undermines the sustainability of the economic system.

It is against this background that TEEB: The Economics of Ecosystems and Biodiversity project was set up in 2007 and led by the United Nations Environment Programme to provide a comprehensive global assessment of economic aspects of these issues. This book, written by a team of international experts, represents the scientific state of the art, providing a comprehensive assessment of the fundamental ecological and economic principles of measuring and valuing ecosystem services and biodiversity, and showing how these can be mainstreamed into public policies.

This volume, along with the subsequent TEEB outputs, provides the authoritative knowledge and guidance to drive forward the biodiversity conservation agenda for the next decade.

This volume is an output of **TEEB: The Economics of Ecosystems and Biodiversity** study and has been edited by **Pushpam Kumar**, Reader in Environmental Economics, University of Liverpool, UK. TEEB is hosted by the United Nations Environment Programme (UNEP) and supported by the European Commission, the German Federal Ministry for the Environment (BMU) and the UK Department for Environment, Food and Rural Affairs (DEFRA), recently joined by Norway's Ministry for Foreign Affairs, The Netherlands' Ministry of Housing (VROM), the UK Department for International Development (DFID) and also the Swedish International Development Cooperation Agency (SIDA). The study leader is Pavan Sukhdev, who is also Special Adviser – Green Economy Initiative, UNEP.

The Economics of Ecosystems and Biodiversity

Ecological and Economic Foundations

Edited by
Pushpam Kumar

Routledge
Taylor & Francis Group

LONDON AND NEW YORK

First published 2010 by Earthscan
First published in paperback 2012
by Routledge
2 Park Square, Milton Park, Abingdon, Oxon OX14 4RN

Simultaneously published in the USA and Canada
by Routledge
711 Third Avenue, New York, NY 10017

Routledge is an imprint of the Taylor & Francis Group, an informa business

The recommended full citation for this volume is as follows: TEEB (2012), The Economics of Ecosystems and Biodiversity: Ecological and Economic Foundations. Edited by Pushpam Kumar. Routledge, Abingdon and New York.

Disclaimer
The designations employed and the presentation of the material in this publication do not imply the expression of any opinion whatsoever on the part of the United Nations Environment Programme concerning the legal status of any country, territory, city or area or of its authorities, or concerning de-limitation of its frontiers or boundaries. Moreover, the views expressed do not necessarily represent the decision or the stated policy of the United Nations Environment Programme, nor does citing of trade names or commercial processes constitute endorsement.

British Library Cataloguing in Publication Data
A catalogue record for this book is available from the British Library

Library of Congress Cataloging-in-Publication Data
The economics of ecosystems and biodiversity : ecological and economic foundations / edited by Pushpam Kumar.
    p. cm.
  "An Output of TEEB: The Economics of Ecosystems and Biodiversity."
  Includes bibliographical references and index.
  1. Ecology–Economic aspects. 2. Ecosystem services. 3. Biodiversity–Economic aspects. 4.
Environmental economics. I. Kumar, Pushpam. II. Economics of Ecosystems and Biodiversity (Project)
  QH541.15.E25E36 2010
  333.95–dc22
            2010028008

ISBN13: 978-1-84971-212-5 (hbk)
ISBN13: 978-0-415-50108-8 (pbk)

Typeset by Domex e-Data Pvt. Ltd

Printed and bound in Great Britain by the MPG Books Group

Contents

List of Figures, Tables and Boxes   *vii*
List of Contributors   *xi*
Acknowledgements   *xv*
Preface   *xvii*
List of Acronyms and Abbreviations   *xxix*
Glossary   *xxxi*

Introduction   1

**1 Integrating the Ecological and Economic Dimensions in Biodiversity
    and Ecosystem Service Valuation**   9
  Introduction   12
  Review of existing frameworks linking ecology and economics   13
  TEEB-conceptual framework   21
  Annex 1 Classification of ecosystems used in TEEB   38
  Annex 2 Ecosystem service classification: Brief literature survey and TEEB
  classification   39

2 Biodiversity, Ecosystems and Ecosystem Services   41
  Introduction   45
  Biodiversity and ecosystems   45
  The links between biodiversity, ecosystem functions and ecosystem services   56
  Managing multiple ecosystem services   81
  Management of ecosystem services: Dealing with uncertainty and change   84
  Biodiversity, ecosystem services and human well-being   91
  Conclusions and further research   95

3 Measuring Biophysical Quantities and the Use of Indicators   113
  Introduction   116
  Existing measures and indicators   119
  In search of relevant indicators for ecosystem services   134
  Link to valuation and further work   141

4 The Socio-cultural Context of Ecosystem and Biodiversity Valuation   149
  Introduction   152
  The trade-offs of valuation   157
  The challenges of valuation: Ecosystems, biodiversity and level of analysis   166
  Final remarks   174

5   The Economics of Valuing Ecosystem Services and Biodiversity   183
     Introduction   187
     Economic valuation of ecosystem services   189
     Valuation methods, welfare measures and uncertainty   196
     Insurance value, resilience and (quasi-)option value   218
     Valuation across stakeholders and applying valuation in developing countries 225
     Benefit transfer and scaling up values   229
     Conclusions   239
     Annex 1 Applied sources for technical support on biodiversity valuation
     for national agency teams   256

6   Discounting, Ethics and Options for Maintaining Biodiversity
     and Ecosystem Integrity   257
     Introduction   260
     The Ramsey discounting equation and intergenerational welfare   264
     Recent behavioural literature on discounting, risk and uncertainty 268
     Ecosystems and biodiversity in the very long run   271
     The total value of ecosystems and biodiversity and the discounting equation 272
     Does a low discount rate promote conservation?   274
     Discounting and safe minimum standards   276
     Summary of the major challenges to discounting biodiversity
     and ecosystem losses   278

7   Key Messages and Linkages with National Policies   285
     Framing of issues for economics of ecosystems and biodiversity   287
     Linkages of ecosystems, ecosystem services and biodiversity   289
     Choice of indicators and value-articulating institutions
     in economic valuation   290
     Economic value, valuation methods, non-linear changes, resilience
     and uncertainty   292
     Discounting as an ethical choice   294
     Identification of knowledge gaps and limitations and mapping them
     into national policies: Challenges and options   295
     Finally   304

Appendix 1 How the TEEB Framework Can be Applied: The Amazon Case   307
     Services and values at the global scale   310
     Services and values at the continental scale   312
     Services and values at the regional (basin) scale   314
     Services and values at the local scale   317
     Limitations and caveats   320

Appendix 2 Matrix Tables for Wetland and Forest Ecosystems   325

Appendix 3 Estimates of Monetary Values of Ecosystem Services   367

Index   403

List of Figures, Tables and Boxes

Figures

1.1	MA conceptual framework: Linking ecosystem services and human well-being	14
1.2	An economic valuation framework: Contrasting states of the world	15
1.3	Ecosystem services: Research agenda	16
1.4	The pathway from ecosystem structure and processes to human well-being	17
1.5	TEEB conceptual framework for linking ecosystems and human well-being	21
1.6	Two examples of degradation pathways showing transition phases between natural and human-dominated (eco)systems	24
2.1	Illustrative relationships between different functional groups in ecosystems	48
2.2	The impact of insertion of the Sub-1 gene on the yield of the rice cultivar Swarna	64
2.3	Organisms may respond differently to increasing human impact	68
2.4	Potential trade-offs between provisioning services and regulating ecosystem services	82
2.5	Wetland trade-off dilemma: Water quality versus climate control	83
2.6	Interactions between provisioning (crops) and regulating services (biological control)	87
2.7	A process-response model of ecosystem functioning and effects of impacts	90
2.8	Deriving the value of biodiversity and the regulating services	94
3.1	Map of ecosystem services of water flows for the Little Karoo region of South Africa	132
3.2	Maps of timber production, measured as dry matter productivity (DMP) in forest areas for (a) the world in 2001, and highlighting change in timber production between 2001 and 2004 for (b) West Africa and (c) Madagascar	135
3.3	Global map of carbon sequestration	136
3.4	Social value of agricultural landscapes in Europe determined by protected agricultural sites, rural tourism and presence of labelled products	138
3.5	Fish stocks outside safe biological limits	140
3.6	Water availability in southern Africa expressed as relative to demand for water	141
4.1	Dimensions for choosing the valuation method	172
4.2	With increasing system complexity and value plurality, monetary valuations become of low scientific quality and doubtful policy relevance	173
5.1	Approaches for the estimation of nature's values	191

5.2	Insurance and output value as part of the economic value of the ecosystem	193
5.3	Value types within the TEV approach	195
5.4	Valuation approaches that have been used to value ecosystem services provided by forests and wetlands	209
5.5	The demand curve for natural capital	238
6.1	Valuing nature: The tree or money in the bank?	260
6.2	Value of loss or gain from a reference point	268
6.3	Hyperbolic discounting	268
6.4	A case in which a rising rate of interest is associated with a rise in the level of investment in human-made capital – a consequence likely to have an adverse impact on biodiversity conservation	275
6.5	A case in which a rise in the rate of interest is associated with a decline in the level of investment in human-made capital. This case is likely to be favourable to biodiversity conservation	275
A1.1	The South American Low-Level Jet (SALLJ) transports water from the central Amazon to the agricultural regions of the Paraguay–Paraná basin	313
A1.2	A: Guri, Brokopondo, and Tucuruí are the three largest hydroelectric facilities in the greater Amazon; B: Controversy about the environmental impacts of river dams surrounds projects planned for the Xingu and Madeira rivers	316
A3.1	Number of monetary values used for this Appendix per biome	369
A3.2	Geographic distribution of the monetary values used in this Appendix	369
A3.3	Number of monetary values used in this Appendix for 22 ecosystem services	370
A3.4	Average estimates of forest benefits at Mediterranean and sub-Mediterranean levels	389

Tables

1.1	Classification of main biomes in TEEB and remaining surface area	22
1.2	Typology of ecosystem services in TEEB	26
2.1a	Some examples of biological and physical processes and interactions that comprise ecosystems functions important for ecosystem services	46
2.1b	Examples of relationships between biodiversity and ecosystem services	46
3.1	Review of existing biophysical measures in terms of their application to measuring biodiversity and ecosystems, their ability to convey information and current data availability at the global scale	120
4.1	Value-articulating institutions and respective normative and epistemological stances	163
5.1	A typology of values	195
5.2	Valuing ecosystem services through the TEV framework	197
5.3	Relationship between valuation methods and value types	204

5.4	Monetary valuation methods and values: Examples from the literature	205
5.5	Use of different valuation methods for valuing ecosystem services in the valuation literature associated with wetlands and forests	206
5.6	Valuation approaches used for valuing ecosystem services in wetlands and forests	206
5.7	Proportion of valuation methods applied across ecosystem services regarding forests and wetlands, based on reviewed literature	207
5.8	Valuation techniques as applied to wetland studies	210
6.1	General observations about life opportunities and discounting	278
A1.1	Characteristics and values of major ecosystem services of the Amazon at varying scales	309
A1.2	Value of carbon stocks in the Amazon forest based on their replacement value in international markets for energy-based carbon credits	311
A1.3	Trade in non timber forest products from the Brazilian Amazon	318
A2.1a	Conceptual matrix based on wetland ecosystem services, benefits/value types and valuation approaches	326
A2.1b	Conceptual matrix based on forest ecosystem services, benefits/value types and valuation approaches	331
A2.2a	Conceptual matrix based on wetland ecosystem services and valuation approaches	338
A2.2b	Conceptual matrix based on forest ecosystem services and valuation approaches	340
A2.3	Matrix linking specific value types, valuation methods and ecosystem services: Examples from wetland and forest ecosystems	344
A3.1	Monetary value of services provided by open oceans	373
A3.2	Monetary value of services provided by coral reefs	375
A3.3	Monetary value of services provided by coastal systems	377
A3.4	Monetary value of services provided by coastal wetlands	380
A3.5	Monetary value of services provided by inland wetlands	382
A3.6	Monetary value of services provided by rivers and lakes	384
A3.7	Monetary value of services provided by tropical forests	386
A3.8	Monetary value of services provided by temperate forests	388
A3.9	Monetary value of services provided by woodlands	391
A3.10	Monetary value of services provided by grasslands	393

Boxes

1.1	Neoclassical economics and its discontents	20
1.2	Spatial explicitness and scale	23
2.1	Biotic communities and their major functions	48
2.2	Biodiversity at the gene level	64
2.3	Trade-offs among ecosystem services	82
4.1	The boom açaí palm fruit in the Amazon	167
4.2	Commodity and symbolic values for wild coffee from Ethiopian forests	169
5.1	The intrinsic *versus* instrumental values controversy	189

5.2	Biophysical approaches to valuation and accounting	192
5.3	Conflicting valuation languages and commensurability of values	193
5.4	Steps for undertaking a contingent valuation study	201
5.5	Example of valuing changes in biodiversity using a choice modelling study	202
5.6	Biodiversity and resilience	219
5.7	Participatory valuation methods	228
6.1	Discounting the Amazon	261
A3.1	Guidance for use of the data in this book, and link with TEEB in National Policy (2011), TEEB in Local Policy (2011) and TEEB in Business (2011)	371
A3.2	Example of TEV case study: Benefit–cost assessment of Marine Conservation Zones (MCZs) in UK	373
A3.3	Example of TEV case study: The total economic value of the coral reefs on Hawaii	376
A3.4	Example of TEV case study: Valuing the services provided by the Peconic Estuary System, USA	378
A3.5	Example of TEV case study: The total economic value of the Muthurajawela Wetland, Sri Lanka	381
A3.6	Two examples of TEV case studies on inland wetlands	383
A3.7	Example of TEV case study: TEV of the River Murray, Australia	385
A3.8	Example of TEV case study: Economic valuation of the Leuser National Park on Sumatra, Indonesia	387
A3.9	Example of TEV case study: Economic valuation of Mediterranean forests	389
A3.10	Example of TEV case study: Goods and services from Opuntia scrublands in Ayacucho, Peru	392
A3.11	Example of TEV case study: The difference in ecosystem services supply before and after restoration in five catchments in dryland areas in South Africa	394

List of Contributors

Coordinating lead authors (CLA)

Eduardo S. Brondízio, Indiana University, USA
Thomas Elmqvist, Stockholm Resilience Centre, Sweden
Franz Gatzweiler, University of Bonn, Germany
John Gowdy, Rensselaer Polytechnic Institute, USA
Rudolf de Groot, Wageningen University, The Netherlands
Timothy J. Killeen, Conservation International, USA
Pushpam Kumar, University of Liverpool, UK
Edward Maltby, University of Liverpool, UK
Roldan Muradian, Centre for International Development Issues, Nijmegen, The Netherlands
Unai Pascual, University of Cambridge, UK
Belinda Reyers, Council for Scientific and Industrial Research (CSIR), South Africa
Pavan Sukhdev, United Nations Environment Programme (UNEP)

Lead authors (LA)

Tom Barker, University of Liverpool, UK
Giovanni Bidoglio, Joint Research Centre (JRC), Milan, Italy
Luke Brander, Vrije University, The Netherlands
Mike Christie, Aberystwyth University, UK
Brendan Fisher, Princeton University, USA
Erik Gómez-Baggethun, Universidad Autónoma de Madrid, Spain
Richard B. Howarth, Dartmouth College, USA
Berta Martín-López, Social-Ecological Systems Laboratory, Spain
Martin Mortimer, University of Liverpool, UK
Patrick O'Farrell, CSIR, South Africa
Manasi Kumar, Manchester Metropolitan University, UK
Charles Perrings, Arizona State University, USA
Sander van der Ploeg, Wageningen University, The Netherlands
Frederik Schutyser, European Environment Agency, Denmark
Rodney B. W. Smith, University of Minnesota, USA
Clem Tisdell, University of Queensland, Australia
Madhu Verma, Indian Institute of Forest Management, India
Christos Zografos, Universitat Autónoma de Barcelona, Spain

Contributing authors (CA)

Claire Armstrong, University of Tromso, Norway
Paul Armsworth, University of Tennessee, USA
James Aronson, Centre d'Ecologie Fonctionnelle et Evolutive (CEFE),
    Centre National de la Recherche Scientifique (CNRS), Montpellier, France
Florence Bernard, World AgroForestry Centre, Kenya
Pieter van Beukering, VU University Amsterdam, The Netherlands

Thomas Binet, University of Portsmouth, UK
James Blignaut, University of Pretoria, South Africa
Leon Braat, Wageningen University, The Netherlands
Luke Brander, VU University Amsterdam, The Netherlands
Mahe Charles, French Marine Protected Areas Agency, Brest, France
Mike Christie, Aberystwyth University, UK
Emmanuelle Cohen-Shacham, Tel-Aviv University, Israel
Hans Cornelissen, Vrije Universiteit, The Netherlands
Neville Crossman, CSIRO, Australia
Jonathan Davies, IUCN, Kenya
Uppeandra Dhar, Hamdard University, New Delhi, India
Lucy Emerton, IUCN, Sri Lanka
Pierne Failler, University of Portsmouth, UK
Josh Farley, University of Vermont, USA
Alistair Fitter, University of York, UK
Naomi Foley, National University of Ireland, Ireland
Andrea Ghermandi, Ca'Foscari University of Venice, Italy
Erik Gómez-Baggethun, Universidad Autónoma de Madrid, Spain
John Gowdy, Rensselaer Polytechnic Institute, New York, USA
Rudolf de Groot, Wageningen University, The Netherlands
Haripriya Gundimeda, Indian Institute of Technology, Bombay, India
Roy Haines-Young, University of Nottingham, UK
Lars Hein, Wageningen University, The Netherlands
Sybille van den Hove, Universitat Autónoma de Barcelona, Spain
Salman Hussain, Scottish Agricultural College, UK
John Loomis, Colorado State University, USA
Georgina Mace, Imperial College London, UK
Myles Mander, Institute of Natural Resources, South Africa
Anai Mangos, Plan Bleu, France
Simone Maynard, SEQ Catchments Ltd, Australia
Jon Norberg, Stockholm University, Sweden
Elisa Oteros-Rozas, Universidad Autónoma de Madrid, Spain
Maria Luisa Paracchini, Joint Research Centre, EC
Leonie Pearson, Commonwealth Scientific and Industrial Research Organisation (CSIRO), Australia
Charles Perrings, Arizona State University, USA
David Pitt, IUCN, Switzerland
Rosimerry Portela, Conservation International, USA
Isabel Sousa Pinto, University of Porto, Portugal
Stephen Polasky, University of Minnesota, USA
Oscar Gomez Prieto, Universitat Autónoma de Barcelona, Spain
Sandra Rajmis, Göttingen University, Germany
Nalini Rao, Conservation International, USA
Irene Ring, UFZ, Germany
Luis C. Rodriguez, CSIRO, Australia
Didier Sauzade, Plan Blue, France
Silvia Silvestri, World Conservation Monitoring Centre, United Nations Environment Programme, Cambridge, UK
Rob Tinch, Environmental Futures Ltd, UK

Yafei Wang, Wageningen University, The Netherlands
Tsedekech Gebre Weldmichael, Wageningen University, The Netherlands

Reviewers

Frank Ackerman, US Center of the Stockholm Environment Institute, USA
Vic Adamowicz, University of Alberta, Canada
Paulus Arnoldus, Economic and Financial Affairs, European Commission, Belgium
Philip Bagnoli, Organisation for Economic Co-operation and Development, USA
Edward B. Barbier, University of Wyoming, USA
Janne Bengtsson, Swedish University of Agricultural Sciences, Sweden
James Blignaut, University of Pretoria, South Africa
Eduardo S. Brondízio, Indiana University, USA
Robert Costanza, Portland State University, USA
Richard Cowling, Nelson Mandela Metropolitan University, South Africa
Arturo Escobar, University of North Carolina-Chapel Hill, USA
Beatriz Gaitan, University of Bern, Switzerland
Volker Grimm, Helmholtz Centre for Environmental Research (UFZ), Germany
Bernd Hansjürgens, UFZ, Germany
Klaus Henle, UFZ, Germany
Cameron Hepburn, University of Oxford, UK
Kurt Jax, UFZ, Germany
Glenn-Marie Lange, World Bank, USA
Rik Leemans, Wageningen University, The Netherlands
Georgina M. Mace, Imperial College London, UK
Karl-Göran Mäler, Royal Swedish Academy of Sciences
Peter H. May, Federal Rural University of Rio de Janeiro, Brazil
Joan Martinez-Alier, University of Barcelona, Spain
Richard B. Norgaard, University of California, Berkeley, USA
Paulo Nunes, Fondazione Eni Enrico Mattei (FEEM), Italy
Jean-Michel Salles, Laboratoire Montpellier ain d'Economie Théorique et
   Appliquée (LAMETA), France
Stanislav Shmelev, University of Oxford, UK
Rehana Siddiqui, Pakistan Institute of Development Economics, Pakistan
R. David Simpson, Environmental Protection Agency, USA
Rodney Smith, University of Minnesota, USA
Simon Stuart, International Union for Conservation of Nature (IUCN), Switzerland
R. Kerry Turner, University of East Anglia, UK
James Vause, Department for Environment, Food and Rural Affairs, UK
Harmen Verbruggen, Vrije Universiteit Amsterdam, The Netherlands
Matt Walpole, World Conservation Monitoring Centre, United Nations Environment
   Programme, Cambridge, UK
Allan D. Watt, Centre for Ecology & Hydrology, UK
Jianchu Xu, ICRAF, Kunmin, China
Jintao Xu, Peking University, China

General reviewers

Gopal K. Kadekodi, Centre for Multi-Disciplinary Development Research, India
Jeffrey A. McNeely, IUCN, Switzerland

Acknowledgements

This volume of TEEB is a tribute to the dedication and strenuous effort of a large number of authors and reviewers from all over the world who provided the best of their knowledge and insight over the last two years (please see pages xi to xiv). We are grateful to TEEB Study Leader, Pavan Sukhdev, for his guidance, support and direction. Heidi Wittmer, Carsten Neßhöver, Augustin Berghöfer, Christoph Schröter-Schlaack and others at UFZ provided us with scientific coordination and support. And we thank Franz W. Gatzweiler (ZEF), Aude Neuville (EC), Florian Eppink (UFZ), Irene Ring (UFZ) and Hans Vos (EEA) for their constant support and inputs as members of the Core Team for this volume.

Thanks also to our TEEB colleagues who coordinated TEEB's other volumes, Patrick ten Brink (IIEP), Heidi Wittmer (UFZ), Haripriya Gundimeda (IITM) and Joshua Bishop (IUCN) for their collaboration and regular inputs.

We were supported by Georgina Langdale (UNEP) in communications, and by Mark Schauer and Raghdan Al-Mallah (UNEP), James Vause (Defra), Benjamin Simmons (UNEP) in administrative and financial management, by Kaavya Varma (GIST) for review coordination, and Paula Loveday-Smith (WCMC) in logistical support. We thank all of them for their support.

We are indebted to members of the TEEB Advisory Board (Joan Martinez-Alier, Giles Atkinson, Edward Barbier, Ahmed Djoghlaf, Jochen Flasbarth, Yolanda Kakabadse, Jacqueline McGlade, Karl-Göran Mäler, Julia Marton-Lefèvre, Peter May, Ladislav Miko, Herman Mulder, Walter Reid, Nicholas Stern and Achim Steiner) for their advice and guidance.

Chris Frid, Andreas Lang, Andy Plater and Tom West (University of Liverpool) provided us with support and encouragement. We thank Michael D. Wood (School of Environmental Sciences, University of Liverpool) for technical editing. And we appreciate the help of Sander van der Ploeg, Mahe Charles, Katrina Borromeo, Nele Steinmetz and Michael Nassl in research support.

Several institutions supported us through the process of writing this volume, including Imperial College London, the Joint Research Centre, Ispra, Milan, The Center for Development Research (ZEF), Bonn, Green India State Trust (GIST), New Delhi, the International Institute for Environment and Development (IIED), London and UNEP's World Conservation Monitoring Centre (WCMC, Cambridge). We are thankful to all of them.

.

Pushpam Kumar, Coordinator,
TEEB: Ecological and Economic Foundations

Preface

Pavan Sukhdev
Study Leader, TEEB

The genesis of TEEB, our global study on the economics of ecosystems and biodiversity, lies in climate change. A meeting of G8+5 environment ministers at Potsdam, 2007 proposed a study to assess the economic impact of the global loss of biodiversity in order to present a convincing economic case for conservation. Their inspiration was the Stern Review, published in the autumn of 2006, which had built upon the science of IPCC and presented a powerful economic case for early action on climate change.

A forest of questions

A veritable forest of questions and doubts quickly grew around this particular proposal from the Potsdam initiative, even while it evolved into a project named The Economics of Ecosystems and Biodiversity (TEEB).

Why extend a logic from the world of climate change to the world of wild Nature? Is it actually ethical to reduce biodiversity, which is about life, to mere economics? And why should the complex web of life, diverse and location-specific in character, lend itself to global economic analysis and modelling? Indeed, why should a Stern-like study be possible at all for biodiversity and ecosystems, when it is obvious that the underlying is irreducible to one variable, unlike greenhouse gases (GHGs) which can be measured in terms of CO_2-equivalents?

And isn't the scientific understanding of ecosystem dynamics, and of the link between biodiversity and ecosystem resilience, too weak to support a study of economic implications? Is it appropriate to isolate ecosystem and biodiversity benefits and value them individually (as in a total economic value (TEV) approach), and assume the whole does not exceed the sum of its parts? Is it appropriate to do so without projecting the effects of expected climate change on the nature and extent of ecosystem services? And even if all these issues were not sufficient deterrents for a study, why should an economic argument work for biodiversity conservation where ethical, spiritual and social arguments had not been sufficient? What could possibly make governments, businesses and society at large internalize such economics and make change happen, when the benefits lost or costs incurred are mostly in the form of public goods and services, which have no markets and no prices?

Furthermore, even if such economic assessment were possible, ethical and worthwhile, how can we actually evaluate costs, when there are no real alternatives to the living fabric of this planet?

The first point to appreciate is that none of the above questions and doubts is either irrelevant or unimportant for TEEB: this particular forest is alive and well. Indeed, it guides our thinking. This Preface is my personal journey through this forest, through the deep-rooted economic, social and political drivers of the problem of biodiversity loss, through the ethical imperatives for TEEB, and its objectives as a synthesis of knowledge presented for a diverse range of end-users in pursuit of the goal of arresting and correcting the accelerating loss of biodiversity and degradation of ecosystems.

The problem and its root causes

The history of post-war economic growth has been one of unsustainable development: unsustainable for the planet's ecosystems, for its species diversity, and indeed for the human race. By some recent yardsticks of sustainability, our global ecological footprint has doubled over the last 40 years (Global Footprint Network, 2009), and now stands at 30 per cent higher than the Earth's biological capacity to produce for our needs.

The ongoing degradation of ecosystems and loss of biodiversity, especially observable in the post-war era, is a well-documented reality. Several reports, culminating in the Millennium Ecosystem Assessment (MA) (2003 and 2005), have presented the evidence of significant degradation, affecting 60 per cent of ecosystem services over the last 40 years (MA, 2005).

These losses are attributed to habitat conversion, habitat fragmentation, climate change, hunting, invasive alien species and so on (see Chapter 3 of C&T Working Group, MA, 2005). These are the 'proximate causes' – or apparent reasons for biodiversity loss – and I distinguish them from 'root causes' – which are the drivers of these causes. Habitat conversion and fragmentation are human-induced land-use changes made to feed and house a growing population with dramatically growing per-capita consumption, and not enough care for the materials-intensity of production. Hunting has a mix of drivers – food, exotic foods, trophies – all meeting human needs. Climate change is now very widely accepted as anthropogenic. And the most destructive examples of loss through invasive alien species are by-products of human intervention, be it deliberate (cane toads introduced in Australia) or accidental (chestnut borers from a Chinese chestnut introduced in America).

Thus the root causes of biodiversity loss lie in the *nature* of the human relationship with nature, and in our dominant economic model. We have not widely understood that our survival depends on co-existence, on living in harmony with nature. And in general, although there are many exceptions that TEEB highlights, our dominant economic model promotes and rewards *more* versus *better* consumption, *private* versus *public* wealth creation, *human-made* capital versus *natural* capital. This is the 'triple-whammy' of self-reinforcing biases that leads us to uphold and promote an economic model in which we tend to extract without fear of limits, consume without awareness of consequences and produce without responsibility for third-party costs, the so-called 'externalities' of business.

Of course, we would not adopt any such damaging behaviours if our relationship with nature were one of co-existence and responsible stewardship, as is still the case with some forest-dependent tribal communities. However, increasing urbanization, which creates both physical and emotional distance from nature, and our dominant 'take–make–waste' economic model with its inherent biases have long ago defeated that possibility. We now enter, in the words of Winston Churchill, a 'period of consequences'. Ecological scarcities, ecosystem degradation, biodiversity loss and climate change are affecting us severely around the world, causing water and food shortages, socio-political stress, economic damage and persistent poverty, as well as increasing the level of ecological, social and economic risks that we as well as future generations will have to manage in our search for well-being for all.

The search for solutions

There is nowadays an increasing level of awareness that something is very wrong, and that human society needs to change in fundamental ways in order to solve any of the problems described above. From many directions, fingers are being pointed at the recent economic crisis, itself a result of crises in fuel, food and finance, and at the parallel crisis in our ecological and climate commons, suggesting that both share a common cause: our failed economic model.

Occasionally, some may conclude (e.g. WEF-GAC summit in Dubai, November 2008) that our systems merely need a 'reboot', and that we do not fundamentally need to change. Many other voices however are arguing for trenchant changes in society and its economic model. There is also a growing view among mainstream political leadership that both the dominant economic model and the accounts of society are in need of serious change (Barosso, Athens, April 2009; Brown, London, July 2009; Sarkozy, Paris, September 2009).

More and more frequently we hear of the need to reform society in fundamental ways: to include natural and human capital formation and destruction in the accounts of society; to expand the reach of markets in order to enable payments for ecosystem services; to tax what we take (resources) and not what we make (profits from goods and services); and so on. These are all big changes, each of which would address the 'root causes' of biodiversity loss and ecosystem degradation.

The challenge, as always, is change and its many dimensions: its nature, its extent and scale, its speed and its unintended consequences. TEEB's review and synthesis of the literature on the economics of ecosystems and biodiversity, our key messages, and our recommendations to end-users are all intended to be a part of that change.

Our approach in recommending changes is to favour pragmatism over perfectionism, discrete planned changes over 'creative destruction' or other adventurous alternatives, common sense and the principle of equity over 'free market fundamentalism' (to borrow a phrase from George Soros), and solutions that have an immediate start and a foreseeable medium-term outcome over solutions that may take ages to negotiate and may not deliver results until after it is too late. Observation and recognition of the value of nature's benefits to society is at the heart of our recommended solutions. Economic valuation, in particular, can help communicate the value of nature to diverse groups of decision makers (TEEB refers to them as the 'end-users' of these economics) using the language of the world's dominant economic and political paradigm. This volume presents the ecological and economic foundations of TEEB. It will be accompanied by four publications for 'end-users' – national and international policy makers (TEEB in National Policy, 2011), subnational policy makers and administrators (TEEB in Local Policy, 2011), business and enterprise (TEEB in Business, 2011) and the individual citizen (a website).

The changing nature of knowledge, economics, valuations and accounts for a changing society are common undercurrents that run through TEEB's 'end-user' deliverables. Some reflection on each of these undercurrents is appropriate to introduce TEEB.

Knowledge for a changing society

While TEEB authors have taken care to consult widely with scientists and economists in order to present a synthesis of scientific knowledge we consider to represent the 'best-of-breed' in each area explored, there is no avoiding the fact that the state knowledge is incomplete. Our understanding of ecosystem dynamics, of the links between biodiversity and ecosystem resilience, and of how ecosystems behave when they are close to thresholds, are all areas of imperfect understanding as of today. Even on measurement issues as fundamental as a set of globally agreed indicators of biodiversity, there remains lively debate on which indicators describing what underlying biodiversity attribute should get selected and why.

Working on the basis of insufficient scientific knowledge about biodiversity and ecosystem functions is certainly a non-trivial concern and a significant challenge. But what constitutes 'scientific proof'? Following Karl Popper's scientific method (Popper, 1959) would suggest that any scientific theory should be falsifiable, and tested and made acceptable through repeated experiments, any one of which could prove it wrong. But applying such scientific method is itself a problem, when the theory in question is (for example) the extent to which the Amazonian rainforest seeds the rainfall cycle that sustains the agriculturally productive plains of central South America. Thus, following Popper's scientific method clinically in this example would entail destroying the Amazonas rainforest, a few times over, to test if the loss of rainforest actually reduced rainfall in central South America – clearly not a socially or environmentally desirable outcome, to say the least.

A less harmful approach derives from applying the 'precautionary principle'. In this example, it would entail assessing whether there is reasonable scientific doubt that rainforests have nothing to do with seeding rainfall and, acting on the absence of reasonable doubt, to then suggest and price an appropriate solution. It might result (for example) in a recommendation encouraging the nations concerned (i.e. Brazil, Argentina, Uruguay, Paraguay) to reduce risks to their rainfall-dependent agricultural economies by collaborating politically and economically to ensure that the so-called 'Amazonian Water Pump' (TEEB in National Policy, 2011) is not damaged. It might include recommendations for appropriate national and international transfers and conservation policies in order to conserve these rainforests. This anecdotal example illustrates a different kind of response to knowledge, and addresses the ethical conundrum of acting on the basis of insufficient scientific *proof*. It is about recognizing and placing a value on future risks, and not just on current certainties.

The level of knowledge among common people on biodiversity and ecosystems is very weak, compared with (for example) their appreciation of climate change. In his poem 'Burnt Norton', from the *Four Quartets* series, T. S. Eliot wrote that 'Human kind ... cannot bear very much reality', and indeed the challenge for our educational systems today if we are really to 'mainstream' a new thinking on nature, knowledge, economics, valuation and so on is no doubt compounded by the human capacity to hear bad news. However, it does still invite an ambitious global campaign of education and persuasion to ensure that governments, corporations, institutions and individuals across all significant societies understand and endorse the need for change as well as TEEB's key initiatives for change. The work undertaken under the banner of 'TEEB for Citizens' was inspired by just such thinking.

Economics for a changing society

TEEB adopts the position that a new awareness of nature can and should be encouraged by describing our economic existence in broader terms than the neoclassical paradigm permits. The familiar 'mantras' of market supremacy, efficiencies of privatization and globalization, trickle-down theory, GDP growth and so on, were the economic toolkit of the 20th century. They worked for a limited time and purpose and have indeed improved the standard of living in many societies, but at the same time, they have created massive negative externalities (i.e. climate change risks and ecological scarcities) which hang over the whole of humanity like the sword of Damocles. The development paradigm of the second half of the 20th century is not a great success story from a humanitarian perspective either: the number of the world's poor increased, not decreased, if 'poverty' is considered in terms of 'well-being', not just being 'well off', and defined to include the various constituents and determinants of human well-being (MA, 2003, chapter 3).

Why did this happen so? In theory, markets should have enabled human choices to be felt by adjusting prices, and if the worsening condition of Earth and its living fabric were not desirable outcomes, then prices and market forces should have engineered a reversal of fortunes? But of course, there are no 'markets' for the largely public goods and services that flow from ecosystems and biodiversity, and no prices. The traditional term for this is 'market failure'. This may strike non-economists as a quaint choice of words, implying that some form of 'market success' eludes us in respect of public goods. The reality is that markets exist only to trade private claims. In order to be of any use for public goods (or bads) we first have to legislate and convert such public goods (or bads) into private claims. Such was the case with the development of intellectual property legislation in the 20th century – before that, knowledge was yet another public good. Legislation can also take the form of allowances and caps, as has been done for carbon markets (Kyoto, EU-ETS, etc.).

In order to flesh out a broader holistic economic approach, which recognizes the existence and significant economic effects of natural capital, we argue that economic valuation of Nature's public goods and service flows is both necessary and ethical, and that shadow prices can and should be calculated and presented, all in the proper context. This requires us to differentiate biomes, recognize differing socio-economic conditions, and evaluate in these contexts a wide range of ecosystem services (such as climate regulation, water provisioning, etc.) and biodiversity benefits (such as crop pollination by bees, citizens' enjoyment from visiting national parks – over and above the cost of travel, profits to pharmaceutical companies from new medication discovered through, for example, bio-prospecting.) Appendix 2 of this volume describes how a 'matrix' of valuations has been assembled by TEEB on this basis.

Indeed, the core of TEEB's content is about assessing and presenting what valid forms economic valuation may take, within what appropriate valuation framework, using which valuation methodologies, and always guided by a paramount consideration: the purpose of such valuation.

Valuation and a changing society

Is valuation an important institution to engender change in the way our society responds to nature?

First, valuation can serve as a tool for self-reflection (see Chapter 4 of this volume), helping us rethink our relationship with the natural world, and alerting us to the consequences of our choices and behaviours on distant places and people. Questions such as what factors influence our relationship with nature, what is the role played by nature in creating social and personal identities, and what are the social and environmental consequences of various ways of relating to and using the natural environment (Clayton and Opotow, 2004; Zavestoski, 2004) become the focus of this self reflection. As such, valuation can work as a 'feedback mechanism' for a society that has increasingly distanced itself from the natural world from which it derives all of its vital resources.

Second, we cannot but recognize the all-pervasiveness of economic valuation. In the words of David Pearce, 'all decisions have costs and hence all decisions to incur that cost imply that benefits exceed costs. All decisions not to incur the costs imply that costs exceed benefits. Economic valuation is always implicit or explicit; it cannot fail to happen at all' (Pearce, 2006, p4). Abstaining from explicit valuation, on apparently valid scientific or ethical grounds, often amounts to no more than an acceptance of someone else's implicit valuation – trade-offs are then made on the basis of that implicit economic valuation.

Last, so deep-seated and widespread is modern society's inherent market-centric mindset (and our almost unequivocal association of 'price' with 'value') that the mere device of demonstrating economic value for the public wealth that nature delivers can itself become an important strategy for the change we seek. The construction of 'shadow prices' for public goods and services can take on a life beyond the quiet workspaces of academic research and enter the turbulent halls of public policy debate. Such valuations can call into question the accepted dogmas of neo-classical economics and the inherent biases of *Homo oeconomicus* mentioned above (i.e. preferences for quantity vs quality of flows; private vs public wealth; human-made vs natural capital), if we can demonstrate significant value flowing from nature to human society in terms of welfare benefits, employment and solutions to poverty. Indeed, TEEB treats such demonstration as an ethical imperative. Commenting in Paris (Wertz-Kanounnikoff and Rankine, November

2008) on our Interim Report, Laurent Mermet described this strategy as the 'political' dimension of TEEB's argument.

TEEB's view is that we should acknowledge the weaknesses of valuation methodology in calculating such shadow prices (not least due to reasons mentioned earlier – insufficient understanding of ecosystem dynamics and of biodiversity's role in ecosystem resilience, valuing single benefits one at a time rather than an ecosystem as a whole, not accounting for the effects of climate change on the nature and extent of ecosystem services and so on) but we should not shy away from stating best available estimates of value using the most appropriate of reviewed methodologies, strictly to help decision makers to make better informed choices. This is because the alternative is in fact ethically worse: to permit the continued absence of prices to seep even further into human consciousness and behaviour as a 'zero' price, and thus no value.

John Gowdy addresses criticisms of valuation by addressing the underlying mathematics used in economics (see Chapter 1, Box 1.1). The purpose of the Walrasian mathematical model was to prove that competitive markets are Pareto optimal. That proof does not work unless economic agents (firms and consumers) act independently of each other. The 'independence' assumption has been repeatedly falsified by empirical tests – it does not make good predictions of real human behaviour. Therefore we need to discard that theoretical model of markets: it is driven solely by the mathematical requirements of constrained optimization and has little or nothing to do with economic reality. And if we do discard the straitjacket of Walrasian mathematics, we can then begin to sort out what can be priced, what can be measured without prices, and what cannot be measured at all but is still valued by society for very good reasons.

In general through the TEEB series of volumes, and in particular in the two volumes for policy makers (TEEB in National Policy, 2011 and TEEB in Local Policy, 2011), we follow a tiered approach in analysing problems and suitable policy responses. We find that at times it suffices just to *recognize* value – be it intrinsic, spiritual or social – to create a policy response favouring conservation or sustainable use (e.g. sacred groves, and the system of Protected Areas for biodiversity conservation). No economic valuation is made as such in these instances, but rather, valuation at a societal level (see Chapter 4, this volume).

At other times we may need to *demonstrate* economic value in order for policy makers to respond – such as a wetland conserved near Kampala (see TEEB in Local Policy, 2011, Chapter 8) for its waste treatment function instead of reclaiming it for agriculture, or river flats maintained for their many ecosystem services instead of converting them for residential use near New Delhi (see TEEB in National Policy, 2011, Chapter 10, Box 10.6). I should caution that it is not a 'risk-free' exercise to demonstrate value by deriving and propagating shadow prices. There is always the risk that misguided decision makers or exploitative interests may want to use these prices for the wrong ends. Therefore, our proposition is that the act of valuing the flows and stocks of nature is ethically valid so long as the purpose of that exercise is, first and foremost, to demonstrate value in order to instigate change of behaviour, and to inform and alert decision makers to damaging trade-offs based on the implicit valuations that are involved in causing the loss of biodiversity and degradation of ecosystems. We have become attuned to giving 'yes' answers for trade-off choices that result in more consumption, more private wealth, more physical capital (as against better consumption, more public wealth, more natural capital), trade-offs that are more informed by inherent biases than by good economics. We also extend that false logic implicitly when we ignore the depletion of forests, fisheries and so on, on a perverted logic of 'promoting growth' or 'promoting development' while not defining these terms in a holistic or equitable manner from either an intra-generational or inter-generational perspective.

Finally, TEEB has also focused considerably on changes that *capture* value by rewarding and supporting good conservation through a variety of means – such as Payments for Environmental Services (PES), international agreements for the same (IPES), establishing new markets, EHS reforms (see TEEB in National Policy, 2011, Chapters 5 and 9, and TEEB in Local Policy, 2011, Chapter 8). In most instances the valuation of services rewarded is an important input for an effective economic solution.

However, we categorically do *not* suggest that putting prices must lead to *tradeability* of the assets or flows being priced. That is a separate societal choice which potentially affects survival of species as well as of forest-dependent and ocean-dependent poor, and such choices cannot be made lightly or on other than an ethical plane, involving as it does both intra-generational and inter-generational equity. Placing blind faith in the ability of markets to optimize social welfare, by privatizing the ecological commons and letting markets discover prices for them, is not at all what TEEB is about. In fact, TEEB is anything *but* a cost–benefit based stewardship model for the Earth and its living fabric of ecosystems and biodiversity.

An important point to appreciate is that the chosen methodology of valuation depends on the purpose of valuation. Is the valuation being used for adjusting national accounts? Or for setting rates for environmental taxes? Or for benchmarking prices to be used in PES or IPES? The purpose of valuation must guide the methodology of valuation. For example, when assessing values to make 'green' adjustments to national accounts, the purpose is to provide a sustainability yardstick with which to assess (*inter alia*) quantitative and qualitative changes in national ecological assets and to internalize these changes in performance measures of the national economy. A conservative or 'floor value' (i.e. which uses that end of a range of valuation assumptions that generates the least deviation from unadjusted accounts) has the simple advantage of being least likely to be challenged, hence most likely to find its way into national planning and budgeting processes supporting sustainable development. A less conservative valuation could be justified for the same ecosystem services from the same biome to the same beneficiaries if the purpose of valuation were, instead, to set benchmark prices for a local or national PES regime.

The use of modelled or shadow prices as inputs to a designed policy response is not without its risks, but we do still advocate their appropriate use. The conservative option of using 'floor values' may likely be much improved if we had more comprehensive means of incorporating future climate change impacts, or of modelling whole systems rather than aggregating single benefits, and indeed we argue that executive actions can and should award higher values for good conservation than 'floor values', but certainly not any lower. Once again, the ethical and pragmatic choice is not to wait interminably for the perfect answer, but to suggest a solution that addresses the purpose of valuation, and serves to correct prevailing biases by making visible the economic value of ecosystem services and biodiversity.

We see therefore that economic valuation can contribute to address our inability, reluctance or ideological intolerance to adjust institutions (including value articulating institutions) to our knowledge of ecosystems, biodiversity and the human being. As such, it can contribute to more inclusive economic planning, management and accounting, and a more inclusive view of non-human beings. In the long run, it may even contribute to internalize a respect for Nature into western cosmology and social life, and thus help address a 'root cause' of the problem of biodiversity loss and ecosystem degradation which, as we have noted above, lies in the *nature* of the human relationship with nature.

Accounts for a changing society

It is a common dictum that 'you cannot manage what you do not measure'. Society generally wishes to manage its development sustainably, mitigate climate risks, reduce ecological scarcity and arrest the extinction of species. However, to be able to achieve any of that, society needs appropriate measures of the underlying variables: the sustainability of economic development, the quantum of GHGs, the extent and quality of our ecological commons, and the richness and variability of species. Other than the second quantity (i.e. measured GHG levels and annual GHG emissions), none of these underlying quantities has a widely accepted standard measure.

'Sustainable development' is still more talk than action, at least partly because for 20 years after the Brundtland Commission's report (which made this term common parlance globally) society has still not matched the talk with a change of metrics. We continue to depend upon archaic measures of progress (in particular, GDP growth) which lead us to ignore significant externalities and bias human activity against the conservation of natural capital. The accounts of society, largely based on the System of National Accounts (SNA) which dates back to the Second World War, do not capture environmental and human factors enough, and the developing world's overwhelming focus on GDP growth as a measure of progress further entrenches the dominant economic model and its failings.

There is a need to design and present alternative metrics, and give them credibility through consensus and standardization. This must be done at the state, corporation and individual level to be truly effective. The question of alternative metrics also opens the issues around ecosystem accounting, with the attendant risks of using existing institutions to make change happen.

At a national level, Bretton Woods and its SNA are part of our old and defective economic compass, and implicit or explicit policy trade-offs based on SNA metrics, such as GDP-optimization strategies to achieve progress, have repeatedly failed in developing countries. However, the problem of wrong metrics does not only affect the national level, but also all levels of decision making in society ranging from global corporations to individuals and households. Significant unaccounted (and unmanaged) externalities of today's corporations make sustainability a tough challenge, as evidenced in the negative impacts of corporations on ecosystems, biodiversity and the quality of individuals' health and life. Unaccounted and untaxed externalities are also at the root of individual behaviour patterns that contribute to unsustainable development, such as unchecked consumerism, excessive materials use and fossil-fuel addiction.

Therefore at the national level, our recommendations (TEEB in National Policy, 2011) are to coordinate and consolidate the major international initiatives and quickly compile a (UN-backed) manual that improves upon and succeeds SEEA-2003, providing a standard *direction* of new metrics for country statistical offices and their governments to follow, but allowing full freedom to these governments to proceed at a *speed* that reflects their institutional capacities and the availability and quality of data needed to compute 'Green GDP', 'Genuine Savings' and 'Inclusive Wealth'.

At the enterprise level, we recognize partial progress (such as optional Green Reporting Initiative sustainability reporting, and optional Carbon Disclosure Project emissions disclosure) but we look to a bolder solution. We argue the case for a move to recognize all the major human capital and natural capital externalities of a corporation and disclose them in appendices to the annual report and accounts of each corporation. The role of the International Accounting Standards Board and national accounting bodies in legislating such disclosure requirements is critical, and we recommend this as a priority. In TEEB in Business (2011), we aim to present research and illustrations of what the elements of a future set of disclosure requirements might look like for a corporation's material externalities.

In summary: 'Mainstreaming' TEEB

To summarize, modern society's predominant focus on market-delivered components of well-being, and its almost total dependence on market prices to indicate value means that we generally do not measure or manage economic value that is exchanged other than through markets, such as the public goods and services that comprise a large part of nature's flows to our economies. Society generally also ignores third-party effects of private exchanges (so-called 'externalities') unless they are actually declared illegal. TEEB has assembled much evidence that the economic invisibility of nature's flows into the economy is a significant contributor to the degradation of ecosystems and the loss of biodiversity. This in turn leads to serious human and economic costs which are being felt now, have been felt for much of the last half-century, and will be felt at an accelerating pace if we continue 'business as usual'.

Lord Stern's review of the Economics of Climate Change (Stern, 2006) showed that there is significant carry in quantitative evaluations (as against just pleas to humanitarianism and common sense, no matter how well argued) which present an argument for change in economic terms. TEEB finds the corresponding case for valuing ecosystems and biodiversity to be more complex and less consensual, multi-layered in terms of services, multi-scaled in terms of beneficiaries, location-specific in terms of the underlying biodiversity, and generally uncertain in terms of our understanding of the dynamics of ecosystems and the links between resilience and biodiversity. However, TEEB argues that the right ethical choice is to compute these imperfect valuations for society to use, illustrated with good examples (which are increasingly being seen) and judicious guidance on how, in what context, and for what purpose to use them.

Valuations are a powerful 'feedback mechanism' for a society that has distanced itself from the biosphere upon which its very health and survival depends. Economic valuation, in particular, communicates the value of Nature to society in the language of the world's dominant economic and political model. Mainstreaming this thinking and bringing it to the attention of policy makers, administrators, businesses and citizens is in essence the central purpose of TEEB.

I wish to thank our funders, the governments of Germany, the Netherlands, Norway, Sweden, the United Kingdom, Belgium and Japan, and the European Union Commission for their commitment to and support of TEEB. I am especially grateful to TEEB's Advisory Board (Joan Martinez-Alier, Giles Atkinson, Edward Barbier, Ahmed Djoghlaf, Jochen Flasbarth, Yolanda Kakabadse, Jacqueline McGlade, Karl-Göran Mäler, Julia Marton-Lefèvre, Peter May, Ladislav Miko, Herman Mulder, Walter Reid, Nicholas Stern and Achim Steiner) for their advice and constant encouragement through the process of compiling the TEEB series. TEEB is very much a community effort that owes much to the dedication and commitment of its authors reviewers, contributors, collaborators, and support and coordination teams. To each member of these, my appreciation and thanks.

References

Clayton, S. and Opotow, S. (eds) (2004) *Identity and the Natural Environment: The Psychological Significance of Nature*, MIT Press, Cambridge, MA

Global Footprint Network (2009) 'How we can bend the curve', Global Footprint Network Annual Report 2009, www.footprintnetwork.org/images/uploads/Global_Footprint_Network_2009_annual_report.pdf (last accessed 21 May 2010)

MA (Millennium Ecosystem Assessment) (2003) *Ecosystems and Human Well-being: A Framework for Assessment*, Island Press, Washington, DC

MA (2005) *Ecosystems and Human Well-being: Synthesis*, Island Press, Washington, DC

Pearce, D. (2006) (ed) *Environmental Valuation in Developed Countries: Case Studies*, Edward Elgar, Cheltenham

Popper, K. (1959) *The Logic of Scientific Discovery*, Hutchinson, London (first published as *Logik der Forschung*, 1935, Verlag von Julius Springer, Vienna)

Stern, N. (2006) *The Economics of Climate Change*, Cambridge University Press, Cambridge

TEEB in National Policy (2011) *The Economics of Ecosystems and Biodiversity in National and International Policy Making* (ed Patrick ten Brink), Earthscan, London

TEEB in Local Policy (2011) *The Economics of Ecosystems and Biodiversity in Local and Regional Policy and Management* (eds Heidi Wittmer and Haripriya Gundimeda), Earthscan, London

TEEB in Business (2011) *The Economics of Ecosystems and Biodiversity in Business and Enterprise* (ed Joshua Bishop), Earthscan, London

Wertz-Kanounnikoff, S. and Rankine, H. (2008) 'Economic and Social: How can governments promote strategic approaches to payments for environmental services (PES)? An exploratory analysis for the case of Viet Nam', IDDRIS, Paris

Zavestoski, S. (2004) 'Constructing and maintaining ecological identities: The strategies of deep ecologists', in Clayton, S. and Opotow, S. (eds) *Identity and the Natural Environment: The Psychological Significance of Nature*, MIT Press, Cambridge, MA, pp297–316

List of Acronyms and Abbreviations

ATEAM	Advanced Terrestrial Ecosystem Analysis and Modelling
ATS	Antarctic Treaty System
BII	Biodiversity Intactness Index
BT	benefits transfer
CA	Contributing authors
CBA	cost–benefit analysis
CBD	Convention on Biological Diversity
CHG	greenhouse gas
CITES	Convention on International Trade in Endangered Species
CLA	Coordinating lead authors
CM	choice modelling
CR	contingent ranking
CV	coefficient of variation
CV(M)	contingent valuation (method)
DMP	dry matter productivity
DMV	deliberative monetary valuation
EASAC	European Academies Science Advisory Council
EC	European Communities
EDF	expected damage function
EEA	European Environment Agency
EPA	United States Environmental Protection Agency
ESA	Ecological Society of America
ESS	ecosystem service
EVRI	Environmental Valuation Research Inventory
FAO	Food and Agriculture Organization of the United Nations
FOE	Friends of the Earth
GDP	gross domestic product
GEEM	general equilibrium ecosystem model
GEF	Global Environmental Facility
GEOBON	Global Earth Observation Biodiversity Observation Network
GIS	geographical information system
GNP	gross national product
HANPP	Human Appropriated Net Primary Productivity
HGMU	hydrogeomorphic unit
HI	headline indicator
HK	human capital
HP	hedonic pricing
IO	input–output
IPY	International Polar Year
LA	Lead authors
LPI	Living Planet Index
MA	Millennium Ecosystem Assessment
MCZ	Marine Conservation Zone
MF	manufactured capital

MSA	Mean Species Abundance (Index)
MTI	marine trophic index
NCE	net carbon exchange
NCI	Natural Capital Index
NERC	Natural Environmental Research Council
NIA	national income account
NK	natural capital
NNP	net national product
NOAA	National Oceanic and Atmospheric Administration
NPP	net primary production
NPV	net present value
NRC	National Research Council
NTFP	non-timber forest products
OECD	Organisation for Economic Co-operation and Development
PA	protected area
PE	preventive expenditure
PES	payment for ecosystem service
PF	production function
POP	persistent organic pollutant
PV	present value
REDD	reducing emissions from deforestation and forest degradation
RLC	relocation cost
RLI	Red List Index
RPC	replacement cost
RSC	restoration cost
SALLJ	South American Low Level Jet
SAM	social accounting matrix
SER	Society for Ecological Restoration
SM	simulated market
SMS	safe minimum standard
SNA	System of National Accounts
SPU	service-providing unit
TC(M)	travel cost (method)
TEM	terrestrial ecosystem model
TEV	total economic value
TFP	total factor productivity
UNEP	United Nations Environment Programme
UNFCCC	United Nations Framework Convention on Climate Change
USFWS	US Fish and Wildlife Service
WCED	World Commission on Environment and Development
WFP	wood forest product
WTA	willingness-to-accept
WTP	willingness-to-pay
WRI	World Resources Institute

Glossary

Adaptation: Adjustment in natural or human systems to a new or changing environment. Various types of adaptation can be distinguished, including anticipatory and reactive adaptation, private and public adaptation, and autonomous and planned adaptation (MA, 2005a).

Adaptive capacity: The general ability of institutions, systems and individuals to adjust to potential damage, to take advantage of opportunities, or to cope with the consequences (MA, 2005a).

Adaptive management: A systematic process for continually improving management policies and practices by learning from the outcomes of previously employed policies and practices. In active adaptive management, management is treated as a deliberate experiment for purposes of learning (MA, 2005a).

Altruistic value: The importance which individuals attach to a resource that can be used by others in the current generation, reflecting selfless concern for the welfare of others (intragenerational equity concerns).

Anthropocentric perspectives: Viewing humans as the most important entities.

Anthropogenic impacts: Impacts resulting from human activities.

Appropriation: The process of capturing some or all of the demonstrated and measured values of ecosystem services so as to provide incentives for their sustainable provision.

Assets: Economic resources.

Avoided cost: The costs that would have been incurred in the absence of ecosystem services.

Benefit sharing: Distribution of benefits between stakeholders.

Benefits: Positive change in wellbeing from the fulfilment of needs and wants.

Benefits-only approach: An evaluation focusing on the benefits of different alternatives.

Benefits transfer approach: Economic valuation approach in which estimates obtained (by whatever method) in one context are used to estimate values in a different context (MA, 2005a).

Bequest value: The importance individuals attach to a resource that can be passed on to future generations, reflecting intergenerational equity concerns.

Biocentric perspectives: Recognizing the importance of non-human life.

Biodiversity (a contraction of biological diversity): The variability among living organisms from all sources, including terrestrial, marine and other aquatic ecosystems and the ecological complexes of which they are part. Biodiversity includes diversity within species, between species and between ecosystems (MA, 2005a). Biodiversity may be described quantitatively, in terms such as richness, rarity and uniqueness.

Biological control services: The control of pests through biological rather than chemical means.

Biological diversity: See *Biodiversity*.

Biome: The largest unit of ecological classification that is convenient to recognize below the entire globe. Terrestrial biomes are typically based on dominant vegetation structure (e.g. forest grassland). Ecosystems within a biome function in a broadly similar way, although they may have very different species composition. For example, all forests share certain properties regarding nutrient cycling, disturbance and biomass that are different from the properties of grasslands. Marine biomes are typically based on biogeochemical properties. TEEB has adopted a typology of 12 main biomes, sub-divided into a larger number of ecosystems.

Biophysical valuation: A method that derives values from measurements of the physical costs (e.g. in terms of labour, surface requirements, energy or material inputs) of producing a given good or service.

Biotope: An ecological area that supports a particular range of biological communities.

Carbon sequestration: The process of increasing the carbon content of a reservoir other than the atmosphere (MA, 2005a).

Choice-conjoint analysis: A stated-preference technique to determine which combination of attributes are most preferred by consumers.

Choice modelling: A technique that models the decision process of an individual in a given context.

Composite indices: Indicators comprised of a number of measures combined in a particular way to increase their sensitivity, reliability or ease of communication.

Consumer surplus: The benefits enjoyed by consumers as a result of being able to purchase a product for a price that is less than the most that they would be willing to pay.

Contingent valuation: Stated preference-based economic valuation technique based on a survey of how much respondents would be willing to pay for specified benefits (MA, 2005a).

Cost–benefit analysis: A technique designed to determine the feasibility of a project or plan by quantifying its costs and benefits (MA, 2005a).

Cost-effectiveness approach: Analysis to identify the least cost option that meets a particular goal (MA, 2005a).

Cross-scale resilience: Response to the same environmental variable at different scales by different species (MA, 2005a).

Cultural ecosystem services: The nonmaterial benefits people obtain from ecosystems through spiritual enrichment, cognitive development, reflection, recreation, and aesthetic experience, including, e.g. knowledge systems, social relations and aesthetic values (MA, 2005a).

Deliberative monetary valuation: The use of formal deliberation concerning an environmental impact to express value in monetary terms for policy purposes (Spash, 2001).

Demand function transfer: The use of demand functions estimated through valuation applications (travel cost, hedonic pricing, contingent valuation or choice modelling) for a study site, in conjunction with information on parameter values for the policy site, to transfer values.

Density compensation: Negative co-variance among species' abundances (MA, 2005a).

Diminishing returns to scale: Adding an additional unit of area to a large ecosystem increases the total value of ecosystem services less than an additional unit of area to a smaller ecosystem.

Direct driver: A driver that unequivocally influences ecosystem processes and can therefore be identified and measured to differing degrees of accuracy (MA, 2005a).

Direct use value (of ecosystems): The benefits derived from the services provided by an ecosystem that are used directly by an economic agent. These include consumptive uses (e.g. harvesting goods) and nonconsumptive uses (e.g. enjoyment of scenic beauty). Agents are often physically present in an ecosystem to receive direct use value (MA, 2005a).

Discount rate: A rate used to determine the present value of future benefits.

Discounted utility: Including the future discounted value of a good in its present value.

Disservices: Undesired negative effects resulting for the generation of ecosystem services.

Disturbed ecosystems: Ecosystems that have been altered as a result of anthropogenic activities or natural disasters.

Double counting of services: Erroneously including the same ecosystem service more than once in an economic analysis.

Driver: Any natural or human-induced factor that directly or indirectly causes a change in an ecosystem (MA, 2005a).

Dynamic equilibrium: An ecosystem state in which the dynamic processes of plant and animal populations leads to a stable system.

Ecological equilibrium: See *Dynamic equilibrium*.

Ecological footprint: An index of the area of productive land and aquatic ecosystems required to produce the resources used and to assimilate the wastes produced by a defined population at a specified material standard of living, wherever on Earth that land may be located (MA, 2005a).

Ecological infrastructure: Any area which delivers services such as freshwater, micro climate regulation, recreation, etc, to a large proximate population, usually cities. This is sometimes referred to as green infrastructure.

Ecological production function: Relationship between environmental inputs and outputs of goods and services.

Ecological stability: See *Ecosystem health*.

Ecological threshold: The point at which the conditions of an ecosystem result in change to a new state.

Ecological threshold of irreversibility: A degree of impairment to an ecosystem, which, when it is surpassed, is too severe to allow recovery of that ecosystem to its former intact state without human intervention.

Ecological value: Non-monetary assessment of ecosystem integrity, health or resilience, all of which are important indicators to determine critical thresholds and minimum requirements for ecosystem service provision.

Economic behaviour: The way in which economic agents reveal their preferences through economic activity.

Economic growth: An increase in economic prosperity measured, for example, as an increase in per capita gross domestic product (GDP).

Economic valuation: The process of expressing a value for a particular good or service in a certain context (e.g. decision making) in monetary terms.

Eco-regional planning: Planning that is undertaken on an eco-regional rather than national basis.

Ecosystem: A dynamic complex of plant, animal and microorganism communities and their non-living environment interacting as a functional unit (MA, 2005a). For practical purposes it is important to define the spatial dimensions of concern.

Ecosystem accounting: The process of constructing formal accounts for ecosystems.

Ecosystem capital: See *Natural capital*.

Ecosystem degradation: A persistent reduction in the capacity to provide ecosystem services (MA, 2005a).

Ecosystem function: A subset of the interactions between ecosystem structure and processes that underpin the capacity of an ecosystem to provide goods and services.

Ecosystem health: A state or condition of an ecosystem that expresses attributes of biodiversity within 'normal' ranges, relative to its ecological stage of development. Ecosystem health depends inter alia on ecosystem resilience and resistance.

Ecosystem integrity: Implies completeness or wholeness and infers capability in an ecosystem to maintain all its components as well as functional relationships when disturbed.

Ecosystem management: An approach to maintaining or restoring the composition, structure, function and delivery of services of natural and modified ecosystems for the goal of achieving sustainability. It is based on an adaptive, collaboratively developed vision of desired future conditions that integrates ecological, socio-economic and institutional perspectives, applied within a geographic framework, and defined primarily by natural ecological boundaries (MA, 2005a).

Ecosystem process: Any change or reaction which occurs within ecosystems, either physical, chemical or biological. Ecosystem processes include decomposition, production, nutrient cycling and fluxes of nutrients and energy (MA, 2005a).

Ecosystem services: The direct and indirect contributions of ecosystems to human well-being. The concept 'ecosystem goods and services' is synonymous with ecosystem services.

Ecosystem structure: The biophysical architecture of an ecosystem. The composition of species making up the architecture may vary.

Ecotourism: Travel undertaken to access sites or regions of unique natural or ecologic quality, or the provision of services to facilitate such travel.

Elasticity: A measure of responsiveness of one variable to a change in another, usually defined in terms of percentage change. For example, own-price elasticity of demand is the percentage change in the quantity demanded of a good for a 1 per cent change in the price of that good. Other common elasticity measures include supply and income elasticity (MA, 2005a).

Endowment effect: An increase in the value that people place on a good or service once their property right has been established.

Environmental envelope: The environmental boundary conditions within which ecosystems exist.

Environmental regulation services: See *Regulating services*.

Equity: Fairness of rights, distribution and access. Depending on context, this can refer to resources, services or power (MA, 2005a).

Existence value: The value that individuals place on knowing that a resource exists, even if they never use that resource (also sometimes known as conservation value or passive use value) (MA, 2005a).

Externality: A consequence of an action that affects someone other than the agent undertaking that action and for which the agent is neither compensated nor penalized through the markets. Externalities can be positive or negative (MA, 2005a).

Extinction: The point at which an organism within a species can no longer reproduce to create subsequent generations and the species dies out.

Factor income: Returns received on factors of production.

Functional diversity: Value, range and abundance of functional traits of organisms in a given ecosystem.

Functional groups: Groups of organisms that respond to the environment or affect ecosystem processes in a similar way. Examples of plant functional types include nitrogen-fixer versus non-fixer, stress-tolerant versus ruderal versus competitor, resprouter versus seeder, deciduous versus evergreen. Examples of animal functional types include granivorous versus fleshy-fruit eater, nocturnal versus diurnal predator, browser versus grazer (MA, 2005a).

Functional redundancy: A characteristic of ecosystems in which more than one species in the system can carry out a particular process. Redundancy may be total or partial – that is, a species may not be able to completely replace the other species or it may compensate only some of the processes in which the other species are involved (MA, 2005a).

Functional traits: A feature of an organism, which has demonstrable links to the organism's function.

Genetic diversity: The value, range and relative abundance of genes present in the organisms in an ecological community.

Governance (of ecosystems): The process of regulating human behaviour in accordance with shared ecosystem objectives. The term includes both governmental and nongovernmental mechanisms.

Group valuation: An approach combining stated preference techniques with elements of deliberative processes from political science.

Habitat service: The importance of ecosystems to provide living space for resident and migratory species (thus maintaining the gene pool and nursery service).

Hedonic pricing: An economic valuation approach that utilizes information about the implicit demand for an environmental attribute of marketed commodities.

Human well-being: A context- and situation-dependent state, comprising basic material for a good life, freedom and choice, health and bodily well-being, good social relations, security, peace of mind and spiritual experience (MA, 2005a).

Hyperbolic discounting: A discount rate reflecting the fact that people generally show more impatience in discounting the near future than the distant future.

Indicator: Information based on measured data used to represent a particular attribute, characteristic or property of a system (MA, 2005a).

Indirect driver: A driver that operates by altering the level or rate of change of one or more direct drivers (MA, 2005a).

Indirect use value: The benefits derived from the goods and services provided by an ecosystem that are used indirectly by an economic agent. For example, an agent at some distance from an ecosystem may derive benefits from drinking water that has been purified as it passed through the ecosystem (MA, 2005a).

Institutional failure: A situation in which institutions create inefficiencies in the use of goods and services.

Institutions: The rules that guide how people within societies live, work and interact with each other. Formal institutions are written or codified rules. Examples of formal institutions would be the constitution, the judiciary laws, the organized market and property rights. Informal institutions are rules governed by social and behavioural norms of the society, family or community. Also referred to as organizations (MA, 2005a).

Instrumental value: Value as a means to acquiring something else.

Interventions: See *Responses*.

Intrinsic value: The value of someone or something in and for itself, irrespective of its utility for someone else (MA, 2005a).

Loss aversion: People tend to prefer to avoid losses rather than to acquire gains.

Low-input systems: Agricultural systems with little or no subsidies of energy, fertilizer or pesticides.

Management (of ecosystems): An approach to maintaining or restoring the composition, structure, function and delivery of services of natural and modified ecosystems for the goal of achieving sustainability. It is based on an adaptive, collaboratively developed vision of desired future conditions that integrates ecological, socio-economic and institutional perspectives, applied within a geographic framework, and defined primarily by natural ecological boundaries (MA, 2005a).

Marginal efficiency of capital: The rate of discount that equates the price of a fixed capital asset with its present discounted value of expected income.

Marginal utility of consumption: The utility gained (or lost) from a small increase (or decrease) in the consumption of a good or service.

Market failure: The inability of a market to capture the correct values of ecosystem services (MA, 2005a).

Measure (or measurement): Information which refers to the actual measurement of a state, quantity or process derived from observations or monitoring.

Meta-analytic function transfer: Using value functions estimated from multiple study results, in conjunction with information on parameter values for the policy site, to estimate values.

Mitigation (or restoration) cost: The cost of mitigating the effects of the loss of ecosystem services or the cost of getting those services restored.

Monetary valuation: See *Economic valuation.*

Natural capital: An economic metaphor for the limited stocks of physical and biological resources found on earth (MA, 2005b).

Non-economic techniques: Techniques that do not require relationships among economic variables to be measured empirically.

Non-use or passive use: Benefits which do not arise from direct or indirect use.

Open access: Accessible to all.

Opportunity cost: The benefits forgone by undertaking one activity instead of another (MA, 2005a).

Option price: The largest sure payment that an individual will pay for a policy before uncertainty is resolved.

Over-exploitation: Use in excess of a sustainable use level.

Potential use (of ecosystem services): The use(s) to which ecosystem services may be put in the future.

Poverty: The pronounced deprivation of well-being. Income poverty refers to a particular formulation expressed solely in terms of per capita or household income (MA, 2005a).

Precautionary principle: The management concept stating that in cases 'where there are threats of serious or irreversible damage, lack of full scientific certainty shall not be used as a reason for postponing cost-effective measures to prevent environmental degradation', as defined in the Rio Declaration (MA, 2005a).

Primary valuation studies: Empirical valuation studies rather than those that rely on the transfer of values or value functions from other studies.

Production, economic: Output of a system (MA, 2005a).

Production function: A function used to estimate how much a given ecosystem service (e.g. regulating service) contributes to the delivery of another service or commodity which is traded on an existing market.

Productivity: Rate of biomass produced by an ecosystem, generally expressed as biomass produced per unit of time per unit of surface or volume. Net primary productivity is defined as the energy fixed by plants minus their respiration (MA, 2005a).

Provisioning services: The products obtained from ecosystems, including, for example, genetic resources, food and fibre, and fresh water (MA, 2005a).

Public goods: A good or service in which the benefit received by any one party does not diminish the availability of the benefits to others, and where access to the good cannot be restricted (MA, 2005a).

Quasi-option value: The value of preserving options for future use of an environmental resource that may be lost irreversibly given expected growth of knowledge.

Range of tolerance: The range of a given parameter within which an organism can function (e.g. temperature tolerance range).

Regulating services: The benefits obtained from the regulation of ecosystem processes, including, for example, the regulation of climate, water and some human diseases (MA, 2005a).

Replacement cost: The costs incurred by replacing ecosystem services with artificial technologies.

Resilience: The ability of an ecosystem to recover from disturbance without human intervention.

Resistance: The ability of an ecosystem to withstand or tolerate disturbance and stay within certain boundary conditions, or states, without human intervention.

Resource: Any physical or virtual entity of limited availability that provides a benefit.

Response diversity: Differential response to environmental variables among species (MA, 2005a).

Responses: Human actions, including policies, strategies and interventions, to address specific issues, needs, opportunities or problems. In the context of ecosystem management, responses may be of legal, technical, institutional, economic and behavioural nature and may operate at various spatial and time scales (MA, 2005a).

Returns to scale: Changes in outputs from a proportional change in inputs. Returns to scale can be constant (if the outputs change by the same proportion), increasing (if the outputs increase by more than the same proportion), or decreasing (if the outputs increase by less than the same proportion).

Revealed preference: A method to assess possible value options or to define utility (consumer preferences) based on the observation of consumer behaviour.

Scale: The measurable dimensions of phenomena or observations. Expressed in physical units, such as metres, years, population size or quantities moved or exchanged. In observation, scale determines the relative fineness and coarseness of different detail and the selectivity among patterns these data may form (MA, 2005a).

Services and benefits of ecosystems: See *Ecosystem services*.

Social costs and benefits: Costs and benefits as seen from the perspective of society as a whole. These differ from private costs and benefits in being more inclusive (all costs and benefits borne by some member of society are taken into account) and in being valued at social opportunity cost rather than market prices, where these differ; sometimes termed 'economic' costs and benefits (MA, 2005a).

Social value: See *Social costs and benefits*.

Societal choice: Collective decisions based on individual preferences.

Socioecological system: An ecosystem, the management of this ecosystem by actors and organizations, and the rules, social norms and conventions underlying this management (MA, 2005a).

Species diversity: Biodiversity at the species level, often combining aspects of species richness, their relative abundance and their dissimilarity (MA, 2005a).

Species richness: The number of species within a given sample, community or area (MA, 2005a).

Stakeholder: A person, group or organization that has a stake in the outcome of a particular activity.

Stated preference: Consumer preferences are understood through questions regarding willingness to pay or willingness to accept.

Substitutability: The extent to which human-made capital can be substituted for natural capital (or vice versa).

Supporting services: Ecosystem services that are necessary for the maintenance of all other ecosystem services. Some examples include biomass production, production of atmospheric oxygen, soil formation and retention, nutrient cycling, water cycling and provisioning of habitat (MA, 2005a).

Sustainability: A characteristic or state whereby the needs of the present and local population can be met without compromising the ability of future generations or populations in other locations to meet their needs (MA, 2005a).

Sustainable flow (of ecosystem services): The availability of ecosystem services to yield a continuous benefit to present generations while maintaining its potential to meet the needs and aspirations of future generations (MA, 2005a).

Sustainable use (of ecosystems): Using ecosystems in a way that benefits present generations while maintaining the potential to meet the needs and aspirations of future generations.

Threshold: A point or level at which new properties emerge in an ecological, economic or other system, invalidating predictions based on mathematical relationships that apply at lower levels. For example, species diversity of a landscape may decline steadily with increasing habitat degradation to a certain point, then fall sharply after a critical threshold of degradation is reached. Human behaviour, especially at group levels, sometimes exhibits threshold effects. Thresholds at which irreversible changes occur are especially of concern to decision makers (MA, 2005a).

Total economic value: The value obtained from the various constituents of utilitarian value, including direct use value, indirect use value, option value, quasi-option value and existence value.

Trade-offs: Management choices that intentionally or otherwise change the type, magnitude and relative mix of services provided by ecosystems (MA, 2005a).

Trade-offs of ecosystem services: The way in which one ecosystem service relates to or responds to a change in another ecosystem service.

Travel cost method: A revealed preference valuation method that infers the value of a change in the quality or quantity of a recreational site (e.g. resulting from changes in biodiversity) from estimating the demand function for visiting the site.

Unsustainable use (of ecosystems): Using ecosystems in a way that benefits present generations but negatively impacts on the potential to meet the needs and aspirations of future generations.

Utility: A measure of satisfaction.

Valuation: The process of expressing a value for a particular good or service in a certain context (e.g. decision making) usually in terms of something that can be counted, often money, but also through methods and measures from other disciplines (sociology, ecology and so on) (MA, 2005a).

Value: The contribution of an action or object to user-specified goals, objectives or conditions (MA, 2005a).

Value function transfer: Value functions estimated through valuation applications (travel cost, hedonic pricing, contingent valuation or choice modelling) for a study site are used in conjunction with information on parameter values for the policy site to transfer values.

Viable populations: Organism populations that can survive in the wild.

Vulnerability: Exposure to contingencies and stress, and the difficulty in coping with them. Three major dimensions of vulnerability are involved: exposure to stresses, perturbations and shocks; the sensitivity of people, places, ecosystems and species to the stress or perturbation, including their capacity to anticipate and cope with the stress; and the resilience of the exposed people, places, ecosystems and species in terms of their capacity to absorb shocks and perturbations while maintaining function (MA, 2005a).

Willingness to accept: The minimum amount that a person is willing to receive to give up a good in their possession.

Willingness to pay: The maximum amount that a person is willing to pay for a good they do not have.

References

MA (2005a) *Ecosystems and Human Well-being: Current State and Trends,* Volume 1, Island Press, Washington, DC

MA (2005b) *Ecosystems and Human Well-being: Synthesis,* Island Press, Washington, DC

Spash, C. (2001) 'Deliberative monetary valuation', 5th Nordic Environmental Research Conference, University of Aarhus, Denmark

Introduction

Pushpam Kumar

Coordinator, TEEB Ecological and Economic Foundations, University of Liverpool, UK

The demand for economic analysis of drivers of change and impacts on ecosystems, ecosystem services and biodiversity has never been as profound as it stands now in 2010. Decision makers at all levels are increasingly asking for the rationale for investment in restoration activities and they are willing to embrace economics-based response policies for the management of ecosystem services. The momentum in favour of economic analysis of change in ecosystems has accelerated in recent years owing to factors such as new evidence on declining ecosystem services and its linkages with apparatus such as monetary and fiscal policies of mainstream economic management.

On the one hand, economists have been grappling with the issues of forestry, fisheries, mining and other types of exhaustible and non-exhaustible resources to determine the optimal rate of harvest or extraction at appropriate temporal and spatial scales for quite some time (Faustmann, 1849; Hotelling, 1931; Gordon, 1954). But they were based on single-resource fragmented biological models. On the other, ecologists have also been deriving insights from the science of economics. Recently Tilman et al (2005) used microeconomic theory to study the competition for scarce resources in ecological sciences. In the predominant thinking on the economics of ecosystems and biodiversity, the questions that should be asked are: Why economics? What can economics deliver? and Where can economics fail? Understanding the economics of ecosystems and biodiversity can inform decisions on where to stop and how much to conserve in the world of conflicting choices and competing demands for resources. Alternatively, economics on the margin can help decision makers to evaluate the implications of one further step for either economic activity or conservation goals. Credible and transparent valuations of ecosystem services are useful in this context. Secondly, economics can indicate how indirect drivers are affecting the flow of services from forests, wetlands, marine and other ecosystems. There are many examples where a change in exchange rate has impacted soil erosion (Coxhead and Jaisurya, 1994), and where agricultural subsidies have caused eutrophication of lakes or caused overfishing in the coast. These events are typically obscure to the natural and physical scientists who are quick enough to point out the direct drivers like introduction of species or habitat fragmentation affecting the ecosystem services. Economic tools can be helpful when applied in a positive analytical framework (understanding and predicting outcomes) but it could be quite challenging if the preferred framework is a normative one (evaluating and ranking outcomes). Integration of ecology and economy remains a cornerstone for both the frameworks, although the normative framework may raise issues like why people value nature, the reliability of criteria for valuation and so on (Kumar and Kumar, 2008; Polasky and Segerson, 2009).

Since the 1990s, five influential publications have shaped decision makers' thinking about the whole approach to the economics of ecosystems and biodiversity.

The first was the *Global Biodiversity Assessment* of 1995 (Heywood, 1995). This was a state-of-art analysis of current knowledge and understanding of biodiversity and human intervention. This comprehensive survey, with the help of more than 1000 international experts, focused on biodiversity and its conservation. The report also discussed the economics of biodiversity with special emphasis on valuation methodology (Perrings, 1995). As the name of the report suggests, it could not say much about ecosystems or ecosystem services.

The second was a paper in *Nature*. In 1997 a group of researchers led by Bob Costanza published a paper on economic value of the world's ecosystems (Costanza et al, 1997). Probably for the first time, not only academic researchers but policy makers in general were exposed to the empirical value of the world's ecosystems, which was estimated to be in the range of USD18–33 trillion at the current price. In many senses it was a path-breaking study, as it highlighted the importance of ecosystems in quantified and monetary terms. This valuation study was severely criticized by the economists for its simplistic approach to total economic value (TEV), and its other assumptions were questioned (Arrow, 1997; Toman, 1998; Pearce et al, 2003; Simpson, 2010). Although policy makers came to know the economic value of ecosystems and ecosystem services, they were reluctant to subscribe to the sanctity of the global 'big number'. In a decision-making framework where trade-off is a reality and decisions are guided by the rationale of going one step further in terms of incremental costs and benefits, such global estimates could not provide any clue except creating awareness about the economic importance of ecosystems for the public.

Third, the publication of *Nature's Services: Societal Dependence on Natural Ecosystems* made a significant leap forward in terms of impact on the way ecosystem services should be seen in social and economic contexts (Daily, 1997).

Fourth, a comprehensive assessment of the world's ecosystems – Millennium Ecosystem Assessment (MA) – was made by more than 1300 natural and social scientists from 95 countries. MA nearly provided a final direction on the state and condition of ecosystems. They not only came out with the performance chart for the world's ecosystem and its services but reflected the future scenarios and assessed the response policies in terms of what policies are best suited to manage the ecosystem of the world in a way that human well-being is improved. 'Any progress achieved in addressing the goals of poverty and hunger eradication, improved health, and environmental protection is unlikely to be sustained if most of the ecosystem services on which humanity relies continue to be degraded' (MA, 2005). It specifically stated that the ongoing degradation of ecosystem services is a roadblock to the Millennium Development Goals agreed to by the world leaders at the United Nations in 2000.

Although evidence remains incomplete, there is enough for the experts to warn that the ongoing degradation of 15 of the 24 ecosystem services examined is increasing the likelihood of potentially abrupt changes that will seriously affect human well-being (MA, 2005). This includes the emergence of new diseases, sudden changes in water quality, creation of 'dead zones' along the coasts, the collapse of fisheries, and shifts in regional climate. 'Only by understanding the environment and how it works can we make the necessary decisions to protect it. Only by valuing all our precious natural and human resources can we hope to build a sustainable future,' said Kofi Annan, then secretary general of the United Nations, in a message launching the MA reports. 'The Millennium Ecosystem Assessment is an unprecedented contribution to our global mission for development, sustainability and peace.' Probably the largest ever interdisciplinary assessment orchestrated by the United Nations Environment Programme (UNEP) came out with clear cut findings (summarized below) in its four reports: 'Condition and Trends', 'Scenarios', 'Response Policies' and 'Sub Global Assessment'.

1   Humans have changed ecosystems more rapidly and extensively in the last 50 years than in any other period. This was done largely to meet rapidly growing demands for food, fresh water, timber, fibre and fuel. More land was converted to agriculture since 1945 than in the 18th and 19th centuries combined. More than half of all the synthetic nitrogen fertilizers, first made in 1913, ever used on the planet have been used since 1985. Experts say that this resulted in a substantial and largely irreversible loss in diversity of life on Earth, with some 10 to 30 per cent of the mammal, bird and amphibian species currently threatened with extinction.

2   Ecosystem changes that have contributed substantial net gains in human well-being and economic development have been achieved at growing costs in the form of degradation of other services. Only four ecosystem services have been enhanced in the last 50 years: increases in crop, livestock and aquaculture production, and increased carbon sequestration for global climate regulation. Two services – capture fisheries and fresh water – are now well beyond levels that can sustain current, much less future, demands. Experts say that these problems will substantially diminish the benefits for future generations.

3   The degradation of ecosystem services could grow significantly worse during the first half of this century and is a barrier to achieving the UN Millennium Development Goals. In all the four plausible futures explored by the scientists, they project progress in eliminating hunger, but at far slower rates than needed to halve number of people suffering from hunger by 2015. Experts warn that changes in ecosystems such as deforestation influence the abundance of human pathogens such as malaria and cholera, as well as the risk of emergence of new diseases. Malaria, for example,

accounts for 11 per cent of the disease burden in Africa, and had it been eliminated 35 years ago the continent's gross domestic product would have increased by $100 billion (MA, 2005).

4   The challenge of reversing the degradation of ecosystems while meeting increasing demands can be met under some scenarios involving significant policy and institutional changes. However, these changes will be large and are not currently under way. The report mentions options that exist to conserve or enhance ecosystem services that reduce negative trade-offs or that will positively impact other services. Protection of natural forests, for example, not only conserves wildlife but also supplies fresh water and reduces carbon emissions.

The MA was indeed a pioneering effort and it did its best, considering its mandate and scope. It could not, however, provide a sufficient guide on economic aspects of ecosystem services. Although it provided numerous reasons to carry out economic analysis, it could not make recommendations on scale and unit for accounting and valuation. It somehow struggled for clarity on recommended methodologies for economic valuation in situations of threshold and non-linear changes. In spite of highlighting the impact of indirect drivers like trade and investment, exchange rate and domestic price structure on the flow of ecosystem services, the evidence base to show those relationships was not very strong.

The fifth influential work was published in autumn of 2006, a year after the publication of the MA reports, when the UK treasury came out with the *The Economics of Climate Change: The Stern Review* under the leadership of Lord Nicholas Stern (Stern, 2007). This report, although dealing exclusively with climate change, organized the complexities of trade-offs between costs of action and inaction and conveyed them in an effective language to decision makers.

At the meeting of the G8+5 Environment Ministers in Potsdam, Germany in March 2007, it was proposed that a global study on 'the economic significance of the global loss of biological diversity' should be undertaken as part of a 'Potsdam Initiative' for biodiversity. The proposal was subsequently endorsed by the G8+5 leaders at the Heiligendamm Summit in June 2007. This global study, which was entitled, 'The Economics of Ecosystems and Biodiversity' (TEEB), was initiated by the European Commission (EC) and Germany in 2007. An interim report (TEEB, 2008) of the study was presented at the 9th Conference of the Parties to the Convention on Biological Diversity (CBD COP-9) in Bonn, Germany in May 2008. The interim findings concluded that significant global and local economic costs and human welfare impacts were attributable to the ongoing losses of biodiversity and degradation of ecosystems.

The Interim Report of TEEB was successful in providing a broad foundation where evidence and examples were collated, elements of a biodiversity/ecosystem valuation framework identified, and long-standing issues such as ethics in making economic choices re-emphasized. At the CBD COP-9 meeting, however, delegates pointed out that major scientific challenges still remain to be addressed. They stressed the need for further inputs from the scientific community to elaborate the valuation framework and methodologies used in 'Phase I' of TEEB and further focus on engaging end-users – namely, policy makers, business executives, consumers and local communities.

The purpose of the TEEB is to build on the results of TEEB Phase I with the overarching aim of addressing the continued and rapid decline of biodiversity and degradation of ecosystems at the global level, as documented in the Millennium Ecosystem Assessment. TEEB is producing the following books in Phase II:

1   *The Economics of Ecosystems and Biodiversity: Ecological and Economic Foundations*
2   *The Economics of Ecosystems and Biodiversity in National and International Policy Making*
3   *The Economics of Ecosystems and Biodiversity in Business and Enterprise*
4   *The Economics of Ecosystems and Biodiversity in Local and Regional Policy and Management.*

The current volume discusses the scientific basis of the economics of ecosystems and biodiversity, whereas other TEEB products are dedicated to specific audiences, including policy makers, administrators, business or consumers. 'TEEB Foundations' (this volume) attempts to synthesize the state-of-the-art knowledge on: framing of issues in economic analysis of ecosystem services and biodiversity; relationships among ecosystems, ecosystem services, and biodiversity; indicators for ecosystem services so that these can be made amenable to economic analysis; social and cultural context of economic valuation, recommended methodologies for economic valuation and suggested rates of discount for projects having impacts on ecosystem services and biodiversity.

Chapter 1 summarizes recent developments and describes our TEEB framework, building upon TEEB 2008 to further operationalize the economics of biodiversity and ecosystem services. Each step within the framework roughly coincides with a chapter in the entire TEEB Foundations report.

Chapters 2 and 3 explore the ecological basis of the assessment. Chapter 2 presents our current state of knowledge on the relationships among biodiversity, ecosystems and ecosystem services. It provides an elaboration of relevant ecological concepts, and highlights the uncertainties and risks associated with ecosystem change caused by humans at an ever-increasing pace. Once biodiversity is lost and ecosystems have irreversibly changed, it can be very expensive – and may be impossible – to restore these systems and recover associated ecosystem services.

Chapter 3 provides a review of existing biophysical measures and indicators that are used to quantify and map current knowledge on biodiversity and ecosystem services, including their merits and shortcomings. Research efforts are needed towards better indicators, especially for measuring changes in biodiversity and the provision of services to serve as a basis for economic valuation.

Chapter 4 establishes the basis for a much-needed encompassing of the understanding of valuation, including ecological, economic and social values, before it more specifically discusses the social and cultural contexts of biodiversity and ecosystem service valuation. *Chapter 5* then provides a detailed discussion of the merits, issues and challenges regarding (i) monetary valuation techniques and then (ii) benefits transfer in the context of this assessment. In

Chapter 6, some of the ethical issues for economic valuation are explored, in particular the use and selection of discount rates that have to be critically reconsidered both with respect to ecological uncertainties and distributional equity.

In general, a higher discount rate applied to specific cases will lead to the long-term degradation of biodiversity and ecosystems. However, a low discount rate for the entire economy might favour more investment and growth and more environmental destruction. In terms of the discounting equation, estimates of how well-off those in the future will be is the key factor as to how much we should leave for the future. Policy makers must decide whether to use income or subjective well-being, or some guess about basic needs. A critical factor in discounting is the importance of environmental draw-down (destruction of natural capital) to estimates of g (as GDP growth). The rich and poor differ greatly in their direct dependence on biodiversity and ecosystem services and bear different responsibilities for their protection.

Chapter 7 summarizes the key lessons from ecological and economic foundation and links it with the needs of national-level policy makers. This chapter also identifies the main gaps in knowledge and discusses the future research agenda.

'TEEB Foundations' attempts to clarify some generic confusions about the relationship between ecosystem services, ecosystems and biodiversity, about what is to be valued and what is not, and the context of economic valuation. In TEEB, we consider how the production of ecosystem services confers value on all components of the biosphere, including biodiversity. The value of biodiversity derives from its role in the provision of ecosystem services, and from people's demand for those services. Economists have typically sought to value the individual components of ecosystems or specific services yielded by ecosystems, rather than ecosystems themselves. In most of the cases the potential for markets for ecosystem services and especially for regulating and cultural services is under doubt (Chapter 1 in Kumar and Wood, 2010). And even where markets for specific services do exist, derivation of the value of individual components of ecosystems is hard (Chapter 2 in this volume). There could be a situation where various types of biodiversity provide the same ecosystem service, and in that situation the marginal value of a particular component of biodiversity may be small or insignificant. The marginal value appearing as small may be due to the role of individual species in the ecological functioning which produces small human benefits. They are typically known only for the well studied and highly controlled processes that yield marketed foods, fuels and fibres. Understanding of the economic value of the ecosystem essentially requires exploring and identifying the ecological production function, initial condition and how a small force (driver) changes the flow of services and creates perturbances impacting the constituents and determinants of human well-being. This volume attempts to organize those complexities.

TEEB is not a cost–benefit analysis of 'Spaceship Earth'. It organizes the complexities of economic valuation, suggests the pathways when confronted with situations of non-linear changes, dynamics of ecosystem changes (non-linear), resilience of biodiversity and its loss. TEEB provides enough places for an ethical element in the valuation of ecosystems and biodiversity and embraces methodological pluralism. Instead of ignoring those complexities, TEEB rather acknowledges and organizes them so that decision makers develop credible ways to resolve them and make them acceptable to society in a cost-effective manner. However, TEEB does not intend to contribute to an artificial separation of people and nature further by oversimplifying its meaning and value to human societies. In this balancing act, one hopes valuation approaches will not be taken as panaceas, but as tools which may contribute in the long run to internalize and promote a respect for nature into social life (Chapter 4 in this volume).

References

Arrow, K. J., Bolin, B., Costanza, R., Dasgupta, P., Folke, C., Holling, C. S., Janssen, B.-O., Levin, S., Mäler, K., Perrings, C. and Pimental, D. (1995) 'Economic growth, carrying capacity, and the environment', *Science*, vol 268, pp520–521

Costanza, R., d'Arge, R., Groot, R. de, Farber, S., Grasso, M., Hannon, B., Limburg, K., Naeem, S., O'Neill, R. V., Paruelo, J., Raskin, R. G., Sutton, P. and Belt, M. v. d. (1997) 'The value of the world's ecosystem services and natural capital', *Nature*, vol 387, pp253–260

Coxhead, I. and Jayasurya, S. (1994) 'Technical change in agriculture and land degradation in developing countries: A general equilibrium analysis', *Land Economics*, vol 70, no 1, pp20–37

Daily, G. (1997) *Nature's Services: Societal Dependence on Natural Ecosystems*, Island Press, Washington DC

Faustmann, M. (1849) *On the Determination of the Value Which Forest Land and Immature Stands Possess for Forestry*, English translation in 'Martin Faustmann and the evolution of discounted cash flow' (translated by W. Linnard; with editing and introduction by M. Gane) (1968), Commonwealth Forestry Institute Paper No. 42. University of Oxford, Oxford [Translation republished with permission from Commonwealth Forestry Association in *Journal of Forest Economics*, vol 1, no 1 (1995)]

Gordon, H. (1954) 'The economic theory of a common property resource: The fishery', *Journal of Political Economy*, vol 62, pp124–142

Heywood, V. H. (ed) (1995) *Global Biodiversity Assessment*, Cambridge University Press, Cambridge

Hotelling, H. (1931) 'The theory of exhaustible resources', *Journal of Political Economy*, vol 39, no 2, pp137–175

Kumar, M. and Kumar, P. (2008) 'Valuation of ecosystem services: Psychological and cultural perspective', *Ecological Economics*, vol 64, no 4, pp808–819

Kumar, P. and Wood, M. D. (eds) (2010) *Valuation of Regulating Services: Theory and Applications*, Routledge, London

MA (2005) *Ecosystems and Human Well-being: Findings from the Conditions and Trends Working Group*, Island Press, Washington, DC

Pearce, D. W., Groom, B., Hepburn, C. and Koundouri, C. (2003) 'Valuing the future: Recent advances in social discounting', *World Economics*, vol 4, pp121–141

Perrings, C. (1995) 'Economics of biodiversity', in V. H. Heywood (ed) *Global Biodiversity Assessment*, Cambridge University Press, Cambridge

Polasky, S. and Segerson, K. (2009) 'Integrating ecology and economics in the study of ecosystem services: Some lessons learned', *Annual Review of Resource Economics*, vol 1, pp409–434

Simpson, D. (2010) 'The "Ecosystem Service Framework": A critical assessment', in P. Kumar and M. D. Wood (eds) *Valuation of Regulating Services: Theory and Applications*, Routledge, London

Stern, N. H. (2007) *The Economics of Climate Change: The Stern Review*, Cambridge University Press, Cambridge

The Economics of Ecosystems and Biodiversity (TEEB) (2008) 'Interim report', European Communities, Brussels.

TEEB in National Policy (2011) The Economics of Ecosystems and Biodiversity in National and International Policy Making (ed Patrick ten Brink), Earthscan, London

Tilman, D., Polasky, S. and Lehman, C. (2005) 'Diversity, productivity and temporal stability in the economies of humans and nature', *J. Environ. Econ. Manag.*, vol 49, pp405–426

Toman, M. (1998) 'Why not to calculate the value of the world's ecosystem services and natural capital', *Ecol. Econ.*, vol 25, pp57–60

Chapter 1

Integrating the Ecological and Economic Dimensions in Biodiversity and Ecosystem Service Valuation

Coordinating lead author
Rudolf de Groot

Lead authors
Brendan Fisher, Mike Christie

Contributing authors
James Aronson, Leon Braat, John Gowdy, Roy Haines-Young,
Edward Maltby, Aude Neuville, Stephen Polasky,
Rosimeiry Portela, Irene Ring

Reviewers
James Blignaut, Eduardo Brondízio, Robert Costanza, Kurt Jax,
Gopal K. Kadekodi, Peter H. May, Jeffrey A. McNeely,
Stanislav Shmelev

Review editor
Gopal K. Kadekodi

Contents

Key messages   11

1   Introduction   12

2   Review of existing frameworks linking ecology and economics   13
     2.1   Ecosystem services: Early developments and recent frameworks   13
     2.2   The TEEB Interim Report and further recent frameworks   15
     2.3   Defining ecosystem functions, services and benefits   16
            2.3.1   From biophysical structure and process to
                     ecosystem services and benefits   18
            2.3.2   From ecosystem services to (economic) value   19

3   TEEB-conceptual framework   21
     3.1   Ecosystem structure, processes and functions   24
     3.2   Typology of ecosystem services   25
     3.3   Human well-being: Typology of benefits and values   27
            3.3.1   Ecological benefits and values   28
            3.3.2   Socio-cultural benefits and values   28
            3.3.3   Economic benefits and values   28
     3.4   Governance and decision making   29
     3.5   Scenarios and drivers of change   31
     3.6   Linking ecosystem service values to decision making:
            The TEEB guidance reports   32

References   33

Annex 1 Classification of ecosystems used in TEEB   38

Annex 2 Ecosystem service classification: Brief literature survey
        and TEEB classification   39

Key messages

- Linking biophysical aspects of ecosystems with human benefits through the notion of ecosystem services is essential to assess the trade-offs (ecological, socio-cultural, economic and monetary) involved in the loss of ecosystems and biodiversity in a clear and consistent manner.

- Any ecosystem assessment should be spatially and temporally explicit at scales meaningful for policy formation or interventions, inherently acknowledging that both ecological functioning and economic values are context, space and time specific.

- Any ecosystem assessment should first aim to determine the service delivery in biophysical terms, to provide solid ecological underpinning to the economic valuation or measurement with alternative metrics.

- Clearly delineating between functions, services and benefits is important to make ecosystem assessments more accessible to economic valuation, although no consensus has yet been reached on the classification.

- Ecosystem assessments should be set within the context of contrasting scenarios – recognizing that both the values of ecosystem services and the costs of actions can be best measured as a function of changes between alternative options.

- In assessing trade-offs between alternative uses of ecosystems, the total bundle of ecosystem services provided by different conversion and management states should be included.

- Any valuation study should be fully aware of the 'cost' side of the equation, as focus on benefits only ignores important societal costs like missed opportunities of alternative uses; this also allows for a more extensive range of societal values to be considered.

- Ecosystem assessments should integrate an analysis of risks and uncertainties, acknowledging the limitations of knowledge on the impacts of human actions on ecosystems and their services and on their importance to human well-being.

- In order to improve incentive structures and institutions, the different stakeholders – that is, the beneficiaries of ecosystem services, those who are providing the services, those involved in or affected by the use, and the actors involved at different levels of decision-making – should be clearly identified, and decision-making processes need to be transparent.

1 Introduction

In spite of the growing awareness of the importance of ecosystems and biodiversity to human welfare, loss of biodiversity and degradation of ecosystems still continue on a large scale. Fundamental changes are needed in the way biodiversity, ecosystems and their services are viewed and valued by society. A major difficulty is that many ecosystem[1] services[2] are (mixed) public goods, and use levels are therefore difficult to regulate, even when they are at or near the point of exhaustion. Although many people benefit from ecosystem services, individuals or groups usually have insufficient incentives to maintain ecosystems for continued provisioning of services. For example, open access fisheries provide valuable harvests but often suffer from over-exploitation that leads to decline in fish populations and lowered future harvests.

The problems of management and governance of ecosystems stem from both poor information and institutional failures. In some cases, knowledge is lacking about the contribution of ecosystem processes and biodiversity to human welfare and how human actions lead to environmental change with impacts on human welfare. In other cases institutions, notably markets, provide the wrong incentives.

These two types of failures, and the complex dynamics between the ecology–economy interface, often lead to large-scale and persistent degradation of the natural environment and accelerating loss of ecosystem services and biodiversity. Given the large scale of human activities on the planet, the point has been reached where the cumulative losses in ecosystem services are forcing society to rethink how to incorporate the value of these services into societal decision making.

The release of the Millennium Ecosystem Assessment (MA, 2005a) helped foster use of the concept of ecosystem services by policy makers and the business community. However, progress in its practical application in land-use planning and decision making has been slow (e.g. Naidoo et al, 2008; Daily et al, 2009).

This lack of progress stems not only from failures of markets and systems of economic analysis and accounting (notably GDP) to capture values of ecosystem services, but also from our limited understanding of: (a) how different services are interlinked with each other and to the various components of ecosystem functioning and the role of biodiversity; (b) how different human actions that affect ecosystems change the provision of ecosystem services; (c) the potential trade-offs among services; (d) the influence of differences in temporal and spatial scales on demand and supply of services; and (e) what kind of governance and institutions are best able to ensure biodiversity conservation and the sustainable flow of ecosystem services in the long term.

Without changes in institutions and incentives, further declines in natural capital are likely, as those who gain from actions that deplete natural capital will continue to avoid paying the full costs of their actions and pass these costs to poor societies and future generations (Srinivasan et al, 2008). Although such estimations are fraught with difficulties, it can be argued that the cumulative loss of 'natural capital' (see further) over the past decades has cost, and still costs, the global community large sums of money in terms of damage, repair and replacement costs (Bartelmus, 2009).

One of the aims of the TEEB study is to provide more and better data and understanding of the (economic) significance of these losses and the consequences of policy inaction on halting biodiversity loss at various scales (global, regional and local). Although emphasis is on the economic, notably monetary, effects of the loss of ecosystem services, TEEB will give due attention to the underlying changes in ecological 'values' (ecosystem integrity and life-support functions) and socio-cultural implications.

2 Review of existing frameworks linking ecology and economics

Over the past few decades many attempts have been made to systematically link the functioning of ecosystems with human well-being. Central elements in this 'link' are the intertwined notions of natural capital 'stocks' and the ecosystem services that flow like interest or dividends from those stocks. According to the Millennium Ecosystem Assessment (MA, 2005a), natural capital is 'an economic metaphor for the limited stocks of physical and biological resources found on earth'. The continuing depletion and degradation of natural capital has generated concerns and debate over the capacity of the economic system to substitute for these losses with human-made capital, and the conditions for sustainable development, defined as non-declining welfare over generations (Pearce et al, 1989; Pezzey, 1992). While the degree of substitutability is ultimately an empirical question, it is generally recognized that substitution has limits (Barbier, 1994; Daly, 1996; Prugh et al, 1999; Daly and Farley, 2004), and that a critical amount of natural capital has to be preserved (see also Chapters 4, 5 and 6 for the implications of this debate for the TEEB study).

This section provides a brief overview of the development of the theory and practice of ecosystem functions and services and discusses some key insights and challenges from the literature and the TEEB Interim Report (2008).

2.1 Ecosystem services: Early developments and recent frameworks

Thinking about people–environment interactions and their effects on human welfare stretches back centuries and includes writings from Roman times on the increase in population and decline in what we now call ecosystem services (Johnson, 2000). Early modern writers on the subject include Marsh (1874), Leopold (1949), Carson (1962) and Krutilla and Fisher (1975) to mention but a few. In 1977, Westman published a paper in *Science* examining the link between ecological and economic systems entitled 'How much are nature's services worth?' (Westman, 1977). Ehrlich and Ehrlich (1981) later coined the term 'ecosystem services' and in the following decade ecologists and economists further elaborated the notion of ecosystems as life-support systems, providers of ecosystem services and economic benefits (see, for example, Hueting, 1980; Ehrlich and Mooney, 1983; De Groot, 1987; Odum, 1989; Folke et al, 1991; De Groot, 1992). But it was not until the late 1990s that the concept got widespread attention with the publications by Costanza et al (1997) and Daily (1997). At the same time, the interdisciplinary field of ecological economics developed the concept of natural capital (Costanza and Daly, 1992; Jansson et al, 1994; Dasgupta et al, 2000), which includes non-renewable resources, renewable resources and ecosystem services, to demonstrate the significance of ecosystems as providing the biophysical foundation for societal development and all human economies (Common and Perrings, 1992; Arrow et al, 1995). In an attempt to facilitate discussion and systematic analysis of ecosystem services, De Groot et al (2002) created a classification system specifying the relationship between, and transitions from ecosystem processes and components, and their transition to goods and services.

Based on these and other studies,[3] the Millennium Ecosystem Assessment (MA, 2005a) recognized four categories of services: supporting (e.g. nutrient cycling, soil formation and primary production); provisioning (e.g. food, fresh water, wood, fibre and fuel); regulating (e.g. climate regulation, flood and disease regulation and water purification); and cultural (aesthetic, spiritual, educational and recreational) (see Figure 1.1).

The introduction of the concept of ecosystem services on the global agenda by the MA provides an important bridge between the imperatives of

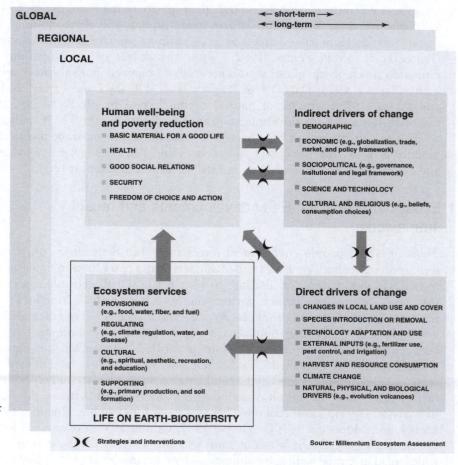

Figure 1.1 *MA conceptual framework: Linking ecosystem services and human well-being*

Source: MA (2005a)

maintaining biodiversity and the challenges in meeting the Millennium Development Goals.

2.2 The TEEB Interim Report and further recent frameworks

The Millennium Assessment, purposely, did not pay much attention to the economics of ecosystem change and in the preparation phase of the TEEB study (TEEB, 2008) a framework was therefore proposed (see Figure 1.2) for articulating the ecological and economic aspects of the analysis necessary for the valuation of biodiversity loss and ecosystem degradation (Balmford et al, 2008).

This scheme stresses the need to rely on counterfactual scenarios that differ through specific actions aimed at addressing the main drivers of loss. Changes in the delivery of services need first to be estimated and mapped in biophysical terms, which requires a sufficient understanding of the factors that drive their production and how they are affected by the actions put in place. Economic valuation should then be applied to the changes in services, which requires a good understanding of the service flows and of the determinants of demand.

Being spatially explicit is important in order to take into account the spatial heterogeneity of service flows and of the economic values that can be assigned to them, as well as the variability of conservation costs. It also allows the identification of mismatches of scales as well as analysing the distributional implications of decisions that affect ecosystems, and exploring trade-offs.

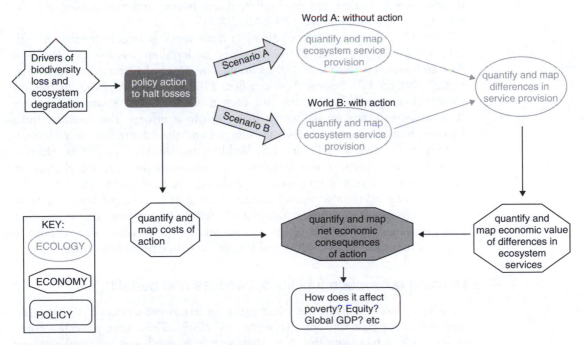

Figure 1.2 *An economic valuation framework: Contrasting states of the world*

Source: Modified after Balmford et al (2008) and TEEB (2008)

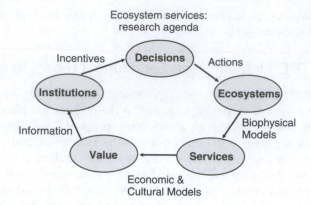

Figure 1.3 *Ecosystem services: Research agenda*

Source: Daily et al (2009)

Marginal valuation in economic thinking assumes substitutability between services and is therefore only applicable within certain ecological limitations, requiring that no irreversible ecosystem changes occur (see Chapters 2 and 4 for more detail). Next to these ecological limitations, socio-cultural considerations may delimit the range of valid cases for marginal valuation (Turner et al, 2003). Therefore, any valuation of biodiversity and ecosystem services needs to take account of the range of ecological and socio-cultural values that are not covered by economic valuation, but need different approaches and methodologies to be reflected in decision making (EPA-SAB, 2009).

The TEEB Interim report's valuation framework is largely consistent with others recently proposed in the analysis undertaken by the US National Research Council (NRC, 2005), including the Natural Capital Project (Daily et al, 2009), the EPA Science Advisory Board (EPA-SAB, 2009), Valuing the Arc (Mwakalila et al, 2009) and the French Council for Strategic Analysis (Chevassus-au-Louis et al, 2009). In all of these efforts, the essential links between human actions, ecosystems, services and their contributions to human welfare are shown (see Figure 1.3, building on Daily et al, 2009). Human decisions lead to actions that have impacts on ecosystems, causing changes in ecosystem structure and function. These changes in turn lead to changes in the provision of ecosystem services. Changes in ecosystem services have impacts on human welfare. A clear understanding of these links can provide information that can lead to the reform of institutions and better decisions that ultimately improve the state of ecosystems and the services they provide to society.

2.3 Defining ecosystem functions, services and benefits

Research efforts regarding the investigation of ecosystem services have increased strongly in the past ten years (Fisher et al, 2009). They have provided much insight in how to ensure that ecosystem service research is scientifically robust and credible, and also conveys a clear message to decision makers in both the public and private sectors.

In spite of the work done so far, there is still much debate about definitions and classifications (e.g. Daily, 1997; Boyd and Banzhaf, 2007; Costanza, 2008; Fisher and Turner, 2008; Wallace, 2008; Fisher et al, 2009; Granek et al, 2009) and perhaps we should accept that no final classification can capture the myriad of ways in which ecosystems support human life and contribute to human well-being. Yet for a global assessment like TEEB, it is essential to be clear about the terminology and classifications used. When dealing with complex relationships like coupled social–ecological systems, we need a rich language to describe their different features and interactions. While accepting that no fundamental categories or completely unambiguous definitions exist for such complex systems, and that any systematization is open to debate, it is still important to be clear about the meaning of the core terms used.

Figure 1.4 gives a schematic representation of the way TEEB proposes to disentangle the pathway from ecosystems and biodiversity to human well-being. A central concept in this diagram is the notion of (ecosystem) service which the MA defined simply as 'the benefits humans derive from nature' (MA, 2005a).

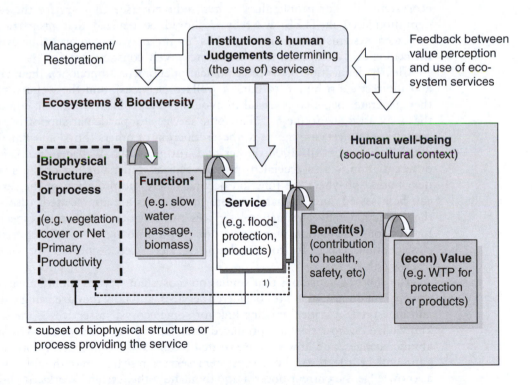

Figure 1.4 *The pathway from ecosystem structure and processes to human well-being*

Note: 1) One function is usually involved in the provision of several services and the use of services usually affects the underlying biophysical structures and processes in multiple ways. Ecosystem service assessments should take these feedback-loops into account.

Source: Adapted from Haines-Young and Potschin (2010) and Maltby (2009)

2.3.1 From biophysical structure and process to ecosystem services and benefits

As Figure 1.4 shows, a lot goes on before services and benefits are provided, and decision makers need to understand what this involves. It is therefore helpful to distinguish 'functions' from the even deeper ecological structures and processes in the sense that the functions represent the *potential* that ecosystems have to deliver a service which in turn depends on ecological structure and processes. For example, primary production (= process) is needed to maintain a viable fish population (= function) which can be used (harvested) to provide food (= service); nutrient cycling (= process) is needed for water purification (= function) to provide clean water (= provisioning service).[4] The benefits of these services are manifold. For example, food provides nutrition but also pleasure and sometimes even social identity (as part of cultural traditions); clean water can be used for drinking but also for swimming (pleasure) and other activities aimed at satisfying needs and wants. Thus, the role of woodlands in slowing the passage of water through a catchment is a function which has the potential of delivering a service (water flow regulation → reduced flood risk) if some beneficiary exists to enjoy the benefit (safety).

Services are actually conceptualizations ('labels') of the 'useful things' ecosystems 'do' for people, directly *and* indirectly (see Glossary for the exact definition used in TEEB) whereby it should be realized that properties of ecological systems that people regard as 'useful' may change over time even if the ecological system itself remains in a relatively constant state.

Clearly delineating between ecological phenomena (functions), their direct and indirect contribution to human welfare (services), and the welfare gains they generate (benefits) is useful in avoiding the problem of double counting that may arise due to the fact that some services (in particular supporting and regulating services) are inputs to the production of others (Boyd and Banzhaf, 2007; Balmford et al, 2008; Fisher and Turner, 2008; Wallace, 2008). Such differentiation is also crucial to provide a clear understanding of the spatial distribution of where the function occurs, where the provision of the service can be assessed, and ultimately where the benefits are appreciated. Although the distinction between functions, services and benefits is important, especially for economic valuation, it often is not possible to make a fully consistent classification, especially for regulating services (see Section 3 for further discussion).

The short conclusion is that studies on ecosystem services should always be transparent on just what are considered services, and how they are being valued and measured. A critical missing link for some ecosystem services is the scant knowledge on how they are produced and maintained, affected by system or abiotic changes, and how they are related to levels of biodiversity. Information gaps will be rife throughout ecosystem service research and should always acknowledge the current uncertainty about how the 'system' works. It should also be realized that many people benefit from ecosystem services without realizing it, and thus fail to appreciate their value (importance). To make the dependence of human well-being on ecosystem services more clear, valuation studies should therefore not only include direct benefits (direct use values) but take due account of all the indirect benefits (indirect use values) and non-use values derived from ecosystem services.

Another issue is how to deal with potential benefits or the 'likelihood of (future) use', e.g. currently functions like wildlife (as potential food source), water purification (keeping rivers clean) or attractive scenery in a remote area may not be used but may have great (economic) potential for future use. Finally, it should also be recognized that ecosystems may provide *disservices* – for example, when they facilitate reproduction and dispersal of species that damage crops or human health.[5] In trade-off analysis, these disservices must be considered and, ultimately, the notion of benefits and 'dis-benefits' should be looked at within a consistent ecosystem accounting framework (e.g. EEA, 2010).

2.3.2 From ecosystem services to (economic) value

Since the functioning of ecosystems and their services affect so many aspects of human welfare, a broad set of indicators can and should be used to measure the magnitude ('value') of their impact. As with the interpretation of the terms 'function', 'service' and 'benefits' (see above), much debate still surrounds the use of the term 'value' in assessing the benefits of ecosystems to human well-being. The Oxford English Dictionary defines value as 'the worth, usefulness, importance of something'. The Millennium Ecosystem Assessment defined value as 'the contribution of an action or object to user-specified goals, objectives, or conditions' (after Farber et al, 2002), the measurement of which could include any kind of metric from the various scientific disciplines, for example ecology, sociology, economics (MA, 2003).

In economics, 'value' is always associated with trade-offs – that is, something only has (economic) value if we are willing to give up something in order to get or enjoy it. The common metric in economics is monetary valuation and some critics say the reliance on this metric has plagued many ecosystem service assessments, failing to incorporate several types of value that are critical to understanding the relationship between society and nature (e.g. Norgaard et al, 1998; Wilson and Howarth, 2002; MA, 2005a; Christie et al, 2006). See also Box 1.1 and Chapter 4 for further discussion.

In addition to economic valuation, other ways to analyse the importance of ecosystem services include livelihoods assessments, capabilities approaches that emphasize the opportunities available to people to make choices (e.g. Sen, 1993), and vulnerability assessments. Such considerations are necessary for integrating into the analysis some dimensions of human well-being that cannot (or should not) be measured in terms of money, such as freedom of choice, human rights and intrinsic values. They are also important for measuring the services and benefits that are of a cultural and philosophical (spiritual) nature. However, while monetary assessments only partially capture the total importance – that is, value – of ecosystem services, they are vitally important for internalizing so-called externalities in economic accounting procedures and in policies that affect ecosystems, thereby influencing decision making at all levels.

Box 1.1 Neoclassical economics and its discontents (by John Gowdy)

There is a long history of antagonism between traditional neoclassical economists and those advocating a more pluralistic approach to economic theory and policy. The debate has been less fruitful than it might have been because of the failure of many on both sides to be specific as to what is being criticized or defended.

Those of us who are critical of standard economic valuation methods need to be precise in what we are criticizing. The current debates raging in economics over the Stern Review, the current financial crisis, and the significance of the findings of behavioural economics, have shown that the problem with neoclassical economics is not valuation *per se* but with the assumptions of the core Walrasian model (named after the Swiss economist Leon Walras). The purpose of that model is to prove that competitive markets achieve Pareto efficiency, that is, no one can be made better off without making someone else worse off. This is called the First Fundamental Theorem of Welfare Economics. That proof does not work unless economic agents (firms and consumers) act independently of each other. That is, my economic decisions are based on self-regarding preferences and my decisions are in no way affected by how others think, behave or how much they have. Likewise, the production and pricing decisions of one firm are independent of the actions of other firms. The independence assumption has been falsified by thousands of empirical tests. It does not make good predictions of real economic behaviour and offers a poor guide for economic policy. We need to replace 'rational economic man' with a science-based model of human behaviour, and the model of the perfectly competitive firm with one that includes competitive institutions, cultural norms and biophysical transformations. The characterization of consumers and firms in the Walrasian model is driven by the mathematical requirements of constrained optimization and has little to do with real-world economic behaviour.

But this doesn't mean that markets are always inefficient or that prices have no meaning. It simply means that economic policy debates need to be decided on the basis of merit and evidence, not arbitrary equations or lines on a piece of paper. The effect of minimum wage laws is a good example. It's easy to 'prove' that they raise the unemployment rate by drawing a simple graph. But the real-world evidence is much more complicated.

Economists frequently use a kind of 'bait and switch' technique to justify their models. We begin with the proposition that 'people do the best they can with the limited means at their disposal', which is reasonable. But in the Walrasian framework this becomes 'People with well-defined, stable and self-regarding preferences maximize a smooth and continuous single-valued function that is twice differentiable...', and so on. Using the mathematical relationships in this model we can calculate shadow prices for items such as natural resources, elasticities of substitution, and total factor productivity. But it is not clear whether these estimates are based on empirical evidence or by the mathematical assumptions used to calculate them.

Regarding discounting future costs and benefits, we can reasonably say that individuals in general would rather have something now than in the distant future (but not always). But that is not the same as using a single precise discount rate number to value everything from biodiversity loss to the effects of climate change decades or even centuries in the future.

If we discard the straitjacket of Walrasian mathematics we can begin to sort out what can be priced, what can be measured without prices, and what cannot be measured at all but still valued.

3 TEEB-conceptual framework

Following the considerations discussed in Section 2, and building upon the work done in the TEEB preparation phase, this section presents the framework adopted for the TEEB study, which also forms the 'backbone' for the subsequent chapters in this book (Figure 1.5).

To analyse the 'Economics of Ecosystems and Biodiversity' a practical and consistent definition and typology of ecosystems (and biodiversity) is essential. In the TEEB assessment, we largely follow the definitions of the United Nations'

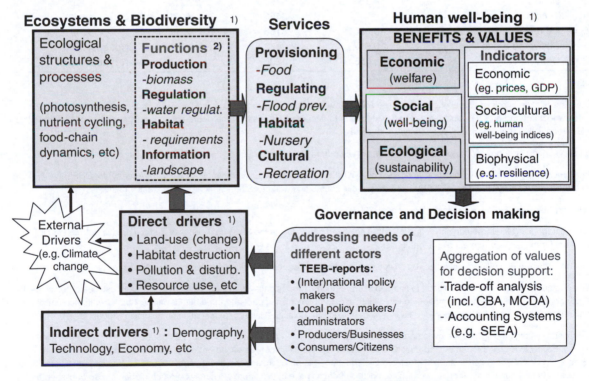

Figure 1.5 *TEEB Conceptual framework for linking ecosystems and human well-being*

Notes: 1) The four bold-lined boxes coincide with the overall MA-Framework.

2) subset of ecosystem processes & components that is directly involved in providing the service.

Table 1.1 Classification of main biomes in TEEB and remaining surface area

Biome type[a]	Surface area remaining (in 1000km²)[f]			Of which in more or less natural state[c]
	MODIS LC 2005[b]	Global cover 2005[b]	Land cover in 2000[c]	
1 Marine / open ocean	416,546			10–15%[g]
2 Coastal systems				40%[h]
3 Wetlands		1799		? %[i]
4 Lakes & rivers		6713		? %[i]
5 Forests	28,936	46,652		
Wooded tundra			2596	93%
Boreal forest			17,611	85%
Cool coniferous forest			3130	72%
Temperate mixed forest			5914	49%
Temp. deciduous forest			4718	43%
Warm mixed forest			5835	52%
Tropical forest			9149	76%
6 Woodland & shrubland	35,829	9766	7870	67%
			8773	44%
Mediterranean shrub[e]			1741	38%
7 Grass & rangeland[d]	23,883	8879	19,056	50%
Savanna only[e]			15,604	57%
8 Desert	18,154	34,753	22,174	83%
9 Tundra		6453	6375	94%
10 Ice/rock/polar	15,930	3166	2290	100%
11 Cultivated areas	20,617	26,472		Not applicable
12 Urban areas	656	336		Not applicable

Notes:

a This classification is based on various sources (see Annex 1, which also gives a more detailed list of ecosystems for each biome). The forest, woodland and grassland biomes are subdivided here to accommodate data on the degree of human impact (last column) and this subdivision is therefore not completely identical with Annex 1.

b Data on surface area provided by Rosimeiry Portela, with help from Marc Steininger and Fabiano Godoy, all Conservation International.

c Data provided by Leon Braat, based on work done by PBL/NEEA (Netherlands Environmental Assessment Agency) for COPI-I on terrestrial systems only (Braat et al, 2008). According to this source, the world total terrestrial area is 132,836,113km².

d Including Steppe in PBL/NEEA data set (Braat et al, 2008).

e These categories (Mediterranean shrub and savanna) are listed separately in the RIVM data set; their surface area is *not* included in sum-total for the respective main biome categories.

f Data on surface areas differ substantially by source due to different interpretations of biome (land cover) classes.

g Data on aquatic systems is more difficult to find and interpret than for terrestrial systems, but Halpern et al (2008) estimated that at least 40 per cent of ocean systems are medium to very highly affected by human impact and the other 60 per cent face low to medium impact. Only 10–15 per cent can be considered to be in a more or less pristine state (Halpern, personal communication, August 2009).

h For coastal systems the figures are even harder to estimate, but according to Halpern et al (2009) 60 per cent of the global coastline experience low to high impact from land-based human activities. This estimate was based on four of the most pervasive land-based impacts on coastal ecosystems: nutrient input; organic and inorganic pollution; and the direct impact of coastal human populations. If we add ocean-based human impact (i.e. over-fishing, pollution from ships, etc) this figure will surely be much higher: a map published by UNEP (http://maps.grida.no/go/graphic/trends-in-sea-level-1870-2006) shows that only about 40 per cent of the coasts face 'little or no' impact from human actions.

i For wetlands, rivers and lakes, no reliable (global) data were found in this phase of the TEEB study but it will be attempted to further verify and complete this table in the coming months.

1992 Convention on Biological Diversity. Thus we see an *ecosystem* as the complex of living organisms and the abiotic environment with which they interact at a specified location. *Biodiversity* is the sum total of organisms including their genetic diversity and the way in which they fit together into communities and ecosystems (see Glossary for exact wording).

Based on various sources, TEEB proposes a typology of 12 main *biomes* (see Table 1.1), subdivided into a much larger number of ecosystem types (see Annex 1).

As Table 1.1 indicates, most of the biomes and associated ecosystems have been converted to human-dominated systems (agriculture, aquaculture, plantations, etc) to a greater or lesser extent (on average approximately one-third of the area) or are otherwise affected by human activity, for example through over-exploitation and pollution of marine systems and damming of rivers. Thus, 'biomes' or other ecology-based land categories have actually become a 'construct' (e.g. Kareiva et al, 2007; Ellis and Ramankutty, 2008). Because of the predominance of so-called 'socio-ecological mosaics' (i.e. a patchwork of landscape units that range from intensively managed to unmanaged areas, all within the same landscape), fine-grained spatial analysis should be a core of any ecosystem service assessment (see Box 1.2).

Box 1.2 Spatial explicitness and scale

A major critique of early ecosystem service valuation work was the rudimentary treatment of ecological systems at the scale of biomes, and the extrapolation of site-specific values across the entire globe (Bockstael et al, 2000; Naidoo et al, 2008). At the other end of the spectrum, the utility of plot-scale experiments for policy formation is questionable. Recognizing this trade-off, advanced research in ecosystem services has focused on spatially explicit economic and ecological models, moving away from standard look-up tables assuming constant marginal values and utilizing benefit transfer based on ecosystem type (Bateman et al, 2002; Naidoo and Ricketts, 2006; Barbier et al, 2008; Polasky et al, 2008; Nelson et al, 2009).

Working at both ecologically understandable and policy-relevant scales also allows researchers to more fully understand the values and perceptions of the relevant stakeholders (Hein et al, 2006; Fisher et al, 2008; Granek et al, 2009). Another major reason why spatial explicitness is important is that the production and use of services from ecosystems vary spatially, as along with the economic benefits they generate (many of which are local in nature), and of course the costs of action, so it matters to human well-being where conservation actions are implemented. A spatially explicit assessment of the impacts of action and quantification of benefits and costs is also helpful to show the possible mismatch between the ecological and socio-economic scales of decision making, service provision and use, and between winners and losers in different scenarios. It is thus essential for designing effective and equitable policy interventions (Balmford et al, 2008).

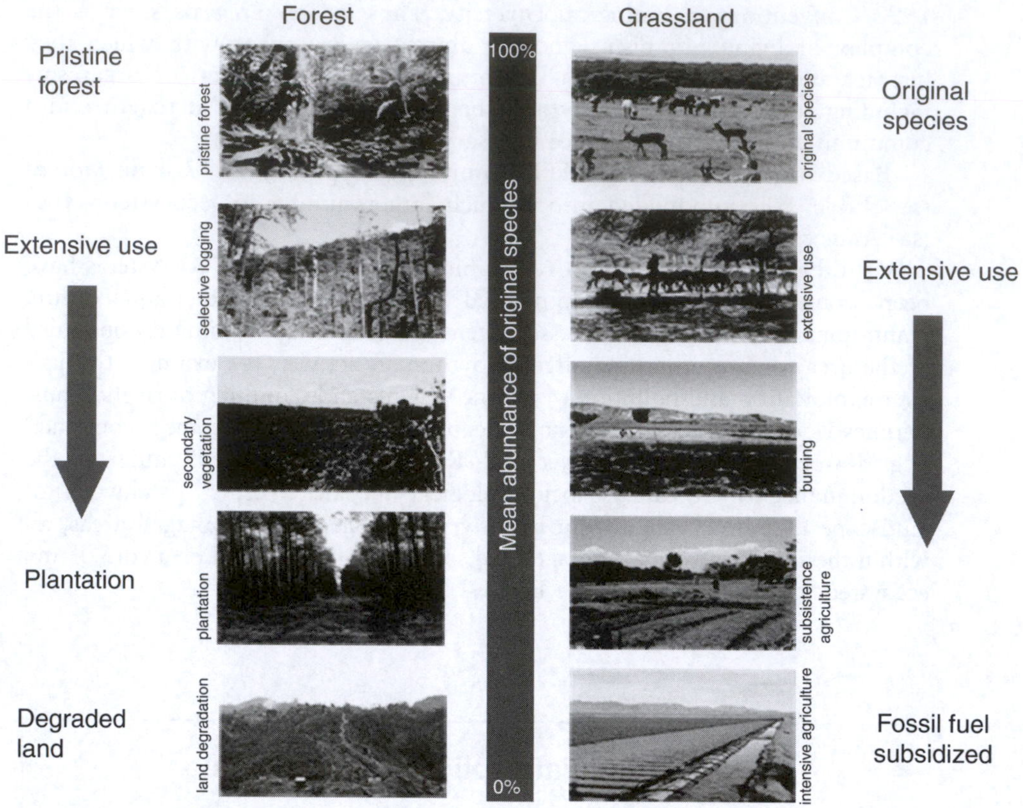

Figure 1.6 *Two examples of degradation pathways showing transition phases between natural and human-dominated (eco)systems*

Source: Braat et al (2008)

In trade-off analysis of land-use change, ideally the costs and benefits of the transitions, and all or at least the main intermediate states (see Figure 1.6), should be based on the economic value of the total bundle of services provided by each transition or management state. This level of detail is impossible within this phase of the TEEB assessment, both for time limitations and given the paucity of studies that compare the provision of services by an ecosystem under alternative management states (Balmford et al, 2002; ICSU-UNESCO-UNU, 2008), but it should be a high priority subject for follow-up studies.

The recognition of tangible ecological or physical boundaries of ecosystems, however arbitrary it may sometimes be, provides an important basis for adaptive and practical management through the mapping of particular functions and landscape units, or even so-called 'service-providing units' (see Chapter 2).

3.1 Ecosystem structure, processes and functions

The TEEB framework (Figure 1.5) starts with the upper left-hand box which distinguishes ecosystem structure, processes and functions. *Ecosystem functions* are defined as a subset of the interactions between ecosystem structure and processes that underpin the capacity of an ecosystem to provide goods and services. The building blocks of ecosystem functions are the interactions between structure and processes, which may be physical (e.g. infiltration of water, sediment movement), chemical (e.g. reduction, oxidation) or biological (e.g. photosynthesis and denitrification), whereby 'biodiversity' is more or less involved in all of them, although the precise detail of the relationship is often unclear or limited (see Chapter 2).

The fundamental challenge is the extent to which it is possible to fully predict the actual functioning of any defined ecosystem unit when relatively few (and rarely replicated) studies worldwide are available. It is often necessary to rely on various combinations of seemingly appropriate indicators of ecosystem condition and function (see Chapter 3) which can in theory be applied more generally than in just individual cases.

3.2 Typology of ecosystem services

Ecosystem services are defined in TEEB as 'the direct and indirect contributions of ecosystems to human well-being'. This basically follows the MA definition except that it makes a finer distinction between services and benefits and explicitly acknowledges that services can benefit people in multiple and indirect ways (see Section 3.3 for a more detailed discussion).

Based on the TEEB preparatory phase and other assessments and meta-analysis (see Section 2), TEEB proposes a typology of 22 ecosystem services divided into four main categories: provisioning, regulating, habitat, and cultural and amenity services, mainly following the MA classification (see Table 1.2 and Annex 2 for a more detailed list and comparison with the main literature).

An important difference we adopt here, as compared to the MA, is the omission of Supporting Services such as nutrient cycling and food-chain dynamics, which are seen in TEEB as a subset of ecological processes. Instead, the Habitat Service has been identified as a separate category to highlight the importance of ecosystems to provide habitat for migratory species (e.g. as nurseries) and gene-pool 'protectors' (e.g. natural habitats allowing natural selection processes to maintain the vitality of the gene pool). The availability of these services is directly dependent on the state of the habitat (habitat requirements) providing the service. In case commercial species are involved, such as fish and shrimp species that spawn in mangrove systems (= nursery service) but of which the adults are caught far away, this service has an economic (monetary) value in its own right. Also the importance of the gene-pool protection service of ecosystems is increasingly recognized, both as 'hot spots' for conservation (in which money is increasingly invested) and to maintain the original gene-pool of commercial species. Mankind is increasingly trying to imitate this service through the creation of botanic gardens, zoos and gene banks, at high cost.

Before economic valuation can be applied, the performance or availability of ecosystem services has to be measured in biophysical terms (see Chapters 2 and 3). In some cases the state of ecological knowledge and the data availability allow using some direct measures of services, while in other cases it is necessary to make use of proxies.

Table 1.2 Typology of ecosystem services in TEEB

	Main service types
	PROVISIONING SERVICES
1	**Food** (e.g. fish, game, fruit)
2	**Water** (e.g. for drinking, irrigation, cooling)
3	**Raw materials** (e.g. fibre, timber, fuelwood, fodder, fertilizer)
4	**Genetic resources** (e.g. for crop-improvement and medicinal purposes)
5	**Medicinal resources** (e.g. biochemical products, models and test-organisms)
6	**Ornamental resources** (e.g. artisan work, decorative plants, pet animals, fashion)
	REGULATING SERVICES
7	**Air quality regulation** (e.g. capturing (fine) dust, chemicals, etc.)
8	**Climate regulation** (incl. C-sequestration, influence of vegetation on rainfall, etc.)
9	**Moderation of extreme events** (e.g. storm protection and flood prevention)
10	**Regulation of water flows** (e.g. natural drainage, irrigation and drought prevention)
11	**Waste treatment** (especially water purification)
12	**Erosion prevention**
13	**Maintenance of soil fertility (incl. soil formation) and nutrient cycling**
14	**Pollination**
15	**Biological control** (e.g. seed dispersal, pest and disease control)
	HABITAT SERVICES
16	**Maintenance of life cycles of migratory species** (incl. nursery service)
17	**Maintenance of genetic diversity** (especially through gene pool protection)
	CULTURAL and AMENITY SERVICES
18	**Aesthetic information**
19	**Opportunities for recreation and tourism**
20	**Inspiration for culture, art and design**
21	**Spiritual experience**
22	**Information for cognitive development**

Source: Based on/adapted (mainly) from Costanza et al (1997), De Groot et al (2002), MA (2005a), Daily et al (2009). See Annex 2 for details

Actual measurements of ecosystem services should be split into (a) the capacity of an ecosystem to provide a service (e.g. how much fish can a lake provide on a sustainable basis), and (b) the actual use of that service (e.g. fish harvesting for food or for use in industrial processing). Measurement of the importance (value) of that fish in terms of nutrition value, a source of income and/or way of life is then part of the 'human value domain'.

When applying valuation, it is necessary to clearly distinguish between potential and actual use of services with direct use value (notably provisioning and some cultural services), and services that have indirect use (notably regulating, habitat and some services). Since most ecosystems provide a bundle of services, and the use of one service often affects the availability of other services, (economic) valuation should consider not only (marginal) values from the flows of individual services but also take due account of the 'stock value' (i.e. the entire ecosystem) providing the total bundle of services.[6] When applying economic valuation the actual management regime of the ecosystem (which is determined by the institutional arrangements) should be taken into account. This regime will influence the expected value of future flows of services, which will differ depending on whether it leads to sustainable or unsustainable uses (Mäler et al, 2008).

3.3 Human well-being: Typology of benefits and values

Following the MA approach, the TEEB framework (Figure 1.5) makes a distinction between ecological, socio-cultural and economic benefits and values. The reason for separating benefits and values is because people have needs which, when fulfilled, are translated into (more or less objectively measurable) benefits. For example, catching fish from the ocean gives us food (health), but also cultural identity (as a fisherman/woman) and income. How we value these benefits is subjective: some people will value the income much higher than their cultural identity (social ties, etc.) and may be willing to give up one aspect of their well-being (cultural identity) over another (e.g. material wealth). Thus, different values can be attached to a particular benefit.

Although the TEEB study focuses primarily on the measurement of economic values and the assessment of costs and benefits in a welfare economics approach, it includes equity considerations in particular for the aggregation of benefits over time and over groups of people. It specifically analyses the relationships between ecosystems and poverty ('GDP of the poor'), because of the higher dependence of the poor on ecosystem services for their livelihood (TEEB, 2008).

Of course, it should also be acknowledged that many native communities ('ecosystem people') still entirely, and directly, depend on ecosystems and their services for their survival, as well as the importance of ecosystems for providing people with the ability to choose certain ways of life that they may value.

The three main types of benefits (well-being aspects) and related values and valuation metrics are briefly introduced below (for more detailed information, see Chapter 3 (biophysical indicators – linked to ecological 'values'), Chapter 4 (socio-cultural values) and Chapter 5 (economic values)).

3.3.1 Ecological benefits and values

The ecological importance (value) of ecosystems has been articulated by natural scientists in reference to the causal relationships between parts of a system such as, for example, the value of a particular tree species to control erosion, or the value of one species to the survival of another species or of an entire ecosystem (Farber et al, 2002). At a global scale, different ecosystems and their constituent species play different roles in the maintenance of essential life-support processes (such as energy conversion, biogeochemical cycling, and evolution) (MA, 2003).

Ecological measures of value (importance) are, for example, integrity, 'health' or resilience, which are important indicators to determine critical thresholds and minimum requirements for ecosystem service provision. These measures of value should be distinguished from what can be included in economic values because although they contribute to welfare, they cannot readily be taken into account in the expression of individual preferences, as they are too indirect and complex, albeit they may be critical for human survival. The related value paradigm could be formulated as the importance people attach to a healthy, ecologically stable environment, both as a contribution to human survival (instrumental value) and for intrinsic reasons (values). Although the notion of ecological value is still much debated, the 'value' of natural ecosystems and their components should be recognized in terms of their contribution to maintaining life on Earth, including human survival in its own right (Farber et al, 2002).

3.3.2 Socio-cultural benefits and values

For many people, biodiversity and natural ecosystems are a crucial source of nonmaterial well-being through their influence on mental health and their historical, national, ethical, religious and spiritual values. While conceptual and methodological developments in economic valuation have aimed at covering a broad range of values, including intangible ones (see the concept of total economic value below), it can be argued that socio-cultural values cannot be fully captured by economic valuation techniques (see Chapters 4 and 5) and have to be complemented by other approaches in order to inform decision making. This is notably the case where some ecosystem services are considered essential to a people's very identity and existence. To obtain at least a minimum (baseline) measure of importance of socio-cultural benefits and values several metrics have been developed, such as the Human Wellbeing Index.

3.3.3 Economic benefits and values

Biodiversity and ecosystem services are important to humans for many reasons. In economic terms, this can be considered as contributing to different elements of 'total economic value', which comprises both use values (including direct use such as resource use, recreation, and indirect use from regulating services) and non-use values, such as the value people place on protecting nature for future use (option values) or for ethical reasons (bequest and existence values). The economic importance of most of these values can be measured in monetary terms, with varying degrees of accuracy, using various techniques (including market pricing, shadow pricing and questionnaire based). Chapter 5 gives a detailed overview of economic values and monetary valuation techniques.

3.4 Governance and decision making

In making decisions at any level (private, corporate or government), decision makers are faced with the dilemma of how to balance (weigh) ecological, socio-cultural and economic values. Preferably, the importance of each of these value-components should be weighted on its own (qualitative and quantitative) dimension, for example through multi-criteria decision analysis. However, since TEEB is focusing on the economic, notably monetary, consequences of the loss of biodiversity, it concentrates on aggregation (1) and economic trade-off issues (2). To make the link with standard macroeconomic indicators, the role of ecosystem services in environmental–economic accounting (3) should also be mentioned as a promising field of analysis to inform economic decisions (EEA, 2009). Finally, awareness raising and positive incentives (4) are essential tools for better decision making.

1 Aggregating monetary values

Aggregation involves bringing together all the information on the monetary values of ecosystem services by ecosystem type into a single matrix to attain an aggregate monetary value of all delivered ecosystem services. This is the task of Chapter 7. Effective aggregation is challenging. Key issues requiring consideration include:

- *Accounting for uncertainties in the monetary valuation of individual services,* including possible biases due to the use of different valuation methods (see Chapter 5 for discussion).
- *Interdependencies between ecosystem services at the ecosystem scale,* including issues of double counting, competing services, bundled services, etc.
- *Aggregation of values over individuals and groups of people:* The relative importance of ecosystem services will vary between different groups of people, e.g. regarding income level or dependence on ecosystem services. To integrate such considerations some adjustments can be applied such as equity weightings (Anthoff et al, 2009).
- *Aggregation of values over spatial scales:* Different ecosystem services may be best considered at different spatial scales. For example, water regulation is best considered at a watershed scale, while carbon sequestration can be considered on a national or global scale. Aggregation should take these differences into account.
- *Aggregation of values over time:* Protecting biodiversity today may have costs and benefits to future generations. In economics, discounting is a common practice to compare these future costs and benefits with current values. An important issue is the selection of the most appropriate discount rate in different decision making contexts. Chapter 6 will further explore these issues.

2   Trade-off analysis

A trade-off occurs when the extraction of an ecosystem service has a negative impact on the provision of other services. For example, timber extraction from a forest will affect, among others, vegetation structure and composition, visual quality and water quality, which will preclude or at least affect the continuous provision of other services (e.g. wildlife harvesting, carbon sequestration, recreation) over time, since loss of structure implies loss of function, and consequently of other services and their derived benefits. Approaches to trade-off analysis include multi-criteria (decision) analysis, cost–benefit analysis and cost-effectiveness analysis.

The foundational strength of *cost–benefit analysis* (CBA) is finding the 'net' benefit of an activity. Since the costs and benefits of an activity (or scenario) have different functional relationship in different circumstances – utilizing a 'benefits only' approach could greatly mislead decision making (Naidoo et al, 2006). This benefits-only approach was common in early ecosystem service assessments (Balmford et al, 2002). A notable early exception is research on the fynbos in South Africa, where researchers enumerated the benefits and costs of both an invasive species eradication campaign and a do-nothing approach (van Wilgen et al, 1996). An understanding of costs is also crucial in ecosystem service research since the complexity of benefit delivery might preclude a full understanding of service delivery. In these cases a *cost-effectiveness approach* can be highly informative, especially where the costs vary more than the benefits (Ando et al, 1998; Balmford et al, 2003; Naidoo et al, 2006, EEA, 2010).

3   Systems of ecological–economic accounting: Macroeconomic implications

A growing number of governments recognize the need to include ecosystem services in economic accounts in order to ensure that their contribution to well-being is recorded in the macroeconomic indicators that are the most widely acknowledged and used in policy making. If ecosystems are regarded as assets that provide services to people, then accounts can be used to describe the way they change over time in terms of stocks and flows. These changes can be described both in physical terms, using various indicators of ecosystem quantity and quality, and ultimately in monetary values (Weber, 2007; EEA, 2010). Ecosystem accounting, linked to geographical information systems and to socio-economic data, can thus offer a useful framework for systematically collecting and analysing data to support assessments of changes in the production and use of ecosystem services, taking into account their spatial heterogeneity.

Several relevant initiatives are currently under way. For example, the European Environment Agency is developing a framework for land and ecosystem accounts for Europe, building on land cover data and following the System of Environmental and Economic Accounts (SEEA) guidelines of the United Nations.

The development of ecosystem accounting will have to be gradual, integrating progressively more ecosystem services, and build on existing information in different countries. This is addressed in more detail in the TEEB report for national and international policy makers (TEEB in National Policy, 2011). An analysis of how the value of some ecosystem services can be recorded at macroeconomic level for some economic sectors is presented in Chapter 9 of this report.

4 Awareness raising and positive incentives

Of special importance in the TEEB context are the numerous decisions by producers and consumers affecting ecosystems (TEEB in Business, 2011, and TEEB for citizens), and the policy changes necessary to ensure that decisions taken at various governmental levels (TEEB in National Policy, 2011 and TEEB in Local Policy, 2011) do not lead to greater degradation of ecosystems and even improve their condition (see Section 3.6).

An important step towards the conservation and sustainable use of biodiversity and ecosystem services lies in accounting for the positive and negative externalities associated with human activities. Rewarding the benefits of conservation through *payments for environmental services* (e.g. Landell-Mills and Porras, 2002; Wunder, 2005) or ecological fiscal transfers (Ring, 2008) is as important as the realignment of perverse subsidies that all too often incentivize unsustainable behaviours (TEEB in National Policy, 2011, Chapters 5 and 6).

A growing societal awareness of the need for research and development, and for changes in policy, practice and law, can help us pursue sustainable ecosystem management and resource use, and engage in eco-regional planning and large-scale restoration and rehabilitation of renewable and cultivated natural capital (Aronson et al, 2007).

3.5 Scenarios and drivers of change

Efforts aimed at changing behaviour towards and impact on ecosystems and biodiversity must take into account that ecosystems have always been dynamic, both internally and in response to changing environments.

The importance of using scenarios in ecosystem service assessments is beginning to be realized as early assessments presented a static picture in a rapidly changing world. The necessity of providing counter-factuals is now being demanded of conservation research (Ferraro and Pattanayak, 2006) and should become the norm in ecosystem service research as well. The generation of scenarios is particularly important for monetary valuation, since scenarios enable analysis of changes in service delivery which are required to obtain marginal values. Making an analysis in incremental terms avoids (or at least reduces) the methodological difficulties, which vary depending on the magnitude of the changes. Such difficulties arise when attempting to estimate total values, related to the non-constancy of marginal values associated with the complete loss of an ecosystem service. Such approaches are also in general more relevant for decision making in real-life circumstances.

In the TEEB context, comparing the outputs under several scenarios will inform decision makers of the welfare gains and losses of alternative possible futures and different associated policy packages. This is also important for non-monetary valuation changes, but more from a social understanding aspect than for analytical robustness. For each scenario to be elaborated, we must analyse the likely consequences of drivers that directly affect the status, current management and future trajectories of ecosystems and biodiversity (and thus of the services and values they represent).

Indirect drivers of ecosystem change include demographic shifts, technology innovations, economic development, legal and institutional frameworks, including policy instruments, the steady loss of traditional knowledge and cultural diversity and many other factors that influence our collective decisions (OECD, 2003; MA, 2005b; OECD, 2008). These (indirect) drivers affect the way people directly use and manage ecosystems and their services.

Direct drivers can be organized in negative, neutral and positive categories. *Negative drivers* include, among others, habitat destruction, over-use of resources, such as largely unrestrained overfishing of the oceans of the world, and pollution (leading among others to climate change). Examples of *neutral drivers* would be land-use change (which can have positive or negative consequences for ecosystems and biodiversity, depending on the context and management regime). Increasing intensification and industrialization of agriculture and animal husbandry should also be placed in a broader context: intensification (provided it is done in a sustainable manner), can provide extra space for natural habitat. Finally, *positive drivers* for enhancing natural capital would include ecosystem conservation and restoration, development of sustainable management regimes and use of environmental-friendly technologies, aimed at reducing human pressure on ecosystems and biodiversity (e.g. organic farming, eco-tourism, renewable energy, etc.). Clearly, even 'positive drivers' can have negative impacts on ecosystems and biodiversity, when applied in the wrong place or context, so the effects of any direct driver on ecosystems need to be carefully analysed through the TEEB framework.

3.6 Linking ecosystem service values to decision making: The TEEB guidance reports

TEEB brings together state-of-the-art research on assessing and valuing ecosystem services to help policy makers, local authorities, companies and individuals in making decisions with respect to their responsibilities in safeguarding biodiversity. Decision makers at different organizational levels, both public and private, affect drivers of ecosystem change such as demographic, economic, socio-political, scientific and technological as well as cultural and religious drivers, which in turn affect ecosystem services and human well-being. Building on a more refined valuation framework and methodology that is more suitable for capturing economic values and policy-relevant information, TEEB will develop specific guidance documents or 'deliverables' addressing decision making at different levels in different contexts by different actors.

The first guidance document addresses *policy makers* (TEEB in National Policy, 2011). It explores the consequences of international and national policies on biodiversity and ecosystems and presents a TEEB policy toolkit for decision makers at various governmental levels. By demonstrating the value attached to ecosystem services and considering them in concrete policies, instruments and measures (e.g. subsidies and incentives, environmental liability, market creation, national income accounting standards, trading rules, reporting requirements, eco-labelling), it aims to enhance biodiversity and ecosystem protection as a prerequisite for maintaining natural service levels.

Local policy makers are addressed by the second TEEB deliverable (TEEB in Local Policy, 2011). It incorporates values of ecosystem services in location-specific, cost–benefit and cost-effectiveness analysis, and their use in methods and guidelines for implementing payments for ecosystem services, as well as equitable access and benefit-sharing arrangements for genetic resources and protected areas.

The third TEEB deliverable focuses on the *business* end-user (TEEB in Business, 2011). It aims to provide a framework for assessing the business impacts on biodiversity and ecosystems, both for measuring and managing risks and identifying and grasping new market opportunities for private enterprises.

Last, but not least, *individuals and consumer organizations* are addressed by the fourth TEEB deliverable. It covers how to reduce their impacts on wild nature while influencing producers through private purchasing decisions. This will include steps to improve consumer information on the land, water and energy resources used in producing foods and consumer goods.

Notes

1   To avoid having to use both the terms ecosystems and biodiversity simultaneously all the time, the term 'ecosystem' is used to include 'biodiversity' throughout the chapter unless indicated otherwise (see Glossary for further explanation of these terms, and Chapter 2 for a more in-depth discussion).

2   All key terms used in TEEB are included in the Glossary, usually indicated in italics in the text.

3   Acknowledging that it is quite impossible to mention all who contributed to the development of the concept of ecosystem services, some key authors and initiatives are listed in Annex 5 of the 'Scoping the Science' report by Balmford et al (2008).

4   Note that water purification is also listed as a regulating service in Annex 2 to this chapter, in case the benefit is related to waste treatment. As mentioned at the beginning of Section 2.3 a fully unambiguous classification system probably does not exist because the mix of ecosystem structure – process – function that provides the service changes depending on the benefit pursued.

5   It should also be realized that many of these disservices are the result of bad planning or management and thus often human-made. For example 'normalizing' rivers (leading to floods), cutting forest on hill slopes (causing erosion and landslides), and disturbing natural food webs (leading to outbreaks of pests).

6   In this context the ecosystem can be seen as the 'factory' providing (a bundle of) services. It is normal that, for example, car factories include the costs of maintaining the machines and buildings in the price of the car but for timber or fish coming from a forest or lake the maintenance costs of the natural capital (stock) providing the service are usually excluded.

References

Ando, A., Camm, J., Polasky, S. and Solow, A. (1998) 'Species distributions, land values, and efficient conservation', *Science*, vol 279, pp2126–2128

Anthoff, D., Hepburn, C. and Tol, R. S. J. (2009) 'Equity weighting and the marginal damage costs of climate change', *Ecological Economics*, vol 68, no 3, pp836–849

Aronson, J., Milton, S. J. and Blignaut, J. N. (eds) (2007) *Restoring Natural Capital: The Science, Business, and Practice*, Island Press, Washington, DC

Arrow, K., Bolin, B., Costanza, R., Dasgupta, P., Folke, C., Holling, C. S., Jansson, B. O., Levin, S., Maler, K.-G., Perrings, C. and Pimentel, D. (1995) 'Economic growth, carrying capacity, and the environment', *Science*, vol 268, pp520–521

Balmford, A., Bruner, A., Cooper, P., Costanza, R., Farber, S., Green, R., Jenkins, M., Jefferiss, P., Jessamay, V., Madden, J., Munro, K., Myers, N., Naeem, S., Paavola, J., Rayment, M., Rosendo, S., Roughgarden, J., Trumper, K. and Turner, R. K. (2002) 'Economic reasons for conserving wild nature', *Science*, vol 297, pp950–953

Balmford, A., Gaston, K. J., Blyth, S., James, A. and Kapos, V. (2003) 'Global variation in terrestrial conservation costs, conservation benefits, and unmet conservation needs', *PNAS*, vol 100, no 3, pp1046–1050

Balmford, A., Rodrigues, A., Walpole, M. J., ten Brink, P., Kettunen, M., Braat, L. and de Groot, R. (2008) *Review of the Economics of Biodiversity Loss: Scoping the Science*, European Commission, Brussels

Barbier, E. B. (1994) 'Natural Capital and the Economics of Environment and Development', in Jansson, A.-M., Hammer, M., Folke, C. and Costanza, R. (eds) *Investing in Natural Capital*, Island Press, Washington DC, 505pp

Barbier, E. B., Koch, E. W., Silliman, B. R., Hacker, S. D., Wolanski, E., Primavera, J., Granek, E. F., Polasky, S., Aswani, S., Cramer, L. A., Stoms, D., Kennedy, C. J., Bael, D., Kappel, C. V., Perillo, G. M. E. and Reed, D. J. (2008) 'Coastal ecosystem-based management with non-linear ecological functions and values', *Science*, vol 319, pp321–323

Bartelmus, P. (2009) 'The cost of natural capital consumption: Accounting for a sustainable world economy', *Ecological Economics*, vol 68, no 6, pp1850–1857

Bateman, I. J., Jones, A. P., Lovett, A. A., Lake, I. R. and Day, B. H. (2002) 'Applying geographical information systems (GIS) to environmental and resource economics', *Environmental and Resource Economics*, vol 22, no 1, pp219–269

Bockstael, N., Freeman, A. M. III, Kopp, R. J., Portney, P. R. and Smith, V. K. (2000) 'On measuring economic values for nature', *Environmental Science and Technology*, vol 34, pp1384–1389

Boyd, J. and Banzhaf, S. (2007) 'What are ecosystem services? The need for standardized environmental accounting units', *Ecological Economics*, vol 63, nos 2–3, pp616–626

Braat, L. and ten Brink, P. (eds) with Bakkes, J., Bolt, K., Braeuer, I., ten Brink, B., Chiabai, A., Ding, H., Gerdes, H., Jeuken, M., Kettunen, M., Kirchholtes, U., Klok, C., Markandya, A., Nunes, P., van Oorschot, M., Peralta-Bezerra, N., Rayment, M., Travisi, C. and Walpole, M. (2008) *The Cost of Policy Inaction (COPI): The Case of not Meeting the 2010 Biodiversity Target*, European Commission, Brussels

Carson, R. (1962) *Silent Spring*, Fawcett Publications, Greenwich, CT

Chevassus-au-Louis, B., Salles, J.-M. and Pujol, J.-L. (2009) 'Approche économique de la biodiversité et des services liés aux écosystèmes: Contribution à la décision publique', Report to the Prime Minister, April 2009, Centre d'analyse stratégique, Paris

Christie, M., Hanley, N., Warren, J., Murphy, K., Wright, R. and Hyde, T. (2006) 'Valuing the diversity of biodiversity', *Ecological Economics*, vol 58, no 2, pp304–317

Common, M. and Perrings, C. (1992) 'Towards an ecological economics of sustainability', *Ecological Economics*, vol 6, pp7–34

Costanza, R. (2008) 'Ecosystem services: Multiple classification systems are needed', *Biological Conservation*, vol 141, pp350–352

Costanza, R. and Daly, H. (1992) 'Natural capital and sustainable development', *Conservation Biology*, vol 6, pp37–46

Costanza, R., d'Arge, R., de Groot, R., Farber, S., Grasso, M., Hannon, B., Limburg, K., Naeem, S., O'Neill, R. V., Paruelo, J., Raskin, R. G., Sutton, P. and van den Belt, M. (1997) 'The value of the world's ecosystem services and natural capital', *Nature*, vol 387, pp253–259

Daily, G. (ed) (1997) *Nature's Services: Societal Dependence on Natural Ecosystems*, Island Press, Washington, DC

Daily, G., Polasky, S., Goldstein, J., Kareiva, P. M., Mooney, H. A., Pejchar, L., Ricketts, T. H., Salzman, J. and Shallenberger, R. (2009) 'Ecosystem services in decision-making: Time to deliver', *Frontiers in Ecology and the Environment*, vol 7, no 1, pp21–28

Daly, H. (1996) 'Introduction to Essays Toward a Steady-State Economy', in Daly, H. and Townsend, K. N. (eds) *Valuing the Earth: Economics, Ecology, Ethics*, The MIT Press, Cambridge, MA, pp11–47

Daly, H. and Farley, J. (2004) *Ecological Economics: Principles and Applications*, Island Press, Washington, DC

Dasgupta, P., Levin, S. and Lubchenko, J. (2000) 'Economic pathways to ecological sustainability'. *BioScience*, vol 50, pp339–345

De Groot, R. S. (1987) 'Environmental functions as a unifying concept for ecology and economics', *The Environmentalist*, vol 7, no 2, pp105–109

De Groot, R. S. (1992) *Functions of Nature: Evaluation of Nature in Environmental Planning, Management and Decision-making*, Wolters Noordhoff BV, Groningen

De Groot, R. S., Wilson, M. A. and Boumans, R. M. J. (2002) 'A typology for the classification, description and valuation of ecosystem functions, goods and services', *Ecological Economics*, vol 41, pp393–408

EEA (European Environment Agency) (2010) 'Ecosystem accounting and the costs of biodiversity losses: The case of coastal Mediterranean wetlands', Haines-Young, R., Potschin, M., Kumar, P. and Weber, J. L. (eds), EEA Technical Report No. 3/2010, available at www.eea.europa.eu/publications/ecosystem-accounting-and-the-cost

Ehrlich, P. R. and Ehrlich, A. H. (1981) *Extinction: The Causes and Consequences of the Disappearance of Species*, 1st edn, Random House, New York

Ehrlich, P. R. and Mooney, H. A. (1983) 'Extinction, substitution, and ecosystem services', *Bioscience*, vol 33, pp248–254

Ellis, E. C. and Ramankutty, N. (2008) 'Putting people in the map: Anthropogenic biomes of the world', *Frontiers in Ecology and the Environment*, vol 6, no 8, pp439–447

EPA-SAB (US Environmental Protection Agency – Science Advisory Board) (2009) 'Valuing the protection of ecological systems and services', US Environmental Protection Agency, Washington, DC

Farber, S. C., Costanza, R. and Wilson, M. A. (2002) 'Economic and ecological concepts for valuing ecosystem services', in 'The dynamics and value of ecosystem services: Integrating economic and ecological perspectives', *Ecological Economics*, vol 41, pp375–392

Ferraro, P. J. and Pattanayak, S. K. (2006) 'Money for nothing? A call for empirical evaluation of biodiversity conservation investments', *Plos Biology*, vol 4, pp482–488

Fisher, B. and Turner, R. K. (2008) 'Ecosystem services: Classification for valuation', *Biological Conservation*, vol 141, pp1167–1169

Fisher, B., Turner, R. K. and Morling, P. (2009) 'Defining and classifying ecosystem services for decision making', *Ecological Economics*, vol 68, pp643–653

Fisher B., Turner, R. K., Zylstra, M., Brouwer, R., de Groot, R. S., Farber, S., Ferraro, P. J., Green, R. E., Hadley, D., Harlow, J., Jefferiss, P., Kirkby, C., Morling, P., Mowatt, S., Naidoo, R., Paavola, J., Strassburg, B., Yu, D. and Balmford, A. (2008) 'Ecosystem services and economic theory: Integration for policy-relevant research', *Ecological Applications*, vol 18 no 8, pp2050–2067

Folke, C., Hammer, M. and Jansson, A. M. (1991) 'Life-support value of ecosystems: A case study of the Baltic region', *Ecological Economics*, vol 3, no 2, pp123–137

Granek, E. F., Polasky, S., Kappel, C. V., Reed, D. J., Stoms, D. M., Koch, E. W., Kennedy, C. J., Cramer, L. A., Hacker, S. D., Barbier, E. B., Aswani, S., Ruckelshaus, M., Perillo, G. M. E., Silliman, B. R., Muthiga, N., Bael, D. and Wolanski, E. (2009) 'Ecosystem services as a common language for coastal ecosystem-based management', *Conservation Biology*, vol 24, no 1, pp207–216

Haines-Young, R. and Potschin, M. (2010) 'The links between biodiversity, ecosystem services and human well-being', in Raffaelli, D. and Frid, C. (eds) *Ecosystem Ecology: A New Synthesis*, BES Ecological Reviews series, Cambridge University Press, Cambridge, pp110–139

Halpern, B. S., Ebert, C. M., Kappel, C. V., Madin, E. M. P., Micheli, F., Perry, M., Selkoe, K. A. and Walbridge, S. (2009) 'Global priority areas for incorporating land-sea connections in marine conservation', *Conservation Letters*, vol 2 (2009), pp189–196

Halpern, B. S., Walbridge, S., Selkoe, K. A., Kappel, C. V., Micheli, F., D'Agrosa, C., Bruno, J. F., Casey, K. S., Ebert, C., Fox, H. E., Fujita, R., Heinmenann, D., Lenihan, H. S., Madin, E. M. P., Perry, M. T., Sellig, E. R., Spalding, M., Steneck, R. and Watson, R. (2008) 'A global map of human impact on marine ecosystems', *Science*, vol 319, pp948–952; also available at www.sciencemag.org/cgi/content/full/319/5865/ 948/DC1

Hein, L., van Koppen, K., de Groot, R. S. and van Ierland, E. C. (2006) 'Spatial scales, stakeholders and the valuation of ecosystem services', *Ecological Economics*, vol 57, pp209–228

Hueting, R. (1980) *New Scarcity and Economic Growth: More Welfare Through Less Production?* North Holland Publ. Co., Amsterdam/New York, Oxford

ICSU-UNESCO-UNU (2008) *Ecosystem Change and Human Well-being: Research and Monitoring Priorities Based on the Millennium Ecosystem Assessment*, International Council for Science, Paris

Jansson, A.-M., Hammer, M., Folke, C., and Costanza, R. (1994) *Investing in Natural Capital: The Ecological Economics Approach to Sustainability*, Island Press, Washington, DC

Johnson, D. G. (2000) 'Population, food, and knowledge', *American Economic Review*, vol 90, no 1, pp1–14

Kareiva, P., Watts, S., McDonald, R. and Boucher, T. (2007) 'Domesticated nature: Shaping landscapes and ecosystems for human welfare', *Science*, vol 316, pp1866–1869

Krutilla, J. and Fisher, A. C. (1975) *The Economics of Natural Environments: Resources for the Future*, Johns Hopkins University Press, Washington, DC

Landell-Mills, N. and Porras, I. (2002) *Silver Bullet or Fools' Gold? A Global Review of Markets for Forest Environmental Services and Their Impact on the Poor*, Instruments for Sustainable Private Sector Forestry series, International Institute for Environment and Development, London

Leopold, A. (1949) *A Sand County Almanac and Sketches Here and There*, Oxford University Press, Oxford

MA (Millennium Ecosystem Assessment) (2003) *Ecosystems and Human Well-being: A Framework for Assessment*, Island Press, Washington, DC

MA (2005a) *Ecosystems and Human Well-being: Synthesis*, Island Press, Washington, DC

MA (2005b) *Ecosystems and Human Well-being: Current State and Trends*, Volume 1, Island Press, Washington, DC

Mäler, K. G., Aniyar, S. and Jansson, A. (2008) 'Accounting for ecosystem services as a way to understand the requirements for sustainable development', *Proceedings of the National Academy of Sciences of the United States of America*, vol 105, pp9501–9506

Maltby, E. (ed) (2009) *Functional Assessment of Wetlands: Towards Evaluation of Ecosystem Services*, Woodhead Publ., Abington, Cambridge

Marsh, G. F. (1874) *The Earth as Modified by Human Action*, Arno, New York

Mwakalila, S., Burgess, N., Ricketts, T., Olwero, N., Swetnam, R., Mbilinyi, B., Marchant, R., Mtalo, F., White, S., Munishi, P., Malimbwi, R., Smith, C., Jambiya, G., Marshall, A., Madoffe, S., Fisher, B., Kajembe, G., Morse-Jones, S., Kulindwa, K., Green, R., Turner, R. K., Green, J. and Balmford, A. (2009) 'Valuing the Arc: Linking science with stakeholders to sustain natural capital', *The Arc Journal*, vol 23, pp25–30

Naidoo, R. and Ricketts, T. H. (2006), 'Mapping the economic costs and benefits of conservation', *Plos Biology*, vol 4, pp2153–2164

Naidoo, R., Balmford, A., Costanza, R., Fisher, B., Green, R. E., Lehner, B., Malcolm, T. R. and Ricketts, T. H. (2008) 'Global mapping of ecosystem services and conservation priorities', *PNAS*, vol 105 no 28, pp9495–9500

Naidoo, R., Balmford, A., Ferraro, P. J., Polasky, S., Ricketts, T. H. and Rouget, M. (2006) 'Integrating economic cost into conservation planning', *Trends in Ecology and Evolution*, vol 21, no 12, pp681–687

Nelson, E., Mendoza, G., Regetz, J., Polasky, S., Tallis, H., Cameron, D. R., Chan, K. M. A., Daily, G., Goldstein, J., Kareiva, P., Lonsdorf, E., Naidoo, R., Ricketts, T. H. and Shaw, M. R. (2009) 'Modeling multiple ecosystem services, biodiversity conservation, commodity production, and trade-offs at landscape scales', *Frontiers in Ecology and the Environment*, vol 7, no 1, pp4–11

Norgaard, R. B. and Bode, C., with the Values Reading Group (1998) 'Next, the value of God, and other reactions' (a response to 'The value of the world's ecosystem services and natural capital' by Costanza et al), *Ecological Economics*, vol 25, no 1, pp37–39

NRC (National Research Council) (2005) *Valuing Ecosystem Services: Towards Better Environmental Decision-making*, National Academies Press, Washington, DC

Odum, E. P. (1989) *Ecology and our Endangered Life-Support Systems*, Sinauer Ass., North Scituate, MA

OECD (2003) *OECD Environmental Indicators: Development, Measurement and Use*, Organisation for Economic Co-operation and Development, Paris

OECD (2008) *Environmental Outlook to 2030*, Organisation for Economic Co-operation and Development, Paris

Pearce, D., Markandya, A. and Barbier, E. B. (1989) *Blueprint for a Green Economy*, Earthscan, London

Pezzey, J. (1992) *Sustainable Development Concepts: An Economic Analysis*, The World Bank Environment Paper, No. 2, The World Bank, Washington, DC

Polasky, S., Nelson, E., Camm, J., Csuti, B., Fackler, P., Lonsdorf, E., Montgomery, C., White, D., Arthur, J., Garber-Yonts, B., Haight, R., Kagan, J., Starfield, A. and Tobalske, C. (2008) 'Where to put things? Spatial land management to sustain biodiversity and economic returns', *Biological Conservation*, vol 141, no 6, pp1505–1524

Prugh, T., with Costanza, R., Cumberland, J. H., Daly, H. E., Goodland, R. and Norgaard, R. B. (1999) *Natural Capital and Human Economic Survival*, Lewis Publishers, Boca Raton, FL

Ring, I. (2008) 'Integrating local ecological services into intergovernmental fiscal transfers: The case of the ecological ICMS in Brazil', *Land Use Policy*, vol 25, no 4, pp485–497

Sen, A. (1993) 'Capability and Well-being', in Nussbaum, M. C. and Sen, A. (eds) *The Quality of Life*, Oxford University Press, Oxford, pp30–53

Srinivasan, U. T., Carey, S. P., Hallstein, E., Higgins, P. A. T., Kerr, A. C., Koteen, L. E., Smith, A. B., Watson, R., Harte. J. and Norgaard, R. B. (2008) 'The debt of nations and the distribution of ecological impacts from human activities', *Proceedings of the National Academy of Sciences of the United States of America*, vol 105, pp1768–1773

TEEB (2008) 'The Economics of Ecosystems and Biodiversity: An Interim report', available at www.teebweb.org, accessed 2 March 2010

TEEB in National Policy (2011) *The Economics of Ecosystems and Biodiversity in National and International Policy Making* (ed Patrick ten Brink), Earthscan, London

TEEB in Local Policy (2011) *The Economics of Ecosystems and Biodiversity in Local and Regional Policy and Management* (ed Heidi Wittmer and Haripriya Gundimeda), Earthscan, London

TEEB in Business (2011) *The Economics of Ecosystems and Biodiversity in Business and Enterprise* (ed Joshua Bishop), Earthscan, London

Turner, R. K., Paavola, J., Cooper, P., Farber, S., Jessamy, V. and Georgiou, S. (2003) 'Valuing nature: Lessons learned and future research directions', *Ecological Economics*, vol 46, pp493–510

van Wilgen, B. W., Cowling, R. M. and Burgers, C. J. (1996) 'Valuation of ecosystem services', *Bioscience*, vol 46, pp184–189

Wallace, K. J. (2008) 'Classification of ecosystem services: Problems and solutions', *Biological Conservation*, vol 139, pp235–246

Weber, J.-L. (2007) 'Implementation of land and ecosystem accounts at the European Environment Agency', *Ecological Economics*, vol 61, no 4, pp695–707

Westman, W. (1977) 'How much are nature's services worth?', *Science*, vol 197, pp960–964

Wilson, M. A. and Howarth, R. B. (2002) 'Valuation techniques for achieving social fairness in the distribution of ecosystem services', *Ecological Economics*, vol 41, pp431–443

Wunder, S. (2005) *Payments for Environmental Services: Some Nuts and Bolts*, CIFOR Occasional Paper No. 42, Center for International Forestry Research, Jakarta

Annex 1 Classification of ecosystems used in TEEB

LEVEL 1 (biomes)		LEVEL 2 (ecosystems)	
1	Marine/Open ocean	1.0	Marine/open ocean
		1.1	Open ocean
		1.2	Coral reefs[1,2]
2	Coastal systems	2.0	Coastal systems (excluding wetlands)
		2.1	– Seagrass/algae beds
		2.2	– Shelf sea
		2.3	– Estuaries
		2.4	– Shores (rocky & beaches)
3	Wetlands	3.0	Wetlands – general (coastal & inland)
			(Coastal wetlands)
		3.1	– Tidal marsh (coastal wetlands)
		3.2	– Mangroves[2]
			(Inland wetlands)
		3.3	– Floodplains (incl. swamps/marsh)
		3.4	– Peat-wetlands (bogs, fens, etc.)
4	Lakes/Rivers	4.0	*Lakes/rivers*
		4.1	– Lakes
		4.2	– Rivers
5	Forests	5.0	Forests – all
			(Tropical forest)
		5.1	– Tropical rain forest[2]
		5.2	– Tropical dry forest
			(Temperate forests)
		5.3	– Temperate rain/Evergreen
		5.4	– Temperate deciduous forests
		5.5	– Boreal/Coniferous forest
6	Woodland & shrubland	6.0	Woodland & shrubland ('dryland')
		6.1	– Heathland
		6.2	– Mediterranean scrub
		6.3	– Various scrubland
7	Grass/Rangeland	7.0	Grass/Rangeland
		7.1	– Savanna etc.
8	Desert	8.0	Desert
		8.1	– Semi-desert
		8.2	– True desert (sand/rock)
9	Tundra	9.0	Tundra

LEVEL 1 (biomes)		LEVEL 2 (ecosystems)	
10	Ice/Rock/Polar	10.0	Ice/rock/polar
11	Cultivated	11.0	Cultivated
		11.1	Cropland (arable land, pastures, etc.)
		11.2	Plantations/orchards/agro-forestry, etc.
		11.3	Aquaculture/rice paddies, etc.
12	Urban	12.0	Urban

Notes: 1 usually placed under 'coastal' but it is proposed to put this under 'marine'.

2 These three ecosystems are dealt with separately in the monetary valuation (Appendix 3, this volume).

Source: Based on mix of classifications, mainly MA (2005a) and Costanza et al (1997), which in turn are based on classifications from US Geol. Survey, IUCN, WWF, UNEP and FAO

Annex 2 Ecosystem service classification: Brief literature survey and TEEB classification

Various sources[1]	Millennium Ecosystem Assessment (2005a)	Daily et al (2009)[2]		TEEB classification
PROVISIONING	**PROVISIONING**			**PROVISIONING**
Food (fish, game, fruit)	Food	Seafood, game	1	Food
Water availability (RS)[3]	Fresh water		2	Water[3]
Raw materials (e.g. wood)	Fibre	Timber, fibres	3	Raw materials
Fuel & energy (fuelwood, organic matter, etc.)	Fibre	Biomass fuels		
Fodder & fertilizer	Fibre	Forage		
Useful genetic material	Genetic resources	– industrial products	4	Genetic resources
Drugs & pharmaceutical	Biochemicals	Pharmaceuticals	5	Medicinal resources
Models & test organisms	–	– industrial products		
Resources for fashion, handicraft, decorative, etc.	Ornamental resources	–	6	Ornamental resources
REGULATING	**REGULATING**			**REGULATING**
Gas regulation/air quality	Air quality regulation	Air purification	7	Air purification
Favourable climate (incl. C-sequestration)	Climate regulation	Climate stabilization	8	Climate regulation (incl. C-sequestration)
Storm protection	–	Moderation of extremes	9	Disturbance prevention or moderation
Flood prevention	Water regulation	Flood mitigation		
Drainage & natural irrigation (drought prevention)	Water regulation	Drought mitigation	10	Regulation of water flows
Clean water (waste treatment)	Water regulation	Water purification	11	Waste treatment (esp. water purification)

Annex 2 (*cont'd*)

Various sources[1]	Millennium Ecosystem Assessment (2005a)	Daily et al (2008)[2]		TEEB classification
Erosion prevention	Erosion regulation	Erosion protection	12	Erosion prevention
Maintenance of productive and 'clean' soils	Soil formation [supporting service]	Soil generation and preservation	13	Maintenance of soil fertility (incl. soil formation) and nutrient cycling
Pollination	Pollination	Pollination	14	Pollination
(biol. control)		Seed dispersal	15	Biological control
Pest & disease control	Pest regulation	Pest control		
	Human disease regulation			
HABITAT/SUPPORT	**SUPPORTING**			**HABITAT**
Nursery-service	e.g. Photosynthesis, primary production, nutrient cycling		16	Lifecycle maintenance
Maintenance of biodiversity		Maintenance of biodiversity	17	Gene pool protection
CULTURAL (& Amenities)	**CULTURAL**			**CULTURAL** & Amenity
Appreciated scenery (incl. tranquility)	Aesthetic values	Aesthetic beauty	18	Aesthetic information
Recreation & tourism	Recreation & eco-tourism		19	Recreation & tourism
Inspiration for art, etc.	–		20	Inspiration for culture, art and design
Cultural heritage	Cultural diversity			
Spiritual & religious use	Spiritual & religious values		21	Spiritual experience
Use in science & education	Knowledge systems Educational values	Intellectual stimulation	22	Information for cognitive development

Notes: 1 Mainly based on/adapted from Costanza et al (1997) and de Groot et al (2002).

2 Daily et al (2009) do not use main categories and also included detoxification and decomposition of waste, nutrient cycling, and UVb-protection as services.

3 Water is often placed under Regulating Services (RS) but in TEEB the consumptive use of water is placed under provisioning services.

– means the service was not recognized by the authors of the corresponding column.

Chapter 2

Biodiversity, Ecosystems and Ecosystem Services

Coordinating lead authors
Thomas Elmqvist, Edward Maltby

Lead authors
Tom Barker, Martin Mortimer, Charles Perrings

Contributing authors
James Aronson, Rudolf de Groot, Alastair Fitter, Georgina Mace,
Jon Norberg, Isabel Sousa Pinto, Irene Ring

Reviewers
Volker Grimm, Kurt Jax, Rik Leemans,
Jean-Michel Salles

Review editor
Jean-Michel Salles

Contents

Key messages   44

1   Introduction   45

2   Biodiversity and ecosystems   45
    2.1   Theory and definitions   45
    2.2   The role of diversity in ecosystem functioning   51
          2.2.1   Species diversity and productivity: Terrestrial systems   51
          2.2.2   Species diversity and productivity: Marine systems   52
    2.3   Functional groups and functional diversity   53
    2.4   The complexity of finding quantitative links between biodiversity
          and ecosystem services   54

3   The links between biodiversity, ecosystem functions and ecosystem services   56
    3.1   Provision of food   56
    3.2   Water provision, including regulation of water flows (3.10) and water
          purification (3.11)   59
    3.3   Fuels and fibres   61
    3.4   Genetic resources   63
    3.5   Medicinal and other biochemical resources   65
    3.6   Ornamental resources   66
    3.7   Air quality regulation and other urban environmental quality regulation   67
    3.8   Climate regulation   69
    3.9   Moderation of extreme events   71
    3.12 Erosion prevention   72
    3.13 Maintenance of soil fertility (including soil formation) and nutrient cycling   73
    3.14 Pollination services   74
    3.15 Biological control   75
    3.16 Maintenance of life cycles of migratory species   77
    3.17 Maintenance of genetic diversity   78
    3.18–22   Cultural services: Aesthetic information, opportunities for recreation
          and tourism, inspiration for culture, art and design, spiritual experience,
          information for cognitive development   79

4   Managing multiple ecosystem services   81
    4.1   Bundles of ecosystem services   81
    4.2   Trade-offs   81
    4.3   Scales of provision   84

5   Management of ecosystem services: Dealing with uncertainty and change   84
    5.1   Ecosystems, services and resilience   85
          5.1.1   Thresholds, recovery and ecological restoration   88
    5.2   Resilience thinking in policy and practice   89

6   Biodiversity, ecosystem services and human well-being   91

7   Conclusions and further research   95

References   97

Key messages

- All ecosystems are shaped by people, directly or indirectly and all people, rich or poor, rural or urban, depend on the capacity of ecosystems to generate essential ecosystem services. In this sense, people and ecosystems are interdependent social-ecological systems.

- The ecosystem concept describes the interrelationships between living organisms (people included) and the non-living environment and provides a holistic approach to understanding the generation of services from an environment that both delivers benefits to and imposes costs on people.

- Variation in biological diversity relates to the operations of ecosystems in at least three ways (Hooper et al, 2005): (1) increase in diversity often leads to an increase in productivity due to complementary traits among species for resource use, and productivity itself underpins many ecosystem services; (2) increased diversity leads to an increase in response diversity (the range of traits of species in the same functional group in their response to environmental drivers) resulting in less variability in functioning over time as environment changes; (3) idiosyncratic effects due to keystone species properties and unique trait-combinations which may result in a disproportional effect of losing one particular species compared to the effect of losing individual species at random.

- Ecosystems produce multiple services and these interact in complex ways, different services being interlinked, both negatively and positively. Delivery of many services will therefore vary in a correlated manner, but when an ecosystem is managed principally for the delivery of a single service (e.g. food production) other services are nearly always affected negatively.

- Ecosystems vary in their ability to buffer and adapt to both natural and anthropogenic changes as well as recover after changes. When subjected to severe stress, ecosystems may cross thresholds and move into different and often less desirable ecological states or trajectories. A major challenge is how to manage environmental drivers to protect ecosystems so that they can maintain resilience and avoid crossing undesirable thresholds.

- There is clear evidence for a central role of high biodiversity in the delivery of many – but not all – services, when viewed individually. However, ecosystems need to be managed to deliver multiple services to sustain human well-being. Management at larger (landscape/seascape) scales should be appropriate for avoidance of dangerous tipping points. We can state with high certainty that maintaining functioning ecosystems capable of delivering multiple services requires a general approach to sustaining biodiversity, in the broad environment. This is as true for single as for multiple services.

1 Introduction

This chapter explores current understanding of the relationships between biodiversity, the structure and functioning of ecosystems, and the provision of ecosystem services. It aims specifically to clarify:

- the nature of and evidence for the links between biodiversity, ecosystems and ecosystem services;
- ecosystem responses to anthropogenic impacts;
- the risks and uncertainties inherent in managing ecosystems, which developed long before the evolution of *Homo sapiens*.

A basic level of understanding of ecosystem functioning is an essential prerequisite to the appropriate application of economic analysis. This chapter highlights the complexities of the concepts of biodiversity and ecosystems. The interactions among the various assemblages of biotic and abiotic components into ecosystems are assessed based on our current scientific knowledge. This evidence is further discussed in the context of how to help inform the policy agenda on the connections between biodiversity and ecosystem services.

The chapter gives a review of the individual ecosystem services themselves with commentary and analysis on the important factors underpinning the services, gaps in knowledge and uncertainties. Recognizing that in reality, ecosystems generate multiple services, we examine the complications arising from 'bundles' of ecosystem services, where strategic priorities may result in trade-offs in service provision. The need for practical approaches to the recognition, quantification and mapping of ecosystem services is examined, and a synthesis presented of the alteration of biodiversity and ecosystems and their functioning with increasing known impacts of global change. Analysis of the growing biophysical knowledge base is essential to help economists understand and interpret the dynamics and complex interactions among living organisms, the abiotic environment and diverse cultural and socio-economic contexts.

2 Biodiversity and ecosystems

2.1 Theory and definitions

Biodiversity reflects the hierarchy of increasing levels of organization and complexity in ecological systems; namely at the level of genes, individuals, populations, species, communities, ecosystems and biomes. Communities of organisms interacting with the abiotic environment comprise and characterize ecosystems. Ecosystems are varied both in size and complexity, and may be nested one within another.

Application of the ecosystem model (Tansley, 1935; Odum, 1969) implies comprehensive understanding of the interactions responsible for distinctive ecosystem types, but unfortunately this knowledge is rarely available. As a result, the use of the term ecosystem, when describing entities such as forests, grasslands, wetlands or deserts is more conceptual than based on any distinct spatial configuration of interactions.

Where communities of organisms persist in dynamic equilibrium over long periods of time, and occupy the same physical space, ecosystems may appear to have discrete physical boundaries, but these boundaries are porous to organisms and materials. Boundaries are, of course, most noticeable when there are major differences in the physical environment (e.g. lakes grasslands) and certainly some terrestrial ecosystems still extend over very large areas of the planet, for example savanna and tropical rainforests. Nevertheless, species abundance and composition within these ecosystems always varies temporally and spatially. The population dynamics of species create temporal and spatial heterogeneity, while gradients in abiotic variables add to the latter (Whittaker, 1975), often over orders of magnitude (Ettama and Wardle, 2002).

Ecosystem processes (Table 2.1a) result from the life processes of multi-species assemblages of organisms and their interactions with the abiotic environment, as well as the abiotic environment itself. These processes ultimately generate services when they provide utilities to humans (see Table 2.1b).

Table 2.1a Some examples of biological and physical processes and interactions that comprise ecosystems functions important for ecosystem services

Ecosystem function	Processes
Primary production:	Photosynthesis
	Plant nutrient uptake
Decomposition:	Microbial respiration
	Soil and sediment food web dynamics
Nitrogen cycling:	Nitrification
	Denitrification
	Nitrogen fixation
Hydrologic cycle:	Plant transpiration
	Root activity
Soil formation:	Mineral weathering
	Soil bioturbation
	Vegetation succession
Biological control:	Predator–prey interactions

Source: From Virginia and Wall (2000)

Table 2.1b Examples of relationships between biodiversity and ecosystem services

Component of biodiversity	Example of ecosystem service (see also Section 3)	Sources
Genetic variability	Medicinal products	Chai et al (1989)
Population sizes and biomass	Food from crops and animals	Kontoleon et al (2008)
Species assemblages, communities and structures	Habitat provision and recreation	Rosenberg et al (2000)
Interactions between organisms and their abiotic environment	Water purification	Hefting et al (2003)
Interactions between and among individuals and species	Pollination and biological control	Messelink et al (2008)

Alterations in biodiversity can result in very noticeable changes in ecosystem functioning: for example individual genes may confer stress tolerance in crops and increased productivity in agricultural ecosystems, and invasive species may transform fundamental ecosystem processes such as the nitrogen cycle (see Section 3). The dimensions of biodiversity and its relationships to human well-being have been extensively addressed by Levin (2000), including both the services that biodiversity supports and the evolutionary genesis of biodiversity together with the ecological processes underlying patterns and trends.

The relationship between biodiversity and ecosystem functioning cannot be revealed by ecological studies of communities that focus on the structure and behaviour of species and populations at a location. What is needed in addition are studies that address the flux of energy and matter through the ecosystem. The measures used may be different: for example, community studies may employ indices measuring aspects of biodiversity, whereas ecosystem studies utilize measures of standing crop, or flux of nutrients. Both are important in the evaluation of ecosystem services. Services directly linked to primary plant productivity, for example provisioning of food, are measured in biomass per unit area, or nutrient content per unit biomass, whereas cultural services may require a measure of complexity of biodiversity at a suitable scale, for example species richness in spatial units within the landscape (Srivastava and Vellend, 2005). However, this is not to say that such measures are mutually exclusive. For example, the service of biological pest control is best estimated both by measures of biodiversity in terms of insect predator guilds, and their temporal relative abundance.

In any community of organisms, some groups make the principal contribution to a particular process, and so contribute to the overall functioning of the ecosystem of which they are a part. Thus, the critical functions of communities of soil organisms are decomposition and nutrient and elemental cycling, whereas plant communities contribute biomass production through photosynthesis. Communities in the soil are intimately interlinked (through root–microbe interrelations) with vegetation, and faunal communities depend not only on primary plant production *per se* but on the composition and physical structure of plant communities for habitat. This linkage between above-ground and below-ground parts of ecosystems is fundamental in all cases, as exemplified by provisioning ecosystem services in low-input agriculture by the role of legumes within cropping cycles.

Box 2.1 illustrates some of the linkages between different communities of organisms in relation to their major functions. These interactions contribute both to the regulation of biomass in an ecosystem and to the diversity of species assemblages within communities.

Spatial interconnectedness maintains links and genetic interchange between populations of species, and underpins ecosystem functioning directly through physical connections. This is evident when considering energy and nutrient budgets; for example where nutrients 'spiral' downstream (Newbold et al, 1981) or move between floodplain wetlands and riverine ecosystems, especially due to flood 'pulses' (Junk et al, 1989). In this way, fish populations of African rivers benefit from the organic matter and nutrients deposited by both wild and domesticated herbivores grazing the floodplains during the dry season (Drijver

Box 2.1 Biotic communities and their major functions

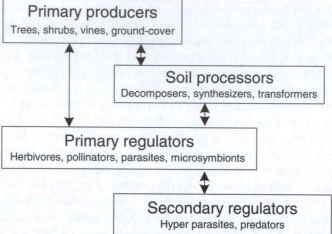

Figure 2.1 *Illustrative relationships between different functional groups in ecosystems*

Source: Following Swift et al (2004)

Primary producers

Classification of plants into functional groups has an extensive history. Groupings can be based on a variety of reproductive, architectural and physiological criteria, but scale and efficiency of resource capture is often suggested as the main criterion. This will be determined by features of both architecture (e.g. position and shape of the canopy and depth and pattern of the rooting system) and physiological efficiency (see Smith et al, 1997). In some agro-ecosystems photosynthetic microorganisms may constitute a significant group, for example lowland rice.

Soil processors

This is a very diverse community of organisms, involved in decomposition of organic matter (decomposers), soil synthesis (synthesizers) and nutrient cycling (transformers).

Decomposers

This is a group of enormous diversity that can be subdivided taxonomically into bacteria, fungi, invertebrates, and others, having functional roles in the breakdown and mineralization of organic materials of plant or animal origin.

Synthesizers

These are species that change the structure of soil and its porosity to water by burrowing, transport of soil particles among soil horizons, and formation of aggregate structures. Many of these species also contribute to decomposition.

Transformers

This includes a range of autotrophic bacteria that utilize sources of energy other than organic matter (and therefore are not classifiable as decomposers) and play key roles in nutrient cycles as transformers of elements (carbon, nitrogen, phosphorus, sulphur, etc.). Some heterotrophs that have a decomposer function also carry out elemental transformations beyond mineralization (e.g. free-living di-nitrogen fixers).

Primary regulators

Organisms that have a significant regulatory effect on primary production and therefore influence the goods and services provided by plants.

Pollinators

Pollinators are a taxonomically very disparate group of organisms that includes many insect groups and vertebrates such as birds and bats.

Herbivores

Vertebrate grazers and browsers are readily distinguished from invertebrate herbivores, although their impacts may be functionally similar and significant at the ecosystem level. The balance of effects of different types of herbivore can influence the structure of plant cover.

Parasites

Microbial and fungal infections of plants may limit primary production in analogous manner to herbivory. Parasitic associations can also influence the growth pattern of plants and hence their architecture and physiological efficiency.

Micro-symbionts

Mutualistic plant-microbial associations, such as di-nitrogen-fixing bacteria and mycorrhizal fungi.

Secondary regulators

Hyper-parasites and predators

This is a diverse group of microbial parasites and vertebrate and invertebrate predators that feed on organisms in other groups and at other trophic levels.

and Marchand, 1985). 'Allochthonous' organic matter (i.e. dead organic matter produced outside and transported into an ecosystem) is significant for the stability of ecosystems. At local scales dissolved or particulate organic matter may be dispersed by rivers during flooding (Junk et al, 1989). At larger scales, the annual migration of Pacific salmon (*Oncorhynchus* spp.) plays a key role in marine–freshwater nutrient recycling over vast distances (Mitchell and Lamberti, 2005), with known dependencies for aquatic insect communities in Alaskan streams (Lessard and Merritt, 2006), for brown bears (*Ursus arctos*) and for predatory birds (Hilderbrand et al, 1999; Helfield and Naiman, 2006) and surrounding forest ecosystems. Polis et al (1997) have highlighted the importance of understanding the impacts of nutrient transfers across ecosystem boundaries to the understanding of the dynamics of these systems.

The interactions within communities of organisms at population and community level play a key role in determining the stability and resilience of the ecosystem as a whole. Communities are structured by multiple biotic processes, and external conditions may strongly influence the outcome. Mouritsen et al (1998) for example describe the dramatic impact of elevated summer temperatures on parasitic infections (by microphallid trematodes) on the mud snail *Hydrobia uvae* and amphipod *Corophium volutator* in Danish mudflats. High ambient temperatures in 1990 elevated the infection rate, which in turn led to the complete collapse of the amphipod population. The local extinction of this sediment-stabilizing population subsequently led to significant mudflat erosion and changes in topography. The result was substantive community depauperation, especially in macro-invertebrates, resulting in a change to the ecosystem (see also Griffin et al, 2009).

Understanding the role of biodiversity in ecosystem functioning has been considerably advanced by complementary studies of both the flow of energy and matter through trophic networks and the functional diversity of species within ecosystems (see Diaz and Cabido, 2001; Diaz et al, 2007a; Suding et al, 2008; Srivastava et al, 2009). Villéger et al (2008) have recently explored functional diversity indices that seek to encompass findings from both types of study. De Leo and Levin (1997) made a useful distinction between these two approaches. In practice, they are not mutually exclusive, and both underpin the ability of the ecosystem to support services of value to society. However, an increasing body of scientific evidence indicates that functional diversity, rather than species diversity *per se*, enhances ecosystem functions such as productivity (Tilman et al, 1997a; Hooper and Dukes, 2004; Petchey et al, 2004), resilience to perturbations or invasion (Dukes, 2001; Bellwood et al, 2004) and regulation of the flux of matter (Waldbusser et al, 2004).

Some species have a disproportionate influence on ecosystem functioning relative to their biomass and abundance, and the loss of such a 'keystone' species has cascading effects on community diversity and ecosystem functioning (Bond, 1993). For example, the removal of the Pacific sea otter (*Enhydra lutris*) from Californian coastal ecosystems has led to the loss of the kelp community and many fish species; removal of fish-eating caiman from some areas of the Amazon resulted in a decline in the fish population and catch because of reduced nutrient cycling in the food chain (Williams and Dodd, 1980); large changes in African elephant (*Loxodonta africana*) numbers have substantial effects on plant productivity, soil nutrient cycles and vegetation diversity in savanna woodlands and forests; and the impacts of herbivores on savanna plant communities are altered in ecosystems dominated by tsetse flies (*Glossina* spp.).

A detailed discussion of functional traits, functional groups and functional diversity is provided by Hooper et al (2005), who concluded that:

- Species functional characteristics strongly influence ecosystem properties. An increase in diversity leads to an increase in productivity due to complementary traits among species for resource use.

- Increased biodiversity leads to an increase in response diversity (range of traits of species in the same functional group in response to environmental drivers) resulting in less variability in functioning over time (Hughes et al, 2002; Elmqvist et al, 2003).
- Idiosyncratic effects due to keystone species properties and unique trait-combinations may result in a disproportional effect of losing one particular species compared to the effect of losing one 'average' species.

2.2 The role of diversity in ecosystem functioning

In this section, we discuss issues of diversity and productivity and the roles of functional diversity before examining factors in ecosystem stability and change and the maintenance and generation of services.

2.2.1 Species diversity and productivity: Terrestrial systems

Species dominating a community are generally major controllers of ecosystem function, yet evidence suggests that less obvious or abundant species have major roles in the functioning of ecosystems. These 'ecosystem engineers' (Swift et al, 2004), and 'keystone species' (Lyons et al, 2005), may be uncommon species that greatly influence community dynamics, for example through enhancing resistance to species invasions (Lyons and Schwartz, 2001) or through their role as pollinators and seed dispersers (Cox et al, 1991). The population of an uncommon species may change dramatically in abundance and importance in response to particular conditions (Hobbs et al, 2007) – for example, in temperate lakes, species of plankton respond to seasonal changes in water temperature, mixing and the associated availability of nutrients, resulting in rapid successional changes of species (Abrantes et al, 2006).

The diversity of functional types in soils is strongly linked to productivity. Many experiments have shown significant enhancements of plant production owing to the presence of soil animals, and specifically their diversity in the case of earthworms (Lavelle et al, 2006). The enhancement of primary production might be the result of increased release of nutrients from decomposition, enhancement of mutualistic micro-organisms (van der Heijden et al, 1998), protection against diseases, and effects on soil physical structure. However, experimentally removing key taxonomic groups from soil food webs may have little impact on rates of processes such as soil respiration and net ecosystem production (Ingham et al, 1985; Liiri et al, 2002; Wertz et al, 2006), possibly because the exceptional diversity of soil organisms and the relatively low degree of specialization in many groups means that many different species can perform similar processes (Bradford et al, 2002; Fitter et al, 2005).

The role of biodiversity in maintaining productivity has been studied in theoretical, controlled-environment and small- and large-scale field studies (see, for example, Naeem et al, 1995; Tilman et al, 1996, 1997b; Lawton et al, 1998), but few data are from 'mature' natural ecosystems. Grace et al (2007) compared a large set of natural ecosystems and suggested that the influence of diversity on productivity was weak when examined at small spatial scales. Nevertheless, a meta-analysis of published studies found clear evidence of a positive effect of biodiversity on productivity at the same trophic level where biodiversity was measured (Balvanera et al, 2006). Furthermore, Balvanera et al (2006) draw the following conclusions based on the review of current data:

- Plant diversity appears to enhance below-ground plant and microbial biomass.
- Plant diversity has positive effects on decomposer activity and diversity, and both plant and mycorrhizal diversity increase nutrients stored in the plant compartment of the ecosystem.
- Increasing the diversity of primary producers contributes to a higher diversity of primary consumers.
- Higher plant diversity contributes to lowering plant damage by pest organisms.
- Abundance, survival, fertility and diversity of invasive species is reduced when plant diversity increases.

At large spatial scales, Costanza et al (2007) showed that over half of the spatial variation in net productivity in North America could be explained by patterns of biodiversity if the effects of temperature and precipitation were taken into account.

In intensively managed and disturbed ecosystems, maximum productivity is typically achieved in systems of very low diversity, for example heavily fertilized monocultures. However, these systems require large inputs of resources, including fertilizers, biocides and water, which generally are not environmentally or economically sustainable (Wright, 2008). Sustained high production without anthropogenic resource augmentation is normally associated with high levels of biodiversity in mature ecosystems. In an eight-year study, Bullock et al (2007) reported positive effects of increased species richness on ecosystem productivity in restored grasslands on a range of soil types across southern England. Similarly, Potvin and Gotelli (2008) reported higher productivity in biologically diverse tree plantations in the tropics, suggesting that increasing diversity in timber plantations may be a viable strategy for both timber yields and biodiversity conservation.

2.2.2 Species diversity and productivity: Marine systems

Biodiversity is also associated with enhanced productivity in marine systems (Worm et al, 2006). Arenas et al (2009) examined how different components of biodiversity influence the performance of macroalgal assemblages in natural communities. They found positive relationships for biomass and species richness with productivity but also relationships of spatial aggregation and species evenness with some of the productivity-related variables analysed. In a meta-analysis of published experimental data Balvanera et al (2006) found that increased biodiversity of both primary producers and consumers enhanced the ecosystem processes examined; the restoration of marine ecosystems has also been shown to increase productivity substantially. Overfishing together with climate change and other pressures are producing impacts of unprecedented intensity and frequency on marine ecosystems, causing changes in biodiversity, structure and organization of marine assemblages directly and indirectly

(Worm et al, 2006). Numbers and diversity of large pelagic predators have been sharply reduced and the impacts of this loss can cascade through marine communities (Heithaus et al, 2008). Predictions about how communities will respond to marine predator declines have to consider the risk effects and behaviourally mediated indirect interactions. In the case of vertebrate predators and long-lived prey species in particular, a sole focus on direct predation might greatly underestimate the community effects of predator loss (Heithaus et al, 2008).

Although evidence from numerous experiments has very often shown a positive, but near universal saturating relationship between biodiversity and ecosystem functioning (Loreau, 2008), analysis of deep-sea ecosystems has shown a very different pattern. A recent global-scale study based on 270 datasets from 116 deep-sea sites showed that functioning of these ecosystems is not only positively but also exponentially related to biodiversity in all the deep-sea regions investigated (Danovaro et al, 2008). Three independent indicators of ecosystem efficiency were used: (1) the meiofaunal biomass to organic C fluxes ratio, to estimate the system's ability to use the photic's zone primary production; (2) the prokaryote C production to organic C flux ratio, to estimate the system's ability to use and recycle organic matter deposited on the sea floor; and (3) the total ratio of benthic meiofaunal biomass to sediment's biopolymeric C content, to estimate the system's ability to channel detritus to higher trophic levels. Significant and exponential relationships were found between biodiversity and each of these three independent indicators. Results suggest that higher biodiversity supports higher rates of ecosystem processes and an increased efficiency with which these processes are performed (Danovaro et al, 2008). These exponential relationships support the hypothesis that mutually positive functional interactions (ecological facilitation) are prevalent in these deep-sea ecosystems. Although there is still no full understanding of all the processes regulating deep-sea food webs and the ecological role of each species, it is hypothesized that the increase in bioturbation of the seafloor may increase benthic fluxes and the redistribution of food within the sediment, leading to an increase in ecosystem functioning. These results suggest that biodiversity loss in deep-sea ecosystems might be associated with significant reductions in functioning. Deep-sea sediments cover 65 per cent of the world's surface, and deep-sea ecosystems play a key role in ecological and biogeochemical processes at a global scale. The importance of deep-sea biodiversity in maintaining the sustainable functioning of the worlds' oceans may still be grossly underestimated (Danovaro et al, 2008).

2.3 Functional groups and functional diversity

Functional groups are groups of organisms that perform particular operations in an ecosystem. They might, for example, produce biomass, pollinate, fix nitrogen, disperse seeds, consume other organisms, decompose biomass, mix soils, modify water flows, or facilitate reorganization and colonization. Loss of a major functional group may cause drastic alterations in ecosystem functioning (Chapin et al, 1997; Jackson et al, 2001). Hooper et al (2005) concluded that certain combinations of species are complementary in their patterns of resource use and can increase average rates of productivity and nutrient retention, making diversity of functional traits one of the key controls on ecosystem properties.

Redundancy or *contingency* (i.e. more than one species performing the same process role) in functional traits and responses in ecosystems may act as an 'insurance' against the loss of individual species. This is enhanced if the diversity of species in the ecosystem encompasses a variety of functional response types (Hooper et al, 2005; Winfree and Kremen, 2009). *Response diversity* (i.e. different responses to environmental change among species that contribute to the same ecosystem function) has been argued to be critical in ecosystem resilience (Elmqvist et al, 2003). Such species may replace each other over time, contributing to the maintenance of ecosystem function over a range of environmental conditions. Regional losses of such species increase the risk of large-scale catastrophic ecosystem change because external species sources of for ecosystem recovery after disturbance are lost (O'Neill and Kahn, 2000; Bellwood et al, 2004). This is a poorly understood area, but nonetheless current ecological theory predicts that when an ecosystem service is provided jointly by many species, it will be stabilized against disturbance by a variety of 'stabilizing mechanisms'. Few studies have investigated the occurrence of stabilizing mechanisms in landscapes affected by human disturbance. Winfree and Kremen (2009) used two datasets on crop pollination by wild native bees to assess three potential stabilizing mechanisms: density compensation (negative co-variance among species' abundances); response diversity (differential response to environmental variables among species); and cross-scale resilience (response to the same environmental variable at different scales by different species). They found evidence for response diversity and cross-scale resilience, but not for density compensation, concluding that these mechanisms may contribute to the stability of pollination services, thus emphasizing the insurance value of seemingly 'redundant' species.

2.4 The complexity of finding quantitative links between biodiversity and ecosystem services

In principle it should be straightforward to relate biodiversity measures to ecosystem service delivery, but in practice it is complicated by several factors (see also Chapter 3). First, biodiversity is a multidimensional concept and its description and measurement therefore takes many forms. Descriptions of biodiversity include classifications of the various hierarchical levels (communities, species, individuals, genes) but also of other dimensions such as interaction webs (trophic, host–parasite, pollinator), evolutionary diversity based on phylogenetic trees, trait diversity based on species-specific traits, or composite measures that attempt to summarize multiple measures. Some of these measures have been developed with a particular purpose in mind, others are attempts to simplify the complexity.

The second problem relates to the diverse set of purposes for the various measures of biodiversity that have been developed. Most available measures have been developed for specific purposes, and may not be appropriate for a particular need. For example, many available datasets that show large-scale (global, continental, major biome) distributions of biodiversity are measures of species richness, primarily derived for conservation reporting and planning, and tend to be counts of species richness or measures of population trends for large-bodied animals and plants. At smaller spatial and geographical scales, information is more varied, but again it is often gathered for particular purposes (e.g. national reporting to international bodies for food and agricultural production and trade, conservation reporting, environmental quality monitoring). Therefore, most of the available data have been collected for another purpose, and are not obviously applicable to measures of biodiversity change that can inform analyses of ecosystem service delivery.

The third problem is that, although ecosystem service delivery often increases in quality, quantity or resilience with increasing biodiversity, the strength and the form of the relationship, and the measure of biodiversity that is the best predictor of ecosystem service quality or quantity, varies widely according to the ecosystem service being considered.

The above considerations mean that it is not yet possible to account accurately for the role of biodiversity, nor the probable impact of its decline, on ecosystem service delivery in general. On the one hand, measures of species richness (and subsets such as endemism, rarity, threat, etc.), which are available globally for vertebrates and some plant groups, are hard to link directly to ecosystem functions and processes. On the other hand, locally available, ecosystem-specific or taxon-specific measures of functional type or functional diversity may relate well to certain specific ecosystem functions, but may not be generally applicable to other valued services in that ecosystem. Unfortunately, these local measures cannot be scaled-up to larger areas or transferred to other ecosystem types.

The extent to which biodiversity metrics can be used for ecosystem service assessments is therefore a direct consequence of whether the measures are correct for the context. Unfortunately, because the understanding of the role of biodiversity is still incomplete, one can only be confident about a few cases where good data are available that are known to support ecosystem service valuations. For example:

- The productivity of terrestrial and aquatic systems for marketed foods, fuels or fibres can be measured using production statistics. The relevant measures of diversity in arable systems, for example, relate to crop genetic diversity, the diversity of land races and wild relatives, and the diversity of pests, pathogens, predators and symbionts. The most relevant biodiversity metric for crops is genetic diversity.
- The ecosystem service of food production depends in many cases on pollinators. Here the relationship between the service and biodiversity is strong, and the relevant metric is pollinator species richness. While the form of these relationships may be quite general, it appears that the resistance of different areas to pollinator loss varies quite widely according to the nature of the plant-pollinator interaction web in that ecosystem, and the recent history of pollinator and plant decline.
- Many cultural services depend primarily on species diversity, and tend to concentrate on the large-bodied, charismatic plants, birds and mammals. The relationships between the service and biodiversity in these cases are very strongly dominated by diversity measures that never saturate. In fact

the values increase with the addition of more, rare forms. For these purposes, the global conservation species datasets are useful and highly relevant. However, the relationships do not scale down simply within countries or local areas.

• The ecosystem service of freshwater quality shows a weak but rapidly saturating relationship with biodiversity and is strongly focused on a few functional types that are likely to be generally applicable across both scales and systems.

Some work done on ecosystem processes such as primary productivity or decomposition (referred to as supporting services in the Millennium Ecosystem Assessment (MA, 2005)) may also be relevant for many ecosystem services that ultimately depend on them. In studies, plant functional traits such as leaf area or plant size are strong predictors of ecosystem process strength, and measures such as the weighted mean of the plants in the community are the best predictor, though sometimes the presence or absence of particular trait values are also very significant (Diaz et al, 2007b; Suding et al, 2008).

3 The links between biodiversity, ecosystem functions and ecosystem services

The following review of the evidence base for links between biodiversity, ecosystem functions and specific ecosystem services is based on two recent reviews, Balmford et al (2008) and the European Academies Science Advisory Council report 'Ecosystem services and biodiversity in Europe' (EASAC, 2009) and updated with additional studies and reports. Substantial knowledge gaps remain, and understanding of the underlying processes for the generation of several services is limited; the following presentation reflects this variable knowledge. This section follows the general typology of services presented in Chapter 1 and treats the services one by one, with the potential linkages among multiple ecosystem services further discussed in Section 4. The typology where services are classified as *provisioning, regulating, habitat and cultural* is mainly used as a way of structuring information and does not reflect the inherent complexity where, for example, a provisioning service, like fish, is not just representing a protein source, but also carries a strong cultural dimension related to harvesting techniques, preparation, symbolism and so on. To place cultural values in a separate category is thus underestimating the cultural dimension of many of the services in other categories and this should be an area for further development.

Provisioning services

3.1 Provision of food

Context and importance of service

Agro-ecosystems provide food for human consumption and, together with the associated ecosystems supporting marine and freshwater fisheries, underpin global food security. Today 35 per cent of the Earth's surface is used for growing crops or rearing livestock (MA, 2005). Grazing land alone accounts for 26 per cent of the Earth's land surface, and animal feed crops account for a third of all cultivated land (FAO, 1999). Heywood (1999) estimated that well over 6000 species of plants are known to have been cultivated at some time or another, and many thousands that are grown locally are scarcely or only partly domesticated, while as many, if not more, are gathered from the wild. Despite this, only about 30 crop species provide 95 per cent of humanity's food (Williams and Haq, 2002) and it has been argued that the world is currently over-dependent on a few plant species.

Plants and animals derived directly from marine biodiversity provide a significant part of the human diet. Fisheries and aquaculture produced 110 million tonnes of food fish in 2006, a *per capita* supply of 16.7kg (FAO, 2009). Almost half of this (47 per cent) was produced by aquaculture. For nearly 3 billion people, fish represent at least 15 per cent of their average *per capita* animal protein intake. Whereas official statistics estimate that in low-income food-deficit countries, the contribution of fish to the total animal protein intake was <20 per cent, the true proportion is probably higher in view of the under-recorded contribution of small-scale and subsistence fisheries (FAO, 2009).

Sensitivity of service to variation in biodiversity: Terrestrial agro-ecosystems

Harlan (1975) argued that the increasing dependence on fewer species for crops was leading to the loss of native genetic resources, and higher yielding modern varieties were displacing 'landraces' uniquely adapted to local conditions. In genetic terms, landraces are typically heterozygous at many loci, and this *in-situ* gene pool, together with that in wild crop relatives, remains an essential source of genetic diversity for plant breeders for new varieties. Failure to maintain sufficient genetic diversity in crops can incur high economic and social costs. The potato famine in Ireland in the 19th century is generally attributed to the low genetic diversity of the potatoes cultivated there, making the entire crop susceptible to potato blight fungus, a problem resolved by using resistant varieties from original gene pools in South America. Mixtures of varieties may successfully reduce disease incidence and increase yields, as for example with the case of barley in Europe (Hajjar et al, 2008; see general review in de Vallavieille-Pope, 2004), although there is much variation and often conflicting conclusions are drawn.

Hooper et al (2005) argue that maintenance of high productivity over time in monocultures almost invariably requires heavy and unsustainable subsidies of chemicals, energy and financial capital (EASAC, 2009). They suggest that, from both economic and ecological perspectives, diversity must become increasingly important as a management goal. Organic farming can increase biodiversity (species richness and abundance), but with inconsistent effects among organisms and landscapes (Bengtsson et al, 2005). Even though crop yields may be 20 per cent lower in organic farming systems, inputs of fertilizer and energy may be reduced by 30–50 per cent, and pesticide input by >90 per cent, suggesting that the enhanced soil fertility and higher biodiversity found in organic plots may render these systems less dependent on external inputs (Mader et al, 2002). In addition, they may be as profitable, or more so, than conventional agro-industrial systems. However, reduced yields in organic farming result in a trade-off between land for agriculture and land for maintaining wild biodiversity. Biodiversity could be promoted by using intensive agriculture and devoting spare land to biodiversity or by extending 'organic' or integrated farming systems that promote biodiversity (Fischer et al, 2008), but the outcomes of these two approaches would be very different.

The value of biodiversity is evident in permanent grassland and pasture ecosystems, where increased species richness often enhances biomass productivity and ecosystem functioning (Naeem et al, 1995; Tilman et al, 1996, 1997a, 1997b; Bullock et al, 2007). Such gains appear to exploit species complementarity (Cardinale et al, 2007), but may also reflect the 'sampling effect' (McNaughton, 1993) – that is, the relative higher frequency of the more productive species in a mixture.

Sensitivity of service to variation in biodiversity: Marine systems and aquaculture

With dwindling marine fish stocks worldwide, aquaculture is thought to be the way to increase fish production necessary to feed an increasing human population. But this activity, which has been growing rapidly and accounts now for half of global fish production, is still very dependent on wild fish for seed and feed (FAO, 2009) and thus on functioning natural ecosystems and biodiversity. Intensively cultured fish and shrimp are fed on fish meal and fish oil that comes mainly from fishing (Deutsch et al, 2007). Furthermore, most aquaculture uses other ecosystem services, especially nutrient recycling and water purification. Since they are concentrated in coastal areas, strong impacts are already being felt in some places (e.g. Chile, Thailand) and this has made the expansion of aquaculture difficult. Although much research has been devoted to the replacement of fish meal and fish oils with land plant-based materials (e.g. soy meal and other cereals), with very good results (Carter and Hauler, 2000; Clayton et al, 2008), provision of these foodstuffs themselves has important environmental impacts (Fearnside, 2001; Steinfeld et al, 2006; FOE, 2008), and their diversion to fish food has nutritional costs for many poor people (Delgado et al, 2003) with high social costs. The use of seaweeds harvested from natural ecosystems or cultivated in seawater (e.g. Valente et al, 2006) may be a way to produce feed for herbivorous fish without burdening fisheries or agricultural land.

Where are services generated?

Food is produced principally in intensively managed agro-ecosystems, but apart from areas devoted to wildlife conservation or recreation, and those used for other production systems (e.g. forestry), most landscapes/seascapes are involved in food production to some extent. Urban and suburban areas have allotment and other forms of gardens that are used for food production, particularly in developing countries. The ubiquity of agricultural production also means that other ecosystems are frequently adjacent to food-producing land, and processes and practices of agriculture may therefore have a broader impact. This may involve spray drift of pesticides, nutrient pollution and barriers to the migration and dispersal of organisms among remaining patches of non-agricultural land, with negative consequences for the ability of distributed populations to withstand environmental change.

Uncertainties in delivery of service

At current levels of consumption, global food production will need to increase by 50 per cent within the next four decades to meet the demands of a growing human population (UN, 2009) and as consumption levels and world food prices rise, pressure to maximize the area under production will grow. Given the rapidly growing demands on the planetary ecosystems (Rockström et al, 2009), it is becoming critical to understand how a dramatic increase in agricultural production and shifting land use in combination with climate change will affect natural processes of the biosphere and levels of key regulating ecosystem services (e.g. CO_2, nitrogen flow, freshwater consumption). Large uncertainties remain about the outcome of these complex interactions. Increasing offshore aquaculture for the production of fish and seaweeds for food will result in substantial intensification of the use of the sea for food production and since the open sea is usually poor in nutrients, these will have to be added (with deep-sea water or artificial fertilization). The effects of these practices for the open sea ecosystems and processes are poorly understood.

3.2 Water provision, including regulation of water flows (3.10) and water purification (3.11)

Context and importance of service: Water provisioning

Ecosystems play important roles in the global hydrological cycle, contributing to water provision (quantity, defined as total water yield), regulation (timing, the seasonal distribution of flows) and purification (quality, including biological purity as well as sediment load) (Dudley and Stolton, 2003; Bruijnzeel, 2004; Brauman et al, 2007). Global water use is dominated by agricultural withdrawals (70 per cent of all use and 85 per cent of consumptive use), including livestock production, followed by industrial and domestic applications. Vegetation, particularly forests, significantly influences the quantity of water circulating in a watershed. It is commonly assumed that forests generate rainfall and, in comparison with pasture and agriculture, promote higher rates of evapotranspiration and greater aerodynamic roughness, leading to increased atmospheric humidity and moisture convergence, and thus to higher probabilities of cloud formation and rainfall generation. Although evidence is increasing (Bruijnzeel, 2004) that large-scale land-use conversions affect cloud formation and rainfall patterns, this effect is highly variable and specific. The hypothesis of a 'biotic pump' has been elaborated by Makarieva et al (2006) and Makarieva and Gorshkov (2007) as an explanation of high rainfall in continental interiors of the Amazon and Congo river basins. Marengo et al (2004) discussed the role of the Amazonian 'water pump' (see Chapter 1, Figure 7), assumed to sustain rain-fed agriculture and other ecological systems elsewhere in the continent. Shiel and Murdiyarso (2009) reviewed the mechanisms and proposed that if the 'water pump' hypothesis proves accurate, modest forest loss may transform conditions in continental interiors from moist to arid, and forest biodiversity may be an underestimated factor in regional rainfall regulation.

Context and importance: Water regulation and purification

In areas with seasonal rainfall, the distribution of stream flow throughout the year is often of greater importance than total annual water yield. This is particularly important to agricultural production, as irrigation is most important during the dry season. The same conditions that increase water infiltration also result in lower surface run-off. The link between regulation of water supply and water quality is strong because rapid flows of water through soil or ecosystems reduce the time in which transformations can occur; extreme weather events thereby lead to poorer water quality.

Sensitivity of services to variation in biodiversity

Although vegetation is a major determinant of water flows and quality, and micro-organisms play an important role in the quality of groundwater, the relationship of water regulation and purification to biodiversity is poorly understood, except insofar as the states of soil and vegetation determine water flows and storage. The activity of soil organisms has a large and direct impact on soil structure and hence on infiltration and retention rates. Ecosystems such as forest and wetlands with intact groundcover and root systems are considered very effective at regulating water flow and improving water quality. Vegetation, microbes and soils remove pollutants from overland flow and from groundwater through various means, including: physically trapping water and sediments; adhering to contaminants; reducing water speed to enhance infiltration; biochemical transformation of nutrients; absorbing water and nutrients from the root zone; stabilizing eroding banks; and diluting contaminated water (Brauman et al, 2007). Changes to water quality that occur in soil include the transformations of persistent organic pollutants (POPs), sequestration and conversion of inorganic ions (nitrate, phosphate, metals), and removal of disease-causing microbes such as *Cryptosporidium* (Lake et al, 2007). Similar processes, including nutrient uptake and consumption of pathogens, occur in water bodies, including lakes and rivers of good ecological quality.

Where are services generated?

Water reaches freshwater stores (lakes, rivers, aquifers) by a variety of routes, including direct precipitation, surface and subsurface flows, and human intervention. In all cases, the water quality is altered by the addition and removal of organisms and substances. Ecosystems therefore play a major role in determining water quality. In particular, the passage of water through soil has a profound impact, both through the dissolution of inorganic (e.g. nitrate, phosphate) and organic (dissolved organic carbon compounds, pesticides) compounds and the modification of many of these by soil organisms. This service is therefore relevant to all terrestrial ecosystems, but may be of particular significance in urban and intensively managed ecosystems.

Uncertainties in delivery of service

Most changes to the capacity of ecosystems to regulate and provide freshwater seem to derive from, and be generally proportional to, land-use change. However, in some situations a relatively small additional change may trigger a disproportionate – and sometimes difficult to reverse – response from ecosystems' hydrological function (Gordon et al, 2008). For example, human-induced eutrophication can lead to sudden shifts in water quality from clear to turbid conditions, due to algal blooms (Scheffer et al, 1993) which affect water quality for potable supply, freshwater fisheries and recreational use of water bodies. Reduction of nutrient concentrations alone is insufficient to restore the original state, with restoration if possible at all necessitating very substantially lower nutrient levels than those at which the regime shift occurred (see Section 5.1 below). Another example is represented by cloud forest loss, which also results in a regime shift that may be largely irreversible. In some areas, such forests were established under a wetter rainfall regime, thousands of years previously. Moisture is supplied through condensation of water from clouds intercepted by the canopy. If the trees are cut, this water input stops and the resulting conditions can be too dry for recovery of the forest (see Folke et al, 2004). In addition, climate change could trigger sudden changes, particularly in regions where ecosystems are already highly water-stressed.

3.3 Fuels and fibres

Context and importance of service

The provision of fuels and fibres – such as timber, cotton, jute, sisal, sugars and oils – has historically been an important ecosystem service. Natural systems provide a great diversity of materials for construction and fuel, notably oils and wood that are derived directly from wild or cultivated plant species. Production of wood and non-wood forest products is the primary commercial function of 34 per cent of the world's forests, while more than half of all forests are used for such production in combination with other functions, such as soil and water protection, biodiversity conservation and recreation. Yet only 3.8 per cent of global forest cover corresponds to forest plantations, indicating that a substantial fraction of natural forests is used for productive uses (FAO, 2006).

There is currently intense interest and strong policy direction to increase the proportion of energy derived from renewable sources, of which biological materials are a part. At present, this is being achieved partly by the cultivation of biomass crops and partly by diversion of materials otherwise useable as food for people or animals, including wheat and maize, to manufacture ethanol as a replacement for petrol and other oil-derived fuels. Recently efforts have been put into the cultivation of algae for biofuels. Although most have selected microalgae known to have high oil content, some studies using macroalgal biomass are also under way (Ross et al, 2008; Adams et al, 2009). This production, which does not need arable land or freshwater, may be a way to produce clean energy without the social costs of terrestrial alternatives. The wider environmental impacts of these cultivations, however, will have to be determined since they would be large-scale operations. In this context, Hill et al (2006) have argued that biodiesel, in comparison to bioethanol, returns such significant environmental advantages that it deserves subsidy.

Sensitivity of service to variation in biodiversity

As in the case of food production, the mix of species cultivated in production forests is selected to maximize the rate of return on timber production, and does not generally reflect the range of ecosystem services that are co-produced with timber – watershed protection, habitat provision, climate amelioration and so on. Managed forests, like farms, typically depend upon a small number of species. The question of whether forests are more productive in terms of biomass if they have higher tree species diversity has been addressed by a few studies, with mixed results. For example, tree species diversity was found to have a negative relationship with above-ground biomass in natural forests of Central Europe (Szwagrzyk and Gazda, 2007), no relationship with productivity in Aleppo pine and Pyrenean Scots forests of Spain (Vilà et al, 2003), and a positive effect on wood production in early successional Mediterranean type forests (Vilà et al, 2007). Although species diversity might lead to higher productivity in the forest, the proportion of commercial species in more diverse sites is typically lower (FAO, 2006). On the other hand, species richness has been found to increase yields in tropical tree plantations, due to increased growth of individual trees (Potvin and Gotelli, 2008), and it may reduce the impact of pests on timber species. At present, however, commercial timber production is dominated by a small number of species.

For biofuels, it seems unlikely that biodiversity of the crop will play a direct role in most production systems, although all land-based biofuel production will still rely on the supporting and regulating services, such as nutrient and water cycling, for which biodiversity of soil organisms is important. The exception is the proposal to use mown grassland as a second-generation biofuel. Sustained production in such a system may well be best achieved by a diverse mixture of plant species. Biofuel production with algae is dependent on aquatic biodiversity for the provision of species adapted to the different places where cultivations would be held.

Where are services generated?

Most ecosystems are important, including forests, savannas, grasslands and marine and coastal systems, in delivering this service. Ecosystems likely to be used for biofuel production include forests, arable land generally and grasslands. There is likely to be strong pressure to bring land currently regarded as marginal for agriculture into production for biofuel production, because time-to-market issues are less important than for food production systems. Remote and relatively inaccessible areas where land values are low may be targets for biofuel systems, introducing conflicts with recreation, biodiversity conservation and subsistence food production.

Uncertainties in delivery of service

It is likely that a decline in the provision of wild timber, plant fibres and fuelwood will take place in proportion to the decline in the forested area. Fragmentation, however, may result in a much quicker decline in forest productivity than what would be expected given the total area of remaining forest (Laurance et al, 2001). Climate change has also been implicated in increasing forest fire risk (e.g. Westerling et al, 2006) and the combined effects of fragmentation and climate change may conspire to prompt an abrupt increase in fire risk, which may be particularly devastating (and less likely to be reversible) in tropical rain forests, as species are not ecologically adapted to fire, and each fire event tends to increase the likelihood that future fires will take place.

3.4 Genetic resources

Context and importance of service

Genetic diversity of crops increases production and decreases susceptibility to pests and climate variation (Ewel, 1986; Altieri, 1990; Zhu et al, 2000). In low-input systems especially, locally adapted varieties often produce higher yields or are more resistant to pests than varieties bred for high performance under optimal conditions (Joshi et al, 2001). In agriculture, the diversity of genetic resources comprises the traditional resources (wild types and the older domesticated landraces) together with modern cultivars. Genetic resources will be increasingly important in support of improved breeding programmes (e.g. for crop plants, farm animals, fisheries and aquaculture), with a wide range of objectives for increasing yield, resistance to disease, optimization of nutritional value, and adaptation to local environment and climate change. Advances in genomics research are opening up a new era in breeding, where the linkage of genes to traits (marker-assisted selection) provides a more efficient and predictable route than conventional breeding programmes to improved strains.

Sensitivity of service to variation in biodiversity

This is a service for which biodiversity is of central importance, because genetic diversity is inevitably lost when biodiversity declines. The greatest focus on genetic diversity as a service is in the protection of gene pools for agriculture. The Food and Agriculture Organization of the United Nations (FAO) has done much significant work at the global level to support characterization of genetic resources in the food crop, livestock, fisheries/aquaculture and forestry sectors, but quantifiable data on trend analysis in genetic resources are very limited and have been collected only for relatively brief periods. There are now numerous initiatives to collect, conserve, study and manage genetic resources *in situ* (e.g. growing crops) and *ex situ* (e.g. seed and DNA banks) worldwide. New techniques using molecular markers are providing new precision in characterizing biodiversity (at the level of molecular systematics and taxonomy) and the genetic diversity within collections – a significant aid to developing management strategy to identify gaps and redundancy (Fears, 2007). Box 2.2 highlights the fundamental importance (option/insurance value) of this reservoir of genetic diversity to crop improvement for stress tolerance.

Where are services generated?

All ecosystems are important for their genetic resources. Agricultural biodiversity can be considered to have a special status because of previous human efforts to improve varieties, hence the specific focus of the International Treaty on Plant Genetics Resources to conserve resources for food and agriculture. The replacement of landraces by high-yielding food crop varieties, taken together with other changes in agricultural practice, has accelerated the erosion of genetic variation in cultivated material. The loss of genetic diversity associated with more intensive agriculture may also have deleterious impacts on the non-domesticated plants and animals (and micro-organisms) in the ecosystem. A decline in crop genetic diversity has consequences for their genetic vulnerability and their plasticity, for example to respond to biotic and abiotic stress.

Box 2.2 Biodiversity at the gene level

A success story

In low-lying agricultural regions of the world, in Bangladesh and India for example, farmers suffer annual crop losses because of flooding of up to 4 million tons of rice (*Oryza sativa*) – enough to feed 30 million people – and the costs across the vast rain-fed lowland areas of Asia, as a whole, amount to about a billion dollars. Flood tolerance originally observed in a traditional Indian variety FR13A, and subsequently located with molecular markers and transferred into modern cultivars by conventional plant breeding (Xu et al, 2006), is conferred by a particular gene, the Sub1A-1 gene at the polygenic 'Submergence-1' (Sub1) locus. This gene halts the elongation of rice stems as a response to flooding, ensuring carbohydrate conservation for further growth when flood waters recede, and enhances yield over susceptible varieties (see Figure 2.2). Phylogenetic analysis has shown that this particular gene is also present in wild relatives *O. rufipogon* and *O. nivara* that persist in the wetlands of south and south-east Asia. These wetlands, such as the Plain of Reeds in southern Vietnam, not only provide ecosystem services in regulation of water flow and quality but also act as a habitat for the evolution of genetic variation among *Oryza* species.

A current threat

The evolution of a new race (Ug99) of wheat stem rust (*Puccinia graminis*) in 1999 in the East African Highlands, and its subsequent range expansion from Kenya to Ethiopia has followed the predominant west–east airflows dispersing spores. It

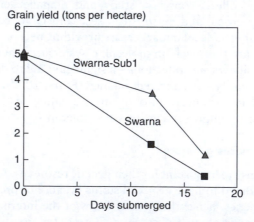

Figure 2.2 *The impact of insertion of the Sub-1 gene on the yield of the rice cultivar Swarna*

Note: This gene confers tolerance to early submergence in water. Plants were completely submerged 14 days after the transplanting of 14-day-old seedlings in field trials at the International Rice Research Institute.

Source: Mackill, 2006

threatens global wheat production because of the absence of resistance in most modern cultivars. The potential migration path from East Africa via the Arabian peninsular to the Middle East into the rice-wheat belt of the Indo-Gangetic plains represents a major threat to food security in South Asia. Strategies to mitigate the risks of loss of yield in a crop that underpins the livelihoods of millions of people requires the breeding of durable resistance into cultivars locally adapted for yield potential. Incorporating different combinations of race-specific resistance genes into new cultivars is one way forward. Such genetic diversity is present in germ plasm of wild relatives of wheat (e.g. *Triticum speltoides* and *T. monococcum*) and traditional Kenyan landraces (Singh et al, 2006).

Uncertainties in delivery of service

Given the likely non-linear relationship between area of natural habitat, or of traditional agricultural lands and genetic diversity, in some cases a small change in area may result in a disproportionate loss in genetic diversity of crops or livestock. This is probably more likely in areas that have already suffered extensive habitat loss and land conversion where the remaining populations of particular varieties and breeds are quite small. Climate change may also have non-linear effects on genetic diversity of crops and livestock.

3.5 Medicinal and other biochemical resources

Context and importance of service

Biochemicals encompass a broad range of chemicals of high value, for example metabolites, pharmaceuticals, nutrients, crop protection chemicals, cosmetics and natural products for industrial use (e.g. enzymes, gums, essential oils, resins, dyes, waxes) and as a basis for biomimetics that may become increasingly important in nanotechnology applications as well as in wider contexts (Ninan, 2009). Some of the best-characterized examples are pharmaceuticals, the value of which has been long recognized in indigenous knowledge. It has been estimated that 'of the top 150 prescription drugs used in the U.S., 118 originate from natural sources: 74% from plants, 18% from fungi, 5% from bacteria, and 3% from one vertebrate (snake species)' (ESA, 2000). In addition to these high-value biochemical products, there is an important related consideration in the use of biomass for chemical feedstocks in addition to bioenergy, where development of integrated biorefineries will generate the building blocks (platform chemicals) for industrial chemistry. A report from the US Environmental Protection Agency (2007) concludes that economically competitive products (compared with oil-derived) are within reach, for example for celluloses, proteins, polylactides, plant oil-based plastics and polyhydroxyalkanoates (Ahmann and Dorgan, 2007). High product values may make the use of biomass economically viable, leading to conflicts over land use.

Sensitivity of service to variation in biodiversity

Biodiversity is the fundamental resource for bioprospecting, but it is rarely possible to predict which species or ecosystem will become an important source. A wide variety of species – microbial, plant and animal – have been valuable sources of biochemicals, but the achievements so far are assumed to be only a very small proportion of what could be possible by more systematic screening. The impact of the current global decline in biodiversity on the discovery of novel biochemicals and applications is probably grossly underestimated. Biodiversity loss resulting from relatively low-value activities such as logging may compromise future high-value activities (as yet undiscovered) associated with the search for novel biochemicals and chemicals.

Where are services generated?

All ecosystems are potential sources of biochemicals. Numerous examples can be cited from the oceans and shoreline, freshwater systems, forests, grasslands and agricultural land. Species-rich environments such as tropical forests have often been assumed to supply the majority of products. However, the problem of the general lack of a robust and reliable measure to assess the commercial or other value of an ecosystem is compounded by the expectation that most biochemical resources have yet to be discovered and exploited. Microbes seem likely to be especially rich in undiscovered metabolic capacities, and the complexity of soil ecosystems indicates the potential in searching for novel biochemicals there.

Uncertainties in delivery of service

Species richness may be quickly reduced as habitat destruction progresses in highly diverse regions (e.g. Forest et al, 2007), and the sources of biochemicals may change abruptly, for example in coral reefs going through a phase shift.

3.6 Ornamental resources

Context and importance of service

Biodiversity has played an iconic, ornamental role throughout the development of human society. Uses of plant and animal parts, especially plumage of birds, have been important in conferring individual status, position and influence. Ornamental plants are typically grown for the display of their flowers but other common ornamental features include leaves, scent, fruit, stem and bark. Considerable exploration effort, and some of the rationale of the voyages of discovery, was underpinned by the search for and transfer of species to be enjoyed in parks, gardens, private greenhouses and zoos by wealthy members of societies less endowed with biodiversity.

A modern example is provided by the statement by the Zoological Society of London that aquarium fish are the most popular pets in the world, representing an industry which in 1999 was worth $3 billion in annual retail sales. About 10 per cent of the species are caught from the wild, causing concerns over the viability of stocks (ZSL, 2006). Over 20 million freshwater fish are exported each year from the Brazilian Amazon and this generated $3 million in 2006 (Prang, 2007). Birds are another focus of the ornamental value of biodiversity. In 1992, the trade in CITES (Convention on International Trade in Endangered Species)-listed wild birds was banned in the US, 'leaving the EU responsible for 87% of the trade' (RSPB, 2007). Because of fears for animal and human health, the EU issued a trade ban from July 2007, saving probably up to 2 million wild birds annually from the pet trade. Following the ban, the Royal Society for the Protection of Birds estimated that trade in CITES-listed threatened birds may drop from ca. 800,000 per year to a few hundred, because 'import of small numbers of wild birds into the EU by zoos and some pet owners will still be allowed' (RSPB, 2007).

Sensitivity of service to variation in biodiversity

The service is related completely to individual species and is highly sensitive to maintenance of viable populations.

Where are services generated?

The same applies as for service 3.5.

Uncertainties in delivery of service

The same applies as for service 3.5.

Regulating services

3.7 Air quality regulation and other urban environmental quality regulation

Context and importance of service

Ecosystems contribute to several environmental regulation services of importance for human well-being, particularly in urban areas where vegetation may significantly reduce air pollution and noise, mitigate the 'urban heat island' effect (e.g. Santamouris, 2001), and reduce impacts related to climate change (Bolund and Hunhammar, 1999). This potential is often substantial (e.g. Pickett et al, 2008). For example, in the Chicago region, trees were found to remove some 5500 tonnes of air pollutants per year, providing a substantial improvement in air quality (McPherson et al, 1997). Vegetation reduces noise levels, and dense shrubs (at least 5m wide) can reduce noise levels by 2dB(A), while a 50m-wide plantation can lower noise levels by 3–6dB(A) (Bolund and Hunhammar, 1999). Evergreen trees are preferred because they contribute to noise reduction year round (Ozer et al, 2008). Urban parks and vegetation reduce the urban heat island effect and have an important potential for lowering urban temperatures when the building envelope is covered with vegetation, such as green roofs and green walls, with the largest effect in a hot and dry climate (Alexandri and Jones, 2008). In relation to overall climate change mitigation, urban ecosystems may assimilate non-negligible quantities of carbon; for example, in Stockholm County ecosystems assimilate about 17 per cent of total anthropogenic CO_2 (Jansson and Nohrstedt, 2001), and residential trees in the continental United States may sequester 20–40 teragrams C per year (Jenkins and Riemann, 2003).

Green areas, vegetation and trees, also have direct health benefits. For example, in a study from New York, presence of street trees was associated with a significantly lower prevalence of early childhood asthma (Lovasi et al, 2008). Green area accessibility has also been linked to reduced mortality

(Mitchell and Popham, 2008) and improved perception of general health (e.g. Maas et al, 2006). In a review by Bird (2007), links were noted between access to green spaces and a large number of health indicators, for example coping with anxiety and stress, treatment for children with poor self-discipline, hyperactivity and Attention Deficit Hyperactivity Disorder (ADHD), benefiting elderly care and treatment for dementia, concentration ability in children and office workers, healthy cognitive development of children, strategies to reduce crime and aggression, strengthened communities, and increased sense of well-being and mental health. The distribution and accessibility of green space to different socio-economic groups, however, often reveals large inequities in cities (e.g. Pickett et al, 2008), contributing to inequity in health among socio-economic groups, although confounding effects are not always possible to separate (Bird, 2007).

Sensitivity of service to variation in biodiversity

To what extent biodiversity and variation in species composition plays a role in the generation of environmental quality services is still poorly investigated (Elmqvist et al, 2008). For air quality, filtering capacity increases with leaf area, and is thus higher for trees than for bushes or grassland (Givoni, 1991). Coniferous trees have a larger filtering capacity than trees with deciduous leaves (Givoni, 1991). Figure 2.3 illustrates a hypothesized distribution of species richness in relation to degree of anthropogenic impact. The urban core has fewer species and often very different species involved in generation of ecosystem services than in more rural areas. Interestingly, the number of plant species in urban areas often correlates with human population size, and plant diversity may correlate positively with measures of economic wealth, as shown for example, in Phoenix, USA (Kinzig et al, 2005).

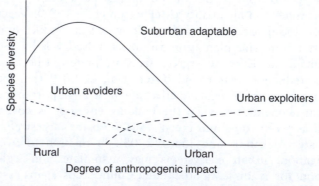

Figure 2.3 *Organisms may respond differently to increasing human impact*

Note: Urban avoiders are large-bodied species or species linked to late successional stages. These species might be very sensitive and show a decline already at moderate human impacts. Suburban adaptable species may, to various degrees, utilize human modifications of the landscape; a large number of plant and animal species are likely to belong to this group. Urban exploiters directly benefit from human presence for food, reproduction or protection, and may often be cosmopolitan, generalist species.

Source: Elmqvist et al (2008)

Where are services generated?

Urban ecosystem services may be generated in a diverse set of habitats, including parks, cemeteries, vacant lots, streams, lakes, gardens and yards, campus areas, golf courses, bridges, airports and landfills. To what extent exotic species contribute to reduced or enhanced flow of ecosystem services is virtually unknown for any urban area, but since introduced species make up a large proportion of the urban biota, it is important to know not only to what extent introduced species are detrimental, but also to what degree some of the introduced species may enhance local diversity and maintain important functional roles.

Uncertainties in delivery of service

Considerable knowledge gaps remain about uncertainties and dynamics of urban ecosystem services. The Millennium Ecosystem Assessment (MA, 2005), which covered almost every other ecosystem in the world, largely neglected urban systems, while on the other hand, the World Development Report (World Bank, 2009), the world's largest assessment of urbanization, has left out ecosystems. Considerable uncertainties relate to the extent that isolation and fragmentation in the urban landscape influence the sustained generation of environmental quality services, and to the effects of climate change and rapid turnover of species on ecological functions of importance for these services.

3.8 Climate regulation

Context and importance of service

Climate is regulated on Earth by a natural 'greenhouse effect' that keeps the surface of the planet at a temperature conducive to the development and maintenance of life. Numerous factors interact in the regulation of climate, including the reflection of solar radiation by clouds, dust and aerosols in the atmosphere. In recent years the climate has been changing and the Earth is becoming warmer. Current change is driven largely by increases in the concentrations of trace gases in the atmosphere, principally as a result of changes in land use and rapidly rising rates of combustion of fossil fuels. The major greenhouse gas (CO_2) is absorbed directly by water and indirectly (through photosynthesis) by vegetation, leading to storage in biomass and in soils as organic matter; the ability of soils to store carbon is a major regulator of climate. Other greenhouse gases, notably methane (CH_4) and nitrous oxide (N_2O) are regulated by soil microbes. Organisms in the marine environment play a significant role in climate control through their regulation of carbon fluxes, by acting as a reserve or sink for CO_2 in living tissue and by facilitating burial of carbon in seabed sediments (Beaumont et al, 2007). The capacity of the marine environment to act as gas and climate regulator is very dependent on its biodiversity.

An additional issue is the impact of vegetation on albedo – the reflection of incident radiation by land surfaces. Dark surfaces, especially those covered by evergreen forest, absorb more radiation than light surfaces, especially snow. Consequently, afforestation of boreal zones may lead to greater levels of warming, potentially outweighing the reduction expected from enhanced carbon sequestration by new trees.

Aerosols have a profound effect on climate, by intercepting and scattering radiation, and by acting as cloud condensation nuclei, thus reducing the amount of solar radiation reaching the Earth's surface. The production of aerosols by marine systems is well understood and has been taken into account in climate models. However, evidence is increasing that forests emit substantial amounts of biogenic volatile organic compounds, which can form aerosol particles. Forests are therefore simultaneously sinks for CO_2, sources of aerosol particles and determinants of albedo (Kulmala et al, 2004).

Sensitivity of service to variation in biodiversity

The interplay between biodiversity and climate regulation is poorly understood. The largest single store of carbon in terrestrial ecosystems globally is in the peat soils of the boreal and cool temperate zones of the northern hemisphere. The response of peatlands to climate change is crucial to predicting potential feedbacks on the global carbon cycle (Belyea and Malmer, 2004). The climate-regulating function of peatlands also depends on land use because intensification of land use is likely to have profound impacts on soil carbon storage and on the emission of trace gases. Considering the area of drained and mined peatlands, restoration on abandoned mined peatlands may represent an important biotic offset through enhanced carbon sequestration (Waddington and Warner, 2001). However, mires are also major sources of potent greenhouse gases and the biodiversity of soil microbes is likely to play an important role in trace gas (methane) production (Roulet, 2000). Current evidence is weak for the role played by soil biodiversity in key processes leading either to carbon sequestration or to the release of trace gases.

The exchange of CO_2 between atmosphere and ocean is larger than that between atmosphere and terrestrial ecosystems. Some of this occurs by physical processes, involving the equilibrium between CO_2 and carbonate, but a significant proportion is accounted for by biological processes. Although oceanic macrophytes account for less than 1 per cent of global biomass carbon, the net primary productivity of the oceans is roughly equal to that of all terrestrial systems.

Where are services generated?

All soils store carbon, but to widely varying extents. The largest stores are in peatlands, but soils rich in organic matter occur in many ecosystems, especially where low temperature, low pH or waterlogging inhibit decomposition. Forests are the only major ecosystems where the amount of carbon stored in biomass of the plants exceeds that in the soil; deforestation therefore also affects climate regulation. Agricultural ecosystems currently have low soil carbon stores owing to intensive production methods, and there is scope for enhancing those stores. Marine ecosystems also play a major role in climate regulation through carbon sequestration and aerosol emission.

Uncertainties in delivery of service

Many uncertainties are associated with this service, particularly related to large time lags in the feedbacks between changes in ecosystem processes and the atmosphere. The global carbon cycle is strongly buffered, in that much of the

CO_2 discharged by human activities into the atmosphere is absorbed by oceans and terrestrial ecosystems (Janzen, 2004). However, the rate of emissions increasingly exceeds absorption capacity, and this capacity is at the same time reduced still further by anthropogenic damage to ecosystems. The complex interactions and long time lags make it very difficult to forecast eventual outcomes or if and when important thresholds will be passed.

3.9 Moderation of extreme events

Context and importance of service

Extreme events or 'natural hazards' are defined here as infrequent phenomena that may pose a high level of threat to life, health or property. Living organisms can form and create natural barriers or buffers, such as forests (including mangroves), coral reefs, seagrasses, kelp forests, wetlands and dunes, and these can mitigate the effects of some natural hazards such as coastal storms (Wells et al, 2006), hurricanes (Costanza et al, 2006), catchment-borne floods (Bradshaw et al, 2007), tsunamis (Kathiresan and Rajendran, 2005), avalanches (Gruber and Bartelt, 2007), wild fires (Guenni et al, 2005) and landslides (Sidle et al, 2006). The available evidence for some of these effects is still scarce, and in some cases controversial. Many hazards arise from human interaction with the natural environment and are sensitive to environmental change. Examples include:

- flash floods due to extreme rainfall events on heavily managed ecosystems that cannot retain rainwater;
- landslides and avalanches;
- storm surges due to sea-level rise and the increasing use of hard coastal margins;
- air pollution due to intensive use of fossil fuels combined with extreme summer temperatures;
- fires caused by prolonged drought, with or without human intervention.

Sensitivity of service to variation in biodiversity

The role of biodiversity in delivering protection from natural hazards is generally small, but it has a role in facilitating recovery from such perturbations. In some particular cases, the ecological integrity of the affected ecosystem is of central importance, and it is likely that loss of biodiversity reduces resilience. Biodiversity plays a key role in the preservation of wetlands and coastal systems such as mangroves that deliver significant ecosystem services. For example, sea-level rise places intense selective pressures on halophytic vegetation, the fate of which is critical to the survival of salt marshes and other transition ecosystems (Marani et al, 2004). In mountain forests, increasing tree diversity is believed to enhance the protection value against, for example, rock fall (see, for example, Dorren et al, 2004).

Where are services generated?

Flooding is a problem in a wide range of ecosystems, including steep deforested catchments, flat alluvial plains and urban ecosystems with constrained water flows.

Flooding can also occur because of exceptionally high tides and storm surges, a problem that will be exacerbated by rising sea levels; coastal wetlands are known to play a major part in defence against tidal flooding. Wind breaks from managed or natural woods are a traditional means of protecting crops and habitations against both violent storms and general damage from exposure to high winds. In all these cases the role of vegetation is structural, and the part played by species diversity is in controlling the stability and resilience of the system.

Marine flora and fauna can play a valuable role in the defence of coastal regions, and dampen or prevent the impact of tidal surges, storms and floods. This disturbance alleviation service is provided mainly by a diverse range of species which bind and stabilize sediments and create natural sea defences, for example salt marshes, mangrove forests, kelp forests and seagrass beds (Rönnbäck et al, 2007). Natural hazard regulation services show a declining trend due to loss of natural buffers such as wetlands and mangroves. For example, 20 per cent or 3.6 million ha have been lost from the 18.8 million ha of mangrove forests covering the planet in 1980 (FAO, 2007); 20 per cent of coral reefs have been seriously degraded in the past two decades (Wilkinson et al, 2006); coastal wetland loss is extremely rapid, reaching 20 per cent annually in some areas. On the other hand, the value of the regulation that is provided by these ecosystems is likely to be escalating, given an increase in human vulnerability to natural hazards.

Uncertainties in delivery of service

The effect of ecosystems on natural hazard mitigation is still poorly understood and it is uncertain to what extent abrupt changes in this service may be associated with abrupt changes in ecosystem extension and condition, for example the degradation of coral reefs or forests due to climate change. If the relationship between hazard regulation and ecosystem extension is an inverse asymptotic relationship, then regions where past ecosystem loss has been extensive may suffer a disproportionate future decline in the provision of this service.

3.12 Erosion prevention

Context and importance of service

Vegetation cover is the key factor preventing soil erosion, as classic historical examples such as the American dust bowl of the 1930s demonstrate, where lack of vegetation cover combined with drought resulted in unprecedented wind erosion, destroying farmland and livelihoods (Cooke et al, 1936). Landslide frequency seems to be increasing, and it has been suggested that land-use change, particularly deforestation, is one of the causes. In steep terrain, forests protect against landslides by modifying the soil moisture regime (Sidle et al, 2006). Increased variability in water flows, together with transport of eroding soil as silt can be devastating to ecosystems and communities downstream (Juo, 2001).

Sensitivity of service to variation in biodiversity

This ecosystem service is not specifically dependent on biodiversity, though in areas of high rainfall, forests may be more effective than grasslands.

Uncertainties in delivery of service

The same apply as for service 3.9.

3.13 Maintenance of soil fertility (including soil formation) and nutrient cycling

Context and importance of service

The process of soil formation is governed by the nature of the parent materials, biological processes, topography and climate. It involves the conversion of a mineral matrix, which has limited capacity to support nutrient cycles, into a complex medium with both inorganic and organic components, and solid, liquid and gas phases in which chemical and biological transformations take place. The progressive accumulation of organic materials is characteristic of the development of most soils, and depends on the activity of a wide range of microbes, plants and associated organisms (Lavelle and Spain, 2001; Brussaard et al, 2007). Soil quality is underpinned by nutrient cycling, which occurs in all ecosystems and is strongly linked to productivity. A key element is nitrogen, which occurs in enormous quantities in the atmosphere and is converted to a biologically useable form (ammonium) by bacteria. Nitrogen fertilizer is increasingly expensive (about 90 per cent of the cost is energy, typically from fossil gas) and supplies are therefore not sustainable. Nitrogen fixation by organisms accounts for around half of all nitrogen fixation worldwide, and sustainable agricultural systems will have to rely on this process increasingly in future.

Sensitivity of service to variation in biodiversity

A large part of the organic material in many soils derives from the faeces of soil animals, and both the gross and fine structure of the soil is determined by biological activity. At a fine scale, structure may depend on fungal mycelia and the activities of mycorrhizal fungi, symbiotic with plant roots, which are the most abundant fungi in most soils (Miller and Jastrow, 2000).

Many different species are implicated in nutrient cycling, which includes numerous transformations of elements often involving complex biochemistry. Nitrogen cycling may depend on diversity of plant communities and particularly on the presence of particular functional groups. Soil biodiversity has a particularly strong impact on nutrient cycling. Barrios (2007), in reviewing the importance of the soil biota for ecosystem services and land productivity, emphasized positive impacts of microbial symbionts on crop yields, as a result of increases in plant available nutrients, especially nitrogen, through biological nitrogen fixation by soil bacteria such as *Rhizobium*, and phosphorus through arbuscular mycorrhizal fungi.

Only 5–10 per cent of added phosphate is recovered in crops, owing to its strong fixation by soils. In natural ecosystems, symbiotic mycorrhizal fungi are the main route of phosphorus transfer from soil to plant, and the diversity of mycorrhizal fungi can regulate both plant diversity and nutrient efficiency, and possibly water-use efficiency (Brussaard et al, 2007). Sustainable agricultural systems will need to make greater use of mycorrhizal fungi, whose diversity is currently very low in arable systems (Helgason et al, 1998). It seems that functional diversity (and its influence on trophic interactions) rather than species diversity alone, is key to the decomposition, nutrient cycling and stability of soil processes.

Where are services generated?

Soil formation is a continuous process in all terrestrial ecosystems, but is particularly important and active in the early stages after land surfaces are exposed (e.g. after glaciation).

Uncertainties in delivery of service

Agricultural expansion into new areas often occupies terrains that are not particularly suitable for agriculture, and soil fertility may decline very quickly as crops effectively mine the soil nutrients (Carr et al, 2006).

3.14 Pollination services

Context and importance of service

In some estimates, over 75 per cent of the world's crop plants, as well as many plants that are source species for pharmaceuticals, rely on pollination by animal vectors (Nabhan and Buchmann, 1997). While the extent to which staple food crops depend on pollinator services has been questioned (e.g. Ghazoul, 2005), Klein et al (2007) found that, for 87 out of 115 leading global crops (representing up to 35 per cent of the global food supply), fruit or seed numbers or quality were increased through animal pollination. In many agricultural systems, pollination is actively managed through the establishment of populations of domesticated pollinators, particularly the honey bee (*Apis mellifera*). However, the importance of wild pollinators for agricultural production is being increasingly recognized (e.g. Westerkamp and Gottsberger, 2000; Kremen et al, 2007) and wild pollinators may also interact synergistically with managed bees to increase crop yields (Greenleaf and Kremen, 2006).

Sensitivity of service to variation in biodiversity

Bees are the dominant taxon providing crop pollination services, but birds, bats, moths, flies and other insects can also be important. Studies in agricultural landscapes commonly show that increasing distances from forest fragments result in a decrease in both abundance and species-richness of flower-visiting bees (e.g. Steffan-Dewenter and Tscharntke, 1999) and a recent quantitative review of 23 studies (Ricketts et al, 2008) found an exponential decay in pollinator richness and native pollinator visitation rate with distance to natural or semi-natural habitats. Hajjar et al (2008) argue that the loss of biodiversity in agro-ecosystems through agricultural intensification and habitat loss negatively affects the maintenance of pollination systems, and causes the loss of pollinators worldwide (Kearns et al, 1998; Kremen and Ricketts, 2000; Richards, 2001; Kremen et al, 2004). Richards (2001) reviewed well-documented cases where low fruit or seed set by crop species, and the resulting reduction in crop yields, has been attributed to the impoverishment of pollinator diversity. Increasing evidence indicates that conserving wild pollinators in habitats adjacent to agriculture improves both the level and the stability of pollination services, leading to increased yields and income (Klein et al, 2003). Furthermore, a diverse assemblage of native pollinators provides insurance against year-to-year population variability or loss of specific pollinator species (Ricketts, 2004; Tscharntke et al, 2005; Hoehn et al, 2008), and might better serve flowers because of pollinator-specific spatial preferences to a flowering plant or crop field (Klein et al, 2007). Given current declines in populations of managed honey bees (Johnson, 2007), and abandonment of beekeeping in regions affected by 'Africanization' of honey bees (Brosi et al, 2008), the importance of wild pollination is likely to increase.

Where are services generated?

This service is important in all ecosystems, though possibly least important in species-poor boreal and arctic systems, where most species are wind-pollinated. Pollinator species often depend on natural or semi-natural habitats for the provisioning of nesting (e.g. tree cavities, suitable soil substrates) and floral resources that cannot be found within crop fields (Kremen et al, 2004). Consequently, the available area of natural habitat has a significant influence on pollinator species richness (Steffan-Dewenter, 2003), abundance (Heard et al, 2007; Morandin et al, 2007), and pollinator community composition (Steffan-Dewenter et al, 2002; Brosi et al, 2007). Loss of suitable habitat is a key driver of declines in pollination services by wild pollinators, and habitat degradation through agricultural intensification leads to scarcity in critical floral and nesting resources for many species. In southern China, large areas of fruit orchards now need to be pollinated by hand since wild pollinators have disappeared, with approximately ten people needed to do the work previously done by one bee colony.

Uncertainties in delivery of service

It is possible that a threshold in pollinator species functional diversity exists, below which pollination services become too scarce or too unstable to persist (Klein et al, 2007). Such a tipping point might occur when, at a landscape context, sufficient habitat is destroyed that the next marginal change causes a population crash in multiple pollinators. Alternatively, a threshold in habitat loss may lead to the collapse of particularly important pollinators, leading to a broader collapse in pollination services. Supporting this prediction, Larsen et al (2005) found that large-bodied pollinators tended to be both most extinction-prone and most functionally efficient, contributing to rapid functional loss with habitat loss. Increased uncertainty is also represented by climate change, as phenological shifts may result in asynchrony and disruption of plant–pollinator interactions (Memmott et al, 2007).

3.15 Biological control

Context and importance of service

Pests and diseases are regulated in ecosystems through the actions of predators and parasites as well as by the defence mechanisms of their prey. Natural control of plant pests is provided by generalist and specialist predators and parasitoids, including birds, bats, spiders, beetles, mantises, flies and wasps, as well as entomopathogenic fungi (Way and Heong, 1994; Naylor and Ehrlich, 1997; Zhang et al, 2007). In the short term, this process suppresses pest damage and improves yields, while in the long term it maintains an ecological equilibrium that prevents populations of herbivorous insects from reaching pest status (Heong et al, 2007; Zhang et al, 2007). Agricultural pests cause significant economic losses worldwide. Globally, more than 40 per cent of food production is being lost to insect pests, plant pathogens and weeds, despite the application of more than 3 billion kilograms of pesticides to crops, plus other means of control (Pimentel, 2008). The services of regulation are expected to be more in demand in future as climate change brings new pests and increases susceptibility of species to parasites and predators.

Sensitivity of service to variation in biodiversity

The diversity of natural enemies seems to improve biological control through a variety of mechanisms, including:

- species complementarity, when more than one type of predator or parasitoid adds to the control of a pest species;
- the sampling effect, whereby a particularly effective natural enemy is more likely by chance alone to occur when more species are present;
- redundancy, where more species will buffer against disturbance or ecosystem change;
- synergy, when the whole is greater than the sum of the parts owing to interactions among species (Tscharntke et al, 2005; Kremen and Chaplin-Kramer, 2007).

A diverse soil community will not only help prevent losses due to soil-borne pests and diseases but also promote other key biological functions of the soil (Wall and Virginia, 2000). Soil-borne pests and diseases such as root-rot fungi cause enormous annual crop losses globally (Haas and Défago, 2005), but bacteria in the rhizosphere (the soil surrounding roots) can protect plant roots from diseases caused by root-rot fungi (Haas and Keel, 2003); similarly, symbiotic mycorrhizal fungi can protect roots from pathogenic fungi (Newsham et al, 1995). Plant-parasitic nematodes represent a major problem in agricultural soils because they reduce the yield and quality of many crops and thus cause great economic losses. However, nematodes have a variety of microbial antagonists that include nematophagous and endophytic fungi, actinomycetes and bacteria (Dong and Zhang, 2006).

Where are services generated?

The natural control of diseases and invasions occurs in all ecosystems. Those heavily influenced by human activity incur the greatest risk of both disease outbreaks and invasion. Data on populations of biological control agents are scarce but the trends are presumed to be negative owing to habitat transformation associated with agricultural intensification (agricultural expansion, enlargement of field size and removal of non-crop habitat, which results in a loss of the natural landscape features required for maintaining their populations) and increasing pesticide use. On the other hand, the increase in organic farming worldwide may help to reverse this trend (Bengtsson et al, 2005; Willer et al, 2008).

Uncertainties in delivery of service

The relationship between densities of natural enemies and the biological control services they provide is unlikely to be linear (Losey and Vaughan, 2006) and biological control functions may decline disproportionately when a tipping point in natural enemy diversity is passed. Empirical evidence in support of this logic is scarce, but the importance of natural enemy assemblage composition in some instances of biological control (Shennan, 2008) indicates that changes in composition can lead to disproportionately large, irreversible and often negative shifts in ecosystem services (Díaz et al, 2006).

Habitat services

The habitat 'service' was identified in Chapter 1 as a distinct category to highlight (a) the interconnectedness of ecosystems in the sense that different ecosystems provide unique and crucial habitats for particular life-cycle stages of migratory species; and (b) that certain ecosystems have been identified that exhibit particularly high levels of species and genetic diversity, which are of major importance for maintenance of life and continued genetic diviersity on Earth, as well as for the capacity for natural adaptation to change. Both of these features underpin all, or most, provisioning, regulating and cultural services (which is why they are often called 'supporting services') but they are distinct services in their own right, as explained below, and depend on particular spatial conditions within ecosystems.

3.16 Maintenance of life cycles of migratory species

Context and importance of service

The life cycle of any species is supported in its entirety or in part by the products and behaviour of many others as well as by the nature of the abiotic environment. Products of ecosystems (e.g. nutrients, seeds) may be exported by wind, water or animals (including humans) to support life cycles of species elsewhere. These interactions between ecosystems should be taken into account when assessing the ecological or economic importance of a given area.

Migratory species, for example some species of fish, birds, mammals and insects, might use an ecosystem for just part of their life cycle. For example, salmonid fish use clean, aerated, shallow areas of flowing water for courtship and egg-laying, and are dependent on these ecosystems to supply clean water and food for juvenile fish (e.g. Kunz, 2004). The adult salmon supports other predatory species, including humans and, on death, contribute significant quantities of organic matter to the river ecosystem. Migrating birds such as geese rely on ecosystems for availability of grazing on their migration 'flyways', and can shape vegetation community composition, affecting competitive interactions and potentially increasing spatial heterogeneity by means of selective feeding (van den Wyngaert and Bobbink, 2009). Some migratory species have commercial value, in which case the ecosystem providing the reproduction habitat provides an important so-called 'nursery-service' which is (economically) valued in its own right (e.g. mangroves, providing reproduction habitat to many species of fish and crustaceans, which are harvested as adults far away from their spawning areas). When economically valuing mangrove-ecosystems, this nursery service should be taken into account.

Sensitivity of service to variation in biodiversity

A high level of interdependency exists among species, and any species loss has consequences, some of which remain unnoticed by human observers, while some will be significant for functioning and provision of ecosystem services for migrating species. Loss of biodiversity will inevitably result in loss of functioning, and consequently, loss or degradation of these ecosystem services (Naeem et al, 1995).

3.17 Maintenance of genetic diversity

Context and importance of service

Genetic diversity, both within and between species populations, is characteristic of all ecosystems and, through natural selection, results in evolution and adaptive radiation of species to particular habitats. The degree of genetic diversity present within a species (which can be expressed in a variety of ways (Nei, 1987)) will depend on individual species' breeding behaviour, the extent to which gene flow occurs between populations, and the biotic and abiotic forces driving selection, in addition to mutation events. Micro-evolution (e.g. of metals tolerance in grasses) can occur over remarkably short distances of a few metres and within a few generations (Antonovics and Bradshaw, 1970). On the other hand, certain species are endemic to particular ecosystems and regions of the world (Morrone, 1994), reflecting macro-evolution. Ecosystems that exhibit particularly high levels of biodiversity (biodiversity hotspots) with exceptional concentrations of endemic species are undergoing dramatic habitat loss. 'As many as 44% of all species of vascular plants and 35% of all species in four vertebrate groups are confined to 25 hotspots comprising only 1.4% of the land surface of the Earth' (Myers et al, 2000). In addition to the overall importance of these 'hotspots' in maintaining genetic diversity, this service is of particular and immediate importance in preserving the gene pool of most of our commercial crops and livestock species. Gene banks, which represent a mechanism of conservation, do not include the processes that generate new genetic diversity and adaptations to environmental change through natural selection.

Sensitivity of service to variation in biodiversity

Preservation of this (remaining) genetic diversity in these hotspots is of strategic value to the provision of ecosystem services, since the hotspots themselves contain not only species richness and genetic diversity within species, but represent the natural laboratory in which evolution can occur. The relationships between biodiversity hotspots, endemism and extinction threat, however, remain a continuing debate in conservation biology (see Prendergast et al, 1993; Orme et al, 2005). The debate about *in-situ* versus *ex-situ* conservation of genetic resources has equivalent prominence in the preservation of sources of both crop and animal germplasm for breeding purposes (see earlier sections). Vavilov (1992) originally promoted the concept of centres of origin of cultivated plants, which recognized that particular temperate and tropical ecosystems were the source of genetic diversity from which crop domestication occurred. The loss of the genetic diversity within habitats in these ecosystems can be only partially balanced by *ex-situ* conservation in gene banks (Nevo, 1998), which by their very nature prohibit the continued evolution among wild, feral and domesticated species in the field.

Cultural and amenity services

3.18 –22 Cultural services: Aesthetic information, opportunities for recreation and tourism, inspiration for culture, art and design, spiritual experience, information for cognitive development

Context and importance of service

Cultural and amenity services refer to the aesthetic, spiritual, psychological and other benefits that humans obtain from contact with ecosystems. Such contact need not be direct, as illustrated by the popularity of the virtual experience of distant ecosystems through books, art, cinema and television. Nor need such contact be of a wild or exotic nature, as shown by the ubiquity of, for example, urban gardens (Butler and Oluoch-Kosura, 2006). The classification here largely follows the one in the Millennium Ecosystem Assessment (MA, 2005) although considerable debate remains about how the wide range of benefits derived from these services should be classified. It has been proposed that many of these services should more appropriately be placed under provisional services, being of similar importance to food, water and so on for human well-being (K. Tidball, pers. comm.). For convenience, these services are here considered as falling into two main groups: (i) spiritual, religious, aesthetic, inspirational and sense of place; and (ii) recreational, ecotouristic, cultural heritage and educational services.

An economic value is hard to apply to those in the first group, while the second group is more amenable to traditional valuation approaches. Although all societies value the spiritual and aesthetic 'services' that ecosystems provide, these may have different significance in affluent, stable and democratic societies. Nevertheless, biodiversity plays an important role in fostering a sense of place in most societies and has considerable intrinsic cultural value. Although recent high-profile research suggests that nature recreation is declining *per capita* in US and Japan (Pergams and Zaradic, 2008), this trend is not mirrored in much of the rest of the world, where growth in visitation to protected areas is growing at least as fast as international tourism as a whole. Fewer data are available for other types of outdoor activity, though it has been estimated that each year over half the population of the UK makes over 2.5 billion visits to urban green spaces (Woolley and Rose, 2004), and 87 million Americans participated in wildlife-related recreation in 2006, an increase of 13 per cent over the decade (USFWS, 2007). Wildlife-based marine tourism, like whale and dolphin watching, is also a profitable activity that is highly dependent on a functioning ecosystem (Wilson and Tisdell, 2003).

Many cultural services are associated with urban areas, and strong evidence demonstrates that biodiversity in urban areas plays a positive role in enhancing human well-being (see Section 3.7). For example, Fuller et al (2007) have shown that the psychological benefits of green space increase with biodiversity, whereas a green view from a window increases job satisfaction and reduces job stress (Lee et al, 2009). This may have a strongly positive effect on economic productivity and hence regional prosperity. Several studies have shown an increased value of properties (as measured by hedonic pricing) with proximity to green areas (Tyrväinen, 1997; Cho et al, 2008). Ninan (2009) and Shu, Yang et al (2004) have also pointed to the role of ecosystems in providing design features that can be utilized in the context of eco-design in architecture and urban and community planning

Sensitivity of service to variation in biodiversity

The role of biodiversity varies greatly among these services but is likely to be particularly large for ecotourism and educational uses of ecosystems. However, in many cases biodiversity may not be the typical identifier of the value being placed on the ecosystem, but nevertheless underlies the character recognized by the visitor.

Where are services generated?

Cultural and recreational services based on biodiversity are most strongly associated with less intensively managed areas, where semi-natural biotopes dominate, although in urban areas this may vary. Low-input agricultural systems are also likely to support cultural services, with many local traditions based on the management of land and its associated biological resources. Newly created or restored green spaces are becoming an increasingly important component of the urban environment providing this service.

Uncertainties in delivery of service

Uncertainty may be assessed for tourism, where abrupt changes in the provision of tourism benefits can occur for a range of reasons. Some of these may be ecological, as systems reach tipping points. Key wildlife populations may collapse through disease or other factors, fire may destroy picturesque landscapes, corals may bleach with sudden temperature shifts, ecosystems may suddenly change from one (attractive) to another (less desirable) stable state. Some of these will be reversible, others will be permanent. Abrupt shifts may also (and perhaps more often) be socially instigated. War, terrorism, socio-political disruption, natural disasters and health crises all tend to rapidly and negatively affect international tourism demand. Likewise, events such as the foot and mouth disease outbreak in the UK in 2001 had dramatic impacts as people were prevented from visiting the countryside for recreation. The current volability in oil prices (and thus aviation fuel costs) and potential carbon taxes may have similar impacts on international tourism if such changes are too sudden and result in an increase in recreational visits in areas closer to urban centres (for urban recreational services see Section 3.7).

4 Managing multiple ecosystem services

4.1 Bundles of ecosystem services

Functioning ecosystems produce multiple services and these interact in complex ways, different services being interlinked or 'bundled' together, and therefore affected negatively or positively as one service (e.g. food) increases (e.g. Bennet et al, 2009). Most studies so far have focused on one or a few services such as pollination, or food versus water quality and quantity. Characterizing multiple ecosystem services as well as biodiversity across the same region has only recently emerged as a field of study (e.g. Schröter et al, 2005), and the little quantitative evidence available to date has led to mixed conclusions (e.g. Bohensky et al, 2006). Scientists have tended to use land use or land cover as a proxy for the provision of services (Nelson et al, 2009) even though the relationships between land use, land cover and service provision are largely untested for most services in most regions of the world (Naidoo et al, 2008). Finding ways of assessing how multiple ecosystem services are interconnected and coupled to each other in 'bundles' is one of the major research gaps on ecosystem services identified by the MA (Carpenter et al, 2009). Furthermore, finding ways to target and implement payments for biodiversity conservation with 'bundles' of ecosystem services, e.g. carbon and water services, also is a major priority (Wendland et al, 2009) that will be discussed in Section 5.2 below.

4.2 Trade-offs

Some ecosystem services co-vary positively (more of one means more of another), for example maintaining soil quality may promote nutrient cycling and primary production, enhance carbon storage and hence climate regulation, help regulate water flows and water quality, and improve most provisioning services, notably food, fibre and other chemicals. Other services co-vary negatively (more of one means less of another) such as when increasing provisioning services may reduce many regulating services, for example provision of agricultural crops may reduce carbon storage in soil, water regulation, cultural services and so on.

Provisioning and regulating ecosystem services can have a range of possible trade-offs. Depending on the type of trade-off (A, B or C in Figure 2.4), the supply of regulating services can be low, intermediate or high for similar levels of provisioning services. This will have very different implications for the design and management of landscapes. For example, it has been suggested that major ecosystem degradation tends to occur as simultaneous failures in multiple ecosystem services (Carpenter et al, 2006). The dry lands of sub-Saharan Africa provide one of the clearest examples of these multiple failures, causing a combination of failing crops and grazing, declining quality and quantity of fresh water, and loss of tree cover. However, a synthesis of over 250 cases of investments in organic agriculture in developing countries around the world (both dry lands and non-dry lands) showed that the implementation of various novel agricultural techniques and practices could result in a reduction of ecosystem service trade-offs, and increased levels of regulating

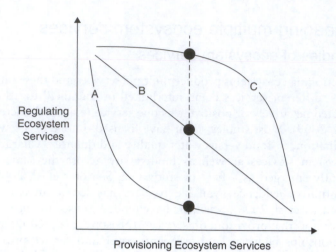

Figure 2.4 *Potential trade-offs between provisioning services and regulating ecosystem services*

Notes: A: Shifting an ecosystem to an increase in provisioning services produces a rapid loss of regulating services. B: Regulating services linearly decrease with increases in provisioning services. C: Provisioning services can increase to quite high levels before regulating services decline.

Source: Elmqvist et al (2010)

services, even as crop yields were maintained (Pretty et al, 2006) (corresponding to B or even C in Figure 2.4).

The generation of some services may also result in other less desired effects, sometimes referred to as disservices, for example, the foods, fuels and fibres grown to satisfy basic human needs for nutrition and shelter may be highly valued, but the pests and pathogens deriving from the same ecosystems have a negative value. Both are products of the way in which the underlying ecosystems are managed, with the result that trade-off decisions have to be made (see Box 2.3). Knowledge of these relationships is essential if policy decisions are to translate into operationally effective and predictable outcomes.

Box 2.3 Trade-offs among ecosystem services

Several different types of trade-off can be identified, and are not mutually exclusive:

1. *Temporal trade-offs: Benefits now – costs later*

Temporal trade-offs represent the central tenet of sustainable development '... that meets the needs of the present generation without compromising the needs of future generations...' (WCED, 1987).

2. *Spatial trade-offs: Benefits here – costs there*

Spatial trade-offs are behind much deliberation between communities and countries (especially water) and also occur between ecosystems and production landscapes. An example of a landscape-level trade-off is between improved water productivity (evapotranspiration used per tonne of grain) up-stream and consequential down-stream problems with deteriorating water quality associated with the use of agricultural inputs.

3. *Beneficiary trade-offs: Some win – others lose*

These trade-offs are real but it is possible to move towards 'winning more and losing less' by improving access to information on ecosystem services and their valuation, framing and using appropriate incentives and/or markets, and clarifying and strengthening rights of local people over their resources.

4. *Service trade-offs: Manage for one service – lose another*

Manipulation of an ecosystem to maximize one particular service risks reducing others, for example maintaining monocultures of a single species (for production of food, fibre and energy) will reduce the delivery of services dependent on the maintenance of biodiversity, including pollination and disease regulation (see Figures 2.4 and 2.5).

Many wetland soils support denitrifier microorganisms which convert nitrate to di-nitrogen gas in a two-stage process with nitrous oxide as the intermediary product. This may result in a major service of water purification, protecting the biodiversity of adjacent waters (Barker et al, 2008). However the balance of N_2O or N_2 production, which is controlled by soil ecosystem properties, may generate a major disservice though release of a potent greenhouse gas (N_2O) as well as a potential source of atmospheric N deposition if full denitrification is not achieved.

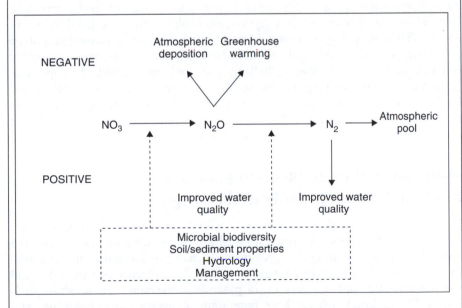

Figure 2.5 *Wetland trade-off dilemma: Water quality versus climate control*

4.3 Scales of provision

A number of key requirements need to be satisfied if knowledge of ecosystem services is to be effectively translated into operational practice. The need for a verifiable evidence base and understanding of the trade-offs resulting from interactions requires knowledge of the scale, and the temporal and spatial dynamics and distribution, of ecosystem service delivery. This will enable key questions to be addressed, such as 'Where and to what extent are services being provided?' and 'How much of a particular ecosystem or individual component is necessary to deliver a particular service or combination of services?'

While some services may be realized on the same temporal or spatial scale as the system that generates them, notwithstanding the importance for ecosystem resilience of ecological connections with other ecosystems, others may be realized on completely different scales. These include: pollination, which operates at a local scale and can be managed by ensuring that there are areas of land that maintain populations of pollinators in a mosaic of land-use types; hydrological services, which function at a catchment or river basin scale and which require co-operation among land managers at that scale; and carbon sequestration in soil organic matter, which operates at regional and global scales and necessitates policy decisions by governments and international bodies to ensure that appropriate incentives are in place to ensure necessary behaviour by local land managers.

Attempts at quantifying spatial aspects of multiple services include that of the service-providing unit (SPU), defined by Luck et al (2003) as 'ecosystem structures and processes that provide specific services at a particular spatial scale'. For example, an SPU might comprise all those organisms contributing to pollination of a single orchard, or all those organisms contributing to water purification in a given catchment area (Luck et al, 2003, 2009). This is a parallel approach to that of the prediction of functioning and service provision in wetland ecosystems using a hydrogeomorphic approach (Maltby et al, 1994). This concept uses spatially defined units to assess functioning at a range of landscape scales, and could feasibly be extended for assessment of other ecosystems. One of the major challenges in applying the SPU concept is to translate the unit into tangible and ideally mappable units of ecosystems and landscape/seascape, but the concept potentially offers an approach that focuses on multiple services and where changes to key species or population characteristics have direct implications for service provision.

5 Management of ecosystem services: Dealing with uncertainty and change

In an increasingly globalized world, social conditions, health, culture, democracy and matters of security, survival and the environment are interwoven and subject to accelerating change. Although change is inevitable, it is essential to understand the nature of change, especially the existence of thresholds and the potential for undesirable and, in practice, irreversible regime shifts. It is impossible to know where these potentially dangerous thresholds lie, and current efforts of adapting to climate change and other stressors will require a precautionary approach and a much deeper understanding of resilience and the combined capacity in both social and ecological systems if society is to cope with and benefit from change – that is, social-ecological resilience (Folke et al, 2004). As the UN Secretary General has observed: 'Building "resilience thinking" into policy and practice will be a major task for all of the world's citizens throughout the new century' (UN Climate Summit, 24 September 2007).

5.1 Ecosystems, services and resilience

Physical influences on ecosystems include geology, climate, topography, hydrology, connectivity with other ecosystems, and the results of human activities. Anthropogenic influences such as atmospheric deposition of chemicals (Vitousek et al, 1997; Phoenix et al, 2006) have ensured that no pristine environments remain on Earth (Lawton, 1997). Frequent minor disturbances are characteristic of ecosystem functioning. Typically, these may be seasonal influxes of nutrients or organisms, variations in temperature or hydrology, or weather or age damage to structuring organisms, for example trees, to which the resident species are adapted (e.g. Titlyanova, 2009). Large and less frequent disturbances may follow geological disturbances, anthropogenic eutrophication (increased nutrient loading) or toxic pollution, habitat loss, disconnection from adjacent ecosystems, species invasions, climate change and other external drivers of ecosystem change (see later). These larger disturbances can drive permanent or long-term ecosystem change by altering the physical structure of the ecosystem, and through removal of species and alteration of species interactions. Grazing pressure from elephants, for example, can result in the long-term replacement of woodland by grassland (de Knegt et al, 2008).

Ecosystem responses to changes in key variables such as temperature, nutrient loading, hydrology or grazing may, for example, lead to an increase in productivity (e.g. Aberle et al, 2007), or alter competition between species (Rahlao et al, 2008) by tipping the balance in favour of one species over another as a function of the response diversity. This type of change may be reversible and in proportion to the degree of change in either direction. For example, eutrophication of a normally nutrient-poor ecosystem typically leads to increased production and greater species diversity until a point is reached of high nutrient loading, when fewer, robust species come to dominate (Grime, 1988; Badia et al, 2008). Over-grazing or cultivation of a forested ecosystem might alter the vegetation by halting recruitment of new trees and by favouring herbaceous species tolerant of grazing and trampling (Mysterud, 2006). If the eutrophication or grazing driver is removed, the site may revert to its former state, unless key species have been eliminated.

A given ecosystem state may be maintained during moderate environmental changes by means of buffering mechanisms. These are negative feedbacks, which maintain the prevailing ecosystem state by containing the potentially exponential growth of some species. For example, in shallow lowland temperate lakes, the increase of fast-growing phytoplanktonic algae is controlled by competition from macrophytes (plants and large algae), which store nutrients, making them unavailable to the algae, and also by invertebrate zooplankton, which grazes the algae. These zooplankters hide from predators in the macrophytes, while predatory fish such as pike (*Esox lucius*) lurk in the macrophyte beds to ambush the smaller fish that consume zooplankton. Together, these buffering mechanisms serve to reinforce the clear-water status of the lake (Scheffer et al, 1993; Jeppesen et al, 2007).

The capacity of an ecosystem to withstand perturbations without losing any of its functional properties is often referred to as *ecosystem resilience*. In practice, minor disturbances to ecosystem stability can serve to increase resilience overall because they impose the necessity for flexibility on species interactions (Gunderson, 2000), hence Holling's original (1973) definition of the term as 'the capacity of a system to absorb and utilize or even benefit from perturbations and changes that attain it, and so to persist without a qualitative change in the system'. Westman (1978) described resilience as the ability of an ecosystem to recover from disturbance without human intervention. Today the most common interpretation of resilience is that it represents the capacity of a system (e.g. a community, society or ecosystem) to cope with disturbances (e.g. financial crises, floods or fire) without shifting into a qualitatively different state (Gunderson and Holling, 2002). A resilient system has the capacity to withstand shocks and surprises and, if damaged, to rebuild itself. Hence, resilience is the capacity of a system to deal deal with change and continue to develop (see also Brand, 2005; Brand and Jax, 2007).

Where environmental drivers are persistent or strong, ecosystems may pass a threshold and undergo sudden and catastrophic structural change (Thom, 1969; Loehle, 1989; Walker and Meyers, 2004). This can shift the ecosystem to an alternative state (Holling, 1973; May, 1977; Scheffer et al, 2001), which is also sometimes termed a '*regime shift*' (Folke et al, 2004). Such regime shifts can produce large, unexpected, changes in ecosystem services. Examples at local and regional levels include state change in lakes, degradation of rangelands, shifts in fish stocks, breakdown of coral reefs and extinctions due to persistent drought (Folke et al, 2004). Environmental drivers may not instigate the regime shift directly, but may increase the susceptibility of the ecosystem to change following some disturbance. This has been elaborated particularly in shallow lake ecology (Irvine et al, 1989; Scheffer et al, 1993; Moss, 2001). Continuing the lake example above, once an ecosystem is placed under stress from eutrophication, the loss of its macrophytes (perhaps through physical or chemical damage) paves the way for algal dominance, resulting in turbidity, because it removes the refuge of zooplankton from predation and the shelter needed by predatory fish that formerly kept zooplanktivorous fish numbers low. In addition, plant loss increases mixing and re-suspension, and removes competition for nutrients, leaving phytoplankton to dominate the ecosystem (Ibelings et al, 2007). Once these buffering feedbacks of the clear-water state are removed, the ecosystem is subject to the prevailing eutrophication driver, and new buffering feedback mechanisms reinforce the degraded ecosystem state.

Crucially, the clear and turbid states are alternatives under similar nutrient regimes. Each is held in place by its own buffering feedback mechanisms (Jeppesen et al, 2007). This means that a simple reduction in nutrient loading to the lake will not result in a reversion to its former clear water status. The change is thus said to be non-linear. Overcoming the buffering mechanisms is neither easy nor cheap nor often possible (see e.g. Phillips et al, 1999). Similar examples have been recorded in coastal systems (Palumbi et al, 2008) and in terrestrial field ecosystems (Schmitz et al, 2006) and woodlands (Walker et al, 1981) among others.

A hypothetical example is provided by a farm that uses most of its land for agriculture, providing a basic provisioning service. Assume that insectivorous birds provide a regulating service in preventing insect pest outbreaks. As long as bird abundances are high, a good crop is produced every year, given schematically as the horizontal line in Figure 2.6. If insufficient bird predation on insects occurs there will be a pest outbreak and crop production will be largely reduced (lower horizontal line). Since insect abundance is then too high for bird predation capacity there is a response delay (hysteresis effect) making it non-linear. The year-to-year abundance of all bird species that eat insects varies over time, yielding a certain probability distribution for total bird predation every year. The probabilities of crossing from one state into the other are given in Figure 2.6 as **a** and **b** respectively.

An important characteristic of this system is the shape of the probability function for the regulating service. Since this service is provided by a functional group of species, insectivorous birds, it is useful to examine how the species richness of this group of species would influence its performance. First, number

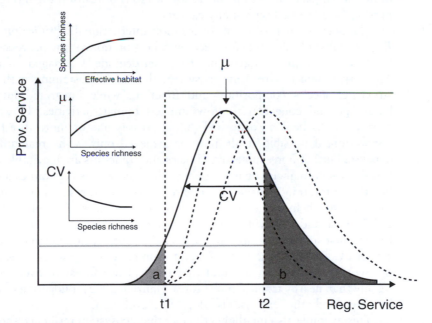

Figure 2.6 *Interactions between provisioning (crops) and regulating services (biological control)*

Notes: Upper line – high generation of a biological control (insectivorous birds) leads to a high yield of crops. Lower line – decreased supply of biological control means a decline in crop yield. The characteristics of the larger landscape (inserted graphs) may give rise to non-linearities and thresholds (**a** and **b**) and the dynamics of the provisioning service being determined by management in the surrounding landscape (for details see text).

of species may depend on the area of suitable habitat for birds, according to standard species-area relationships (upper inset graph). Species richness is generally positively correlated to total abundance due to complementary resource use among different bird species as shown in the middle inset graph. Higher species richness also results in lower coefficient of variation (CV) in the total bird abundance if there is some degree of negative autocorrelation between different species (Hughes et al, 2002). This negative autocorrelation can be thought of as species having different response functions and the effect on total bird abundance CV is shown in the lowest inset graph. The result of these effects is a change in the probability distribution of the regulating service, consumption of insects, as shown as dashed lines. A consequence of increasing land available for natural bird populations is that the probability of falling into the undesired state with insect outbreaks (lower line) is reduced. At the same time the probability of recovering if this should happen increases. One consequence of this is that the expected long-term value of the provisioning service largely depends on the management actions in the surrounding area.

5.1.1 Thresholds, recovery and ecological restoration

Although in many cases it may be possible to restore 'mildly' degraded ecosystems back to some defined earlier state, ecosystems can be so altered that restoration in the strict sense of the term is no longer possible. Given the extent of human impacts on the biosphere, the notions of restoration and restorability need to be expressed with many caveats.

The Society for Ecological Restoration International's *Primer on Ecological Restoration* (SER, 2002) defines ecological restoration as 'the process of assisting the recovery of an ecosystem that has been degraded, damaged, or destroyed'. The target state is a resilient ecosystem that is self-sustaining with respect to structure, species composition and function, while integrated into a larger landscape and congenial to 'low impact' human activities. However, if an ecosystem has been so disturbed that it crosses one or more thresholds, then restoration, if possible at all, may be achieved only with great difficulty and expense. Furthermore, subjective choices and trade-offs are inevitable and will be based on non-financial or marketable values as well as economics and ecology. For the restoration manager, the awareness of past threshold crossings in these cases should help guide the restoration programmes (Clewell and Aronson, 2007). Ease and cost will also vary among ecosystems, which impose the need for pragmatism. For example, in the Area de Conservación Guanacaste, in north-western Costa Rica, one of the longest running and largest scale restorations in the world, scientists have found that tropical dry forest recovers much more readily than nearby tropical moist forest (Janzen, 2002). Budgeting of investment in labour and other expenses is allocated accordingly.

This example also highlights the fact that ecosystem resilience should not be interpreted in a normative way. Undesirable ecosystem states, such as cow pastures seeded with exotic grasses, may become very resilient to change, and restoration will need an understanding of how to erode undesirable resilient states. Managers should also not always seek to restore in terms of an original or 'pre-disturbance' ecosystem state or trajectory. Recovery of ecosystem *services* through revitalization of ecosystem *processes* may be better options. Placing emphasis on restoring *process* – and thus, ultimately, ecosystem services – rather than restoring a specific species inventory (Falk et al, 2006) also facilitates valuation and financing (de Groot et al, 2007; Holmes et al, 2007; see Section 5.2 below). This is consistent with the first principle in applying the 'ecosystem approach' under the Convention on Biological Diversity (CBD, 2000–2008).

5.2 Resilience thinking in policy and practice

In order to develop a deeper resilience thinking of relevance for policy and practice, there are at least three factors that need to be understood:

1   *Depletion of non-renewable resources:* A historic or geological legacy of environmental conditions may be supporting current patterns of use, but these are not being renewed on human time scales. Aside from minerals and fossil fuels, examples include groundwater resources and aquifers effectively containing 'fossil' water built up under different climatic conditions in previous millennia (Foster and Loucks, 2006), and carbon storage in peat-based ecosystems developed since the end of the last glacial period, where net accumulation of peat no longer occurs. These represent resources that may be exhausted through use.

2   *The changing environmental 'envelope':* The environmental envelope within which organisms evolve and patterns and processes of biodiversity and ecosystems develop is changing because of human activity. This raises far-reaching questions of reliance on biodiversity and ecosystems and their viability when their baseline of environmental support and pressure of use is shifting. Coined by Pauly (1995) the related term 'shifting baselines' highlights the fact that successive generations adjust to the state of the environment they find themselves in – that is, an ecosystem state which is already degraded may be accepted as 'normal'. Jackson et al (2001) collated worldwide data to demonstrate that in marine systems, humans have had such a prominent impact of successively reducing species richness for so long that previous levels of biodiversity are today difficult to imagine. Shifting baselines have major implications for the sustainability of resource use.

3   *The effects of environmental shocks and disturbances:* Both natural (e.g. climate, flood, fire, landslide) and human-induced (e.g. climate, sea-level change, deforestation, overgrazing, overfishing, river-regulation, impoundment, pollution) impacts may be unpredictable and uncertain, producing major step changes, surprises and regime shifts. When faced with change through environmental stress, ecosystems may pass a critical threshold where the existing ecosystem structure collapses (Folke et al, 2004). Erosion of resilience may be an effect of variables such as human-induced environmental changes and loss of biodiversity.

A simple process-response schema is used to represent these relationships (Figure 2.7). It represents an ecosystem as a functional entity and a result of interactions between its structure and biological composition and processes.

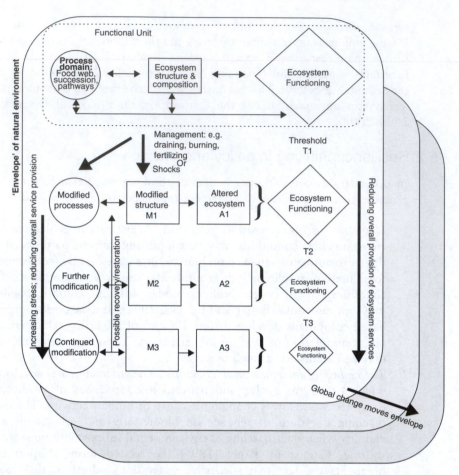

Figure 2.7 *A process-response model of ecosystem functioning and effects of impacts.*
The changing environmental envelope of global environmental conditions alters the predictability
of ecosystem responses to perturbations

Source: Adapted from Maltby et al (1994)

The ecosystem includes biological components representing particular genetic, species and community-scale elements, all within a particular 'envelope' of prevailing environmental conditions. Both direct and indirect human influences as well as natural environmental shocks can modify ecosystem structure or the process domain, so altering ecosystem functioning. A sequence of increased modification resulting from increasing intensity of impact is shown as reducing the total combination of functions (although an individual function may actually increase, such as in the case of agricultural productivity). More or less distinct 'tipping points' may indicate the transition or shift from one state to another. The possibilities for recovery to previous ecosystem conditions will depend partly on external drivers discussed above, but mostly on the intrinsic properties and ecological integrity of the ecosystem, as well as time scale. However, erosion of resilience may make it impossible to recover a particular condition of functioning, structure or process because it no longer can occur within the boundary of the new envelope (i.e. due to changes in ecosystem dynamics).

This framework contests models and policies that are based on assumptions of linear dynamics, with a focus on optimal solutions. Applications of such theory and world views tend to develop governance systems that invest in controlling a few selected ecosystem processes, causing loss of key ecological support functions, in the urge to produce particular resources to fulfil economic or social goals (Holling and Meffe, 1996). An alternative approach is based on ecosystems viewed as complex and adaptive, characterized by historical (path) dependency, non-linear regime shifts, and limited predictability. A dynamic view of nature and society has major implications for valuations of nature. If a system is discontinuous, the basic theorems of welfare economics are not valid and the result of resource allocation may be very far from the optimum, even if there are well-defined property rights (Mäler, 2000). This has major implications for production, consumption and international trade, and also major implications for economic policy. Optimal management will often, because of the complex dynamics, be extremely difficult to implement.

6 Biodiversity, ecosystem services and human well-being

Since ecosystem services are the benefits that people get from ecosystems, it follows that changes in ecosystem services associated with changes in biodiversity will have implications for human well-being. Subsequent chapters explore the methods economists use to estimate the value of non-marketed ecosystem services, and summarize the results of existing valuation studies. Here we consider not how ecosystem services are valued, but how the production of ecosystem services confers value on all components of the biosphere, including biodiversity. The value of biodiversity derives from its role in the provision of ecosystem services, and from peoples' demand for those services. Economists have typically sought to value the individual components of ecosystems or specific services yielded by ecosystems, rather than ecosystems themselves. In some cases – where well-functioning markets exist – the valuation of specific services is straightforward. In most cases it is not. And even where markets for specific services do exist, derivation of the value of individual components of ecosystems is hard. The 'bundling' of services (Section 4.1), and the fact that particular species may contribute to the production of many different services, mean that their marginal contribution to a particular service will be, at best, a partial measure of their value. In addition, the precise role of individual species in the ecological functioning that produces human benefits are typically known only for the well studied and highly controlled processes that yield marketed foods, fuels and fibres. Yet without this knowledge it is not possible to derive the value of either the basic building blocks of individual ecosystem services (however they might be defined) or of the functioning ecosystems that support an array of services. There may be numerous different pathways by which a particular function is generated and a resulting service delivered. Only exceptionally are all these pathways known – a challenge epitomized in the whole question of species 'redundancy'.

In principle, the value of ecosystems derives from the set of services – the discounted stream of benefits – they produce (Barbier, 2007; Barbier et al, 2009). So if we define B_t to be the social benefits from the set of all services provided by an ecosystem at time t, then the present (discounted) social value of that system is:

$$V_0 = \int_0^\infty e^{-\delta t} B_t dt \tag{1}$$

where δ is the social rate of discount. For each time period, B_t is the sum of all benefits deriving from the ecosystem. That is, $B_t = \sum_i B_{it}$. Since those benefits depend upon sets of ecosystem services that, in turn, depend upon biodiversity, the value of of biodiversity can be derived from them. For example, if $B_t = f\left(S_t\left(X_t\right)\right)$ where S_t is the set of services produced, and X_t is the set of species, then the marginal value of the it species is given by the derivative: $\dfrac{\partial B_t}{\partial S_t}\dfrac{\partial S_t}{\partial x_{it}}$. The main challenge for the calculation of the stream of benefits from ecosystems is that, while a number of the services in an economy are marketed, many ecosystem services supported by biodiversity are not. Some benefits that contribute to human well-being do not have a price attached to them, and are therefore neglected in normal market transactions (Freeman, 2003; Heal et al, 2005). Ecosystems are invariably multifunctional. Except in the case of managed systems (such as agro-ecosystems) their structure and function may be consistent with environmental conditions and historic patterns, but not the purposeful delivery of services. But even managed systems typically yield a range of benefits, and the value of the system depends not only on the value of the benefits that are the primary goal of management, but also on the ancillary services delivered as by-products of the primary services (Perrings et al, 2009).

How bundles of ecosystem services are configured matters. The beneficiaries of services may be spread among quite different stakeholder interests, and be distributed both off-site and on-site. Thus the value of freshwater quality improvement may be realized at various points downstream from the ecosystem performing the work and may be particularly significant even for the estuarine, coastal and more distant marine waters and the services they, in turn, support.

Uncovering the value of ecosystem components requires an understanding of the ways in which they contribute to the production of ecosystem services. Neither individual species nor the ecosystems of which they are a part are exactly comparable or identical. The spectrum from microbial to charismatic top carnivore species encompasses a wide range of processes and functioning. The most charismatic species may be excellent indicators of ecosystem condition but not necessarily be of greatest functional importance. Ecosystem properties vary in detail according to both spatial and temporal factors. To derive the value of ecosystem components from their marginal impact on the production of valued goods and services, we need to know the shape of the ecological production functions that define the relationship between environmental inputs and outputs of goods and services. Ecological production functions thus capture the biophysical relationships between ecological systems and the services they provide, as well as interrelated processes and functions such as sequestration, predation and nutrient cycling. They accordingly include both well-understood inputs over which humans have direct control, and poorly understood inputs over which humans have variable and often limited control. Identification of ecological production functions requires: (i) specification of the ecosystem services of interest, and (ii) development of a complete mapping from the structure and function of the ecological system to the provision of the relevant ecosystem services. Although we are making progress in understanding and defining ecological production functions for certain ecosystem services, such as carbon sequestration, the specification of production functions for many important ecosystem services is still rudimentary (Perrings et al, 2009).

Nevertheless, certain things are well understood. Conversion of ecosystems for the production of particular services generally reduces their capacity to provide other services. Whether specialization of this kind enhances the value of the ecosystem depends on the value of the forgone services (Balmford et al, 2002). Converted lands may gain value in terms of provisioning services, but lose value in terms of other types of services, such as water regulation, erosion control, habitat provision, fire regulation and so on. Conversion of natural forest to rice paddies and mangrove forest to shrimp ponds in many parts of south-east Asia has led to a reduction in a range of regulatory functions, from storm buffering to silt entrapment (Barbier, 2007). In the Mekong Delta, for example, acidification of potential acid sulphate soil materials, resulting from lowering of the water table and oxidation of the marine sediments, reduces the crop yield and harvest after just a few years, and often results in abandonment (Maltby et al, 1996). Such ecosystem alteration yields no obvious compensating gains. In such cases, the cost of reduced water quality, storm and flood protection, wildlife habitat and shrimp or fish recruitment from wild populations have still not been factored in to the decisions that lead to ecosystem change (Barbier, 2007). Understanding and valuing the changes in the regulating ecosystem services involved is probably the biggest challenge to the economics of biodiversity at the moment.

The valuation of the contribution of biodiversity to regulating services poses particular challenges. The regulating services provide value through their role in assuring the reliability of service supply over space or time – sometimes expressed in terms of the resilience of the system to environmental shocks. That is, they moderate the variability or uncertainty of the supply of provisioning and cultural services. Estimation of the contribution of individual species to this service is, however, problematic. A small subset of species and their accompanying symbionts, mutualists or commensalists supply the ecosystem services required for human survival. While an increase in biodiversity may increase production, experimental data indicate that for given environmental conditions this effect is small. The productivity of some biologically diverse communities, for example, has been found to be about 10 per cent higher than the productivity of monocultures, but the effect often saturates at fewer than ten species. If environmental conditions are not constant, however, the effect may increase with the number of species, providing that they have different niches and hence different responses to disturbances or changes in environmental conditions. For instance, the regulation of pest and disease outbreaks is affected by foodweb

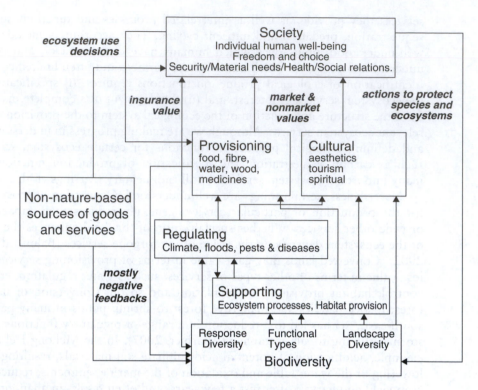

Figure 2.8 *Deriving the value of biodiversity and the regulating services*

Source: Kinzig et al (2009)

complexity. Simple predator–prey systems are prone to 'boom-and-bust' epidemiology, whereas the presence of multiple predators and prey operating at several trophic levels, and including prey-switching, involves much more stable dynamics (Thebault and Loreau, 2006).

The value of biodiversity in regulating the provisioning and cultural services is illustrated in Figure 2.8. Since people care about the reliability (or variability) in the supply of these services (people are generally risk averse), anything that increases reliability (reduces variability) will be valued. The value of regulating services accordingly lies in their impact on the variability in the supply of the provisioning and cultural services. An important factor in this is the diversity of the functional groups responsible for the services involved. The greater the specialization or niche differentiation of the species within a functional group, the wider the range of environmental conditions that group is able to tolerate. In some cases greater diversity with a functional group both increases the mean level and reduces the variability of the services that group supports. Indeed, this portfolio effect turns out to be one of the strongest reasons for maintaining the diversity of functional groups.

The general point here is that the value of ecosystem components, including the diversity of the biota, derives from the value of the goods and services they produce. For each of the ecosystem services described in this chapter we have identified its sensitivity to changes in biodiversity. If greater diversity enhances mean yields of valued services, it is transparent that diversity will have value.

However, it is also true that if greater diversity reduces the variance in the yield of valued services, that will also be a source of value. Since people prefer reliability over unreliability, certainty over uncertainty, and stability over variability, they typically choose wider rather than narrower portfolios of assets. Biodiversity can be thought of as a portfolio of biotic resources, the value of which depends on its impact on both mean yields and the variance in yields.

It follows that there is a close connection between the value of biodiversity in securing the regulating services, and its value in securing the resilience of ecosystems. Since resilience is a measure of the capacity of ecosystems to function over a range of environmental conditions, a system that is more resilient is also likely to deliver more effective regulating services. The economics of resilience are considered in more detail in Chapter 5.

The various forms of natural capital (see MA, 2005) provide and regulate flows of ecosystem services essential to life and economic production (de Groot et al, 2002). However, with the exception of agricultural land, it is currently undervalued, and sometimes even invisible, both in our national and international systems of economic analysis, and in indicators like gross domestic product (GDP) (Arrow et al, 1995; Dasgupta et al, 2000; TEEB, 2008, TEEB in National Policy, 2011). Furthermore, global society is making withdrawals of natural capital stocks far in excess of its yield in interest (ecosystem services, e.g. carbon sequestration), and societal re-investments in natural capital are, to date, limited. Yet increasing evidence shows that investing in the restoration and replenishment of renewable and cultivated natural capital 'pays' in economic and political terms (e.g. Goldstein et al, 2008).

As shown in Chapter 1, the concept of restoring natural capital is a relevant concept defined as all investments in renewable and cultivated natural capital stocks and their maintenance in ways that improve the functions of both natural and human-managed ecosystems, while contributing to the socio-economic well-being of people (Aronson et al, 2007). It is thus a broader concept than ecological restoration (Section 5.1.1), can be applied at landscape or regional scales, and can generate significant economic savings. An example is given by the integrated programmes seeking to restore degraded natural systems and rehabilitate production systems in the Drakensberg Mountain Range Project (Blignaut et al, 2008).

7 Conclusions and further research

We now have a reasonable understanding of the intricacies and outcomes of ecological dynamics as well as the expressions of these processes in the provision of goods and services to human society. Significant gaps in our knowledge remain, but there is an emerging scientific consensus on the need to sustain biological diversity to protect the delivery of ecosystem services. Nevertheless, if we wish, for example, to predict the impact of biodiversity change on variability in the supply of ecosystem services, we need to measure the impact of biodiversity conservation over a range of environmental conditions. In the same way, we need to be able to identify the effect of biodiversity change on the capacity of social-ecological systems to absorb anthropogenic and environmental stresses and shocks without loss of value (Scheffer et al, 2000; Kinzig et al, 2006; see Figure 2.8). To do so requires comprehensive analysis of the myriad linkages among biodiversity change, ecological functioning, ecosystem processes and the provision of valued goods and services. To understand or enhance the resilience of such complex, coupled systems, therefore, would need robust models of every link between biodiversity and ecosystem services, and between biodiversity change and human well-being (Perrings, 2007).

A major gap in knowledge is how different ecosystems interact in the delivery of services. Ecosystems are rarely homogeneous. For example, extensive forest ecosystems often contain rivers, lakes and wetlands as well as patches of land which may be farmed or managed as open habitat for wildlife. It is important to know how the various combinations of ecosystems operate together to generate services, which may be enhanced or impeded by interactions. Equally we need urgently to develop evidence-based management practices that maximize the delivery of a broad range of services from individual ecosystems, especially where these are managed intensively for food or fuel.

Existing knowledge is also sufficient to develop more effective instruments for ecosystem service-based biodiversity conservation, including the payments for ecosystem service (PES) systems discussed elsewhere in this report (TEEB in National Policy 2011). These instruments offer a mechanism to translate external, non-market values of ecosystem services into real financial incentives for local actors to provide such services (Ferraro and Kiss, 2002; Engel et al, 2008). Similarly, existing knowledge is sufficient to develop more effective governance institutions, including property rights regimes and regulatory structures. Once such mechanisms are established, their effectiveness can be increased by improving the quality of available information on the effect of conservation on ecosystem service provision.

Major questions that future research needs to address include:

1   *Understanding links between biodiversity, ecosystems and resilience*

- What are the roles of species interactions and functional diversity for ecosystem resilience?
- What are the drivers behind loss of resilience and how do they interact across scales?
- What are the impacts of climate and related environmental changes on ecosystem functioning through effects on species (re)distribution, numbers and process rates?

2   *Understanding the dynamics of ecosystem services*

- How can we better analyse effects on regulating ecosystem services of an increase in provisioning services?
- Are tools available to effectively map landscape and seascape in terms of functioning and service support / provision?
- What specific tools could contribute to better assessment of spatial and temporal dynamics of service provision, especially in relation to defining who benefits, where and to what extent?

3   *Understanding the dynamics of governance and management of ecosystems and ecosystem services*

- If all ecosystem services are taken into account, what is the appropriate balance between 'more diverse landscapes generating bundles of ecosystem services' and more intensively managed ecosystems like monocultures for food production?

- What are the trade-offs and complementarities involved in the provision of bundles of ecosystem services, and how do changes in the configuration of ecosystems affect their value?
- What are the most effective mechanisms for the governance of non-marketed ecosystem services, and how can these be designed so as to exploit future improvements in our understanding of the relationships between biodiversity, ecosystem functioning and ecosystem services?

References

Aberle, N., Lengfellner, K. and Sommer, U. (2007) 'Spring bloom succession, grazing impact and herbivore selectivity of ciliate communities in response to winter warming', *Oecologia*, vol 150, no 4, pp668–681

Abrantes, N., Antunes, S. C., Pereira, M. J. and Gonçalves, F. (2006) 'Seasonal succession of cladocerans and phytoplankton and their interactions in a shallow eutrophic lake (Lake Vela, Portugal)', *Acta Oecologica*, vol 29, no 1, pp54–64

Adams, H. D., Guardiola-Claramonte, M., Barron-Gafford, G. A., Camilo Villegas, J., Breshears, D. D., Zou, C. B., Troch, P. A. and Huxman, T. E. (2009) 'Temperature sensitivity of drought-induced tree mortality portends increased regional die-off under global-change-type drought', *Proceedings of the National Academy of Sciences*, vol 106, no 17, pp7063–7066

Ahmann, D. and Dorgan, J. R. (2007) *Bioengineering for Pollution Prevention through Development of Biobased Energy and Materials*, State of the Science Report, U.S. Environmental Protection Agency, Office of Research and Development, National Center for Environmental Research, Report No. 600/R-07/028, Washington, DC

Alexandri, E. and Jones, P. (2008) 'Temperature decreases in an urban canyon due to green walls and green roofs in diverse climates', *Building and Environment*, vol 43, no 4, pp480–493

Altieri, M. A. (1990) 'Agroecology and Rural Development in Latin America', in Altieri, M. A. and Hecht, S. B. (eds) *Agroecology and Small Farm Development*, CRC Press, Florida, pp113–118

Antonovics, J. and Bradshaw, A. D. (1970) 'Evolution in closely adjacent plant populations VIII: Clinal patterns at a mine boundary', *Heredity*, vol 25, pp349–362

Arenas, F., Rey, F. and Sousa-Pinto, I. (2009) 'Diversity effects beyond species richness: Evidence from intertidal macroalgal assemblages', *Marine Ecology Progress Series*, vol 381, pp99–108

Aronson, J., Milton, S. J. and Blignaut, J. N. (eds) (2007) *Restoring Natural Capital: The Science, Business, and Practice*, Island Press, Washington, DC

Arrow, K., Bolin, B., Costanza, R., Dasgupta, P., Folke, C., Holling, C. S., Jansson, B. O., Levin, S., Mäler, K.-G., Perrings, C. and Pimentel, D. (1995) 'Economic growth, carrying capacity, and the environment', *Science*, vol 268, pp520–521

Badia, D., Marti, C., Sánchez, J. R., Fillat, F., Aguirre, J. and Gómez, D. (2008) 'Influence of livestock soil eutrophication on floral composition in the Pyrenees mountains', *Journal of Mountain Science*, vol 5, no 1, pp63–72

Balmford, A., Bruner, A., Cooper, P., Costanza, R., Farber, S., Green, R. E., Jenkins, M., Jefferiss, P., Jessamy, V., Madden, J., Munro, K., Myers, N., Naeem, S., Paavola, J., Rayment, M., Rosendo, S., Roughgarden, J., Trumper, K. and Turner, R. K. (2002) 'Economic reasons for conserving wild nature', *Science*, vol 297, pp950–953

Balmford, A., Rodrigues, A. S. L., Walpole, M., ten Brink, P., Kettunen, M., Braat, L. and de Groot, R. (2008) *The Economics of Ecosystems and Biodiversity: Scoping the Science*, European Commission, Cambridge, UK

Balvanera, P., Pfisterer, A. B., Buchmann, N., He, J. S., Nakashizuka, T., Raffaelli, D. and Schmid, B. (2006) 'Quantifying the evidence for biodiversity effects on ecosystem functioning and services', *Ecology Letters*, vol 9, no 10, pp1146–1156

Barbier, E. B. (2007) 'Valuing ecosystems services as productive inputs', *Economic Policy*, vol 22, pp177–229

Barbier, E. B., Baumgärtner, S., Chopra, K., Costello, C., Duraiappah, A., Hassan, R., Kinzig, A., Lehman, M., Pascual, U., Polasky, S. and Perrings, C. (2009), 'The Valuation of Ecosystem Services', in Naeem S., Bunker, D., Hector, A., Loreau, M. and Perrings, C. (eds) *Biodiversity, Ecosystem Functioning, and Human Wellbeing: An Ecological and Economic Perspective*, Oxford University Press, Oxford, pp248–262

Barker, T., Hatton, K., O'Connor, M., Connor, L. and Moss, B. (2008) 'Effects of nitrate load on submerged plant biomass and species richness: Results of a mesocosm experiment', *Fundamental and Applied Limnology/Archiv für Hydrobiologie*, vol 173, no 2, pp89–100

Barrios, E. (2007) 'Soil biota, ecosystem services and land productivity', *Ecological Economics*, vol 64, pp269–285

Beaumont, N. J., Austen, M. C., Atkins, J., Burdon, D., Degraer, S., Dentinho, T. P., Derous, S., Holm, P., Horton, T., van Ierland, E., Marboe, A. H., Starkey, D. J., Townsend, M. and Zarzycki, T. (2007), 'Identification, definition and quantification of goods and services provided by marine biodiversity: Implications for the ecosystem approach', *Marine Pollution Bulletin*, vol 54, pp253–265

Bellwood, D. R., Hughes, T. P., Folke, C. and Nyström, M. (2004) 'Confronting the coral reef crisis', *Nature*, vol 429, pp827–833

Belyea, L. R. and Malmer, N. (2004) 'Carbon sequestration in peatland: Patterns and mechanisms of response to climate change', *Global Change Biology*, vol 10, pp1043–1052

Bengtsson, J., Ahnstrom, J. and Weibull, A.-C. (2005) 'The effects of organic agriculture on biodiversity and abundance: A meta-analysis', *Journal of Applied Ecology*, vol 42, pp261–269

Bennett, E. M., Peterson, G. D. and Gordon, L. J. (2009) 'Understanding relationships among multiple ecosystem services', *Ecology Letters*, vol 12, pp1–11

Bird, W. (2007) *Natural Thinking: Investigating the Links between the Natural Environment, Biodiversity and Mental Health*, Royal Society for the Protection of Birds, Sandy, Bedfordshire

Blignaut, J. N., Aronson, J., Mander, M. and Marais, C. (2008) 'Investing in natural capital and economic development: South Africa's Drakensberg Mountains', *Ecological Restoration*, vol 26, pp143–150

Bohensky, E. L., Reyers, B. and Van Jaarsveld, A. S. (2006) 'Future ecosystem services in a Southern African river basin: A scenario planning approach to uncertainty', *Conservation Biology*, vol 20, pp1051–1061

Bolund, P. and Hunhammar, S. (1999) 'Ecosystem services in urban areas', *Ecological Economics*, vol 29, pp293–301

Bond, W. J. (1993) 'Keystone Species', in Schulze, E.-D. and Mooney, H. A. (eds) *Biodiversity and Ecosystem Function*, Springer Verlag, New York, pp237–253

Bradford, M. A., Jones, T. H., Bardgett, R. D., Black, H. I. J., Boag, B., Bonkowski, M., Cook, R., Eggers, T., Gange, A. C., Grayston, S. J., Kandeler, E., McCaig, A. E., Newington, J. E., Prosser, J. I., Setälä, H., Staddon, P. L., Tordoff, G. M., Tscherko, D. and Lawton, J. H. (2002) 'Impacts of soil faunal community composition on model grassland ecosystems', *Science*, vol 298, pp615–618

Bradshaw, C. J. A., Sodhi, N. S., Peh, K. S. H. and Brook, B. W. (2007) 'Global evidence that deforestation amplifies flood risk and severity in the developing world', *Global Change Biology*, vol 13, pp1–17

Brand, F. (2005) *Ecological Resilience and Its Relevance Within a Theory of Sustainable Development*, UFZ-Report 03/2005, UFZ Centre for Environmental Research, Leipzig, Germany

Brand, F. S. and Jax, K. (2007) 'Focusing the meaning(s) of resilience: Resilience as a descriptive concept and a boundary object', *Ecology and Society*, vol 12, no 1, p23

Brauman, K. A., Daily, G. C., Duarte, T. K. and Mooney, H. A. (2007) 'The nature and value of ecosystem services: An overview highlighting hydrologic services', *The Annual Review of Environment and Resources*, vol 32, pp6.1–6.32

Brosi, B. J., Daily, G. and Ehrlich, P. (2007) 'Bee community shifts with landscape context in a tropical countryside', *Journal of Applied Ecology*, vol 17, pp418–430

Brosi, B. J., Daily, G. C., Shih, T. M., Oviedo, F. and Duran, G. (2008) 'The effects of forest fragmentation on bee communities in tropical countryside', *Journal of Applied Ecology*, vol 45, no 3, pp773–783

Bruijnzeel, L. A. (2004) 'Hydrological functions of tropical forests: Not seeing the soil for the trees?', *Agriculture, Ecosystems & Environment*, vol 104, pp185–228

Brussaard, L., de Ruiter, P. C. and Brown, G. G. (2007) 'Soil biodiversity for agricultural sustainability', *Agriculture, Ecosystems and Environment*, vol 121, no 3, pp233–244

Bullock, J. M., Pywell, R. F. and Walker, K. J. (2007) 'Long-term enhancement of agricultural production by restoration of biodiversity', *Journal of Applied Ecology*, vol 44, no 1, pp6–12

Butler, C. D. and Oluoch-Kosura, W. (2006) 'Linking future ecosystem services and future human well-being', *Ecology and Society*, vol 11, no 1, p30

Cardinale, B. J., Wright, J. P., Cadotte, M. W., Carroll, I. T., Hector, A., Srivastava, D. S., Loreau, M. and Weis, J. J. (2007) 'Impacts of plant diversity on biomass production increase through time because of species complementarity', *Proceedings of the National Academy of Sciences*, vol 104, pp18123–18128

Carpenter, S. R., DeFries, R., Dietz, T., Mooney, H. A., Polasky, S., Reid, W. V. and Scholes, R. J. (2006) 'Millennium Ecosystem Assessment: Research needs', *Science*, vol 314, pp257–258

Carpenter, S. R., Mooney, H. A., Agard, J., Capistrano, D., DeFries, R. S., Diaz, S., Dietz, T., Duraiappah, A. K., Oteng-Yeboah, A., Pereira, H. M., Perrings, C., Reid, W. V., Sarukhan, J., Scholes, R. J. and Whyte, A. (2009) 'Science for managing ecosystem services: Beyond the Millennium Ecosystem Assessment', *Proceedings of the National Academy of Sciences*, vol 106, no 5, pp1305–1312

Carr, D., Barbieri, A., Pan, W. and Iranavi, H. (2006) 'Agricultural Change and Limits to Deforestation in Central America', in Brouwer, F. and McCarl, B. A. (eds) *Agriculture and Climate Beyond 2015*, Springer, Dordrecht, Netherlands, pp91–107

Carter, C. G. and Hauler, R. C. (2000) 'Fish meal replacement by plant meals in extruded feeds for Atlantic salmon, *Salmo salar* L', *Aquaculture*, vol 185, pp299–311

CBD (2000–2008) The Convention on Biological Diversity web pages: The Ecosystem Approach homepage. Decision V/6: Ecosystem approach, COP5 2000; Decision VI/12: Ecosystem approach, COP6 2002; Decision VII/11: Ecosystem approach, COP7 2004; Decision VIII/15: Ecosystem approach, COP8 2006; Decision IX/7: Ecosystem approach, COP9 2008. www.biodiv.org/programmes/cross-cutting/ecosystem/, last accessed 2 September 2009

Chai, P. P. K., Lee, B. M. H. and Ismawi, H. O. (1989) *Native Medicinal Plants of Sarawak* (Report FB1), Forestry Department, Sarawak

Chapin, F. S., Walker, B. H., Hobbs, R. J., Hooper, D. U., Lawton, J. H., Sala, O. E. and Tilman, D. (1997) 'Biotic control over the functioning of ecosystems', *Science*, vol 277, no 5325, pp500–504

Cho, S. H., Poudyal, N. C. and Roberts, R. K. (2008) 'Spatial analysis of the amenity value of green open space', *Ecological Economics*, vol 66, nos 2–3, pp403–416

Clayton, R. D., Morris, J. E. and Summerfelt, R. C. (2008) 'Comparison of soy and fish oils in practical diets for fingerling walleyes', *North American Journal of Aquaculture*, vol 70, pp171–174

Clewell, A. F. and Aronson, J. (2007) *Ecological Restoration: Principles, Values, and Structure of an Emerging Profession*, Island Press, Washington, DC

Cooke, M. L., Bennett, H. H., Fowler, F. H., Harrington, F. C., Moore, R. C., Page, J. C., Wallace, H. A. and Tugwell, R. G. (1936) *Report of the Great Plains Drought Area Committee*, Hopkins Papers, Box 13, Franklin D. Roosevelt Library, New York

Costanza, R., Mitsch, W. J. and Day, J. (2006) 'Creating a sustainable and desirable New Orleans', *Ecological Engineering*, vol 26, pp317–320

Costanza, R. Graumlich, L., Steffen, W., Crumley, C., Dearing, J., Hibbard, K., Leemans, R., Redman, C. and Schimel, D. (2007) 'Sustainability or collapse: What can we learn from integrating the history of humans and the rest of nature', *Ambio*, vol 36, no 7, pp522–527

Cox, P. A., Elmqvist, T., Rainey, E. E. and Pierson, E. D. (1991) 'Flying foxes as strong interactors in South Pacific Island ecosystems: A conservation hypothesis', *Conservation Biology*, vol 5, pp448–454

Danovaro, R., Gambi, C., Dell'Anno, A., Corinaldesi, C., Fraschetti, S., Vanreusel, A., Vincx, M. and Gooday, A. J. (2008) 'Exponential decline of deep-sea ecosystem functioning linked to benthic biodiversity loss', *Current Biology*, vol 18, no 1, pp1–8

Dasgupta, P., Levin, S. and Lubchenko, J. (2000) 'Economic pathways to ecological sustainability', *BioScience*, vol 50, pp339–345

de Groot, R. S., Wilson, M. A. and Boumans, R. M. J. (2002) 'A typology for the classification, description and valuation of ecosystem functions, goods and services', *Ecological Economics*, vol 41, pp393–408

de Groot, R., de Wit, M., Brown Gaddis, E. J., Kousky, C., McGhee, W. and Young, M. D. (2007) 'Making Restoration Work: Financial Mechanisms', in Aronson, J., Milton, S. J. and Blignaut

J. N. (eds) *Restoring Natural Capital: Science, Business, and Practice*, Island Press, Washington, DC, pp286–293

de Knegt, H. J., Groen, T. A., van de Vijver, C. A. D. M., Prins, H. H. T. and van Langevelde, F. (2008) 'Herbivores as architects of savannas: Inducing and modifying spatial vegetation patterning', *Oikos*, vol 117, no 4, pp543–554

de Leo, G. A. and Levin, S. (1997) 'The multifaceted aspects of ecosystem integrity', *Conservation Ecology*, vol 1, no 1, p3

Delgado, C. L., Wada, N., Rosegrant, M. W., Meijer, S. and Mahfuzuddin, A. (2003) *Fish to 2020: Supply and Demand in Changing Global Markets*, World Fish Center Technical Report 62, International Food Policy Research Institute, The WorldFish Center, Penang

Deutsch, L., Gräslund, S., Folke, C., Huitric, M., Kautsky, N., Troell, M. and Lebel, L. (2007) 'Feeding aquaculture growth through globalization; Exploitation of marine ecosystems for fishmeal', *Global Environmental Change*, vol 17, pp238–249

de Vallavieille-Pope, C. (2004) 'Management of disease resistance diversity of cultivars of a species in single fields: Controlling epidemics', *Comptes Rendus Biologies*, vol 327, pp611–620

Díaz, S. and Cabido, M. (2001) 'Vive la difference: Plant functional diversity matters to ecosystem processes', *Trends in Ecology and Evolution*, vol 16, pp646–655

Díaz S., Fargione J., Chapin, F. S. III. and Tilman, D. (2006) 'Biodiversity loss threatens human well-being', *PLoS Biology*, vol 4, no 8, pp1300–1305

Díaz, S., Lavorel, S., Chapin, F. S. III., Tecco, P. A., Gurvich, D. E. and Grigulis, K. (2007a) 'Functional Diversity: At the Crossroads between Ecosystem Functioning and Environmental Filters', Chapter 7, in Canadell, J. G., Pataki, D. E. and Pitelka, L. F. (eds) *Terrestrial Ecosystems in a Changing World, Part B, Global Change*, The IGBP Series, Springer, Berlin and Heidelberg, pp81–91

Diaz, S., Lavorel, S., de Bello, F., Quetier, F., Grigulis, K. and Robson, M. (2007b) 'Incorporating plant functional diversity effects in ecosystem service assessments', *Proceedings of the National Academy of Sciences*, vol 104, no 52, pp20684–20689

Dong, L. Q. and Zhang, K. Q. (2006) 'Microbial control of plant-parasitic nematodes: A five-party interaction', *Plant and Soil*, vol 288, pp31–45

Dorren, L. K. A., Berger, F., Imeson, A. C., Maier, B. and Rey, F. (2004) 'Integrity, stability and management of protection forests in the European Alps', *Forest Ecology and Management*, vol 195, pp165–176

Drijver, C. A. and Marchand, M. (1985) *Taming the Floods: Environmental Aspects of Floodplain Development in Africa*, Centre for Environmental Studies, State University of Leiden, Netherlands

Dudley, N. and Stolton, S. (2003) *Running Pure: The Importance of Forest Protected Areas to Drinking Water*, World Bank/WWF Alliance for Forest Conservation and Sustainable Use, Gland, Switzerland

Dukes, J. S. (2001) 'Biodiversity and invasibility in grassland microcosms', *Oecologia*, vol 126, pp563–568

EASAC (European Academies Science Advisory Council) (2009) *Ecosystem Services and Biodiversity in Europe*, EASAC policy report 09, The Royal Society, London

Elmqvist, T., Alfsen, C. and Colding, J. (2008) 'Urban Systems', in Jørgensen, S. E. and Fath, B. D. (eds) 'Ecosystems', *Encyclopedia of Ecology, Vol 5*, Elsevier, Oxford, pp3665–3672

Elmqvist, T., Folke, C., Nyström, M., Peterson, G., Bengtsson, J., Walker, B. and Norberg, J. (2003) 'Response diversity, ecosystem change, and resilience', *Frontiers in Ecology and the Environment*, vol 1, no 9, pp488–494

Elmqvist, T., Tuvendal, M., Krishnaswamy, J. and Hylander, K. (2010) 'Ecosystem Services – Managing Trade-offs between Provisioning and Regulating Services', in Kumar, P. and Wood, M. D. (eds) *Valuation of Regulating Services of Ecosystems: Methodology and Applications*, Routledge, London

Engel, S., Pagiola, S. and Wunder, S. (2008) 'Designing payments for environmental services in theory and practice: An overview of the issues', *Ecological Economics*, vol 65, pp663–674

ESA (Ecological Society of America) (2000) *Ecosystem Services: A Primer*, www.actionbioscience. org/environment/esa.html, accessed 1 September 2009

Ettama, C. H. and Wardle, D. A. (2002) 'Spatial soil ecology', *Trends in Ecology and Evolution*, vol 17, pp177–183

Ewel, J. (1986) 'Designing agricultural systems for the humid tropics', *Annual Review of Ecology and Systematics*, vol 17, pp245–271

Falk, D. A., Palmer, M. A. and Zedler, J. B. (eds) (2006) *Foundations of Restoration Ecology*, Island Press, Washington, DC

FAO (Food and Agriculture Organization) (1999) *Sustaining Agricultural Biodiversity and Agro-Ecosystem Functions: Opportunities, Incentives and Approaches for the Conservation and Sustainable Use of Agricultural Biodiversity in Agro-ecosystems and Production Systems*, Food and Agriculture Organization of the United Nations, Rome, Italy

FAO (2006) *Global Forest Resources Assessment 2005: Progress Towards Sustainable Forest Management*, Food and Agriculture Organization of the United Nations, Rome, Italy

FAO (2007) *The World's Mangroves 1980–2005*, Food and Agriculture Organization of the United Nations. Rome, Italy

FAO (2009) *State of World Fisheries and Aquaculture, 2008*, Food and Agriculture Organization of the United Nations, Rome, Italy

Fearnside, P. M. (2001) 'Soybean cultivation as a threat to the environment in Brazil', *Environmental Conservation*, vol 28, no 1, pp23–38

Fears, R. (2007) *Genomics and Genetic Resources for Food and Agriculture*, Background Study Paper 34, Commission on Genetic Resources for Food and Agriculture, Food and Agriculture Organization of the United Nations, Rome, Italy

Ferraro, P. and Kiss, A. (2002) 'Direct payments to conserve biodiversity', *Science*, vol 298, pp1718–1719

Fischer, J., Brosi, B., Daily, G. C., Ehrlich, P. R., Goldman, R., Goldstein, J., Lindenmayer, D. B., Manning, A. D., Mooney, H. A., Pejchar, L., Ranganathan, J. and Tallis, H. (2008) 'Should agricultural policies encourage land sparing or wildlife-friendly farming?', *Frontiers in Ecology and the Environment*, vol 6, no 7, pp380–385

Fitter, A. H., Gilligan, C. A., Hollingworth, K., Kleczkowski, A., Twyman, R. M., Pitchford, J. W. and the Members of the NERC Soil Biodiversity Programme (2005) 'Biodiversity and ecosystem function in soils', *Functional Ecology*, vol 19, pp369–377

FOE (2008) *What's Feeding Our Food? The Environmental and Social Impacts of the Livestock Sector*, Friends of the Earth, London, www.foe.co.uk/resource/briefings/livestock_impacts.pdf

Folke, C., Carpenter, S., Walker, B., Scheffer, M., Elmqvist, T., Gunderson, L. and Holling, C. S. (2004) 'Regime shifts, resilience, and biodiversity in ecosystem management', *Annual Review of Ecology, Evolution, and Systematics*, vol 35, pp557–581

Forest, F., Grenyer, R., Rouget, M., Davies, T. J., Cowling, R. M., Faith, D. P., Balmford, A., Manning, J. C., Proches, S., van der Bank, M., Reeves, G., Hedderson, T. A. J. and Savolainen, V. (2007) 'Preserving the evolutionary potential of floras in biodiversity hotspots', *Nature*, vol 445, pp757–760

Foster, S. and Loucks, D. P. (eds) (2006) *Non-renewable Groundwater Resources: A Guidebook on Socially-Sustainable Management for Water Policy Makers*, IHP-VI Series on Groundwater No. 10, UNESCO, Paris

Freeman, A. M. III. (2003) *The Measurement of Environmental and Resource Values: Theory and Methods*, 2nd edn, Resources for the Future, Washington, DC

Fuller, R. A., Irvine, K. N., Devine-Wright, P., Warren, P. H. and Gaston, K. J. (2007) 'Psychological benefits of greenspace increase with biodiversity', *Biology Letters*, vol 3, pp390–394

Ghazoul, J. (2005) 'Buzziness as usual? Questioning the global pollination crisis', *Trends in Ecology and Evolution*, vol 20, no 7, pp367–373

Givoni, B. (1991) 'Impact of planted areas on urban environmental quality: A review', *Atmospheric Environment*, vol 25B, no 3, pp289–299

Goldstein, J. H., Pejchar L. and Daily, G. C. (2008) 'Using return-on-investment to guide restoration: A case study from Hawaii', *Conservation Letters*, vol 1, pp236–243

Gordon, L. J., Peterson, G. D. and Bennett, E. (2008) 'Agricultural modifications of hydrological flows create ecological surprises', *Trends in Ecology and Evolution*, vol 23, pp211–219

Grace, J. B., Anderson, T. M., Smith, M. D., Seabloom, E., Andelman, S. J., Meche, G., Weiher, E., Allain, L. K., Jutila, H., Sankaran, M., Knops, J., Ritchie, M. and Willig, M. R. (2007) 'Does species diversity limit productivity in natural grassland communities?', *Ecology Letters*, vol 10, pp680–689

Greenleaf, S. S., and Kremen, C. (2006) 'Wild bees enhance honey bees' pollination of hybrid sunflower', *Proceedings of the National Academy of Sciences*, vol 103, no 37, pp13890–13895

Griffin, J. N., O'Gorman, E. J., Emmerson, M. C. Jenkins, S. R., Klein, A.-M., Loreau, M. and Symstad, A. (2009) 'Biodiversity and the Stability of Ecosystem Functioning', in Naeem, S.,

Bunker, D., Hector, A., Loreau, M. and Perrings, C. (eds) *Biodiversity, Ecosystem Functioning, and Human Wellbeing: An Ecological and Economic Perspective*, Oxford University Press, Oxford, pp78–93

Grime, J. P. (1988) *Comparative Plant Ecology: A Functional Approach to Common British Species*, Unwin Hyman, London

Gruber, U. and Bartelt, P. (2007) 'Snow avalanche hazard modelling of large areas using shallow water numerical methods and GIS', *Environmental Modelling and Software*, vol 22, no 10, pp1472–1481

Guenni, L. B., Cardoso, M., Goldammer, J., Hurtt, G., Mata, L. J., Ebi, K., House, J., Valdes, J. and Norgaa, R. (2005) 'Regulation of Natural Hazards: Floods and Fires', in Hassan, R., Scholes, R. and Ash, N. (eds) *Millennium Ecosystem Assessment. Ecosystems and Human Wellbeing: Current States and Trends*, Island Press, Washington, DC, pp441–454

Gunderson, L. H. (2000) 'Ecological resilience: In theory and application', *Annual Review of Ecology and Systematics*, vol 31, pp425–439

Gunderson, L. H. and Holling, C. S. (2002) *Panarchy: Understanding Transformations in Human and Natural Systems*, Island Press, Washington, DC

Haas, D. and Défago, G. (2005) 'Biological control of soil-borne pathogens by fluorescent pseudomonads', *Nature Reviews in Microbiology*, vol 3, pp307–319

Haas, D. and Keel, C. (2003) 'Regulation of antibiotic production in root-colonizing *Pseudomonas* spp. and relevance for biological control of plant disease', *Annual Reviews in Phytopathology*, vol 41, pp117–153

Hajjar, R., Jarvis, D. I. and Gemmill-Herren, B. (2008) 'The utility of crop genetic diversity in maintaining ecosystem services', *Agriculture, Ecosystems and Environment*, vol 123, pp261–270

Harlan, J. R. (1975) *Crops and Man*, American Society of Agronomy, Madison, WI

Heal, G. M., Barbier, E. B., Boyle, K. J., Covich, A. P., Gloss, S. P., Hershner, C. H., Hoehn, J. P., Pringle, C. M., Polasky, S., Segerson, K. and Shrader-Frechette, K. (2005) *Valuing Ecosystem Services: Toward Better Environmental Decision Making*, The National Academies Press, Washington, DC

Heard, M. S., Carvell, C., Carreck, N. L., Rothery, P., Osborne, J. L., and Bourke, A. F. G. (2007) 'Landscape context not patch size determines bumble-bee density on flower mixtures sown for agri-environment schemes', *Biology Letters*, vol 3, pp638–641

Hefting, M., Bobbink, R. and Janssens, M. (2003) 'Nitrous oxide emission and denitrification in chemically nitrate-loaded riparian buffer zones', *Journal of Environmental Quality*, vol 32, pp1194–1203

Heithaus, M. R., Frid, A., Wirsing, A. J. and Worm, B. (2008) 'Predicting ecological consequences of marine top predator declines', *Trends in Ecology and Evolution*, vol 23, pp202–210

Helfield, J. H. and Naiman, R. J. (2006) 'Keystone interactions: Salmon and bear in riparian forests of Alaska', *Ecosystems*, vol 9, no 2, pp167–180

Helgason, T., Daniell, T. J., Husband, R., Fitter, A. H. and Young, J. P. W. (1998) 'Ploughing up the wood-wide web?', *Nature*, vol 394, p431

Heong, K. L., Manza, A., Catindig, J., Villareal, S. and Jacobsen, T. (2007) 'Changes in pesticide use and arthropod biodiversity in the IRRI research farm', *Outlooks in Pest Management*, October

Heywood, V. H. (1999) *Use and Potential of Wild Plants in Farm Households*, Food and Agriculture Organization, Rome

Hilderbrand, G. V., Hanley, T. A., Robbins, C. T. and Schwartz, C. C. (1999) 'Role of brown bears (*Ursus arctos*) in the flow of marine nitrogen into a terrestrial ecosystem', *Oecologia*, vol 121, no 4, pp546–550

Hill, J., Nelson, E., Tilman, D., Polasky, S. and Tiffany, D. (2006) 'Environmental, economic, and energetic costs and benefits of biodiesel and ethanol biofuels', *PNAS*, vol 103, no 30, pp11206–11210

Hobbs, R. J., Yates, S. and Mooney, H. A. (2007) 'Long-term data reveal complex dynamics in grassland in relation to climate and disturbance', *Ecological Monographs*, vol 77, no 4, pp545–568

Hoehn, P., Tscharntke, T., Tylianakis, J. M. and Steffan-Dewenter, I. (2008) 'Functional group diversity of bee pollinators increases crop yield', *Proceedings of the Royal Society B – Biological Sciences*, vol 275, no 1648, pp2283–2291

Holling, C. S. (1973) 'Resilience and stability of ecological systems', *Annual Review of Ecology and Systematics*, vol 4, pp1–23

Holling, C. S. and Meffe, G. K. (1996) 'Command and control and the pathology of natural resource management', *Conservation Biology*, vol 10, pp328–337

Holmes, P. M., Richardon, D. M. and Marais, C. (2007) 'Costs and Benefits of Restoring Natural Capital Following Alien Plant Invasions in Fynbos Ecosystems in South Africa', in Aronson, J., Milton, S. J. and Blignaut, J. N. (eds) *Restoring Natural Capital: Science, Business, and Practice*, Island Press, Washington, DC, pp88–197

Hooper, D. U. and Dukes, J. S. (2004) 'Overyielding among plant functional groups in a long-term experiment', *Ecology Letters*, vol 7, pp95–105

Hooper, D. U., Chapin III, F. S., Ewel, J. J., Hector, A., Inchausti, P., Lavorel, S., Lawton, J. H., Lodge, D. M., Loreau, M., Naeem, S., Schmid, B., Setälä, H., Symstad, A. J., Vandermeer, J. and Wardle, D. A. (2005) 'Effects of biodiversity on ecosystem functioning: A consensus of current knowledge', *Ecological Monographs*, vol 75, no 1, pp3–35

Hughes, J. B., Anthony, R. Ives, A. R. and Norberg, J. (2002) 'Do Species Interactions Buffer Environmental Variation (In Theory)?', in Loreau, M., Naeem, S. and Inchausti, P. (eds) *Biodiversity and Ecosystem Functioning*, Oxford University Press, Oxford, pp92–101

Ibelings, B. W., Portielje, R., Lammens, E. H. R. R., Noordhuis, R., van den Berg, M. S., Joose, W. and Meijer, M. L. (2007) 'Resilience of alternative stable states during the recovery of shallow lakes from eutrophication: Lake Veluwe as a case study', *Ecosystems*, vol 10, pp4–16

Ingham, R. E., Trofymov, J. A., Ingham, E. R. and Coleman, D. C. (1985) 'Interaction of bacteria, fungi, and their nematode grazers: Effects on nutrient cycling and plant growth', *Ecological Modelling*, vol 55, pp119–140

Irvine, K., Moss, B. and Balls, H. R. (1989) 'The loss of submerged plants with eutrophication II: Relationships between fish and zooplankton in a set of experimental ponds, and conclusions', *Freshwater Biology*, vol 22, pp89–107

Jackson, J. B. C., Kirby, M. X., Berger, W. H., Bjorndal, K. A., Botsford, L. W., Bourque, B. J., Bradbury, R. H., Cooke, R., Erlandson, J., Estes, J. A., Hughes, T. P., Kidwell, S., Lange, C. B., Lenihan, H. S., Pandolfi, J. M., Peterson, C. H., Steneck, R. S., Tegner, M. J. and Warner, R. R. (2001) 'Historical overfishing and the recent collapse of coastal ecosystems', *Science*, vol 293, pp629–638

Jansson, Å. and Nohrstedt, P. (2001) 'Carbon sinks and human freshwater dependence in Stockholm County', *Ecological Economics*, vol 39, pp361–370

Janzen, D. H. (2002) 'Tropical Dry Forest: Area de Conservacion Guancaste, Northwestern Costa Rica', in Perrow, M. R. and Davy, A. J. (eds) *Handbook of Ecological Restoration*, Cambridge University Press, Cambridge, pp 559–583

Janzen, H. H. (2004) 'Carbon cycling in earth systems: A soil science perspective', *Agriculture, Ecosystems and Environment*, vol 104, pp399–417

Jenkins, I. C. and Riemann, R. (2003) 'What Does Nonforest Land Contribute to the Global C Balance?', in McRoberts, R. E., Reams, G. A., van Deusen, P. C. and Moser, J. W. (eds) *Proceedings of the Third Annual Forest Inventory and Analysis Symposium*, US Department of Agriculture, Forest Service, pp173–179

Jeppesen, E., Søndergaard, M., Meerhoff, M., Lauridsen, T. L. and Jensen, J. P. (2007) 'Shallow lake restoration by nutrient loading reduction: Some recent findings and challenges ahead', *Hydrobiologia*, vol 584, no 1, pp239–252

Johnson, R. (2007) *Recent Honey Bee Colony Declines*, Congressional Research Service Report for Congress, RL 33938, Washington, DC

Joshi, J., Schmid, B., Caldeira, M. C., Dimitrakopoulos, P. G., Good, J., Harris, R., Hector, A., Huss-Danell, K., Jumpponen, A., Minns, A., Mulder, C. P. H., Pereira, J. S., Prinz, A., Scherer-Lorenzen, M., Siamantziouras, A.-S. D., Terry, A. C., Troumbis, A. Y. and Lawton, J. H. (2001) 'Local adaptation enhances performance of common plant species', *Ecology Letters*, vol 4, no 6, pp536–544

Junk, W. J., Bayley, P. B. and Sparks, R. E. (1989) 'The flood-pulse concept in river-floodplain systems', *Canadian Special Publications in Fisheries and Aquatic Sciences*, vol 106, pp110–127

Juo, A. S. R. (2001) 'Technologies for sustainable management of steep lands in Asia: Harmonizing economic and ecological sustainability; in Partap, T. (ed) *Sustainable Farming Systems in Upland Areas*, Report of the APO study meeting on Sustainable Farming Systems in Upland Areas, held in New Delhi, India, 15–19 January 2001, Asian Productivity Organisation, Tokyo

Kathiresan, K. and Rajendran, N. (2005) 'Coastal mangrove forests mitigated tsunami', *Estuarine, Coastal and Shelf Science*, vol 65, pp601–606

Kearns, C. A., Inouye, D. W. and Waser, N. M. (1998) 'Endangered mutualisms: The conservation of plant-pollinator interactions', *Annual Review of Ecology and Systematics*, vol 29, pp83–112

Kinzig, A. P., Ryan, P., Etienne, M., Allyson, H., Elmqvist, T. and Walker, B. H. (2006) 'Resilience and regime shifts: Assessing cascading effects', *Ecology and Society*, vol 11, no 1, p20

Kinzig, A. P., Warren, P. S. Martin, C., Mope, D. and Katti, M. (2005) 'The effects of human socioeconomic status and cultural characteristics on urban patterns of biodiversity', *Ecology and Society*, vol 10, p23

Klein, A. M., Steffan-Dewenter, I. and Tscharntke, T. (2003) 'Fruit set of highland coffee increases with the diversity of pollinating bees', *Proceedings of the Royal Society B – Biological Sciences*, vol 270, no 1518, pp955–961

Klein, A. M., Vaissière, B. E., Cane, J. H., Steffan-Dewenter, I., Cunningham, S. A., Kremen, C. and Tscharntke, T. (2007) 'Importance of pollinators in changing landscapes for world crops', *Proceedings of the Royal Society B – Biological Sciences*, vol 274, pp303–313

Kontoleon, A., Pascual, U. and Smale, M. (eds) (2008) *Agrobiodiversity, Conservation and Economic Development*, Taylor and Francis, New York

Kremen, C. and Chaplin-Kramer, R. (2007) 'Insects as Providers of Ecosystem Services: Crop Pollination and Pest Control', in Stewart, A. J. A., New, T. R. and Lewis, O. T. (eds) *Insect Conservation Biology*, Royal Entomological Society, London, pp349–382

Kremen, C. and Ricketts, T. (2000) 'Global perspectives on pollination disruptions', *Conservation Biology*, vol 14, no 5, pp1226–1228

Kremen, C., Williams, N. M., Aizen, M. A., Gemmill-Herren, B., LeBuhn, G., Minckley, R., Packer, L., Potts, S. G., Roulston, T., Steffan-Dewenter, I., Vazquez, D. P., Winfree, R., Adams, L., Crone, E. E., Greenleaf, S. S., Keitt, T. H., Klein, A. M., Regetz, J. and Ricketts, T. H. (2007) 'Pollination and other ecosystem services produced by mobile organisms: A conceptual framework for the effects of land-use change', *Ecology Letters*, vol 10, no 4, pp299–314

Kremen, C., Williams, N. M., Bugg, R. L., Fay, J. P. and Thorp, R. W. (2004) 'The area requirements of an ecosystem service: Crop pollination by native bee communities in California', *Ecology Letters*, vol 7, pp1109–1119

Kulmala, M., Suni, T., Lehtinen, K. E. J., Dal Maso, M., Boy, M., Reissell, A., Rannik, Ü., Aalto, P., Keronen, P., Hakola, H., Bäck, J., Hoffmann, T., Vesala, T. and Hari, P. (2004) 'A new feedback mechanism linking forests, aerosols, and climate', *Atmospheric Chemistry and Physics*, vol 4, pp557–562

Kunz, Y. W. (2004) *Developmental Biology of Teleost Fishes*, Springer, Heidelberg, Germany

Lake, I. R., Harrison, F. C. D., Chalmers, R. M., Bentham, G., Nichols, G., Hunter, P. R., Kovats, R. S. and Grundy, C. (2007) 'Case-control study of environmental and social factors influencing cryptosporidiosis', *European Journal of Epidemiology*, vol 22, pp805–811

Larsen, T. H., Williams, N. M. and Kremen, C. (2005) 'Extinction order and altered community structure rapidly disrupt ecosystem functioning', *Ecology Letters*, vol 8, pp538–547

Laurance, W., Salicrup, P., Delamônica, P., Fearnside, P., D'Angelo, S., Jerozolinksi, A., Pohl, L. and Lovejoy, T. (2001) 'Rain forest fragmentation and the structure of Amazonian liana communities', *Ecology*, vol 82, pp105–116

Lavelle, P. and Spain, A. V. (2001) *Soil Ecology*, Kluwer Academic Publishers, Netherlands

Lavelle, P., Decaëns, T., Aubert, M., Barota, S., Blouina, M., Bureau, F., Margerieb, P., Mora, P. and Rossi, J.-P. (2006) 'Soil invertebrates and ecosystem services', *European Journal of Soil Biology*, vol 42 (suppl 1), ppS3–S15

Lawton, J. (1997) 'The science and non-science of conservation biology', *Oikos*, vol 79, no 1, pp3–5

Lawton, J. H., Naeem, S., Thompson, L. J., Hector, A. and Crawley, M. J. (1998) 'Biodiversity and ecosystem function: Getting the Ecotron experiment in its correct context', *Functional Ecology*, vol 12, pp848–852

Lee, J., Park, B.-J., Tsunetsugu, Y., Takahide, K. and Miyazaki, Y. (2009) 'Restorative effects of viewing real forest landscapes, based on a comparison with urban landscapes', *Scandinavian Journal of Forest Research*, vol 24, no 3, pp227–234

Lessard, J. L. and Merritt, R. W. (2006) 'Influence of marine-derived nutrients from spawning salmon on aquatic insect communities in southeast Alaskan streams', *Oikos*, vol 113, pp334–343

Levin, S. A. (ed) (2000) *Encyclopedia of Biodiversity*, Five-Volume Set, 2nd edn, Academic Press San Diego

Levin, S.A., Carpenter, S., Godfray, C., Kinzig, A., Loreau, M., Losos, J., Walker, B. and Wilcove, D. (eds) *Princeton Guide to Ecology*, Princeton University Press, Princeton

Liiri, M., Setälä, H., Haimi, J., Pennanen, T. and Fritze, H. (2002) 'Soil processes are not influenced by the functional complexity of soil decomposer food webs under disturbance', *Soil Biology and Biochemistry*, vol 34, pp1009–1020

Loehle, C. (1989) 'Catastrophe theory in ecology: A critical review and an example of the butterfly catastrophe', *Ecological Modelling*, vol 49, pp125–152

Loreau, M. (2008) 'Biodiversity and ecosystem functioning: The mystery of the deep sea', *Current Biology*, vol 18, no 3, ppR126–R128

Losey, J. E. and Vaughan, M. (2006) 'The economic value of ecological services provided by insects', *Bioscience*, vol 56, pp331–323

Lovasi, G. S., Quinn, J. W., Neckerman, K. M., Perzanowski, M. S. and Rundle, A. (2008) 'Children living in areas with more street trees have lower prevalence of asthma', *Journal of Epidemiology and Community Health*, vol 62, pp647–649

Luck, G. W., Daily, G. C. and Ehrlich, P. R. (2003) 'Population diversity and ecosystem services', *Trends in Ecology and Evolution*, vol 18, no 7, pp331–336

Luck, G. W., Harrington, R., Harrison, P. A., Kremen, C., Berry, P. M., Bugter, R., Dawson, T. P., de Bello, F., Diaz. S., Feld, C. K., Haslett, J. R., Hering, D., Kontogianni, A., Lavorel, S., Rounsevell, M., Samways, M. J., Sandin, L., Settele, J., Sykes, M. T., van den Hove, S., Vandewalle, M. and Zobel, M. (2009) 'Quantifying the contribution of organisms to the provision of ecosystem services', *Bioscience*, vol 59, pp223–235

Lyons, K. G. and Schwartz, M. W. (2001) 'Rare species loss alters ecosystem function: Invasion resistance', *Ecology Letters*, vol 4, pp358–365

Lyons, K. G., Brigham, C. A., Traut, B. H. and Schwartz, M. W. (2005) 'Rare species and ecosystem functioning', *Conservation Biology*, vol 19, no 4, pp1019–1024

MA (Millennium Ecosystem Assessment) (2005) *Ecosystems and Human Well-being: Synthesis*, Island Press, Washington, DC

Maas, J., Verheij, R. A., Groenewegen, P. P., de Vries, S. and Spreeuwenberg, P. (2006) 'Green space, urbanity, and health: How strong is the relation?', *Journal of Epidemiology and Community Health*, vol 60, no 7, pp587–592

Mackill, D. (2006) 'From genes to farmer's fields', *Rice Today*, October–December, pp28–31

Mader, P., Fliessbach, A., Dubois, D., Gunst, L., Fried, P. and Niggli, U. (2002) 'Soil fertility and biodiversity in organic farming', *Science*, vol 296, pp1694–1697

Makarieva, A. M. and Gorshkov, V. G. (2007) 'Biotic pump of atmospheric moisture as driver of the hydrological cycle on land', *Hydrology and Earth Systems Science*, vol 11, pp1013–1033

Makarieva, A. M., Gorshkov, V. G. and Bai-Lian, Li (2006) 'Conservation of water cycle on land via restoration of natural closed-canopy forests: Implications for regional landscape planning', *Ecological Research*, vol 21, no 6, pp897–906

Mäler, K.-G. (2000) 'Development, ecological resources and their management: A study of complex dynamic systems', *European Economic Review*, vol 44, nos 4–6, pp645–665

Maltby, E., Burbridge, P. and Fraser, A. (1996) 'Peat and Acid Sulphate Soils: A Case Study from Vietnam', in Maltby, E., Immirzi, C. P. and Safford, R. J. (eds) *Tropical Lowland Peatlands of Southeast Asia*, International Union for Conservation of Nature, Gland, Switzerland

Maltby, E., Hogan, D. V., Immirzi, C. P., Tellam, J. H. and van der Peijl, M. J. (1994) 'Building a New Approach to the Investigation and Assessment of Wetland Ecosystem Functioning', in Mitsch, W. J. (ed) *Global Wetlands: Old World and New*, Elsevier, Amsterdam, pp637–658

Marani, M., Lanzoni, S., Silvestric, S. and Rinaldo, A. (2004) 'Tidal landforms, patterns of halophytic vegetation and the fate of the lagoon of Venice', *Journal of Marine Systems*, vol 51, pp191–210

Marengo, J. A., Soares, W. R., Saulo, C. and Nicolini, M. (2004) 'Climatology of the low-level jet east of the Andes as derived from the NCEP–NCAR reanalyses: Characteristics and temporal variability', *Journal of Climate*, vol 17, no 12, pp2261–2280

May, R. M. (1977) 'Thresholds and breakpoints in ecosystems with a multiplicity of stable states', *Nature*, vol 269, pp471–477

McNaughton, S. J. (1993) 'Biodiversity and Function of Grazing Ecosystems', in Schulze, E. D. and Mooney, H. A. (eds) *Biodiversity and Ecosystem Function*, Springer-Verlag, Berlin, pp361–383

McPherson, E. G., Nowak, D., Heisler, G., Grimmond, S., Souch, C., Grant, R. and Rowntree, R. (1997) 'Quantifying urban forest structure, function and value: The Chicago Urban Forest Climate Project', *Urban Ecosystems*, vol 1, pp49–61

Memmott, J., Craze, P. G., Waser, N. M. and Price, M. V. (2007) 'Global warming and the disruption of plant-pollinator interactions', *Ecology Letters*, vol 10, pp710–717

Messelink, G. J., van Maanen, R., van Steenpaal, S. E. F. and Janssen, A. (2008) 'Biological control of thrips and whiteflies by a shared predator: Two pests are better than one', *Biological Control*, vol 44, no 3, pp372–379

Miller, R. M. and Jastrow, J. D. (eds) (2000) *Mycorrhizal Fungi Influence Soil Structure. Arbuscular Mycorrhizas: Molecular Biology and Physiology*, Kluwer Academic Press, Dordrecht, Netherlands

Mitchell, N. L. and Lamberti, G. A. (2005) 'Responses in dissolved nutrients and epilithon abundance to spawning salmon in southeast Alaska streams', *Limnology and Oceanography*, vol 50, pp217–227

Mitchell, R. and Popham, F. (2008) 'Effect of exposure to natural environment on health inequalities: An observational population study', *Lancet*, vol 372, no 9650, pp1655–1660

Morandin, L. A., Winston, M. L., Abbott, V. A. and Franklin, M. T. (2007) 'Can pastureland increase wild bee abundance in agriculturally intense areas?', *Basic and Applied Ecology*, vol 8, pp117–124

Morrone, J. J. (1994) 'On the identification of areas of endemism', *Systematic Biology*, vol 43, no 3, pp438–441

Moss, B. (2001) *The Broads: The People's Wetland*, The New Naturalist Series, Harper Collins, London

Mouritsen, K. N., Mouritsen, L. T. and Jensen, K. T. (1998) 'Change of topography and sediment characteristics on an intertidal mud-flat following mass-mortality of the amphipod Corophium volutator', *Journal of the Marine Biological Association of the United Kingdom*, vol 78, pp1167–1180

Myers, N., Mittermeier, R. A., Mittermeier, C. G., da Fonseca, G. A. B. and Kent, J. (2000) 'Biodiversity hotspots for conservation priorities', *Nature*, vol 403, pp853–858

Mysterud, A. (2006) 'The concept of overgrazing and its role in management of large herbivores', *Wildlife Biology*, vol 12, no 2, pp129–141

Nabhan, G. P. and Buchmann, S. L. (1997) 'Services Provided by Pollinators', in Daily, G. C. (ed) *Nature's Services: Societal Dependence on Natural Ecosystems*, Island Press, Washington, DC, pp133–150

Naeem, S., Thompson, L. J., Lawler, S. P., Lawton, J. H. and Woodfin, R. M. (1995) 'Empirical evidence that declining species diversity may alter the performance of terrestrial ecosystems', *Philosophical Transactions: Biological Sciences*, vol 347, no 1321, pp249–262

Naidoo, R., Balmford, A., Costanza, R., Fisher, B., Green, R. E., Lehner, B., Malcolm, T. R. and Ricketts, T. H. (2008) 'Global mapping of ecosystem services and conservation priorities', *Proceedings of the National Academy of Sciences*, vol 105, pp9495–9500

Naylor, R. and Ehrlich, P. (1997) 'Natural Pest Control Services and Agriculture', in Daily, G. C. (ed) *Nature's Services: Societal Dependence on Natural Ecosystems*, Island Press, Washington, DC, pp151–174

Nei, M. (1987) *Molecular Evolutionary Genetics*, Columbia University Press, Irvington, New York

Nelson, E., Mendoza, G., Regetz, J., Polasky, S., Tallis, H., Cameron, D. R., Chan, K. M. A., Daily, G. C., Goldstein, J., Kareiva, P. M., Lonsdorf, E., Naidoo, R., Ricketts, T. H. and Shaw, M. R. (2009) 'Modeling multiple ecosystem services, biodiversity conservation, commodity production, and tradeoffs at landscape scales', *Frontiers in Ecology and the Environment*, vol 7, pp4–11

Nevo, E. (1998) 'Genetic diversity in wild cereals: Regional and local studies and their bearing on conservation ex situ and in situ', *Genetic Resources and Crop Evolution*, vol 45, no 4, pp355–370

Newbold, J. D., Elwood, J. W., O'Neill, R. V. and van Winkle, W. (1981) 'Nutrient spiralling in streams: The concept and its field measurements', *Canadian Journal of Fisheries and Aquatic Sciences*, vol 38, pp860–863

Newsham, K. K., Fitter, A. H. and Watkinson, A. R. (1995) 'Arbuscular mycorrhiza protect an annual grass from root pathogenic fungi in the field', *Journal of Ecology*, vol 83, pp991–1000

Ninan, K. N. (ed) (2009) *Conserving and Valuing Ecosystem Services and Biodiversity*, Earthscan, London

Odum, E. P. (1969) 'The strategy of ecosystem development', *Science*, vol 164, pp262–270

O'Neill, R. V. and Kahn, J. R. (2000) '*Homo economus* as a keystone species', *BioScience*, vol 50, no 4, pp333–337

Orme, C. D. L., Davies, R. G., Burgess, M., Eigenbrod, F., Pickup, N., Olson, V. A., Webster, A. J., Ding, T.-S., Rasmussen, P. C., Ridgely, R. S., Stattersfield, A. J., Bennett, P. M., Blackburn, T. M., Gaston, K. J. and Owens, I. P. F. (2005) 'Global hotspots of species richness are not congruent with endemism or threat', *Nature*, vol 436, pp1016–1019

Ozer, S., Irmak, M. A. and Yilmaz, H. (2008) 'Determination of roadside noise reduction effectiveness of *Pinus sylvestris* L. and *Populus nigra* L. in Erzurum, Turkey', *Environmental Monitoring and Assessment*, vol 144, pp191–197

Palumbi, S. R., McLeod, K. L. and Grünbaum, D. (2008) 'Ecosystems in action: Lessons from marine ecology about recovery, resistance, and reversibility', *BioScience*, vol 58, no 1, pp33–42

Pauly, D. (1995) 'Anecdotes and the shifting baseline syndrome of fisheries', *Trends in Ecology and Evolution*, vol 10, no 10, p430

Pergams, O. R. W. and Zaradic, P. A. (2008) 'Evidence for a fundamental and pervasive shift away from nature-based recreation', *Proceedings of the National Academy of Sciences*, vol 105, pp2295–2300

Perrings, C. (2007) 'Going beyond panaceas: Future challenges', *Proceedings of the National Academy of Sciences*, vol 104, pp15179–15180

Perrings, C., Baumgärtner, S., Brock, W. A., Chopra, K., Conte, M., Costello, C., Duraiappah, A., Kinzig, A. P., Pascual, U., Polasky, S., Tschirhart, J. and Xepapadeas, A. (2009) 'The Economics of Biodiversity and Ecosystem Services', in Naeem, S., Bunker, D., Hector, A., Loreau, M. and Perrings, C. (eds) *Biodiversity, Ecosystem Functioning, and Human Wellbeing: An Ecological and Economic Perspective*, Oxford University Press, Oxford, pp230–247

Petchey, O. L., Hector, A. and Gaston, K. J. (2004) 'How do different measures of functional diversity perform?', *Ecology*, vol 85, pp847–857

Phillips, G., Bramwell, A., Pitt, J., Stansfield, J. and Perrow, M. (1999) 'Practical application of 25 years' research into the management of shallow lakes', *Hydrobiologia*, vol 395/396, pp61–76

Phoenix, G. K., Hicks, W. K., Cinderby, S., Kuylenstierna, J. C. I., Stock, W. D., Dentener, F. J., Giller, K. E., Austin, A. T., Lefroy, R. D. B., Gimeno, B. S., Ashmore, M. R. and Ineson, P. (2006) 'Atmospheric nitrogen deposition in world biodiversity hotspots: The need for a greater global perspective in assessing N deposition impacts', *Global Change Biology*, vol 12, no 3, pp470–476

Pickett, S. T. A., Cadenasso, M. L., Grove, J. M., Groffman, P. M., Band, L. E., Boone, C. G., Burch, W. R., Grimmond, C. S. B., Hom, J., Jenkins, J. C., Law, N. L., Nilon, C. H., Pouyat, R. V., Szlavecz, K., Warren, P. S. and Wilson, M. A. (2008) 'Beyond urban legends: An emerging framework of urban ecology, as illustrated by the Baltimore Ecosystem Study', *BioScience*, vol 58, no 2, pp139–150

Pimentel, D. (2008) 'Conservation biological control', *Biological Control*, vol 45, p171

Polis, G. A., Anderson, W. B. and Holt, D. R. (1997) 'Toward an integration of landscape and food web ecology: The dynamics of spatially subsidized food webs', *Annual Review of Ecology and Systematics*, vol 28, pp289–316

Potvin, C. and Gotelli, N. J. (2008) 'Biodiversity enhances individual performance but does not affect survivorship in tropical trees', *Ecology Letters*, vol 11, pp217–223

Prang, G. (2007) 'An industry analysis of the freshwater ornamental fishery with particular reference to supply of Brazilian freshwater ornamentals to the UK market', *UAKARI*, vol 3, no 1, pp7–51

Prendergast, J. R., Quinn, R. M., Lawton, J. H., Eversham, B. C. and Gibbons, D. W. (1993) 'Rare species, the coincidence of diversity hotspots and conservation strategies', *Nature*, vol 365, pp335–337

Pretty, J. N., Noble, A. D., Bossio, D., Dixon, J., Hine, R. E., de Vries, F. W. T. P. and Morison, J. I. L. (2006) 'Resource-conserving agriculture increases yields in developing countries', *Environmental Science & Technology*, vol 40, no 4, pp1114–1119

Rahlao, S. J., Hoffman, M. T., Todd, S. W. and McGrath, K. (2008) 'Long-term vegetation change in the Succulent Karoo, South Africa following 67 years of rest from grazing', *Journal of Arid Environments*, vol 72, no 5, pp808–819

Richards, A. J. (2001) 'Does low biodiversity resulting from modern agricultural practice affect crop pollination and yield?', *Annals of Botany*, vol 88, pp165–172

Ricketts, T. H. (2004) 'Tropical forest fragments enhance pollinator activity in nearby coffee crops', *Conservation Biology*, vol 18, pp1262–1271

Ricketts, T. H., Regetz, J., Steffan-Dewenter, I., Cunningham, S. A., Kremen, C., Bogdanski, A., Gemmill-Herren, B., Mayfield, M. M., Klein, A. M., Morandin, L. A., Greenleaf, S. S., Ochieng, A. and Viana, B. F. (2008) 'Landscape effects on crop pollination services: Are there general patterns?', *Ecology Letters*, vol 11, no 5, pp499–515

Rockström, J., Steffen, W., Noone, K., Persson, Å., Chapin, F. S., Lambin, E., Lenton, T. M., Scheffer, M., Folke, C., Schellnhuber, H. J., Nykvist, B., de Wit, C. A., Hughes, T., van der Leeuw, S., Rodhe, H., Sörlin, S., Snyder, P. K., Costanza, R., Svedin, U., Falkenmark, M., Karlberg, L., Corell, R. W., Fabry, V. J., Hansen, J., Walker, B., Liverman, D., Richardson, K., Crutzen, P. and Foley, J. (2009) 'Planetary boundaries: Exploring the safe operating space for humanity', *Ecology and Society*, vol 14, no 2, art 32, available at www.ecologyandsociety.org/vol14/iss2/art32/

Rönnbäck, P., Kautsky, N., Pihl, L., Troell, M., Söderqvist, T. and Wennhage, H. (2007) 'Ecosystem goods and services from Swedish coastal habitats: Identification, valuation, and implications of ecosystem shifts', *AMBIO*, vol 36, pp534–544

Rosenberg, A., Bigford, T. E., Leathery, S., Hill, R. L. and Bickers, K. (2000) 'Ecosystem approaches to fishery management through essential fish habitat', *Bulletin of Marine Science*, vol 66, no 3, pp535–542

Ross, A. B., Jones, J. M., Kubacki, M. L. and Bridgeman, T. (2008) 'Classification of macroalgae as fuel and its thermochemical behaviour', *Bioresource Technology*, vol 99, pp6494–6504

Roulet, N. T. (2000) 'Peatlands, carbon storage, greenhouse gases, and the Kyoto Protocol: Prospects and significance for Canada', *Wetlands*, vol 20, no 4, pp605–615

RSPB (Royal Society for the Protection of Birds) (2007) 'Trade ban will save two million wild birds', www.rspb.org.uk/ourwork/policy/wildbirdslaw/birdtradeban.asp, accessed 1 September 2009

Santamouris, M. (ed) (2001) *Energy and Climate in the Urban Built Environment*, James and James, London

Scheffer, M., Brock, W. and Westley, F. (2000) 'Socioeconomic mechanisms preventing optimum use of ecosystem services: An interdisciplinary theoretical analysis', *Ecosystems*, vol 3, pp451–471

Scheffer, M., Carpenter, S. R., Foley, J. A., Folke, C. and Walker, B. (2001) 'Catastrophic shifts in ecosystems', *Nature*, vol 413, pp591–596

Scheffer, M., Hosper, S. H., Meijer, M.-L., Moss, B. and Jeppesen, E. (1993) 'Alternative equilibria in shallow lakes', *Trends in Ecology and Evolution*, vol 8, pp275–279

Schmitz, O. J., Kalies, E. L. and Booth, M. G. (2006) 'Alternative dynamic regimes and trophic control of plant succession', *Ecosystems*, vol 9, no 4, pp659–672

Schröter, D., Cramer, W., Leemans, R., Prentice, I. C., Araujo, M. B., Arnell, N. W., Bondeau, A., Bugmann, H., Carter, T. R., Gracia, C. A., de la Vega-Leinert, A. C., Erhard, M., Ewert, F., Glendining, M., House, J. I., Kankaanpaa, S., Klein, R. J. T., Lavorel, S., Lindner, M., Metzger, M. J., Meyer, J., Mitchell, T. D., Reginster, I., Rounsevell, M., Sabate, S., Sitch, S., Smith, B., Smith, J., Smith, P., Sykes, M. T., Thonicke, K., Thuiller, W., Tuck, G., Zaehle, S. and Zierl, B. (2005) 'Ecosystem service supply and vulnerability to global change in Europe', *Science*, vol 310, pp1333–1337

SER (Society for Ecological Restoration) (2002) *The SER Primer on Ecological Restoration*, SER Science and Policy Working Group, Tucson, AZ, www.ser.org/, accessed 1 September 2009

Sheil, D. and Murdiyarso, D. (2009) 'How forests attract rain: An examination of a new hypothesis', *Bioscience*, vol 59, no 4, pp341–347

Shennan, C. (2008) 'Biotic interactions, ecological knowledge and agriculture', *Philosophical Transactions of the Royal Society B*, vol 363, no 1492, pp717–739

Shu-Yang, F., Freedman, B. and Cote, R. (2004) 'Principles and practice of ecological design', *Environ. Rev.*, vol 12, no 2, pp97–112

Sidle, R. C., Ziegler, A. D., Negishi, J. N., Nik, A. R., Siew, R. and Turkelboom, F. (2006) 'Erosion processes in steep terrain: Truths, myths, and uncertainties related to forest management in Southeast Asia', *Forest Ecology and Management*, vol 224, nos 1–2, pp199–225

Singh, R. P., Hodson, D. P., Jin, Y., Huerta-Espino, J., Kinyua, M. G., Wanyera, R., Njau, P. and Ward, R. W. (2006) 'Current status, likely migration and strategies to mitigate the threat to wheat production from race Ug99 (TTKS) of stem rust pathogen', *CAB Reviews: Perspectives in Agriculture, Veterinary Science, Nutrition and Natural Resources*, vol 1, no 054

Smith, T. M., Shugart, H. H. and Woodward, F. I. (1997) *Plant Functional Types: Their Relevance to Ecosystem Properties and Global Change*, Cambridge University Press, Cambridge

Srivastava, D. S and Vellend, M. (2005) 'Biodiversity-ecosystem function research: Is it relevant to conservation?', *Annual Review of Ecology, Evolution, and Systematics*, vol 36, pp267–294

Srivastava, D. S., Cardinale, B. J., Downing, A. L., Duffy, J. E., Jouseau, C., Sankaran, M. and Wright, J. P. (2009) 'Diversity has stronger top–down than bottom–up effects on decomposition', *Ecology*, vol 90, no 4, pp1073–1083

Steffan-Dewenter, I. (2003) 'Importance of habitat area and landscape context for species richness of bees and wasps in fragmented orchard meadows', *Conservation Biology*, vol 17, no 4, pp1036–1044

Steffan-Dewenter, I. and Tscharntke, T. (1999) 'Effects of habitat isolation on pollinator communities and seed set', *Oecologia*, vol 121, no 3, pp432–440

Steffan-Dewenter, I., Münzenberg, U., Bürger, C., Thies, C. and Tscharntke, T. (2002) 'Scale-dependent effects of landscape context on three pollinator guilds', *Ecology*, vol 83, no 5, pp1421–1432

Steinfeld, H., Gerber, P., Wassenaar, T., Castel, V., Rosales, N. and de Haan, C. (2006) *Livestock's Long Shadow, Environmental Issues and Options*, Food and Agriculture Organization of the United Nations, Rome, www.fao.org/docrep/010/a0701e/a0701e00.htm

Suding, K. N., Lavorel, S., Chapin, F. S., Cornelissen, J. H. C., Diaz, S., Garnier, E., Goldberg, D., Hooper, D. U., Jackson, S. T. and Navas, M. L. (2008) 'Scaling environmental change through the community-level: A trait-based response-and-effect framework for plants', *Global Change Biology*, vol 14, no 5, pp1125–1140

Swift, M. J., Izac, A.-M. N. and van Noordwijk, M. (2004) 'Biodiversity and ecosystem services in agricultural landscapes: Are we asking the right questions?', *Agriculture, Ecosystems and Environment*, vol 104, pp113–134

Szwagrzyk, J. and Gazda, A. (2007) 'Above-ground standing biomass and tree species diversity in natural stands of Central Europe', *Journal of Vegetation Science*, vol 18, no 4, pp555–562

Tansley, A. G. (1935) 'The use and abuse of vegetational concepts and terms', *Ecology*, vol 16, pp284–307

TEEB (2008) 'The economics of ecosystems and biodiversity: An interim report', available at www.teebweb.org, accessed 1 November 2009

TEEB in National Policy (2011) *The Economics of Ecosystems and Biodiversity in National and International Policy Making* (ed Patrick ten Brink), Earthscan, London

Thebault, E. and Loreau, M. (2006) 'The relationships between biodiversity and ecosystem functioning in food webs', *Ecological Research*, vol 21, pp17–25

Thom, R. (1969) 'Topological models in biology', *Topology*, vol 8, pp313–335

Tilman, D., Knops, J., Weldin, D., Reich, P., Ritchie, M. and Siemann, E. (1997a) 'The influence of functional diversity and composition on ecosystem processes', *Science*, vol 277, pp1300–1302

Tilman, D., Lehman, C. L. and Thomson, K. T. (1997b) 'Plant diversity and ecosystem productivity: Theoretical considerations', *Proceedings of the National Academy of Sciences*, vol 94, pp1857–1861

Tilman, D., Wedin, D. and Knops, J. (1996) 'Productivity and sustainability influenced by biodiversity in grassland ecosystems', *Nature*, vol 379, pp718–720

Titlyanova, A. A. (2009) 'Stability of grass ecosystems', *Contemporary Problems of Ecology*, vol 2, no 2, pp119–123

Tscharntke, T., Klein, A. M., Kruess, A., Steffan-Dewenter, I. and Thies, C. (2005) 'Landscape perspectives on agricultural intensification and biodiversity: Ecosystem service management', *Ecology Letters*, vol 8, pp857–874

Tyrväinen, L. (1997) 'The amenity value of the urban forest: An application of the hedonic pricing method', *Landscape and Urban Planning*, vol 37, nos 3–4, pp211–222

UN (2009) *World Population Prospects: The 2008 Revision*, UN Population Division Policy Brief No. 2009/1, United Nations, New York, www.un.org/esa/population/unpop.htm, accessed 1 September 2009

US Environmental Protection Agency (2007) *Bioengineering for Pollution Prevention Through Development of Biobased Materials and Energy*, State-of-the-science report, US Environmental Protection Agency, Washington, DC

USFWS (US Fish and Wildlife Service) (2007) *2006 National Survey of Fishing, Hunting, and Wildlife-Associated Recreation: State Overview (Preliminary Findings)*, US Fish and Wildlife Service, Washington, DC

Valente, L. M. P., Gouveia, A., Rema, P., Matos, J., Gomes, E. F. and Pinto, I. S. (2006) 'Evaluation of three seaweeds *Gracilaria bursa-pastoris*, *Ulva rigida* and *Gracilaria cornea* as dietary ingredients in European sea bass (*Dicentrarchus labrax*) juveniles', *Aquaculture*, vol 252, pp85–96

van der Heijden, M. G. A., Klironomos, J. N., Ursic, M., Moutoglis, P., Streitwolf-Engel, R., Boller, T., Wiemken, A. and Sanders, I. R. (1998) 'Mycorrhizal fungal diversity determines plant biodiversity, ecosystem variability and productivity', *Nature*, vol 396, pp69–72

van den Wyngaert, I. J. J. and Bobbink, R. (2009) 'The Influences of Vertebrate Herbivory on Ecological Dynamics in Wetland Ecosystems', in Maltby, E. and Barker, T. (eds) *The Wetlands Handbook*, Wiley-Blackwell, Oxford, pp304–325

Vavilov, N. I. (1992) *Origin and Geography of Cultivated Plants* (translated by Doris Love), Cambridge University Press, Cambridge

Vilà, M., Vayreda, J., Comas, L., Ibanez, J. J., Mata, T. and Obon, B. (2007) 'Species richness and wood production: A positive association in Mediterranean forests', *Ecology Letters*, vol 10, pp241–250

Vilà, M., Vayreda, J., Gracia, C. and Ibanez, J. J. (2003) 'Does tree diversity increase wood production in pine forests?', *Oecologia*, vol 135, no 2, pp299–303

Villéger, S., Mason, N. W. H. and Mouillot, D. (2008) 'New mullti-dimensional functional diversity indices for a multifaceted framework in functional ecology', *Ecology*, vol 89, pp2290–2301

Virginia, R. A. and Wall, D. H. (2000) 'Ecosystem Function, Basic Principles of', in Levin, S. A. (ed) *Encyclopedia of Biodiversity Vol 2*, Academic Press, San Diego pp345–352

Vitousek, P. M., Mooney, H. A., Lubchenco, J. and Melillo, J. M. (1997) 'Human domination of Earth's ecosystems', *Science*, vol 277, no 5325, pp494–499

Waddington, J. M. and Warner, K. D. (2001) 'Atmospheric CO_2 sequestration in restored mined peatlands', *Ecoscience*, vol 8, pp359–368

Waldbusser, G. G., Marinelli, R. L., Whitlatch, R. B. and Visscher, P. T. (2004) 'The effects of infaunal biodiversity on biogeochemistry of coastal marine sediments', *Limnology and Oceanography*, vol 49, pp1482–1492

Walker, B. and Meyers, J. A. (2004) 'Thresholds in ecological and social-ecological systems: A developing database', *Ecology and Society*, vol 9, no 2, p3

Walker, B. H., Ludwig, D., Holling, C. S., and Peterman, R. M. (1981) 'Stability of semi-arid savanna grazing systems', *Journal of Ecology*, vol 69, pp473–498

Wall, D. H. and Virginia, R. A. (2000) 'The World Beneath Our Feet: Soil Biodiversity and Ecosystem Functioning', in Raven, P. and Williams, T. A. (eds) *Nature and Human Society: The Quest for a Sustainable World*, National Academy of Sciences Press, pp225–241

Way, M. J. and Heong, K. L. (1994) 'The role of biodiversity in the dynamics and management of insect pests of tropical irrigated rice: A review', *Bulletin of Entomological Research*, vol 84, pp567–587

WCED (World Commission on Environment and Development) (1987) *Our Common Future*, Oxford University Press, Oxford

Wells, S., Ravilious, C. and Corcoran, E. (2006) *In the Front Line: Shoreline Protection and Other Ecosystem Services from Mangroves and Coral Reefs*, UNEP World Conservation Monitoring Centre, Cambridge, UK

Wendland, K. J., Honzák, M., Portela, R., Vitale, B., Rubinoff, S. and Randrianarisoa, J. (2009) 'Targeting and implementing payments for ecosystem services: Opportunities for bundling biodiversity conservation with carbon and water services in Madagascar', *Ecological Economics*, doi:10.1016/j.ecolecon.2009.01.002

Wertz, S., Degrange, V., Prosser, J., Poly, F., Commeaux, C., Freitag, T., Guillaumaud, N. and Xavier Le, R. (2006) 'Maintenance of soil functioning following erosion of microbial diversity', *Environmental Microbiology*, vol 8, pp2162–2169

Westerkamp, C. and Gottsberger, G. (2000) 'Diversity pays in crop pollination', *Crop Science*, vol 40, pp1209–1222

Westerling, A. L., Hidalgo, H. G., Cayan, D. R. and Swetnam, T. W. (2006) 'Warming and earlier Spring increase western U.S. forest wildfire activity', *Science*, vol 313, pp940–943

Westman, W. E. (1978) 'Measuring the inertia and resilience of ecosystems', *BioScience*, vol 28, pp705–710

Whittaker, R. H. (1975) *Communities and Ecosystems*, 2nd edn, Macmillan, London

Wilkinson, C., Caillaud, A., DeVantier, L. and South, R. (2006) 'Strategies to reverse the decline in valuable and diverse coral reefs, mangroves and fisheries: The bottom of the J-Curve in Southeast Asia?', *Ocean & Coastal Management*, vol 49, nos 9–10, pp764–778

Willer, H., Yussefi-Menzler, M. and Sorensen, N. (eds) (2008) *The World of Organic Agriculture: Statistics and Emerging Trends 2008*, IFOAM (International Federation of Organic Agriculture Movements) Bonn, Germany and FiBL (Research Institute of Organic Agriculture), Frick, Switzerland

Williams, J. D. and Dodd, C. K. Jr. (1980) 'Importance of Wetlands to Endangered and Threatened Species', in Greeson, P. E., Clark, J. R. and Clark, J. E. (eds) *Wetland Functions and Values: The State of Our Understanding*, American Water Resources Association, Minneapolis, MN, pp565–575

Williams, J. and Haq, N. (2002) *Global Research on Underutilized Crops: An Assessment of Current Activities and Proposals for Enhanced Cooperation*, International Centre for Underutilized Crops (ICUC), Southampton

Wilson, C. and Tisdell, C. (2003) 'Conservation and economic benefits of wildlife-based marine tourism: Sea turtles and whales as case studies', *Human Dimensions of Wildlife*, vol 8, pp49–58

Winfree, R. and Kremen, C. (2009) 'Are ecosystem services stabilized by differences among species? A test using crop pollination', *Proceedings of the Royal Society B – Biological Sciences*, vol 276, no 1655, pp229–237

Woolley, H. and Rose, S. (2004) *The Value of Public Space*, CABE Space, London

World Bank (2009) *Reshaping Economic Geography*, World Development Report, World Bank, Washington, DC

Worm, B., Barbier, E. B., Beaumont, N., Duffy, J. E., Folke, C., Halpern, B. S., Jackson, J. B. C., Lotze, H. K., Micheli, F., Palumbi, S. R., Sala, E., Selkoe, K. A., Stachowicz, J. J. and Watson, R. (2006) 'Impacts of biodiversity loss on ocean ecosystem services', *Science*, vol 314, pp787–790

Wright, J. (2008) *Sustainable Agriculture and Food Security in an Era of Oil Scarcity: Lessons from Cuba*, Earthscan, London

Xu, K., Xu, X., Fukao, T., Canlas, P., Maghirang-Rodriguez, R., Heuer, S., Ismail, A. M., Bailey-Serres, J., Ronald, P. C. and Mackill, D. J. (2006) 'Sub1A is an ethylene-response-factor-like gene that confers submergence tolerance to rice', *Nature*, vol 442, pp705–708

Zhang, W., Ricketts, T. H., Kremen, C., Carney, K. and Swinton, S. M. (2007) 'Ecosystem services and dis-services to agriculture', *Ecological Economics*, vol 64, pp253–260

Zhu, Y. Y., Chen, H., Fan, J., Wang, Y., Li, Y., Chen, J., Fan, J. X., Yang, S., Hu, L., Leung, H., Mew, T. W., Teng, P. S., Wang, Z. and Mundt, C. C. (2000) 'Genetic diversity and disease control in rice', *Nature*, vol 406, pp718–722

ZSL (Zoological Society of London) (2006) *Ornamental Fish in the Brazilian Amazon*, www.zsl. org/conservation/regions/americas/fish-amazon/, accessed 1 September 2009

Chapter 3
Measuring Biophysical Quantities and the Use of Indicators

Coordinating lead author
Belinda Reyers

Lead authors
Giovanni Bidoglio, Patrick O'Farrell, Frederik Schutyser

Contributing authors
Uppeandra Dhar, Haripriya Gundimeda,
Maria Luisa Paracchini, Oscar Gomez Prieto

Reviewers
Klaus Henle, Jeffrey A. McNeely, Georgina M. Mace, Simon Stuart,
Matt Walpole, Allan D. Watt

Review editor
Allan D. Watt

Contents

Key messages   115

1   Introduction   116
    1.1 Aim and scope of this chapter   116
    1.2. Why are indicators needed?   116
    1.3. What makes a good indicator?   117

2   Existing measures and indicators   119
    2.1 Indicators of diversity   127
    2.2 Indicators of quantity   127
    2.3 Indicators of condition   129
    2.4 Indicators of pressures   130
    2.5 Indicators of ecosystem services   131
    2.6 Lessons   133

3   In search of relevant indicators for ecosystem services   134
    3.1 Developing relevant indicators   134
    3.2 A provisioning service: Timber production   134
    3.3 A regulating service: Global carbon sequestration   136
    3.4 A cultural service: Social appreciation of the agricultural landscape   137
    3.5 Relevant indicators at local scales   138
    3.6 The way forward   139

4   Link to valuation and further work   141

References   142

Key messages

- A lack of relevant information at different scales has hampered the ability to assess the economic consequences of the loss of ecosystems and biodiversity.

- Most of the current measures and indicators of biodiversity and ecosystems were developed for purposes other than the economic assessment outlined by TEEB. They are therefore unable to show clear relationships between components of biodiversity and the services or benefits they provide to people, making them less relevant to the audience and aims of TEEB.

- A reliance on these existing measures will in all likelihood capture the value of only a few species and ecosystems relevant to food and fibre production, and will miss out the role of biodiversity and ecosystems in supporting the full range of benefits, as well as their resilience into the future.

- A set of indicators is needed that is not only relevant and able to convey the message of the consequences of biodiversity loss, but must also be based on accepted methods that reflect the aspects of biodiversity involved and the service that is of interest, capture the often non-linear and multi-scale relationships between ecosystems and the benefits that they provide, and be convertible into economic terms.

- While it is possible to obtain preliminary estimates of the consequences of biodiversity and ecosystem loss using existing data and measures, these must be complemented with active research and development into the measurement of biodiversity and ecosystem change, their links to benefit flows and the value of these flows so as to realize the full value of biodiversity and ecosystem management.

1 Introduction

1.1 Aim and scope of this chapter

Changes in biodiversity, ecosystems and their services ultimately affect all people (MA, 2005b). Global declines in biodiversity and ecosystems, the ongoing degradation and unsustainable use of ecosystem services, and the resultant effects on human well-being have led to many international and national responses focused on halting and reversing these trends (Balmford et al, 2005).

However, attempts to halt or reverse these declines in ecosystems and biodiversity are confounded by a lack of information on the status and changes in ecosystems and biodiversity, the drivers of change, and the consequences of management responses (Pereira and Cooper, 2006). The information that does exist remains fragmented, not comparable from one place to another, highly technical and unsuitable for policy makers, or simply unavailable (Schmeller, 2008; Scholes et al, 2008).

Over the past decade, several programmes have sought to fill some of these information gaps, from local to global levels (Royal Society, 2003; Pereira and Cooper, 2006; Scholes et al, 2008). The purpose of TEEB and this chapter is twofold: to provide guidance to interested stakeholders on the strengths and weaknesses of available measures and indicators of biodiversity and ecosystem status and change, with a focus on those which can put an economic value on these changes (TEEB, 2008); and to outline what is needed to improve the existing science base of biodiversity and ecosystem indicators to better meet the needs of TEEB and associated efforts.

The chapter also describes in detail a set of global and subglobal indicators to highlight the opportunities and challenges associated with developing indicators which can be used in assessing the economic consequences of changes in biodiversity and ecosystems.

1.2 Why are indicators needed?

Ecosystem and biodiversity indicators serve multiple purposes which can broadly be categorized into three key functions: (1) tracking performance; (2) monitoring the consequences of alternative policies; and (3) scientific exploration (Failing and Gregory, 2003). This chapter will focus mostly on the first two roles. Indicators are defined here as variables communicating something of interest or relevance to policy or decision makers with some logical connection to the object or the process being measured. They reflect, in an unambiguous and usually quantitative way, the status, causes (drivers) or outcome of the process or object (Ash et al, 2009). Indicators simplify and quantify information so that it can be easily communicated and intuitively understood, allowing policy and decision makers to base their decisions on evidence (Layke, 2009).

It is useful to distinguish between measures, indicators and indices, the key terms used in this chapter. The term *measure* (or measurement) is used to refer to the actual measurement of a state, quantity or process derived from observations or monitoring. For example, bird counts are a measure derived from an observation. An *indicator* serves to indicate or give a suggestion of something of interest and is derived from measures. For example bird counts compared over time show a trend which can indicate the success of conservation actions for a specific group of species. Indicators are typically used for a specific purpose, for example to provide a policy maker with information about progress towards a target. An *index* or multiple *indices* comprise a number of measures combined in a particular way to increase their sensitivity, reliability or ease of communication. These are useful in the context of biodiversity assessment where multiple attributes and measurements, related to a wide variety of policies, have resulted in long lists of measures and indicators. To communicate these trends in a small number of simple and meaningful indices is sensible (Balmford et al, 2005). For example, in the Red List Index for birds, changes in threat status over time are expressed as a number, obtained through a specific formula. A concern with composite indices is that the underlying measures often become obscured. Ideally they should be disaggregatable and traceable back to the original measures (Scholes and Biggs, 2005).

1.3 What makes a good indicator?

The Convention on Biological Diversity (CBD, 2003), as well as a number of other publications (Royal Society, 2003; Mace and Baillie, 2007; Ash et al, 2009), list multiple criteria to consider when selecting and developing indicators and measures of ecosystems and biodiversity. Of these criteria, perhaps the most pertinent to this chapter and its readers is the need to make the indicators relevant to the purpose. This not only requires setting clear goals and targets in the indicator development process, but also a thorough understanding of the target audience and their needs (Mace and Baillie, 2007).

Vagueness in current targets, the diversity of target audiences and their needs, the resources required to turn measures into effective indicators, and the reliance of most current measures and indicators on available data have posed substantial obstacles in the development of relevant and useful indicators (Royal Society, 2003; Green et al, 2005; Mace and Baillie, 2007; Layke, 2009).

Much of the current effort in indicator development has arisen from the CBD's Biodiversity 2010 Target and regional or national responses to this target (e.g. EEA, 2009), as well as the work of the Millennium Ecosystem Assessment (MA) (MA, 2005b). While the latter did not aim to develop indicators, the global and subglobal assessment of ecosystem status and trend collated many measures of ecosystems and ecosystem services (Layke, 2009). Both of these initiatives have resulted in substantial effort and resources invested in indicator development and the collation of measures, with good progress in some aspects of the assessment of biodiversity, ecosystem and ecosystem service status and trends (Mace et al, 2005; Mace and Baillie, 2007; EEA, 2009; Layke, 2009; http://twentyten.net; www.unep-wcmc.org/collaborations/BINU/). However, many gaps and substantial challenges remain for scientists and policy makers in ensuring that the measures and indicators are sensitive, realistic and useful (MA, 2005b; Mace and Baille, 2007; Scholes et al, 2008; Layke, 2009).

In the context of TEEB it is important to recognize that its objectives and audience differ from existing programmes like the Biodiversity 2010 Target and the MA. TEEB moves beyond the measurement of biodiversity and ecosystem status and change to an assessment of the economic implications of changes in biodiversity and ecosystems (TEEB, 2008). It is therefore possible that existing indicators and measures developed mainly for the Biodiversity 2010 Target and for the MA's purposes may not best address the objectives of TEEB.

The intended audience of TEEB is wider and more varied than previous biodiversity and ecosystems indicator programme audiences and comprises stakeholders at different levels, including individuals whose livelihoods directly depend on harvesting natural resources, resource managers, decision makers at all levels, and civil society in general. The scientific community is also a stakeholder as scientists are involved in the monitoring and observation of a broad range of biodiversity and ecosystem measures over a variety of scales (Schmeller, 2008). This varied audience will require different sets of indicators relevant and understandable within and across sectors and scales. Taking a sectoral perspective also implies combining measures that provide a broad integrated time series of ecosystem status at the relevant scale with relevant socio-economic indicators related to issues such as employment or trade.

TEEB's focus on the economic consequences of changes in biodiversity and ecosystems brings with it new challenges to the science and practice of biodiversity and ecosystem indicator development. First, TEEB is interested in the measurement of *biodiversity change*. This is a concept with which the Biodiversity 2010 Target indicator development has struggled. Not only is biodiversity a multifaceted, multi-attribute concept of a hierarchy of genes, species and ecosystems, with structural, functional and compositional aspects within each hierarchical level (Noss, 1990). Change in biodiversity is also multifaceted and can include loss of quantity (abundance, distribution), quality (ecosystem degradation) or variability (diversity of species or genes) within all levels and aspects (Balmford et al, 2008). As Mace et al (2005) highlight, different facets of change will have different implications for different ecosystem services, for example changes in functional and structural variability in species will have broad-ranging impacts on most services, while changes in the quantity and distribution of populations and ecosystems will be important for many provisioning and regulating services. Therefore the most appropriate measures and indicators will involve a consideration of both the aspects of biodiversity involved and the service that is of interest.

Second, in order to assess the consequences of change in biodiversity TEEB is targeted at the *links* between biodiversity, ecosystem services and human well-being. While there may be good progress in the development of indicators to measure the status and trends of biodiversity, ecosystem services and human well-being, TEEB needs measures that can capture the often non-linear and multi-scale relationships between ecosystems and the benefits that they provide (van Jaarsveld et al, 2005; Fisher and Turner, 2008). This is an area of very little current development and investment, especially at global scales.

Finally, TEEB is interested in the *economic* consequences of biodiversity change. Therefore indicators and measures used in TEEB must be convertible into economic terms and suitable for economic analyses. This implies more than the generation of monetary values, and requires the inclusion of livelihood conditions, risk and access to resources, benefit sharing and poverty considerations

(Balmford et al, 2008) (see Chapters 4 and 5). Since TEEB's ultimate aim is to make the use of natural resources more sustainable, indicators should address the sustainability of the use patterns measured. TEEB, although acknowledging the importance of nature's intrinsic worth, does not explicitly address intrinsic values of nature, including the ethical considerations regarding the rights of all species. At this stage, TEEB also does not cover the economic value of the interactions between species that structure ecological processes, though this is relevant to the assessment of ecosystem services and may be attempted in future.

This chapter aims to take these challenges into account and, through an assessment of existing measures and indicators, to identify which of the available measures are the most appropriate for the purposes of assessing the economic consequences of biodiversity and ecosystem change. In this context, good measures would be measured with known precision and should sample across relevant places or systems; they ideally would be repeatable and have a history, and would have a clear relationship to some benefit that people receive from biodiversity or ecosystems. In addition to these general characteristics, indicators and measures need to have an appropriate temporal and geographical coverage, and ideally be spatially explicit.

The importance of being spatially explicit has been emphasized in TEEB by Balmford et al (2008). The production, flow and use of the benefits of biodiversity and ecosystems varies spatially, as do the impacts of policy interventions. Making available data and information spatially explicit helps make assumptions explicit, and also identifies needs for further information. The production and use of the benefits of ecosystems and biodiversity often take place in different geographical areas, so a spatially explicit approach is essential to fully evaluate the importance of ecosystem services and the impacts of related policy actions.

2 Existing measures and indicators

Biodiversity, ecosystem and ecosystem service indicators and measures have proliferated over the past several years, largely in response to the setting of the CBD Biodiversity 2010 Target and the Millennium Ecosystem Assessment and its subglobal activities. An exhaustive review of all these indicators and measures is not intended here (for in-depth reviews of indicator groups, see Mace and Baillie, 2007; Layke, 2009); rather, this section highlights what types of indicators and measures are available and reviews their relative strengths and weaknesses in an effort to guide the selection and development of appropriate indicators and measures that can be used to assess and predict the economic consequences of biodiversity and ecosystem change.

Biodiversity and the ecosystems that it structures are notoriously complex entities to measure and assess, and this can be undertaken in a variety of different ways. The MA (2005a) and Balmford et al (2008) highlighted that biodiversity indicators are available for assessing all the different levels of the biodiversity hierarchy (genes, species, ecosystems), as well as measuring several attributes at these levels, namely *diversity, quantity* and *condition*. These three categories of attributes are used to structure this review and Table 3.1.

Table 3.1 Review of existing biophysical measures in terms of their application to measuring biodiversity and ecosystems, their ability to convey information and current data availability at the global scale

Broad category of origin	Category	Examples	Application	Ability to convey information	Data quality and availability
Biodiversity measures and indicators	Measures of diversity	Species diversity, richness and endemism Beta-diversity (turnover of species) Phylogenetic diversity Genetic diversity Functional diversity	To biodiversity: These measures are used to identify areas of high biodiversity value and conservation priority at global and subglobal scales. Seldom used to measure change at global scales, but have been used to indicate functional and structural shifts associated with declines in diversity at subglobal scales. Trends in genetic diversity of species is a headline indicator (HI) for Biodiversity 2010 Target To ecosystem services: Not easily linked to specific provisioning or regulating ecosystem services, with the exception of proposed measures of functional diversity. Analysis of congruence between diversity and service levels shows mixed support. Studies demonstrate importance of species and genetic diversity in promoting ecosystem resilience across ecosystem services. Genetic diversity also linked to options for bio-prospecting and food security. Cultural values of diversity, especially education, research and aesthetic values, provide these measures with a link to cultural ecosystem services To valuation: Not easily valued due to general rather than specific role in providing benefits. Some valuation of bioprospecting and genetic diversity of crop species possible. Also possible to value the cultural values attached to diversity, although not yet common practice	Measures and maps of areas of high species diversity and endemism easily understood by wide audience, based on agreed methods and data. Not sensitive to short-term change	Species measures for some taxa available globally, but not as a time series Other measures not available globally

Table 3.1 (*continued*)

Broad category of origin	Category	Examples	Application	Ability to convey information	Data quality and availability
	Measures of quantity	Extent and geographic distribution of species and ecosystems Abundance / population size Biomass / net primary production (NPP)	To biodiversity: Descriptive measure of biodiversity used in baseline studies and descriptions; when available over temporal scales they can feed into indicators of biodiversity status and trends, and prioritization and risk assessment protocols. Trends in selected ecosystems and species are HIs of the Biodiversity 2010 Target To ecosystem services: Measure of status and trends for ecosystems (e.g. forest, wetlands, coral reefs) and species (medicinal plants, food) which have clear links to provisioning services have been used as measures of stocks and flows of ecosystem services. Similarly useful for ecosystems and species with social and cultural values which have links to cultural services. Some use in measuring regulating services that rely on biomass or a particular habitat / vegetation cover (e.g. carbon sequestration, pollination, erosion control, water flow regulation) To valuation: Measures of provisioning, cultural and regulating services can be valued using the variety of approaches listed in Chapter 5 (e.g. market price, contingent valuation, factor income or replacement cost)	Measures and indicators of trends in habitat area and species populations are intuitive to a wide audience (e.g. deforestation rates). Measures of biomass and NPP less intuitive. Most measures are based on accepted methods and are sensitive to change (data dependent)	Global datasets of broad ecosystems and some taxa available for a single time period. For some species and populations there are good time series data. NPP and Biomass measures available at global scales and can be modelled over multiple time series

Table 3.1 (continued)

Broad category of origin	Category	Examples	Application	Ability to convey information	Data quality and availability
	Measures of condition	Threatened species/ ecosystems Red List Index (RLI) Ecosystem connectivity/ fragmentation (Fractal dimension, Core Area Index, Connectivity, Patch Cohesion) Ecosystem degradation Trophic integrity (Marine Trophic Index (MTI)) Changes in disturbance regimes (human-induced ecosystem failure, changes in fire frequency and intensity) Population integrity / abundance measures (Mean Species Abundance (MSA), Biodiversity Intactness Index (BII), Natural Capital Index (NCI))	To biodiversity: These measures are used to assess and indicate the status and trends of biodiversity and ecosystems. Change in status of threatened species, Marine Trophic Index, connectivity/fragmentation, human-induced ecosystem failure are HIs of Biodiversity 2010 Target To ecosystem services: While providing an indication of the status and trend of ecosystems and their services, these indicators are seldom linked to quantified changes in ecosystem service levels. They are however useful indicators of sustainability, thresholds and the scale of human impacts on ecosystems, particularly where clear and demonstrable linkages exist To valuation: Not currently converted into monetary values, although potentially useful in determining risk of economic loss	Threatened species status, RLI and MTI used and understood indicators of biodiversity loss, based on acceptable methods and data and sensitive to change. Other measures less intuitive and quite technical, little consensus on methods and data	Threatened species status and trends available for limited taxa at a global scale. Most other measures only available at a subglobal scale and often only for one period of time

Table 3.1 (*continued*)

Broad category of origin	Category	Examples	Application	Ability to convey information	Data quality and availability
	Measures of pressures	Land cover change Climate change Pollution and eutrophication (Nutrient level assessment) Human footprint indicators (e.g. Human Appropriated Net Primary Productivity (HANPP), Living Planet Index (LPI), ecological debt) Levels of use (harvesting, abstraction) Alien invasive species	To biodiversity: These are measures of the pressures or threats facing biodiversity. They do not measure the status and trends of biodiversity, but are an indication of the size and trends of the pressures on biodiversity and often feed into biodiversity assessments at national scales in State of Environment Reports. They are frequently used in communicating biodiversity status and trends and many are relevant to Biodiversity 2010 Target To ecosystem services: When linked to particular species (e.g. fish) or ecosystems (e.g. wetlands) which provide or support ecosystem services, these measures are useful indicators of ecosystem service levels and declines. They are also used to indicate the sustainability of ecosystem service use and supply To valuation: Changes in ecosystem service levels lend themselves to valuation of the losses or gains in services. If information is available on threshold effects for particular services then these indicators can be useful in determining economic risk	Many of these measures and indicators are used to communicate the status of biodiversity to a wide audience (public and policy), consensus methods are in development, most are sensitive to change Composite footprint indicators are increasingly disaggregatable	Land cover data available at global scales, but not as a time series Climate change models are globally available for a range of future time periods; linking these pressures to biodiversity changes remains a gap Some measures of pollution available globally and over time (e.g. nitrogen deposition) Composite footprint indicators available globally and over time periods Use levels and alien species under development

Table 3.1 (*continued*)

Broad category of origin	Category	Examples	Application	Ability to convey information	Data quality and availability
Ecosystem service measures & indicators[a]	Provisioning service measures	Timber, fuel and fibre production Livestock production Fisheries production Wild animal products Harvested medicinal plants	To biodiversity: Measures of provisioning services currently used to indicate use and sustainability of use on biodiversity and ecosystems. More recently used to indicate the value of biodiversity and ecosystems To ecosystem services: Direct measures of ecosystem service levels and changes. When calculated as sustainable production measures can be used as indicators for monitoring and managing ecosystem services, contrasting sustainable production with actual To valuation: Most indicators expressed as biophysical units which can be converted into monetary values where markets exist.	Simple and compelling indicators where they do exist. Methods of modelling and development not yet agreed upon. Sensitive to change	Timber and livestock production available globally. Most data only available at subglobal scales and for single time period. Possibility of upscaling and modelling for some (see Section 3) Total production and direct use values more common than sustainable production indicators
	Regulation service measures	Carbon sequestration Water flow regulation and production Air quality regulation Natural hazard regulation Waste assimilation Erosion regulation / soil protection Disease regulation Pollination Maintenance of genetic diversity Pest control	To biodiversity: Many of these measures of measurements of ecological processes important to the persistence of ecosystems and so can be used to indicate functional biodiversity condition and trends. Recently used to indicate the value of biodiversity and ecosystems To ecosystem services: Direct measures of ecosystem service levels and changes To valuation: Regulating services are more difficult to value but see Chapter 5 for progress in valuing through avoided / replacement or restoration and other costs. Double counting remains an issue with some of these services	Less intuitive to a wide audience than the provisioning measures, excluding water and carbon which are increasingly understood. Limited consensus on methods of measurement and modelling. Less sensitive to short term changes	Most measures only at subglobal scales, although many identified as possible global indicators for development Carbon sequestration available globally Where data exist possible to model over time, but not common

Table 3.1 (*continued*)

Broad category of origin	Category	Examples	Application	Ability to convey information	Data quality and availability
	Cultural service measures	Recreational use Tourism numbers or income Spiritual values Aesthetic values	To biodiversity: Many of these measures are specific to particular ecosystems or species of cultural value, although tourism can often be linked to habitat and species diversity. More recently been suggested as indicative of the value of biodiversity and ecosystems To ecosystem services: Direct measures of ecosystem service levels and changes To valuation: Most cultural services are poorly understood and often difficult to value. Tourism and recreation services, as well as existence value more amenable to valuation. Some debate over the economic valuation of spiritual and religious values. See Chapter 5 for progress in valuing	No such measures yet available globally. At sub global levels some measures intuitive e.g. tourism numbers or recreational values Other measures poorly understood No consensus on measurement and modelling. Not sensitive to change	Most measures only at subglobal scales, although tourism identified as possible global indicator for development

Note: [a] The data availability and ability to convey messages for ecosystem service measures and indicators are reviewed in detail by Layke (2009).

A fourth category of indicators is one that measures *pressures* exerted on the environment. This chapter also includes an additional category focused on *ecosystem service* measures and indicators, in recognition of the large amount of data and measures made available through the MA and its follow-up activities, as well as the importance of these measures in linking biodiversity to economic valuation. The ecosystem service measures are separated into *provisioning*, *regulating* and *cultural service* categories due to the different relationships between these groups of services and ecosystem elements (see Chapter 2), as well as the different tools available for valuing different ecosystem service groups (see Chapter 5). TEEB in National Policy (2011, Chapter 3) provides a list of examples of ecosystem service indicators, but this review focuses on only those measures and indicators that are already in use and thus available for review.

This chapter does not propose a specific set of indicators and measures; as discussed earlier, different sets of indicators will be required for different audiences. Rather, the chapter provides an overview of existing indicators and measures of biodiversity and ecosystems and their potential use in economic valuation exercises like those adopted by TEEB. The chapter focuses on existing spatially explicit indicators and measures (with some mention of those known to be in development). It assesses their current application in biodiversity and ecosystem service measurement and in valuing change, their ability to convey information and their data availability. These last two criteria were developed and applied in the World Resources Institute (WRI) review of the MA measures and indicators (Layke, 2009). In this review indicators are ranked based on their ability to convey information as a combination of their intuitiveness, sensitivity and acceptability, and their data availability based on the presence of adequate monitoring systems, availability of processed data and whether the data are normalized and disaggregated. This chapter does not provide an evaluation of use, access or human well-being indicators.

An examination of Table 3.1 shows that there are a large number of measures and indicators available across geographic scales and regions for assessing biodiversity and ecosystem services. As in previous reviews of measures and indicators of biodiversity and ecosystem services (Royal Society, 2003; Mace and Baillie, 2007; Layke, 2009), much of the existing data and indicators were collected and developed for purposes other than the one TEEB is interested in and are therefore not necessarily the right measures for assessing the economic consequences of biodiversity and ecosystem change. Furthermore most of the existing indicators are developed and applied within specific contexts resulting in some good biodiversity indicators and some progress in the development of ecosystem service indicators, but the current lack of measures and indicators that span contexts and show clear relationships between components of biodiversity and the services or benefits they provide to people is a key gap, making existing measures and indicators less relevant to the audience and aims of TEEB. The categories of indicators presented in Table 3.1 are reviewed below with two objectives: (1) to identify existing measures useful for economic valuation in the short term; and (2) to highlight the work still required to develop key fit-for-purpose indicators in the longer term.

2.1 Indicators of diversity

At a global level, measures and maps of species diversity, endemism and richness are available for some taxa, for example mammals and amphibians (Myers et al, 2000; MA, 2005a), while at subglobal scales these are supplemented by measures and indicators of genetic and ecosystem diversity (e.g. Bagley et al, 2002). Although these indicators are the focus of many conservation agencies and policies and good at conveying their message of high biodiversity value, these measures are seldom used to assess the benefits provided by the diversity of genes, species and ecosystems to people and economies. This is probably a result of the complex and tenuous relationships between diversity and ecosystem services (Balvanera et al, 2001; Hooper et al, 2005; Mace et al, 2005). While some evidence exists that diversity is important in resilience and adaptive capacity of biodiversity and ecosystems (Johnson et al, 1996; Naeem, 1998; Swift et al, 2004; Balvanera et al, 2006; Diaz et al, 2006), this 'insurance value' is seldom calculated (see Chapter 2 for a detailed explanation). A frequently cited example of the importance of diversity is the value of genetic diversity in agriculture and bioprospecting (Esquinas-Alcázar, 2005); however, these benefits are complex given their option-based nature and are therefore hard to quantify and value. Other benefits of diversity include cultural services associated with enjoyment and appreciation of diversity which may be more amenable to valuation, using for example willingness-to-pay approaches (e.g. Esquinas-Alcázar, 2005), but the reliability of these approaches has not been demonstrated (see Chapter 5). Finally, functional diversity (i.e. the diversity of functional groups or types) is said to be important for regulating services (Bunker et al, 2005; Diaz et al, 2006, Chapter 2), but challenges with developing indicators of functional diversity, as well as the challenges associated with valuing regulating services (Chapter 5), limit the numbers and application of these indicators in valuation assessments.

These measures of diversity have good potential to convey a message in that they are intuitive, already widely in circulation, and largely based on accepted and rigorous methods and data. However, their sensitivity to change over policy-relevant periods is weak because of data gaps, and because change would require local or global extinctions of species or ecosystems, which as Balmford et al (2003) point out, is often a longer term process insensitive to short-term change.

With the exception of genetic diversity, this category of measures is not the current focus of many indicator or valuation efforts, but a need remains for further research into quantifying the currently tenuous links between diversity and human well-being.

2.2 Indicators of quantity

Indicators and measures of quantity can be developed at the population, species and ecosystem level. They can express the total number or changes in number at these levels. Widely used indicators of quantity include those that highlight changes in ecosystem extent (e.g. forest area: FAO, 2001) and those that demonstrate changes in species abundances (e.g. number of waterbirds: Revenga and Kura, 2003). Many of these indicators focus on functional groups rather than taxonomic groupings (e.g. waterbirds, pelagic fish, wetland ecosystems).

When these measures or indicators exist for ecosystems, species or functional groups, and are coupled with good data on the benefit flows and associated economic value of those features being assessed (e.g. fish stocks (FAO, 2000) or wetland services (Finlayson et al, 2005)), then these measures form a valuable indicator for demonstrating the economic impacts of biodiversity change. At the global scale changes in important fish stocks have been directly valued (e.g. Wood et al, 2005), while at local scales temporal changes in ecosystem extent have been used to quantify declines in water, erosion control, carbon storage and nature-based tourism (Reyers et al, 2009).

Indicators of quantity also include measures of primary productivity and biomass. These may be seen as undiscerning indicators of biodiversity, in that they do not measure taxonomic or functional units of species or ecosystems (but see Costanza et al, 2007). However, they are potentially useful indicators of ecosystem production which have been linked to several benefits including carbon storage (Naidoo et al, 2008), timber production (Balmford et al, 2008) and grazing (O'Farrell et al, 2007). They currently do not differentiate between natural / indigenous production and human-enhanced production, and must therefore be carefully interpreted when calculating the economic consequences of ecosystem and biodiversity change for a specific area.

Data gaps include clear geographical and taxonomic selection biases towards popular, well-known and easy-to-measure species and ecosystems, for example mammals, birds, forest ecosystems (Royal Society, 2003; Collen et al, 2008; Schmeller et al, 2009). Further gaps in knowledge and data on the abundance of, for example, useful plants and animals, limit the development of these indicators and may result in a significant underestimation of the economic impacts of species and ecosystem losses.

In reviewing their ability to convey their message, strengths of indicators include their intuitiveness (especially measures of well-known species and ecosystems, e.g. fish and forests), the general consensus on methods and data, and their sensitivity to change. Weaknesses exist around the methods, use and communication of measures of productivity and biomass, but good progress is being made (Imhoff et al, 2004).

Due to the clear links to easily valued provisioning services, this category of measures and indicators holds much promise for measuring and predicting some of the economic consequences of change in biodiversity and ecosystem services. At a local scale this is already possible where data on ecosystem extent and species abundances exist (Balmford et al, 2002; Reyers et al, 2009); at a global scale this will require the rapid development and collation of global databases on ecosystem extent and information on the abundance of a wide range of useful species, and changes in these measures. Current ability to model changes in ecosystem extent (Czúcz et al, 2009), as well as changes in species abundances (Scholes and Biggs, 2005; Diaz et al, 2006; Alkemade et al, 2009) make this a useful focus for TEEB. A focus on functional types or groups could prove highly useful and help avoid the challenges associated with the issue of redundancy, where more than one species or ecosystem is capable of providing a service (Diaz et al, 2006).

2.3 Indicators of condition

These measures reflect changes in the condition or quality of ecosystems and biodiversity, reflecting the degradation of components of biodiversity from the population level to the ecosystem. While they are closely linked to the previous category, these indicators focus less on the quantity of species or ecosystems, and more on the quality or integrity of the element being assessed. Examples include species and ecosystems at risk of extinction (Mace and Lande, 1991; EEA, 2009), levels of nutrients (e.g. soil condition, nitrogen deposition and depletion (MA 2005b)), degree of fragmentation of an ecosystem (Rodriguez et al, 2007), trophic level changes (Pauly et al, 1998), population integrity measures (Scholes and Biggs, 2005) and alteration of disturbance regimes (Carpenter et al, 2008).

Changes in species abundances in relation to thresholds (Mace and Lande, 1991), and more recently changes in ecosystem extent in relation to thresholds (Rodriguez et al, 2007), have been used to develop risk assessment protocols that highlight biodiversity features with a high risk of extinction. The Red List Index, a composite measure summarizing the overall rate at which a group of species is moving towards extinction, for example European birds (EEA, 2009), has been widely applied and used in measuring progress towards the Biodiversity 2010 Target. These approaches could prove useful in valuing the economic risk of biodiversity loss, especially if the species and ecosystems under assessment have a high risk of extinction and are clearly linked to benefits, but this has yet to be explored.

Indicators of population integrity include recently developed composite indices focused on changes in abundance. Examples of these are the Biodiversity Intactness Index (BII) (Scholes and Biggs, 2005) and the Mean Species Abundance (MSA) Index (Alkemade et al, 2009). These indices use data and expert input on land cover and use impacts on populations of species, and together with information on historic or predicted land-use change, model the aggregated impact of change at a population level. While useful tools for assessing the population level consequences of land-use change, these mean or summed aggregated measures make it hard to link these changes to shifts in benefit flows (which are usually linked to only a few species, functional types or populations within the set modelled). The disaggregatable and traceable nature of the BII makes this a useful indicator of biodiversity condition, and with more research and data could be extended to measure functional group integrity – providing a clearer link to benefits.

MSA is an index that captures the average effect of anthropogenic drivers of change on a set of species. This measure provides insight into the effects of disturbance, particularly land-cover change on species numbers, with the focus on determining the average numbers of species for disturbed versus undisturbed environments. It is also linked to various global scenarios, useful in the context of TEEB. This indicator is not an independently verifiable measure and is strongly influenced by the assumed species assemblages at the outset. Because it is a measure of the average population response, the same MSA values can result from very different situations. Furthermore, this average effect is unable to deal with changing species composition such as extinction or invasion and will miss important functional changes associated with the loss of particular species. This, together with an inability to incorporate changes in ecosystem functions resulting from biodiversity loss, makes the index's links to ecosystem services potentially tenuous.

Many of these measures and indicators have been applied at global and sub-global scales (e.g. MA, 2005a; Biggs et al, 2006; EEA, 2009) and appear to provide a clear and relevant message on the condition and trends of biodiversity. Some data and methodological gaps exist for determining ecosystem fragmentation or alteration of disturbance regimes and limit these indicators to use at mostly subglobal scales. Generally, these indicators are data- and knowledge-intensive (but can be supplemented by expert input), and are often only available at subglobal scales.

As they currently stand, few of these condition measures are amenable to the aims of TEEB, but their wide uptake, ease of application and available data and models will make them central to most assessments of biodiversity and ecosystems. However, their links to benefit provision are tenuous and complicated by inadequate knowledge of the relationship between ecosystem integrity and benefit flow, as well as gaps in our knowledge of functional thresholds.

2.4 Indicators of pressures

In many cases the measurement and modelling of ecosystem and biodiversity change relies on measures of the pressures facing biodiversity and ecosystems as an indicator of biodiversity loss or ecosystem change. These pressures include many of the direct drivers of change highlighted by the MA as the most important factors affecting biodiversity and ecosystems: habitat destruction, introduction of alien invasive species, over-exploitation, disease and climate change (Mace et al, 2005). These measures rely on land cover and use data, climate change models, distribution and density data on alien species and data on levels of use. Some indicators are composite indices which incorporate several pressures to indicate human impacts on ecosystems. Chief examples include the Living Planet Index (www.panda.org/livingplanet), the Ecological Footprint (www.ecologicalfootprint.com), and Human Appropriated Net Primary Productivity (HANPP) (Imhoff et al, 2004; Erb et al, 2009; and, with specific reference to biodiversity, Haberl et al, 2007; for maps see www.uni-klu.ac.at/socec/inhalt/1191.htm) which are all available at a global scale over a period of time. Many of these composite measures also include thresholds of carrying capacity or total annual productivity to provide an indication of the sustainability of these impacts.

Land-cover change is a widely used measure, where remote sensing and satellite imagery have made such data available for all parts of the world (e.g. Global Land Cover (GLC2000); Bartholomé and Belward, 2005). Time series data on land cover, as well as models of future land-cover change have been used to assess biodiversity and ecosystem service change at all scales from global (Mace et al, 2005) to local (Fox et al, 2005). Levels of pollutants and eutrophication are commonly used measures of human pressures at a global scale (MA, 2005b; EEA, 2009).

The history and widespread use of many of these pressure measures demonstrates their sound ability to convey the message of human pressures on biodiversity. The recent additions of composite indices relative to some threshold capacity have proven a useful and relevant communication tool.

While land cover should not be confused with ecosystems, these data can still be useful for broad assessments of changes in benefit flows associated with particular classes of land cover. Some of the earliest work on quantifying the economic consequences of land-cover change was done in this fashion by Costanza et al (1997). A few local-scale studies which attempt to measure change in ecosystem services rely on this approach using land-cover change data (derived from remote sensing) and ecosystem service value coefficients (usually extracted from Costanza et al, 1997) (Kreuter et al, 2001; Zhao et al, 2004; Viglizzo and Frank, 2006; Li et al, 2007). Case studies and simulations of land-cover change have also been used to examine the effects on single ecosystem services or processes (nitrogen levels: Turner et al, 2003; pollination: Priess et al, 2007; livestock production services: O'Farrell et al, 2007; soil organic carbon: Yadav and Malanson, 2008). Recent advances in ecosystem mapping (Olson et al, 2001), earth observation (Bartholomé and Belward, 2005) and valuation (Chapter 5) should make this kind of approach a complementary and practical way to evaluate the economic consequences of biodiversity and ecosystem change. The ability to use data on drivers of change to predict future change provides a further compelling reason for the adoption of these indicators (e.g. Schröter et al, 2005).

2.5 Indicators of ecosystem services

Several measures of ecosystem services are already in existence and a recent review by Layke (2009) of the indicators used in the Millennium Ecosystem Assessment and its subglobal assessments highlighted that current ecosystem service indicators are limited by insufficient data and an overall low ability to convey information. Of the indicators available, Layke (2009) found them inadequate in characterizing the diversity and complexity of the benefits provided by ecosystem services. Layke (2009) found that regulating and cultural services fare worse than provisioning services in all findings.

Provisioning services were found to have a high ability to convey information for services of food, raw materials, fuel and water provision, but data availability was average and in the case of wild food, capture fisheries and aquaculture it was poor. Genetic resources and biochemicals were found to be poor at conveying information and poor in terms of data availability.

For the cultural services Layke (2009) found no measures of spiritual or religious values and the measures of tourism, recreation and aesthetic value available showed poor data availability and poor ability to convey information. Balmford et al (2008) highlight this shortcoming and point to a need to focus on cultural services that better lend themselves to measurement and assessment. They suggest a focus on services like bird watching and scuba diving, where the links between biodiversity and the cultural or recreational benefit are simple and clearly defined, and where valuation studies already exist (e.g. Losey and Vaughan, 2006; Tapsuwan and Asafu-Adjaye, 2008; Lee et al, 2009). Protected area visitor numbers and values are also a potential indicator. However, these indicators are not yet available at global or regional scales.

For regulating services measures are limited to just more than half of the ecosystem services listed by Layke (2009) and where measures do exist data availability and ability to convey information are poor. Water regulation and water purification are listed as the only measures with a high ability to convey information, but are limited by data availability, while climate, air quality and natural hazard regulation were all found to have an average ability to convey information but were also hampered by an average (in the case of climate) to poor data availability.

These shortcomings in all services, but particularly in cultural and regulating services will have serious consequences for the comprehensive economic valuation of all ecosystem services, limiting the valuation to a few provisioning and even fewer regulating services.

However, the review presented in Balmford et al (2008) as well as some recent studies (e.g. Troy and Wilson, 2006; Naidoo et al, 2008; Wendland et al, 2009) indicate that the spatially explicit measurement of ecosystem services at regional and global scales is a rapidly growing research area. Projects such as those of the Heinz Center in the USA (Heinz Center, 1999; Clark et al, 2002; Heinz Center, 2006) and the European-based Advanced Terrestrial Ecosystem Analysis and Modelling (ATEAM) have made good progress in the development of indicators and the mapping of ecosystem services, even to the point of including scenarios of future change (Metzger et al, 2006).

Furthermore, the development of several international programmes advancing the measurement and valuation of ecosystem services will help to fill these gaps in the future (e.g. The Natural Capital Project (Nelson et al, 2009); The Global Earth Observation Biodiversity Observation Network (GEOBON) (Scholes et al, 2008); The World Resources Institute Mainstreaming Ecosystem Services Initiative: www.wri.org/project/mainstreaming-ecosystem-services/tools). These programmes are developing tools and approaches to model, map and value the production of particular ecosystem services based on abiotic, biotic (often from measures listed above) and anthropogenic factors, as well as knowledge of relationships between these factors (Figure 3.1 presents an

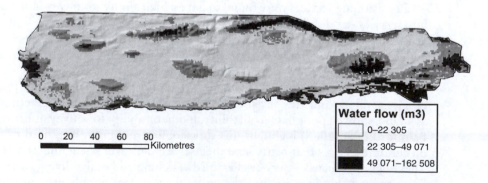

Figure 3.1 *Map of ecosystem services of water flows for the Little Karoo region of South Africa*

Note: These data were used by Reyers et al (2009) to assess changes in ecosystem services supply over time.

example from South Africa where data on rainfall, geology (lithology), vegetation type, recharge, groundwater-quality (electrical conductivity) and land-use activities were used to map water flows.) Very complex measures relying on species diversity, abundance, distribution and landscape pattern have also been developed at local scales (e.g. pollination: Kremen, 2005).

However, Naidoo et al (2008) observed that evidence of the spatial estimation of ecosystem services and the flow of benefits to near and distant human populations is limited to a few local case studies. Most of the existing quantitative analyses still tend to provide aggregated values for large regions, and data availability and disaggregation of spatial data are still a limitation to the mapping of ecosystem services. Furthermore, the multivariate nature of these ecosystem service indicators makes it hard to isolate the role of biodiversity in ecosystem service supply, which in turn makes the economic consequences of biodiversity loss hard to untangle from the other biotic, abiotic and anthropogenic factors involved in service supply. These are further explored in the following sections.

In summary, few indicators at present move beyond the quantification of a stock or flow of a service to the actual valuing of the service, and despite developments, calculating the contribution of biodiversity and effects of changes in its state to these values remains a challenge.

2.6 Lessons

Despite the array of biodiversity and ecosystem service indicators available, few lend themselves to a direct application of determining the economic consequences of biodiversity and ecosystem change. We will need a representative set of indicators to ensure that all relevant aspects of biodiversity and ecosystem change are captured and valued – from diversity to condition. A reliance on existing indicators will in all likelihood capture the value of a few species and ecosystems relevant to food and fibre production, and will miss out the role of biodiversity and ecosystems in supporting the full range of ecosystem services, as well as their resilience in the future.

An alternative avenue is to focus on pressures and their use in models of the economic consequences of policy options in the arena of land-cover or climate change. This approach bypasses the actual measurement or modelling of biodiversity and ecosystem change, and investigates the implications of land-cover and climate change on ecosystem services directly (e.g. Schröter et al, 2005; Metzger et al, 2006). However, this approach will not necessarily advance the case for biodiversity and ecosystem governance which is the key purpose of TEEB, but it will perhaps highlight the need for land-use and climate policy and action in the context of ecosystem service governance.

While it is important to use available tools to meet short-term policy and decision-making needs, it is critical to marry these measures of quantity and pressures with measures of diversity and condition in order to ensure a full accounting of the value of biodiversity and ecosystems in decision making. So the current focus on synthesizing existing data must be complemented with active research and development into the measurement of biodiversity and ecosystem change, their links to benefit flows and the value of these flows.

Many of the measures currently available are primarily determined by the existing information, which does not necessarily make them good measures or good indicators. TEEB and other assessments of the economic value and consequences of biodiversity loss will need fit-for-purpose indicators and new data with which to populate them. These fit-for-purpose indicators must address the challenges outlined in Section 3 and must not only be relevant and effective in conveying their message, but must also be precise, applicable across relevant systems and places, repeatable and defensible, and demonstrate a clear link between the benefit and the component of biodiversity delivering that benefit.

3 In search of relevant indicators for ecosystem services

3.1 Developing relevant indicators

It is clear from the previous section that most existing measures of biodiversity, ecosystems and ecosystem services were not developed for the purpose of TEEB and similar projects: to examine the economic consequences of changes in biodiversity and ecosystem services, and in particular the marginal loss of biodiversity. The InVEST model of the Natural Capital Project does allow for the quantification of economic values and changes in these values under future scenarios and is a powerful tool being explored by many global and subglobal programmes (Daily et al, 2009). Rather than argue for a single unified methodology that can apply to all possible circumstances, several parallel approaches and ways of modelling are needed. To support the development of indicators relevant to the aims of TEEB and other projects interested in the economic consequences of biodiversity loss, a few potential indicators are explored below, to highlight key opportunities and constraints in these indicators. These include a readily measured provisioning service of timber production, a published model and map of the regulating service of carbon sequestration, and a preliminary assessment of the methods for measuring a less easily measured cultural service of social value of agricultural landscapes. The section also discusses advances made at local scales in indicator development, and ends with some discussion on the importance of baselines and thresholds in indicator development.

3.2 A provisioning service: Timber production

Provisioning services (with clear production functions) appear to have received most of the attention in ecosystem service mapping exercises (Balmford et al, 2008; Naidoo et al, 2008). A popular provisioning service, timber production, can be modelled and mapped using estimates of dry matter productivity (DMP) in forest areas by combining remote sensing imagery with meteorological data (for more information see http://geofront.vgt.vito.be/geosuccess/relay. do?dispatch=DMP_info). The service's production function includes measures of ecosystem extent (forest area) and measures of biological quantity (dry matter). The DMP index provides a measure of the vegetation growth in kilograms of dry matter per hectare. This is the annual amount of new dry matter created by the ecosystems and can be understood as the new timber offered by the ecosystems each year. Comparing DMP across different years can show areas with different vegetation activity, enabling it to be used to derive changes in DMP and find those areas where natural timber production has increased or decreased.

The maps in Figure 3.2 show a world map which illustrates where the DMP is more intense (darker shading). The country-scale maps show the difference between the years 2001 and 2004 for the vegetation activity in West Africa and in Madagascar. In the case of Madagascar, the total DMP dropped by 6 per cent between 2001 and 2004 due to deforestation.

This measure provides good opportunities to measure and model the impacts of changes in forest area and natural timber production (for measures of the quantity: see Table 3.1) on the production service. However, it still falls short of the ideal TEEB indicators in that some development is still required in converting DMP units into economic value (i.e. determining commercially

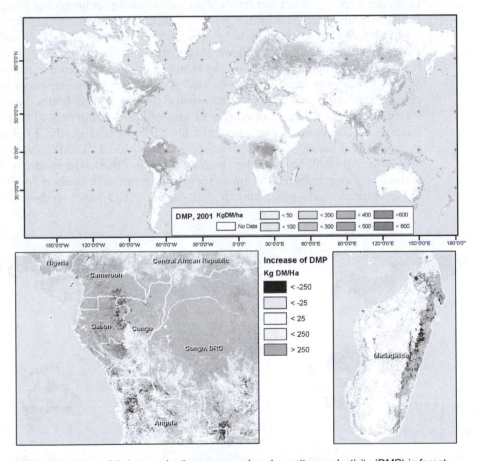

Figure 3.2 *Maps of timber production, measured as dry matter productivity (DMP) in forest areas for (a) the world in 2001, and highlighting change in timber production between 2001 and 2004 for (b) West Africa and (c) Madagascar*

Data source: JRC/MARS remote sensing database – European Commission – JRC important species, use and access). Further useful development could also include information on levels of sustainable production by using, for example, the weight of dry matter per hectare grown in a specific year. Disentangling the role of biodiversity from the anthropogenic factors associated with timber production will be a challenge.

Forests provide a bundle of ecosystem services including carbon sequestration, scenic values, watershed protection and cultural services. These services interact with one another in a dependent and non-linear fashion. Harvesting timber will cause declines in many other services from forest (which are more challenging to measure). Quantifying and managing these trade-offs is a key challenge to sustainable development. By taking a single-service approach – like the timber production service described here – the other services and their values are ignored. This highlights the importance of taking a multi-service approach to economic valuation taking account of trade-offs over ecosystem services, space and time.

3.3 A regulating service: Global carbon sequestration

Ecosystems play an important role in determining atmospheric chemistry, acting as both sources and sinks for many atmospheric constituents that affect air quality or that affect climate by changing radiative forcing. This ability of ecosystems to modify the climate forms the ecosystem services of climate regulation. Carbon sequestration, the removal of carbon from the atmosphere by the living phytomass of ecosystems, is an important component of this climate regulation service. In the map below (Figure 3.3) carbon sequestration was modelled as the net annual rate of atmospheric carbon added to existing biomass carbon pools, using a proxy of net carbon exchange (NCE) produced in simulations using the Terrestrial Ecosystem Model (TEM) developed by McGuire et al (2001) and applied by Naidoo et al (2008). The model simulates carbon exchange between the atmosphere and terrestrial biosphere on the basis of vegetation types, soils, climate, atmospheric CO_2 and land-use history.

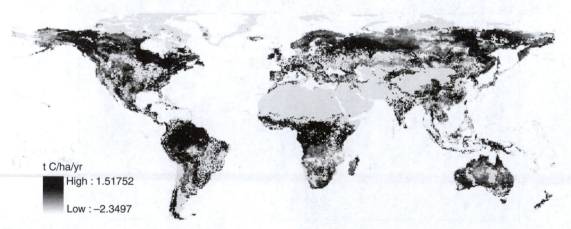

t C/ha/yr
High : 1.51752

Low : −2.3497

Figure 3.3 *Global map of carbon sequestration*

Source: Developed by Naidoo et al (2008) using the Terrestrial Ecosystem Model (TEM) developed by McGuire et al (2001). Copyright (2008) National Academy of Sciences, USA

Naidoo et al (2008) point to the limitations of using a model-based rather than observational approach and the reliance on assumptions, time series and input variables. However, together with the possibility of assigning economic values to the tons of carbon sequestered, Balmford et al (2008) point to the possibilities presented by these land-use-coupled models to estimate differences in carbon storage, emissions and sequestration under different scenarios (e.g. McGuire et al, 2001). This would make it possible to map the economic value of these services of global climate regulation, and how they might change under different scenarios of ecosystem and land-use change.

3.4 A cultural service: Social appreciation of the agricultural landscape

Cultural ecosystem services refer to the aesthetic, spiritual, recreational, educational and other non-material benefits that humans obtain from contact with ecosystems (MA, 2005b; Butler and Oluoch-Kosura, 2006). Little progress has been made in mapping cultural services. Even in the case of the popular cultural service of nature-related outdoor tourism, Balmford et al (2008) point out that these services or their benefits cannot yet be mapped due to both a lack of knowledge of the links between biodiversity and tourism demand or use and the subjective and context-specific nature of perception and appreciation. Nevertheless, attempts can be made to quantify and map cultural services on the basis of proxies that describe societal interest for cultural ecosystem services in specific landscape types. This example represents an attempt to derive an index of social value of the agricultural landscape.

It is currently not possible, in the context of a global or regional assessment, to address landscape perception through targeted enquiries and the use of questionnaires to record people's preferences. Instead in this example three variables were identified as representative of societies' preferences – protected agricultural sites, rural tourism and presence of labelled products – and combined in the map shown in Figure 3.4. This example of a spatially explicit cultural service, although a novel demonstration of the distribution of regional social value, is still some distance from a fit-for-purpose indicator that can be used to measure and model the economic consequences of biodiversity and ecosystem change. Methods for mapping cultural services are not yet developed or agreed and therefore this model has to be carefully interpreted, in order to avoid the risk of confounding different values or assuming direct transfer of values. Trade-offs and synergies in the input components must be understood and correctly taken into consideration, and underlying measures would have to be made available in a format that can be disaggregated and traceable. Furthermore, assigning economic values to social values will be a challenge (see Chapter 5 for developments in this area), while determining the changing contribution of biodiversity and determining past and future trends in the service are also not yet possible. As Balmford et al (2008) suggest, it might be best to start with cultural services where the links between biodiversity and the cultural or recreational benefit are simple and clearly defined and where valuation studies already exist (e.g. bird watching: Lee et al, 2009). Protected

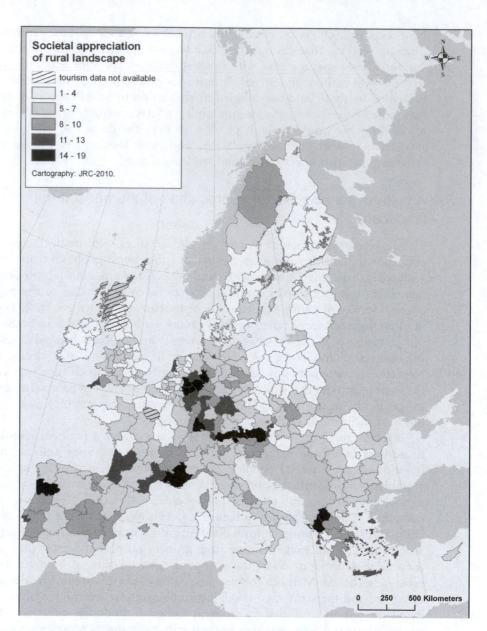

Figure 3.4 *Social value of agricultural landscapes in Europe determined by protected agricultural sites, rural tourism and presence of labelled products*

area visitor numbers and values are also a potential indicator which should be explored at regional and global scales.

3.5 Relevant indicators at local scales

The above global- and regional-scale indicators highlight some of the opportunities and challenges faced in the search for indicators of the economic consequences of changes in biodiversity and ecosystems, and in particular indicators that are convertible into economic values. At the local scale recent publications highlight the progress made in ecosystem service indicator development. Chan et al (2006), Nelson et al (2009) and Reyers et al (2009) used data from a variety of sources on ecosystems and biodiversity (especially functional types), land cover, population, access, hydrology and economic value to model and map multiple ecosystem services at a local scale in the USA and South Africa. These maps were used to investigate trade-offs and planning options by Chan et al (2006), to quantify the consequences of land-use change on ecosystem services by Reyers et al (2009) and to investigate the consequences of future scenarios on ecosystem services by Nelson et al (2009). While some of the indicators are expressed in biophysical quantities, these quantities (litres of water, tons of carbon) are convertible into economic terms. This conversion is clearly demonstrated in another local-scale study by Naidoo and Ricketts (2006) in Paraguay, where the value of ecosystem services was modelled and made spatially explicit to assess the costs and benefits of biodiversity conservation in the region.

3.6 The way forward

This review has highlighted the following lessons for mapping ecosystem services for economic valuation and for use in scenarios of the marginal costs and benefits of ecosystem change and biodiversity loss:

- The need to be spatially explicit while not resorting to large regional aggregations reduces the set of ecosystem services which currently can be mapped to mostly provisioning services at global and regional scales.
- Global datasets of primary productivity and vegetation cover have played a significant role in most of the global maps of services now available (e.g. Naidoo et al, 2008).
- Ecosystem service mapping needs to progress beyond the production of maps that show biophysical quantities or biological stocks of services such as grazing resources to an approach that includes regulating and cultural services and the relationships between these services (i.e. an approach that is cognisant of trade-offs).
- Spatially explicit data on the flow of services and their use at global scales are rare, proving a major obstacle to moving from maps of biophysical quantities to maps of economic value. This is less of an issue at local and regional scales.
- Few of the existing global, regional and local maps of ecosystem services demonstrate clear and indisputable connections between biodiversity and the final benefit quantity or value.
- Investment in spatially explicit data at local and regional scales is a first necessary step in improving ecosystem service mapping and in turn economic valuation.
- Alignment between available maps of ecosystem services and existing models or scenarios of future change is limited, making it difficult for the assessment of change in service levels and values.

Finally, a lesson emerging from this chapter is that using global maps of service production, and changes in these services, as a proxy of value and value change

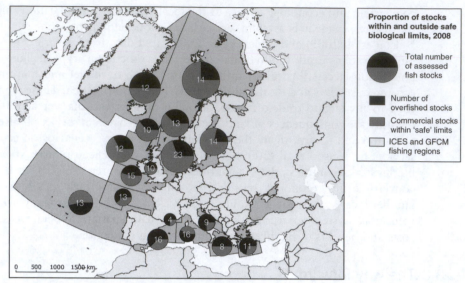

Figure 3.5 *Fish stocks outside safe biological limits*

Note: The chart shows the proportion of assessed stocks which are overfished (dark grey) and stocks within safe biological limits (mid grey). Number in circle is the number of stocks assessed within the given region. The size of the circles is scaled proportional to the magnitude of the regional catch.

Source: Extracted from http://themes.eea.europa.eu/IMS/ISpecs/ISpecification20041007132227/IAssessment1199788344728/view_content

may miss out on two crucial facets related to ecosystem management thresholds of sustainability and vulnerability. The challenge of thresholds of sustainability can be highlighted in the case of fisheries, where Figure 3.5 shows fish stocks outside safe biological limits (from http://themes.eea.europa.eu/IMS/ISpecs/ISpecification20041007132227/IAssessment1199788344728/view_content) which would not necessarily be captured by a map of trophic biomass. This highlights the crucial importance of thresholds in ecosystem service measures and indicators.

In demonstrating the challenge of depicting thresholds of vulnerability, Figure 3.6 shows a map of southern Africa where provision of water has been displayed as a proportion of demand for water (Scholes and Biggs, 2004). This map highlights areas of high vulnerability where water supplies do not currently meet water demand. In global or regional maps of this service, high-value areas do not accurately depict important areas with a low water supply where social thresholds and local demand are not met. Even small changes in water supply in these important and vulnerable areas would have significant impacts on human well-being in those areas, impacts that would not necessarily be illustrated in an assessment of monetary value and changes in that value. Closer examination and differentiation of the demand for services, which should theoretically be linked with supply, may provide a more socially realistic assessment of services.

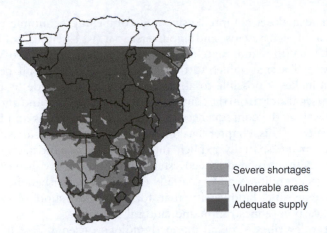

Figure 3.6 *Water availability in southern Africa expressed as relative to demand for water*

Source: Extracted from Scholes and Biggs (2004)

Both of these examples reflect the importance of thresholds highlighted in the MA. Ecosystem service change is seldom linear or independent and can often be accelerating, abrupt and potentially irreversible (MA, 2005b). The loss of biodiversity and increasing pressures from drivers of ecosystem change increase the likelihood of these non-linear changes. While science is increasingly able to predict some of these risks and non-linearities, predicting the thresholds at which these changes will happen generally is not possible. Users of indicators and assessments of ecosystem change and its consequences need to bear this in mind, and where possible to reflect known or possible ecological and social thresholds and not to assume linear relationships between biodiversity loss and its consequences.

4 Link to valuation and further work

The flow of ecosystem services from point of production to point of use is influenced by both biophysical (e.g. currents, migration) and anthropogenic (e.g. trade, access) processes which influence the scale of service flow from locally produced and used services (e.g. soil production) to globally distributed benefits (e.g. carbon sequestration for climate regulation). The flow of benefits and scale of flows influences the value of the service due to changes in demand and supply which vary spatially and temporally. Use of the service is intrinsically a human-centred process relying largely on socio-economic data and to a lesser degree on biophysical information. Information will include the distribution of users, the socio-economic circumstances of users, governance systems, human pressure on ecosystems and other social measures like willingness and perceptions. Spatial data are likely to include maps of population distribution and economic status, maps of land use, trade data and other spatial data on political units and administrative boundaries.

In order to make a comprehensive and compelling economic case for the conservation of ecosystems and biodiversity it is essential to be able to understand, quantify and map the benefits received from ecosystems and biodiversity, and assign values to those benefits. This must all be done in a fashion that makes it possible to assess the contribution made by biodiversity to this value (separately from the contribution made by abiotic and anthropogenic factors), as well as the consequences of changes in ecosystems and biodiversity for these values. This chapter has focused on reviewing current ability to quantify and make spatially explicit the biophysical quantities (water, food, timber) or benefits provided by ecosystems and biodiversity. It has also aimed to review current ability to make spatially explicit the other beneficial processes from ecosystems and biodiversity that form our life support systems (e.g. pollination, carbon sequestration and cultural services).

Chapter 5 describes in detail the methodologies used and challenges faced when attempting the valuation of biodiversity and ecosystem services. In economic valuation, the focus has been on flows of ecosystem services (the 'interest' from the capital stock). Chapter 5 acknowledges that the valuation literature currently does not consider biodiversity in detail. It is indeed not straightforward to assign a value to the actual diversity in a system, as opposed to the biomass present. At the same time, the diversity is linked to production, so measurements of this aspect need to be built in. The instruments described in this chapter, on the other hand, have traditionally focused on biological resources, the capital itself.

Biophysical measurements are important since biodiversity underpins the delivery of many ecosystem services and thus forms the underlying basis of value. The framework of total economic value (TEV) (see Figure 5.3 – Value types within the TEV approach) is useful to help analyse where indicators need to be further developed. Ecosystem accounting is also addressed in Chapter 3 of TEEB in National Policy (2011), where several elements of the accounting framework (e.g. data issues, valuation approaches, socio-ecological accounting units) are examined for the three interconnected governance levels – Global/Continental, National/Regional and Local.

References

Alkemade, R., van Oorschot, M., Miles, L., Nellemann, C., Bakkenes, M., ten Brink, B. (2009) 'GLOBIO3: A framework to investigate options for reducing global terrestrial biodiversity loss', *Ecosystems*, vol 12, pp374–390

Ash, N., Blanco, H., Brown, C., Garcia, K., Hendrichs, T., Lucas, N., Ruadsepp-Hearne, C., Simpson, R. D., Scholes, R., Tomich, T., Vira, B. and Zurek, M. (2009) *Ecosystems and Human Well-being: A Manual for Assessment Practitioners*, World Resources Institute, Washington, DC

Bagley, M. J., Franson, S. E., Christ, S. A., Waits, E. R. and Toth, G. P. (2002) *Genetic Diversity as an Indicator of Ecosystem Condition and Sustainability Utility for Regional Assessments of Stream Condition in the Eastern United States*, US Environmental Protection Agency, EPA/600/R-03/056, September 2002

Balmford, A., Bennun, L., Ten Brink, B., Cooper, D., Cote, I. M., Crane, P., Dobson, A., Dudley, N., Dutton, I., Green, R. E., Gregory, R. D., Harrison, J., Kennedy, E. T., Kremen, C., Leader-Williams, N., Lovejoy, T. E., Mace, G., May, R., Mayaux, P., Morling, P., Phillips, J., Redford, K., Ricketts, T. H., Rodriguez, J. P., Sanjayan, M., Schei, P. J., van Jaarsveld, A. S. and Walther, B. A. (2005) 'The Convention on Biological Diversity's 2010 Target', *Science*, vol 307, pp212–213

Balmford, A., Bruner, A., Cooper, P., Costanza, R., Farber, S., Green, R. E., Jenkins, M., Jefferiss, P., Jessamy, V., Madden, J., Munro, K., Myers, N., Naeem, S., Paavola, J., Rayment, M., Rosendo, S., Roughgarden, J., Trumper, K. and Turner, R. K. (2002) 'Economic reasons for conserving wild nature', *Science*, vol 297, pp950–953

Balmford, A., Green, R. E. and Jenkins, M. (2003) 'Measuring the changing state of nature', *Trends in Ecology & Evolution*, vol 18, no 7, pp326–330

Balmford, A., Rodrigues, A. S. L., Walpole, M., ten Brink, P., Kettunen, M., Braat, L. and de Groot, R. (2008) *The Economics of Biodiversity and Ecosystems: Scoping the Science*, European Commission, ENV/070307/2007/486089/ETU/B2, Cambridge, UK

Balvanera, P., Daily, G. C., Ehrlich, P. R., Ricketts, T. H., Bailey, S. A., Kark, S., Kremen, C., Pereira, H. (2001) 'Conserving biodiversity and ecosystem services', *Science*, vol 291, no 5511, p2047

Balvanera, P., Pfisterer, A. B., Buchmann, N., He, J. S., Nakashizuka, T., Raffaelli, D. and Schmid, B. (2006) 'Quantifying the evidence for biodiversity effects on ecosystem functioning and services', *Ecology Letters*, vol 9, no 10, pp1146–1156

Bartholomé, E. and Belward, A. S. (2005) 'GLC2000: A new approach to global land cover mapping from Earth observation data', *Int. J. Remote Sens.*, vol 26, no 9, pp1959–1977

Biggs, R., Reyers, B. and Scholes, R. J. (2006) 'A biodiversity intactness score for South Africa', *South African Journal of Science*, vol 102, pp277–283

Bunker, D. E., DeClerck, F., Bradford, J. C., Colwell, R. K., Perfecto, I., Phillips, O. L., Sankaran, M. and Naeem, S. (2005) 'Species loss and above-ground carbon storage in a tropical forest', *Science*, vol 310, pp1029–1031

Butler, C. D. and Oluoch-Kosura, W. (2006) 'Linking future ecosystem services and future human well-being', *Ecology and Society*, vol 11, no 1, www.ecologyandsociety.org/vol11/iss1/art30/

Carpenter, S. R., Brock, W. A., Cole, J. J., Kitchell, J. F. and Pace, M. L. (2008) 'Leading indicators of trophic cascades', *Ecology Letters*, vol 11, pp128–138

CBD (2003) *Monitoring and Indicators: Designing National-level Monitoring Programmes and Indicators*, UNEP/CBD/SBSTTA/9/10, Convention on Biological Diversity, Montreal

Chan, K. M. A., Shaw, M. R., Cameron, D. R., Underwood, E. C. and Daily, G. C. (2006) 'Conservation planning for ecosystem services', *PLoS Biology*, vol 4, no 11, e379, doi:10.1371/journal.pbio.0040379

Clark, W. C., Jorling, T., Lovejoy, T. E. and O'Malley, R. (2002) *The State of The Nation's Ecosystems: Measuring the Lands, Waters, and Living Resources of the United States. Summary and Highlights*, The H. John Heinz III Center For Science, Economics and the Environment, Washington, DC

Collen, B., Loh, J., Whitmee, S., McRae, L., Amin, R. and Baillie, J. E. M. (2008) 'Monitoring change in vertebrate abundance: The Living Planet Index', *Conservation Biology*, vol 23, no 2, pp317–327

Costanza, R., d'Arge, R., de Groot, R., Farber, S., Grasso, M., Hannon, B., Limburg, K., Naeem, S., O'Neill, R. V., Paruelo, J., Raskin, R. G., Sutton, P. and van den Belt, M. (1997) 'The value of the world's ecosystem services and natural capital', *Nature*, vol 387, pp253–260

Costanza, R., Fisher, B., Mulder, K., Liu, S. and Christopher, T. (2007) 'Biodiversity and ecosystem services: A multi-scale empirical study of the relationship between species richness and net primary production', *Ecological Economics*, vol 61, nos 2–3, pp478–491

Czúcz, B., Horváth, F., Botta-Dukát, Z. and Molnár Z. (2009) 'Modelling changes in ecosystem service supply based on vegetation projections', IOP Conf. Series: *Earth and Environmental Science*, vol 6, 302011 doi:10.1088/1755-1307/6/0/302011

Daily, G. C., Polasky, S., Goldstein, J., Kareiva, P. M., Mooney, H. A., Pejchar, L., Ricketts, T. H., Salzman, J. and Shallenberger, R. (2009) 'Ecosystem services in decision making: Time to deliver', *Front. Ecol. Environ.*, vol 7, no 1, pp21–28

Diaz, S., Fargione, J., Chapin, F. S. and Tilman, D. (2006) 'Biodiversity loss threatens human well-being', *PLoS Biology*, vol 4, no 8, pp1300–1305

EEA (2009) *Progress towards the European 2010 Biodiversity Target*, European Environment Agency, Copenhagen, available at www.eea.europa.eu/publications/progress-towards-the-european-2010-biodiversity-target/

Erb, K.-H., Krausmann, F., Gaube, V., Gingrich, S., Bondeau, A., Fischer-Kowalski, M. and Haberl, H. (2009) 'Analyzing the global human appropriation of net primary production – processes, trajectories, implications: An introduction', *Ecological Economics*, vol 69, pp250–259

Esquinas-Alcázar, J. (2005) 'Protecting crop genetic diversity for food security: Political, ethical and technical challenges', *Nature Reviews Genetics*, vol 6, no 12, pp946–953

Failing, L. and Gregory, R. (2003) 'Ten common mistakes in designing biodiversity indicators for forest policy', *Journal of Environmental Management*, vol 68, pp121–132

FAO (2000) *Forest Resources of Europe, CIS, North America, Australia, Japan and New Zealand*, Main Report, ECE/TIM/SP/17, UN, NEW York and Geneva

FAO (2001) Forest Resources Assessment homepage, available at www.fao.org/forestry/fo/fra/index/jsp

Finlayson, C. M., D'Cruz, R., Aladin, N., Barker, D. R., Beltram, G., Brouwer, J., Davidson, N., Duker, L., Junk, W., Kaplowitz, M. D., Ketelaars, K., Kreuzberg-Mukhina, E., de la Lanza Espino, G., Lévêque, C., Lopez, A., Milton, R. G., Mirabzadeh, P., Pritchard, D., Revenga, C., Rivera, M., Hussainy, A. S., Silvius, M., Steinkamp, M., Aparin, V., Bykova, E., Calderón, J. L. G., Gorelkin, N., Hagemeijer, W., Kreuzberg, A., Rodríguez, E. M., Mirabdullaev, I., Mumba, M., Plotnikov, I., Talskykh, V. and Toryannikova, R. (2005) 'Inland Water Systems', in R. Hassan, R. J. Scholes and N. Ash (eds) *Ecosystems and Human Well-being: Current State and Trends (Volume 1)*. Findings of the Conditions and Trends, Working Group of the Millennium Ecosystem Assessment, Island Press, Washington, DC, pp551–583

Fisher, B. and Turner, R. K. (2008) 'Ecosystem services: Classification for valuation', *Biological Conservation*, vol 141, no 5, pp1167–1169

Fox, S. C., Hoffman, M. T. and Hoare, D. (2005) 'The phenological pattern of vegetation in Namaqualand, South Africa and its climate correlates using NOAA-AVHRR data', *S. Afr. Geogr. J.*, vol 87, no 2, pp85–94

Green, R. E., Balmford, A., Crane, P. R., Mace, G. M., Reynolds, J. D. and Turner, R. K. (2005) 'A framework for improved monitoring of biodiversity: Responses to the World Summit on Sustainable Development', *Conservation Biology*, vol 19, pp56–65

Haberl, H., Erb, K. H., Krausmann, F., Gaube, V., Bondeau, A., Plutzar, C., Gingrich, S., Lucht, W. and Fischer-Kowalski, M. (2007) 'Quantifying and mapping the human appropriation of net primary production in earth's terrestrial ecosystems', *Proceedings of the National Academy of Sciences*, vol 104, no 31, pp12942–12947, available online at www.pnas.org/content/104/31/12942.full.pdf+html, accessed 17 February 2010

The Heinz Center (1999) *Designing a Report on the State of the Nation's Ecosystems*, The H. John Heinz III Center for Science, Economics and the Environment, Washington, DC

The Heinz Center (2006) *Filling the Gaps: Priority Data Needs and Key Management Challenges for National Reporting on Ecosystem Condition*, a Report of the Heinz Center's State of the Nation's Ecosystems Project, May 2006, The H. John Heinz III Center for Science, Economics and the Environment, Washington, DC

Hooper, D. U., Chapin III, F. S., Ewel, J. J., Hector, A., Inchausti, P., Lavorel, S., Lawton, J. H., Lodge, D. M., Loreau, M., Naeem, S., Schmid, B., Setala, H., Systad, A. J., Vandermeer, J. and Wardle, D. A. (2005) 'Effects of biodiversity on ecosystem functioning: A consensus of current knowledge', *Ecological Monographs*, vol 75, no 1, pp3–35

Imhoff, M. L., Bounoua, L., Ricketts, T., Loucks, C., Harriss, R. and Lawrence, W. T. (2004) 'Global patterns in human consumption of net primary production', *Nature*, vol 429, pp870–873

Johnson, K. H., Vogt, K. A., Clark, H. J., Schmitz, O. J. and Vogt, D. J. (1996) 'Biodiversity and the productivity and stability of ecosystems', *Trends in Ecology & Evolution*, vol 11, pp372–377

Kremen, C. (2005) 'Managing ecosystem services: What do we need to know about their ecology?', *Ecology Letters*, vol 8, pp468–479

Kreuter, U. P., Harris, H. G., Matlock, M. D. and Lacey, R. E. (2001) 'Change in ecosystem service values in the San Antonio area, Texas', *Ecological Economics*, vol 39, pp333–346

Layke, C. (2009) *Measuring Nature's Benefits: A Preliminary Roadmap for Improving Ecosystem Service Indicators*, World Resources Institute, Washington, DC

Lee, C. K., Lee, J. H., Mjelde, J. W., Scott, D. and Kim, T. K. (2009) *Assessing the Economic Value of a Public Birdwatching Interpretative Service Using a Contingent Valuation Method*, International Journal of Tourism Research, published online in Wiley InterScience, www.interscience.wiley.com/ DOI: 10.1002/jtr.730

Li, R.-Q., Dong, M., Cui, J.-Y., Zhang, L.-L., Cui, Q.-G. and He, W.-M. (2007) 'Quantification of the impact of land-use changes on ecosystem services: A case study in Pingbian County, China', *Environmental Monitoring and Assessment*, vol 28, pp503–510

Losey, J. E. and Vaughan, M. (2006) 'The economic value of ecological services provided by insects', *BioScience*, vol 56, no 4, pp311–323

MA (Millennium Ecosystem Assessment) (2005a) *Ecosystems and Human Well-being: Biodiversity Synthesis*, World Resources Institute, Washington, DC

MA (2005b) *Millennium Ecosystem Assessment Synthesis Report*, Island Press, Washington, DC

Mace, G. M. and Baillie, J. (2007) 'The 2010 biodiversity indicators: Challenges for science and policy', *Conservation Biology*, vol 21, no 6, pp1406–1413

Mace, G. M. and Lande, R. (1991) 'Assessing the extinction threats: Towards a reevaluation of IUCN threatened species categories', *Conservation Biology*, vol 5, no 2, pp148–157

Mace, G. M., Masundire, H., Baillie, J., Ricketts, T. H., Brooks, T. M., Hoffmann, M. T., Stuart, S., Balmford, A., Purvis, A., Reyers, B., Wang, J., Revenga, C., Kennedy, E., Naeem, S., Alkemade, J. R. M., Allnutt, T. F., Bakarr, M., Bond, W. J., Chanson, J., Cox, N., Fonseca, G., Hilton-Taylor, C., Loucks, C. J., Rodrigues, A., Sechrest, W., Stattersfield, A. J., Janse van Rensburg, B., Whiteman, C., Abell, R., Cokeliss, Z., Lamoreux, J. F., Pereira, H., Thönell, J. and Williams, P. (2005) 'Biodiversity', in R. Hassan, R. J. Scholes and N. Ash (eds) *Ecosystems and Human Well-being: Current State and Trends (Volume 1)*, Findings of the Conditions and Trends Working Group of the Millennium Ecosystem Assessment. Island Press, Washington, DC, pp79–112

McGuire, A. D., Sitch, S., Clein, J. S., Dargaville, R., Esser, G., Foley, J., Heimann, M., Joos, F., Kaplan, J., Kicklighter, D. W., Meier, R. A., Melillo, J. M., Moore III, B., Prentice, I. C., Ramankutty, N., Reichenau, T., Schloss, A., Tian, H., Williams, L. J. and Wittenberg, U. (2001) 'Carbon balance of the terrestrial biosphere in the twentieth century: Analyses of CO_2, climate and land use effects with four process-based ecosystem models', *Global Biogeochem Cycles*, vol 15, pp183–206

Metzger, M. J., Rounsevell, M. D. A., Acosta-Michlik, L., Leemans, R. and Schröter, D. (2006) 'The vulnerability of ecosystem services to land use change', *Agriculture, Ecosystems & Environment*, vol 114, pp69–85

Myers, N., Mittermeier, R. A., Mittermeier, C. G., da Fonseca, G. A. B. and Kent, J. (2000) 'Biodiversity hotspots for conservation priorities', *Nature*, vol 403, no 6772, pp853–858

Naeem, S. (1998) 'Species redundancy and ecosystem reliability', *Conservation Biology*, vol 12, pp39–45

Naidoo, R. and Ricketts, T. H. (2006) 'Mapping the economic costs and benefits of conservation', *PLoS Biology*, vol 4, no 11, e360, DOI: 10.1371/journal.pbio.0040360

Naidoo, R., Balmford, A., Costanza, R., Fisher, B., Green, R. E., Lehner, B., Malcolm, T. R. and Ricketts, T. H. (2008) 'Global mapping of ecosystem services and conservation priorities', *Proceedings of the National Academy of Sciences*, vol 105, no 28, pp9495–9500

Nelson, E., Mendozam, G., Regetz, J., Polasky, S., Tallis, H., Cameron, D., Chan, K. M., Daily, G. C., Goldstein, J., Kareiva, P. M., Lonsdorf, E., Naidoo, R., Ricketts, T. H. and Shaw, M. (2009) 'Modeling multiple ecosystem services, biodiversity conservation, commodity production, and tradeoffs at landscape scales', *Frontiers in Ecology and the Environment*, vol 7, pp4–11, doi:10.1890/080023

Noss, R. F. (1990) 'Indicators for monitoring biodiversity: A hierarchical approach', *Conservation Biology*, vol 4, no 4, pp355–364

O'Farrell, P. J., Donaldson, J. S. and Hoffman, M. T. (2007) 'The influence of ecosystem goods and services on livestock management practices on the Bokkeveld Plateau, South Africa', *Agriculture, Ecosystem and Environment*, vol 122, pp312–324

Olson, D. M. D., Wikramanayake, E. D., Burgess, N. D., Powell, G. V. N., Underwood, E. C., D'Amico, J. A., Itoua, I., Strand, H. E., Morrison, J. C., Loucks, C. J., Allnutt, T. F., Ricketts, T. H., Kura, Y., Lamoreux, J. F., Wettengel, W. W., Hedao, P. and Kasseem, K. R. (2001) 'Terrestrial ecoregions of the world: A new map of life on Earth', *BioScience*, vol 51, pp933–938

Pauly, D., Christensen, V., Dalsgaard, J., Froese, R. and Torres, F. (1998) 'Fishing down marine food webs', *Science*, vol 279, pp860–863

Pereira, H. and Cooper, H. D. (2006) 'Towards the global monitoring of biodiversity change', *Trends in Ecology & Evolution*, vol 21, pp123–129

Priess, J. A., Mimler, M., Klein, A., Schwarze, S., Tscharntke, T. and Steffan-Dewenter, I. (2007) 'Linking deforestation scenarios to pollination services and economic returns in coffee agroforestry systems', *Ecological Applications*, vol 17, no 2, pp407–417

Revenga, C. and Kura, Y. (2003) *Status and Trends of Biodiversity of Inland Water Ecosystems*, Technical Series no.11, Secretariat of the Convention on Biological Diversity, Montreal

Reyers, B., O'Farrell, P. J., Cowling, R. M., Egoh, B. N., Le Maitre, D. C. and Vlok, J. H. J. (2009) 'Ecosystem services, land-cover change, and stakeholders: Finding a sustainable foothold for a semiarid biodiversity hotspot', *Ecology and Society*, vol 14, no 1, art 38, available at www.ecologyandsociety.org/vol14/iss1/art38/

Rodriguez, J. P., Balch, J. K. and Rodriguez-Clark, K. M. (2007) 'Assessing extinction risk in the absence of species-level data: Quantitative criteria for terrestrial ecosystems', *Biodiversity and Conservation*, vol 16, pp183–209

Royal Society (2003) *Measuring Biodiversity for Conservation*, Royal Society, London

Schmeller, D. S. (2008) 'European species and habitat monitoring: Where are we now?', *Biodiversity & Conservation*, vol 17, pp3321–3326

Schmeller, D. S., Henry, P. Y., Julliard, R., Gruber, B., Clobert, J., Dziock, F., Lengyel, S., Nowicki, P., Deri, E., Budrys, E., Kull, T., Tali, K., Bauch, B., Settele, J., van Swaay, C., Kobler A., Babij, V., Papastergiadou, E., Henle, K. (2009) 'Advantages of volunteer-based biodiversity monitoring in Europe', *Conservation Biology*, vol 23, pp307–316

Schröter, D., Cramer, W., Leemans, R., Prentice, I. C., Araujo, M. B., Arnell, N. W., Bondeau, A., Bugmann, H., Carter, T. R., Gracia, C. A., de la Vega-Leinert, A. C., Erhard, M., Ewert, F., Glendining, M., House, J. I., Kankaanpaa, S., Klein, R. J. T., Lavorel, S., Lindner, M., Metzger, M. J., Meyer, J., Mitchell, T. D., Reginster, I., Rounsevell, M., Sabate, S., Sitch, S., Smith, B., Smith, J., Smith, P., Sykes, M. T., Thonicke, K., Thuiller, W., Tuck, G., Zaehle, S. and Zierl, B. (2005) 'Ecosystem service supply and vulnerability to global change in Europe', *Science*, vol 310, pp1333–1337

Scholes, R. J. and Biggs, R. (2004) *Ecosystem Services In Southern Africa: A Regional Assessment*, Council for Scientific and Industrial Research, Pretoria, South Africa

Scholes, R. J. and Biggs, R. (2005) 'A biodiversity intactness index', *Nature*, vol 434, no 7029, pp45–49

Scholes, R. J., Mace, G. M., Turner, W., Geller, G. N., Jürgens, N., Larigauderie, A., Muchoney, D., Walther, B. A. and Mooney, H. A. (2008) 'Toward a global biodiversity observing system', *Science*, vol 321, pp1044–1045

Swift, M. J., Izac, A. M. N. and van Noordwijk, M. (2004) 'Biodiversity and ecosystem services in agricultural landscapes: Are we asking the right questions?', *Agriculture Ecosystems & Environment*, vol 104, no 1, pp113–134

Tapsuwan, S. and Asafu-Adjaye, J. (2008) 'Estimating the economic benefit of SCUBA diving in the Similan Islands, Thailand', *Coastal Management*, vol 36, pp431–442

TEEB (2008) 'The economics of ecosystems and biodiversity: An interim report', available at www.teebweb.org, accessed 2 March 2010

TEEB in National Policy (2011) *The Economics of Ecosystems and Biodiversity in National and International Policy Making* (ed Patrick ten Brink), Earthscan, London

Troy, A. and Wilson, M. A. (2006) 'Mapping ecosystem services: Practical challenges and opportunities in linking GIS and value transfer', *Ecological Economics*, vol 60, pp435–449

Turner, B. L. II, Matson, P. A., McCarthy, J., Corell, R. W., Christensen, L., Eckley, N., Hovelsrud-Broda, G. K., Kasperson, J. X., Kasperson, R. E., Luers, A., Martello, M. L., Mathiesen, S., Naylor, R., Polsky, C., Pulsipher, A., Schiller, A., Selink, H. and Tyler, N. (2003) 'Illustrating the coupled human–environment system for vulnerability analysis: Three case studies', *Proceedings of the National Academy of Sciences*, vol 100, pp8080–8085

van Jaarsveld, A. S., Biggs, R., Scholes, R. J., Bohensky, E., Reyers, B., Lynam, T., Musvoto, C. and Fabricius, C. (2005) 'Measuring conditions and trends in ecosystem services at multiple scales: The Southern African Millennium Ecosystem Assessment (SAfMA) experience', *Philosophical Transactions of the Royal Society B-Biological Sciences*, vol 360, no 1454, pp425–441

Viglizzo, F. and Frank, F. C. (2006) 'Land-use options for Del Plata Basin in South America: Tradeoffs analysis based on ecosystem service provision', *Ecological Economics*, vol 57, pp140–151

Wendland, K. J., Honzák, M., Portela, R., Vitale, B., Rubinoff, S. and Randrianarisoa, J. (2009) 'Targeting and implementing payments for ecosystem services: Opportunities for bundling biodiversity conservation with carbon and water services in Madagascar', *Ecological Economics*, doi:10.1016/j.ecolecon.2009.01.002

Wood, S., Ehui, S., Alder, J., Benin, S., Cassman, K. G., Cooper, H. D., Johns, T., Gaskell, J., Grainger, R., Kadungure, S., Otte, J., Rola, A., Watson, R., Wijkstrom, U., Devendra, C., Kanbar, N. et al (2005) 'Food', in *Millennium Ecosystem Assessment. Ecosystems and Human Well-being: Current States and Trends*, World Resources Institute, Washington, DC, pp209–241

Yadav, V. and Malanson, G. (2008) 'Spatially explicit historical land use, land cover and soil organic carbon transformations in Southern Illinois', *Agriculture, Ecosystems and Environment*, vol 123, pp280–292

Zhao, B., Kreuter, U., Li, B., Ma, Z., Chen, J. and Nakagoshi, N. (2004) 'An ecosystem service value assessment of land-use change on Chongming Island, China', *Land Use Policy*, vol 21, pp139–148

Chapter 4
The Socio-cultural Context of Ecosystem and Biodiversity Valuation

Coordinating lead authors
Eduardo S. Brondízio, Franz W. Gatzweiler

Lead authors
Christos Zografos, Manasi Kumar

Reviewers
Gopal K. Kadekodi, Jeffrey A. McNeely, Jianchu Xu

Review editor
Joan Martinez-Alier

Contents

Key messages   149

1   Introduction   150

2   The trade-offs of valuation   155
    2.1   The long-term implications of valuation: The changing concept
          of ownership and property   155
    2.2   Intrinsic value of Nature and value-articulating institutions   158
    2.3   Valuation as a feedback mechanism   162

3   The challenges of valuation: ecosystems, biodiversity and level of analysis 164
    3.1   The problem of transformative value and economic return of resource use 164
    3.2   Complexity and functional interdependencies underlying valuations   168
    3.3   How to choose how to value   169

4   Final remarks   172

Acknowledgements   173

References   174

Key messages

- Valuation, including economic valuation, functions as a system of cultural projection which imposes a way of thinking and a form of relationship with the environment and reflects particular perceived realities, worldviews, mind sets and belief systems. However, it can also serve as a tool for self-reflection and a feedback mechanism which helps people to rethink their relations to the natural environment and increase their knowledge about the consequences of consumption, choices and behaviour.

- Because of the multidimensional and socio-cultural embeddedness of value any exercise of valuation is relative to a given individual or group of people. In a multicultural and democratic context of biodiversity valuation, this makes the question of choosing a value-articulating institution more important than that of finding a correct value.

- Economic valuation influences the notion of ownership and property applied to biodiversity and over the long term may change human relationship to the environment in significant ways.

- Intrinsic values are culturally embedded moral truths. They can be taken into account by choosing the appropriate institutions which allow their articulation in addition to utilitarian values.

- Valuation processes can be seen as a form of regulatory adaptation by serving as a mechanism to provide feedback in a system where production and consumption, trade and exchange are so distant and complex that they undermine perceptions of the impacts of habits and behaviour on the environment.

- Value change along the commodity chain has implications for the distribution of benefits, affects the level of incentives for conservation and represents an important methodological challenge for economic valuation.

- Economic valuation may contribute to addressing our inability, reluctance or ideological intolerance to adjust institutions (also those that are value articulating) to our knowledge of ecosystems, biodiversity and the human being.

- Economic valuation is a complex, spatial and institutional cross-scale problem. Many efforts focusing on particular parts of ecosystems or species, while effective at one level, lack the scope to control the pressure of commodity markets for land resources surrounding them. As such, and depending on their biophysical context, they may be limited to capturing the linkages created by a growing functional interdependency of resource-use systems nested within larger ecosystems.

1 Introduction

Economic valuation of ecosystems, their services and biodiversity represents a balancing act. On the one hand, valuation can function as a system of cultural projection which imposes a way of thinking and a form of relationship with the environment,[1] a particular notion of property and ownership, and view of development and what constitutes human well-being. Side by side with contributions from several distinguished scholars such as Arrow, Sen's liberal paradox has shown the inadequacy of this worldview (Sen, 1973; Arrow, 1982). On the other hand, valuation can serve as a tool for self-reflection which helps people rethink their relations to the natural environment and increase knowledge about the consequences of consumption choices and behaviour for distant places and people. Questions such as what factors influence human relationships with nature, what is the role played by nature in the formation of social and personal identity and what are the social and environmental consequences of various ways of relating to and using the environment (Clayton and Opotow, 2004; Zavestoski, 2004) become the focus of this self reflection.

As such, valuation can work as a feedback mechanism for a society that derives its resources from the environment but has distanced itself from the consequences of its actions. Further, economic valuation can help communicate the value of nature to different people using a language that speaks to dominant economic and political views around the world. The outcomes of any valuation exercise depend on what the various interest groups value, whose values count, who benefits, and how we account for the growing interdependencies of social and ecological systems. In that context the question of how to value ecosystem services and biodiversity and the choice of a valuation method are as challenging as the attempt to attach a particular value to them. Valuation entails conceptual and methodological challenges to account not only for different dimensions of value and their interconnections, but assimilating different cultural perspectives and levels of analysis.

Across disciplines, scholars have recognized cultural differences as very fundamental in the way people conceive and relate to the environment. While it is not the intention of this chapter to compare and review these attempts, a brief overview may offer insights that are particularly relevant to the exercise of environmental valuation. For instance, Descola (1996) proposes a three-tier analytical model to characterize implicit schemes of praxis [practical and applied knowledge] used by different societies to objectify their relationship to nature: (1) modes of identification including animism (i.e. social character of relations between humans and non-humans, thus the space between nature and society as being social), totemism (metaphoric conceptualization of social distinctions based on the relationship between nature and culture) and naturalism (the relations between nature and society as functioning according to natural and biological laws); (2) modes of interaction (i.e. based on reciprocity, predation, protection between species), and (3) modes of categorization (i.e. metaphoric similarities based on morphological resemblances, analogy, and/or contrast as in totemic structures, and metonymic such as classification based on properties of use and differences in nature as exemplified differently by animistic and naturalistic associations between habitats and species). His approach helps to place the western perspective (i.e. scientific, naturalist and protectionist) as rooted within not only a Judaeo–Christian tradition of control and utilitarianism, but also in the context of the historical separation of social and biological sciences and the consequent epistemological distinction between culture and nature. This contrasts with indigenous understandings of the human–nature relationship that acknowledge a continuum between human and non-human as part of a large chain of reciprocity and predation. In contrast, for instance, the conservation movement, as Descola puts it, 'fetishing nature as a transcendental object, the control of which would be displaced from predatory capitalism to the rational management of modern economics, the conservationist movement, far from questioning the foundation of Western cosmology, tends rather to perpetuate the ontological dualism [culture–nature] typical of modern ideology' (1996, p97). Descola goes further, however, predicting that in the long run this agenda may shift completely the relationship of people to nature:

> However, the program set forth by environmental activists will perhaps lead, unintentionally, to dissolution of naturalism, since the survival of a whole range of non-humans, now increasingly protected from anthropic damage, will shortly depend almost exclusively upon social conventions and human action. The conditions of existence for blue whales, the ozone layer or the Antarctic will thus be no more 'natural' than they are presently for wild species in zoos or for genes in biological data banks. Drifting away from its time-honored definition, nature is less and less the product of an autonomous principle of development; its foreseeable demise, as a concept, will probably close a long chapter of our own history. (1996, pp97–98)

Along similar lines, Palsson (1996) distinguishes three kinds of paradigms representing particular forms of human–environment interaction: orientalism, paternalism and communalism. While the first two are based on different degrees of separating nature and society, the latter 'rejects the radical separation of nature and society, object and subject, emphasizing a notion of dialogue' (1996, p65). Ellen (1996), on the other hand, proposes a model to interpret cultural variations on the relationship between people and nature based on a comparative perspective to human cognitive imperatives: how people identify things based on senses, context and value; which code systems people use to contrast self and others; and the different ways people recognize some inner force and essence in nature. However, calling attention to the danger of 'infinite relativity', Ellen's model seeks to understand the implications of different systems of thinking to our current environmental challenges. In other words (paraphrasing Ellen), how particular ways of conceiving the environment serve the interest of particular groups, whether these are the conservation movement, industries, churches, political parties, academics, indigenous people or governments. Whether reinventing an image of the noble ecological savage, or defining nature with a price tag, or constructing a shared image of the global environment, these models carry political and social goals and have long far-reaching consequences (Ellen, 1996, p28). An important message for TEEB studies is that approaches to understanding nature and environment originally driven by naturalism have drifted away to a utilitarian-led paradigm of economics as a social choice. But the limitations of a utilitarian approach is not fully understood by societies; after all a utilitarian approach is essentially individualistic, from which there is no way to deduce a social welfare unless very strict conditions are laid (Arrow, 1963; Sen, 1970a).

Yet, while some scholars tend to focus on the contexts of the people–nature relationship, others have proposed that our modes of relation to nature are also innate to human evolutionary history (Wilson, 1984; Kellert and Wilson, 1993). The biophilia hypothesis, for instance, articulates that all humans have an innate need and connection to nature, including spiritual and emotional, as well as utilitarian dimensions. These relationships, however, are not ahistorical and change in level of importance as a function of the different degrees of interaction and dependency on them. Kellert (1996) presents nine dimensions intrinsic to the way people and environment relate, some of which can dominate depending on our experience and context, and the balance between them influences well-being: utilitarian; naturalistic; scientific/ecologic; aesthetic; symbolic; humanistic; moralistic; dominionistic; and negativistic (1996, p38). As in other domains of science and philosophy, dichotomies and typologies defining how people vary in the way they value and relate to nature can be useful or misleading, not necessarily true or false. Following the approach suggested by Ellen, the intention here in recognizing cultural differences and perspectives on nature is to find synergies between them, the utilitarian and aesthetic, the pragmatic and the symbolic (Ellen, 1996).

The epistemological tradition of economics has also evolved from a specific socio-cultural context which presumes that economic values are predefined, held by people as preferences and can be derived by analysis, via either stated or revealed preference methods. Economics is built on this 'belief system' as manifested in the Cartesian and Newtonian tradition of modern science, and Descola's referred naturalism, according to which the world works mechanistically as a giant clockwork. Understanding the complexity of the world requires taking it apart to its individual components or according to the Cartesian worldview, even if implying separating the mind from the body, culture from nature, so the latter can be understood objectively, free of values. In this sense, one can see this particular context, and the pre-analytic assumptions of how ecosystems function and humans behave, as part of TEEB's constructed reality and values, nevertheless based on perceived social demands and scientific methods. Gowdy (1998, pxvi) expressed this by stating that, 'My own particular tribe, that of academic economists has its own belief system to explain and justify the world of commerce we have created, typified by the notion of "economic man".' Within the western socio-cultural context 'economic man' stems from the Judaeo–Christian conception of human nature: because of Adam's original sin, inherited by humanity, humans are viewed as 'scarcity-driven creature(s) of need' and 'as ever imperfect and suffering beings with wants ever beyond their powers' (Sahlins, 1996, p397). Others have argued that, 'In Hebrew religion, the ancient bond between God and nature was destroyed' (Frankfort, 1948, p343), and that, 'Christianity continued to widen the rift between man and nature by its opposition to pantheism' (Sahhins, 1996, p411) (the belief that nature/the universe is a manifestation of god or spirits), thereby desacralizing nature and reframing it as a natural resource (Gatzweiler, 2003, p61).

As such, economic values and processes of valuation, although grounded in a shared scientific methodology, are socially and culturally constructed, as are concepts such as ecosystems and biodiversity. Economic values are not objective facts nor do they reflect universal truths; instead they reflect the culturally constructed realities, worldviews, mindsets and belief systems of particular societies and/or sectors of society (Wilk and Cliggett, 2006). They are not exogenous, but rather shaped by the social interactions of everyday life (Henrich et al, 2001) as well as political and power relations operating within a system of local, regional and global interdependencies (Hornborg et al, 2007). They derive from a belief system of how economists and others view the world and what they think the role of humans in it should be. Mainstream economic beliefs of values of ecosystems and biodiversity are defined by people's willingness to pay for them and the existence or creation of markets, but they have to be understood as part of the broader historical and geopolitical context which gave rise to contemporary environmental conservation and valuation.

The rise of the so-called new environmentalism during the 1960s marked a shift from environmental concerns based on the protection of 'empty' spaces and particular species to concerns with the human environment (McCormick, 1989; Caldwell, 1990). This is well represented by the 1972 United Nations Stockholm conference on 'The Human Environment'. Since then, although many efforts have aimed at regulating development and reconciling economic growth and conservation, the most striking outcome of these processes has been the exponential rise of protected areas (Zimmerer, 2006). Some have referred to this process as the globalization of conservation, for its generalized world distribution and impact on local populations (West et al, 2006). Even today, more political emphasis is placed on protecting and isolating ecosystems from economic development and commodity markets, than on redefining and regulating the latter.

During the 1980s, the now landmark Brundtland Commission of the United Nations 'Our Common Future' report (Brundtland, 1987) marked more directly an effort to internalize the environment in the economy, slowly opening space for new conceptions of development based on the principle of intergenerational responsibility. The latest Global Environmental Outlook (GEO 4) of the United Nations Environment Programme (UNEP), for instance, which started as a periodic assessment exercise since 'Our Common Future', positively acknowledges the mainstreaming of environmental issues in government and corporate agendas during the past 20 years – that is, 'from periphery to the core of decision making' (UNEP, 2007; King et al, 2007).

Reflecting these larger trends in conservation, the Convention on Biological Diversity (CBD), one of the lasting high-profile agreements resulting from the 1992 Rio UN Earth Summit, represented a shift from species-based conservation, championed by some international conservation organizations, to the conservation of ecosystems and biomes. It also gave heightened importance to local populations as stewards of nature and as a source of knowledge relevant to conservation and sustainable development. Not unlike TEEB, it has put significant emphasis on the value, including economic value, of biodiversity and local knowledge, such as through incentives for bioprospecting (Reid et al, 1993), a process which triggered diverse social consequences, many of which are still unfolding (Moran et al, 2001).

The Millennium Ecosystem Assessment (MA) represented another important shift towards efforts to view the environment on a global scale and internalize it in policy and economic thinking. Its core concept of ecosystem services, for instance, while emphasizing an anthropocentric and utilitarian approach, proposes a framework centred on human dependency not only on resources, but also on ecosystem functioning itself, contributing to make visible a broad array of ecological and biophysical functions taken for granted by society (MA, 2005). In doing so, the MA has contributed to a broader understanding of the overwhelming scale of human impacts and their footprints, and their current and future economic and social consequences.

Valuation exercises have not shied away from the challenges of valuing biodiversity and ecosystems from different social and cultural perspectives, and levels of analysis. Many recognize the multiple dimensions and concepts of value embedded in ecosystems and biodiversity, and that any exercise of valuation is relative to a given individual or group of people (Turner et al, 2003; Shmelev, 2008). A comprehensive report from the United States Environmental Protection Agency (EPA), for instance, proposes an approach of multiple methods to help capture different dimensions of biodiversity and ecosystem services, as well as the perspectives of different stakeholders. The underlying idea is that an integrated and multidimensional approach will be more likely to capture the full range of contributions, thus the broader value, of biodiversity and ecosystems, including values that may be context-specific (global, national, regional, local) (EPA, 2009). It adopts a broad definition of value to incorporate aspects based on human preference (e.g. attitudes and judgements, economic value, community-based value, and constructed preferences) and on the biophysical environment (bio-ecological and energy-based values). In order to capture these dimensions, the report recommends that the EPA should not only use economic models and tools, but also methods to capture social attitudes, preferences and intentions, such as civic valuation, a decision science approach, ecosystem benefit indicators, biophysical ranking methods, and cost as a proxy for value (EPA, 2009).

A similar recognition of the multidimensional and context-dependent nature of valuing biodiversity and ecosystems has been adopted by the UK Natural Environmental Research Council (NERC, 2009). Based on the OECD (2002) typology, it distinguishes several types of value (e.g. direct-use consumptive value, direct-use non-consumptive value, indirect-use value, insurance value, option value and bequest value) and proposes a series of eight pathways for valuation, each defined in terms of specific assessment frameworks and disciplinary expertise, but which together aim at presenting a more comprehensive picture of the valuation process. These pathways include valuation of ecosystem services, existence value, recreation and amenities, well-being, direct resource use, genetic and bio-prospecting value, and conservation and energy values (NERC, 2009).

In spite of these advances, it is important to recognize some limitations of economic valuation. The inclusion of social and cultural criteria, for instance, while desirable, is difficult to attain and constrained by methodological limitations (Shmelev, 2008; see also Chapter 5), as are studies examining the longitudinal aspects of different attempts to value biodiversity and ecosystem services. In particular, valuation studies face the challenge of recognizing the interdependency among the many types of ecosystem services and that of different interest groups competing or associated with different parts of the same ecosystem (Turner et al, 2003).

Considering the issues above, how a middle ground can be found for various implications of economic valuation, including an appraisal of the limitations of what should and should not be valued, is a significant challenge before us. Beyond proposing definitive solutions, this chapter aims at contributing to these discussions and to TEEB by raising questions about the trade-offs and challenges of valuation. Valuation represents one particular way of thinking and a perspective that is based on a rational management approach to the environment, and it can play an important role in calling attention to the value of biodiversity and to intangible ecosystem services vis-à-vis other forces competing for use and control of particular resources to the detriment of others (e.g. standing forest vs land for agricultural expansion). Although this requires some level of objective measurement and some imposition of a value system, it is one way to confront the pressures of market forces which see the environment strictly as a commodity. However, finding a middle ground will imply shifting attention from the question of the value of nature to second-order questions of when, how and what to value, and whose values count.

The following section continues the discussion of the socio-cultural context of valuation by referring to the trade-offs of valuation as well as its challenges. The discussion of trade-offs of valuation includes (2.1) changing notions of property and property relations induced by valuation, (2.2) the role of intrinsic values, and (2.3) the importance of valuation as a social and economic feedback mechanism. The chapter concludes by focusing on methodological challenges such as (3.1) the problem of equity and the transformation of resource value along the value chain, (3.2) the growing complexity and interdependency of ecosystems and the limitations of valuing 'islands' of resources, and finally (3.3) the importance of considering value-articulating institutions.

2 The trade-offs of valuation

2.1 The long-term implications of valuation: The changing concept of ownership and property

In spite of efforts to acknowledge value of biodiversity and ecosystem services as multidimensional, contested and context-specific, exercises of valuation represent an effort to promote some universal notion of the environment, and as such, they carry broad and long-term consequences. By acknowledging the value of benefits derived from biodiversity and ecosystems, perhaps the most important consequence of economic valuation is the way it contributes to change the notion of ownership and property applied to the environment in general, and biodiversity in particular. In this context, to use a reference from Polyani (1944, p73), valuation contributes to create a 'commodity fiction'. Or, as Sahlins (1996, p411) says, '... a purely Western (construct) that nature is pure materiality'. The danger with the commodity fiction is that the commoditized environment becomes a contrived artefact of itself: 'Ecosystems and biodiversity can be owned and traded in the market system for dollars' (Vatn and Bromley, 1994, p137).

As such, environmental valuation creates a means for valuing biodiversity monetarily, and thus implies and/or imposes new notions of ownership and property. However, people do not necessarily have previously defined monetary values for non-market goods (Cummings et al, 1986; Mitchell and Carson, 1989) such as biodiversity or biological processes such as carbon uptake, and the process of valuation can trigger negotiations between and within endogenous and exogenous systems of value (Hanemann, 1994; Sagoff, 1998). This suggests that environmental valuation creates a framework that can induce not only previously ignored monetary appreciation of biodiversity and ecosystem functioning but new utilitarian frames of appreciating them. Gowdy and Erickson (2005) explain that behaviours such as cooperative consensus building and collective decision making become difficult to pursue in a decision-making framework where only individual preferences count. In other words, the institutional setting influences preferences in a choice situation by activating particular motivations and rationalities (Vatn, 2005).

There are two separate though interrelated lines of critique worth pointing here: (a) institutional and (b) psychological. While cultural and social anthropology points towards flaws in the structural and institutional outlook of economic valuation (Descola's theory points to fundamentally different cultural approaches in conceptualizing human–environment relationship), psychological critique centres on the de-psychologizing of human behaviour as seen in stated or revealed preference theory where there is little appreciation of intrapsychic or interpersonal origins of human behaviour. The relationship between economics and psychology has been quite fraught. Several authors, notably Sen (1973), Lewin (1996), Johansson-Stenman (2002) and Muramatsu (2009) voice a common criticism that economics has chosen to use psychological theories and constructs in an inconsistent way to explain economic behaviour mainly through championing the rational-choice paradigm. Sen (1973, 1979) pointed out that despite seeking motivations behind their actions, economists choose to focus solely on the outcome, that is, resultant behaviour or have chosen to aggregate the behavioural outcomes as if these were prices and physical quantities. Psychological reasoning, understanding affects, feelings and thoughts underpinning different states of mind, interactions between individual and group, groups and social institutions has been compromised in this process. This is despite the fact that empirical research in behavioural economics, anthropology, psychology and moral philosophy have time and again rejected the standard economic assumptions with respect to people's preferences and behaviours (Sen, 1973; Wilk, 1993; Nussbaum, 2001; Kahneman, 2003; Muramatsu, 2009) and in terms of theoretical advancement what resulted over time is a corpus of (unsuccessful) non-psychological preference theory proven to be ineffective, counter-intuitive and limited in explanatory potential (Lewin, 1996).

More recent developments in behavioural economics suggest that utility and emotions cannot be divorced from each other; 'utility arises from emotions and emotions arise from changes, and people's judgements and choices have more intuitive than rational/logical origins (Kahneman, 2003; see also Bernoulli, 1954; Kahneman, 2000). Further Kahneman (2003) argues that 'a theory of choice that completely ignores feelings such as the pain of losses and the regret of mistakes is not only descriptively unrealistic, it also leads to incorrect prescriptions that do not. It maximize the utility of outcomes as they are actually experienced – that is, utility as Bentham conceived it' (p1457).

A discussion on the implications of attaching new forms and concepts of property to nature and culture (e.g. ethnic affiliation and markers, knowledge systems) is ongoing in anthropology (e.g. Dove, 2006; Hames, 2007; Commaroff and Commaroff, 2009), but this is still an overdue discussion in environmental sciences and conservation policy. Since the late 1980s, and concomitant with the rise of protected areas in previously populated regions, numerous policies have focused on granting resource-use rights and ownership to indigenous groups and rural populations considered 'traditional'. These policies are changing significantly local relationships within and between indigenous and rural populations in terms of rights to control, exclude and derive monetary value based on distinct ancestry, ethnic affiliation and knowledge of resource use. Martinez-Alier (pers. comm., 2007) directs attention to a phenomenon he calls 'fetishism of fictitious commodities', referring to those environmental commodities that are not even in the market and yet are valued in monetary terms.

Hale (2002) has described these processes in Latin America as a form of 'neoliberal multiculturalism', one which has come about during the rise of neoliberalism since the 1980s in part as a response to demands for rights by the culturally oppressed and excluded, in part a move away from universalist policies towards multicultural policies. Despite having opened new political spaces, an overemphasis on ethnic-based policies are contributing to the fragmentation of society into multiple identity groups with few perceived common interests and characteristics. These changes have represented a form of commodification of intangible goods such as ethnic identity usually associated with a repackaged version of the 'noble savage' where local populations are expected to behave as stewards of nature (Dove, 2006; Hames, 2007; Pedrosa and Brondízio, 2008). Not only ought the needs and rights of the local populations be recognized, but also their unique interdependence and attachment to nature needs to be better understood. The association of multicultural policies and environmental conservation has set the stage for competing ownership of natural resources and knowledge systems (Escobar, 1998; Kohler, 2008). In parallel, critical theory and its influence in disciplines such as anthropology, psychoanalysis, sociology and ecology have challenged dominance of largely patriarchal, educated, logico-positivist structures of thought and reasoning over voices of weaker, marginalized sections of society (see Martinez-Alier and Thrupp, 1992; Roughgarden, 2004; Martinez-Alier, 2008) and towards alternative discursive, hermeneutic paradigms (Howarth and Farber, 2000; Zografos and Howarth, 2008).

Nazarea (1998, 2006) called attention to the value of biodiversity, particularly but not only agrodiversity (e.g. identification of varieties and their specific qualities), as depending in large part on having cultural memory and knowledge associated with it: 'Local knowledge and cultural memory are crucial for the conservation of biodiversity because both serve as repositories of alternative choices that keep cultural and biological diversity flourishing' (Nazarea, 2006, p318). The value of medicinal plants, crop varieties or forest resources, for instance within the perspective of bioprospecting, gains meaning as valuable only when associated with knowledge to identify and recognize how to use and manage a resource (Brush and Stabinsky, 1997; Jarvis et al, 2007). In other words, these knowledge systems associated with biodiversity are held collectively and intergenerationally and change processually as local systems and practices co-evolve with changing environments (e.g. Pinedo-Vasquez et al, 2002).

Bioprospecting programmes based on the association of corporations (e.g. pharmaceutical, agronomic), governments and local populations have flourished around the world with the 'promise of selling biodiversity to protect it' (Reid et al, 1993; Hayden, 2003). While the economic benefits of these experiments have been minimal or null in the majority of cases, internal conflicts within and between communities, governments and corporations have abounded (Hayden, 2003; Greene, 2004). Some have raised the questions of bioprospecting as another form of colonialism, a 'bioimperialism' which appropriates resources and knowledge from marginal groups to powerful corporations using social and environmental discourse (Moran et al, 2001). The key issue, however, is that in doing so, biodiversity and knowledge about it becomes 'no longer considered "common heritage", the pre-CBD paradigm that provided open access to bioresources' (Moran et al, 2001, p501). It has become clear that the commodification of knowledge, which evolved historically from a collective base, does not lend itself to the application of 'conventional' legal–economic tools of property rights, such as industrial patent, intellectual property and royalties. Examples in Mexico (Hayden, 2003), Peru (Greene, 2004) and South Africa (Commaroff and Commaroff, 2009), among many others, illustrate some of the trade-offs of the valuing and selling-to-protect approach, at least when it comes to the distribution of benefits. The unfolding lessons of bioprospecting programmes started during the 1980s and 1990s can serve as powerful examples for other programmes of economic valuation to reflect on their long-term and potentially negative implications.

2.2 Intrinsic value of nature and value-articulating institutions

Among the values of ecosystems are cultural values perceived by specific cultures (e.g. the belief in holy trees). But, all values are culturally constructed and contextualized. Values are institutions and as such (contribute to) define behaviour. Values can be made visible by applying specific valuation methods and the valuation methods themselves are socio-cultural constructs which define the rules for eliciting or articulating values. Choosing the socio-cultural context of valuation also implies a choice of the respective valuation method. The design of valuation methods themselves emerges from the understanding of what values are or should be, and how they can be elicited. Valuation methods, for example, imply certain models of humans, nature and their interactions and they define whether values are revealed, discovered, constructed or evolve during the process of valuation (Vatn and Bromley, 1994). Vatn (2005) refers to valuation methods as value-articulating institutions. Values for the same ecosystem service therefore vary across institutional settings.

The question of the value of nature also raises the opposite question of the nature of values (Gatzweiler, 2003). Values, as well as norms, beliefs and conventions of society are an essential part of our culture. Values derive from the worldviews and fundamental perceptions of a society of, for example, what is right or wrong, good or bad, valuable or worthless. They are deep manifestations of a culture of which not all can be directly observed or predicted through models of rational choice (Wilk and Cliggett, 2006). A large number of empirical studies based on experimental games as well as experimental social psychology have shown that apart from being egoistic utility maximizers, as assumed to be the case for the *Homo economicus*, 'people tend to be more altruistic than the economic model predicts' (Gowdy et al, 2003, p469) and that they act both selfishly and cooperatively (Etzioni, 1986; Güth and Tietz, 1990; Ostrom, 1990; Fehr and Tougareva, 1995; Caporael, 1997; Alesina and Ferrara, 2000; Gintis, 2000; Kahneman, 2000, 2003; Manski, 2000; Nowak et al, 2000). The model of *Homo reciprocans* presented by Bowles and Gintis (2004) suggests that people behave altruistically to those who reciprocate their altruistic behaviour. Depending on whether they perceive the behaviour of others as being beneficial or harmful, they will respond in kind.

Gowdy et al (2003), however, have presented yet another type of behaviour observed in a rural Nigerian village, where fairness was an important predictor of economic behaviour, but not retaliation. Their case demonstrates that non-cooperative behaviour elicits a cooperative response and that 'retaliation is much less common in traditional cultures than in Western societies' (p477). An important implication of those findings is that behavioural differences among cultures are large and they are often correlated with group norms and values, and not with attributes of the individual. This should be clearly articulated in the context of our attempt to value ecosystem services and biodiversity according to a model evolved from the very particular cultural tradition of the industrialized world.

The view of nature and humans being distinct from each other, as discussed above, shows itself in the neglect of intrinsic values in economics – values of nature simply for the sake of its existence, independent of any current or future usefulness to humans (Gatzweiler, 2008). The Newtonian conception of reality, however, has fundamentally changed with quantum physics, the philosophical substance of which tells us that no clear distinction can be drawn between observer (subject) and observed (object), or human and nature. This has consequences for human cognition, because it entails that there is a close connection between human software and hardware: the way people perceive their environment (software) and the way they measure, value and construct it (hardware). From that holistic perspective, 'what we observe is not nature itself, but nature exposed to our method of questioning... The observer decides how he is going to set up the measurement and this arrangement will determine, to some extent, the properties of the observed object' (Capra, 1991, p140; see also Heisenberg, 1958).

In this context, the methods used to elicit values define the values actually elicited. If individuals are asked about their willingness to pay for ecosystems and biodiversity, it is likely that people actually state their willingness to pay for ecosystems and biodiversity and the method requires the individual to articulate its values according to a consistent logic and specific rationality. Other methods allow for communication and deliberation, and value statements then emerge from a social process.

The issue of intrinsic values is helpful to reflect on the relationship between nature and humans. It proposes that nature has value in itself and is valued as an end in itself, independent of its usefulness to achieve some higher end. The question whether intrinsic value can or should exist or not, directly relates to how we perceive human–nature relationships and the way people relate to nature is not only reflected by their actions but also by the rules they apply to articulate values for nature. Therefore, acknowledging intrinsic values of nature acknowledges the fact that people are part of nature and 'it is how we choose to perceive people and biodiversity that determines choices of how to (value and eventually) conserve biodiversity' (Gatzweiler, 2008).

The point made here is that the approach to eliciting values from people for ecosystems reflects understandings, perceptions and normative stances of what values are and how values are generated and held: the pre-analytic conceptions of those asking questions. And just these pre-analytic conceptions define the values the researcher wishes to discover or create. Two extremes are to ask individuals about their willingness to pay or allowing people to deliberate. Asking individuals about their willingness to pay thereby reflects different pre-analytic conceptions than allowing them to deliberate. The former assumes that people:

- hold these values in advance or can easily generate them;
- have sufficient information and understanding of what they are valuing;
- can decide (alone) on the values they attribute to ecosystems;
- behave according to the cost–benefit rule;
- value consistently;
- value according to individual rationality.

On the other hand, deliberative valuation methods do not assume pre-existing values for ecosystems and biodiversity. Given the fact that values are part of the institutional and cultural context people live in and that this societal context has co-evolved over long time periods it is likely that values are not held in advance and that people need to communicate and deliberate on issues that require valuation. In such deliberative processes values emerge from a communicative social process (O'Connor, 2000; Zografos and Paavola, 2008). Commonly known techniques such as Participatory Rural Appraisals (Chambers, 1991), Citizen Juries or Roundtables can be suitably modified to facilitate these processes.

The foregoing discussion makes a case for environmental valuation as a value-articulating institution (Jacobs, 1997), that is, a framework that is invoked in the process of expressing values and which influences which values come forward and what sort of conclusions can be reached on the basis of those values. Vatn (2005) defines a value-articulating institution as a 'constructed set of rules or typifications' which specifies the conditions under which values will be expressed, such as what type of data will be deemed relevant (e.g. environmental valuation considers only monetary bids as relevant data), who participates in valuation (similar concerns raised by feminist economics, Agarwal et al, 2005) and in what capacity (e.g. environmental valuation asks individuals to participate as consumers). He further explains that different value-articulating institutions 'tend to give different outcomes or preferred solutions', which implies that 'the choice of such institutions is certainly non-trivial' (Vatn, 2005, p211).

As a value-articulating institution, environmental valuation is not particularly inclusive of plural environmental values, given that values of some ecosystem services cannot be monetarized. However, as also discussed in Chapter 5, alternative value-articulating institutions such as multi-criteria evaluation and deliberative processes (e.g. citizen juries, etc.) try to reflect environmental values and motivational plurality (Table 4.1). These alternatives also attempt to consider the criticism of environmental valuation, namely that people may want to participate as citizens instead of consumers in environmental decision making (Sagoff, 1988).

Deliberative methods stem from an awareness of the need to acknowledge and legitimize plural values in public policy and decision making. Deliberative democracy scholars require that beyond other outcomes policy generates a public domain where reflection upon preferences is stimulated in a non-coercive manner, by means of information provision and deliberation (Dryzek, 2000). As deliberative democracy's aim to pursue such public spheres is in tune with environmental value plurality, deliberative forums (e.g. citizen juries) seem to provide a desirable model of a value-articulating institution. However, the potential of deliberative decision making has sceptics. For example, advocates of deliberative planning are reproached for paying 'insufficient attention to the practical context of power relations in which planning practice is situated'

Table 4.1 Value-articulating institutions and respective normative and epistemological stances

Value-articulating institution	Normative and epistemological stance
Contingent valuation method	Cartesianism: Value is pre-existing and needs to be discovered. Separation between values and facts, human and nature. Substitutability between money and ecosystem goods and services. Values are revealed.
Deliberative or social process methods	Democracy stance: Value is constructed in social processes. Previously unknown values evolve from deliberation and debate. Prioritizes each member of society to contribute to knowledge and judgement.
Multi-criteria methods	Complexity: Value understood in terms of ranked importance. Irreducible plurality of analytical perspectives.

Source: Modified from O'Connor et al (1998)

(McGuirk, 2001, p196). Likewise, others argue that 'a deliberative and democratic praxis of sustainability may be effective only if and when underpinned by substantive changes to the exercise of power and leadership' (Stratford and Jaskolski, 2004, p311). Similar concerns have been raised as regards biodiversity management through deliberative decision-making processes (O'Riordan, 2002).

Valuation scholars have attempted to integrate deliberative processes in environmental valuation by means of developing deliberative methods of environmental valuation (Sagoff, 1998). This practice can be seen as a response to criticisms of contingent valuation (CV); those criticisms postulate that environmental value is a group value and should not be sought as an aggregate of individual values. The practice also tries to take on board criticisms that environmental preferences do not exist ex-ante but are socially constructed (Vatn, 2005) and that values are sensitive to changes in issue framing and information brought to the attention of the public during the process of value elicitation (Slovic et al, 1990). Basically, deliberative valuation tries to turn the value elicitation process into a preference-constructing process in order to deal with the issue that people do not hold pre-determined preferences towards the environment and that such preferences should be well-informed and deliberatively derived (Zografos and Howarth, 2008). However, critics of deliberative environmental valuation point out that in practice it has been applied as a means for justifying stated preference methods by adding often superficial forms of deliberation or discussion, and that in essence the relevant studies establish that the economic model they use is unsuitable for understanding particular sets of social values as regards the environment (Spash, 2008).

2.3 Valuation as a feedback mechanism

Exercises of valuation can play an important role in calling attention to the value of biodiversity and to intangible ecosystem services vis-à-vis other forces competing for use of particular resources to the detriment of others. Although this requires some level of objective measurement and some imposition of a value system, it is also a way to confront the pressures of market forces which treat the environment as commodity. Further, valuation of ecosystem services can create incentives for land-use change, such as promoting what has been called an agro-ecological transition aiming at reconciling the value of production and environmental services (Mattos et al, 2009). While several parts of this chapter have called attention to the potential negative implications of economic valuation, its value as a decision-making and awareness mechanism to society are also clear. One can argue that in the long run this approach actually will lead to the internalization of the environment into western thinking and economics. In this context, valuation methods can serve as a mechanism to provide feedback in a system where production and consumption, trade and exchange are so distant and complex that they undermine perceptions of the impacts of habits and behaviour on the environment (Wilk, 2002; Moran, 2006). One can see these processes as a form of regulatory adaptation where behavioural responses within particular cultural and social contexts are taken progressively to cope with environmental changes perceived as detrimental (Moran, 2000). In this context, valuation can be seen as a feedback mechanism that confronts the problems of market demand for commodities and lack of accounting for externalities with the same tools and language, that is, values and costs. However, the processes that mediate perceptions of value and actions to conserve biodiversity and ecosystems carry a time lag between behavioural responses at the levels of the individual and whole populations, in which the actions of the former can be overwhelmed by the inactions of the latter. In this context, as other processes affecting society, the impact of valuation on behavioural changes are functions of cultural context (e.g. perceived notions of value, whether changes are culturally accepted), society and economics (e.g. degree of participation of the larger society, available institutional arrangements facilitating collective action) and the perceived environmental benefits (e.g. availability of resources or access to desirable landscapes) (Brondízio and Moran, 2008). Furthermore, adaptation to environmental change depends on forms of institutional arrangements that facilitate these activities within and across levels.

The socio-cultural construction of economic value is not static, but evolves in a processual way as behavioural actions respond (or not) to feedbacks. It co-evolves with changing perceptions of society's environmental reality (Norgaard, 1984, p165; 1987). This process of co-evolution is underpinned by a cognitive performance of mutual specification and co-determinism (Maturana and Varela, 1928; Varela, 1999): humans bring forth their own domain of (environmental) problems and solve them according to their ability to order interactions with nature. This process of ordering interactions between humans and nature is also facilitated by institutions, because 'institutions pattern lives' (Tool, 1986, p51). Therefore, ecosystems are degraded and biodiversity is lost, attitudes and values towards nature (must) change. The institutions according to which people pattern their lives will then change as a consequence, but the time lag may be long.

The values attached to ecosystems and biodiversity (or anything else) are not only determined by a constructed ethical environment and the respective institutions. They also depend on social emotions and feelings. The extinction of the blue whale might be deemed economically rational by some (Clark, 1973). Ethically and culturally, however, the extinction of blue whale would make many people feel incensed and react in extremely angry ways. Because of the complexity of the issue, those people may not be able to reason scientifically and logically why the blue whale should not be hunted until extinction; they could merely express their unease about it. Both stances employ their very own ethics: The economic stance is based on an ethics of individual rationality (which also defines 'good' and 'bad' decisions) and the 'ethical stance' is one that is based on some feeling of what is 'good' and 'bad'.

Damasio identifies feeling as the 'embryo of ethical behavior' and part of 'an overall program of bioregulation'. He defines feelings as homeostatic devices to keep the body–brain system in balance, just as institutions are rules to keep social and socio-ecological interactions in balance. Damasio says that ethical behaviour depends on the working of certain brain systems that are not exclusively dedicated to ethics but also to biological regulation, memory, decision making and creativity. On those grounds, the role of feelings can be tied to natural, life-monitoring functions:

> Ever since feelings began, their natural role would have been to keep the condition of life in mind and to make the condition of life count in the organization of behavior. Our life must be regulated not only by our own desires and feelings but also by our concern for the desires and feelings of others expressed as social conventions and rules of ethical behavior ... feelings remain essential to maintaining those goals, the cultural group considers unavoidable and worthy of perfecting. Feelings also are a necessary guide to the invention and negotiation of ways and means that somehow, will not clash with basic life regulation and distort the intention behind the goal. [They] remain as important today as when humans first discovered that killing other humans was a questionable action. (Damasio, 2003, p162)

Feelings are important for decision making to enable people to deal with the uncertainty inherent in all complex decision-making situations. Although abstract, they are located where communicative interactions, social rationality and complex system properties are taken into account; thus, as an important aspect of human behaviour, they remain a central component for valuation.

3 The challenges of valuation: Ecosystems, biodiversity and level of analysis

The scope of this section is to present, on the one hand, the main challenges of addressing various levels of analysis using valuation methodology and accounting, and, on the other hand, the required attention to complexity embedded in resource-use systems today. It is divided into three parts, each of which is built upon issues raised above.

3.1 The problem of transformative value and economic return of resource use

Indigenous and rural populations, although often considered stewards of biodiversity, share an unequal position, usually at the lower end, in larger commodity chains of resources. Around the world, the value of resources increases along the market chain usually far from their areas of origin, thus creating unequal distribution of benefits and weak incentives for conservation and management. As a resource moves from a state of raw material to various levels of industrial transformation, its economic values are increasingly attached to market symbols aimed at different groups of consumers (Brondízio, 2008). This is a classic situation for many valuable resources coming from tropical forests or aquatic systems around the world. On the one side, the producer of tropical forest fruits who manages standing forests receives the minimum price for a basket of fruit *in natura* while on the other side a consumer in the United States pays high prices for products which in some cases contain only traces of the same fruit, but which, in some cases, make bold, albeit unsupported, claims about health benefits and sustainable development. Thus, what parameters should be used to value specific resources? Which basis can we use to estimate the value of a resource as it changes in price as much as 70-fold along a commodity chain? If valuing biological resources is a tool to improve in-situ conservation, it assumes that local stakeholders have sufficient incentives to maintain a given ecosystem against other competing uses. The symbolic value embedded in resources as commodities mediates its economic value along a commodity chain (e.g. Appadurai, 1986; Haugerud et al, 2000; Brondízio, 2008). The economic value of forest resources, for instance, becomes dependent not only on their demand as raw material, but the level of industrial transformation and, most importantly, the symbolic meaning attached to their marketing symbols as end products to consumers. The pragmatic dimension of this discussion, as illustrated by the case of açaí palm fruit of the Amazon presented in Box 4.1 and Ethiopian wild coffee in Box 4.2, is the importance of aggregating value to resources locally as a form of creating incentives for local management vis-à-vis conversion to other uses because of market pressures. The Amazon illustrates well this tension. The combination of limited global availability of arable land, increased demand for vegetable (e.g. soy bean) and animal protein (e.g. beef), with government priority to export surplus, and the low value of forest resources at a regional level explains the majority of Amazonian deforestation during the past two decades.

Box 4.1 The boom açaí palm fruit in the Amazon

There is possibly no better example of an economic prospect for reconciling forest conservation and development in Amazonia than the case of the açaí fruit (*Euterpe oleracea* Mart.) production system (Brondízio, 2008). Emerging from the initiative of local producers to supply a growing market demand for açaí fruit, using locally developed technology and knowledge with respect to forest management, açaí fruit production embodies the social and environmental principles that permeate the discourse of sustainable development for the Amazon region. At the same time, the formation of this production system poses important questions concerning the spread and duration of benefits resulting from booming tropical forest economies. To what extent are production and market opportunities to value forest resources diminished by a history of socio-cultural prejudice, land-tenure insecurity, and differential access to economic incentives and markets? The expansion of the açaí fruit economy occurs as a combination of both endogenous and exogenous factors associated with the region as a whole, and in association with its consumption basis. These include rural out-migration and urban expansion since the 1970s, the organization and marketing strategies developed for the export of other Amazonian fruits during the 1980s, and the growth of the 'green products' industry during the 1990s. The growth of açaí fruit consumption is driven by various claims relating to its healthy and invigorating qualities, rainforest conservation, respect for indigenous causes and products, and its representation as an icon of the sustainable development agenda proposing alternative forms of land use in the Amazon. Açaí fruit's secure position at the regional level as a staple food favourite, as well as its expanding national and international markets, has transformed açaí fruit into a symbol of cultural identity and regional pride for Amazonian small farmers, particularly in the Amazon estuary. Today, it has been industrialized into a range of products of popular consumption, such as yogurts, concentrated juices, ice creams, energy beverages and vitamin pills, as well as products such as shampoos and soaps.

Overall, for most of the history of açaí economy producers have received better prices than the average price of most agricultural and husbandry products of the region. Analysing the evolution of prices, it becomes clear that açaí producers had an incentive to manage forests for açaí production. As a result, during the past 30 years, the Amazon estuary has experienced, contrary to elsewhere in the Amazon, a forest transition, that is, high rates of regrowth, increasing forest cover and minimum deforestation. Emerging from a local rural economy, the açaí fruit industry is now functioning as a complex multilevel economic structure. As part of this process, forest managers and producers of açaí fruit negotiate a position amid regional and international investors and companies, although suffering from the lack of infrastructure to commercialize their product and incentives to participate in value aggregation. This creates a paradoxical situation where the açaí fruit economy continues to grow in scale, but the proportion of revenues retained locally decreases. Although producers have been benefiting from the expansion of this market, they have been unable to participate in new sectors of the economy associated with the commercialization and control of fruit stock, its transformation and its value aggregation along the chain. Producers suffer from the stigma of extractivism and the invisibility of their intensive agroforestry management system (still widely referred as an extractivist system), a situation which continues to maintain them as suppliers of raw material (Brondízio and Siqueira, 1997). New entrepreneurs and large regional producers have come to occupy the most profitable niches of the market and assume greater control over production, commercialization, processing and marketing. Estimates of the current economic impact of the açaí fruit market in the region range from R$100 to 500 million/yr, but it is much larger depending on how, what, where and how far along the commodity chain one counts (Brondízio, 2008).

Most of this economy, however, aggregates value away from production areas. For instance, the value of açaí fruit pulp resulting from the harvest of one hectare of managed forest at the farmer's gate (i.e. fruit in nature) ranges from around US$1000 to US$1200. The same amount (in equivalent processed pulp) will increase 20- to 50-fold (depending on the end product) when reaching consumers in southern Brazil and up to 70-fold or more (depending on the end product) when reaching international consumers (Brondízio, 2008). Further, the increasing competition from new areas of production and corporate plantations seeking to control supply are leading, progressively, to increasingly monocultural systems (vis-à-vis forest management). The lack of transformation industries installed locally and accessible to producers that could help to aggregate value locally (to producers and municipalities) is progressively decreasing incentive for managing and maintaining diverse standing forests where small farmers manage several species vis-à-vis other land uses.

Box 4.2 Commodity and symbolic values for wild coffee from Ethiopian forests

Despite Ethiopia being the largest Coffea arabica producing and exporting country in Africa, 98 per cent of the national coffee production comes from smallholdings which are less than a hectare in size and 95 per cent of that coffee is produced in forest, semi-forest and garden systems. The commodity chain involves producers, cooperatives, exporters, importers, roasters, retailers and consumers. Coffee is bought and sold as a tradable commodity and the farm gate prices of coffee in Ethiopia are connected to price fluctuations on the New York Commodity Exchange. Although some specialty coffees, like wild forest coffee, are connected to retail prices, the largest price margins are still achieved between the roaster and the retailer and between the retailer and the consumer. Once the coffee has reached the consumer it is no longer just a commodity which is valued for its quality as raw material, and by the forces of supply and demand. It is now a lifestyle product for which consumers are willing to pay because it responds to their needs, wants, beliefs or convictions. Whereas in 2006/7 an Ethiopian farmer in Yayu received US$0.5–1(=0.4–0.8 Euro) per kg green wild forest coffee, when he delivered it to the cooperative, 1kg of packaged, roasted wild forest coffee is now sold for 38 Euro/kg. If a kg of coffee is sold in the form of 100 warm cups of coffee at 2–3 Euro/cup, its value has already increased to 200–300 Euro/kg.

On the other hand, although valuing biodiversity can be a tool for in-situ conservation, the increasing economic value of forest resources along the value chain can also be a disincentive for biodiversity conservation. Seyoum (2009) shows that higher incomes for households in Ethiopia close to coffee forest areas can be an incentive to intensify coffee management inside the forest and thereby reduce the wild coffee and forest diversity. However, the discussion of whether intensification of land use leads to deforestation is still poorly understood (Angelsen and Kaimowitz, 2001), in part because this relationship is mediated, on the one hand, by the role of markets and their distributive benefits (i.e. the degree of value aggregation at a local level), and on the other hand, by the effectiveness of institutions regulating use of resources. The two examples presented here illustrate well the problem of value aggregation and the counter-forces of intensification.

The recognition that value change along the commodity chain has implications for the distribution of benefits and affects the level of incentives for conservation represents an important methodological challenge for economic valuation. The inability of conservation and development programmes to create incentive systems to aggregate value locally (and thus employment in rural areas) represents a widespread problem not only for developed countries, but around the world. Initiatives such as certification and *terroir* recognition are expanding with diverse success in different parts of the world. In general, however, the lack of policy frameworks to promote local value aggregation and reduce distances between producers and consumers fuels an economic logic, whereas the market for monocultural plantation and/or cleared land is many-fold higher for the [valuable] resources of standing forests or the rich agrodiversity passed down through generations.

3.2 Complexity and functional interdependencies underlying valuations

Economic valuation is a complex, spatial and institutional cross-scale problem (Turner et al, 2003). As also pointed out in Chapter 5, Section 3, values of ecosystem goods and services differ with changing ecological features and with differing size and characteristics of groups of beneficiaries. Whereas recreational values of a site may be valued for its direct use at local scale by visitors to the site, high levels of biodiversity may be valued for option, bequest, existence and altruistic benefits at a global scale by the global community.

Many efforts focusing on particular parts of ecosystems or species, such as the creation of protected areas, while effective at one level, lack the scope to control the pressure of commodity markets for land resources surrounding them. As such, and depending on their biophysical context, they are limited to capturing the linkages and vertical interplay created by a growing functional interdependency of resource-use systems nested within larger ecosystems (Young, 2006; Brondízio et al, 2009). Increasingly common around the world, as described in the Introduction, 'islands of protected ecosystems' are nested within and affected by systems at higher or lower levels, and thus have substantial long-term limitations to guarantee conservation. Furthermore, they illustrate the importance of understanding the diversity of cultural perspectives to the environment. Take for instance the case of an indigenous group which values and has successfully protected forests within a given territory, an area/ecosystem which is, however, nested within a larger watershed (Brondizio et al, 2009). Assume the larger watershed is occupied by very different groups of people who have very different perspectives of the environment and who are closely responding to global markets for agricultural commodities. The result is that rampant deforestation outside reserves will systemically undermine the (protected) environment through water pollution, soil erosion and forest fire, including the possibility of reaching thresholds that may lead to unpredictable ecosystem changes. As the authors describe, recently arrived farmers may see the forest as a threat and the environment as sets of resources to be transformed. On the other hand, the environment as a whole is an intrinsic part of indigenous cosmology and an organic part of their economy. Indigenous groups carry detailed intergenerational knowledge about forest and water resources, cultural attachment to place, and customary rules of use and resource appropriation which tend to hinder members of the group from carrying out short-term and large-scale transformations that are characteristic of large (and small scale) corporative farmers aiming at seizing immediate opportunities on commodity markets. The authors stress that, 'we should build social capital that enhances the long-term sustainability of natural capital at multiple levels on scales of relevance to particular ecological resources'. In other words, it points to the role of institutions in facilitating cross-level environmental governance as an important form of social capital that is essential for the long-term protection of ecosystems and the well-being of different populations (pp258–259). This scenario illustrates the challenges of conservation and development in the Brazilian Amazon during the past two decades and currently. The creation of a record number of protected areas and indigenous reserves, today corresponding close to around 30 per cent of the region, happened concomitantly with the period of highest rates of deforestation ever observed. Increasingly, the region is observing the formation of 'islands' of forests and forest fragments (Carneiro Filho and Souza, 2009). This scenario represents the trend in many regions around the world and raises the issue of social and environmental interdependency and the limitations of valuation methods that may account for valuing resources at one level but neglect at other levels affecting its long-term sustainability.

The situation of vertical interplay of institutions (Young, 2006) representing groups competing or cooperating for authority over resources requires one to look at questions of subtractability (i.e. whether resource appropriation by one user reduces availability to others) and exclusion (i.e. how costly it is to keep potential beneficiaries out of the benefit stream) from a multiscale perspective (Brondízio et al, 2009; Ostrom, 2009). Local forms of use and regulation of a resource (e.g. based on customary rules of use and exclusion), while potentially effective at a local level, are affected and in some cases overwhelmed by resource use in a different part of the larger ecosystem. As called to attention by the MA, one of the biggest challenges of contemporary environmental governance is to promote conservation outside protected areas (Bhattacharya et al, 2005).

Along these lines, valuing resources and protecting an ecosystem requires attention to the value of connectivity at a landscape level. An overemphasis on conservation focused on carbon storage, for instance, with metrics based on stocks of carbon may downplay the role of connectivity of habitats, habitat and species diversity, or the water quality within a watershed. Interconnected social-ecological systems are dynamic, thus requiring constant monitoring and institutional adjustments, but most institutions and forms of incentives are designed to be applied at a given level. Görg (2007) calls attention to multilevel decision making as a pressing issue for environmental governance. He proposes the concept of landscape governance as an approach based on the notion of society relationship to nature to bridge what he calls the 'politics of scale' ('socially constructed spaces') and the biophysical interconnection between places. In this context, the challenge for valuation is to function as part of a larger process of co-evolution and adaptive management which stresses, on the one hand, the value of flows and connectivity within and between ecosystems, and on the other hand, facilitates the dissemination of knowledge and responses of institutions and social groups across levels.

3.3 How to choose how to value

One relevant question for decision makers is how to decide which valuation method is to be used to guide decisions. According to Arrow (1963) and Sen (1970b), the social choice problem is to make decisions for a society composed of a variety of members having non-identical interests and values.

Ostrom (1990), McGinnis (1999), Ostrom et al (1994), among others, have tried to answer the question of how to design institutions for the governance of complex resource regimes (such as water, forests or knowledge). Their proposed design principles for successful governance of common pool resources have proven very useful to policy making, particularly when applied to specific local-level situations. They were guided by a rule defined by Ashby (1952) 'Law of Requisite Variety'. This law says that any regulatory system needs as much variety in the actions it can take as exists in the system it is regulating. Ostrom and Parks (in McGinnis, 1999, p284) concluded: 'the more social scientists preach the need for simple solutions to complex problems, the more harm we can potentially cause in the world' (see also Ostrom, 2007, 2009).

There is today considerable evidence that putting a monetary value on an environmental change is a cognitively very demanding task for which people tend to use various simplified context-dependent choice rules, thereby implying that the responses are often difficult to interpret (Schkade and Payne, 1994; Vatn and Bromley, 1994) and psychologists like Kahneman and Tversky spent nearly 40 years trying to show that people have developed preferences for very few familiar good rules and for most circumstances employ various heuristic choice rules (Johansson-Stenman, 2002).

Making decisions in situations of high complexity and incomplete knowledge is characteristic for decision situations related to ecosystems and biodiversity. According to Ashby's law such situations require methods that are able to capture value plurality, ecosystem complexity and biodiversity. This would require a move from aggregating individual values to reasoning over a common set of priorities. Because '... to handle the common goods aspect social rationality and some form of communicative process must be taken in account. It is the only institutional structure that can be true to the choice problem at hand' (Vatn, 2005, p421). Strategies for the management of complex systems have been developed (Malik, 2008) (see Figure 4.1).

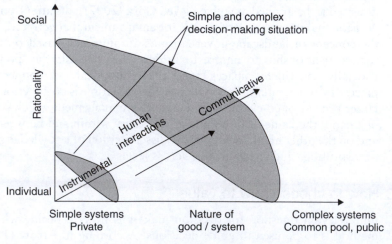

Figure 4.1 *Dimensions for choosing the valuation method*

Source: Adapted from Vatn (2005, p419)

Applied to the complex problem of biodiversity conservation, this would require matching the complexity of the problem situation with the organization of public engagement, which is (principally) able to capture as much variety (value plurality, types of rationality, etc.) as in the system it aims to conserve. Neglecting socio-ecological complexity (e.g. by limiting discussion to the rationality of economic humans and the market system) leads to increasing system vulnerability and increasing danger of system collapse. Applying valuation methods that apply simplified models of the complex systems being addressed by, for example, monetary valuation, would consequently not only be less useful, it would also reduce value plurality from the start.

O'Connor and Frame (2008) therefore suggest, 'that the logic of valuation [...] is: 1. make the proposition to sustain/conserve the forms of community or environmental features in question (e.g. avoid the production of toxic wastes, preserve a designated forest system or other feature of nature), and then, 2. investigate what commitments this does or might entail for – and on the interfaces between – the various communities of interest involved.' To engage methodologically with this hydra-like problem, O'Connor and Frame introduce a sequence of strong dialectical simplifications. First, they propose two main types of thresholds beyond which assessing trade-offs or the consequences of choices on the basis of monetary measures alone are of questionable pertinence. Either the estimation is scientifically very difficult, or the proposition of a 'trade-off' implied by the opportunity cost considerations is deemed morally inappropriate (Figure 4.2).

Recognizing the fact that valuation methods are 'value articulating institutions' and that the choice of a method can strongly influence the outcome of a valuation exercise and thereby actual behaviour, supports Atlee's (2003) argument that people are co-producers or 'co-creators' of institutional change: (global) environmental change is a collective process, the consequences of

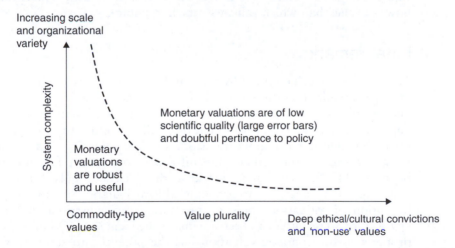

Figure 4.2 *With increasing system complexity and value plurality, monetary valuations become of low scientific quality and doubtful policy relevance*

Source: Redrawn from O'Connor and Frame (2008)

which individuals cannot comprehend in its entire range, depth and detail. Therefore, better ways are needed to perceive and reflect the state of the Earth and to facilitate integration of the individual diversity of perceptions and values. Atlee defines co-intelligence as a human capacity and ability to generate creative responses.

Therefore, the choice of value-articulating institution (= valuation method) will define the outcome of the valuation exercise. For instance:

- the private good side (instead of common pool and public features) of ecosystems and biodiversity;
- simple (instead of complex) systems;
- the individual and egoistic (instead of social) side of human behaviour and rationality; and
- the instrumental (instead of communicative) type of human interaction.

In other words, the choice of approach will bring forth values of a world as understood and seen by the eye of the beholder. That means, the way ecosystems and biodiversity are perceived determines the way they are valued, and the way they are valued determines the human interaction with, and (mis)use of, the natural environment. The decision situations with ecosystems and biodiversity are not simply a matter of value exclusion, meaning that some values of ecosystems and biodiversity have not been considered. The decision-making situation is about applying (what one thinks is) the right valuation frame of reference for the valuation of ecosystems and biodiversity. Valuing biodiversity, and the ecosystems to conserve it, requires more than attaching additional values to nature by appreciating its goods and services. The choice of the value-articulating institution becomes more important than valuing nature in order to prevent market failure. That is, one may assume that if markets do not fail, ecosystems and biodiversity will be conserved. We do not know that and we cannot know that for sure. Therefore one may argue that it is more important how we value than which value we attach to nature.

4 Final remarks

Trying to put a value on biodiversity and ecosystem services involves trade-offs. The broader literature on economic valuation recognizes these challenges and problems, and the multidimensional and contested nature of these approaches. The social sciences literature calls attention to some pitfalls and the potential long-term implications of economic valuation. Many challenges remain ahead; among others: the difficulty to account for inter-linkages between different ecosystem services, the lack of tools for cross-level valuation and mechanisms to promote value-articulating institutions, and the limitation of valuation tools to promote equity distribution and value aggregation to resources and ecosystems at the local level. On the other hand, properly used, economic valuation has the potential to serve as a tool of awareness and as a feedback mechanism for a society that has distanced itself from the resources it uses and from the impacts of its uses on distant ecosystems and people.

Economists know and have known all along (not just since the rise of ecological economics) that their value-articulating institutions are not all-inclusive. Therefore, valuation is essentially a matter of choosing how to perceive the human being itself, how to perceive human's place in nature, and how to perceive nature itself. This is because the way we perceive our natural environment determines the way we value and change it. One way of incorporating a multilayered understanding of human–environment relations and understanding the value and motivational linkages between the two is to address the large gap that exists between the language in which the preference of the people for ecosystem services is elicited and the language in which people feel more at home. The languages of research and policy show similar dissonance. The more the discourse moves away from the common lives and real life concerns to abstruse quantification and reductionism, the more people are likely to be confused and to give preferences that are, themselves, fudged and confused, merely because the choices we offer are far from adequate (Kumar and Kumar, 2008, p814). Valuation approaches aiming at addressing complex socio-ecological systems require attention to the challenge of understanding problems of credibility, saliency and legitimacy at the intersection of different knowledge systems, and access to information at different levels and by different groups (Cash et al, 2006). In this sense, valuation mechanisms should be seen as part of a broader range of diagnostic and assessment tools and political–institutional mechanisms that facilitate the understanding of complex socio-ecological systems (Ostrom, 2009), as well as coproduction, mediation, translation and negotiation of information and knowledge within and across levels (Cash et al, 2006; Brondízio et al, 2009). The main lesson that comes across when one reviews valuation literature is to avoid a 'one size fits all' approach, or as Ostrom (2007) puts it when proposing a framework for the analysis of complex social-ecological systems, we need to move beyond panaceas.

Economic valuation may contribute to address our inability, reluctance or ideological intolerance to adjust institutions (also those which are value articulating) to our knowledge of ecosystems, biodiversity and the human being. As such, it can contribute to more inclusive economic accounting and planning, and a more inclusive view of non-human beings. In other ways, however, it can also contribute to separating people and nature further apart by simplifying its meaning and value to human societies. In this balancing act, one hopes valuation approaches will not be taken as panaceas, but as tools which may contribute in the long run to internalize a respect for nature into western cosmology and social life.

Note

1   For all purposes, we use environment and nature as interchangeable terms, unless referring to their use by particular authors. For a comprehensive review of these terms, particularly the concept of nature, see the volume edited by Ellen and Fukui (1996) and, in particular, Ellen (1996).

Acknowledgements

We are thankful for the constructive comments and suggestions provided by Pushpam Kumar, Irene Ring, Jeffrey McNeely, Luciano Mattos, Roldan Muradian, Florian Eppink,

Erik Gómez-Baggethun, Unai Pascual, Jianchu Xu, Joan Martinez-Alier and Gopal K. Kadekodi. We are thankful for the support of the Laboratoire d'Anthropologie Sociale (Collège de France), the Department of Anthropology and the Anthropological Center for Training and Research on Global Environmental Change (ACT) at Indiana University-Bloomington, and the Center for Development Research (ZEF Bonn) at the University of Bonn.

References

Agarwal, B. Humphries, J. and Robeyns, I. (2005) *Amartya Sen's Work and Ideas: A Gender Perspective*, Routledge, New York

Alesina, A. and Ferrara, F. (2000) 'Participation in heterogeneous communities', *The Quarterly Journal of Economics*, vol 105, pp847–904

Angelsen, A. and Kaimowitz, D. (eds) (2001) *Agricultural Technologies and Tropical Deforestation*, CAB International, Wallingford

Appadurai, A. (ed) (1986) *The Social Life of Things: Commodities in Cultural Perspective*, Cambridge University Press, Cambridge

Arrow, K. (1963) *Individual Values and Social Choice*, 2nd edn, Wiley, New York

Arrow, K. (1982) 'Risk Perception in psychology and economics', *Economic Inquiry*, vol 20, no 1, pp1–9

Ashby, W. R. (1952) *Design For a Brain*, 1st edn, Chapman and Hall, London

Atlee, T. (2003) *The Tao of Democracy: Using Co-Intelligence to Create a World that Works for All*, The Writer's Collective, Cranston, RI

Bernoulli, D. (1954) 'Exposition of a new theory on the measurement of risk', *Econometrica*, vol 22, no 1, pp23–36 (Original work published 1738)

Bhattacharya, D. K., Brondízio, E. S., Spiemberg, M., Ghosh, A., Traverse, M., Castro, F., Morsello, C. and Siqueira, A. (2005) 'Cultural Services of Ecosystems', in Chopra, K. et al (eds) *Ecosystems and Human Well-Being: Policy Responses*, Findings of the Responses Working Group of the Millennium Ecosystem Assessment, Island Press, London, pp401–422

Bowles, S. and Gintis, H. (2004) 'The evolution of strong reciprocity', *Theoretical Population Biology*, vol 65, pp17–28

Brondízio, E. S. (2008) *The Amazonian Caboclo and the Açaí Palm: Forest Farmers in the Global Market*, New York Botanical Garden Press, New York

Brondízio, E. S. and Moran, E. F. (2008) 'Human dimensions of climate change: The vulnerability of small farmers in the Amazon', *Philosophical Transactions of the Royal Society*, vol 363, pp1803–1809

Brondízio, E. S. and Siqueira, A. D. (1997) 'From extractivists to forest farmers: Changing concepts of agricultural intensification and peasantry in the Amazon estuary', *Research in Economic Anthropology*, vol 18, pp233–279

Brondízio, E. S., Ostrom, E. and Young, O. (2009) 'Connectivity and the governance of multilevel socio-ecological systems: The role of social capital', *Annual Review of Environment and Resource*, vol 34, pp253–278

Bruntland, G. (ed) (1987) *Our Common Future: The World Commission on Environment and Development*, Oxford University Press, Oxford

Brush, S. and Stabinsky, D. (1997) *Valuing Local Knowledge: Indigenous People and Intellectual Property Rights*, Island Press, Washington, DC

Caldwell, L. K. (1990) *International Environmental Policy: Emergence and Dimensions*, 2nd edn, Duke University Press, Durham

Capra, F. (1991) *The Tao of Physics*, Shambhala, Boston, MA

Caporael, I. (1997) 'The evolution of truly social cognition: The core configurations model', *Personality and Social Cognition Review*, vol 1, pp276–298

Carneiro Filho, A. and Souza, O. B. (2009) *Atlas of Pressures and Threats to Indigenous Lands in the Brazilian Amazon*, Instituto SocioAmbiental, São Paulo

Cash, D. W., Adger, W. N., Berkes, F., Garden, P., Lebel L., Olsson, P., Pritchard, L. and Young, O. (2006), 'Scale and cross-scale dynamics: Governance and information in a multilevel world', *Ecology and Society*, vol 11, no 2, p8, www.ecologyandsociety.org/vol11/iss2/art8/

Chambers, R. (1991) 'Shortcut and Participatory Methods for Gaining Social Information for Projects', in Cernea, M. M. (ed) *Putting People First: Sociological Variables in Rural Development*, 2nd edn, pp515–537, Johns Hopkins University Press, Baltimore, MA

Clark, C. W. (1973) 'Profit maximization and the extinction of animal species', *Journal of Political Economy*, vol 81, no 4, pp950–961

Clayton, S. and Opotow, N. (eds) (2004) *Identity and the Natural Environment: The Psychological Significance of Nature*, The MIT Press, Cambridge, MA

Comaroff, J. and Comaroff, J. (2009) *Ethnicity, Inc.*, The University of Chicago Press, Chicago, IL

Cummings, R., Brookshire, D. and Schultze, W. (1986) *Valuing Environmental Goods: An Assesment of the Contingent Valuation Method*, Roman and Allenheld, Totowa, NJ

Damasio, A. (2003) *Looking for Spinoza: Joy, Sorrow and the Feeling Brain*, Harcourt, London

Descola, P. (1996) 'Constructing Natures: Symbolic Ecology and Social Practice', in Descola, P. and Palsson, G. (eds) *Nature and Society: Anthropological Perspectives*, Routledge, New York, pp81–102

Dove, M. (2006) 'Indigenous People and Environmental Politics', *Annual Review of Anthropology*, vol 35, pp191–208

Dryzek, J. (2000) *Deliberative Democracy and Beyond: Liberals, Critics and Contestations*, Oxford University Press, Oxford

Ellen, R. F. (1996) 'Introduction', in Ellen, R. F. and Fukui, K. (eds) *Redefining Nature: Ecology, Culture, and Domestication*, Berg, Oxford and Washington, DC

Ellen, R. F. and Fukui, K. (eds) (1996) *Redefining Nature: Ecology, Culture, and Domestication*, Berg, Oxford and Washington, DC

EPA (Environmental Protection Agency) (2009) *Valuing the Protection of Ecological Systems and Services*, a Report of the EPA Science Advisory Board, Washington, DC, EPA-SAB-09-012, May 2009, www.epa.gov/sab

Escobar, A. (1998) 'Whose knowledge, whose nature? Biodiversity, conservation, and the political ecology of social movements', *Journal of Political Ecology*, vol 5, pp53–82

Etzioni, A. (1986) 'The case for a multiple utility concept', *Economics and Philosophy*, vol 2, pp159–183

Fehr, E. and Tougareva, E. (1995) 'Do high stakes remove reciprocal fairness? Evidence from Russia', Working Paper, Department of Economics, University of Zürich

Frankfort, H. (1948) *Kingship and the Gods: A Study of Ancient Near-eastern Religion as the Integration of Society and Nature*, University of Chicago Press, Chicago

Gatzweiler, F. W. (2003) *The Changing Nature of Economic Value: Indigenous Forest Garden Values in Kalimantan, Indonesia*, Shaker, Aachen

Gatzweiler, F. W. (2008) 'Beyond economic efficiency in biodiversity conservation', *Journal of Interdisciplinary Economics*, vol 19, nos 2 and 3, pp215–238

Gintis, H. (2000) *Game Theory Evolving*, Princeton University Press, Princeton, NJ

Görg, C. (2007) 'Landscape governance: The "politics of scale" and the "natural" conditions of places', *Geoforum*, vol 38, no 5, pp954–966

Gowdy, J. (1998) *Limited Wants, Unlimited Means: A Reader on Hunter-Gatherer Economics and the Environment*, Island Press, Washington, DC

Gowdy, J. and Erickson, J. (2005) 'The approach of ecological economics', *Cambridge Journal of Economics*, vol 29, pp207–222

Gowdy, J., Iorgulescu, R. and Onyeiwu, S. (2003) 'Fairness and retaliation in a rural Nigerian village', *Journal of Economic Behavior & Organization*, vol 52, pp469–479

Greene, L. S. (2004) 'Indigenous people incorporated? Culture as politics, culture as property in pharmaceutical bioprospecting', *Current Anthropology*, vol 45, no 2, pp211–237

Güth, W. and Tietz, R. (1990) 'Ultimatum bargaining behavior: A survey and comparison of experimental results', *Journal of Economic Psychology*, vol 11, pp417–449

Hale, C. (2002) 'Does multiculturalism menace? Governance, cultural rights and the politics of identity in Guatemala', *Journal of Latin American Studies*, vol 34, pp485–524

Hames, R. (2007) 'The ecologically noble savage debate', *Annual Review of Anthropology*, vol 36, pp177–190

Hanemann, W. M. (1994) 'Valuing the environment through contingent valuation', *The Journal of Economic Perspectives*, vol 8, no 4, pp19–43

Haugerud, A., Stone, M. P. and Little, P. D. (eds) (2000) *Commodities and Globalization: Anthropological Perspectives*, Rowman & Littlefield, Lanham, MD

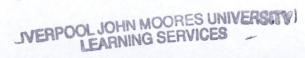

Hayden, C. (2003) *When Nature Goes Public: The Making and Unmaking of Bioprospecting in Mexico*, Princeton University Press, Princeton and Oxford

Heisenberg, W. (1958) *Physics and Philosophy*, Harper, New York

Henrich, J., Boyd, R., Bowles, S., Camerer, C., Fehr, E., Gintis, H. and McElreath, R. (2001) 'In search of *Homo economicus*: Behavioral experiments in 15 small-scale societies', *The American Economic Review*, vol 91, no 2, pp73–78

Hornborg, A., McNeill, J. and Martinez-Alier, J. (2007) *Rethinking Environmental History: World-System History and Global Environmental Change*, Altamira Press, Lanham, MD

Howarth, R. and Farber, S. (2000) 'Accounting for the value of ecosystem services', *Ecological Economics*, vol 41, pp421–429

Jacobs, M. (1997) 'Environmental valuation, deliberative democracy, and public decision-making', in J. Foster (ed) *Valuing Nature ? Economics, Ethics and Environment*, Routledge, London, pp211–231

Jarvis, D. I., Padoch, C. and Cooper, H. D. (2007) *Managing Biodiversity in Agricultural Ecosystems*, Columbia University Press/Bioversity International, New York

Johansson-Stenman, O. (2002) 'What to Do With Inconsistent, Non-welfaristic, and Undeveloped Preferences?', in Bromley, D. W. and Paavola, J. (eds) *Economics, Ethics and Environmental Policy: Contested Choices*, Wiley Blackwell, Oxford

Kahneman, D. (2000) 'Evaluation by Moments: Past and Future', in Kahneman, D. and Tversky, A. (eds) *Choices, Values, and Frames*, Cambridge University Press, New York, pp 693–708

Kahneman, D. (2003) 'Maps of bounded rationality: Psychology for behavioral economics', *The American Economic Review*, vol 93, no 5, pp1449–1475

Kellert, S. R. (1996) *The Value of Life: Biological Diversity and Human Society*, Island Press/Shearwater Books, Washington, DC

Kellert, S. R. and Wilson, E. O. (eds) (1993) *The Biophilia Hypothesis*, Island Press, Washington, DC

King, P. N., Levy, M. A., Varughese, G. C., Al-Ajmi, A., Brzovic, F., Castro-Herrera, G., Clark, B., Diaz-Lara, E., Kamal Gueye, M., Jacob, K., Jalala, S., Mori, H., Rensvik, H., Ullsten, O., Wall, C., Guang Xia, Ambala, C., Anderson, B., Barr, J., Baste, I., Brondízio, E., Chenje, M., Chernyak, M., Clements-Hunt, P., Dankelman, I., Draggan, S., Kameri-Mbote, P., Karlsson, S., Lagos, C., Mehta, V., Narain, V., Peters, H., Salem, O., Rabesahala, V., Rumbaitis del Rio, C., Sabet, M., Simpson, J. and Stanners, D. (2007) 'From the Periphery to the Core of Decision Making: Options for Action', *Global Environmental Outlook 4* (GEO-4), United Nations Environmental Programme, Nairobi, pp455–496

Kohler, F. (2008) 'Effets collatéraux des programmes de conservation sur le littoral brésilien', *Etudes Rurales*, janvier–juin, vol 181, pp75–88

Kumar, M. and Kumar, P. (2008) 'Valuation of ecosystem services: A psychocultural perspective', *Ecological Economics*, vol 64, pp808–819

Lewin, S. (1996) 'Economics and psychology: Lessons for our own day from the early twentieth century', *Journal of Economic Literature*, vol 34, pp1293–1323

Malik, F. (2008) *Strategie des Managements komplexer Systeme: Ein Beitrag zur Management Kybernetik evolutionärer Systeme*, Haupt Verlag, Bern

Manski, C. F. (2000) 'Economic analysis of social interactions', *Journal of Economic Perspectives*, vol 14, pp115–136

Martinez-Alier, J. (2008) 'Social metabolism, ecological distribution conflicts and languages of valuation', opening lecture at Conference on 'Common Ground, Converging Gazes: Integrating the Social and Environmental in History', EHEES, Paris, 11–13 September

Martinez-Alier, J. and Thrupp. L. A. (1992) 'Review of "Ecologia y capital: Hacia una perspectiva ambiental del desarrollo", by Enrique Leff', *Latin American Perspectives*, vol 19, no 1, pp148–152

Mattos, L., Romeiro, A. R. and Hercowit, M. (2009) 'Economia do meio ambiente', in Mattos, L. and Hercowitz, M. (org) *Parte I – Economia do meio ambiente e serviços ambientais no contexto de populações tradicionais e povos indígenas*. Capítulo 3, in Novion, H. and Valle, R. (eds) *É pagando que se preserva? Subsídios para políticas de compensação por serviços ambientais*, Documentos ISA, No 10

Maturana, H. and Varela, F. J. (1928) *Autopoeiesis and Cognition*, New Holland, Dordrecht

McCormick, J. (1989) *Reclaiming Paradise: The Global Environmental Movement*, Indiana University Press, Bloomington, IN

McGinnis, M. (1999) 'Polycentricity and Local Public Economies', Readings from the Workshop in Political Theory and Policy Analysis, University of Michigan Press, Ann Arbor, MI

McGuirk, P. M. (2001) 'Situating communicative planning theory: Context, power, and knowledge', *Environment and Planning A*, vol 33, pp195–217

Millennium Ecosystem Assessment (MA) (2005) *Ecosystems and Human Well-being: Synthesis*, Island Press, Washington, DC

Mitchell, R. and Carson, R. (1989) *Using Surveys to Value Public Goods: The Contingent Valuation Method*, Resources for the Future, Washington, DC

Moran, E. F. (2000) *Human Adaptability*, 2nd edn, Westview Press, Boulder, CO

Moran, E. F. (2006) *People and Nature: An Introduction to Human Ecological Relations*, Blackwell Publishers, Cambridge

Moran, K., King, S. R. and Carlson, T. (2001) 'Biodiversity prospecting: Lessons and prospects', *Annual Review of Anthropology*, vol 30, pp505–526

Muramatsu, M. (2009) 'The death and resurrection of "economics with psychology": Remarks from a methodological standpoint', *Brazilian Journal of Political Economy*, vol 29, no 1 (113), pp62–81

Nazarea, N. (1998) *Cultural Memory and Biodiversity*, The University of Arizona Press, Tucson, AZ

Nazarea, V. (2006) 'Local knowledge and memory in biodiversity conservation', *Annual Review of Anthropology*, vol 35, pp317–335

NERC (Natural Environment Research Council) (2009) *Valuation of Biodiversity: A NERC Scoping Study*, Final Report, Natural Environment Research Council, UK

Norgaard, R. B. (1984) 'Co-evolutionary development potential', *Land Economics*, vol 60, pp160–173

Norgaard, R. B. (1987) 'Economics as mechanics and the demise of biological diversity', *Ecological Modeling*, vol 38, pp107–121

Nowak, M. A., Page, K. M. and Sigmund, K. (2000) 'Fairness versus reason in the ultimatum game', *Science*, vol 289, pp1773–1775

Nussbaum, M. C. (2001) *Women and Human Development: A Capabilities Approach*, Cambridge University Press, Cambridge

O'Connor, M. (2000) 'The VALSE project: An introduction', *Ecological Economics*, vol 34, pp165–174

O'Connor, M. and Frame, B. (2008) *In a Wilderness of Mirrors: Complexity, Confounded Meta-narratives and Sustainability Assessment. Centre d'Economie et d'Ethique pour l'Environnement et le Développement* (C3ED), Cahiers du C3ED, France

O'Connor, M., Funtowicz, S., Aguiler-Klink, F., Spash, C. L. and Holland, A. (1998) *Valuation for Sustainable Environments*, The VALSE Project Full Final Report, Ispra: European Commission, Joint Research Centre

OECD (2002) *Handbook of Biodiversity Valuation: A Guide for Policy Makers*, Organisation for Economic Co-operation and Development, Paris

O'Riordan, T. (ed) (2002) *Biodiversity, Sustainability and Human Communities: Protecting Beyond the Protected*, Cambridge University Press, Cambridge

Ostrom, E. (1990) *Governing the Commons*, Cambridge University Press, Cambridge

Ostrom, E. (2007) 'A diagnostic approach for going beyond panaceas', *PNAS*, vol 104, pp15181–15187

Ostrom, E. (2009) 'A general framework for analyzing sustainability of social-ecological systems', *Science*, vol 325, pp419–422

Ostrom, E., Gardner, R. and Walker, J. (1994) *Rules, Games, and Common Pool Resources*, The University of Michigan Press, Ann Arbor, MI

Palsson, G. (1996) 'Human–Environmental Relations: Orientalism, Paternalism and Communalism', in Descola, P. and Palsson, G. (eds) *Nature and Society: Anthropological Perspectives*, Routledge, New York, pp65–81

Pedrosa, R. P. F. and Brondízio, E. S. (2008) 'The risks of commodifying poverty: Rural communities, Quilombola identity, and nature conservation in Brazil', *Habitus Pedrosa and Brondizio Habitus*, vol 5, no 2, pp355–373

Pinedo-Vasquez, M., Pasquale, J. B., Del Castillo Torres, D. and Coffey, K. (2002) 'A tradition of change: The dynamic relationship between biodiversity and society in sector Muyuy, Peru', *Environmental Science and Policy*, vol 5, pp43–53

Polyani, K. (1944) *The Great Transformation*, Beacon, Boston, MA

Reid, W. V., Laird, S. A., Meyer, C. A., Gamez, R., Sittenfield, A., Janzen, D., Gollin, M. A. and Juma, C. (1993) *Biodiversity Prospecting: Using Genetic Resources for Sustainable Development*, World Resources Institute, Washington, DC

Roughgarden, J. (2004) *Evolution's Rainbow: Diversity, Gender and Sexuality in Nature and People*, University of California, Los Angeles, CA

Sagoff, M. (1988) *The Economy of the Earth*, Cambridge University Press, Cambridge

Sagoff, M. (1998) 'Aggregation and deliberation in valuing environmental public goods: A look beyond contingent pricing', *Ecological Economics*, vol 24, nos 2–3, pp213–230

Sahlins, M. (1996) 'The native anthropology of western cosmology', *Current Anthropology*, vol 37, no 3, pp395–428

Schkade, D. A. and Payne, J. W. (1994) 'How people respond to contingent valuation questions: A verbal protocol analysis of willingness to pay for an environmental regulation', *Journal of Environmental Economics and Management*, vol 26, pp88–109

Sen, A. K. (1970a) *Collective Choice and Social Welfare*, Holden-Day, San Francisco

Sen, A. K. (1970b) 'The impossibility of a Paretian liberal', *Journal of Political Economy*, vol 78, pp152–157

Sen, A. K. (1973) 'Behaviour and the concept of preference', *Economica*, vol 40, no 159, pp241–259

Sen, A. K. (1979) 'Issues in the measurement of poverty', *Scandinavian Journal of Economics*, vol 81, no 2, pp285–307

Seyoum, A. (2009) 'Microeconomics of wild coffee genetic resources conservation in Southwestern Ethiopia', PhD Thesis, Division of Resource Economics, Department of Agricultural Economics, Humboldt University of Berlin, Germany

Shmelev, S. E. (2008) *Multicriteria Analysis of Biodiversity Compensation Schemes: Review of Theory and Practice with a Focus on Integrating Socioeconomic and Ecological Information*, Environment Europe, UK

Slovic, P., Kraus, N. and Covello, V. (1990) 'What should we know about making risk comparisons?', *Risk Analysis*, vol 10, pp389–392

Spash, C. L. (2008) 'Deliberative monetary valuation (DMV) and evidence for a new theory of value', *Land Economics*, vol 84, no 3, pp469–488

Stratford, E. and Jaskolski, M. (2004) 'In pursuit of sustainability? Challenges for deliberative democracy in a Tasmanian local government', *Environment and Planning B*, vol 31, pp311–324

Tool, M. R. (1986) *Essays in Social Value Theory: A Neoclassical Contribution*, Armonk, New York

Turner, R. K., Paavola, J., Cooper, P., Farber, S., Jessamy, V. and Georgiou, S. (2003) 'Valuing nature: Lessons learned and future research directions', *Ecological Economics*, vol 46, pp493–510

UNEP (2007) *Global Environmental Outlook 4 (GEO-4)*, United Nations Environmental Programme, Nairobi

Varela, F. J. (1999) *Ethical Know-how: Action, Wisdom, and Cognition*, Stanford University Press, Stanford, CA

Vatn, A. (2005) *Institutions and the Environment*, Edward Elgar, Cheltenham

Vatn, A. and Bromley, D. (1994) 'Choices without prices without apologies', *Journal of Environmental Economics and Management*, vol 26, pp129–148

West, P., Igoe, J. and Brockington, D. (2006) 'Parks and peoples: The social impact of protected areas', *Annual Review of Anthropology*, vol 25, pp251–277

Wilk, R. (1993) 'Towards a Unified Anthropological Theory of Decision Making', in Barry, I. (ed) *Research in Economic Anthropology*, JAI Press, Greenwich, CT, pp191–212

Wilk, R. (2002) 'Consumption, human needs, and global environmental change', *Global Environmental Change*, vol 12, no 1, pp5–13

Wilk, R. and Cliggett, L. (2006) *Economies and Cultures: Foundations of Economic Anthropology*, 2nd edn, Westview Press, Boulder, CO

Wilson, E. O. (1984) *Biophilia*, Harvard University Press, Cambridge, MA

Young, O. R. (2006) 'Vertical interplay among scale-dependent environmental and resource regimes', *Ecology and Society*, vol 11, no 1, p27, available at www.ecologyandsociety.org/vol11/iss1/art27/

Zavestoski, S. (2004) 'Constructing and Maintaining Ecological Identities: The Strategies of Deep Ecologists', in Clayton, S. and Opotow, S. (eds) *Identity and the Natural Environment: The Psychological Significance of Nature*, The MIT Press, Cambridge, MA, pp297–316

Zimmerer, K. S. (ed) (2006) *Globalization and New Geographies of Conservation*, University of Chicago Press, Chicago, IL

Zografos, C. and Howarth, R. B. (eds) (2008) *Deliberative Ecological Economics*, Oxford University Press, Oxford

Zografos, C. and Paavola, J. (2008) 'Critical Perspectives on Human Action and Deliberative Ecological Economics', in Zografos, C. and Howarth, R. B. (eds) *Deliberative Ecological Economics*, Oxford University Press, Delhi, pp146–166

Chapter 5
The Economics of Valuing Ecosystem Services and Biodiversity

Coordinating lead authors
Unai Pascual, Roldan Muradian

Lead authors
Luke Brander, Erik Gómez-Baggethun, Berta Martín-López, Madhu Verma

Contributing authors
Paul Armsworth, Michael Christie, Hans Cornelissen, Florian Eppink, Joshua Farley, John Loomis, Leonie Pearson, Charles Perrings, Stephen Polasky

Reviewers
Jeffrey A. McNeely, Richard Norgaard, Rehana Siddiqui, R. David Simpson, R. Kerry Turner

Review editor
R. David Simpson

Contents

Key messages   186

1   Introduction   187

2   Economic valuation of ecosystem services   189
    2.1   Why valuation?   190
    2.2   Valuation paradigms   191
    2.3   The TEV framework and value types   192

3   Valuation methods, welfare measures and uncertainty   196
    3.1   Valuation methods under the TEV approach   196
          3.1.1   Direct market valuation approaches   197
          3.1.2   Revealed preference approaches   199
          3.1.3   Stated preference approaches   200
          3.1.4   Choosing and applying valuation methods: Forests and wetlands   206
    3.2   Acknowledging uncertainty in valuation   212
          3.2.1   Supply uncertainty   212
          3.2.2   Preference uncertainty   214
          3.2.3   Technical uncertainty   216
          3.2.4   Data enrichment models as the way forward   217

4   Insurance value, resilience and (quasi-)option value   218
    4.1   What is the value of ecosystem resilience?   221
    4.2   Main challenges of valuing ecosystem resilience   222
    4.3   Dealing with (quasi-)option value   224

5   Valuation across stakeholders and applying valuation in developing countries   225
    5.1   Valuation across stakeholders   225
    5.2   Applying monetary valuation in developing countries   227

6   Benefit transfer and scaling up values   229
    6.1   Benefit transfer as a method to value ecosystem services   229
    6.2   Challenges in benefit transfer for ecosystem services at individual
          ecosystem sites   231
          6.2.1   Transfer errors   231
          6.2.2   Aggregation of transferred values   232
          6.2.3   Challenges related to spatial scale   232
          6.2.4   Variation in values with ecosystem characteristics and context   233
          6.2.5   Non-constant marginal values   234
          6.2.6   Distance decay and spatial discounting   235
          6.2.7   Equity weighting   236
          6.2.8   Availability of primary estimates for ecosystem service values   236
    6.3   Scaling-up the values of ecosystem services   237

7   Conclusions   239

References   244

Annex 1 Applied sources for technical support on biodiversity valuation
     for national agency teams   256

Key messages

- In the Total Economic Value (TEV) framework, ecosystems may generate output values (the values generated in the current state of the ecosystem, for example food production, climate regulation and recreational value) as well as insurance values. The latter, closely related to 'option value', is the value of ensuring that there is no regime shift in the ecosystem with irreversible negative consequences for human well-being. Even if an ecosystem or some component of it currently generates no output value, its option value may still be significant.

- Estimating the value of the various services and benefits that ecosystems and biodiversity generate may be done with a variety of valuation approaches. All of these have their advantages and disadvantages. Hybridizing approaches may overcome disadvantages of particular valuation methods.

- Valuation techniques in general and stated preference methods specifically are affected by uncertainty, stemming from gaps in knowledge about ecosystem dynamics, human preferences and technical issues in the valuation process. There is a need to include uncertainty issues in valuation studies and to acknowledge the limitations of valuation techniques in situations of radical uncertainty or ignorance about ecosystem dynamics.

- Valuation results will be heavily dependent on social, cultural and economic contexts, the boundaries of which may not overlap with the delineation of the relevant ecological system. Better valuation can be achieved by identifying and involving relevant stakeholders.

- Despite the difficulties of transferring valuation approaches and results between world regions, Benefits Transfer can be a practical, swift and cheaper way to get an estimate of the value of local ecosystem services, particularly in the context of a large number of diverse ecosystems. Values will vary with the characteristics of the ecosystem and the beneficiaries of the services it provides. Correcting values accordingly is advised when there are significant differences between the sites where the primary values are taken from and the sites to which values are to be transferred. Transfer errors are unavoidable and if highly precise estimates are needed, primary valuation studies should be commissioned.

- Monetary valuation can provide useful information about changes to welfare that will result from ecosystem management actions, but valuation techniques have limitations that are as yet unresolved. Valuation practitioners should present their results as such, and policy makers should interpret and use valuation data accordingly.

- The limitations of monetary valuation are especially important as ecosystems approach critical thresholds and ecosystem change is irreversible or reversible only at prohibitive cost. Under conditions of high or radical uncertainty and existence of ecological thresholds, policy should be guided by the 'safe-minimum-standard' and 'precautionary approach' principles.

1 Introduction

Economics, as the study of how to allocate limited resources, relies on valuation to provide society with information about the relative level of resource scarcity. The value of ecosystem services and biodiversity is a reflection of what we, as a society, are willing to trade off to conserve these natural resources. Economic valuation of ecosystem services and biodiversity can make explicit to society in general and policy making in particular that biodiversity and ecosystem services are scarce and that their depreciation or degradation has associated costs to society. If these costs are not imputed, then policy would be misguided and society would be worse off due to misallocation of resources.

Economically speaking, an asset is scarce if its use carries opportunity costs. That is, in order to obtain one additional unit of the good one must give up a certain amount of something else. In economic terms, quantifying and valuing ecosystem services are no different from quantifying and valuing goods or services produced by humans. In practice, however, valuing ecosystem services is problematic. There are reasonable estimates of the value of many provisioning services – in cases where well-developed markets exist – but there are few reliable estimates of the value of most non-marketed cultural and regulating services (Carpenter et al, 2006; Barbier et al, 2009). The problem is that since most ecosystem services and biodiversity are public goods, they tend to be overconsumed by society.

From an economic point of view, biodiversity (and ecosystems) can broadly be seen as part of our natural capital, and the flow of ecosystem services is the 'interest' on that capital that society receives (Costanza and Daly, 1992). Just as private investors choose a portfolio of capital to manage risky returns, we need to choose a level of biodiversity and natural capital that maintains future flows of ecosystem services in order to ensure enduring environmental quality and human well-being, including poverty alleviation (Perrings et al, 2006).

The basic assumption underlying the present chapter is that society can assign values to ecosystem services and biodiversity only to the extent that these fulfil needs or confer satisfaction to humans either directly or indirectly (although different forms of utilitarianism exist; see Goulder and Kennedy, 1997). This approach to valuing ecosystem services is based on the intensity of changes in people's preferences under small or marginal changes in the quantity or quality of goods or services. The economic conception of value is thus anthropocentric and for the most part instrumental in nature, in the sense that these values provide information that can guide policy making. This valuation approach, as discussed in Chapter 4, should be used to complement, but not to substitute for, other legitimate ethical or scientific reasoning and arguments relating to biodiversity conservation (see Turner and Daily, 2008).

Valuation plays an important role in creating markets for the conservation of biodiversity and ecosystem services, for instance through Payments for Ecosystem Services (Engel et al, 2008; Pascual et al, 2010). Such market creation process requires three main stages: demonstration of values, appropriation of values and sharing the benefits from conservation (Kontoleon and Pascual, 2007). Demonstration refers to the identification and measurement of the flow of ecosystem services and their values (see also Chapters 2 and 3).

Appropriation is the process of capturing some or all of the demonstrated and measured values of ecosystem services so as to provide incentives for their sustainable provision. This stage in essence 'internalizes', through market systems, demonstrated values of ecosystem services so that those values affect biodiversity resource use decisions. Internalization is achieved by *correcting* markets when they are 'incomplete' and/or *creating* markets when they are altogether missing. In the benefit-sharing phase, appropriation mechanisms must be designed in such a manner that the captured ecosystem services benefits are distributed to those who bear the costs of conservation.

The concept of *total economic value* (TEV) of ecosystems and biodiversity is used thoughout this chapter. It is defined as the sum of the values of all service flows that natural capital generates both now and in the future – appropriately discounted. These service flows are valued for marginal changes in their provision. TEV encompasses all components of (dis)utility derived from ecosystem services using a common unit of account: money or any market-based unit of measurement that allows comparisons of the benefits of various goods. Since in many societies people are already familiar with money as a unit of account, expressing relative preferences in terms of money values may give useful information to policy makers.

This chapter reviews the variety of taxonomies and classifications of the components of TEV and valuation tools that can be used to estimate such components for different types of ecosystem services. Given the complex nature of ecosystem services, economic valuation faces important challenges, including the existence of ecological thresholds and non-linearities, how to incorporate the notion of resilience of socio-ecological systems, the effects of uncertainty and scaling up estimated values of ecosystem services. This chapter reviews these challenges and from best practice provides guidelines for dealing with them when valuing ecosystems, ecosystem services and biodiversity.

An important note that should be kept in mind when reading this chapter is that while it follows the previous chapters in its conceptual approach to ecosystem services (see Chapters 1 and 2), it also acknowledges that ecologists have multiple ways of framing and understanding ecosystems and that only some of these are compatible with a stock-flow model, or capital and interest analogy, of economics as it is presented here.

The chapter is structured as follows: Section 2 starts by asking the basic question of why we need to value ecosystem services and what types of values may be estimated that can have an effect in environmental decision making, following the TEV approach.

In Section 3, we look critically at the main methods used to estimate the various components of the TEV of ecosystem services and biodiversity. A summary and a brief description of each of these methods is provided, as well as a discussion of the appropriateness of using certain methods to value particular ecosystem services. We also address various types of uncertainty inherent to valuation techniques.

Section 4 considers the insurance value of ecosystems by discussing related concepts such as resilience, option, quasi-option, and insurance value of biodiversity. Valuation results will vary along social, cultural and economic gradients and institutional scales will rarely correspond to the spatial scale of the relevant ecosystem and its services. Section 5 addresses these topics by covering stakeholder involvement, participatory valuation methods and the particular challenges of performing valuation studies in developing countries.

In Section 6, we turn to benefits transfer, a widely used technique to estimate values when doing primary studies is too costly in time or money. This section will present existing techniques for doing benefits transfer and discuss modifications needed to address problems that may arise when applying it across differing ecological, social and economic contexts. Section 7 concludes and reflects on the role of using value estimates to inform ecosystem policy.

2 Economic valuation of ecosystem services

It is difficult to agree on a philosophical basis for comparing the relative weights of intrinsic and instrumental values of nature. Box 5.1 presents briefly some of the main positions in this debate. Notwithstanding alternative views on valuation as discussed in Chapter 4, this chapter sets the background and methods of economic valuation from the utilitarian perspective. Economic value refers to the value of an asset, which lies in its role in attaining human goals, be it spiritual enlightenment, aesthetic pleasure or the production of some marketed commodity (Barbier et al, 2009). Rather than being an inherent property of an asset such as a natural resource, value is attributed by economic agents through their willingness to pay for the services that flow from the asset. While this may be determined by the objective (e.g. physical or ecological) properties of the asset, the willingness to pay depends greatly on the socio-economic context in which valuation takes place – on human preferences, institutions, culture and so on (Pearce, 1993; Barbier et al, 2009).

Box 5.1 The intrinsic *versus* instrumental values controversy

Ethical and aesthetic values have so far constituted the core of the rationale behind modern environmentalism, and the recent incorporation of utilitarian arguments has opened an intense debate in the conservation community. Whereas ecologists have generally advocated biocentric perspectives based on intrinsic ecological values, economists adopt anthropocentric perspectives that focus on instrumental values. A main issue in this debate is the degree of complementarity or substitutability of these two different approaches when deciding on the conservation of biodiversity and ecosystem services. Some authors consider these two rationales to be complementary and see no conflict in their simultaneous use (e.g. Costanza, 2006). Others argue that adopting a utilitarian perspective may induce societal changes that could result in an instrumental conception of the human–nature relationship based increasingly on cost–benefit rationales (McCauley, 2006). Findings from behavioural experiments suggest that whereas some complementarity is possible, economic incentives may also undermine moral motivations for conservation (Bowles, 2008).

2.1 Why valuation?

One overarching question is why we need to value ecosystem services and biodiversity. Economics is about choice and every decision is preceded by a weighing of values among different alternatives (Bingham et al, 1995). Ecological life-support systems underpin a wide variety of ecosystem services that are essential for economic performance and human well-being. Current markets, however, only shed information about the value of a small subset of ecosystem processes and components that are priced and incorporated in transactions as commodities or services. This poses structural limitations on the ability of markets to provide comprehensive pictures of the ecological values involved in decision processes (MA, 2005). Moreover, an information failure arises from the difficulty of quantifying most ecosystem services in terms that are comparable with services from human-made assets (Costanza et al, 1997). From this perspective, the logic behind ecosystem valuation is to unravel the complexities of socio-ecological relationships, make explicit how human decisions would affect ecosystem service values, and to express these value changes in units (e.g. monetary) that allow for their incorporation in public decision-making processes (Mooney et al, 2005).

Economic decision making should be based on understanding the changes to economic welfare from small or marginal changes to ecosystems due to, for example, the logging of trees in a forest or the restoration of a polluted pond (Turner et al, 2003). Value thus is a *marginal* concept insofar that it refers to the impact of small changes in the state of the world, and not the state of the world itself. In this regard, the value of ecological assets, like the value of other assets, is individual-based and subjective, context-dependent, and state-dependent (Goulder and Kennedy, 1997; Nunes and van den Bergh, 2001). Estimates of economic value thus reflect only the current choice pattern of all human-made, financial and natural resources given a multitude of socio-ecological conditions such as preferences, the distribution of income and wealth, the state of the natural environment, production technologies, and expectations about the future (Barbier et al, 2009). A change in any of these variables affects the estimated economic value.

In summary, there are at least six reasons for conducting valuation studies:

- missing markets;
- imperfect markets and market failures;
- for some biodiversity goods and services, it is essential to understand and appreciate its alternatives and alternative uses;
- uncertainty involving demand and supply of natural resources, especially in the future;
- Governments may like to use valuation rather than restricted, administered or operating market prices for designing biodiversity/ecosystem conservation programmes;
- in order to arrive at natural resource accounting, for methods such as Net Present Value methods, valuation is a must.

2.2 Valuation paradigms

Since there are multiple theories of value, valuation exercises should ideally: (i) acknowledge the existence of alternative, often conflicting, valuation paradigms; and (ii) be explicit about the valuation paradigm that is being used and its assumptions. A review on the approaches to valuation makes it possible to identify two well-differentiated paradigms for valuation: *biophysical* methods, constituted by a variety of biophysical approaches, and *preference-based* methods, which are more commonly used in economics. These methods are summarized in Figure 5.1.

Biophysical valuation uses a 'cost of production' perspective that derives values from measurements of the physical costs (e.g. in terms of labour, surface requirements, energy or material inputs) of producing a given good or service. In valuing ecosystem services and biodiversity, this approach would consider the physical costs of maintaining a given ecological state. Box 5.2 provides a short discussion about biophysical approaches to valuation and accounting as an alternative to the dominant preference-based methods.

In contrast to biophysical approaches to valuation, preference-based methods rely on models of human behaviour and rest on the assumption that values arise from the subjective preferences of individuals. This perspective assumes that ecosystem values are commensurable in monetary terms, among themselves as well as with human-made and financial resources, and that subsequently, monetary measures offer a way of establishing the trade-offs involved in alternative uses of ecosystems.

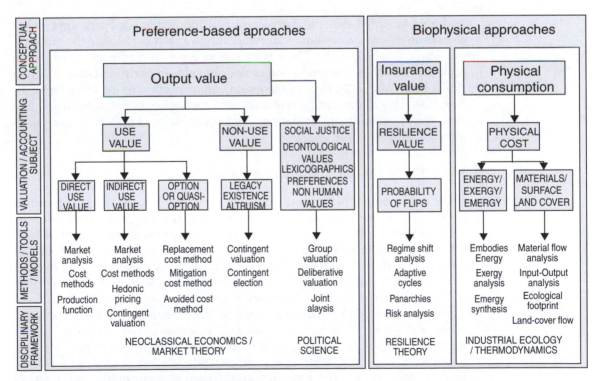

Figure 5.1 *Approaches for the estimation of nature's values*

Source: Drafted from Gómez-Baggethun and de Groot (2010) (in press)

Box 5.2 Biophysical approaches to valuation and accounting

A number of economists have advocated biophysical measurements as a basis for valuation exercises. In contrast to preference-based approaches, biophysical valuation methods use a 'cost of production' approach, as did some value theories in classical economics (e.g. the Ricardian and Marxist embodied labour theory of value). Biophysical approaches assess value based on the intrinsic properties of objects by measuring underlying physical parameters (see Patterson, 1990 for a review). Biophysical measures are generally more useful for the valuation of natural capital stocks than for valuation at the margin of flows of ecosystem services. This is particularly true when ecosystem services have no direct biophysical expression, as in the case of some cultural services. In particular, biophysical measures can be especially useful for calculating depreciation of natural capital within a strong sustainability framework (which posits that no substitution is possible between human-made and natural resources). Examples of biophysical methods for the valuation or accounting of natural capital are embodied in energy analysis (Costanza, 1980), emergy analysis (Odum, 1996), exergy analysis (Naredo, 2001; Valero et al, in press), ecological footprint (Wackernagel et al, 1999), material flow analysis (Daniels and Moore, 2002), land-cover flow (EEA, 2006), and Human Appropriation of Net Primary Production (HANPP) (Schandl et al, 2002).

It should be noted that the biophysical and the preference-based approaches stem from different axiomatic frameworks and value theories, and therefore are not generally compatible. There is an ongoing debate about the need to use multiple units of measurement and notions of value in environmental valuation (for a brief overview of controversies on commensurability of value types see Box 5.3). This chapter deals primarily with *preference-based approaches*, and the terms economic valuation and monetary valuation are used interchangeably.

2.3 The TEV framework and value types

From an economic viewpoint, the value (or system value) of an ecosystem should account for two distinct aspects. The first is the aggregated value of the ecosystem service benefits provided in a given state, akin to the concept of TEV. The second aspect relates to the system's capacity to maintain these values in the face of variability and disturbance. The former has sometimes been referred to as 'output' value, and the latter has been named 'insurance' value (Gren et al, 1994; Turner et al, 2003; Balmford et al, 2008) (Figure 5.2).

It should be emphasized that 'total' in 'total economic value' is summed across categories of values (i.e. use and non-use values) measured under marginal changes in the socio-ecological system, and not over ecosystem or biodiversity (resource) units in a constant state. Recent contributions in the field of ecosystem services have stressed the need to focus on the end products

Box 5.3 Conflicting valuation languages and commensurability of values

Controversies remain concerning the extent to which different types or dimensions of value can be reduced to a single rod of measure. Georgescu-Roegen (1979) criticized monism in applying theories of value, either preference-based or biophysical, as being a form of reductionism. Similarly, Martínez-Alier (2002) states that valuation of natural resources involves dealing with a variety of conflicting languages of valuation – e.g. economic, aesthetic, ecological, spiritual – that cannot be reduced to a single rod of measure. This perspective emphasizes 'weak comparability' of values (O'Neill, 1993; Martínez-Alier et al, 1998) that puts values in a relation of 'incommensurability' with each other. According to this view, decision support tools should allow for the integration of multiple incommensurable values. Multi-criteria analysis (MCA) makes possible the formal integration of multiple values after each of them has been assigned a relative weight (Munda, 2004). Like in monetary analysis, the output of MCA is a ranking of preferences that serve as a basis for taking decisions among different alternatives, but without the need to convert all values to a single unit (the result is an ordinal and not a cardinal ranking). MCA thus is a tool that accounts for complexity in decision-making processes. A weakness of this method is that the weighing of values can be easily biased by the scientists, or if the process is participatory, by power asymmetries among stakeholders. Transparent deliberative processes can reduce such risks, but also involve large amounts of time and resources that are not generally available to decision makers (Gómez-Baggethun and de Groot, 2007).

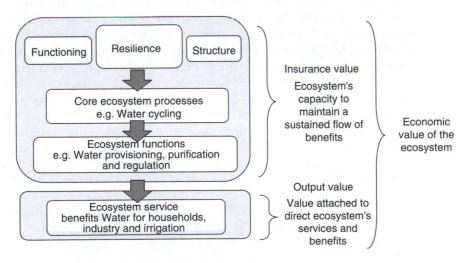

Figure 5.2 *Insurance and output value as part of the economic value of the ecosystem*

Note: The figure poses *insurance value* (related to the ecosystem's resilience) and *output value* (related to ecosystem service benefits) as the two main components of the economic value of the ecosystem.

(benefits) when valuing ecosystem services. This approach helps to avoid double counting of ecosystem functions, intermediate services and final services (Boyd and Banzhaf, 2007; Fisher et al, 2009).

The insurance value of ecosystems is closely related to the system's resilience and self-organizing capacity. The notion of resilience relates to the ecosystems' capacity to absorb shocks and reorganize so as to maintain its essential structure and functions, that is, the capacity to remain at a given ecological state or avoid regime shifts (Holling, 1973; Walker et al, 2004). Securing ecosystem resilience involves maintaining minimum amounts of ecosystem infrastructure and processing capability that allows 'healthy' functioning. Such minimum ecological infrastructure can be approached through the concept of 'critical natural capital' (Deutsch et al, 2003; Brand, 2009). The status of critical natural capital and related insurance values are sometimes recognized by the precautionary conservation of stocks, or setting safe minimum standards. However, the question remains how to measure resilience and critical natural capital in economic terms. These thorny issues are further discussed in more detail in Section 4 of this chapter.

Benefits corresponding to the 'output value' of the ecosystem can span from disparate values such as the control of water flows by tropical cloudy forests or the mitigation of damages from storms and other natural hazards by mangroves. The elicitation of these kinds of values can generally be handled with the available methods for monetary valuation based on direct markets, or, in their absence, on revealed or stated preferences techniques as will be discussed later.

Within the neoclassical economic paradigm, ecosystem services that are delivered and consumed in the absence of market transactions can be viewed as a form of positive externalities. Framing this as a market failure, the environmental economics literature has developed since the early 1960s a range of methods to value these 'invisible' benefits from ecosystems, often with the aim of incorporating them into extended cost–benefit analysis and internalizing the externalities. In order to comprehensively capture the economic value of the environment, different types of economic values neglected by markets have been identified, and measurement methods have been progressively refined. In fact, valuation of non-marketed environmental goods and services is associated with a large and still expanding literature in environmental economics.

Since the seminal work by Krutilla (1967), total (output) value of ecosystems has generally been divided into use- and non-use value categories, each subsequently disaggregated into different value components (Figure 5.3). A summary of the meaning of each component is provided in Table 5.1 based on Pearce and Turner (1990), de Groot et al (2002), de Groot et al (2006) and Balmford et al (2008).

Use values can be associated with private or quasi-private goods, for which market prices usually exist. Use values are sometimes divided further into two categories:

1   *Direct use value*, related to the benefits obtained from direct use of ecosystem service. Such use may be extractive, which entails consumption (for instance of food and raw materials), or non-extractive use (e.g. aesthetic benefits from landscapes).

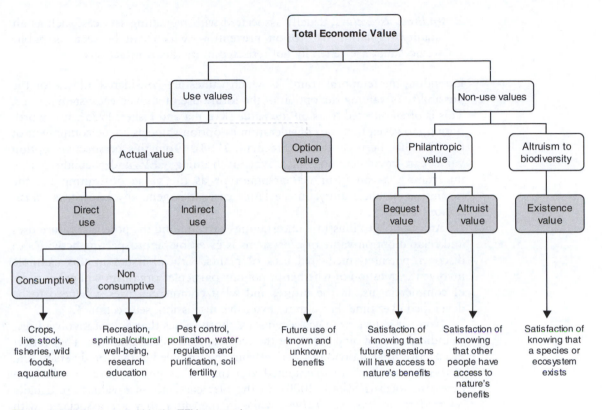

Figure 5.3 *Value types within the TEV approach*

Note: The figure reviews the value types that are addressed in the literature on nature valuation. Boxes in dark grey and the examples below the arrows are those that are directly addressed by value elicitation methods related to the TEV framework.

Table 5.1 A typology of values

Value type	Value sub-type	Meaning
Use values	Direct use value	Results from direct human use of biodiversity (consumptive or non-consumptive).
	Indirect use value	Derived from the regulation services provided by species and ecosystems.
	Option value	Relates to the importance that people give to the future availability of ecosystem services for personal benefit (option value in a strict sense).
Non-use values	Bequest value	Value attached by individuals to the fact that future generations will also have access to the benefits from species and ecosystems (intergenerational equity concerns).
	Altruist value	Value attached by individuals to the fact that other people of the present generation have access to the benefits provided by species and ecosystems (intragenerational equity concerns).
	Existence value	Value related to the satisfaction that individuals derive from the mere knowledge that species and ecosystems continue to exist.

2   *Indirect use values*, usually associated with regulating services, such as air quality regulation or erosion prevention, which can be seen as public services that are generally not reflected in market transactions.

Extending the temporal frame in which values are considered allows for the possibility of valuing the option of the future use of a given ecosystem service. This is often referred to as *option value* (Krutilla and Fisher, 1975). It is worth noting, however, that the consideration of option value as a true component of the TEV has been contested (Freeman, 1993). From this perspective, option value can be understood as a way of framing TEV under conditions of uncertainty, as an insurance premium or as the value of waiting for the resolution of uncertainty. In the latter case, it is generally known as *quasi-option value*.

An example to illustrate uncertainties surrounding the potential future uses and related option value of ecosystems is given by bioprospecting activities to discover potential medicinal uses of plants. Crucial issues in this example involve the question of whether or not any particular organism will prove to be of commercial use in the future; and what commercial uses will need to be developed over time. For a more extensive discussion, see Section 4.

Non-use values from ecosystems are those values that do not involve direct or indirect uses of biodiversity or the ecosystem service in question. They reflect satisfaction that individuals derive from the knowledge that biodiversity and ecosystem services are maintained and that other people have or will have access to them (Kolstad, 2000). In the first case, non-use values are usually referred to as *existence values*, while in the latter they are associated with *altruist values* (in relation to intra-generational equity concerns) or *bequest values* (when concerned with inter-generational concerns).

It should be noted that non-use values involve greater challenges for valuation than do use values since non-use values are related to moral, religious or aesthetic properties, for which markets usually do not exist. This is different from other services which are associated with the production and valuation of tangible *things* or *conditions*. Cultural services and non-use values in general involve the production of *experiences* that occur in the valuer's mind. These services are therefore co-produced by ecosystems and people in a deeper sense than other services (Chan et al, in press). Table 5.2 provides an overview of the links between different categories of values of ecosystem services. The aggregation of these value categories is reflected in the TEV.

3 Valuation methods, welfare measures and uncertainty

3.1 Valuation methods under the TEV approach

Within the TEV framework, values are derived, if available, from information of individual behaviour provided by market transactions relating directly to the ecosystem service. In the absence of such information, price information must be derived from parallel market transactions that are associated indirectly with the good to be valued. If both direct and indirect price information on ecosystem

Table 5.2 Valuing ecosystem services through the TEV framework

Group	Service	Direct use	Indirect use	Option value	Non-use value
Provisioning	Includes: food; fibre and fuel; biochemicals; natural medicines, pharmaceuticals; fresh water supply	✓	NA	✓	NA
Regulating	Includes: air-quality regulation; climate regulation; water regulation; natural hazard regulation, carbon storage, nutrient recycling, micro-climatic functions etc.	NA	✓	✓	NA
Cultural	Includes: cultural heritage; recreation and tourism; aesthetic values	✓	NA	✓	✓
Habitat	Includes: primary production; nutrient cycling; soil formation	*Habitat services are valued through the other categories of ecosystem services*			

Note: NA = Non applicable.

services are absent, hypothetical markets may be created in order to elicit values. These situations correspond to a common categorization of the available techniques used to value ecosystem services: (a) direct market valuation approaches, (b) revealed preference approaches and (c) stated preferences approaches, respectively (Chee, 2004). Below, a brief description of each method is provided together with a discussion of its strengths and weaknesses. We also discuss the adequacy of each method for different valuation conditions, purposes, ecosystem service types and value types to be estimated.

3.1.1 Direct market valuation approaches

Direct market valuation approaches are divided into three main approaches: (a) market price-based approaches, (b) cost-based approaches and (c) approaches based on production functions. The main advantage of using these approaches is that they use data from actual markets, and thus reflect actual preferences or costs to individuals. Moreover, such data – prices, quantities and costs – exist and thus are relatively easy to obtain.

Market price-based approaches are most often used to obtain the value of provisioning services, since the commodities produced by provisioning services are often sold on, for example, agricultural markets. In well-functioning markets preferences and marginal cost of production are reflected in a market price, which implies that these can be taken as accurate information on the value of commodities. The price of a commodity times the marginal product of the ecosystem service is an indicator of the value of the service. Consequently, market prices can also be good indicators of the value of the ecosystem service that is being studied especially in the absence of distortions such as taxes or subsidies.

Cost-based approaches are based on estimations of the costs that would be incurred if ecosystem service benefits needed to be recreated through artificial means (Garrod and Willis, 1999). Different techniques exist, including: (a) the *avoided cost method*, which relates to the costs that would have been incurred in the absence of ecosystem services, (b) the *replacement cost method*, which estimates the costs incurred by replacing ecosystem services with artificial technologies and (c) the *mitigation* or *restoration cost method*, which refers to the cost of mitigating the effects of the loss of ecosystem services or the cost of getting those services restored.

Production function-based approaches (PF) estimate how much a given ecosystem service (e.g. regulating service) contributes to the delivery of another service or commodity which is traded on an existing market. In other words, the PF approach is based on the contribution of ecosystem services to the enhancement of income or productivity (Mäler et al, 1994; Pattanayak and Kramer, 2001). The idea thus is that any resulting 'improvements in the resource base or environmental quality' as a result of enhanced ecosystem services, 'lower costs and prices and increase the quantities of marketed goods, leading to increases in consumers' and perhaps producers' surpluses' (Freeman, 2003, p259). The PF approach generally consists of the following two-step procedure (Barbier, 1994). The first step is to determine the physical effects of changes in a biological resource or ecosystem service on an economic activity. In the second step, the impact of these changes is valued in terms of the corresponding change in marketed output of the traded activity. A distinction should be made then between the gross value of output and the value of the marginal product of the input.

Hence, the PF approach generally uses scientific knowledge on cause–effect relationships between the ecosystem service(s) being valued and the output level of marketed commodities. It relates to objective measurements of biophysical parameters. As Barbier et al (2009) note, for many habitats where there is sufficient scientific knowledge of how these link to specific ecological services that support or protect economic activities, it is possible to employ the production function approach to value these services.

Limitations of direct market valuation approaches

Direct market valuation approaches rely primarily on production or cost data, which are generally easier to obtain than the kinds of data needed to establish demand for ecosystem services (Ellis and Fisher, 1987). However, when applied to ecosystem service valuation, these approaches have important limitations. These are mainly due to ecosystem services not having markets or markets being distorted.

The direct problems that arise are two fold. If markets do not exist either for the ecosystem service itself or for goods and services that are indirectly related, then the data needed for these approaches are not available. In cases where markets do exist but are distorted, for instance because of a subsidy scheme (see TEEB in National Policy, 2011) or because the market is not fully competitive, prices will not be a good reflection of preferences and marginal costs. Consequently, the estimated values of ecosystem services will be biased and will not provide reliable information to base policy decisions on.

Some direct market valuation approaches have specific problems. Barbier (2007) illustrates that the replacement cost method should be used with caution, especially under uncertainty. The PF approach has the additional problem that adequate data on and understanding of the cause–effect linkages between the ecosystem service being valued and the marketed commodity are often lacking (Daily et al, 2000; Spash, 2000). In other words, 'production functions' of ecosystem services are rarely understood well enough to quantify how much of a service is produced, or how changes in ecosystem condition or function will translate into changes in the ecosystem services delivered (Daily, 1997). Furthermore, the interconnectivity and interdependencies of ecosystem services may increase the likelihood of double-counting ecosystem services (Barbier, 1994; Costanza and Folke, 1997).

3.1.2 Revealed preference approaches

Revealed preference techniques are based on the observation of individual choices in existing markets that are related to the ecosystem service that is the subject of valuation. In this case it is said that economic agents 'reveal' their preferences through their choices. The two main methods within this approach are:

(a) The *travel cost method* (TC), which is mostly relevant for determining recreational values related to biodiversity and ecosystem services. It is based on the rationale that recreational experiences are associated with a cost (direct expenses and opportunity costs of time). The value of a change in the quality or quantity of a recreational site (resulting from changes in biodiversity) can be inferred from estimating the demand function for visiting the site that is being studied (Bateman et al, 2002; Kontoleon and Pascual, 2007).

(b) The *hedonic pricing* (HP) approach utilizes information about the implicit demand for an environmental attribute of marketed commodities. For instance, houses or property in general consist of several attributes, some of which are environmental in nature, such as the proximity of a house to a forest or whether it has a view of a nice landscape. Hence, the value of a change in biodiversity or ecosystem services will be reflected in the change in the value of property (either built-up or land that is in a (semi-)natural state). By estimating a demand function for property, the analyst can infer the value of a change in the non-marketed environmental benefits generated by the environmental good.

The main steps for undertaking a revealed preference valuation study are:

1   determining whether a surrogate market exists that is related to the environmental resource in question;
2   selecting the appropriate method to be used (travel cost, hedonic pricing);
3   collecting market data that can be used to estimate the demand function for the good traded in the surrogate market;

4   inferring the value of a change in the quantity/quality of an environmental resource from the estimated demand function;
5   aggregating values across the relevant population;
6   discounting values where appropriate.

Limitations of revealed preference approaches

In revealed preferences methods, market imperfections and policy failures can distort the estimated monetary value of ecosystem services. Scientists need good quality data on each transaction, large data sets, and complex statistical analysis. As a result, revealed preference approaches are expensive and time-consuming. Generally, these methods have the appeal of relying on actual/observed behaviour but their main drawbacks are the inability to estimate non-use values and the dependence of the estimated values on the technical assumptions made on the relationship between the environmental good and the surrogate market good (Kontoleon and Pascual, 2007).

3.1.3 Stated preference approaches

Stated preference approaches simulate a market and demand for ecosystem services by means of surveys on hypothetical (policy-induced) changes in the provision of ecosystem services. Stated preference methods can be used to estimate both use and non-use values of ecosystems and/or when no surrogate market exists from which the value of ecosystems can be deduced. The main types of stated preference techniques are:

- *Contingent valuation method* (CV): Uses questionnaires to ask people how much they would be willing to pay to increase or enhance the provision of an ecosystem service, or alternatively, how much they would be willing to accept for its loss or degradation.
- *Choice modelling* (CM): Attempts to model the decision process of an individual in a given context (Hanley et al, 1998; Philip and MacMillan, 2005). Individuals are faced with two or more alternatives with shared attributes of the services to be valued, but with different levels of those attributes (one of the attributes being the money people would have to pay for the service).
- *Group valuation*: Combines stated preference techniques with elements of deliberative processes from political science (Spash, 2001; Wilson and Howarth, 2002), and are being increasingly used as a way to take into account important issues such as value pluralism, incommensurability, non-human values or social justice (Spash, 2008).

As pointed out by Kontoleon and Pascual (2007), the main difference between CV and CM is that CV studies usually present one option to respondents. This option is associated with some (varying across respondents) price-tag. Respondents are then asked to vote on whether they would be willing to support this option and pay the price or if they would support the status quo (and not pay the extra price).[1] The distinction between voting as a market agent versus voting as a citizen has important consequences for the interpretation of CV results (Blamey et al, 1995).

In a CM study, respondents within the survey are given a choice between several options, each consisting of various attributes, one of which is either a price or subsidy. Respondents are then asked to consider all the options by balancing (trading off) the various attributes. Either of these techniques can be used to assess the TEV from a change in the quantity of biodiversity or ecosystem services. Though the CV method is less complicated to design and implement, the CM approach is more capable of providing value estimates for changes in specific characteristics (or attributes) of an environmental resource. Box 5.4 provides the steps for undertaking a CV study and Box 5.5 gives an example of a CM study that aimed to value biodiversity.

Box 5.4 Steps for undertaking a contingent valuation study (Kontoleon and Pascual, 2007)

1   *Survey design*
   - Start with focus group sessions and consultations with stakeholders to define the good to be valued.
   - Decide the nature of the market, that is, determine the good being traded, the status quo, and the improvement or deterioration level of the good that will be valued.
   - Determine the quantity and quality of information provided over the traded 'good', who will pay for it, and who will benefit from it.
   - Set allocation of property rights (determines whether a willingness-to-pay (WTP) or a willingness-to-accept (WTA) scenario is presented).
   - Determine credible scenario and payment vehicle (tax, donation, price).
   - Choose elicitation method (e.g. dichotomous choice vs. open-ended elicitation method).

2   *Survey implementation and sampling*
   - Interview implementation: on site or face-to-face, mail, telephone, internet, groups, consider inducements to increase the response rate.
   - Interviewers: private companies, researchers themselves.
   - Sampling: convenience sample, representative and stratified sample.

3   *Calculate measures of welfare change*
   - Open-ended – simple mean or trimmed mean (with removed outliers; note that this is a contentious step).
   - Dichotomous choice – estimate expected value of WTP or WTA.

4   *Technical validation*
   - Most CV studies will attempt to validate responses by investigating respondents WTP (or WTA) bids by estimating a bid function.

5   *Aggregation and discounting*
   - Calculating total WTP from mean/median WTP over relevant population – for example by multiplying the sample mean WTP of visitors to a site by the total number of visitors per annum.
   - Discount estimated values as appropriate.

6   *Study appraisal*
   - Testing the validity and reliability of the estimates produced.

Box 5.5 Example of valuing changes in biodiversity using a choice modelling study

In a study by Christie et al (2007) the value of alternative biodiversity conservation policies in the UK was estimated using the CM method. The study assessed the *total* value of biodiversity under alternative conservation policies as well as the *marginal* value of a change in one of the attributes (or characteristics) of the policies. The policy characteristics explored were familiarity of species conserved, species rarity, habitat quality and type of ecosystem services preserved. The policies would be funded by an annual tax. An example of the choice options presented to individuals is presented below.

	POLICY LEVEL 1	POLICY LEVEL 2	DO NOTHING (Biodiversity degradation will continue)
Familiar species of wildlife	Protect *rare* familiar species from further decline	Protect *both rare and common* familiar species from further decline	Continued decline in the populations of familiar species
Rare, unfamiliar species of wildlife	Slow down the rate of decline of rare, unfamiliar species.	Stop the decline and ensure the recovery of rare unfamiliar species	Continued decline in the populations of rare, unfamiliar species
Habitat quality	Habitat restoration, e.g. by better management of existing habitats	Habitat re-creation, e.g. by creating new habitat areas	Wildlife habitats will continue to be degraded and lost
Ecosystem process	Only ecosystem services that have a direct impact on humans, e.g. flood defences are restored.	*All* ecosystem services are restored	Continued decline in the functioning of ecosystem processes
Annual tax increase	£100	£260	No increase in your tax bill

Respondents had to choose between Policy 1, Policy 2 and the status quo (do nothing). Studies such as these can provide valuable information in an integrated assessment of the impacts of trade policies on biodiversity. Consider a change in EU farmer subsidization policies which will probably affect the agricultural landscape in the UK. The network of hedgerows that exists in the UK countryside and which hosts a significant amount of biodiversity and yields important biodiversity services will be affected by such a revised subsidization policy. Using results from the aforementioned CV study, policy makers can obtain an approximation of the value of the loss in biodiversity that might come about from a change in the current hedgerow network.

Group valuation approaches have been acknowledged as a way to tackle shortcomings of traditional monetary valuation methods (de Groot et al, 2006). Main methods within this approach are *deliberative monetary valuation* (DMV), which aims to express values for environmental change in monetary terms (Spash, 2007, 2008), and *mediated modelling*.

In the framework of stated preference methods, it is easy to obtain other important data types for the assessment of ecosystem services, such as stated perceptions, attitudinal scales, previous knowledge and so on. All of these pieces of information have been shown to be useful in understanding choices and preferences (Adamowicz, 2004). Stated preference methods could be a good approximation of the relative importance that stakeholders attach to different ecosystem services (Nunes, 2002; Martín-López et al, 2007; García-Llorente et al, 2008), and sometimes could reveal potential conflicts among stakeholders and among alternative management options (Nunes et al, 2008).

Limitations of stated preference approaches

Stated preference techniques are often the only way to estimate non-use values. Concerning the understanding of the *objective of choice*, it is often asserted that the interview process 'assures' understanding of the object of choice, but the hypothetical nature of the market has raised numerous questions regarding the validity of the estimates (Kontoleon and Pascual, 2007). The major question is whether respondents' hypothetical answers would correspond to their behaviour if they were faced with costs in real life.

One of the main problems that have been flagged in the literature on stated preference methods is the divergence between willingness-to-pay (WTP) and willingness-to-accept (WTA) (Hanneman, 1991; Diamond, 1996). From a theoretical perspective, WTP and WTA should be similar in perfectly competitive private markets (Willing, 1976; Diamond, 1996). However, several studies have demonstrated that for identical ecosystem services, WTA amounts systematically exceed WTP (Vatn and Bromley, 1994). This discrepancy may have several causes: faulty questionnaire design or interviewing technique; strategic behaviour by respondents and psychological effects such as 'loss aversion' and the 'endowment effect' (Garrod and Willis, 1999).

Another important problem is the 'embedding', 'part-whole bias' or 'insensitivity to scope' problem (Veisten, 2007). Kahneman (1986) was among the first to claim that respondents in a CV survey were insensitive to scope – he observed from a study that people were willing to pay the same amount to prevent the drop in fish populations in one small area of Ontario as in all Ontario (see also Kahneman and Knetsch, 1992; Desvousges et al, 1993; Diamond and Hausman, 1993; Diamond et al, 1993; Boyle et al, 1994, 1998; Svedsäter, 2000).

There is also a controversy on whether non-use values are commensurable in monetary terms (Martínez-Alier et al, 1998; Carson et al, 2001). The problem here is whether, for instance, the religious or bequest value that may be attributed to a forest can be considered within the same framework as the economic value of logging or recreation in that forest. Such an extreme range of values may not be equally relevant to all policy problems, but the issue has remained largely unresolved for now.

Furthermore, the application of stated preference methods to public goods that are complex and unfamiliar has been questioned on the grounds that respondents cannot give accurate responses as their preferences are not fully defined (Svedsäter, 2003). Sometimes stated preference methods incorporate basic upfront information in questionnaires (e.g. Wilson and Tisdell, 2005; Tisdell and Wilson, 2006; García-Llorente et al, 2008). Christie et al (2006) argue that valuation workshops that provide respondents with opportunities to discuss and reflect on their preferences help to overcome some of the potential cognitive and knowledge constraints associated with stated preference methods. Typically, deliberative monetary valuation methods will provide upfront information to stakeholders as well. The bias in deliberative monetary valuation approaches is supposedly less than in individual CV studies (de Groot et al, 2006). Such methods may further reduce non-response rates and increase respondents' engagement.

3.1.4 Choosing and applying valuation methods: Forests and wetlands

The main purpose of this section is to provide examples about how valuation methods have been applied to elicit different kinds of ecosystem values. Here we present results, summarized in tables, from an extensive literature review about the application of valuation techniques to estimate a variety of values, particularly in forests and wetlands. The information here presented may help valuation practitioners to choose the appropriate valuation methods, according to the concerned values. This section is short in scope because numerous previous publications have dealt already with classification and applications of techniques..

As discussed extensively elsewhere (NRC, 1997, 2004; Chee, 2004; Turner et al, 2004), some valuation methods are more appropriate than others for valuing particular ecosystem services and for the elicitation of specific value components. Table 5.3 shows the links between specific methods and value components.

Table 5.3 Relationship between valuation methods and value types

Approach		Method	Value
Market valuation	Price-based	Market prices	Direct and indirect use
	Cost-based	Avoided cost	Direct and indirect use
		Replacement cost	Direct and indirect use
		Mitigation / Restoration cost	Direct and indirect use
	Production-based	Production function approach	Indirect use
		Factor income	Indirect use
Revealed preference		Travel cost method	Direct (indirect) use
		Hedonic pricing	Direct and indirect use
Stated preference		Contingent valuation	Use and non-use
		Choice modelling / Conjoint analysis	Use and non-use
		Contingent ranking	Use and non-use
		Deliberative group valuation	Use and non-use

Table 5.4 provides insight into and comments on some of the potential applications of methods in ecosystem services valuation and some illustrative references from the literature.

Regulation services have been mainly valued through avoided cost, replacement and restoration costs, or contingent valuation; cultural services through travel cost (recreation, tourism or science), hedonic pricing (aesthetic information), or contingent valuation (spiritual benefits – i.e. existence value); and provisioning services through methods based on the production function approach and direct market valuation approach (Martín-López et al, 2009a).

Table 5.4 Monetary valuation methods and values: Examples from the literature

Method			Comment /example	References
Market valuation	Market prices		Mainly applicable to the 'goods' (e.g. fish) but also some cultural (e.g. recreation) and regulating services (e.g. pollination).	Brown et al, 1990; Kanazawa, 1993
	Cost based	Avoided cost	The value of the flood control service can be derived from the estimated damage if flooding would occur.	Gunawardena and Rowan 2005; Ammour et al, 2000; Breaux et al, 1995; Gren, 1993
		Replacement cost	The value of groundwater recharge can be estimated from the costs of obtaining water from another source (substitute costs).	
		Mitigation/ restoration costs	For example: cost of preventive expenditures in absence of wetland service (e.g. flood barriers) or relocation.	
	Production function/ factor income		How soil fertility improves crop yield and therefore the income of the farmers, and how water quality improvements increase commercial fisheries catch and thereby incomes of fishermen.	Pattanayak and Kramer, 2001
Revealed preferences	Travel Cost Method		For example: part of the recreational value of a site is reflected in the amount of time and money that people spend while travelling to the site.	Whitten and Bennet, 2002; Martín-López et al, 2009b
	Hedonic Pricing Method		For example: clean air, presence of water and aesthetic views will increase the price of surrounding real estate.	Bolitzer and Netusil, 2000; Garrod and Willis, 1991
Simulated valuation	Contingent Valuation Method (CVM)		It is often the only way to estimate non-use values. For example, a survey questionnaire might ask respondents to express their willingness to increase the level of water quality in a stream, lake or river so that they might enjoy activities like swimming, boating or fishing.	Wilson and Carpenter, 1999; Martín-López et al, 2007
	Choice modelling		It can be applied through different methods, which include choice experiments, contingent ranking, contingent rating and pair comparison.	Hanley et al, 1998; Li et al, 2004; Philip and MacMillan, 2005
	Group valuation		It allows addressing shortcomings of revealed preference methods such as preference construction during the survey and lack of knowledge of respondents about what they are being asked to allocate values to.	Wilson and Howarth, 2002; Spash, 2008

Source: Compiled after Wilson and Carpenter (1999), King and Mazotta (2001), de Groot et al (2006)

Drawn from a review of 314 peer-reviewed valuation case studies (see Appendix 2 for references), Tables 5.5 and 5.6 provide quantitative information on valuation approaches and specific valuation techniques that have been used for the estimation of particular categories and types of ecosystem services. Table 5.7 and Figure 5.4 focus on values of wetlands and forests, following a review of valuation studies in these biomes.

Table 5.5 Use of different valuation methods for valuing ecosystem services in the valuation literature associated with wetlands and forests

Valuation method	Cultural	Provisioning	Regulating	Supporting
Avoided cost	1	2	26	0
Benefits transfer	9	3	4	6
Bio-economic modelling	0	1	0	0
Choice modelling	16	4	7	17
Consumer surplus	1	0	0	0
Contingent ranking	1	2	0	0
Conversion cost	0	1	0	0
CVM	26	10	9	33
Damage cost	0	0	6	0
Factor income/Production function	1	33	9	0
Hedonic pricing	5	1	0	0
Market price	0	7	3	0
Mitigation cost	0	2	3	0
Net price method	0	1	0	0
Opportunity cost	1	17	1	6
Participatory valuation	2	3	3	0
Public investments	0	1	1	28
Replacement cost	2	3	20	11
Restoration cost	1	2	6	0
Substitute goods	0	4	0	0
Travel cost method	32	3	3	0
Grand total	**100%**	**100%**	**100%**	**100%**

Table 5.6 Valuation approaches used for valuing ecosystem services in wetlands and forests

Type of valuation approach	Cultural	Provisioning	Regulating	Supporting
Benefits transfer	9	3	4	6
Cost based	5	27	61	17
Production based	1	33	9	0
Revealed preference	38	18	7	28
Stated preference	46	19	19	50
Grand total	**100%**	**100%**	**100%**	**100%**

Note: The data pertains to valuation studies published in peer reviewed literature. The total number of valuation studies is 314. See Appendix 2 for references.

Table 5.7 Proportion of valuation methods applied across ecosystem services regarding forests and wetlands, based on reviewed literature (see Appendix 2 for references)

Row labels	Forests					Wetlands					Grand total
	Cultural	Provisioning	Regulating	Supporting	Forests total	Cultural	Provisioning	Regulating	Supporting	Wetlands total	
Benefits transfer	2	1	5	0	2	16	6	3	25	9	5
Cost based	2	30	69	14	30	9	24	52	25	25	28
Avoided cost	0	2	33	0	8	2	2	16	0	5	7
Conversion cost	0	0	0	0	0	0	2	0	0	1	0
Damage cost	0	0	10	0	2	0	0	0	0	0	1
Mitigation cost	0	4	3	0	2	0	0	3	0	1	2
Opportunity cost	0	20	3	7	10	2	13	0	0	6	8
Replacement cost	0	2	18	7	6	4	4	23	25	9	7
Restoration cost	2	1	3	0	2	0	4	10	0	4	3
Production based	2	30	8	0	16	0	39	10	0	18	17
Bio-economic modelling	0	0	0	0	0	0	2	0	0	1	0
Factor income/Prod function	2	30	8	0	16	0	37	10	0	17	16
Revealed preference	57	27	13	36	32	20	4	0	0	8	22
Consumer surplus	0	0	0	0	0	2	0	0	0	1	0
Hedonic pricing	7	2	0	0	3	4	0	0	0	1	2

Table 5.7 (continued)

Row labels	Forests				Forests total	Wetlands				Wetlands total	Grand total
	Cultural	Provisioning	Regulating	Supporting	total	Cultural	Provisioning	Regulating	Supporting	total	total
Market price	0	12	5	0	7	0	0	0	0	0	4
Net price method	0	1	0	0	1	0	0	0	0	0	0
Public investments	0	0	3	36	3	0	4	0	0	1	3
Substitute goods	0	6	0	0	3	0	0	0	0	0	2
Travel cost method	50	5	5	0	16	13	0	0	0	4	11
Stated preference	**37**	**12**	**5**	**50**	**20**	**56**	**28**	**35**	**50**	**40**	**28**
Choice modelling	11	0	0	14	4	22	9	16	25	16	9
Contingent ranking	2	2	0	0	2	0	2	0	0	1	1
CVM	22	9	5	36	13	31	11	13	25	19	16
Participatory valuation	2	1	0	0	1	2	6	6	0	4	3
Grand total	**100%**	**100%**	**100%**	**100%**	**100%**	**100%**	**100%**	**100%**	**100%**	**100%**	**100%**

The tables in Appendix 2 provide an extensive overview of the valuation literature regarding the use of valuation methods to estimate different types of economic values of ecosystem services. The review covers only wetlands and forests, two biomes for which most studies could be found. Appendix 2 contains a summary of the ecosystem services provided by these biomes and the techniques applied to them, as well as a table to summarize this information according to the typology of values from Table 5.1.

Tables A2.1 (a, b) show benefits/value types within each major (a) wetland and (b) forest ecosystem services categories, that is, provisioning, regulating, cultural and supportive services. It also identifies valuation approaches used to estimate economic values. Table A2.2 (a, b) provides a complementary view that associates the ecosystem services from these two biomes with valuation approaches. Table A2.3 associates the benefits/value types in wetlands (a) and forest (b) ecosystem services per type of value (across various use/non-use values).

In sum, each of the methods explained herewith has its own strengths and shortcomings (Hanley and Spash, 1993; Pearce and Moran, 1994), and each can be particularly suitable for specific ecosystem services and value types. Table 5.8 summarizes the advantages and disadvantages of different techniques using the case of wetlands, but the information can also be used for other biomes.

Lastly, it should also be mentioned that there are 'hybrid' valuation methods that can also be considered. For instance, it is theoretically possible to link a production function approach to stated preference method to estimate the economic value of, for example, cultural services offered by totemic species. Allen and Loomis (2006) use such an approach to derive the value of species at lower trophic levels from the results of surveys of willingness to pay for the conservation of species at higher trophic levels. Specifically, they derive the implicit WTP for the conservation of prey species from direct estimates of WTP for top predators.

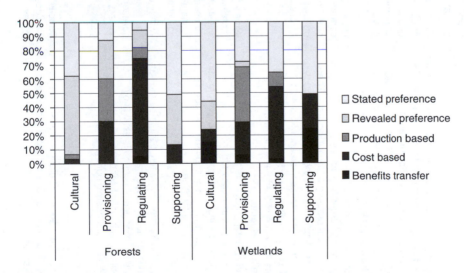

Figure 5.4 *Valuation approaches that have been used to value ecosystem services provided by forests and wetlands*

Table 5.8 Valuation techniques as applied to wetland studies

Valuation technique	Advantage	Disadvantages
Market prices method. Use prevailing prices for goods and services traded in domestic or international markets.	Market prices reflect the private willingness to pay for wetland costs and benefits that are traded (e.g. fish, timber, fuelwood, recreation). They may be used to construct financial accounts to compare alternative wetland uses from the perspective of the individual or company concerned with private profit and losses. Price data are relatively easy to obtain.	Market imperfections and/or policy failures may distort market prices, which will therefore fail to reflect the economic value of goods or services to society as a whole. Seasonal variations and other effects on prices need to be considered when market prices are used in economic analysis.
Efficiency (shadow) prices method. Use of market prices but adjusted for transfer payments, market imperfections and policy distortions. May also incorporate distribution weights, where equality concerns are made explicit. Shadow prices may also be calculated for non-marketed goods.	Efficiency prices reflect the true economic value or opportunity cost, to society as a whole, of goods and services that are traded in domestic or international markets (e.g. fish, fuelwood, peat).	Derivation of efficiency prices is complex and may require substantial data. Decision makers may not accept 'artificial' prices.
Hedonic pricing method. The value of an environmental amenity (such as a view) is obtained from property or labour markets. The basic assumption is that the observed property value (or wage) reflects a stream of benefits (or working conditions) and that it is possible to isolate the value of the relevant environmental amenity or attribute.	Hedonic pricing has the potential to value certain wetland functions (e.g. storm protection, ground-water recharge) in terms of their impact on land values, assuming that the wetland functions are fully reflected in land prices.	Application of hedonic pricing to the environmental functions of wetlands requires that these values are reflected in surrogate markets. The approach may be limited where markets are distorted, choices are constrained by income, information about environmental conditions is not widespread and data are scarce.
Travel cost approach. The travel cost approach derives willingness to pay for environmental benefits at a specific location by using information on the amount of money and time that people spend to visit the location.	Widely used to estimate the value of recreational sites including public parks and wildlife services in developed countries. It could be used to estimate willingness to pay for eco-tourism to tropical wetlands in some developing countries.	Data intensive; restrictive assumptions about consumer behaviour (e.g. multifunctional trips); results highly sensitive to statistical methods used to specify the demand relationship.
Production function approach. Estimates the value of a non-marketed resource or ecological function in terms of changes in economic activity by modelling the physical contribution of the resource or function to economic output.	Widely used to estimate the impact of wetlands and reef destruction, deforestation and water pollution etc., on productive activities such as fishing, hunting and farming.	Requires explicit modelling of the 'dose–response' relationship between the resources and some economic output. Application of the approach is most straightforward in the case of single-use systems but becomes more complicated with multiple-use systems. Problems may arise from multi-specification of the ecological–economic relationship or double counting.
Constructed market techniques. Measure of willingness to pay by directly eliciting consumer preferences.	Directly estimates Hicksian welfare measure – provides best theoretical measure of willingness to pay.	Practical limitations of constructed market techniques may detract from theoretical advantages, leading to poor estimates of true willingness to pay.

Table 5.8 (*continued*)

Valuation technique	Advantage	Disadvantages
Simulated market (SM) constructs an experimental market in which money actually changes hands.	Controlled experimental setting permits close study of factors determining preferences.	Sophisticated decision and implementation may limit application in developing countries.
Contingent valuation methods (CVM) construct a hypothetical market to elicit respondents' willingness to pay.	Only method that can measure option and existence values and provide a true measure of total economic value.	Results sensitive to numerous sources of bias in survey design and implementation.
Contingent ranking (CR) ranks and scores relative preferences for amenities in quantitative rather than monetary terms.	Generates value estimate for a range of products and services without having to elicit willingness to pay for each.	Does not elicit willingness to pay directly, hence lacks theoretical advantages of other approaches. Being qualitative, cannot be used directly in policies (say for fixing cess, taxes etc.)
Cost-based valuation. Based on assumption that the cost of maintaining an environmental benefit is a reasonable estimate of its value.	It is easier to measure the costs of producing benefits than the benefits themselves, when goods, services and benefits are non-marked. Approaches are less data and resource-intensive.	These second-best approaches assume that expenditure provides positive benefits and net benefits generated by expenditure match the original level of benefits. Even when these conditions are met, costs are usually not an accurate measure of benefits. So long as it's not clear whether it's worth it to replace a lost or damaged asset, the cost of doing so is an inadequate measure of damage.
Restoration cost (RSC) method uses costs of restoring ecosystem goods or services.	Potentially useful in valuing particular environmental functions.	Diminishing returns and difficulty of restoring previous ecosystem conditions make application of RSC questionable.
Replacement cost (RPC) method uses cost of artificial substitutes for environmental goods or services.	Useful in estimating indirect use benefits when ecological data are not available for estimating damage functions with first-best methods.	Difficult to ensure that net benefits of the replacement do not exceed those of the original function. May overstate willingness to pay if only physical indicators of benefits are available.
Relocation cost (RLC) method uses costs of relocating threatened communities.	Only useful in valuing environmental amenities in the face of mass dislocation such as a dam project and establishment of protected areas.	In practice, benefits provided by the new location are unlikely to match those of the original location.
Preventive expenditure (PE) approach uses the costs of preventing damage or degradation of environmental benefits.	Useful in estimating indirect use benefits with prevention technologies	Mismatching the benefits of investment in prevention to the original level of benefits may lead to spurious estimates of willingness to pay.
Damage costs avoided (DCA) approach relies on the assumption that damage estimates are a measure of value. It is not a cost-based approach as it relies on the use of valuation methods described above.	Precautionary principle applied here	Data or resource limitations may rule out first-best valuation methods.

Source: Barbier et al (1997)

3.2 Acknowledging uncertainty in valuation

In addition to the issues discussed in previous sections, uncertainty is another critical issue in the valuation of ecosystem services and biodiversity. This section addresses the role of uncertainty by reviewing the state of the art in the valuation literature. To do so, it is useful to distinguish between risk and uncertainty. Risk is associated with a situation where the possible consequences of a decision can be completely enumerated in terms of states of nature and probabilities assigned to each possibility (Knight, 1921). In a Knightian sense, uncertainty is understood as the situation where the possible consequences of a decision can be fully enumerated but where a decision maker cannot assign probabilities objectively to these states. In addition, there is a more profound type of uncertainty where the decision maker cannot enumerate all of the possible consequences of a decision. This is usually referred to as 'radical uncertainty' or 'ignorance' (Perman et al, 2003) and should be acknowledged when science cannot explain some complex functioning of ecosystems and biodiversity.[2] In this chapter the term 'uncertainty' will refer to the one commonly used in economic valuation of the environment, that is, the conflated risk and uncertainty notion as in Freeman (1993), unless the term 'radical uncertainty' or 'ignorance' is used instead.

Further, it is useful to distinguish three sources of uncertainty and radical uncertainty/ignorance. First, we may face uncertainty or/and ignorance in terms of the nature of the ecosystem services to be valued. Second, we may be uncertain or/and ignorant about the way people form their preferences about ecosystem services, that is, the way they subjectively value changes in the delivery of ecosystem services and biodiversity. Lastly, another layer of uncertainty exists regarding the application of valuation tools. This is acknowledged here as technical uncertainty. In the following sections, these terms will be discussed where relevant, and best-practice solutions discussed.

3.2.1 Supply uncertainty

Beyond the problem of assigning probability distributions, radical uncertainty has tremendous implications for valuing biodiversity and ecosystem services. Science is starting to shed light on the role of biodiversity in terms of the delivery of supporting services, and robust information is still lacking on how biodiversity contributes to the ecological functions that translate into tangible benefits for society. For example, forested riparian corridors in agricultural landscapes clearly improve water quality and reduce sediment loads from upstream erosion, but ecologists have only a limited understanding of how species richness in riparian zones contribute to these ecosystem services (Jackson et al, 2007). In the same light, it is not straightforward to assign values to the services attributable to the diversity of tree species, rather than the stock of tree biomass or to the ecosystem as a whole. Usually valuation studies using stated preference methods rather than focusing on direct evidence about the link between 'biodiversity' (e.g. tree diversity) and peoples' preferences about such diversity have mostly focused on more easily identifiable biological 'resources' or stocks (e.g. forests, wetlands and charismatic species) (Nunes and van den Bergh, 2001).

Beyond the more challenging effect of radical uncertainty, in cases where states of nature are identifiable and probability distributions can be objectively assigned by researchers, it is possible to resort to the use of *expected values* for those variables whose precise values cannot be known in advance. In this way uncertainty is dealt by weighting each potential outcome by the probability of its occurrence. In this case, we are dealing with the more palatable notion of Knightian risk, which is conflated with the standard notion of uncertainty in economic valuation. In this case, the valuation of a change in ecosystem services is based on the weighted outcomes of alternative states of the world. For example, a set of forest tree species could be associated with an *expected* level of carbon capture given various rainfall patterns (states of nature). If probabilities can be assigned to these rainfall patterns, the amount of carbon that the forest can be expected to capture can be estimated by summing up the probability-weighted capture outcomes. Then, what is valued is the expected change in carbon capture associated with tree diversity given an objectively assigned probability distribution to rainfall patterns.

Examples from the literature dealing with ecosystem service valuation under uncertainty include the flow regulation in rivers and surge protection in coastal ecosystems which are fundamentally probabilistic. A promising approach is based on the expected damage function (EDF), akin to a dose–response approach but based on methodologies used in risk analysis. Barbier (2007) applies the EDF approach to value the storm protection service provided by a coastal wetland. The underlying assumption is that changes in wetland area affect the probability and severity of economically damaging storm events (states of nature) in coastal areas. More generally, this approach measures the WTP by measuring the total expected damages resulting from changes in ecosystem stocks. This approach has been used routinely in risk analysis and health economics (e.g. Barbier et al, 2009).

In the case of the coastal wetland example provided by Barbier (2007), a key piece of information becomes critical for estimating the value of wetlands in the face of economically damaging natural disasters: the influence of wetland area on the expected incidence of storm events. Provided that there is sufficient data on the incidence of past natural disasters and changes in wetland area in coastal regions, the first component can be dealt with by employing a *count data model* to estimate whether a change in the area of coastal wetlands reduces the expected incidence of economically damaging storm events. Once the damage cost per event is known, the count data model yields the information to be used to calculate the value of wetlands in terms of protection against natural disasters.

The uncertainty of supply of ecosystem services makes stated preference methods significantly complex. This may be the reason why there are few examples where CV has considered valuation under uncertainty. In a seminal study, Brookshire et al (1983) showed how option prices change when the uncertainty of supply (based on probabilistic risk) is reduced. Their WTP bid schedules were estimated by asking hunters their WTP given different probabilistic scenarios of the supply of threatened species such as grizzly bears and bighorn sheep in Wyoming. In another early application of CV under uncertainty, Crocker and Shogren (1991) valued landscape visibility changes under different accessibility contingencies of the sample of individuals being surveyed. Their approach was based on eliciting the individuals' subjective perceptions about the probabilities of alternative landscape visibility states.

Generally, CV studies have resorted to measure respondents' risk perceptions, especially using so-called 'risk indexes' in order to obtain information about whether respondents feel concerned when considering an uncertain issue. Risk indexes reflect individual beliefs about subjective probabilities of a given event occurring (e.g. the loss of a given species). In another CV application, Rekola and Pouta (2005) measure the value of forest amenities in Finland under uncertainty regarding forest regeneration cuttings. In this study, respondents' risk perceptions are measured and used to calculate the probability density function of expectations. They conclude that surveyed individuals may answer questions about risk perception inconsistently as people have a tendency to overestimate small probabilities, especially when these probabilities are connected with unwanted outcomes. The reason is that individuals may confound the subjective probability of the event occurring with the subjective perception about the severity of the event being perceived (e.g. the *feelings* about the loss of the species). This may undermine the use of risk indexes in CV (see Poe and Bishop, 1999; Rekola, 2004). This is possibly another reason why stated preference practitioners tend to avoid using quantitative information about probabilities of provision of ecosystem services. Such information can undermine the studies in a way similar to how incentive compatible revelation of preferences can affect valuation results (e.g. Carson and Groves, 2007).

3.2.2 Preference uncertainty

Valuation studies often assume that respondents know their preferences with certainty, that is, they are aware how much they would be willing to pay for ecosystem service provision. Empirical evidence in the stated preference literature suggests, however, that respondents are uncertain about their responses (Ready et al, 1995; Champ et al, 1997; Alberini et al, 2003; Akter et al, 2008). This is mainly due to respondents using a heuristic mode when processing information provided in one of several contingent valuation formats (e.g. interview, email), which tends to dominate over more systematic ways of information processing for decision making (Bateman et al, 2008). This is compounded by an unfamiliar hypothetical nature of the market being recreated for sometimes unfamiliar or intangible goods such as the protection of a rare bird species in an unfamiliar location (Champ and Bishop, 2001; Schunn et al, 2003; Bateman et al, 2008).

Often an *ad hoc* way of dealing with preference uncertainty is to assume that people are expected-utility maximizers. This assumption makes it possible to calculate point estimates of expected willingness-to-pay for changes in ecosystem services. These calculations require that a random variable is added to individuals' utility functions, since arguably they do not know their true WTP for the service with certainty (Hanemann et al, 1996). Instead, they perceive that the true value of the service lies within an interval. A similar approach proposes that the level of individual preference uncertainty is determined by the magnitude of difference between a deterministic and a stochastic part of an individual's utility difference function (Loomis and Ekstrand, 1998).

There is no consensus about which approach is more appropriate for measuring preference uncertainty in stated preference methods.[3] There are three main approaches to deal with this kind of uncertainty in CVM. One is to request respondents to state how certain they are about their answer to the WTP question (e.g. Loomis and Ekstrand, 1998). Another one is to introduce uncertainty directly using multiple bounded WTP questions or a polychotomous choice model (e.g. Alberini et al, 2003). The third option is to request respondents to report a range of values rather than a specific value for the change in the provision of an ecosystem service (e.g. Hanley et al, 2009).

The first approach to deal with preference uncertainty in stated preference methods is the most straightforward one but one which does not solve the problem of uncertainty *per se*. It tries to uncover whether individuals' perceptions and attitudes to the good or service being valued are correlated with self-reported 'certainty scores'. The literature suggests some positive association between certainty scores and respondents' prior knowledge about the particular good being valued or respondents' attitudes towards the hypothetical market being confronted (Loomis and Ekstrand, 1998).[4]

The second approach introduces uncertainty directly into the WTP question by including uncertainty options. The idea is to include multiple bids in discrete choices by displaying a panel to respondents with suggested costs (WTP) on the rows and categories of certainty (e.g. from 'extremely unlikely' to 'extremely likely') of whether respondents would be WTP the cost in exchange for a good or service in the columns (e.g. Alberini et al, 2003; Akter et al, 2009). The advantage of this approach is that it is possible to model the ordered structure of the data and identify threshold values, showing at which average bid levels people switch from one uncertainty level to another (Broberg, 2007). However, similar to the problems of using responses to uncertainty questions to reclassify WTP statements in stated preference methods, this polychotomous choice approach suffers from not knowing how respondents interpret concepts such as 'very unlikely' and whether all respondents do so in the same way.[5]

The third approach is a promising alternative to the previous two approaches when people may prefer reporting a range of values rather than a specific value for the change in the provision of an ecosystem service. Hanley et al (2009) suggest using a payment ladder to elicit peoples' WTP for changes in ecosystem services. In their example they value improvements in coastal water quality in Scotland and show that when using value ranges uncertainty is inversely related to the level of knowledge and experience with the good, although this effect only appears once a certain minimal level of experience has been acquired.

From the three approaches described above, the third approach appears to be the most promising for dealing with preference uncertainty. One issue that remains open though is the range of values to be used in this elicitation method. In addition, it is important to note that valuing an ecosystem service using the method presented in Hanley et al (2009) only deals with one aspect of uncertainty about preferences as ecosystem services relevant to local respondents may not match with scientifically described ecosystem functions (Barkmann et al, 2008).

3.2.3 Technical uncertainty

When deciding which valuation tools to use one should also think of the several conceptual, methodological and technical shortcomings associated with all valuation methods which add some further uncertainty to the estimated values. An extensive review of these issues is provided in Kontoleon et al (2002). For the purposes of technical uncertainty that should be acknowledged in TEEB, two sets of issues must be noted: the first concerns the accuracy of valuation estimates and the second concerns the issue of discounting future values. Next we address the problem of the accuracy of valuation estimates elicited using standard valuation approaches, and Section 5 deals with the effect of different discount rates on the range of values that are estimated.

Measurement issues concern at least two key aspects of the problems concerning the accuracy of stated preference studies. One aspect is the *credibility* of the stated preferences. It is usually assumed when using stated preference methods such as CV that respondents answer questions truthfully given the hypothetical nature of the technique. This issue is treated as a debate revolving around whether an upward 'hypothetical bias' (the difference between purely hypothetical and actual statements of value) permeates CV estimates. Interestingly, a meta-analysis based on estimates from CV surveys to estimates with their counterparts based on revealed behaviour techniques found no statistically significant upward hypothetical bias of CV methods (Carson et al, 1996). However the question remains whether estimates of non-use values elicited through stated preference methods are credible, as there is no other approach to directly compare these values.

The second question is whether respondents answer truthfully only when it is in their interest to do so. While this problem is consistent with standard economic theory, this also means that responses depend critically on how well the surveys create incentives for the truthful revelation of preferences (Carson et al, 2009). For example, if an individual wishes to skew the results of the exercise, surveys do not generally include any explicit in-built incentive or mechanism that will constrain this sort of behaviour. Hence the credibility of the results of a survey is a function of the quality of the survey design. The other problem of accuracy concerns the margin of error surrounding the valuation. This error will depend to some extent on the size of the sample and the nature of the good being valued, but it will necessarily remain fairly large and uncertain on account of the technique that is used.

As mentioned in Section 2, it should also be noted that a particularly prevalent error is the general use of WTP-type questions instead of WTA-type ones in stated preference surveys especially when the property rights of the goods or services being valued would warrant the WTA questions. This is so in spite of a sizeable literature establishing the presence of 'endowment effects' (Knetsch, 2005). Careful experiments reveal that even for market goods (e.g. coffee mugs, pens or candybars), WTA typically exceeds WTP (Kahneman et al, 1990). Further there is evidence that stated preference-based studies exhibit a rather substantial divergence between WTP and WTA results. A meta-analysis of 45 studies has found over a seven-fold difference between the two measures, on average (Horowitz and McConnell, 2002). Theoretical arguments against such disparities still are a matter of concern for valuation practitioners. It also provides ammunition against the use of stated preference methods and is taken as evidence that the CVM is a flawed valuation approach as it is inconsistent with neoclassical consumer theory in general and in its ability to measure consumer preferences (e.g. Hausman, 1993; Diamond, 1996). Against these notorious criticisms, practitioners of the CVM (e.g. Mitchell and Carson, 1989) or the members of the NOAA panel (1993) recommend use of the WTP format for practical studies.[6] Their reason is that since WTP generally turns out to be smaller than WTA, this is consistent with applying a 'conservative choice' to be on the safe side (NOAA, 1993). But in this recommendation one may interpret some resignation with respect to the significance of CV results.

Accuracy problems also affect revealed preference and pricing techniques. The first problem has to do with the *availability* of revealed preference and market data that is required to undertake such valuation studies. Market data availability is about both quantity and quality of the data especially in the developing world where market data may suffer from poor quality that misrepresents reality. The second aspect of the accuracy of revealed preference and pricing techniques has to do with the fact that these methods (by their design) *cannot account for non-use values*. Hence, market data can only provide a lower bound estimate of the value of a change in biodiversity or ecosystem services.

In sum, valuation studies using various techniques can suffer from technical uncertainty due to accuracy problems or biases, examples being: (i) the potential (e.g. hypothetical or strategic) biases that arise from the design of questionnaires in stated preference methods (Bateman et al, 2002); (ii) the effect of assigning probabilistic scenarios in production function based approaches; and (iii) the influence of unstable market prices of substitutes or complements to natural resources in revealed preference methods (e.g. travel cost approach).

3.2.4 Data enrichment models as the way forward

One practical way to deal with at least two of the sources of uncertainty, namely technical uncertainty and to a lesser extent preference uncertainty, is the use of the data enrichment or 'data fusion' approach. The idea is to combine revealed and stated preference methods when valuing a given ecosystem service which is at least associated with clear direct-use values. While this approach is not dominant in the valuation literature there are increasing calls from previous studies which have combined data and models to increase the reliability of the valuation estimates, for example to derive values for recreation, environmental amenity, cultural heritage and agrobiodiversity (e.g. Cameron, 1992; Adamowicz et al, 1994; Earnhart, 2001; Haab and McConnell, 2002; Birol et al, 2006). The main advantage of the data enrichment approach involving the combination of revealed and stated preference methods is that it overcomes two of the main problems associated with each of the two methods.

On the one hand while the advantage of using revealed preference methods is that it has a high 'face validity' because the data reflect real choices and take into account various constraints on individual decisions, such as market imperfections, budgets and time (Louviere et al, 2000), it suffers on the grounds that the new policy situation (after the change in the quality or the quantity of ecosystem services) may be outside the current set of experiences, that is, outside the data range. Therefore, simulation of the new situation would involve extrapolation of available data outside the range used when estimating the model. In this case, combining information about the actual behavioural history of individuals with hypothetical changes to their behaviour through stated preference methods is seen as an obvious advantage of data fusion.

On the other hand, the purely hypothetical aspect of the latter can be checked against actual behaviour through revealed preference methods. Using revealed preference data assures that estimation is based on observed behaviour, and combining it with stated preference responses to hypothetical changes of ecosystem services allows the identification of value ranges that otherwise would not be identified. This way, the amount of information increases, and findings can be cross-validated (Haab and McConnell, 2002).

An example of the data-enriching approach is the study by Earnhart (2001) who combines a hedonic analysis (revealed preference approach) with a choice-conjoint analysis (state preference approach), in order to increase the reliability of estimated values regarding the aesthetic benefits generated by improving the quality of coastal wetlands near residential locations. In another example Birol et al (2006) combine a choice experiment model and a discrete-choice farm household model to produce more robust estimates of the value of Hungarian agricultural biodiversity, which comprises private use values of agrobiodiversity managed in home gardens as they accrue to the farmers who manage them.

Another complementary option is the use of a 'preference calibration' approach in which multiple value estimates for ecosystem services and biodiversity arising from different valuation methods such as hedonic property value, travel cost demand and contingent valuation can be used to calibrate a single preference function to reconcile potential differences (Smith et al, 2002). This is akin to the use of specific preference restrictions to link contingent valuation estimates of environmental quality improvements to revealed preference measures for a closely selected value change, taking place for the same biodiversity component or ecosystem service. The idea is to isolate restrictions linking the parameters estimated with the different revealed (and stated preference) methods (e.g. Smith et al, 2002).

4 Insurance value, resilience and (quasi-)option value

The insurance value of an ecosystem (see Section 2.3) is dependent on and related to the system's resilience. A general measure of the resilience of any system is the conditional probability that it will flip from one stability domain to another, given the current state of the system and the current disturbance regime (Perrings, 1998). These regimes are separated by thresholds, which are given by the level of disturbance that triggers a dramatic change in the state of ecosystems and the provision of ecosystem services (Muradian, 2001; Luck, 2005). Resilience relates to the vulnerability of a system, its capacity in a given state to accommodate perturbations without losing functionality (Box 5.6). For this section, ecological resilience is the capacity of a system to remain in a given configuration of states – a regime – in systems where multiple regimes are possible (Walker et al, 2006).

Box 5.6 Biodiversity and resilience

Resilience is a complex ecosystem property that is simultaneously related to the system's inner functioning and to cross-scale interactions (Holling, 2001; Holling and Gunderson, 2002). The semantics of resilience can be confusing, but studies suggest that resilience relates to features such as functional diversity within an ecosystem (Schulze and Mooney, 1993; Folke et al, 1996), and to functional redundancy within a given ecosystem function. Changes in the set of species in an ecosystem affect its capacity to support ecosystem services under various conditions, that is, functional redundancy. The links between biodiversity change and ecosystem functioning constitute a hot research topic in ecology (Loreau et al, 2003; Caldeira et al, 2005; Hooper et al, 2005; Spehn et al, 2005), as does the relationship between biodiversity and the resilience of ecological systems (Scheffer et al, 2001, 2003; Walker et al, 2004; Walker et al, 2006). Despite rising attention to these issues from ecologists, our knowledge about the functioning of regulating services and the capacity of the system to maintain functionality over a range of environmental conditions is still limited.

The literature on ecological resilience offers growing evidence of regime shifts in ecosystems when critical thresholds are reached as a consequence of either discrete disturbances or cumulative pressures (Scheffer et al, 2001; Folke et al, 2004; Walker and Meyers, 2004). This has been studied in a wide range of ecosystems, including among others temperate lakes (Carpenter and Cottingham, 1997), tropical lakes (Scheffer et al, 2003), coastal waters (Jansson and Jansson, 2002) and savannas (Anderies et al, 2002). When such shifts occur, the capacity of the ecosystem to underpin ecosystem services can change drastically and in a non-linear way (Folke et al, 2002).

The distance to an ecological threshold affects the economic value of ecosystem services given the sate of the ecosystem (Limburg et al, 2002). Valuation exercises cannot be carried out reliably without accounting for this distance. The reason is that when the system is *sufficiently* close to a threshold, radical uncertainty or ignorance about the potential and often non-linear consequences of a regime shift becomes a critical issue. This makes standard valuation approaches of little use. In other words, traditional valuation under radical uncertainty is unreliable at best (Pritchard et al, 2000; Limburg et al, 2002). In fact, while it may be possible to develop early warning indicators to anticipate proximity to such tipping points, available scientific knowledge has not yet progressed enough to anticipate shifts with precision (Biggs et al, 2009). This implies the existence of radical uncertainty and hence poses formidable challenges to valuation. The problem is that standard approaches to estimating the total economic value of ecosystem services are based on marginal changes over some non-critical range (Turner et al, 2003). Under such circumstances policy ought to resort to other complementary instruments such as using the safe minimum standard and the precautionary principle (Turner, 2007).

In more palatable situations where science can provide information about ecological resilience, decision makers still need information about the conditions that may trigger regime shifts, the ability of human societies to adapt to these transformations, and their socio-economic implications. There are at least three questions to direct a resilience assessment of ecosystem services (Walker and Pearson, 2007):

- Can major changes in the provision of ecosystem services be triggered by the transition to alternate stable regimes in a particular ecosystem?
- If so, how will the shift to the alternate regime affect people's valuation of ecosystem services? That is, what are the consequences, in terms of economic costs and benefits?
- What is the probability of crossing the threshold? This requires knowledge about where the threshold is, the level of current disturbance, and the properties of the system (see Chapter 2).

The latter question stresses the need to adopt a dynamic approach and to take into consideration the probability of alternative states given a level of disturbance. As resilience is reduced, for example due to human interventions, then the probability of regime shifts (either due to natural or human-induced disturbances) will rise (Scheffer et al, 2001).

One example is the regime shift that took place in Caribbean coral reefs (from pristine coral to algae-dominated systems). A pre-shift stage, characterized by increased nutrient loading combined with intensive fishing, reduced the number of herbivorous fishes. The event that led to the regime shift was a pathogen-induced mass mortality of a species of sea urchin, *Diadema antillarum*. Had the herbivorous fish populations not been so reduced in numbers, they could have replaced the ecological function of the sea urchin in controlling the population of algae (deYoung et al, 2008). The regime shift took place during the 1980s, within a period of one to two years, and the new state (algae-dominated ecosystems) has lasted for more than 20 years.

There are also plenty of cases showing that invasive species, whether introduced accidentally or deliberately, can also alter ecosystems and their services drastically, sometimes leading to a total and costly ecological regime shift (Perrings and Williamson 2000; Pimentel et al, 2005; Maron et al, 2006; Vitule et al, 2009), whether in water (Mills et al, 1993; Knowler, 2005) or on land (Cook et al, 2007). For example, *Miconia calvescens*, introduced as an ornamental tree in the 20th century in Hawaii, has since expanded rapidly. *Miconia* is now referred as 'the purple plague' of Hawaii, where its range covers over 1000km², including extensive mono-specific stands. It threatens watersheds, reduces biodiversity severely by driving endangered native species to local extinction and lowers recreational and aesthetic values (Kaiser, 2006).

One of the features of regime shifts in ecosystems is that the new regime may have a high level of resilience itself. Therefore the costs associated with transitioning back to the previous regime (i.e. restoration costs) may be very high. The increased probability of regime shifts that furthermore may be very hard to remediate has significant implications for the economic valuation of ecosystems. As ecosystems reach thresholds, marginal human impacts on the system will lead to increasingly uncertain non-marginal effects. Under these conditions, the reliable estimation of TEV becomes increasingly difficult – if not impossible.

4.1 What is the value of ecosystem resilience?

The value of the resilience of an ecosystem lies in its ability to maintain the provision of benefits under a given disturbance regime. The role of biodiversity in supporting an ecosystem's functions has been studied by, for example, Perrings and Gadgil (2003) and Figge (2004). Diversity within (Haldane and Jayakar, 1963; Bascompte et al, 2002) and among species (Ives and Hughes, 2002) can contribute to a stable flow of ecosystem service benefits. Ecological systems in which there are redundant species within functional groups experience lower levels of covariance in the 'returns' on members of such groups under varying environmental conditions than do systems that contain no redundant species. A marginal change in the value of ecosystem resilience thus corresponds to the difference in the expected value of the stream of benefits that the ecosystem yields given a range of environmental conditions.

The valuation of system resilience in some state can therefore be viewed to be analogous to the valuation of a portfolio of assets in a given state (Brock and Xepapadeas, 2002). The value of the asset mix – the portfolio – depends on the covariance in the returns on the individual assets it contains. Sanchirico et al (2008) apply financial asset management tools to multi-species fisheries, for example. They show that acknowledging covariance structures between revenues from catches of individual species can achieve a reduction in risk at no cost or loss of overall revenue.

It is worth noting that just as the value of a portfolio of financial assets depends on the risk preferences of the asset holders, so does the value of the ecosystem resilience, which depends on the risk preferences of society. The more risk averse is society, the more weight it will place on strategies that preserve or build ecosystem resilience, and the higher the value it would allocate to ecosystem configurations that are less variance prone (i.e. more resilient) (Armsworth and Roughgarden, 2003).

Currently, environmental economists interested in valuing resilience of ecosystems regard it not as a property but as natural capital (stock) yielding a 'natural insurance' service (flow) which can be interpreted as a benefit amenable for inclusion in cost–benefit analysis (Mäler et al, 2007; Walker et al, 2009). An example will help illustrate how and why to value resilience as an asset.

Irrigated agriculture in many parts of the world is under threat from rising salinity. Indeed, many erstwhile productive regions are now salinized and have little value to agriculture. The cause is rising water tables which are brought about through a combination of land clearing and irrigation. The rising water table brings with it salt from deeper layers in the soil up to the surface. An example in South East Australia shows that original water tables were very deep (30m) (Walker et al, 2009). Fluctuations in rainfall caused variations in water table depth, but these were not problematic. However, there is a critical threshold in the depth of the water table – ca. 2m, depending on soil type. Once the water table reaches this level, the salt is drawn to the surface by capillary action. When the water table is 3m below the surface, the top metre of soil – the 'stock' of topsoil that determines agricultural production – is the same as when the water table was 30m below. But it is much less resilient to water table fluctuations and the risk of salinization increases. Resilience, in this case, can be estimated as the distance from the water table to 2m below the surface. As this distance declines, the value of the stock of productive topsoil diminishes. Therefore any valuation exercise that includes only the status of the topsoil stock and ignores its resilience to water table fluctuations is inadequate and misleading.

Walker et al (2009) have estimated a value of the resilience stock 'salinity', which reflects the expected change in future social welfare from a marginal change in resilience as given by small changes in the water table today. Resilience (X) is equal to the current distance of the water table to the threshold – that is, 2m below the surface. Let $F(X_0,t)$ be the cumulative probability distribution of a flip up to time t if the initial resilience is X_0 based on past water table fluctuations and environmental conditions (i.e. rainfall, land clearing, etc.). It is assumed that the flip is irreversible or at least very costly to reverse. Walker et al (2009b) define $U_1(t)$ as the net present value of all ecosystem service benefits at time t if the system has not shifted at that time and $U_2(t)$ as the net present value of ecosystem service benefits in the alternate regime if the system has shifted before (or at) t. It can then be shown that the expected social welfare of resilience $W(X_0)$ is:

$$W(X_0) = \int_0^\infty [S(X_0,t)U_1(t) + F(X_0,t)U_2(t)]dt \qquad (1)$$

The current regime is one of agriculturally productive land (non-saline) and its ecosystem service value was estimated as the net present value of all current land under production (estimated market value). The alternate regime, saline land, was assumed to yield a minimal value for the land (i.e. U_2 is a small fraction of U_1) as it will lose all agricultural productivity, which is the basis for current regional social and economic conditions. The probability that the current agricultural regime will continue, $S(X_0,t)$ was estimated from past water table fluctuations and known relationships with agricultural practices now and into the future. Estimations showed significant expected loss in welfare due to salinity.

This formulation of resilience is specific to the case study but can be generalized. It may be easily extended to deal with reversible thresholds, multiple regimes (more than two), different denominators (i.e. monetary, etc.) and more than one type of resilience. The challenge lies in determining the accurate ecological and economic data that can be used to estimate probability functions, costs, discount rates etc. which are relevant to management decisions.

4.2 Main challenges of valuing ecosystem resilience

When it comes to economic valuation, at least three issues become salient in relation to non-linear behaviour and resilience of ecosystems. First, the fact that transitions may take place in uncertain, sudden and dramatic ways imposes severe limitations on the marginalist approach that underlies most valuation methods. The majority of methods allocate economic values to changes *at the margin*, assuming that small human disturbances produce proportional changes in the condition of ecosystems and therefore in their capacity to provide ecosystem services. If threshold effects are present, however, then an extrapolation of the economic value based on marginal changes is no longer valid. As Barbier et al (2008, p321) formulate it, the linearity assumption 'can lead to the misrepresentation of economic values inherent in (ecosystem) services' by creating a bias to either side of the conservation–development debate.

Secondly, the capacity of ecologists both to assess the level of resilience and to detect when a system is approaching a threshold is still incipient. Contamin and Ellison (2009) point out that 'prospective indicators of regime shifts exist, but when the information about processes driving the system is incomplete or when intensive management actions cannot be implemented rapidly, many years of advance warning are required to avert a regime shift'. They add that to enhance predictive capacity would normally require considerable resources and time, which usually are not available to decision makers. This is particularly the case in developing countries. In addition, what seems to be clear is that the larger the spatial scale, the higher the complexity and therefore more difficult it is to detect and predict regime shifts (deYoung et al, 2008).

Thirdly, we often fail to learn of the benefits provided by a given species or ecosystem until it is gone (Vatn and Bromley, 1994). For example, the North American passenger pigeon was once the most populous bird species on the planet, and its population was deemed inexhaustible. However, excessive hunting led to its extinction at the beginning of the 20th century. It then became clear that passenger pigeons had been consuming untold tons of acorns. Scientists speculate that with the pigeons demise, acorns were consumed by deer and mice, leading to a boom in their populations, followed by a boom in the populations of ticks that fed on them, and finally in the populations of spirochaetes that lived in the ticks. The result was an entirely unpredictable epidemic in Lyme disease several decades after the loss of the pigeons (Blockstein, 1998).

In summary, standard valuation approaches ought to be used over the non-critical range and far from ecological thresholds. By contrast, serious constraints on traditional economic valuation methods exist when ecological thresholds are identified by science as being 'sufficiently' close and when the potential irreversibility and magnitude of the non-marginal effects of regime shifts are also deemed sufficiently important. Our ability to observe and predict the dynamics of ecosystems and biodiversity will always be limited (Harwood and Stokes, 2003) and ecosystem management strategies need to consider how we live with irreducible sources of uncertainty about future benefits. In situations of radical uncertainty resilience should be approached with the precautionary principle and safe minimum standards.

Economists have traditionally used stated preference and revealed preference techniques to determine monetary values of ecosystems (reviewed in the previous sections). When radical uncertainty is not an issue, thoughts regarding the ability of these methods to handle thresholds and resilience are still being developed and new valuation approaches that account for uncertainty have been attempted, including bioeconomic models that regard resilience as a stock and not just as a property of the ecosystem.

4.3 Dealing with (quasi-)option value

In the context of valuation of expected outcomes, the concepts of 'option value' and 'quasi-option value' are anchored in the expected utility theory (see Section 2.3). Even if an ecosystem (or component of it) has no current use, it may have option value. Barbier et al (2009) point out, for instance, that the future may bring human diseases or agricultural pests that are unknown today. In this case, today's biodiversity would have an option value insofar as the variety of existing plants may already contain a cure against the as yet unknown disease, or a biological control of the as yet unknown pest (Polasky and Solow, 1995; Simpson et al, 1996; Goeschl and Swanson, 2003). In this sense, the option value of biodiversity conservation corresponds to an 'insurance premium' (Perrings, 1998; Baumgärtner, 2008), which one is willing to pay today in order to reduce the potential loss should an adverse event occur in the future. Accordingly, option value can be defined as 'the added amount a risk averse person would pay for some amenity, over and above its current value in consumption, to maintain the option of having that amenity available for the future, given that the future availability of the amenity is uncertain' (Bulte et al, 2002, p151).

The option value assumes supply uncertainty of ecosystem services and derives from risk aversion on the part of the beneficiaries of such services. It is usually measured as the difference between the *option price*, the largest sure payment that an individual will pay for a policy before uncertainty is resolved, and the *expected consumer surplus*, which is the probability-weighted sum of consumer surpluses over all potential states of the world (Pearce and Turner, 1990). The size and sign of the option value have been subject to empirical discussions and it is found to depend on the source of uncertainty (Perman et al, 2003).[7]

If it is possible to reduce supply uncertainty about ecosystem services by acquiring further scientific information on ecosystems over time, the notion of *quasi-option value* becomes more relevant. It is the value of preserving options for future use given expected growth of knowledge. The quasi-option value is generally agreed to be positive if such growth of knowledge is independent of actual changes in the ecosystem (Pearce and Turner, 1990). In this case quasi-option value measures the benefit of information and remaining flexible by avoiding possibly irreversible changes.

Valuation studies that have focused on quasi-option values have largely dealt with the role of bioprospecting. This is so because the uncertainty surrounding the future commercial value of the genetic material present in ecosystems creates an incentive to conserve it (Arrow and Fisher, 1974). It is argued that as uncertainty regarding the ecosystem is resolved (i.e. as the genetic material within the system is screened) the quasi-option value of resource conservation diminishes (Barrett and Lybbert, 2000).[8]

Bulte et al (2002) provide a possible approach to calculating quasi-option value, in the context of non-use values of primary forest in Costa Rica. The provision of ecosystem services of the forest is uncertain but expected to be increasing, and deforestation of primary forest is thought to have an irreversible negative effect on the provision of such services. The quasi-option value of maintaining primary forests is included as a component of investment in natural capital. The uncertainty of ecosystem service supply in this case – as in many others – arises essentially from uncertain income growth rates, which affect preferences and thus demand for forest conservation, as well as from the possible future availability of substitutes for the ecosystem services supplied by the forest.

It should be clear that calculating option and quasi-option values is not straightforward. First the risk preferences of individuals need to be known. While option values are associated with degrees of risk aversion, risk neutrality is assumed to hold for quasi-option values (Bulte et al, 2002). Finding out risk preferences is not trivial, however. Additionally, experimental studies on the relation between risk preferences and economic circumstances do not support simple generalizations, particularly if individuals face extraordinarily risky environments in general (Mosley and Verschoor, 2005).

Calculating option and quasi-option values are thus perhaps one of the most problematic issues surrounding valuation of ecosystem services. However, such values may be significant especially with regard to irreversible changes to natural capital. It is important to know the extent to which ecosystem services may be demanded in the future and which ones may become unavailable. It is this information about future preferences and future availability of the services that is most highly needed to calculate option and quasi-option values.

There is increasing experimental evidence that the theory of expected utility, on which the concepts of option and quasi-option rely, is not an accurate model of economic behaviour. Analysts need to compare results of estimates produced using (modified) expected utility models with estimates based on the prospect theory, the regret theory and other non-expected utility models (e.g. see reviews in Rekola (2004) and Mosley and Verschoor (2005) for detailed discussions). Such alternative theories are gaining more support, and previous ways to estimate (quasi-)option values may need to be revised. Individuals may choose among and value ecosystem services through alternative behavioural rules rather than systematically weighing probabilistic outcomes.

5 Valuation across stakeholders and applying valuation in developing countries

5.1 Valuation across stakeholders

For the economic valuation of ecosystem services, identification of relevant stakeholders is a critical issue (Hein et al, 2006). In almost all steps of the valuation procedure, stakeholder involvement is essential in order to determine main policy and management objectives, to identify the main relevant services and assess their values, and to discuss trade-offs involved in ecosystem services use or enjoyment (de Groot et al, 2006). Here, stakeholders refer to persons, organizations or groups with interest in the way a particular ecosystem service is used, enjoyed or managed.

Stakeholder-oriented approaches in economic valuation connect valuation to possible management alternatives in order to solve social conflicts. Using stakeholder analysis in ecosystem services valuation can support the identification and evaluation of who wins and who loses when possible management strategies are implemented in a social-ecological system. Hence, identifying and characterizing stakeholders and their individual reasons for conserving different ecosystem services could help resolve conflicts and develop better policies.

Socio-cultural characterization of the stakeholders beforehand may be critical to determining these underlying factors. This characterization is, however, a largely unexplored issue in economic valuation research (Manski, 2000). As stated by Adamowicz (2004), economic valuation based on factors that influence monetary value generates more useful information than making a simple inventory of values.

Different stakeholders often attach different values to ecosystem services depending on cultural background and the impact the service has on their living conditions (Kremen et al, 2000; Hein et al, 2006). Further, goods with wider spillovers are more 'public' in nature, and require contributions from a more diverse set of donors. For this reason different types of ecosystem services are valued differently as the spatial scale of the analysis varies (Hein et al, 2006; Martín-López et al, 2007). Local agents tend to attach higher values to provisioning services than national or global agents, who attach more value to regulating or cultural services.

Considering spatial scales and stakeholders enhances the ability of ecosystem service valuation studies to support decision making. The formulation of management plans that are acceptable to all stakeholders requires the balancing of their interests at different scales (Hein et al, 2006). Since different stakeholders have different interests in ecosystem services use and enjoyment (Martín-López et al, 2009b), there is a potential imbalance between the costs that arise at the local level from ecosystem management and the benefits that accrue at the national and international levels. Policy makers who are aware of these differences can implement management measures that limit or even reduce social inequities. One option that is currently widely considered is to compensate people living in or near protected areas through Payment for Ecosystem Services (Ferraro and Kramer, 1997; Muradian et al, 2010). This policy instrument is presented in more detail in TEEB in National Policy (2011) and TEEB in Local Policy (2011).

The stakeholder approach in valuation processes entails a challenge because it requires stakeholder involvement in the entire process. It may lead to identification of knowledge gaps and research needs as the process progresses (Hermans et al, 2006). This involvement can be supported by tools of participatory analysis, as well as by deliberative monetary valuation (Spash, 2007, 2008). In using tools for participatory analysis, all stakeholder types must be fairly represented in order to prevent one stakeholder type dominating the process. Therefore, identifying and selecting organizations and stakeholders representatives is an essential part of economic valuation of ecosystem services.

Future steps of the stakeholder-oriented approach in ecosystem services valuation processes should include: (1) the prioritization of stakeholders based on their degree of influence in the ecosystem services management and their degree of dependence on the ecosystem services (de Groot et al, 2006), and (2) the identification of stakeholders based on their capacity to adapt to disturbances and their governance capacity in order to identify who are able to manage in the long term the ecosystem services provided by biodiversity (Fabricius et al, 2007).

5.2 Applying monetary valuation in developing countries

Biodiversity supports a range of goods and services that are of fundamental importance to people for health, well-being, livelihoods and survival (Daily, 1997; MA, 2005). Often, it is the people from the poorest regions in developing economies that have the greatest immediate dependency on these stocks – such as direct reliance on natural resources for food, fuel, building material and natural medicines. Gaining a better understanding of the role of biodiversity is fundamental for securing the livelihoods and well-being of people in developing countries.

In recent years many studies have examined how people value biodiversity (Nunes and van den Bergh, 2001; Christie et al, 2004, 2007). The majority of this work has been conducted in the developed world with only limited application in developing countries (Abaza and Rietbergen-McCracken, 1998; Georgiou et al, 2006; Van Beukering et al, 2007). In a search of the Environmental Valuation Research Inventory (EVRI) database of valuation studies (www.evri.ca), Christie et al (2008) have recently identified 195 studies that aimed to value biodiversity in developing countries. This number represented approximately one-tenth of all published biodiversity valuation studies at the time. These studies were equally distributed between 'lower middle income' and 'lower income' countries, but no studies were found of valuation in the poorest 'transition economies'. Half the studies identified were conducted in Asia, 18 per cent in Africa and 5 per cent in South America. It is therefore evident that there is great variability in the application of valuation in developing countries, with the poorest countries and some regions having little or no coverage.

The application of economic valuation in developing countries is clearly in its infancy. Further, it is clear that there are significant methodological, practical and policy challenges associated with applying valuation techniques in developing countries. Many of these challenges stem from the local socio-economic, political situation in developing countries which may mean that a direct transfer of methods is not appropriate. Thus, it is likely that some modification of standard approaches may be required to do good valuation studies in developing countries. The Christie et al (2008) review of biodiversity valuation in developing countries highlights many of these challenges. Here we pay special attention to methodological, practical and policy issues.

With regard to methodological issues it should be noted that low levels of literacy and education create barriers to valuing complex environmental goods, as well as creating difficulties for utilizing traditional survey techniques such as questionnaires and interviews. More deliberative and participatory approaches to data collection may overcome these issues (Bourque and Fielder, 1995; Jackson and Ingles, 1998; Asia Forest Network, 2002; Fazey et al, 2007) (see Box 5.6).

Many developing countries have informal or subsistence economies, in which people may have little or no experience of dealing with money. The consequence of this is that they would find it extremely difficult to place a monetary value on a complex environmental good. Some researchers have attempted to address this issue by assessing willingness to pay in terms of other measures of wealth, for example number of bags of rice (Shyamsundar and Kramer, 1996; Rowcroft et al, 2004).

The majority of valuation methods have been developed and refined by researchers from developed countries. There is evidence that the current best-practice guidelines for these methods might not be appropriate for applications in developing countries. For example, the NOAA guidelines for contingent valuation suggest taxation as the most appropriate payment vehicle. However, many people in developing countries do not pay taxes, and may not trust the government to deliver policy (McCauley and Mendes, 2006).

As for implications for practitioners of valuation studies, it should be pointed out that many developing countries are affected by extreme environmental conditions which may affect the researcher's ability to access areas or effectively undertake research (Bush et al, 2004; Fazey et al, 2007). In

---

Box 5.7 Participatory valuation methods

Participatory valuation methods differ from economic valuation methods in several aspects, including the following:

- **Focus**: Participatory valuation methods ought to have a focused perspective that limits data to the needs of valuation. Collecting contextual data can be important to understand local situations but collecting extraneous or unnecessary information can waste time and confuse the purpose of the valuation objective.
- **Flexibility**: It is important to allow for the ability to adapt to changing local conditions, unanticipated setbacks during the valuation study design, and the process of developing and applying specific valuation techniques in conjunction with participants.
  - *Overlapping techniques*: Participatory valuation methods gain in effectiveness when different techniques collect at least some of the same data from different participants as this makes it possible to cross-check valuation results.
  - *Cooperation*: In designing and implementing valuation studies, gaining the full support of local stakeholders is important to obtain reliable information and to develop a sense of learning between all participants.
  - *Sharing*: The outcome of the valuation studies needs to be communicated back to stakeholders in order to strengthen the focus of the valuation approach.

Source: Jarvis et al (2000)

many developing countries there may be a lack of local research capacity to design, administer and analyse research projects. However, the involvement of local people is considered essential within the research process to ensure that local nuances and values are accounted for (Bourque and Fielder, 1995; Whittington, 1998; Alberini and Cooper, 2000).[9]

Lastly, one of the main aspects to be kept in mind when using valuation in developing countries is the lack of local research capacity as this may result in a lack of awareness of valuation methods. A capacity-building programme on these issues is considered important if developing countries are effectively to address biodiversity issues. Much of the existing biodiversity valuation research is extractive, with little input from or influence on local policy (Barton et al, 1997). Incorporating ideas from action research into valuation is seen as being essential if this type of research is to meaningfully influence policy (Wadsworth, 1998).

It is clear that the way people in developing countries think about the natural environment is different to that of people in developed countries. All of the issues discussed above mean that it may be extremely difficult for people from developing countries to express their valuation of ecosystem services and biodiversity as compared to people from more developed economies, who usually hold different value concepts that are more closely related to market economics. Hence, standard approaches to valuation in developing countries should be taken with due caution. These issues further suggest that valuation may be more effective if (i) local researchers are used throughout the research process, and (ii) deliberative, participative and action research approaches are incorporated into the valuation methods.

6 Benefit transfer and scaling up values

6.1 Benefit transfer as a method to value ecosystem services

To estimate the value of ecosystem services one would ideally commission detailed ecological and economic studies of each ecosystem of interest. Undertaking new ecological and economic studies, however, is expensive and time-consuming, making it impractical in many policy settings. Benefit (or value) transfer (BT henceforth) is an approach to overcome the lack of system-specific information in a relatively inexpensive and timely manner. BT is the procedure of estimating the value of an ecosystem service by transferring an existing valuation estimate from a similar ecosystem. The ecosystem to which values are transferred is termed the 'policy site' and the ecosystem from which the value estimate is borrowed is termed the 'study site'. If care is taken to closely match policy and study sites or to adjust values to reflect important differences between sites, BT can be a useful approach to estimate the value of ecosystem services (Smith et al, 2002).[10]

BT methods can be divided into four categories: (i) unit BT, (ii) adjusted unit BT, (iii) value function transfer, and (iv) meta-analytic function transfer.

Unit BT involves estimating the value of an ecosystem service at a policy site by multiplying a mean unit value estimated at a study site by the quantity of that ecosystem service at the policy site. Unit values are generally either expressed as values per household or as values per unit of area. In the former case, aggregation of values is over the relevant population that hold values for the ecosystem in question. In the latter case, aggregation of values is over the area of the ecosystem.

Adjusted unit transfer involves making simple adjustments to the transferred unit values to reflect differences in site characteristics. The most common adjustments are for differences in income between study and policy sites and for differences in price levels over time or between sites.

Value or demand function transfer methods use functions estimated through valuation applications (travel cost, hedonic pricing, contingent valuation or choice modelling) for a study site together with information on parameter values for the policy site to transfer values. Parameter values of the policy site are plugged into the value function to calculate a transferred value that better reflects the characteristics of the policy site.

Lastly, meta-analytic function transfer uses a value function estimated from multiple study results together with information on parameter values for the policy site to estimate values. The value function therefore does not come from a single study but from a collection of studies. This allows the value function to include greater variation in both site characteristics (e.g. socio-economic and physical attributes) and study characteristics (e.g. valuation method) that cannot be generated from a single primary valuation study. Rosenberger and Phipps (2007) identify the important assumptions underlying the use of meta-analytic value functions for BT: First, there exists an underlying meta-valuation function that relates estimated values of a resource to site and study characteristics. Primary valuation studies provide point estimates on this underlying function that can subsequently be used in meta-analysis to estimate it; second, differences between sites can be captured through a price vector; thirdly, values are stable over time, or vary in a systematic way; and lastly, the sampled primary valuation studies provide 'correct' estimates of value.

The complexity of applying these BT methods increases in the order in which they have been presented. Unit BT is relatively simple to apply but may ignore important differences between study and policy sites. Meta-analytic function transfer on the other hand has the potential to control for differences between study and policy sites but can be complex and time-consuming if an existing meta-analytic value function is not available (i.e. primary studies need to be collected, coded in a database, and a value function estimated). The complexity of the BT method does not necessarily imply lower transfer errors. In cases where a high quality primary valuation study is available for a study site with very similar characteristics to the policy site, simple unit BT may result in the most precise value estimate.

BT methods generally transfer values either in terms of value per beneficiary (e.g. value per person or household) or value per unit of area of ecosystem (e.g. value per hectare). The former approach explicitly recognizes that it is people who hold values for ecosystem services, whereas the latter approach emphasizes the spatial extent of ecosystems in the provision of services. In practical terms it is often difficult to identify the beneficiaries of ecosystem services and many valuation methods do not produce value estimates in per person/household terms (e.g. production function approach, net factor income method). It is therefore often more practical to define values for transfer in terms of units of area.

6.2 Challenges in benefit transfer for ecosystem services at individual ecosystem sites

6.2.1 Transfer errors

The application of any of the BT methods described above may result in significant transfer errors, meaning that transferred values may differ significantly from the actual value of the ecosystem under consideration. There are three general sources of error in the values estimated using value transfer:

1   Errors associated with estimating the original measures of value at the study site(s). Measurement error in primary valuation estimates may result from weak methodologies, unreliable data, analyst errors, and the whole gamut of biases and inaccuracies associated with valuation methods.

2   Errors arising from the transfer of study site values to the policy site. So-called generalization error occurs when values for study sites are transferred to policy sites that are different without fully accounting for those differences. Such differences may be in terms of population characteristics (income, culture, demographics, education, etc.) or environmental/physical characteristics (quantity and/or quality of the good or service, availability of substitutes, accessibility, etc.). This source of error is inversely related to the correspondence of characteristics of the study and policy sites. There may also be a temporal source of generalization error in that preferences and values for ecosystem services may not remain constant over time. Using BT to estimate values for ecosystem services under future policy scenarios may therefore entail a degree of uncertainty regarding whether future generations hold the same preferences as current or past generations.

Publication selection bias may result in an unrepresentative stock of knowledge on ecosystem values. Publication selection bias arises when the publication process through which valuation results are disseminated results in an available stock of knowledge that is skewed to certain types of results and that does not meet the information needs of value transfer practitioners. In the economics literature there is generally an editorial preference to publish statistically significant results and novel valuation applications rather than replications, which may result in publication bias.

Given the potential errors in applying BT, it is useful to examine the scale of these errors in order to inform decisions related to the use of value transfer. In making decisions based on transferred values or in choosing between commissioning a BT application or a primary valuation study, policy makers need to know the potential errors involved. In response to this need there is now a sizeable literature that tests the accuracy of BT. Rosenberger and Stanley (2006) and Eshet et al (2007) provide useful overviews of this literature. Evidence from recent studies that examine the relative performance of alternative BT methods for international benefit transfers suggests that value function and meta-analytic function transfers result in lower mean transfer errors (e.g. Lindhjem and Navrud, 2007; Rosenberger and Phipps, 2007).

It is not possible to prescribe a specific acceptable level of transfer error for policy decision making. What can be considered an acceptable level of transfer error is dependent on the context in which the value estimate is used. Precise value estimates that minimize transfer errors are needed to determine compensation for environmental damage. On the other hand, for regional assessments of the value of ecosystem services, higher transfer errors may be acceptable, particularly in cases where site specific errors cancel out when aggregated.

6.2.2 Aggregation of transferred values

Aggregation refers to multiplying the unit value of an ecosystem service by the quantity demanded/supplied to estimate the total value of that service. The units in which values are transferred (either per beneficiary or per unit area) have important implications for the aggregation of values to estimate total value. In the case that values are expressed per beneficiary, aggregation implies the estimation of the total WTP of a population by applying the individual WTP value from a representative sample to the relevant population that hold values for the ecosystem service in question. In order to do this, the analyst needs to assess what the size of the market is for the ecosystem service, that is, identify the population that hold values for the ecosystem. In the case that values are expressed per unit of area, values are aggregated over the total area of the ecosystem in question. This approach focuses more on the supply of ecosystem services than on the level of demand, and care needs to be taken that it is received services and not potential supply that are assessed. In this case, the effect of the market size for an ecosystem service needs to be reflected in the estimated per unit area value.

Aggregation can also refer to summing up the value of different ecosystem services of the same good. Summing across all services provided by a specific ecosystem provides an estimate of the total economic value of that ecosystem. This procedure should be conducted with caution to avoid double counting of ecosystem service values. As long as the ecosystem services are entirely independent, adding up the values is possible. However, ecosystem services can be mutually exclusive, interacting or integral (Turner et al, 2004). The interaction of ecosystem services and values can also be dependent on their relative geographical position, for instance with substitutes that are spatially dependent.

Aggregation of ecosystem service values over a large number of services can result in improbable large numbers (Brown and Shogren, 1998). If the estimated value of maintaining a single ecosystem service is relatively large (say one tenth of one per cent of household wealth) then summing over all ecosystem services that a household might be called upon to support might give implausibly large estimates.

6.2.3 Challenges related to spatial scale

Spatial scale is recognized as an important issue to the transfer of ecosystem service values (Hein et al, 2006). The spatial scales at which ecosystem services are supplied and demanded contribute to the complexity of transferring values between sites. On the supply side, ecosystems themselves vary in spatial scale (e.g. small individual patches, large continuous areas, regional networks) and provide services at varying spatial scales. The services that ecosystems provide can be both on- and off-site. For example, a forest might provide recreational opportunities (on-site), downstream flood prevention (local off-site), and climate regulation (global off-site). On the demand side, beneficiaries of ecosystem services also vary in terms of their location relative to the ecosystem service(s) in question. While many ecosystem services may be appropriated locally, there are also manifold services that are received by beneficiaries at a wider geographical scale.

Spatial scale raises a number of challenges in conducting accurate BT. Most of these challenges are dealt with in separate subsections but are mentioned here to highlight the cross-cutting importance of spatial scale. Consideration of the spatial scale of the provision of ecosystem services and location of beneficiaries is important for the aggregation of values to calculate the total economic value of these services and for dealing with heterogeneity in site and context characteristics. The availability and proximity of substitute and complementary ecosystem sites and services in particular has a clear spatial dimension. Spatial scale is also highly relevant to the issue of distance decay and spatial discounting.

Important spatial variables and relationships for BT can be usefully defined and modelled using geographical information systems (GIS). Socio-economic characteristics of beneficiaries (e.g. income, culture and preferences) that are not spatial variables *per se* can also often be usefully defined in a spatial manner (e.g. by administrative area, region or country) using GIS. There are a growing number of studies that utilize GIS in conducting BT (e.g. Lovett et al, 1997; Bateman et al, 2003).

6.2.4 Variation in values with ecosystem characteristics and context

Values for ecosystem services are likely to vary with the characteristics of the ecosystem site (area, integrity and type of ecosystem), beneficiaries (distance to site, number of beneficiaries, income, preferences, culture), and context (availability of substitute and complementary sites and services). It is therefore important to recognize this variation in values and make appropriate adjustments when transferring values between study sites and policy sites with different characteristics and contexts.

The characteristics of an ecosystem will influence the value of the services it provides. For example, the extent to which vegetation in coastal marshes attenuates waves and provides protection to coastal communities from storm surges depends upon the height of the vegetation in the water column (which varies by time of year and tide), width of the vegetation zone, density of vegetation, height of waves (which varies by storm intensity), coastal bathymetry and other factors (Das and Vincent, 2009; Koch et al, 2009). BT methods therefore need to account for differences in site characteristics. In the case of the unit transfer method, study sites and policy sites need to be carefully matched. In the case of value function transfer and meta-analytic function transfer, parameters need to be included in the functions to control for important site characteristics. Ecosystem size is an important site characteristic and the issue of non-constant marginal values over the size of an ecosystem is discussed in this chapter.

Ecosystems often have multiple and heterogeneous groups of beneficiaries (differing in terms of spatial location and socio-economic characteristics). For example, the provision of recreational opportunities and aesthetic enjoyment by an ecosystem will generally only benefit people in the immediate vicinity, whereas the existence of a high level of biodiversity may be valued by people at a much larger spatial scale. Differences in the size and characteristics of groups of beneficiaries per ecosystem service need to be taken into account in transferring and aggregating values for each service. In conducting BT it is important to control for differences in the characteristics of beneficiaries between the study and policy sites. Again this can be done by either using closely similar sites in unit transfer or by including parameters in value functions that can be used to adjust transferred values. For example, transferred values can be adjusted to reflect differences in income by using estimated elasticities of WTP with respect to income (see for example Brander et al, 2006; Schläpfer, 2006; Brander et al, 2007; Jacobsen and Hanley, 2008).

BT should also account for important differences in context, such as differences in the availability of substitute and complementary sites and services. The availability of substitute (complementary) sites within the vicinity of an ecosystem is expected to reduce (increase) the value of ecosystem services from that ecosystem. For example, in a meta-analysis of wetland valuation studies Ghermandi et al (2007) find a significant negative relationship between the value of wetland ecosystem services and the abundance of wetlands (measured as the area of wetland within a 50km radius of each valued wetland site). This issue is of importance to the scaling-up of ecosystem service values.

6.2.5 Non-constant marginal values

Many ecosystem service values have non-constant returns to scale. Some ecosystem service values exhibit diminishing returns to scale – that is, adding an additional unit of area to a large ecosystem increases the total value of ecosystem services less than an additional unit of area to a smaller ecosystem (Brander et al, 2006, 2007). Diminishing returns may occur either because of underlying ecological relationships (e.g. species–area curves) or because of declining marginal utility by users of services. In contrast, other ecosystem services such as habitat provision may exhibit increasing returns to scale over some range. For example, if the dominant goal is to maintain a viable population of some large predator, habitats too small to do so may have limited value until they reach a size large enough to be capable of supporting a viable population. It is therefore important to account for the size of the ecosystem being valued and the size of the change in this ecosystem by, for example, using estimated value elasticities with respect to size (see for example, Brander et al, 2007). The appropriateness of this approach is limited by complexities in ecosystem service provision related to non-linearities, step changes and thresholds (see Chapter 2). Simple linear adjustments for changes in ecosystem size will not capture these effects.

6.2.6 Distance decay and spatial discounting

The value of many ecosystem services is expected to decline as the distance between beneficiary and ecosystem increases (so called distance decay). The rate at which the value of an ecosystem service declines with distance can be represented by spatial discounting, that is, placing a lower weight on the value of ecosystem services that are further away (or conversely, making a downward adjustment to estimated values held by beneficiaries that are located further from the ecosystem site).

Aggregation of transferred values across beneficiaries without accounting for distance decay may result in serious overestimation of total values. An illustrative example can be found in Bateman et al (2005), who compare different aggregation methods and assess the effect of neglecting distance-effects. Instead of simply aggregating sample means, they apply a spatially sensitive valuation function that takes into account the distance to the site and the socio-economic characteristics of the population in the calculation of values. Thereby, the variability of values across the entire economic market area is better represented in the total WTP. They found that not accounting for distance in the aggregation procedure can lead to overestimations of total benefits of up to 600 per cent.

The rate of distance decay is likely to vary across ecosystem services. Direct-use values are generally expected to decline with distance to an ecosystem but the rate of decay will vary across ecosystem services depending on how far beneficiaries are willing to travel to access each specific service, the differentiated availability of substitute services, or the spatial scale at which ecosystem services are 'delivered' by an ecosystem. The market size or economic constituency for ecosystem services from a specific ecosystem will therefore vary across services. For example, beneficiaries may be willing to travel a large distance to view unique fauna (distance decay of value is low and people in a wide geographic area hold values for the ecosystem and species of interest) whereas beneficiaries may not travel far to access clean water for swimming (distance decay of value is high due to availability of substitute sites for swimming and only people within a short distance of the ecosystem hold values for maintaining water quality to allow swimming). Non-use values may also decline with distance between the ecosystem and beneficiary, although this relationship may be less related to distance than to cultural or political boundaries. The spatial discounting literature suggests that non-use values should have much lower spatial discount rates than use values (Brown et al, 2002). In some cases, non-use values may not decline at all with distance – the rate of spatial discounting is zero. This might be the case for existence values for certain charismatic species that are known worldwide.

Loomis (2000) examines spatial discounting for the preservation of a range of threatened environmental goods in the US (spotted owls, salmon and wetlands, as well as a group of 62 threatened and endangered species). The first finding from this research is that WTP does fall off with distance. However, there are still substantial benefits to households that live more than a thousand miles from the habitat areas for these species. This implies that limiting summation of household benefits to nearby locations results in a large underestimation of the total benefits. These results have two implications for BT. First, WTP is not zero as one moves beyond commonly used political jurisdictions such as states in the USA and possibly within single countries in the European Union. Given the available data there are no means to ascertain how values change across countries. Such cross-country comparison of values of ecosystem services is an important avenue for future research. Second, while values per household do not fall to zero at distances of a thousand miles or more, it is important to recognize that there is a spatial discount, so generalizing values obtained from an area where the species resides to the population in a wider geographic area would overstate WTP values. The limited data discussed above suggest there may be a 20 per cent discount in the values per household at 1000 miles and a 40–50 per cent discount at 2000 miles for high-profile species or habitats.

6.2.7 Equity weighting

In conducting BT between study and policy sites with different socio-economic characteristics it is important to take account of differences in income levels. Generally there is an expectation that WTP for environmental improvements is positively related to income. Adjustments to transferred values can be made using estimated income elasticities (e.g. Brander et al, 2006; Schläpfer, 2006; Brander et al, 2007; Jacobsen and Hanley, 2008). An argument can also be made, however, for the use of equity weighting to reflect the greater dependence of the poor, particularly in developing countries, on ecosystem services, especially provisioning services (food and shelter). Equity weights correspond to the intuition that 'a dollar to a poor person is not the same as a dollar to a rich person'. More formally, the marginal utility of consumption declines as income increases: a rich person will obtain less utility from an extra dollar available for consumption compared to a poor person.

Equity-weighted ecosystem service value estimates take into account that the same decline in ecosystem service provision to someone who is poor causes greater welfare loss than if that change in service had happened to someone who is rich. Using local or regional data instead of national data for such an exercise is important in order to avoid smoothing of income inequalities by using larger regions to calculate average per capita incomes. Use of equity weights is particularly appropriate in the context of transferring values for ecosystem services from developed to developing countries, given the huge difference in income of those affected and the difficulties to assess the true welfare loss (Anthoff et al, 2007).

6.2.8 Availability of primary estimates for ecosystem service values

The scope for using BT for estimating the value of ecosystem services is limited by the availability of high-quality primary valuation studies for all relevant ecosystem types, ecosystem services, and socio-economic and cultural contexts.

Importantly, data from poorly designed empirical studies will compromise the robustness of BT (the phrase '*garbage in, garbage out*' appropriately describes this issue). Some types of ecosystem are well-represented in the economic valuation literature (e.g. wetlands and forests) whereas for others there are relatively few primary valuation studies from which to transfer values (e.g. marine, grassland and mountain ecosystems). Similarly, some ecosystem services are better covered in the valuation literature than others. For example, recreation and environmental amenities are well-represented whereas valuation studies for regulating services are uncommon. There is also a relative dearth of ecosystem service valuation studies conducted in developing countries (Christie et al, 2008). This represents a major gap in the available information base for BT since dependence on and preferences for ecosystem services, and consequently values, are likely to be substantially different between developed and developing countries.

There is also a (understandably) limited availability of primary valuation studies that estimate values for changes in ecosystem services outside of the context of the current availability of substitute and complementary ecosystems. The marginal value of changes in ecosystem service provision in a situation where the overall level of provision is greatly diminished is therefore beyond the domain of general observations and therefore principally unknown. This has implications for the possibilities for scaling-up ecosystem services values across large geographic areas and entire stocks of ecosystems.

6.3 Scaling-up the values of ecosystem services

The challenges encountered in conducting reliable BT, discussed above, relate to the transfer of values to estimate the value of individual ecosystem sites. When using BT to estimate the value of an entire stock of an ecosystem or provision of all ecosystem services within a large geographic area (so-called 'scaling-up'), the value of ecosystem services over an entire region or biome cannot be found simply by adding up estimated values from smaller ecosystem sites, a problem that becomes much worse in the presence of non-linear socio-ecological dynamics. Large-scale changes in the provision of ecosystem services will likely result in changes in the marginal value of services. Therefore, scaling-up to estimate the total economic value in a large geographic area requires taking account of the non-constancy of marginal values. Adjustments to these values can be made using estimated value elasticities with respect to ecosystem scarcity (e.g. Brander et al, 2007).

Conceptually, the economic value of a loss in the provision of an ecosystem service can be expressed as the area under the demand curve for the service that is bounded by the pre-change level of provision and the post-change level of provision, everything else being equal. For some ecosystem services it may be possible to make general assertions about the shape of the demand curve. For example, in cases where ecosystem services can be relatively easily and cheaply provided through human-engineered solutions, or degraded or lost without much loss of utility, the demand curve should be relatively easy to draw. However, for critical services essential to sustain human life and for which no adequate substitutes are available (Ekins et al, 2003; Farley, 2008) such

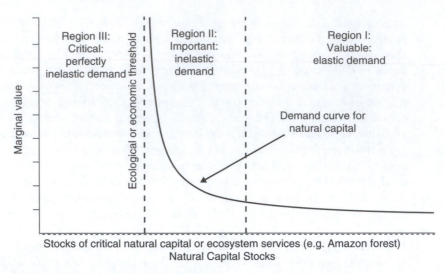

Figure 5.5 *The demand curve for natural capital*

Source: Farley (2008)

estimations are much harder. Therefore, our capacity to predict future demand for scarcer environmental goods or services, whose dynamics moreover are hardly predictable, will likely remain very limited.

Figure 5.5 depicts a stylized demand curve for critical natural capital with an economic or ecological threshold. In region I, where stocks are abundant and marginal value is low, marginal values remain reasonably constant with respect to changes in stocks. Over this range of service provision, the value of changes in supply can be reasonably well estimated using constant marginal values. Monetary valuation may facilitate decisions on allocation between conserving or not natural capital. As the overall level of natural capital declines (region II), marginal value begins to rise steeply and natural capital stocks are less resilient and approaching a threshold beyond which they cannot spontaneously recover from further loss or degradation. Marginal uses are increasingly important, and values are increasingly sensitive to small changes in stocks (inelastic demand). Hence, over this range the use of *constant* marginal values to assess changes in ecosystem service supply could result in large errors in valuation (usually underestimates given that currently observed marginal values are low but rising). It is thus risky to transfer constant values from a site associated with a level of capital in region I to another site associated with region II. Further as Farley (2008) notes, conservation needs should determine the supply of the natural stock available for being exploited and hence its price. In region III, capital stocks have passed critical ecological thresholds. If no close subsitute for such ecosystem exists for those valuing it, marginal values are essentially infinite, and restoration of natural capital stocks essential (Farley, 2008). In region III, standard valuation techniques, including benefit transfer, are not useful any more.

The problem of dealing with non-constant marginal values over large changes in the stock of an ecosystem becomes more difficult in the presence of non-linear ecological dynamics. Similar to the difficulty in accounting for threshold effects in valuing (and transferring values to) individual ecosystem sites, we lack knowledge of how ecosystem service values change following large-scale losses. The difficulties of conventional micro-economic methods in dealing with these complexities call for alternative approaches, such as deliberative and multicriteria methods (Spash and Vatn, 2006), which would aid decision processes at higher scales.

Current available studies measure the value of ecosystem services around present levels of overall provision (studies usually focus on one ecosystem site, with the implicit or explicit assumption that the level of provision of services from the remaining stock of ecosystems is not changed). Large changes in the overall level of provision are therefore beyond the domain of our observations and are thus unknown. This makes the assessment of the value of large or complete loss of an ecosystem service impossible. Crossing ecological thresholds in critical natural capital (region III) may involve large changes to welfare that render the estimation of marginal and total values essentially meaningless since they approach infinity. Scaling-up ecosystem service values across a range of service provision may be possible, particularly if adjustments are made to reflect non-constancy of marginal values over the stock, but it is important to recognize the limitations of this approach to estimate the value of large-scale or complete losses of (critical) natural capital.

7 Conclusions

This chapter has addressed some of the most important theoretical and practical challenges of assessing the economic value of ecosystem services and biodiversity. For example, it has tackled some critical issues regarding the way values may be scaled up geographically to offer total value for ecosystem services for ecosystems, regions, biomes or indeed the entire world, an approach upon which Chapter 7 and Appendix 3 of this book are based. It has also addressed some of the most important challenges for valuation studies, especially with regard to confronting problems such as uncertainty and ignorance and taking into consideration dynamic behaviour of ecosystems.

The role of valuation and the TEV approach

This chapter has provided an overview on the rationale behind economic valuation of ecosystem services, the available methods and tools, and some key challenges. Since many ecosystem services are produced and enjoyed in the absence of market transactions, their value is often underestimated and even ignored in daily decision making. One of the ways to tackle this information failure and make the value of ecosystems explicit in economic decision making is to estimate the value of ecosystem services and biodiversity in monetary terms. We have suggested that the economic value of ecosystems resides basically in two aspects. The first is the total economic value of the ecosystem service benefits at a given ecological state. The second is the insurance value that lies in the resilience of the ecosystem, which provides flows of ecosystem service benefits with stability over a range of variable environmental conditions.

The value of ecosystems is generally estimated using the so-called total economic value (TEV) approach. The TEV of an ecosystem is generally divided into use- and non-use values, each of which can be further disaggregated in several value components. Valuation methods that follow the TEV approach can be divided into three main categories – direct market approaches, revealed preferences and stated preference techniques – the last of which is being increasingly combined with deliberative methods from political science to develop formal procedures for deliberative group valuation of ecosystem values. These have been described briefly, discussing some of their strengths and weaknesses, as well as some of the aspects that have been subject to criticism.

Through the use of synthesis tables, each method has been analysed in terms of its relative capacity to deal with specific value components and types of ecosystem services. An extensive literature database has also been provided specifically for the key biomes forest and wetland ecosystems. Building on a case study database, we have reviewed how these biomes have been treated in the literature on economic valuation of ecosystems and provided quantitative data on which specific methods have been used for specific ecosystems services and value types. This chapter has also addressed several challenges valuation practitioners are faced with when adapting valuation methods to various institutional and ecological scales, such as valuation across stakeholders and applying valuation methods in developing countries.

The role of uncertainty

Regarding uncertainty inherent to valuation methods, this chapter has dealt with various types of uncertainty. The standard notion of uncertainty in valuation conflates risk and Knightian uncertainty. This chapter has also acknowledged the more profound type of uncertainty, here called 'radical uncertainty' or 'ignorance'. This chapter has discussed ways in which the standard concept of uncertainty is applied in the valuation of ecosystem services and biodiversity and the implications of recognizing radical uncertainty especially in the case of dealing with ecological resilience.

In addition, three sources of uncertainty pervading valuation of ecosystem services and biodiversity have been taken into account: (i) uncertainty regarding the delivery or supply of ecosystem services and biodiversity, (ii) preference uncertainty and (iii) technical uncertainty in the application of valuation methods.

The uncertainty regarding the delivery of ecosystem services makes stated preference methods complex. This may be the reason why there are few examples where stated preference approaches have considered the issue of uncertainty in an explicit way. Stated preference methods have generally resorted to measuring respondents' risk perceptions. Other valuation approaches based on expected damage functions are based on risk analysis instead.

Preference uncertainty is inversely related to the level of knowledge and experience with the ecosystem service to be valued. This source of uncertainty has been more widely acknowledged in stated preference approaches, for instance by requesting respondents to report a range of values rather than a specific value for the change in the provision of an ecosystem service.

Lastly, technical uncertainty pervades valuation studies, especially with regard to the credibility of the estimates of non-use values through stated preference methods and the non-conclusive issue of the large disparity between WTP and WTA value estimates. It has been suggested that combining valuation models and a preference calibration approach may be the way forward to minimize technical uncertainty.

The value of ecosystem resilience

The discussions in this chapter mostly address contemporary economic valuation techniques and estimates produced with these techniques. However, it should be borne in mind that these valuation techniques, which assume smooth and small system changes, may produce meaningless results in the context of ecosystems characteristics and dynamics such as ecological thresholds, resilience and regime shifts. Addressing these issues remains an important challenge in environmental valuation. Further advancements in these fields would require both a better knowledge of ecological processes and innovative valuation techniques.

The value of the resilience of an ecosystem is related to the benefits and costs that occur when the ecosystem shifts to another regime. An analogy can be drawn between the valuation of ecosystem resilience and the valuation of a portfolio of assets, in that the value of the asset mix – the ecosystem and its biodiversity – depends on the probability that a shift occurs, as well as the benefits and costs when it does. Current knowledge about biodiversity and ecosystem dynamics at this point is insufficient to implement such portfolio assessment, and monetary analysis will be misleading when ecosystems are near critical thresholds. At the policy level, it is better to address this uncertainty and ignorance by employing a safe minimum standard approach and the precautionary principle.

Using benefit transfer

With regard to the use of secondary data, the approach of value or benefit transfer (BT) has been discussed, both in terms of its main advantages and limitations. BT is the procedure of estimating the value of one ecosystem (the 'policy site') by transferring an existing valuation estimate from a similar ecosystem (the 'study site'). BT methods can be divided into four categories, in increasing order of complexity: (i) unit BT, (ii) adjusted unit BT, (iii) value function transfer and (iv) meta-analytic function transfer. BT using any of these methods may result in estimates that differ from actual values – so-called transfer errors. The acceptable level of transfer error for decision making is context-specific, but if a highly precise value estimate is required it is recommended to commission a primary valuation study.

BT can be a practical, timely and low-cost approach to estimate the value of ecosystem services, particularly for assessing policy scenarios involving a large number of diverse ecosystems. However, since marginal values are likely to vary with ecosystem characteristics, socio-economic characteristics of beneficiaries, and ecological context, care needs to be taken to adjust transferred values when there are important differences between study and policy sites.

Important site characteristics include the type of ecosystem, the services it provides, its integrity and size. Beneficiary characteristics include income, culture and distance to the ecosystem. It is important to account for distance decay effects in determining the market size for an ecosystem service and in aggregating per person values across the relevant population. It should be noted that the market size and rate of distance decay is likely to vary across different ecosystem services from the same ecosystem. It is also important to account for differences in site context in terms of the availability of substitute and complementary ecosystems and services.

In cases where a high-quality primary valuation study is available for a study site with very similar characteristics to the policy site, the unit transfer method may produce the most precise value estimate. In cases where no value information for a closely similar study site is available, value function or meta-analytic function transfer provide a sound approach for controlling for site specific characteristics.

Transferred values are generally expressed either per beneficiary or per unit of area. The former focuses the analysis on the demand for the service and the latter focuses on the supply. Aggregation of transferred unit values across the relevant population or ecosystem area needs to be undertaken carefully to avoid double counting values or misspecifying the market size for an ecosystem service.

Scaling-up refers to the use of BT to estimate the value of an entire stock of an ecosystem or provision of all ecosystem services within a large geographic area. In addition to the other challenges involved in using BT, scaling-up values requires accounting for the non-constancy of marginal values across the stock of an ecosystem. Simply multiplying a constant per unit value by the total quantity of ecosystem service provision is likely to underestimate total value. Appropriate adjustments to marginal values to account for large-scale changes in ecosystem service provision need to be made, for example by using estimated elasticities of value with respect to ecosystem scarcity. This approach may be useful for estimating total values over a certain range of ecosystem service provision but is limited by non-linearities and thresholds in the underlying ecological functions, particularly in the case of critical natural capital.

Final words

It should become clear that techniques to place a monetary value on biodiversity and ecosystem services are fraught with complications, only some of which currently can be addressed. Despite these limitations, demonstrating the approximate contribution of ecosystems to the economy remains urgently needed and the contribution of this chapter should be understood in this light. Valuation exercises can still provide information that is an indispensable component of environmental policy in general. Ignoring information from valuation methods is thus neither a realistic nor a desirable option. Instead, policy makers should interpret and utilize the valuable information provided by these techniques while acknowledging the limitations of this information.

In this context, Chapter 7 and Appendix 3 of this book intend to show policy makers that there is a probability of massive losses due to depletion of natural capital. The closer we believe we are to a threshold, the more important it is to improve valuation methods to estimate what is at stake. This will emphasize the importance of ensuring that natural capital stocks remain far from critical thresholds. It is likely that new techniques and combinations of different methodological approaches (e.g. monetary, deliberative and multicriteria methods) will be needed in order to properly face future challenges and provide more accurate values that would benefit decision-making processes.

Koch et al (2009) call for such a new decision-making approach to ecosystem services management. They recommend a number of actions that have to be taken to move in that direction, including: filling existing data gaps, especially using comparative studies; developing ecological modelling to understand patterns of non-linearity across different spatial and temporal scales; and testing the validity of assumptions about linearity in the valuation of ecosystem services at different scales. A closer collaboration between ecologists and economists would contribute to develop valuation techniques that are better suited to dealing with the complex relationship between ecosystems and the services they provide to the local and global economy. Last but not least, future valuation practitioners of biodiversity and ecosystem services should make explicit the procedures and methods used in their studies as well as openly acknowledging any obstacles that they may have encountered.

Notes

1   If a WTA scenario is involved a policy option is described to respondents as associated with a specific subsidy amount. Respondents have to decide if they would want to support the policy and receive the subsidy or support the status quo and not receive any subsidy.

2   Economists usually conflate risk and uncertainty (in the Knightian sense). For instance Freeman (1993, p220) defines 'individual uncertainty' as 'situations in which an individual is uncertain as to which of two or more alternative states of Nature will be realized'. In this chapter the terms risk and uncertainty are used in a conflated way following Freeman (1993) but the different type of 'radical uncertainty' or 'ignorance' due to science is also acknowledged explicitly.

3   A number of studies have used information on uncertainty with regard to preferences to shed light on the disparity between hypothetical values and actual economic behaviour (e.g. Akter et al, 2008).

4   See Akter et al (2008) for a theoretical framework based on cognitive psychology to select explanatory variables in econometric models aimed at explaining variations in preference uncertainty beyond the more intuitive variables.

5   An alternative strand assumes that there is an 'underlying vagueness of preferences' and uses fuzzy theory to address both lack of accurate understanding of what is the nature of the ecosystem service and uncertainty about the values that have already been measured (Van Kooten et al, 2001, p487).

6   The National Oceanic and Atmospheric Administration (1993), better known as the 'NOAA' panel, was chaired by Nobel laureates in economics such as Kenneth Arrow and Robert Solow.

7   If only the supply of the good is uncertain, the option value is positive if assumed that individuals are risk averse (Pearce and Turner, 1990). If other sources of uncertainty also exist, such as preference uncertainty, the sign of the option value is indeterminate.

8   Most studies that have focused on the value of bioprospecting are based on benefit–cost analysis by allowing explicit weights to various opportunity cost, such as land conservation, as opposed to the option value or expected benefits from the 'discovery' of a useful property of a given genetic material, net of the associated research and development costs such as biological material screenings (Pearce and Purushothaman, 1992; Simpson et al, 1996; Rausser and Small, 2000; Craft and Simpson, 2001).

9   An alternative approach to BT is based on 'preference calibration' but this is a much more information-intensive approach and thus this chapter does not cover it (see Smith et al, 2002).

References

Abaza, J. and Rietbergen-McCracken, J. (eds) (1998) *Environmental Valuation: A Worldwide Compendium of Case Studies*, United Nations Environment Programme

Adamowicz, W. L. (2004) 'What's it worth? An examination of historical trends and future directions in environmental valuation', *The Australian Journal of Agricultural and Resource Economics*, vol 48, pp419–443

Adamowicz, W. L., Louviere, J. and Williams, M. (1994) 'Combining revealed and stated preference methods for valuing amenities', *Journal of Environmental Economics and Management*, vol 26 (May), pp271–292

Akter, S., Bennett, J. and Akhter, S. (2008) 'Preference uncertainty in contingent valuation', *Ecological Economics*, vol 67, no 3, pp345–351

Akter, S., Brouwer, R., Brander, L. and van Beukering, P. (2009) 'Respondent uncertainty in a contingent market for carbon offsets', *Ecological Economics*, vol 68, no 6, pp1858–1863

Alberini, A. and Cooper, J. (2000) *Applications of the Contingent Valuation Method in Developing Countries: A Survey*, FAO Economic and Social Development Paper No. 146, Rome

Alberini, A., Boyle, K. and Welsh, M. (2003) 'Analysis of contingent valuation data with multiple bids: A response option allowing respondents to express uncertainty', *Journal of Environmental Economics and Management*, vol 45, pp40–62

Allen, B. P. and Loomis, J. B. (2006) 'Deriving values for the ecological support function of wildlife: An indirect valuation approach', *Ecological Economics*, vol 56, pp49–57

Ammour, T., Windevoxhel, N. and Sencion, G. (2000) *Economic Valuation of Mangrove Ecosystems and Subtropical Forests in Central America: Sustainable Forest Management and Global Climate Change*, Edward Elgar, Cheltenham, pp166–197

Anderies, J. M., Janssen, M. A., Walter, B. H. (2002) 'Grazing management, resilience and the dynamics of fire driven rangeland system', *Ecosystems*, vol 5, pp23–44

Anthoff, D., Nicholls, R. J. and Tol, R. S. J. (2007) *Global Sea-Level Rise and Equity Weighting*, Working Paper FNU-136, Research Unit, Sustainability and Global Change, Hamburg University

Armsworth, P. R. and Roughgarden, J. E. (2003) 'The economic value of ecological stability', *Proc. Natl. Acad. Sci. USA*, vol 100, pp7147–7151

Arrow, K. J. and Fisher, A. C. (1974) 'Environmental preservation, uncertainty, and irreversibility', *Quarterly Journal of Economics*, vol 88, no 2, pp312–319

Asia Forest Network (2002) *Participatory Rural Appraisal for Community Forest Management: Tools and Techniques*, Asia Forest Network, Santa Barbara, CA

Balmford, A., Rodrigues, A., Walpole, M., ten Brink, P., Kettunen, M., Braat, L. and de Groot, R. (2008) *The Economics of Ecosystems and Biodiversity: Scoping the Science*, European Commission, Cambridge

Barbier, E. B. (1994) 'Valuing environmental functions: Tropical wetlands', *Land Economics*, vol 70, no 2, pp155–173

Barbier, E. B. (2007) 'Valuing ecosystem services as productive inputs', *Economic Policy*, vol 22, no 49, pp177–229

Barbier, E. B., Acreman, M. C. and Knowler, D. (1997) *Economic Valuation of Wetlands: A Guide for Policy Makers and Planners*, Ramsar Convention Bureau, Gland, Switzerland

Barbier, E. B., Baumgärtner, S., Chopra, K., Costello, C., Duraiappah, A., Hassan, R., Kinzig, A., Lehman, M., Pascual, U., Polasky, S. and Perrings, C. (2009) 'The Valuation of Ecosystem Services', in Naeem, S., Bunker, D., Hector, A., Loreau M. and Perrings, C. (eds) *Biodiversity,*

Ecosystem Functioning, and Human Wellbeing: An Ecological and Economic Perspective, Oxford University Press, Oxford, UK, ch 18, pp248–262

Barbier, E. B., Koch, E. W., Silliman, B. R., Hacker, S. D., Wolanski, E., Primavera, J., Granek, E. F., Polasky, S., Aswani, S., Cramer, L. A., Stoms, D. M., Kennedy, C. J., Bael, D., Kappel, C. V., Perillo, G. M. E. and Reed, D. J. (2008) 'Coastal ecosystem-based management with nonlinear ecological functions and values', *Science*, vol 319, pp321–323

Barkmann, J., Glenk, K., Keil, A., Leemhuis, C., Dietrich, N., Gerold, G. and Marggraf, R. (2008) 'Confronting unfamiliarity with ecosystem functions: The case for an ecosystem service approach to environmental valuation with stated preferences', *Ecological Economics*, vol 65, no 1, pp48–62

Barrett, C. B. and Lybbert, T. J. (2000) 'Is bioprospecting a viable strategy for conserving tropical ecosystems?', *Ecological Economics*, vol 34, pp293–300

Barton, T., Borrini-Feyerabend, G., de Sherbin, A. and Warren, P. (1997) *Our People, Our Resources: Supporting Rural Communities in Participatory Action Research on Population Dynamics and the Local Environment*, IUCN, Gland, Switzerland

Bascompte, J., Possingham, H. and Roughgarden, J. (2002) 'Patchy populations in stochastic environments: Critical number of patches for persistence', *American Naturalist*, vol 159, pp128–137

Bateman, I. J., Burgess, D., Hutchinson, W. G. and Matthews, D. I. (2008) 'Contrasting NOAA guidelines with Learning Design Contingent Valuation (LDCV): Preference learning versus coherent arbitrariness', Journal of Environmental Economics and Management, vol 55, pp127–141

Bateman, I. J., Carson, R. T., Day, B., Hanemann, M., Hanley, N., Hett, T., Jones-Lee, M., Loomes, G., Mourato, S., Özdemiroglu, E., Pearce, D. W., Sugden, R. and Swanson, J. (2002) *Economic Valuation with Stated Preference Techniques: A Manual*, Edward Elgar, Cheltenham

Bateman I. J., Lovett, A. A. and Brainard, J. S. (2003) *Applied Environmental Economics: A GIS Approach to Cost–Benefit Analysis*, Cambridge University Press, Cambridge

Bateman, J., Brainard, A., Jones, J. and A. Lovett, A. (2005) *Geographical Information Systems (GIS) as the Last/Best Hope for Benefit Function Transfer, Benefit Transfer and Valuation Databases: Are We Heading in the Right Direction?*, United States Environmental Protection Agency and Environment Canada, Washington, DC

Baumgärtner, S. (2008) 'The insurance value of biodiversity in the provision of ecosystem services,' *Natural Resource Modeling*, vol 20, no 1, pp87–127

Biggs, R., Carpenter, S. R. and Brock, W. A. (2009) 'Turning back from the brink: Detecting an impending regime shift in time to avert it', *PNAS*, vol 106, no 3, pp826–831

Bingham, G., Bishop, R., Brody, M., Bromley, D., Clark, E. T., Cooper, W., Costanza, R., Hale, T., Hayden, G., Kellert, S., Norgaard, R., Norton, B., Payne, J., Russell C. and Suter, G. (1995) 'Issues in ecosystem valuation: Improving information for decision-making', *Ecological Economics*, vol 14, pp73–90

Birol, E., Kontoleon, A. and Smale, M. (2006) 'Combining revealed and stated preference methods to assess the private value of agrobiodiversity in Hungarian home gardens', Discussion Paper 156, Environment and Production Technology Division, International Food Policy Research Institute (IFPRI), Washington, DC

Blamey, R., Common, M. and Quiggin, J. (1995) 'Respondents to contingent valuation surveys: Consumers or citizens?', *Australian Journal of Agricultural Economics*, vol 39, no 3, pp263–288

Blockstein, D. E. (1998) 'Lyme disease and the passenger pigeon?', *Science*, vol 279, p1831

Bourque, L. B. and Fielder, E. P. (1995) *How to Conduct Self-Administered and Mail Surveys*, Sage, London

Bowles, S. (2008) 'Policies designed for self-interested citizens may undermine "the moral sentiments": Evidence from economic experiments', *Science*, vol 320, pp1605–1609

Boyd, J. and Banzhaf, S. (2007) 'What are ecosystem services? The need for standardized environmental accounting units', *Ecological Economics*, vol 63, pp616–626

Boyle, K. J., Bishop, R., Hellerstein, D.,Welsh, M. P., Ahearn, M. C., Laughland, A., Charbonneau, J. and O'Conner, R. (1998) 'Test of scope in contingent-valuation studies: Are the numbers for the birds', Paper presented at the World Congress of Environmental and Resource Economists (AERE/EAERE), Venice, Italy, 25–27 June

Boyle, K. J., Desvousges, W. H., Reed Johnson, F., Dunford, R. W. and Hudson, S. P. (1994) 'An investigation of part–whole biases in contingent-valuation studies', *Journal of Environmental Economics and Management*, vol 27, pp64–83

Brand, F. (2009) 'Critical natural capital revisited: Ecological resilience and sustainable development', *Landscape Ecology*, vol 68, pp605–612

Brander, L. M., Florax, R. J. G. M. and Vermaat, J. E. (2006) 'The empirics of wetland valuation: A comprehensive summary and a meta-analysis of the literature', *Environmental and Resource Economics*, vol 33, pp223–250

Brander, L. M., van Beukering, P. and Cesar, H. S. J. (2007) 'The recreational value of coral reefs: A meta-analysis', *Ecological Economics*, vol 63, pp209–218

Breaux, A., Faber, S. and Day, J. (1995) 'Using natural coastal wetlands systems for wastewater treatment: An economic benefit analysis', *Journal of Environmental Management*, vol 44, pp285–291

Bolitzer, B. and Netusil, N. R. (2000) 'The impact of open spaces on property values in Portland, Oregon', *Journal of Environmental Management*

Broberg, T. (2007) *The Value of Preserving Nature: Preference Uncertainty and Distributional Effects*, Umeå Economic Studies No. 720, PhD Thesis, Department of Economics, Umeå University, Umeå, Sweden

Brock, W. A. and Xepapadeas, A. (2002) 'Biodiversity Management Under Uncertainty: Species Selection and Harvesting Rules', in Kristrom, B., Dasgupta, P. and Löfgren, K.-G. (eds) *Economic Theory for the Environment: Essays in Honour of Karl-Göran Mäler*, Edward Elgar, Cheltenham pp62–97

Brookshire, D. S., Eubanks, L. S. and Randall, A. (1983) 'Estimating option prices and existence values for wildlife resources', *Land Economics*, vol 59, pp1–15

Brown, G. M. and Shogren, J. F. (1998) 'Economics of the endangered species act', *Journal of Economic Perspectives*, vol 12, no 3, pp3–20

Brown, G. M., Reed, P. and Harris, C. C. (2002) 'Testing a place-based theory for environmental evaluation: An Alaska case study', *Applied Geography*, vol 22, no 1, pp49–77

Brown, T. C., Harding B. L. and Payton, E. A. (1990) 'Marginal economic value of streamflow: A case study for the Colorado River Basin', *Water Resources Research*, vol 6, pp2845–2859

Bulte, E., van Soest, D. P., van Kooten, G. C. and Shipper, R. (2002) 'Forest conservation in Costa Rica when nonuse benefits are uncertain but rising', *American Journal of Agricultural Economics*, vol 84, no 1, pp150–160

Bush, G., Nampindo, S., Aguti, C. and Plumptre, A. (2004) *Valuing Uganda's Forests: A Livelihoods and Ecosystems Approach*, Technical Report, European Union Forest Resources Management and Conservation Programme, Uganda

Caldeira, M. C., Hector, A., Loreau, M. and Pereira, J. S. (2005) 'Species richness, temporal variability and resistance of biomass production in a Mediterranean grassland', *Oikos*, vol 110, pp115–123

Cameron, T. A. (1992) 'Combining contingent valuation and travel cost data for the valuation of nonmarket goods', *Land Economics*, vol 68, no 3, pp302–317

Carpenter, S. R. and Cottingham, K. L. (1997) 'Resilience and restoration of lakes', *Conservation Ecology*, vol 1, no 1, p2, www.consecol.org/vol1/iss1/art2/

Carpenter, S. R., DeFries, R., Dietz, T., Mooney, H. A., Polasky, S., Reid, W. V. and Scholes, R. J. (2006) 'Millennium Ecosystem Assessment: Research needs', *Science*, vol 314, pp257–258

Carson, R. and Groves, T. (2007) 'Incentive and information properties of preference questions', *Environment and Resource Economics*, vol 37, pp181–210

Carson, R. T., Flores, N. E., Martin, K. M. and Wright, J. L. (1996) 'Contingent valuation and revealed preference methodologies: Comparing the estimates for quasi-public goods', *Land Economics*, vol 72, no 1, pp80–99

Carson, R. T., Flores, N. E. and Meade, N. F. (2001) 'Contingent valuation: Controversies and evidence', *Environmental and Resource Economics*, vol 19, pp173–210

Carson, R. T., Koundouri, P. and Nauges, C. (2009) 'Arsenic mitigation in Bangladesh: A household labour market approach', TSE Working Papers 09–106, Toulouse School of Economics, Toulouse

Champ, P. and Bishop, R. (2001) 'Donation payment mechanisms and contingent valuation: An empirical study of hypothetical bias', *Environmental and Resource Economics*, vol 19, pp383–402

Champ, P. A., Bishop, R. C., Brown, T. C. and McCollum, D. W. (1997) 'Using donation mechanisms to value nonuse benefits from public goods', *Journal of Environmental Economics and Management*, vol 33, no 1, pp151–162

Chan, K. M. A., Goldstein, J., Satterfield, T., Hannahs, N., Kikiloi, K., Naidoo, R., Vadeboncoeur, N. and Woodside, U. (2010) 'The Theory and Practice of Ecosystem Service Valuation in

Conservation', in Kareiva, P. K., Ricketts, T. H., Daily, G. C., Tallis, H. and Polasky, S. (eds) *The Theory and Practice of Ecosystem Service Valuation in Conservation*, Oxford University Press, Oxford

Chee, Y. E. (2004) 'An ecological perspective on the valuation of ecosystem services', *Biological Conservation*, vol 120, pp459–565

Christie, M., Fazey, D., Cooper, R., Hyde, T., Deri, A., Hughes, L., Bush, G., Brander, L. M., Nahman, A., de Lange, W. and Reyers, B. (2008) *An Evaluation of Economic and Non-economic Techniques for Assessing the Importance of Biodiversity to People in Developing Countries*, Report to the Department for Environment, Food and Rural Affairs, London

Christie, M., Hanley, N., Warren, J., Hyde, T., Murphy, K. and Wright, R. (2007) 'Valuing Ecological and Anthropocentric Concepts of Biodiversity: A Choice Experiments Application', in Kontoleon, A., Pascual, U. and Swanson, T. (eds) *Biodiversity Economics: Principles, Methods and Applications*, Cambridge University Press, Cambridge, pp343–368

Christie, M., Hanley, N., Warren, J., Murphy, K. and Wright, R. E. (2004) *A Valuation of Biodiversity in the UK Using Choice Experiments and Contingent Valuation*, Defra, London

Contamin, R. and Ellison, A. M. (2009) 'Indicators of regime shifts in ecological systems: What do we need to know and when do we need to know it', *Ecological Applications*, vol 19, no 3, pp799–816

Cook, D. C., Thomas, M. B., Cunningham, S. A., Anderson, D. L. and De Barro, P. J. (2007) 'Predicting the economic impact of an invasive species on an ecosystem service', *Ecological Applications*, vol 17, pp1832–1840

Costanza, R. (1980) 'Embodied energy and economic valuation', *Science*, vol 210, pp1219–1224

Costanza, R. (2006) 'Nature: Ecosystems without commodifying them', *Nature*, vol 443, p749

Costanza, R. and Daly, H. (1992) 'Natural capital and sustainable development', *Conservation Biology*, vol 6, pp37–46

Costanza, R. and Folke, C. (1997) 'Valuing Ecosystem Services with Efficiency, Fairness and Sustainability as Goals', in Daily, G. (ed) *Nature's Services: Societal Dependence on Natural Ecosystems*, Island Press, Washington, DC, pp49–68

Costanza, R., d'Arge, R., de Groot, R., Farber, S., Grasso, M., Hannon, B., Limburg, K., Naeem, S., O'Neill, R. V., Paruelo, J., Raskin, R. G., Sutoon, P. and van den Belt, M. (1997) 'The value of the world's ecosystem services and natural capital', *Nature*, vol 387, pp253–260

Craft, A. B. and Simpson, R. D. (2001) 'The value of biodiversity in pharmaceutical research with differentiated products', *Environmental and Resource Economics*, vol 18, no 1, pp1–17

Crocker, T. D. and Shogren, J. F. (1991) 'Ex ante valuation of atmospheric visibility', *Applied Economics*, vol 23, pp143–151

Daily, G. C. (ed) (1997) *Nature's Services: Societal Dependence on Natural Ecosystems*, Island Press, Washington, DC

Daily, G. C., Soderqvist, T., Aniyar, S., Arrow, K., Dasgupta, P., Ehrlich, P. R., Folke, C., Jansson, A., Jansson, B., Kautsky, N., Levin, S., Lubchenko, J., Mäler, K., Simpson, D., Starrett, D., Tilman, D. and Walker, B. (2000) 'The value of nature and the nature of value', *Science*, vol 289, pp395–396

Daniels, P. L. and Moore, S. (2002) 'Approaches for quantifying the metabolism of physical economies', *Journal of Industrial Ecology*, vol 5, no 4, pp69–93

Das, S. and Vincent, J. R. (2009) 'Mangroves protected villages and reduced death toll during Indian super cyclone', *Proceedings of the National Academy of Sciences of the United States of America*, vol 106, no 18, pp7357–7360

De Groot, R. S., Stuip, M., Finlayson, M. and Davidson, N. (2006) *Valuing Wetlands: Guidance for Valuing the Benefits Derived from Wetland Ecosystem Services*, Ramsar Technical Report No. 3, CBD Technical Series No. 27, Ramsar Convention Secretariat, Gland

De Groot, R. S., Wilson, M. and Boumans, R. (2002) 'A typology for the description, classification and valuation of ecosystem functions, goods and services', *Ecological Economics*, vol 41, pp393–408

Desvousges, W. H., Johnson, F. R., Dunford, R. W., Boyle, K. J., Hudson, S. P. and Wilson, K. N. (1993) 'Measuring Natural Resource Damages with Contingent Valuation: Tests of Validity and Reliability', in Hausman, J. A. (ed) *Contingent Valuation: A Critical Assessment*, North-Holland/Elsevier Science Publishers, Amsterdam, pp91–159

Deutsch, L., Folke, C. and Skånberg, K. (2003) 'The critical natural capital of ecosystem performance as insurance for human well-being', *Ecological Economics*, vol 44, pp205–217

DeYoung, B., Barange, M., Beaugrand, G., Harris, R., Perry, R., Scheffer, M. and Werner, F. (2008) 'Regime shift in marine ecosystems: Detection, prediction and management', *Trends in Ecology and Evolution*, vol 23, no 7, pp402–409

Diamond, P. (1996) 'Testing the internal consistency of contingent valuation surveys', *Journal of Environmental Economics and Management*, vol 30, no 3, pp265–281

Diamond, P. A. and Hausman, J. A. (1993) 'On Contingent Valuation Measurement of Nonuse Values', in Hausman, J. A. (ed) *Contingent Valuation: A Critical Assessment*, North-Holland/Elsevier Science Publishers, Amsterdam, pp1–38

Diamond, P. A., Hausman, J. A., Leonard, G. K. and Denning, M. A. (1993) 'Does Contingent Valuation Measure Preferences? Experimental Evidence', in Hausman, J. A. (ed) *Contingent Valuation: A Critical Assessment*, North-Holland/Elsevier Science Publishers, Amsterdam, pp41–85

Earnhart, D. (2001) 'Combining revealed and stated preference methods to value environmental amenities at residential locations', *Land Economics*, vol 77, no 1, pp12–29

EEA (European Environment Agency) (2006) *Land Accounts for Europe 1990–2000: Towards Integrated Land and Ecosystem Accounting*, EEA Report No 11/2006, Copenhagen, Denmark

Ekins, P., Folke, C. and de Groot, R. (2003) 'Identifying critical natural capital', *Ecological Economics*, vol 44, nos 2–3, pp159–163

Ellis, G. M. and Fisher, A. C. (1987) 'Valuing environment as input', *Journal of Environmental Management*, vol 25, pp149–156

Engel, S., Pagiola, S. and Wunder, S. (2008) 'Designing payments for environmental services in theory and practice: An overview of the issues', *Ecological Economics*, vol 62, pp663–674

Eshet, T., Baron, M. G. and Shechter, M. (2007) 'Exploring benefit transfer: Disamenities of waste transfer stations', *Environmental and Resource Economics*, vol 37, pp521–547

Fabricius, C., Folke, C., Cundill, G. and Schultz, L. (2007) 'Powerless spectators, coping actors, and adaptive co-managers: A synthesis of the role of communities in ecosystem management', *Ecology and Society*, vol 12, no 1, p29

Farley, J. (2008) 'The role of prices in conserving critical natural capital', *Conservation Biology*, vol 22, no 6, pp1399–1408

Fazey, I., Latham, I., Hagasua, J. E. and Wagatora, D. (2007) *Livelihoods and Change in Kahua, Solomon Islands*, Aberystwyth University, Aberystwyth

Ferraro, P. J. and Kramer, R. K. (1997) 'Compensation and Economic Incentives: Reducing Pressure on Protected Areas', in Kramer, R. A., van Schaik, C. and Johnson, J. (eds) *Last Stand: Protected Areas and the Defense of Tropical Biodiversity*, Oxford University Press, New York, pp187–211

Figge, F. (2004) 'Bio-folio: Applying portfolio theory to biodiversity', *Biodiversity and Conservation*, vol 13, pp827–849

Fisher, B., Turner, R. K. and Morling, P. (2009) 'Defining and classifying ecosystem services for decision-making', *Ecological Economics*, vol 68, pp643–653

Folke, C., Carpenter, S., Elmqvist, T., Gunderson, L., Holling, C. S., Walker, B., Bengtsson, J., Berkes, F., Colding, J., Dannell, K., Falkenmark, M., Gordon, L., Kasperson, R., Kautsky, N., Kinzig, A., Levin, S., Mäler, K.-G., Moberg, F., Ohlsson, L., Ostrom, E., Reid, W., Rockström, J., Savenije, H. and Svedin, U. (2002) *Resilience and Sustainable Development: Building Adaptive Capacity in a World of Transformations*, Scientific Background Paper on Resilience for the process of The World Summit on Sustainable Development on Behalf of The Environmental Advisory Council to the Swedish Government

Folke, C., Carpenter, S., Walker, B., Scheffer, M., Elmqvist, T., Gunderson, L. and Holling, C. S. (2004) 'Regime shifts, resilience, and biodiversity in ecosystem management', *Annu. Rev. Ecol. Syst.*, vol 35, pp557–581

Folke, C., Holling, C. S. and Perrings, C. (1996) 'Biological diversity, ecosystems and the human scale', *Ecological Applications*, vol 6, no 4, pp1018–1024

Freeman, A. M. (1993) *The Measurement of Environmental and Resource Values*, Resources for the Future Press, Baltimore, MD

Freeman, A. M. (2003) *The Measurement of Environmental and Resource Values*, Resources for the Future Press, Baltimore, MD

García-Llorente, M., Martín-López, B., Gónzalez, J. A., Alcorlo, A. and Montes, C. (2008) 'Social perceptions of the impacts and benefits of invasive alien species: Implications for management', *Biological Conservation*, vol 141, pp2969–2983

Garrod, G. D. and Willis, K. G. (1991) 'Estimating the benefits of environmental enhancement: A case study of the River Darent', *Journal of Environmental Planning and Management*, vol 39, pp189–203

Garrod, G. and Willis, K. G. (1999) *Economic Valuation of the Environment*, Edward Elgar, Cheltenham

Georgescu-Roegen, N. (1979) 'Energy analysis and economic valuation', *Southern Economic Journal*, vol 45, pp1023–1058

Georgiou, S., Whittington, D., Pearce, D. and Moran, D. (2006) *Economic Values and the Environment in the Developing World*, Edward Elgar, Cheltenham

Ghermandi, A., van den Bergh, J. C. J. M., Brander, L. M., de Groot, H. L. F. and Nunes, P. A. L. D. (2007) 'Exploring diversity: A meta-analysis of wetland conservation and creation', Proceedings of the 9th International BIOECON Conference on Economics and Institutions for Biodiversity Conservation, Cambridge, 19–21 September

Goeschl, T. and Swanson, T. (2003) 'Pests, plagues, and patents', *Journal of the European Economic Association*, vol 1, nos 2–3, pp561–575

Gómez-Baggethun, E. and de Groot, R. (2007) 'Natural capital and ecosystem functions: Exploring the ecological grounds of the economy', *Ecosistemas*, vol 16, no 3, pp4–14

Gómez-Baggethun, E. and de Groot, R. (2010) 'Natural Capital and Ecosystem Services: The Ecological Foundation of Human Society', in Hester, R. E. and Harrison, R. M. (eds) *Ecosystem Services*, Issues in Environmental Science and Technology 30, Royal Society of Chemistry, Cambridge, pp105–121 (In press)

Goulder, L. H. and Kennedy, D. (1997), 'Valuing Ecosystem: Philosophical Bases and Empirical Methods', in Daily, G. C. (ed) *Nature's Services: Societal Dependence on Natural Ecosystems*, Island Press, Washington, DC, pp23–48

Gren I.-M. (1993) 'Alternative nitrogen reduction policies in the Malar Region, Sweden', *Ecological Economics*, vol 7, pp159–172

Gren, I.-M., Folke, C., Turner, R. K. and Batman, I.-J. (1994) 'Primary and secondary values of wetland ecosystems', *Environmental and Resource Economics*, vol 4, no 4, pp55–74

Gunawardena, M. and Rowan, J. S. (2005) 'Economic valuation of a mangrove ecosystem threatened by shrimp aquaculture in Sri Lanka', *Environmental Management*, vol 36, no 4, pp535–550

Haab, T. C. and McConnell, K. E. (2002) *Valuing Environmental and Natural Resources: The Econometrics of Non-market Valuation*, Edward Elgar, Cheltenham

Haldane, J. B. S. and Jayakar, S. D. (1963) 'Polymorphism due to selection of varying direction', *Journal of Genetics*, vol 58, pp237–242

Hanneman, M. (1991) 'Willingness to pay and willingness to accept: How much can they differ?', *American Economic Review*, vol 81, pp635–647

Hanemann, W. M., Kriström, B. and Li, C. Z. (1996) 'Nonmarket valuation under preference uncertainty: Econometric models and estimation', Paper 794, CUDARE Working Papers, University of California, Berkeley, CA

Hanley, N. and Spash, C. L. (1993) *Cost–Benefit Analysis and the Environment*, Edward Elgar, Aldershot

Hanley, N., Kriström, B. and Shogren, J. F. (2009) 'Coherent arbitrariness: On value uncertainty for environmental goods', *Land Economics*, vol 85, pp41–50

Hanley, N., Wright, R. E. and Adamowicz, V. (1998) 'Using choice experiments to value the environment', *Environmental and Resource Economics*, vol 11, no 3, pp413–428

Harwood, J. and Stokes, K. (2003) 'Coping with uncertainty in ecological advice: Lessons from fisheries', *Trends in Ecology and Evolution*, vol 18, pp617–622

Hausman, J. A. (ed) (1993) *Contingent Valuation: A Critical Assessment*, Elsevier Science Publishers, Amsterdam

Hein, L., van Koppen, K., de Groot, R. S. and van Ierland, E. C. (2006) 'Spatial scales, stakeholders and the valuation of ecosystem services', *Ecological Economics*, vol 57, pp209–228

Hermans, L., Renault, D., Emerton, L., Perrot-Maître, D., Nguyen-Khoa, S. and Smith, L. (2006) *Stakeholder-oriented Valuation to Support Water Resources Management Processes: Confronting Concepts with Local Practice*, FAO, Rome

Holling, C. S. (1973) 'Resilience and stability of ecological systems', *Annual Review of Ecology and Systematics*, vol 4, pp1–23

Holling, C. S. (2001) 'Understanding the complexity of economic, ecological and social systems', *Ecosystems*, vol 4, no 5, pp390–405

Holling, C. S. and Gunderson, L. H. (2002) 'Resilience and Adaptive Cycles', in Gunderson, L. H. and Holling, C. S. (eds) *Panarchy: Understanding Transformations in Human and Natural Systems*, Island Press, Washington, DC, pp25–62

Hooper, D. U., Chapin III, F. S., Ewel, J. J., Hector, A., Inchausti, P., Lavorel, S., Lawton, J. H., Lodge, D. M., Loreau, M., Naeem, S., Schmid, B., Setälä, H., Symstad, A. J., Vandermeer, J. and Wardle, D. A. (2005) 'Effects of biodiversity on ecosystem functioning: A consensus of current knowledge', *Ecological Monographs*, vol 75, no 1, pp3–35

Horowitz, J. K. and McConnell, K. E. (2002) 'A review of WTA/WTP studies', *Journal of Environmental Economics and Management*, vol 44, no 3, pp426–447

Ives, A. R. and Hughes, J. B. (2002) 'General relationships between species diversity and stability incompetitive systems', *American Naturalist*, vol 159, pp388–395

Jackson, L. E., Pascual, U. and Hodgkin, T. (2007) 'Utilizing and conserving agrobiodiversity in agricultural landscapes', *Agriculture, Ecosystems and the Environment*, vol 121, pp196–210

Jackson, W. and Ingles, A. (1998) 'Participatory Techniques for Community Forestry: A Field Manual', in *Issues in Forest Conservation*, AusAid, IUCN, WWF

Jacobsen, J. B. and Hanley, N. (2008) 'Are there income effects on global willingness to pay for biodiversity conservation?', *Environmental and Resource Economics*, vol 43, no 2, pp137–160

Jannson, B.-O. and Jansson, A. M. (2002) 'The Baltic Sea: Reversibly Unstable or Irreversibly Stable?', in Gunderson, L. H. and Pritchard, L. (eds) *Resilience and the Behaviour of Large Scale Systems*, Island Press, Washington, DC, pp71–110

Jarvis, D. I., Myer, L., Klemick, H., Guarino, L., Smale, M., Brown, A. H. D., Sadiki, M., Sthapit, B. and Hodgkin, T. (2000) *A Training Guide for In Situ Conservation On-farm*, Version 1, International Plant Genetic Resources Institute, Rome, Italy

Kahneman, D. (1986) 'The Review Panel Assessment: Comment', in Cummings, R. G., Brookshire, D. S. and Schulze, W. D. (eds) *Valuing Public Goods: The Contingent Valuation Method*, Rowman and Allanheld, Totowa, NJ

Kahneman, D. and Knetsch, J. L. (1992) 'Valuing public goods: The purchase of moral satisfaction', *Journal of Environmental Economics and Management*, vol 22, pp57–70

Kahneman, D., Knetsch, J. and Thaler, R. (1990) 'Experimental tests of the endowment effect and the Coase Theorem', *The Journal of Political Economy*, vol 98, no 6, pp1325–1348

Kaiser, B. A. (2006) 'Economic impacts of non-indigenous species: *Miconia* and the Hawaiian economy', *Euphytica*, vol 148, pp135–150

Kanazawa, M. (1993) 'Pricing subsidies and economic efficiency: The U.S. Bureau of Reclamation', *Journal of Law and Economics*, vol 36, pp205–234

King, D. M. and Mazotta, M. (2001) www.ecosystemvaluation.org

Knetsch, J. (2005) 'Gains, losses, and the US-EPA Economic Analyses Guidelines: A hazardous product?', *Environmental and Resource Economics*, vol 32, pp91–112

Knight, F. H. (1921) *Risk, Uncertainty, and Profit*, Hart, Schaffner, and Marx Prize Essays, no. 31, Houghton Mifflin, Boston and New York

Knowler, D. (2005) 'Reassessing the costs of biological invasion: *Mnemiopsis leidyi* in the Black Sea', *Ecological Economics*, vol 52, pp187–199

Koch, E. W., Barbier, E. B., Silliman, B. R., Reed, D. J., Perillo, G. M. E., Hacker, S. D., Granek, E. F., Primavera, J. H., Muthiga, N., Polasky, S., Halpern, B. S., Kennedy, C. J., Kappel, C. V. and Wolanski, E. (2009) 'Non-linearity in ecosystem services: Temporal and spatial variability in coastal protection', *Frontiers in Ecology and the Environment*, vol 7, no 1, pp29–37

Kolstad, C. D. (2000) *Environmental Economics*, Oxford University Press, New York and Oxford

Kontoleon, A. and Pascual, U. (2007) *Incorporating Biodiversity into Integrated Assessments of Trade Policy in the Agricultural Sector*, Volume II: Reference Manual, Chapter 7, Economics and Trade Branch, United Nations Environment Programme, Geneva, available at: www.unep.ch/etb/pdf/UNEP%20T+B%20Manual.Vol%20II.Draft%20June07.pdf

Kontoleon, A., Macrory, R. and Swanson, T. (2002) 'Individual preference based values and environmental decision-making: Should valuation have its day in court?', *Journal of Research in Law and Economics*, vol 20, pp179–216

Kremen, C., Niles, J. O., Dalton, M. G., Daily, G. C., Ehrlich, P. R., Fay, J. P., Grewal, D. and Guillery, R. P. (2000) 'Economic incentives for rain forest conservation across scales', *Science*, vol 288, pp1828–1832

Krutilla, J. V. (1967) 'Conservation reconsidered', *American Economic Review*, vol 57, pp777–786

Krutilla, J. V. and Fisher, A. C. (1975) *The Economics of the Natural Environment: Studies in the Valuation of Commodity and Amenity Resources*, Johns Hopkins Press for Resources for the Future, Baltimore, MD

Li, C., Kuuluvainen, J., Pouta, E, Rekola, M. and Tahvonen, O. (2004) 'Using choice experiments to value the Natura 2000 nature conservation programs in Finland', *Environmental and Resource Economics*, vol 29, no 3, pp361–374

Limburg, K. E., O'Neill, R. V., Costanza, R. and Farber, S. (2002) 'Complex systems and valuation', *Ecological Economics*, vol 41, pp409–420

Lindhjem, H. and Navrud, S. (2007) 'How reliable are meta-analyses for international benefit transfer?', *Ecological Economics*, vol 66, nos 2–3, pp425–435

Loomis, J. (2000) 'Vertically summing public good demand curves: An empirical comparison of economic versus political jurisdictions', *Land Economics*, vol 76, no 2, pp312–321

Loomis, J. and Ekstrand, E. (1998) 'Alternative approaches for incorporating respondent uncertainty when estimating willingness to pay: The case of the Mexican Spotted Owl', *Ecological Economics*, vol 27, pp29–41

Loreau, M., Mouquet, N. and Gonzalez, A. (2003) 'Biodiversity as spatial insurance in heterogeneous landscapes', *PNAS*, vol 22, pp12765–12770

Louviere, J. J., Hensher, D. A., Swait, J. D. and Adamowicz, W. L. (2000) *Stated Choice Methods: Analysis and Applications*, Cambridge University Press, Cambridge

Lovett, A. A., Brainard, J. S. and Bateman, I. J. (1997) 'Improving benefit transfer demand functions: A GIS approach', *Journal of Environmental Management*, vol 51, no 4, pp373–389

Luck, G. (2005) 'An introduction to ecological thresholds', *Biological Conservation*, vol 124, pp299–300

MA (Millennium Ecosystem Assessment) (2005) *Ecosystems and Human Well-being: Synthesis*, Island Press, Washington, DC

Mäler, K.-G., Gren, I. and Folke, C. (1994) 'Multiple Use of Environmental Resources: A Household Production Function Approach to Valuing Natural Capital', in Jansson, A., Hammar, M., Folke, C. and Costanza, R. (eds) *Investing in Natural Capital*, Island Press, Washington, DC, pp234–249

Mäler, K.-G., Li, C.-Z. and Destouni, G. (2007) 'Pricing resilience in a dynamic economy-environment system: A capital-theoretical approach', Beijer Discussion Papers, 208

Manski, C. (2000) 'Economic analysis of social interactions', *Journal of Economic Perspectives*, vol 14, pp115–136

Maron, J. L., Estes, J. A., Croll, D. A., Danner, E. M., Elmendorf, S. C. and Buckelew, S. L. (2006) 'An introduced predator alters Aleutian island plant communities by thwarting nutrient subsidies', *Ecological Monographs*, vol 76, pp3–24

Martínez-Alier, J. (2002) *The Environmentalism of the Poor*, Edward Elgar, London

Martínez-Alier, J., Munda, G. and O'Neill, J. (1998) 'Weak comparability of values as a foundation for ecological economics', *Ecological Economics*, vol 26, pp277–286

Martín-López, B., Gómez-Baggethun, E., González, J. A., Lomas, P. L. and Montes, C (2009a) 'The Assessment of Ecosystem Services Provided by Biodiversity: Re-thinking Concepts and Research Needs', in Aronoff, J. B. (ed) *Handbook of Nature Conservation*, Nova Publisher, Hauppauge, NY

Martín-López, B., Gómez-Baggethun, E., Lomas, P. L. and Montes, C. (2009b) 'Effects of spatial and temporal scales on cultural services valuation areas', *Journal of Environmental Management*, vol 90, no 2, pp1050–1059

Martín-López, B., Montes, C. and Benayas, J. (2007) 'The role of user's characteristics on the ecosystem services valuation: The case of Doñana Natural Protected Area (SW Spain)', *Environmental Conservation*, vol 34, pp215–224

McCauley, C. and Mendes, S. (2006) *Socio-Economic Assessment Report*, Montserrat Centre Hills Project

McCauley, D. J. (2006) 'Selling out on nature', *Nature*, vol 443, pp27–28

Mills, E. L., Leach, J. H. and Carlton, J. T. (1993) 'Exotic species in the Great Lakes – a history of biotic crises and anthropogenic introductions', *Journal of Great Lakes Research*, vol 19, pp1–54

Mitchell, R. and Carson, R. (1989) *Using Surveys to Value Public Goods: The Contingent Valuation Method*, Resources for the Future, Washington, DC

Mooney, H., Cooper, A. and Reid, W. (2005) 'Confronting the human dilemma: How can ecosystems provide sustainable services to benefit society?', *Nature*, vol 434, pp561–562

Mosley, P. and Verschoor, A. (2005) 'Risk attitudes and the "vicious circle of poverty"', *European Journal of Development Research*, vol 17, no 1, pp59–88

Munda, G. (2004) 'Social multi-criteria evaluation: Methodological foundations and operational consequences', *European Journal of Operational Research*, vol 158, pp662–677

Muradian, R. (2001) 'Ecological thresholds: A survey', *Ecological Economics*, vol 38, no 1, pp7–24

Muradian, R., Corbera, E., Pascual, U., Kosoy, N. and May, P. (2010) 'Reconciling theory and practice: An alternative conceptual framework for understanding payments for environmental services', *Ecological Economics*, vol 69, no 6, pp1202–1208

Naredo, J. M. (2001) 'Quantifying Natural Capital: Beyond Monetary Value', in Munasinghe, M. and Sunkel, O. (eds) *The Sustainability of Long Term Growth: Socioeconomic and Ecological Perspectives*, Edward Elgar, Cheltenham, and Northampton, MA

NOAA (National Oceanic and Atmospheric Administration) (1993) Report of the NOAA panel on Contingent Valuation, Federal Register 58/10, 4602–4614

NRC (National Research Council) (1997) *Valuing Ground Water: Economic Concepts and Approaches*, Committee on Valuing Ground Water, Water Science and Technology Board, Commission on Geosciences, Environment and Resources, The National Academies Press, Washington, DC

NRC (National Research Council) (2004) *Valuing Ecosystem Services: Toward Better Environmental Decision-making*, The National Academies Press, Washington, DC

Nunes, P. (2002) 'Using factor analysis to identify consumer preferences for the protection of a natural area in Portugal', *European Journal of Operational Research*, vol 140, pp499–516

Nunes, P. and van den Bergh, J. (2001) 'Economic valuation of biodiversity: Sense or nonsense?', *Ecological Economics*, vol 39, no 2, pp203–222

Nunes, P., Silvestri, S., Pellizzato, M. and Voatto, B. (2008) 'Regulation of the fishing activities in the lagoon of Venice, Italy: Results from a socio-economic study', *Estuarine, Coastal and Shelf Science*, vol 80, pp173–180

O'Neill, J. (1993) *Ecology, Policy and Politics*, Routledge, London

Odum, H. T. (1996) 'Economic impacts brought about by alterations to freshwater flow', in Urban, E. R. and Malloy, L. (eds) *Improving Interactions between Coastal Science and Policy. Proceedings of the Gulf of Mexico Symposium*, National Research Council, National Academy Press, Washington, DC, pp239–254

Pascual, U., Muradian, R., Rodríguez, L. and Duraiappah, A. (2010) 'Exploring the links between equity and efficiency in payments for environmental services: A conceptual approach', *Ecological Economics*, vol 69, no 6, pp1237–1244

Pattanayak, S. K. and Kramer, R. A. (2001) 'Worth of watersheds: A producer surplus approach for valuing drought mitigation in Eastern Indonesia', *Environment and Development Economics*, vol 6, no 01, pp123–146

Patterson, K. A. (1990) 'Global distribution of total and total-available soil water-holding capacities', MSc thesis, University of Delaware, 119pp

Pearce, D. W. (1993) *Economic Values and the Natural World*, Earthscan, London

Pearce, D. W. and Moran, D. (1994) *The Economic Value of Biodiversity*, Earthscan, London

Pearce, D. W. and Turner, R. K. (1990) *Economics of Natural Resources and the Environment*, Johns Hopkins University Press, Baltimore, MD

Pearce, D. W. and Purushothaman, S. (1992) 'Preserving biological diversity: The economic value of pharmaceutical plants', Discussion Paper: 92-27, CSERGE, London

Perman, R., Ma, Y., McGilvray, J. and Common, M. (2003) *Natural Resource and Environmental Economics*, 3rd edn, Pearson, Harlow, Essex

Perrings, C. (1998) 'Resilience in the dynamics of economy–environment systems', *Environmental and Resource Economics*, vol 11, nos 3–4, pp503–520

Perrings, C. and Gadgil, M. (2003) 'Conserving Biodiversity: Reconciling Local and Global Public Benefits', in Kaul, I., Conceição, P., le Goulven, K. and Mendoza, R. L. (eds) *Providing Global Public Goods: Managing Globalization*, Oxford University Press, Oxford, pp 532–555

Perrings, C. and Williamson, M. (eds) (2000) *The Economics of Biological Invasions*, Edward Elgar, Cheltenham

Perrings, C., Jackson, L., Bawa, K., Brussaard, L., Brush, S., Gavin, T., Papa, R., Pascual, U. and de Ruiter, P. (2006) 'Biodiversity in agricultural landscapes: Saving natural capital without losing interest', *Conservation Biology*, vol 20, no 2, pp263–264

Philip, L. J. and MacMillan, D. C. (2005) 'Exploring values, context and perceptions in contingent valuation studies: The CV market stall technique and willingness to pay for wildlife conservation', *Journal of Environment Plannning and Management*, vol 48, no 2, pp257–274

Pimentel, D., Zuniga, R. and Morrison, D. (2005) 'Update on the environmental and economic costs associated with alien-invasive species in the United States', *Ecological Economics*, vol 52, pp273–288

Poe, G. L. and Bishop, R. (1999) 'Valuing the incremental benefits of groundwater protection when exposure levels are known', *Environmental and Resource Economics*, vol 13, pp341–367

Polasky, S. and Solow, A. R. (1995) 'On the value of a collection of species', *Journal of Environmental Economics and Management*, vol 29, pp298–303

Pritchard, L., Folke, C. and Gunderson, L. (2000) 'Valuation of ecosystem services in institutional context', *Ecosystems*, vol 3, pp36–40

Rausser, G. C. and Small, A. A. (2000) 'Valuing research leads: Bioprospecting and the conservation of genetic resources', *Journal of Political Economy*, vol 108, no 1, pp173–206

Ready, R. C., Whitehead, J. C. and Blomquist, G. C. (1995) 'Contingent valuation when respondents are ambivalent', *Journal of Environmental Economics and Management*, vol 29, pp181–197

Rekola, M. (2004) *Incommensurability and Uncertainty in Contingent Valuation: Willingness to Pay for Forest and Nature Conservation Policies in Finland*. PhD dissertation, January 2004, Faculty of Agriculture and Forestry, University of Helsinki

Rekola, M. and Pouta, E. (2005) 'Public preferences for uncertain regeneration cuttings: A contingent valuation experiment involving Finnish private forests', *Forest Policy and Economics*, vol 7, no 4, pp634–649

Rosenberger, R. S. and Phipps, T. T. (2007) 'Correspondence and Convergence in Benefit Transfer Accuracy: A Meta-analytic Review of the Literature', in Navrud, S. and Ready, R. (eds) *Environmental Values Transfer: Issues and Methods*, Springer, Dordrecht

Rosenberger, R. S. and Stanley, T. D. (2006) 'Measurement, generalization, and publication: Sources of error in benefit transfers and their management', *Ecological Economics*, vol 60, no 2, pp372–378

Rowcroft, P., Studley, J. and Ward, K. (2004) *Eliciting Forest Values and 'Cultural Loss' for Community Plantations and Nature Conservation*, DFID, London

Sanchirico, J., Smith, M. and Lipton, D. (2008) 'An empirical approach to ecosystem-based fishery management', *Ecological Economics*, vol 64, no 3, pp586–596

Schandl, H., Grünbühel, C. M., Haberl, H. and Weisz, H. (2002) 'Handbook of Physical Accounting. Measuring bio-physical dimensions of socio-economic activities: MFA – EFA – HANPP', Social Ecology Working Paper 73, Vienna, July

Scheffer, M., Carpenter, S., Foley, J. A., Folke, C. and Walker, B. (2001) 'Catastrophic shifts in ecosystems', *Nature*, vol 413, pp591–596

Scheffer, M., Szabo, S., Gragnani, A., van Nes, E. H., Rinaldi, S., Nils Kautsky, N., Norberg, J., Roijackers, R. M. M. and Franken, R. J. M. (2003) 'Floating plant dominance as a stable state', *Proceedings of the National Academy of Sciences*, vol 100, pp4040–4045

Schläpfer, F. (2006) 'Survey protocol and income effects in the contingent valuation of public goods: A meta-analysis', *Ecological Economics*, vol 57, pp415–429

Schulze, E.-D. and Mooney H. A. (ed) (1993) *Biodiversity and Ecosystem Function*, Springer, New York

Schunn, C., Kirschenbaum, S. and Trafton, J. (2003) 'The ecology of uncertainty: Sources, indicators, and strategies for information uncertainty', www.au.af.mil/au/awc/awcgate/navy/nrl_uncertainty_taxonomy.pdf

Shyamsundar, P. and Kramer, R. A. (1996) 'Tropical forest protection: An empirical analysis of the costs borne by local people', *Journal of Environmental Economics and Management*, vol 31, pp129–144

Simpson, R. D., Sedjo, R. A. and Reid, J. W. (1996) 'Valuing biodiversity for use in pharmaceutical research', *Journal of Political Economy*, vol 104, pp163–185

Smith, V. K., Van Houtven, G. and Pattanayak, S. K. (2002) 'Benefit transfer via preference calibration: "Prudential algebra" for policy', *Land Economics*, vol 78, pp132–152

Spash, C. (2000) *The Concerted Action on Environmental Valuation in Europe (EVE): An Introduction*, Policy Research Brief No 1, Environmental Valuation in Europe (EVE), Cambridge Research for the Environment

Spash, C. (2001) 'Deliberative monetary valuation', Conference paper, Fifth Nordic Environmental Research Conference, University of Aarhus, Denmark, available at www.clivespahs.org/2001acp.pdf

Spash, C. (2007) 'Deliberative monetary valuation (DMV): Issues in combining economic and political processes to value environmental change', *Ecological Economics*, vol 63, pp690–699

Spash, C. (2008) 'Deliberative monetary valuation and the evidence for a new value theory', *Land Economics*, vol 83, no 3, pp469–488

Spash, C. and Vatn, A. (2006) 'Transferring environmental value estimates: Issues and alternatives', *Ecological Economics*, vol 60, no 2, pp379–388

Spehn, E. M., Hector, A., Joshi, J., Scherer-Lorenzen, M., Schmid, B., Bazeley-White, E., Beierkuhnlein, C., Caldeira, M. C., Diemer, M., Dimitrakopoulos, P. G., Finn, J. A., Freitas, H., Giller, P. S., Good, J., Harris, R., Högberg, P., Huss-Dannell, K., Jumpponen, A., Koricheva, J., Leadley, P. W., Loreau, M., Minns, A., Mulder, C. P. H., O'Donovan, G., Otway, S. J., Palmborg, C., Pereira, J. S., Pfisterer, A. B., Prinz, A., Read, D. J., Schulze, E.-D., Siamantziouras, A.-S. D., Terry, A. C., Troumbis, A. Y., Woodward, F. I., Yachi, S. and Lawton, J. H. (2005) 'Ecosystem effects of biodiversity manipulations in European grasslands', *Ecological Monographs*, vol 75, no 1, pp37–63

Svedsäter, H. (2000) 'Contingent valuation of global environmental resources: Test of perfect and regular embedding', *Journal of Economic Psychology*, vol 21, pp605–623

Svedsäter, H. (2003) 'Economic valuation of the environment: How citizens make sense of contingent valuation questions', *Land Economics*, vol 79, pp122–135

TEEB in National Policy (2011) *The Economics of Ecosystems and Biodiversity in National and International Policy Making* (ed Patrick ten Brink), Earthscan, London

TEEB in Local Policy (2011) *The Economics of Ecosystems and Biodiversity in Local and Regional Policy and Management* (eds Heidi Wittmer and Haripriya Gundimeda), Earthscan, London

Tisdell, C. and Wilson, C. (2006) 'Information, wildlife valuation, conservation: Experiments and policy', *Contemporary Economic Policy*, vol 24, pp144–159

Turner, K. T., Paavola, J., Cooper, P., Farber, S., Jessamy, V. and Georgiu, S. (2003) 'Valuing nature: Lessons learned and future research directions', *Ecological Economics*, vol 46, pp493–510

Turner, R. K. (2007) 'Limits to CBA in UK and European environmental policy: Retrospects and future prospects', *Environmental and Resource Economics*, vol 37, pp253–269

Turner, R. K. and Daily, G. D. (2008) 'The ecosystem service framework and natural capital conservation', *Environmental and Resource Economics*, vol 39, pp25–35

Turner, R. K, Georgiu, S., Clark, R., Brouwer, R. and Burke, J. (2004) 'Economic valuation of water resources in agriculture', from the sectoral to a functional perspective of natural resource management', Food and Agriculture Organization of the United Nations, Rome, Italy

Valero, A., Uche, J., Valero, A., Martínez, A., Naredo, J. M. and Escriu, J. (2010) 'The Fundamentals of Physical Hydronomics: A Novel Approach for Physico-Chemical Water Valuation', chapter 5 in Pascual, U., Shah, A. and Bandyopadhyay, J. (eds) *Water, Agriculture and Sustainable Well-being*, Oxford University Press, New Delhi

van Beukering, P., Brander, L. M., Tompkins, E. and McKenzie, E. (2007) *Valuing the Environment in Small Islands: An Environmental Economics Toolkit*, Joint Nature Conservation Committee, Peterborough

Van Kooten, G., Kckmar, E. and Bulte, E. (2001) 'Preference uncertainty in non-market valuation: A fuzzy approach', *American Journal of Agricultural Economics*, vol 83, no 3, pp487–500

Vatn, A. and Bromley, D. W. (1994) 'Choices without prices without apologies', *Journal of Environmental Economics and Management*, vol 26, no 2, pp129–148

Veisten, K. (2007) 'Contingent valuation controversies: Philosophic debates about economic theory', *The Journal of Socio-Economics*, vol 36, pp204–232

Vitule, J. R. S., Freire, C. A. and Simberloff, D. (2009) 'Introduction of non-native freshwater fish can certainly be bad', *Fish and Fisheries*, vol 10, pp98–108

Wackernagel, M., Onisto, L., Bello, P., Callejas Linares, A., López Falfán, I. S., Méndez García, J., Suárez Guerrero, A. I. and Suárez Guerrero, M. G. (1999) 'Natural capital accounting with the Ecological Footprint concept', *Ecological Economics*, vol 29, no 3, pp375–390

Wadsworth, Y. (1998) 'What is participatory action research?', *Action Research International*, Paper 2, Institute of Workplace Research, Learning and Development, www.scu.edu.au/schools/gcm/ar/ari/p-ywadsworth98.html

Walker, B. and Pearson, L. (2007) 'A resilient perspective of the SEEA', *Ecological Economics* (special edition), vol 61, no 4, pp708–715

Walker, B. H. and Meyers, J. A. (2004) 'Thresholds in ecological and social-ecological systems: A developing database', *Ecology and Society*, vol 9, no 2, p3

Walker, B. H., Abel, N., Anderies, J. M. and Ryan, P. (2009a) 'Resilience, adaptability, and transformability in the Goulburn-Broken Catchment, Australia', *Ecology and Society*, vol 14, no 1, p12

Walker, B., Barrett, S., Polasky, S., Galaz, V., Folke, C., Engström, G., Ackerman, F., Arrow, K., Carpenter, S., Chopra, K., Daily, G., Ehrlich, P., Hughes, T., Kautsky, N., Levin, S., Mäler, K.-G., Shogren, J., Vincent, J., Xepepadeas, T. and de Zeeuw, A. (2009b) 'Looming global-scale failures and missing institutions', *Science*, vol 325, no 5946, pp1345–1346

Walker, B. H., Gunderson, L. H., Kinzig, A. P., Folke, C., Carpenter, S. R. and Schultz, L. (2006) 'A handful of heuristics and some propositions for understanding resilience in social-ecological systems', *Ecology and Society*, vol 11, no 1, p13

Walker, B. H., Holling, C. S., Carpenter, S. R. and Kinzig, A. P. (2004) 'Resilience, adaptability, and transformability', *Ecology and Society*, vol 9, no 2, p5

Whittington, D. (1998) 'Administering contingent valuation surveys in developing countries', *World Development*, vol 26, no 1, pp21–30

Whitten, S. M. and Bennett, J. W. (2002) 'A travel cost study of duck hunting in the upper south east of South Australia', *Australian Geographer*, vol 33, pp207–221

Willing, R. (1976) 'Consumer's surplus without apology', *American Economic Review*, vol 66, pp589–597

Wilson, C. and Tisdell, C. (2005) 'What role does knowledge of wildlife play in providing support for species' conservation?', *Journal of Social Sciences*, vol 1, pp47–51

Wilson, M. A. and Carpenter, S. R. (1999) 'Economic valuation of freshwater ecosystems services in the United States 1971–1997', *Ecological Applications*, vol 9, no 3, pp772–783

Wilson, M. A. and Howarth, R. B. (2002) 'Valuation techniques for achieving social fairness in the distribution of ecosystem services', *Ecological Economics*, vol 41, pp431–443

Annex 1 Applied sources for technical support on biodiversity valuation for national agency teams

There are two types of readily available sources of technical support on biodiversity valuation for national policy teams:

(a) Applied literature on targeted valuation methods. Indicative non-technical reference manuals on valuation techniques such as:

Dixon, J. Scura, L., Carpenter, R. and Sherman, P. (1994) *Economic Analysis of Environmental Impacts*, Earthscan, London

Bateman, I. et al (2002) *Economic Valuation With Stated Preference Techniques: A Manual*, Edward Elgar, Cheltenham, as well as useful technical support websites such as

www.biodiversityeconomics.org

www.ecosystemvaluation.org/default.htm

http://envirovaluation.org/

(b) Databases of existing valuation studies and data including:

EVRI - Environmental Valuation Reference Inventory: www.evri.ca/

ENVALUE environmental valuation database: www.epa.nsw.gov.au/envalue/

Valuation Study Database for Environmental Change: www.beijer.kva.se/valuebase.htm

The New Zealand Non-Market Valuation DataBase http://learn.lincoln.ac.nz/markval/

RED Data Base: www.red-externalities.net/

Benefit transfer information pages:
www.idrc.ca/en/ev-73300-201-1-DO_TOPIC.html
http://yosemite.epa.gov/EE/epa/eed.nsf/webpages/btworkshop.

Chapter 6
Discounting, Ethics and Options for Maintaining Biodiversity and Ecosystem Integrity

Coordinating lead author
John Gowdy

Lead authors
Richard B. Howarth, Clem Tisdell

Reviewers
Paulus Arnoldus, Bernd Hansjürgens, Cameron Hepburn,
Jeffrey A. McNeely, Karl-Göran Mäler

Review editor
Karl-Gorän Mäler

Contents

Key messages   259

1   Introduction   260

2   The Ramsey discounting equation and intergenerational welfare   264

3   Recent behavioural literature on discounting, risk and uncertainty   268

4   Ecosystems and biodiversity in the very long run   271

5   The total value of ecosystems and biodiversity and the discounting equation   272
    5.1   The economic value of ecosystems and biodiversity   273
    5.2   The socio-cultural value of ecosystems and biodiversity   273
    5.3   The ecological value of biodiversity to ecosystems   273

6   Does a low discount rate promote conservation?   274

7   Discounting and safe minimum standards   276

8   Summary of the major challenges to discounting biodiversity
    and ecosystem losses   278

References   280

Key messages

- There are no purely *economic* guidelines for choosing a discount rate. Responsibility to future generations is a matter of ethics, best guesses about the well-being of those in the future, and preserving life opportunities.

- A variety of discount rates, including zero and negative rates, should be used, depending on the time period involved, the degree of uncertainty and the scope of project or policy being evaluated.

- In general, a higher discount rate applied to specific cases will lead to the long-term degradation of biodiversity and ecosystems. A 5 per cent discount rate implies that biodiversity loss 50 years from now will be valued at only 1/7 of the same amount of biodiversity loss today.

- But a low discount rate for the entire economy might favour more investment and growth and more environmental destruction.

- In terms of the discounting equation, estimates of how well-off those in the future will be is the key factor as to how much we should leave the future. Policy makers must decide whether to use income or subjective well-being or some guess about basic needs.

- A critical factor in discounting is the importance of environmental draw-down (destruction of natural capital) to estimates of g (as GDP growth). Is the current generation living on savings that should be passed to their descendants?

- The rich and poor differ greatly in their direct dependence on biodiversity and ecosystem services and bear different responsibilities for their protection.

1 Introduction

A central issue in the economic analysis of biodiversity and ecosystems is the characterization of the responsibility of the present generation to those who will live in the future. That is, how will our current use of biological resources affect our future life opportunities and those of our descendants? A common approach is to begin with the Brundtland Commission's definition of sustainable development, which emphasizes 'meeting present needs without compromising the ability of future generations to meet their own needs' (WCED, 1987). This definition is very general and has widely different interpretations. In economics, sustainability is often interpreted in terms of maintaining human well-being over intergenerational time scales, though some economists attach special importance to conserving stocks of biodiversity, ecosystem services and other forms of natural capital (see Neumayer, 2003). As discussed in the TEEB interim report (TEEB, 2008) discounting is a key issue in the economics of biodiversity and ecosystems. How should economists account for the future effects of biodiversity and ecosystem losses using a variety of valuation methods? This leaves open the question of how to integrate traditional cost–benefit analysis with other approaches to understanding and/or measuring environmental values.

For most resource allocation problems economists use a capital investment approach. Resources should be allocated to those investments yielding the highest rate of return, accounting for uncertainty, risk and the attitude of the investor toward risk. As illustrated in Figure 6.1, suppose an investor has a choice between letting a valuable tree grow at a rate of 5 per cent per year, or cutting the tree down, selling it and putting the money in the bank. Which decision is best depends on the rate of interest the bank pays. If the bank pays 6 per cent and the price of timber is constant the investor will earn more money by cutting the tree down and selling it, that is, by converting natural capital into financial capital. This simple example is a metaphor for the conversion of biodiversity and ecosystem services into other forms of capital. The shortcomings of this simple approach to valuing biodiversity and ecosystems include: (1) the irreversibility of biodiversity loss; (2) pure uncertainty as to the effects of such losses; (3) the difference between private investment decisions and the responsibilities of citizens of particular societies; (4) the implicit assumption

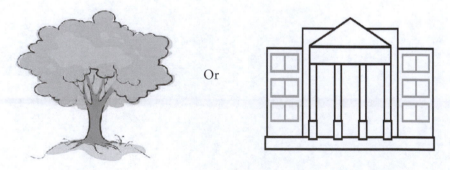

Figure 6.1 *Valuing nature: The tree or money in the bank?*

that all forms of capital are in principle substitutable for one another on a Euro-for-Euro basis; (5) the assumption that reinvestment of natural capital is possible and that future returns on the reinvestment are certain; (6) the assumption that the change being evaluated is marginal, that is, it will not substantially alter existing economic conditions including relative prices (Hepburn, 2006); and (7) assuming that the only value of the tree is its potential as timber, thereby ignoring its role in providing ecosystem services. The discount rate can be seen as a reverse interest rate. In the above example, suppose the tree was not growing at all and the rate of interest on money was 6 per cent. By not cutting down the tree and putting the money earned from selling the tree in the bank, the owner would be losing 6 per cent per year. This would be the discount rate on the tree in the world of financial investment.

The financial model of resource use is enshrined in the theory of optimal economic growth as described in macroeconomics textbooks (see Dasgupta and

---

Box 6.1 Discounting the Amazon

The discussion of the value of the Amazon rainforest illuminates the distinction between economic, cultural and ecosystem values. The services of the Amazon generate large direct market values, including revenue from ecotourism, fishing, rainforest crops and pharmaceuticals. Indirect economic benefits include climate regulation, option values for undiscovered rainforest products, and climate change protection from carbon storage. Cultural values not only include the spiritual and life-giving values the Amazon holds for its indigenous people, but also its existence value to the rest of the world's population. Most of those who know something of the unique and beautiful features of Amazon ecosystems feel a loss when they hear of their destruction even if they have never seen them. But the most important values of the Amazon, as discussed in Chapter 1, may be its role in providing ecosystem services such as regulating weather in the Western Hemisphere and as the world's largest storehouse of biodiversity.

What role should discounting play in each of these layers of value? As the discussion in Chapter 1 shows, when calculating the costs and benefits of a development project, such as a dam, discounting will tend to favour short-term economic benefits such as temporary job creation over the costs of losing environmental services that have smaller annual values but that last indefinitely. Cultural and ecosystems values are difficult or impossible to price and thus are usually excluded by traditional cost–benefit analysis. Referring to Figure 6.1, the direct economic services of the Amazon might be represented by the tree. If a section of the Amazon rainforest yields sustainable economic services equivalent to an annual rate of return of 5 per cent and if the forest could be cut down, sold as timber and invested at a rate of return of 6 per cent, then the economically rational thing to do is to cut down the forest, sell it and put the money in the bank. But this assumes that investments are secure and last indefinitely and that environmental features and economic investments are completely fungible. The tree's role in providing regulating ecosystem services is ignored.

Heal, 1974; Blanchard and Fischer, 1989). This model assumes that society can and should seek to maximize the weighted sum of present and future economic welfare. The weight attached to future welfare declines at ρ per cent per year, reflecting society's impatience, or preference to receive benefits in the short run while deferring costs to the future. In a continuous-time setting with constant population and a single consumption good, this approach employs constrained optimization methods to maximize the social welfare functional:

$$\int_0^\infty U[C(t)]\, e^{-\rho t}\, td \tag{1}$$

subject to the technological, economic and environmental constraints that force decision makers to balance short-run and long-run welfare. In this setting, U is instantaneous utility and C is the flow of consumption goods.[1] This equation characterizes well-being or utility as deriving from the discounted flow of market goods (or pseudo market goods). This characterization of intertemporal choice, particularly in the cases of biodiversity loss and climate change, has been questioned on both theoretical and behavioural grounds (Bromley, 1998; Spash, 2002; DeCanio, 2003; Gowdy, 2004). The model ignores the fact that individuals have finite lifespans and assumes that ρ represents both *individuals'* time preference and *social preferences* regarding trade-offs between the welfare of present and future generations (Howarth and Norgaard, 1992; Burton, 1993). Although it is restrictive, the discounted utility framework is mathematically tractable. It is perhaps this fact that explains the model's widespread use in applied economics. Most important, the framework is useful for illuminating the economic, ethical and cultural aspects of valuing the future impacts of public policies.

Beckerman and Hepburn (2007) argue that the practice of utility discounting is justified by the theory of 'agent relative ethics'. In this perspective, people reasonably attach greater weight to the welfare of themselves and their immediate family than to people who are less proximate to them in space and time. An early contribution by Dasgupta and Heal (1974), however, showed that the discounted utility criterion sometimes generates outcomes that are unsustainable, yielding a moral paradox that has generated a quite substantial literature. This problem arises in economies that depend on an essential, non-renewable resource, such as oil. In this model, short-run economic growth leads to resource depletion that, in turn, leads to long-run economic decline. This occurs because decision makers are too impatient to make the investments in substitute technologies needed to offset the costs of resource depletion.

To address this problem, Solow (1974) proposed the so-called 'maximum' social welfare function, which allocates resources in a way that achieves a constant level of utility over time. Conversely, equation (1) may be maximized, subject to the constraint that utility is constant or increasing over time (Asheim, 1988). In this approach, the utility discount rate represents society's altruistic preferences towards future generations, or willingness to undertake voluntary sacrifices so that future generations may enjoy a better way of life. The non-declining utility constraint, in contrast, is based on a perceived moral duty to ensure that present actions do not jeopardize the life opportunities available to posterity (Howarth, 1995). This approach can be viewed as rational given a rights-based (or 'Kantian') ethical framework in which moral duties complement preference satisfaction in making rational decisions.

In applied studies, the discounted utility criterion is often embraced as a sufficient basis for optimal resource allocation, a fact that puts special emphasis on the choice of the utility discount rate. The release of the Stern Review (Stern, 2007) and the ensuing debate among economists as to its merit did much to illuminate the role of discounting the costs and benefits of policies having very long time spans and very broad spatial scales – climate change and biodiversity loss being the prime examples. At first the Stern debate centred primarily on the 'proper' discount rate to apply to future costs and benefits of climate change mitigation (Dasgupta, 2006; Smith and Mendelson, 2007; Yohe and Tol, 2007; Ackerman, 2008). As the debate progressed it became clear that there was more to the economics of climate change than choosing the 'correct' discount rate. Several prominent environmental economists came to the conclusion that the standard economic model offers an inadequate framework to analyse environmental issues characterized by irreversibilities, pure uncertainty and very long time horizons (Dasgupta, 2008; Weitzman, 2009). The 'key messages' in the Stern Review's economic analysis of climate change (chapter 2, p25) apply with equal force to the economic analysis of biodiversity. The loss of biodiversity and ecosystems has properties that make it difficult to apply standard welfare analysis including discounting the future:

1   It is a phenomenon having global as well as local consequences.
2   Its impacts are long-term and irreversible.
3   Pure uncertainty is pervasive.
4   Changes are non-marginal and non-linear.
5   Questions of inter- and intra-generational equity are central.

These points have been made about environmental resources for decades by economists working outside the neoclassical paradigm (Georgescu-Roegen, 1971; Boulding, 1973; Daly, 1977). Interestingly, it seems that the policy prescriptions of both those using a more conventional welfare economics approach, and those who call for an alternative, heterodox approach to environmental valuation, are converging. Using either standard or alternative approaches, when the services of nature are taken into account, sustaining human welfare in the future implies aggressive conservation and ecosystem restoration policies in the present.

This chapter is organized as follows: Section 2 discusses the economic approach to intergenerational welfare using the Ramsey discounting equation; Section 3 reviews some recent findings from behavioural economics and their relevance to the discounting issue; Section 4 examines the issue of ecosystems and biodiversity preservation in the very long run; Section 5 discusses the discounting equation in the context of the total value of ecosystems and biodiversity; Section 6 examines the macroeconomic implications on biodiversity of a low discount rate; Section 7 looks at the issues of discounting and the safe minimum standard, and of ecosystem services and the poor; and Section 8 presents conclusions.

2 The Ramsey discounting equation and intergenerational welfare

In optimal growth theory, it is common to assume that the utility function presented in equation (1) takes the specific form $U(C) = C^{1-\eta}(1 - \eta)$. Here η is a parameter that reflects the curvature of the utility function. Given this assumption, future *monetary* costs and benefits should be discounted at the rate r that is defined by the so-called 'Ramsey equation':

$$r = \rho + \eta \bullet g \tag{2}$$

The discount rate r is determined by the rate of pure time preference (ρ), η, and the rate of growth of per capita consumption (g). In intuitive terms, people discount future economic benefits because: (a) they are impatient; and (b) they expect their income and consumption levels to rise so that 1 Euro of future consumption will provide less satisfaction than 1 Euro of consumption today.

This equation ignores uncertainty, thereby streamlining the analysis but reducing the model's plausibility and descriptive power. Accounting for uncertainty leads to a more complex specification in which the discount rate equation includes a third term that reflects the perceived risk of the action under consideration (see Starrett, 1988; Blanchard and Fischer, 1989, ch 6). As noted above, the rate of pure time preference (ρ) is supposed to reflect both individuals' time preferences and social preferences regarding the value of the well-being of future generations as seen from the perspective of those living today. More realistic models distinguish between these effects, and blending them together can obscure important aspects of both descriptive modelling and prescriptive analysis (Auerbach and Kotlikoff, 1987; Howarth, 1998; Gerlagh and Keyzer, 2001). A positive value for ρ means that, all other things being equal, the further into the future we go the less the well-being of persons living there is worth to us. The higher the value of ρ the less concerned we are about negative impacts in the future. A large literature exists arguing for a variety of values for pure time preference but it is clear by now that no econometric method is available to determine the value of ρ. Choosing the rate of pure time preference comes down to a question of ethics. Ramsey (1928, p543) asserted that a positive rate of pure time preference was 'ethically indefensible and arises merely from a weakness of the imagination'. On the other side of the debate, Pearce et al (2003) took the position that a positive time preference discount rate is an observed fact since people do in fact discount the value of things expected to be received in the future. Nordhaus (1992, 2007) has consistently argued that the market rate of interest constitutes the appropriate discount rate that reveals individuals' time preference.[2]

Sen's (1961) 'isolation paradox' casts doubt on the argument that the social discount rate should be set equal to the market rate of return. According to Sen (1961), private investments may provide spillover benefits that are not captured by individual investors. Providing bequests to one's daughter, for example, serves to increase the welfare of the daughter's spouse and, by extension, his parents. When preferences are interconnected in this way, individuals underinvest. Correcting this market failure would lead to increased investment, lower interest rates, and therefore a lower discount rate in cost–benefit analysis (Howarth and Norgaard, 1992). But even if it is agreed to use a market rate, which market rate should be used? In the United States, a voluminous literature has focused on the fact that, since the late 1920s, safe financial instruments such as bank deposits and short-run government bonds yield average returns of roughly 1 per cent. Corporate stocks, in contrast, yielded average returns of 7 per cent per year with substantial year-to-year volatility. Assets with intermediate risks (such as corporate bonds and long-term government bonds that carry inflation risks) pay intermediate returns (see Cochrane, 2001, for an authoritative textbook discussion). Choosing a discount rate, then, involves a judgement regarding the perceived riskiness of a given public policy (Starrett, 1988). Low discount rates are appropriate for actions that yield safe benefit streams or provide precautionary benefits – that is, that reduce major threats to future economic welfare.[3]

Biodiversity loss will affect the entire world's population including those from cultures with very different ideas about obligations to the future. Furthermore, Portney and Weyant (1999, p4) point out that '[t]hose looking for guidance on the choice of discount rate could find justification [in the literature] for a rate at or near zero, as high as 20 percent, and any and all values in between' (quoted in Cole, 2008). Frederick et al (2004) report empirical estimates of discount rates ranging from -6 per cent to 96,000 per cent. Others argue that discounting from the perspective of an individual at a point in time is not equivalent to a social discount rate reflecting the long-term interest of the entire human species. An observed positive market discount rate merely shows that market goods received in the future are worth less as evaluated by an individual living now, not that they are worth less at the point in the future that they are received.

The other important factor in the Ramsey equation determining how much we should care about the future is how well-off those in the future are likely to be. As shown in equation (2), the standard model characterizes the well-being of future generations using two components: the growth rate of per capita income in the future (g) and the elasticity of the marginal utility of consumption (η). The elasticity of marginal utility measures how rapidly the marginal utility of consumption falls as the consumption level increases. It is often assumed that η is equal to 1 (Nordhaus, 1994; Stern, 2007). In this case, then ηg corresponds to a Bernoulli (logarithmic) utility function, and 1 per cent of today's income has the same value as 1 per cent of income at some point in the future (since g is a percentage change). So if per capita income today is $10,000 and income in the year 2100 is $100,000, $1000 today has the same value as $10,000 in 2100. Put another way, a $1000 sacrifice today would be justified only if it added at least $10,000 to the average income of people living in the year 2100 (Quiggin, 2008). The higher the value of η, the higher the future pay-off must be for a sacrifice today. For example, with ρ near zero and a positive value for g, increasing η from 1 to 2 would double the discount rate.

Several assumptions are buried in the parameter η as it is usually formulated. It is assumed that η is independent of the level of consumption, that it is independent of the growth rate of consumption, and that social well-being can be characterized by per capita consumption. These assumptions are arbitrary and adopted mainly for convenience (Pearce et al, 2006).

At least three distinct valuation concepts are present in η (Cole, 2008, p18). It contains a measure of risk aversion, a moral judgement about static income inequality among present day individuals, and a moral judgement about dynamic income inequality over time. Weitzman (2009) notes that the values of these components move the discount rate in different directions. On one hand a high value for η (in conjunction with g) would seem to take the moral high ground – a given loss in income has a greater negative impact on a poor person than a rich person. But if we assume, as most economic models do, that per capita consumption g continues to grow in the future, a higher η means a higher value for ηg and the less value economists place on income losses for those in the future.

Assuming a near-zero value for ρ and that $\eta = 1$ (as in Cline, 1992 and Stern, 2007) means that the total discount rate (r) is determined by projections of the future growth rate of per capita income, g. The growth rate of income is derived from projecting past world economic performance and the researcher's judgement. The values of g in the Stern report and in the most widely used climate change models range between 1.5 per cent and 2.0 per cent (Quiggin, 2008, p12). With a high g, discounting the future is justified by the assumption that those living in the future will be better off than those living today (Pearce et al, 2006). In the TEEB interim report (TEEB, 2008, p30) Martinez-Alier argues that assuming constant growth in g leads to the 'optimist's paradox'. The assumption of continual growth justifies the present use of more resources and more pollution because our descendants will be better off. But such growth would leave future generations with a degraded environment and a lower quality of life.

A major step forward in understanding the economics of sustainability was the realization that maintaining a constant or increasing level of consumption or utility depends on maintaining the stock of capital assets generating that welfare (Solow, 1974; Hartwick, 1977, 1997; Dasgupta and Mäler, 2000; Arrow et al, 2004). Thus, maintaining a non-declining g means maintaining (1) productive manufactured physical capital, (2) human capital – knowledge, technical know-how, routines, habits and customs – and the institutions supporting it, and (3) natural capital. Using the terminology in Chapter 1, the biodiversity component of natural capital is, in turn, comprised of three different kinds of value to humans:

1 *Economic*: The direct inputs from nature to the market economy.
2 *Socio-cultural*: The non-market services necessary for maintaining the biological and psychological needs of the human species.
3 *Ecological value*: The value to ecosystems such as preserving evolutionary potential through biological diversity and ecosystem integrity.

These layers of biodiversity value are discussed in more detail in Section 5.

Under certain technical assumptions, g may be interpreted as the growth rate of per capita income adjusted for externalities and other market imperfections. Under these conditions, Dasgupta and Mäler (2000) show that g can be considered as the rate of return on all forms of capital. In a dynamic growth context, g is equivalent to the growth rate of total factor productivity

(TFP) along a balanced growth path. TFP is the rate of growth of economic output not accounted for by the weighted growth rates of productive inputs. In the three input cases used here,

$$TFP = Q - aMK - bHK - cNK, \quad a+b+c = 1 \text{ and the weights} \\ \text{are input cost shares} \tag{3}$$

For example, in a simple model using manufactured capital (MK), human capital (HK) and natural capital (NK) as inputs, if output grows by 5 per cent per year and the weighted average growth rates of inputs increases by 4 per cent, then TFP would be 1 per cent. Environmental economists have long maintained that estimates of TFP (g in the Ramsey model) do not adequately take into account the draw-down of the stock of natural capital (Repetto et al, 1989; Dasgupta and Mäler, 2000; Ayres and Warr, 2006). Vouvaki and Xeapapadeas (2008) found that when the environment (they use CO_2 pollution as a proxy for environmental damage) is not considered as a factor of production TFP estimates are biased upward. They argue that failing to internalize the cost of an environmental externality is equivalent to using an unpaid factor of production. After including as natural capital only the external effects of CO_2 pollution from energy use, they found that TFP estimates for 19 of 23 countries switched from positive to negative. The average of TFP estimates for the 23 countries changed from +0.865 to -0.952. This result implies that when the negative effects of economic production on the ability of natural world to provide productive inputs g could well be negative, so future generations would be worse off. Moreover, when environmental degradation effects beyond CO_2 accumulation are included the case for a negative g becomes even stronger. This has serious implications for long-run economic policies for climate change mitigation and biodiversity loss. Given some reasonable assumptions about pure time preference and the elasticity of consumption, a negative g implies that the present generation should consume less in order to invest more in the well-being of future generations.

If we step back from the assumption that the well-being of future generations can be characterized by per capita consumption – by, for example, considering g as representing subjective well-being (Kahneman et al, 1997) – the case for considering a negative g becomes even stronger. Among the most important findings of the subjective well-being literature are these: (1) traditional economic indicators such as per capita net national product (NNP) are inadequate measures of welfare; (2) the effect of an income change depends on interpersonal comparisons and relative position; (3) humans have common, identifiable biological and psychological characteristics related to their well-being (Frey and Stutzer, 2002; Layard, 2005). These observations have direct bearing on the sustainability debate and have the potential to guide intergenerational welfare and policies to protect biological diversity. People receive economic benefits from biodiversity but the psychological and aesthetic benefits cannot be properly captured by market values (Wilson, 1994). All these contributions of biodiversity are being rapidly reduced and should be taken into account in estimates of future well-being (g). Dasgupta (1995) further identifies self-reinforcing links between environmental degradation, biodiversity loss, poverty and population growth.

3 Recent behavioural literature on discounting, risk and uncertainty

Insights from behavioural economics have greatly broadened understanding of how people compare future costs and benefits. Relevant insights into human behaviour include the following:

1   *Loss aversion*: Losses are given higher values than equivalent gains. Figure 6.2 summarizes the considerable evidence that people are loss averse; that is, they evaluate gains and losses from a reference point and place a higher value on a loss than on a gain of an equal amount of that same thing (Kahneman and Tversky, 1979). This is confirmed in the widely reported discrepancy between willingness to pay (WTP) and willingness to accept (WTA) measures of environmental changes (Brown and Gregory, 1999). The implications for evaluating biodiversity loss are clear. Even in the context of standard utility theory, the required compensation for biodiversity loss (WTA) is likely to be much greater than the estimated market value of that loss (WTP).

2   *Hyperbolic discounting*: Some evidence indicates that people discount the future hyperbolically – that is, as shown in Figure 6.3, the discount rate declines and then flattens out so that after some time the present value of something no longer significantly declines (Laibson, 1997).

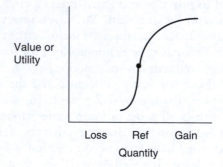

Figure 6.2 *Value of loss or gain from a reference point*

Source: Knetsch (2005)

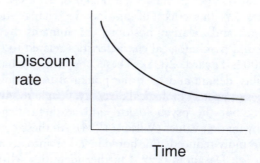

Figure 6.3 *Hyperbolic discounting*

The existence of hyperbolic discounting implies that standard economic analysis may seriously underestimate the long-term benefits of biodiversity protection. If people discount hyperbolically, and if we respect stated preferences, straight-line discounting should not be used to place values on distant-future environmental damages such as those caused by biodiversity loss. Hyperbolic discounting has been widely discussed in the theoretical literature and has had some impact on policy recommendations. Cropper and Laibson (1999) recommend using hyperbolic discounting in the case of global warming and Chichilnisky (1996) uses hyperbolic discounting in her model of sustainable development. One of the positive features of welfare economics is that, in theory, it respects individual choice. If individuals choose to place the same value on biodiversity present 50 years from now as they do on biodiversity 100 years from now, then economists should respect that preference. Of course, just because individuals are observed to discount hyperbolically does not mean that a social discount rate should be hyperbolic.

Beltratti et al (1998) advocate the use of the 'green golden rule' for renewable resources, using something near market discount rates in the short run (so that the present is not exploited) and a rate asymptotically approaching zero in the long run (so that the distant future is not exploited). Similarly, Weitzman (2001) advocates what he terms 'gamma discounting' using a rate of about 4 per cent for the immediate future with a steady decline to near zero in the distant future.

3 *Inconsistent discounting*: Rubinstein (2003) points out that hyperbolic discounting has been accepted by many economists because it can be easily incorporated into the net present value framework of standard economic analysis. He argues that the evidence suggests that the larger problem is inconsistent, not hyperbolic, discounting. People appear to have different discount rates for different kinds of outcomes (Loewenstein, 1987). Considerable evidence exists that people are wildly inconsistent even when discounting similar things. Inconsistent discounting suggests some limits to attempts to placing precise numbers on the general tendency of individuals to prefer something now rather than later.

4 *The equity premium puzzle*: Mehra and Prescott (1985) showed that the discounted utility model is deeply inconsistent with the observed gap between the low returns available on safe investments and the much higher average returns paid provided by risky assets such as corporate stocks. Mankiw and Zeldes (1991) calculate that the level of risk aversion implied by this rate-of-return spread implies that an investor would have to be indifferent between a bet equally likely to pay $50,000 or $100,000 (with an expected value of $75,000) and a certain pay-off of $51,209.

Explaining the low market return on safe assets requires that both η and ρ must assume values near zero (Kocherlakota, 1996). Yet explaining the high risk premium paid by stocks requires that investors must be highly risk averse, which implies that η must attain a high, positive value to be consistent with the data. Scientifically, this suggests that the discounted utility model is in a deep sense inconsistent with empirical observations. This point undercuts reliance on equation (2) to calculate discount rates.

Several approaches have been advanced to address this disparity (see Kocherlakota, 1996; Cochrane, 2001). Some models have extended preferences to distinguish between risk preferences and the elasticity of intertemporal substitution. Others assume that preferences are shaped by habit formation and/or relative consumption effects. A third hypothesis is that investors are loss averse with respect to investment gains and losses (Benartzi and Thaler, 1995). Including this effect in the utility function serves to decouple the social discount rate from the market rate of return (Howarth, 2009). In this case, the public policies should be discounted at a rate that is close to the risk-free rate of return, even for policies that involve significant degrees of uncertainty.

5   *Discounting under uncertainty*: On theoretical grounds, there is reason to believe that greater uncertainty about the future may tend to produce lower certainty-equivalent discount rates (Gollier et al, 2008). This is because investing in safe assets reduces the risks pertaining to future economic welfare, rendering them attractive to investors even at low rates of return. Newell and Pizer (2003) used random walk and mean-reverting models to compute certainty-equivalent discount rates that measure the uncertainty adjusted rate out into the distant future. When applied to climate change scenarios, their results suggested that the present value of mitigation efforts almost doubled. Hepburn et al (2009) extended this result to estimate autoregressive and regime-switching models of US interest rates and also found that uncertainty-adjusted rates declined more rapidly. Although much of the recent literature on discounting an uncertainty deals with climate change, uncertainty is also pervasive in the case of the welfare effects of biodiversity loss and this suggests using lower discount rates in valuing future losses of biodiversity and ecosystem services.

6   *Discounting and relative prices*: The discount rate is applied to an aggregate consumption good and an implicit assumption is that the prices of all goods are changing at the same rate. But biodiversity is not a typical consumption good. For at least two reasons – increasing scarcity and limits to its substitutability – calculating the rate of change of the relative *value* of biodiversity will be different from determining the *price* of a typical consumption good (Cameron Hepburn, pers. comm.). Sterner and Persson (2008, p62) write:

> Briefly, because the rate of growth is uneven across sectors of the economy, the composition of economic output will inevitably change over time. If output of some material goods (e.g. mobile phones) increases, but access to environmental goods and services (e.g. access to clean water, rain-fed agricultural production, or biodiversity) declines, then the relative price of these environmental amenities should rise over time.

This would mean that the estimated damages from biodiversity loss (or the benefits from biodiversity preservation) would rise over time and this might be great enough to offset the effect of the positive discount rate. If this is the case, increasing the amount of biodiversity and ecosystems would be economically justified (Hoel and Sterner, 2007).

7   *Risk aversion and insurance*: A large body of evidence suggests that most people are risk averse (Kahneman and Tversky, 1979). This has major implications for evaluating biodiversity and ecosystem losses. As in the case of climate change there is a real, although unknown, possibility that biodiversity loss will have catastrophic effects on human welfare. Paul and Anne Ehrlich (1997) use the 'rivet popper' analogy to envision the effects of biodiversity loss. A certain number of rivets can pop out of an airplane body without causing any immediate danger. But once a critical threshold is reached the airplane becomes unstable and crashes. Likewise, ecosystems are able to maintain themselves with a certain range of stress, but after a point they may experience a catastrophic flip from a high biodiversity stable state to another, low diversity stable state. Weitzman (2009) uses the evidence for a small, but significant, possibility of a runaway greenhouse effect to argue for aggressive climate change mitigation policies. Weitzman's reasoning might be applied to ecosystem services considering the possibility of ecosystem collapse once a damage threshold is crossed.

4 Ecosystems and biodiversity in the very long run

Many economists (e.g. Spash, 2002, chapters 8, 9) question the appropriateness of discounting as applied to global and far-reaching issues like biodiversity loss. Ultimately, human existence depends on maintaining the web of life within which humans co-evolved with other species and thus the idea of placing a discounted 'price' on total biodiversity is absurd. One may object that the ability to adapt to environmental change is one of the most striking characteristics of *Homo sapiens* (Richerson and Boyd, 2005). But the rapidity of current and projected environmental change is unique in human history. Human activity within the past 100 years or so has drastically altered the course of biological evolution on planet Earth. According to a survey by the International Union for Conservation of Nature, a quarter of mammal species face extinction (Gilbert, 2008). Conservative estimates indicate that 12 per cent of birds are threatened, together with over 30 per cent of amphibians and 5 per cent of reptiles. Particularly alarming is the state of the world's oceans. Human-caused threats to ocean biodiversity are summarized by Jackson (2008, p11458):

> Today, the synergistic effects of human impacts are laying the groundwork for a comparatively great Anthropocene mass extinction in the oceans with unknown ecological and evolutionary consequences. Synergistic effects of habitat destruction, overfishing, introduced species, warming, acidification, toxins and mass runoff of nutrients are transforming once complex ecosystems like coral reefs into monotonous level bottoms, transforming clear and productive coastal seas into anoxic dead zones, and transforming complex food webs topped by big animals into simplified, microbially dominated ecosystems with boom and bust cycles of toxic dinoflagellate blooms, jellyfish, and disease.

If we modelled ecosystems according to the Solow–Hartwick approach for economic sustainability (maintaining the capital stock necessary to ensure that economic output does not decline) it would certainly be clear that the 'ecosystem capital' base for sustaining biodiversity is being rapidly depleted. If the biologists and paleontologists who study the problem are correct, Earth is entering into its sixth mass extinction of complex life on the planet during the past 570 million years or so. Biodiversity recovery from past mass extinctions took between 5 and 20 million years (Ward, 1994; Wilson, 1998). Past mass extinctions irreversibly restructured the composition of the Earth's biota (Krug et al, 2009). Even if the final result of the current mass extinction is a richer, more biologically diverse world, as occurred after past mass extinctions, humans will not be around to see it. Human-induced biodiversity loss will constrain the evolution of humans and other species for as long as humans will have inhabited planet Earth. This prospect raises entirely new kinds of questions about how to value today's impact on future generations. These include:

- Functional transparency (Bromley, 1989): In many cases the role of a particular species in an ecosystem is apparent only after it has been removed. The change may be non-linear and irreversible. The effect on local economies may be catastrophic as in the collapse the Northern Cod fishery due to overharvesting. More than 40,000 people in Newfoundland lost their jobs and the cod fishery has still not recovered 15 years after a total moratorium on cod fishing.
- Preserving genetic and ecosystem diversity (Gowdy, 1997): Evolutionary potential is the ability of a species or ecosystem to respond to changing conditions in the future. Future conditions are largely unpredictable (the effects of climate change on biodiversity, for example) but in general the greater the diversity of an ecosystem, the more resilient that system is (Tilman and Downing, 1994).
- Preserving options for future generations (Page, 1983; Norton, 2005): The financial model of sustainability treats biodiversity as an input for commodity production. Even if the notion of consumer utility is broadened to include concepts like existence values, the model's frame of reference is still the industrial market economy. The effects of present day biodiversity loss and ecosystem service disruption will last for millennia. The question becomes how do societies decide what to leave for future generations if it is impossible to predict what sorts of economies/values/needs they will have?

5 The total value of ecosystems and biodiversity and the discounting equation

The total value of ecosystems and biodiversity is unknown but logically the ultimate value to humans is infinite because if they are reduced beyond a certain point our species could not exist. Biodiversity value can be seen as layers of a hierarchy moving from market value to non-market value to humans to ecosystem value. These various levels of biodiversity value point to the need for a pluralistic and flexible methodology to determine appropriate policies for its use and preservation (Gowdy, 1997).

5.1 The economic value of ecosystems and biodiversity

Economic value includes the direct economic contributions of biodiversity including eco-tourism, recreation and the value of direct biological inputs such as crops, fisheries and forests. These values can be very large. For example, Geist (1994) estimated that the direct economic value of Wyoming's big game animals, from tourism and hunting, exceeded $1 billion or about $1000 for every large animal. Although evidence from contingent valuation, hedonic pricing and other economic valuation tools underscore the importance of biodiversity and ecosystems, these give incomplete, lower-bound estimates of their values (see Nunes and van den Bergh, 2001).

The degree to which an economically valuable biological resource should be exploited is driven by the social discount rate, r in equation (2) above. The rate is a method for determining (in theory) how to split the stock of natural capital between consumption now and consumption in the future.

5.2 The socio-cultural value of ecosystems and biodiversity

The biological world contributes to human psychological well-being in ways that can be empirically measured (Wilson, 1994; Kellert, 1996). But measures of subjective well-being cannot be adequately valued in a traditional social welfare framework (Orr, 2004; Norton, 2005). Spiritual, cultural, aesthetic and other contributions of interacting with nature may be included in a more comprehensive conception of utility such as the Bentham/Kahneman notion of utility as well-being.

Considering non-market values of biodiversity helps to answer the question of what should be left for future generations. Is there any reason to think those in the future will not have the same psychological need for interacting with nature? Is there any reason to believe that a walk in a rainforest is worth more to a person living now than to a person living 1, 50 or 100 years from now? The reasonable answer is no. The appropriate discount rate for this part of biodiversity, the pure time preference of biophilia, is $\rho = 0$. Another interesting interpretation of ρ in this context would be to consider it as the discount rate if a person were behind a Rawlsian veil of ignorance not knowing where in time she would be placed (Dasgupta, 2008).

5.3 The ecological value of biodiversity to ecosystems

Biologically diverse ecosystems seem to be more resilient to environmental shocks than less diverse ones (Tilman and Downing, 1994) although the relationship between resilience and biodiversity is complicated (Robinson et al, 1992). It is also well established that human activity has degraded terrestrial and marine ecosystems across the planet. Suppose the discounting rule is expanded further to include ecosystem integrity itself? This is reasonable since human existence in the long run depends on preserving our biological context. In the discounting equation (2) suppose 'g' is considered to be a change in the stock of the Earth's biodiversity and ecosystems. With climate change, continued land clearance and continued exploitation of the world's fisheries,

g is likely to be negative for decades to come. Let η be the value of a marginal change in the state of an ecosystem. The value of η is likely to be larger the more degraded an ecosystem is (more susceptible to changes in the state of the environment). So the term ηg applied to ecosystems is likely to be negative, large and increasing in the future. This implies making large sacrifices today to improve ecosystems in the future. Today's generation has prospered by spending much of the natural capital it inherited. Ethically, they owe it to future generations to rebuild that inheritance.

6 Does a low discount rate promote conservation?

The discount rate is also relevant to investment and economic performance at the macroeconomic level which in turn affects biodiversity and ecosystems. At the macroeconomic level there is no unambiguous relationship between the rate of interest (the mirror image of the discount rate) and the extent of biodiversity conservation. A low rate of interest can be associated with a high degree of biodiversity loss and so can a high rate of interest. This follows if the level of investment in human-made capital is regarded as a major factor leading to ecosystem disruption and biodiversity (Tisdell, 2005, p250). That the accumulation of manufactured capital is a major factor resulting in species loss has been pointed out for a long time (Harting, 1880, p209; Tisdell, 1982, p378; Swanson, 1994). Manufactured capital is a produced input using 'land' (the direct use of biodiversity and ecosystems, and their indirect destruction) and labour.

For simplicity, assume that the real rate of interest depends only on the demand for loanable funds for investment and on the supply of these funds as a result of savings. Assume further that these demand and supply curves have normal slopes. First, it can be observed that in this case, an increase in the rate of interest can come about either because the demand for loanable funds rises (due to an increase in the marginal efficiency of capital), other things kept constant, or due to fall in the willingness to save, other things unchanged. These two situations are illustrated in Figures 6.4 and 6.5 respectively. In the case shown in Figure 6.4, the demand for loanable funds rises from $D_1 D_1$ to $D_2 D_2$ and the supply curve of these funds remains unaltered as shown by $S_1 S_1$. The equilibrium in the loanable funds market changes from E_1 to E_2 and the rate of interest rises from r_1 to r_2. The amount of funds invested goes up from X_1 to X_2. This result is unfavourable to biodiversity conservation because it results in more capital accumulation and conversion of natural resources into human-made capital. On the other hand, in the case illustrated by Figure 6.5, a rise in the rate of interest is associated with a reduction in the level of investment and therefore is favourable to biodiversity conservation. In this case, the demand curve for loanable funds, $D_1 D_1$ is stationary but the willingness to supply loanable funds declines, as shown by the supply line being initially $S_1 S_1$ and subsequently $S_2 S_2$. Market equilibrium alters from E_1 to E_2 and the rate of interest rises from r_1 to r_2. However, in this case, the level of investment falls from X_1 to X_0, and the result is favourable to biodiversity conservation. Converse results also apply. If the demand curve in the case illustrated in Figure 6.4 shifts downwards rather than upwards, the rate of interest falls but

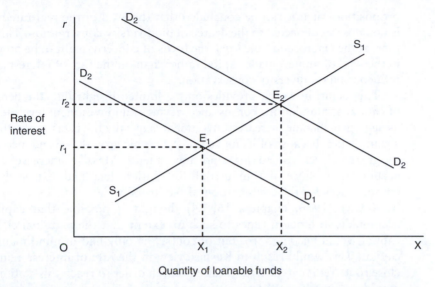

Figure 6.4 *A case in which a rising rate of interest is associated with a rise in the level of investment in human-made capital – a consequence likely to have an adverse impact on biodiversity conservation*

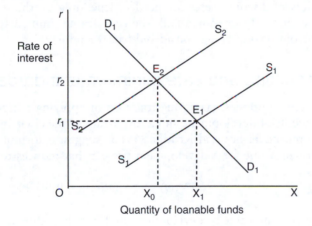

Figure 6.5 *A case in which a rise in the rate of interest is associated with a decline in the level of investment in human-made capital. This case is likely to be favourable to biodiversity conservation*

investment does likewise. On the other hand, if the supply curve of loanable funds moves downwards in the case illustrated by Figure 6.5, the interest rate falls but the level of investment rises. The fall in the interest rate in the former case is favourable to biodiversity conservation but not in the latter one.

Other examples could also be given. The ones above, however, are sufficient to show that at the macro level, changes in the rate of interest can be associated (depending on the circumstances) with an increase or decrease in the level of investment in human-made capital. If investment in human-made capital is seen as the main threat to biodiversity and ecosystem conservation (a reasonable proposition) then it can be concluded that the level of the real rate of interest is not closely connected to the degree of biodiversity conservation. This suggests that, at the macroeconomic level, the focus of concern ought to be on variations in the level of human-made capital rather than on the rate of interest as a major influence on biodiversity conservation.

This point, however, provides only a limited insight into the determinants of capital accumulation. For instance, savings and investment levels tend to rise as aggregate income increases. Investment is usually the basis for further capital accumulation because of its impact on economic growth – rising incomes result in greater levels of saving and investment. Massive increase in capital accumulation since the Industrial Revolution has had extremely adverse consequences for the conservation of biodiversity.

Keynes (1936, chapters 16, 24) thought it possible that capital could accumulate in modern times to such an extent that the marginal efficiency of capital would become zero. But of course, he only had in mind manufactured capital. This would result in Keynes' view in the rate of interest being zero or close to it. Yet it can be hypothesized that in order to reach this stationary state would require a tremendous conversion of natural resources into human-made capital resulting in great biodiversity loss. Consequently, a zero rate of interest can be associated in this instance with major loss of biodiversity. This observation reinforces the position of the TEEB interim report (EC, 2009) that a variety of discount rates are needed depending on the scale (economy-wide, local community or individual), the time frame (immediate or distant future) and income group being considered (rich or poor).

7 Discounting and safe minimum standards

Resource economics has a long tradition of applying a higher discount rate to the benefits of development and a lower rate to the environmental costs of that development. Fisher and Krutilla (1985) suggest a formula for estimating the net present value for a development project that reduces to:

$$NPV(D) = -1 + D/(r+k) - P/(r - h) \qquad (4)$$

where D is the value of development and P is the value of preservation. In this setup, a factor k is added to the discount rate applied to development benefits to reflect the depreciation of development benefits over time. In a similar vein, a factor h is subtracted from the rate of discount applied to the benefits of preservation. Here h is supposed to represent growth in the value of environmental services over time based on increased material prosperity that augments willingness to pay for scarce non-market goods. No hard and fast rules can be applied to determine exactly how much these discount rates should be adjusted.

This status quo bias mentioned above lends support to the notion of a safe minimum standard (SMS) and the precautionary principle. The SMS approach (Bishop, 1978) explicitly recognizes that irreversible environmental damage should be avoided unless the social costs of doing so are 'unacceptably high'. The concept is necessarily vague because it does not rely on a single money metric. It recognizes that a discount premium should be applied to environmental losses, economic gains should be discounted more heavily, a great amount of uncertainty is involved in judging the effects of environmental losses, and there are limits to substituting manufactured goods for environmental resources.

Rights-based or deontological values are widely held, as indicated by numerous valuation surveys (Stevens et al, 1991; Spash, 1997; Lockwood, 1998). A rights-based approach may be especially appropriate for policies affecting future generations (Page, 1983; Howarth, 2007). Do future generations have a right to clean air, clean water and an interesting and varied environment? There is no reason to think that future generations would be any more willing than the current one to have something taken away from them for ever (especially things like a stable climate and biological species) unless they are compensated by something 'of equal value'. A rights-based approach to sustainability moves away from the welfare notions of trade-offs and fungibility towards the two interrelated concerns of uniqueness and irreversibility. As Bromley (1998, p238) writes: 'Regard for the future through social bequests shifts the analytical problem to a discussion about deciding what, rather than how much, to leave for those who will follow.' The question of what to leave also moves away from marginal analysis, and concern only about relative amounts of resources, towards looking at discontinuous changes and the basic biological requirements of the human species in evolutionary context.

It is often argued that only the wealthy have the luxury to be concerned about environmental quality. This is the so-called 'post-materialist' thesis of Inglehart (1990), Krutilla (1967) and others. Martinez-Alier (1995) points out two flaws in this thesis. First, continued material growth implies environmental degradation, and second, the world's poorest receive a large percentage of their livelihoods directly from ecosystems (firewood, water, fish and game). The 'GDP of the poor' (TEEB, 2008) is undervalued because so much of it depends on unpriced inputs from nature. Yet, in general it is the rich who decide whether or not to preserve biodiversity and ecosystems based on market rates of interest and investment opportunities. On one hand, the poor have a larger stake in preserving flows of ecosystem services, but on the other hand a large percentage of the world's poor are in such a desperate position that they have very high discount rates. Cultural differences are also critical, not only between the rich and poor but also among the diverse cultures of the world's poorest. Traditional cultures in general have a reverence for the natural world but specific practices and cultural attitudes toward nature vary considerably. Likewise large variations exist in the environmental attitudes of the wealthy (Bandara and Tisdell, 2004).

Table 6.1 is a broad attempt to translate these general observations into discount rates. Here, 'rich' generally means the middle and upper middle-class population of North America, Japan and Europe. A sizable portion of the world's wealthiest may not fit this category. 'Poor' generally means the 1 billion or so of the world's population living on less than $1 a day (World Bank estimate). This group is also heterogeneous. The bottom line is that characterizing responsibilities to future generations by a 'discount rate' does not do justice to the nuances of human cultures, the heterogeneous nature of the many contributors to well-being, or the pure uncertainty as to the future of *Homo sapiens* on planet Earth.

Table 6.1 General observations about life opportunities and discounting

	Ecosystem services	Manufactured capital
Poor	ρ = low in the case of traditional cultures	ρ = low, maintain capital stock for future generations
	ρ = positive for cultures under severe stress	ρ = positive – cultures under stress may be unable to invest in capital stock maintenance
	η = likely to be very high any increment to consumption will add to	η = very high well-being
	g = for the very poor, likely to be negative (future generations will be worse off because of deteriorating environmental conditions, but this cannot be taken into account in economic decisions).	
	Consider its value to be 1 so that ηg is large.	
Rich	ρ = 0 (ethical responsibility to future generations)	ρ = 0 or (–) maintain or increase natural capital stock for the future
	η = positive but low, higher incomes imply higher income elasticities for environmental goods	η = 0 or negative. More capital means more consumption, but not an increase in well-being
	g = negative for the very rich to compensate for past natural capital destruction; also even if future generations have more material wealth, does this mean they need less biodiversity?	

8 Summary of the major challenges to discounting biodiversity and ecosystem losses

Even a few years ago economists were quite confident about the ability of the standard economic model to capture the future values of environmental features. But recent debates among economists over two of the most pressing issues of our time, biodiversity loss and climate change, have made it clear that no purely *economic* guidelines are available for valuing essential and irreplaceable features of the natural world. Responsibility to future generations is a matter of inter- and intra-generational ethics, best guesses about the well-being of those who will live in the future, and preserving life opportunities for humans and the rest of the living world. Economics can offer valuable insights, as the discussion surrounding the Ramsey equation has shown, but ultimately economic value represents only a small portion of the total value of biodiversity and ecosystems. The practice of discounting applies first and foremost to an individual deciding how to allocate scarce resources at a particular point in time. In general, an individual would prefer to have something 'now' rather than in the future, though with some exceptions (the value of anticipation, for example). This is the main argument for a positive discount rate. But, again in general, a higher discount rate will lead to the long-term degradation of biodiversity and ecosystems. For example, a 5 per cent discount rate implies that biodiversity loss 50 years from now will be valued at only 1/7 of the same amount of biodiversity loss today. This leads to the following observations:

1   There is a fundamental difference between the individual-at-a-point-in-time discount rate and the social discount rate. The Ramsey equation ($r = \rho + \eta$ • g as discussed above) can help to illuminate this difference. Ethical responsibility to future generations is captured, in part, by the term ρ, the rate of pure time preference. Although there is still considerable disagreement among economists, a strong case can be made that ρ should be near zero, indicating that there is no reason to place a lower value on the well-being of a person who happens to be born later in time than another person.

2   In terms of the discounting equation, estimates of how well-off those in the future will be (g) is the key factor as to how much we should leave the future. Should we use income or subjective well-being, or some guess about basic needs? g should encompass everything that gives people utility including intangible benefits of nature (Dasgupta and Mäler, 2000). In practice, however, per capita consumption is usually used as a proxy for well-being (Stern, 2007).

3   A critical factor in discounting is the importance of environmental draw-down (destruction of natural capital) to estimates of the future growth rate of per capita consumption, g. Some evidence indicates that the current generation has prospered by drawing down savings (natural capital) that should have been passed to our descendants. A case can be made that estimates of g (and of the discount rate) should be negative.

4   In contrast to the recommendations of conventional economists, a variety of discount rates, including zero and negative rates, should be used depending on the time period involved, the degree of uncertainty, ethical responsibilities to the world's poorest, and the scope of project or policy being evaluated.

5   A low discount rate for the entire economy might favour more investment and growth and more environmental destruction. Macroeconomic consequences of a particular discount rate should be considered separately from microeconomic ones.

6   The rich and poor differ greatly in their direct dependence on biodiversity and the services of ecosystems. The world's poorest, probably numbering in the billions, live to a large extent directly on ecosystem services and biodiversity (Gundimeda and Sukdev, 2008). These people are suffering disproportionally from the loss of ecosystems and biodiversity.

Acknowledgements

The authors would like to thank Paulus Arnoldus, Bernd Hansjürgens, Cameron Hepburn, Karl-Göran Mäler, Jeffrey A. McNeely, Pushpam Kumar and Mike Wood for comments on an earlier draft.

Notes

1   Equation (1) will take different forms depending on whether we consider discrete or continuous time, whether or not we allow population growth, or whether we consider per capita consumption or total consumption. See the discussion in Dasgupta and Mäler, 2003; Arrow et al, 2004.

2   Hepburn (2006) suggests that the recent literature on 'optimal paternalism' calls for correcting 'internalities', that is, behaviour damaging to the individual. A lower discount rate might be imposed by a paternalistic government to ensure the optimal preservation of biological diversity.

3   On the other hand Lind (1982) argues that the risk and insurance aspects of an investment should not be accounted for by adjusting the social rate of time preference but rather by adjusting the estimates of costs and benefits.

References

Ackerman, F. (2008) 'The New Climate Economics: The Stern Review Versus Its Critics', in Harris, J. M. and Goodwin, N. R. (eds) *Twenty-First Century Macroeconomics: Responding to the Climate Challenge*, Edward Elgar Publishing, Cheltenham, pp32–57

Arrow, K., Dasgupta, P., Goulder, L., Daily, G., Ehrlich, P., Heal, G., Levin, S., Mäler, K.-G., Schneider, S., Starrett, D. and Walker, B. (2004) 'Are we consuming too much?', *Journal of Economic Perspectives*, vol 18, pp147–172

Asheim, G. B. (1988) 'Rawlsian intergenerational justice as a Markov-perfect equilibrium in a resource technology', *Review of Economic Studies*, vol 55, pp469–483

Auerbach, A. J. and Kotlikoff, L. J. (1987) *Dynamic Fiscal Policy*, Cambridge University Press, Cambridge

Ayres, R. and Warr, B. (2006) 'Accounting for growth: The role of physical work', *Structural Change and Economic Dynamics*, vol 16, pp211–220

Bandara, R. and Tisdell, C. (2004) 'The net benefit of saving the Asian elephant: A policy and contingent valuation study', *Ecological Economics*, vol 46, pp93–107

Beckerman, W. and Hepburn, C. (2007) 'Ethics of the discount rate in the Stern Review on the economics of climate change', *World Economics*, vol 8, pp187–210

Beltratti, A., Chichilnisky, G. and Heal, G. (1998) 'Sustainable use of renewable resources', in Chichilnisky, G. and Heal, G. (eds) *Sustainability: Dynamics and Uncertainty*, Kluwer, Dordrecht (chapter 2.1)

Benartzi, S. and Thaler R. (1995) 'Myopic loss aversion and the equity premium puzzle', *Quarterly Journal of Economics*, vol 110, pp73–92

Bishop, R. (1978) 'Endangered species and uncertainty: The economics of a safe minimum standard', *American Journal of Agricultural Economics*, vol 60, pp10–18

Blanchard, O. J. and Fischer, S. (1989) *Lectures on Macroeconomics*, MIT Press, Cambridge, MA

Boulding, K. (1973) 'The Economics of the Coming Spaceship Earth', in Daly, H. (ed) *Toward a Steady State Economy*, W. H. Freeman, San Francisco, CA

Bromley, D. (1989) 'Entitlements, missing markets, and environmental uncertainty', *Journal of Environmental Economics and Management*, vol 17, pp181–194

Bromley, D. (1998) 'Searching for Sustainability: The Poverty of Spontaneous Order', in Cleveland, C., Costanza, R. and Stern, D. (eds) *Changing the Nature of Economics*, Island Press, Washington, DC (chapter 5)

Brown, T. and Gregory, R. (1999) 'Why the WTA–WTP disparity matters', *Ecological Economics*, vol 28, pp323–335

Burton, P. S. (1993) 'Intertemporal preferences and intergenerational equity considerations in optimal resource harvesting', *Journal of Environmental Economics and Management*, vol 24, no 2, pp119–132

Chichilnisky, G. (1996) 'An axiomatic approach to sustainable development', *Social Choice and Welfare*, vol 13, pp231–257

Cline, W. (1992) *The Economics of Global Warming*, Institute for International Economics, Washington, DC

Cochrane, J. H. (2001) *Asset Pricing*, Princeton University Press, Princeton, NJ

Cole, D. (2008) 'The *Stern Review* and its critics: Implications for the theory and practice of benefit–cost analysis', *Natural Resources Journal*, vol 48, pp53–90

Cropper, W. and Laibson. D. (1999) 'The Implications of Hyperbolic Discounting for Project Evaluation', in Portney, P. and Weyant, J. (eds) *Discounting and Intergenerational Equity*, Resources for the Future, Washington, DC

Daly, H. E. (1977) *Steady State Economics*, W. H. Freeman, San Francisco, CA

Dasgupta, P. (1995) 'Population, poverty and the local environment', *Scientific American*, vol 272, pp40–45

Dasgupta, P. (2006) 'Commentary: The Stern Review's economics of climate change', *National Institute Economic Review*, vol 119, pp4–7

Dasgupta, P. (2008) 'Nature in economics', *Environmental and Resource Economics*, vol 39, pp1–7

Dasgupta, P. and Heal, G. (1974) 'The optimal depletion of exhaustible resources', *The Review of Economic Studies*, Symposium Issue, pp3–28

Dasgupta, P. and Mäler, K.-G. (2000) 'Net national product, wealth and social well-being', *Environment and Development Economics*, vol 5, pp69–93

DeCanio, S. (2003) *Economic Models of Climate Change: A Critique*. Palgrave Macmillan, New York

EC (European Communities) (2009) *The Economics of Ecosystems and Biodiversity*, Welzel-Hardt, Wesseling, Germany

Ehrlich, P. and Ehrlich, A. (1997) *Betrayal of Science and Reason: How Anti-Environmental Rhetoric Threatens our Future*, Island Press, Washington, DC

Fisher, A. and Krutilla, J. (1985) *The Economics of Natural Environments*, Resources for the Future, Washington, DC

Frederick, S., Loewenstein, G. and O'Donoghue, T. (2004) 'Time Discounting and Time Preference: A Critical Review', in Camerer, C., Lowenstein, G. and Rabin, M. (eds) *Advances in Behavioral Economics*, Princeton University Press, Princeton, NJ, pp162–222

Frey, B. and Stutzer, A. (2002) *Happiness and Economics: How the Economy and Institutions Affect Well-Being*, Princeton University Press, Princeton, NJ

Geist, V. (1994) 'Wildlife conservation as wealth', *Nature*, vol 368, pp491–492

Georgescu-Roegen, N. (1971) *The Entropy Law and the Economic Process*, Harvard University Press, Cambridge, MA

Gerlagh, R. and Keyzer, M. A. (2001) 'Sustainability and the intergenerational distribution of natural resource entitlements', *Journal of Public Economics*, vol 79, pp315–341

Gilbert, N. (2008) 'A quarter of mammals face extinction', *Nature*, vol 455, p717

Gollier, C., Koundouri, P. and Pantelidis, T. (2008) 'Declining discount rates: Economic justifications and implications for long-run policy', *Economic Policy*, vol 23, no 56, pp757–795

Gowdy, J. (1997) 'The value of biodiversity', *Land Economics*, vol 73, pp25–41

Gowdy, J. (2004) 'The revolution in welfare economics and its implications for environmental valuation and policy', *Land Economics*, vol 80, pp239–257

Gundimeda, H. and Sukdev, P. (2008) 'GDP of the poor', Paper presented at the conference of the International Society for Ecological Economics, Nairobi, Kenya

Harting, J. (1880) *British Animals Extinct in Historic Times, with some Account of British Wild White Cattle*, orginally published by Trubner, London, reprinted (1972) by Paul P. B. Minet, Chicheley, Buckinghamshire

Hartwick, J. (1977) 'Intergenerational equity and the investing of rents from exhaustible resources', *American Economic Review*, vol 67, pp972–974

Hartwick, J. (1997) 'National Wealth, Constant Consumption, and Sustainable Development', in Folmer, H. and Tietenberg, T. (eds) *The International Yearbook of Environmental and Resource Economics*, Edward Elgar, Cheltenham

Hepburn, C. (2006) *Use of Discount Rates in the Estimation of the Costs of Inaction with Respect to Selected Environmental Concerns*, ENV/EPOC/WPNEP(2006)13, Organisation for Economic Co-operation and Development, Paris

Hepburn, C., Koundouri, P., Panopoulou, E. and Pantelidis, T. (2009) 'Social discounting under uncertainty: A cross-country comparison', *Journal of Environmental Economics and Management*, vol 57, pp140–150

Hoel, M. and Sterner, T. (2007) 'Discounting and relative prices', *Climatic Change*, vol 84, pp265–280

Howarth, R. B. (1995) 'Sustainability under uncertainty: A deontological approach', *Land Economics*, vol 71, pp417–427

Howarth, R. B. (1998) 'An overlapping generations model of climate–economy interactions', *Scandinavian Journal of Economics*, vol 100, pp575–591

Howarth, R. B. (2007) 'Towards an operational sustainability criterion', *Ecological Economics*, vol 63, pp656–663

Howarth, R. B. (2009) 'Rethinking the theory of discounting and revealed time preference', *Land Economics*, vol 85, pp24–40

Howarth, R. B. and Norgaard, R. B. (1992) 'Environmental valuation under sustainable development', *American Economic Review*, vol 82, no 2, pp473–477

Inglehart, R. (1990) *Cultural Shift in Advanced Industrial Societies*, Princeton University Press, Princeton, NJ

Jackson, J. (2008) 'Ecological extinction and evolution in the brave new ocean', *Proceedings of the National Academy of Science*, vol 105, pp11458–11465

Kahneman, D. and Tversky, A. (1979) 'Prospect theory: An analysis of decision under risk', *Econometrica*, vol 47, pp263–291

Kahneman, D., Wakker, P. and Sarin, R. (1997) 'Back to Bentham? Explorations of experienced utility', *Quarterly Journal of Economics*, vol 112, pp375–405

Kellert, S. (1996) *The Value of Life: Biological Diversity and Human Society*, Island Press/Shearwater Books, Washington, DC

Keynes, J. M. (1936) *The General Theory of Employment, Interest and Money*, Macmillan Press, London

Knetsch, J. (2005) 'Gains, losses, and the US-EPA *Economic Analyses Guidelines*: A hazardous product', *Environmental & Resource Economics*, vol 32, pp91–112

Kocherlakota, N. R. (1996) 'The equity premium: It's still a puzzle', *Journal of Economic Literature*, vol 34, pp42–71

Krug, A., Jablonski, D. and Valentine, J. (2009) 'Signature of the end-Cretaceous mass extinction in modern biota', *Science*, vol 323, pp767–771

Krutilla, J. (1967) 'Conservation reconsidered', *American Economic Review*, vol 57, pp777–786

Laibson, D. (1997) 'Golden eggs and hyperbolic discounting', *Quarterly Journal of Economics*, vol 112, pp443–477

Layard, R. (2005) *Happiness: Lessons from a New Science*, Penguin Press, New York

Lind, R. (1982) 'A Primer and the Major Issues Relating to the Discount Rate for Evaluating National Energy Options', in Lind, R. (ed) *Discounting for Time and Risk in Energy Policy*, Resources for the Future, Washington, DC, pp21–94

Lockwood, M. (1998) 'Integrated value assessment using paired comparisons', *Ecological Economics*, vol 25, pp73–87

Loewenstein, G. (1987) 'Anticipation and the value of delayed consumption', *Economic Journal*, vol 97, pp666–684

Mankiw, G. and Zeldes, S. (1991) 'The consumption of stockholders and nonstockholders', *Journal of Financial Economics*, vol 29, pp97–112

Martinez-Alier, J. (1995) 'The environment as a luxury good or "too poor to be green"', *Ecological Economics*, vol 13, pp1–10

Mehra, R. and Prescott, E. (1985) 'The equity premium: A puzzle', *Journal of Monetary Economics*, vol 15, pp145–161

Neumayer, E. (2003) *Weak vs. Strong Sustainability*, 2nd edn, Edward Elgar, Cheltenham

Newell, R. and Pizer, W. (2003) 'Discounting the distant future: How much do uncertain rates increase valuations?', *Journal of Environmental Economics and Management*, vol 46, pp52–71

Nordhaus, W. (1992) 'An optimal transition path for controlling greenhouse gases', *Science*, vol 258, pp1315–1319

Nordhaus, W. (1994) *Managing the Global Commons: The Economics of Climate Change*, MIT Press, Cambridge, MA

Nordhaus, W. (2007) 'A review of the *Stern Review on the Economics of Climate Change*', *Journal of Economic Literature*, vol XLV, pp686–702

Norton, B. (2005) *Sustainability: A Philosophy of Adaptive Ecosystem Management*, University of Chicago Press, Chicago

Nunes, P. and van den Bergh, J. (2001) 'Economic valuation of biodiversity: Sense or nonsense', *Ecological Economics*, vol 39, pp203–222

Orr, D. (2004) *Earth in Mind: On Education, Environment, and the Human Prospect*, Island Press, Washington, DC

Page, T. (1983) 'Intergenerational Justice as Opportunity', in MacLean, D. and Brown, P. G. (eds) *Energy and the Future*, Rowman and Littlefield, Totowa, NJ

Pearce, D., Atkinson, G. and Mourato, S. (2006) *Cost Benefit Analysis and the Environment: Recent Developments*, OECD Publishing, Paris

Pearce, D., Groom, B., Hepburn, C. and Koundouri, P. (2003) 'Valuing the future: Recent advances in social discounting', *World Economics*, vol 4, pp121–141

Portney, P. and Weyant, J. (1999) 'Introduction', in Portney, P. and Weyant, J. (eds) *Discounting and Intergenerational Equity*, Resources for the Future, Washington, DC, pp1–11

Quiggin, J. (2008) 'Stern and the critics on discounting and climate change: An editorial essay', *Climatic Change*, vol 89, pp195–205, DOI 10.1007/s10584-008-9434-9

Ramsey, F. (1928) 'A mathematical theory of saving', *Economic Journal*, vol 38, no 152, pp543–549

Repetto, R., Magrath, W., Wells, M., Beer, C. and Rossini, F. (1989) *Wasting Assets: Natural Resources in National Income Accounts*, World Resources Institute, Washington, DC

Richerson, P. and Boyd, R. (2005) *Not by Genes Alone*, University of Chicago Press, Chicago, IL

Robinson, G., Holt, R., Gaines, M., Hamburg, S., Johnson, M., Fitch, H. and Martinko, E. (1992) 'Diverse and contrasting effects of habitat fragmentation', *Science*, vol 257, pp524–525

Rubinstein, A. (2003) '"Economics and psychology"? The case of hyperbolic discounting', *International Economic Review*, vol 44, pp1207–1216

Sen, A. (1961) 'On optimizing the rate of saving', *The Economic Journal*, vol 71, pp479–496

Smith, J. B. and Mendelsohn, R. (eds) (2007) *The Impact of Climate Change on Regional Systems: A Comprehensive Analysis of California*, Edward Elgar, Cheltenham

Solow, R. (1974) 'Intergenerational equity and exhaustible resources', *Review of Economic Studies*, Symposium Issue, pp29–46

Spash, C. (1997) 'Ethics and environmental attitudes with implications for economic valuation', *Journal of Environmental Management*, vol 50, pp403–416

Spash, C. (2002) *Greenhouse Economics: Value and Ethics*, Routledge, London

Starrett, D. A. (1988) *Foundations of Public Economics*, Cambridge University Press, New York

Stern, N. (2007) *The Economics of Climate Change: The Stern Review*, Cambridge University Press, Cambridge

Sterner, T. and Persson, M. (2008) 'An even sterner review: Introducing relative prices into the discounting debate', *Review of Environmental Economics and Policy*, vol 2, pp61–76

Stevens, T., Echeverria, J., Glass, R., Hager, T. and More, T. (1991) 'Measuring the existence value of wildlife: What do CVM estimates really show?', *Land Economics*, vol 67, pp390–400

Swanson, T. (1994) 'The economics of extinction revisited: A generalized framework for the analysis of the problems of endangered species and biodiversity loss', *Oxford Economic Papers*, vol 46, pp800–821

TEEB (2008) 'The Economics of Ecosystems and Biodiversity: An Interim Report', available at www.teebweb.org, accessed 2 March 2010

Tilman, D. and Downing, J. (1994) 'Biodiversity and stability in grasslands', *Nature*, vol 367, pp363–365

Tisdell, C. (1982) *Microeconomics of Markets*, John Wiley & Sons, Brisbane, New York and Chichester

Tisdell, C. (2005) *Economics of Environmental Conservation*, 2nd edn, Edward Elgar, Cheltenham and Northampton, MA

Vouvaki, D. and Xeapapadeas, A. (2009) 'Total factor productivity growth when factors of production generate environmental externalities', *Working Papers*, no 2009.20, Fondazione Eni Enrico Mattei, Milan, http://ideas.repec.org/p/fem/femwpa/2009.20.html

Ward, P. (1994) *The End of Evolution*, Bantam Books, New York

WCED (World Commission on Environment and Development) (1987) *Our Common Future*, Oxford University Press, Oxford

Weitzman, M. (2001) 'Gamma discounting', *American Economic Review*, vol 91, pp260–271

Weitzman, M. (2009) 'On modeling and interpreting the economics of catastrophic climate change', *The Review of Economics and Statistics*, vol XCI, pp1–19

Wilson, E. O. (1994) *Biophilia*, Harvard University Press, Cambridge, MA

Wilson, E. O. (1998) *Consilience: The Unity of Knowledge*, Alfred Knopf, New York

Yohe, G. and Tol, R. (2007) 'The *Stern Review*: Implications for climate change', *Environment*, vol 49, no 2, pp36–42

Chapter 7
Lessons Learned and Linkages with National Policies

Coordinating lead author
Pushpam Kumar

Lead authors
Eduardo Brondízio, Thomas Elmqvist, Franz Gatzweiler, John Gowdy,
Rudolf de Groot, Roldan Muradian, Unai Pascual, Belinda Reyers,
Rodney B. W. Smith, Pavan Sukhdev

Contents

Synthesis		**287**
1	Framing of issues for economics of ecosystems and biodiversity	287
2	Linkages of ecosystems, ecosystem services and biodiversity	289
3	Choice of indicators and value-articulating institutions in economic valuation	290
4	Economic value, valuation methods and non-linear changes	292
5	Discounting as an ethical choice	294
6	National policies: Challenges and options	295
	6.1 Links between biodiversity, ecosystems and resilience	295
	6.2 Dynamics of ecosystem services	296
	6.3 Understanding the dynamics of governance and management of ecosystems and ecosystem services	296
	6.4 Valuation methods and benefit transfer method	296
	6.5 Valuations and its context	297
	6.6 From micro foundation to macro policy	298
References		**304**

Synthesis

One of the major objectives of this TEEB book is to assess current approaches for using ecological sciences and economics for informed choices and decision making. On the one hand TEEB intends to better inform conventional economic policy about its impacts on ecosystem health and biodiversity, on the other it suggests ways to mainstream the valuation of ecosystem services into national and local planning and policies as well as business assessments of their economic impacts and dependencies on biodiversity. The previous six chapters assess the state of art of our scientific understanding underlying economic analysis of ecosystem services and biodiversity. Chapter 1 in this volume identifies several challenges in integrating the disciplines of ecology and economics and organizes the complexities of the problem resulting from the differences in methodological frameworks in relation to variation in temporal and spatial scales. For example, the relevant time horizon for a cost–benefit analysis of afforestation or ecosystem restoration project is 10–20 years while the changes in biodiversity could occur on a time scale ranging from short – a fraction of a second (molecular level) to long – millions of years (biome level). Chapter 2 highlights that ecosystems typically produce multiple services that interact in complex ways. A resilient ecosystem maintains a flow of ecosystem services on a continuous basis, but ecosystems may or may not be resilient to anthropogenic disturbances. Chapter 3 suggests that biodiversity and ecosystems are amenable to economic analysis only if they can be quantified and several approaches for developing indicators are discussed. Chapters 4 and 5 together highlight the socio-cultural embeddedness of ecosystem service and biodiversity valuation, as well as its constraints and limitations. Chapter 4 outlines the role and importance of valuation as a human institution and places in context the role of *economic* valuation. Chapter 5 explains how, for a chosen set of ecosystem indicators and within a structured economic valuation framework, there could be reliable approaches for the economic valuation of ecosystem services. Chapter 5 also highlights commonly practised methods of ecosystem service valuation, and discusses their constraints and limitations. Chapter 6 assesses the basis of choosing appropriate discount rates to be applied to a project with impacts on ecosystems and biodiversity.

In this chapter we attempt to summarize the key lessons learned from the assessments done in Chapters 1–6. The summary can be categorized under the following headings:

1 Framing of issues for economics of ecosystems and biodiversity

The study of the economics of ecosystem services and biodiversity strongly emphasizes the joint effort of ecology and economics. There is a growing need for collaboration between ecologists and economists to have a coherent perspective on the trade-offs reflected in individual and societal choice (Polasky and Segerson, 2009). Even if the outlooks of the two disciplines differ, the scale of the problem requires that solutions can only emerge in making the methodology more porous and fluid in order to embrace each other's take on the problem. We find that:

1   Linking biophysical aspects of ecosystems with human benefits through the notion of ecosystem services is essential to assess the trade-offs involved in the loss of ecosystems and biodiversity in a clear and consistent manner.
2   Economic assessment should be spatially and temporally explicit at scales meaningful for policy formation or interventions, inherently acknowledging that both ecological functioning and economic values are contextual, anthropocentric, individual-based and time-specific.
3   Economic assessment should first aim to determine the service delivery in biophysical terms, to provide ecological underpinning to the economic valuation or measurement with alternative metrics.
4   Clearly distinguishing between functions, services and benefits is important to make ecosystem assessments more accessible to economic valuation, although no consensus has yet been reached on the classification.
5   Ecosystem assessments should be set within the context of contrasting scenarios – recognizing that both the values of ecosystem services and the costs of actions can be best measured as a function of changes between alternative options.
6   In assessing trade-offs between alternative uses of ecosystems, the total bundle of ecosystem services provided by different conversion and management states should be included.
7   Any valuation study should be fully aware of the 'cost' side of the equation, as focus on benefits only ignores important societal costs such as missed opportunities of alternative uses; this also allows for a more extensive range of societal values to be considered.
8   Economic assessments should integrate an analysis of risks and uncertainties, acknowledging the limitations of knowledge on the impacts of human actions on ecosystems and their services and on their importance to human well-being.
9   In order to improve incentive structures and institutions, the different stakeholders – that is, the beneficiaries of ecosystem services, those who are providing the services, those involved in or affected by the use, and the actors involved at different levels of decision making – should be clearly identified, and decision-making processes need to be transparent.
10 Efforts aimed at changing behaviour of individuals and society towards their impact on ecosystems and biodiversity must take into account that ecosystems have always been dynamic, both internally and in response to changing environments.
11 The importance of using scenarios in ecosystem service assessments is beginning to be realized as early assessments presented a static picture in a rapidly changing world. The necessity of providing counter-factual evidence is now being demanded of conservation research (Ferraro and Pattanayak, 2006) and should become the norm in ecosystem service research as well.
12 The generation of scenarios is particularly important for monetary valuation, since scenarios enable analysis of changes in service delivery which are required to obtain marginal values. Making an analysis in

incremental terms avoids (or at least reduces) the methodological difficulties which arise, depending on the relative magnitude of changes, especially when attempting to estimate total values given the non-constancy of marginal values associated with the complete loss of an ecosystem service.

13 In the TEEB context, comparing the outputs under several scenarios will inform decision makers of the welfare gains and losses of alternative possible futures and different associated policy packages.

14 Indirect drivers of ecosystem change include demographic shifts, technology innovations, economic development, legal and institutional frameworks, including policy instruments, the steady loss of traditional knowledge and cultural diversity and many other factors that influence our collective decisions.

15 All ecosystems are shaped by people, directly or indirectly and all people, rich or poor, rural or urban, depend directly or indirectly on the capacity of ecosystems to generate essential ecosystem services. In this sense, people and ecosystems are interdependent social-ecological systems. It is not surprising that around 1.2 billion poor people are located in fragile and vulnerable ecosystems but it is not primarily the actions of the poor that affect those fragile ecosystems but rather the actions of 'rich' people who interfere with them and put in question the dependence of the poor (Barbier, 2008).

2 Linkages of ecosystems, ecosystem services and biodiversity

A clear understanding of the links between ecosystems and ecosystem services, and how variation in biodiversity affects ecosystem dynamics is needed to map the temporal and spatial flow of services. This will not only help in making robust valuations but would avoid double counting and provide necessary caveats while up-scaling the value from local to national and regional scales. We find that:

1 Variation in biological diversity relates to the function of ecosystems in at least three ways: (i) increase in diversity often leads to an increase in productivity due to complementary traits among species for resource use, and productivity itself underpins many ecosystem services; (ii) increased diversity leads to an increase in response diversity (range of traits related to how species within the same functional group respond to environmental drivers) resulting in less variability in functioning over time as environment changes; (iii) idiosyncratic effects due to keystone species properties and unique trait-combinations which may result in a disproportional effect of losing one particular species compared to the effect of losing individual species at random.

2 Ecosystems produce multiple services and these interact in complex ways, different services being interlinked, both negatively and positively. Delivery of many services will therefore vary in a correlated manner, but when an ecosystem is managed principally for the delivery of a single service (e.g. food production) other services are always affected negatively.

3   Ecosystems vary in their ability to buffer and adapt to both natural and anthropogenic changes as well as recover after changes (i.e. resilience). When subjected to severe change, ecosystems may cross thresholds and move into different and often less desirable ecological states or trajectories. A major challenge is how to design ecosystem management in ways that maintain resilience and avoid the passing of undesirable thresholds.

4   There is clear evidence for a central role of biodiversity in the delivery of some – but not all – services, viewed individually. However, ecosystems need to be managed to deliver multiple services to sustain human well-being and also managed at the level of landscapes and seascapes in ways that avoid the passing of dangerous tipping points. We can state with high certainty that maintaining functioning ecosystems capable of delivering multiple services requires a general approach to sustaining biodiversity, in the long term also when a single service is the focus.

5   When predicting the impact of biodiversity change on variability in the supply of ecosystem services, we need to measure the impact of biodiversity conservation over a range of environmental conditions. In the same way, we need to be able to identify the effect of biodiversity change on the capacity of social-ecological systems to absorb anthropogenic and environmental stresses and shocks without loss of value (Scheffer et al, 2001; Kinzig et al, 2006).

6   To understand and enhance the resilience of such complex, coupled systems, we need robust models of the linkages between biodiversity and ecosystem services, and between biodiversity change and human well-being (Perrings, 2007; Perrings et al, 2009).

3 Choice of indicators and value-articulating institutions in economic valuation

Economic analysis, especially the evaluation of changes in ecosystem services due to marginal change in intervention and policies, requires careful choice of indicators and measures. The social and cultural contexts in which value-articulating institutions exist and reveal value must be known to those assigning economic values. Establishing these prerequisites would also provide greater credibility to the estimates that follow. We find that:

1   A lack of relevant information at different scales has hampered the ability to assess the economic consequences of the loss of ecosystems and biodiversity.

2   Most of the current measures and indicators of biodiversity and ecosystems were developed for purposes other than the economic assessment. They are therefore unable to show clear relationships between components of biodiversity and the services or benefits they provide to people.

3   A reliance on these existing measures will in all likelihood capture the value of only a few species and ecosystems relevant to food and fibre production, and will miss out the role of biodiversity and ecosystems in supporting the full range of benefits, as well as their resilience into the future.

4   A set of indicators is needed that is not only relevant and able to convey the message of the consequences of biodiversity loss, but must also be based on accepted methods that reflect the aspects of biodiversity involved and the service that is of interest, that captures the often non-linear and multi-scale relationships between ecosystems and the benefits that they provide, and is convertible into economic terms.

5   While it is possible to obtain preliminary estimates of the consequences of biodiversity and ecosystem loss using existing data and measures, these must be complemented with active research and development into the measurement of biodiversity and ecosystem change, their links to benefit flows and the value of these flows so as to realize the full value of biodiversity and ecosystem management

6   The flow of ecosystem services from point of production to point of use is influenced by both biophysical (e.g. currents, migration) and anthropogenic (e.g. trade, access) processes which influence the scale of service flow from locally produced and used services (e.g. soil production) to globally distributed benefits (e.g. carbon sequestration for climate regulation).

7   In order to make a comprehensive and compelling economic case for the conservation of ecosystems and biodiversity it is essential to be able to understand, quantify and map the benefits received from ecosystems and biodiversity, and assign values to those benefits.

8   Biophysical measurements are important since biodiversity underpins the delivery of many ecosystem services and thus forms the underlying basis of value.

9   Valuation, including economic valuation, functions as a system of cultural projection which imposes a way of thinking and a form of relationship with the environment and reflects particular perceived realities, worldviews, mind sets and belief systems. However, it can also serve as a tool for self-reflection and feedback mechanism which helps people rethink their relations to the natural environment and increase knowledge about the consequences of consumption, choices and behaviour.

10   Due to multidimensional and socio-cultural embeddedness of value any exercise of valuation is relative to a given individual or group of people. In a multicultural and democratic context of biodiversity valuation, this makes the question of choosing a value-articulating institution more important than that of finding a correct value.

11   Economic valuation influences the notion of ownership and property applied to biodiversity and over the long term may change human relationship to the environment in significant ways.

12   Intrinsic values are culturally embedded. They can be taken into account by choosing appropriate institutions, which allow their articulation in addition to utilitarian values.

13   Valuation processes can be seen as a form of regulatory adaptation by serving as a mechanism to provide feedback in an economic system where production and consumption, trade and exchange are so distant from the underlying ecosystem and so complex in their commercial structure that they may undermine perceptions of the impacts of human habits and behaviours on the natural environment.

14 Value change along the commodity chain has implications for the distribution of benefits, affects the level of incentives for conservation and represents an important methodological challenge for economic valuation.

15 Economic valuation may contribute to address our inability, reluctance or ideological intolerance to adjust institutions (also those which are value-articulating) to our knowledge of ecosystems, biodiversity and the human being.

16 Economic valuation is a complex, spatial and institutional cross-scale problem. Many efforts focusing on particular parts of ecosystems or species, while effective at one level, lack the scope to control the pressure of commodity markets for land resources surrounding them. As such, and depending on their biophysical context, they may be limited to capturing the linkages and vertical interplay created by a growing functional interdependency of resource-use systems nested within larger ecosystems.

4 Economic value, valuation methods and non-linear changes

How to value ecosystem services, what are the tools available, and what are the assumptions necessary to arrive at credible and transparent estimates and finally come out with recommended methods to apply in a situation of non-linear changes remain the main mandate of TEEB. The literature on valuation is full of good suggestions (Freeman, 2003; Heal et al, 2005; Barbier, 2007; Hanley and Barbier, 2009; Barbier, 2009; Atkinson, 2010, Bateman et al, 2010). Yet valuation techniques face important challenges especially regarding uncertainty, irreversibility and resilience. They are typically found while valuing the regulating services of ecosystems (Kumar and Wood, 2010). Our assessment suggests that:

1   Estimating the value of the various services and benefits that ecosystems and biodiversity generate may be achieved with a variety of valuation approaches. Applying a combination of approaches may overcome disadvantages of relying solely on an individual method.

2   Valuation techniques in general and stated preference methods specifically are affected by uncertainty stemming from gaps in knowledge about ecosystem dynamics, human preferences and technical issues in the valuation process. There is a need to include uncertainty issues in valuation studies. However, when uncertainty is compounded by ignorance about ecosystem functioning or when there is even a small possibility of disastrous damage, such as complete ecological collapse of ecosystems, current valuation techniques used to estimate values to feed into extended cost–benefit analyses are insufficient.

3   Valuation results will be heavily dependent on social, cultural and economic contexts, the boundaries of which may not overlap with the delineation of the relevant ecological system. It is likely that better valuation can be achieved by identifying and involving relevant stakeholders.

4   Implementation of valuation approaches that may be suitable for some developed regions may be inadequate in developing countries, thus not being immediately transferable. Hence, standard valuation approaches

need to be carefully adapted to account for particular challenges that arise in developing countries.

5   While benefits transfer methods may seem a practical, swift and cheaper way to get an estimate of the value of local ecosystems, particularly when the aim is to assess a large number of diverse ecosystems, due care should be exercised in their use especially when key features of 'sites', such as ecosystem dynamics, socio-economic and cultural contexts, largely differ one from another.

6   Benefit transfer methods can be divided into four categories in increasing order of complexity: (i) unit BT; (ii) adjusted unit BT; (iii) value function transfer; and (iv) meta-analytic function transfer. BT using any of these methods may result in estimates that differ from actual values, so-called transfer errors. The acceptable level of transfer error for decision making is context-specific, but if a highly precise value estimate is required it is recommended to commission a primary valuation study.

7   Economic valuation can provide useful information about changes to welfare that will result from ecosystem management actions, especially with regard to localized impacts that are fairly well known and far from ecological thresholds.

8   Valuation practitioners should acknowledge that valuation techniques face limitations that are as yet unresolved. They should present their results as such, and decision makers should interpret and use valuation data accordingly.

9   The limitations of monetary valuation are especially important as ecosystems approach critical thresholds and ecosystem change is irreversible, or reversible only at extreme cost. In this case and until more understanding of ecological dynamics and techniques to estimate the insurance value of biodiversity or the value of ecosystem resilience become available, under conditions of high uncertainty and existence of ecological thresholds, policy should be guided by the 'safe-minimum-standard' and 'precautionary approach' principles.

10 There are three sources of uncertainty pervading valuation of ecosystem services and biodiversity that have been taken into account: (i) uncertainty regarding the delivery or supply of ecosystem services and biodiversity; (ii) preference uncertainty; and (iii) technical uncertainty in the application of valuation methods. Some promising approaches are being developed to try to account for such types of uncertainty but generally valuation applications disregard the uncertainty factor.

11 The uncertainty regarding the delivery of ecosystem services makes stated preference methods complex. Stated preference methods have generally resorted to measuring respondents' risk perceptions. Other valuation approaches based on expected damage functions are based on risk analysis instead.

12 Preference uncertainty is inversely related to the level of knowledge and experience with the ecosystem service to be valued. This source of uncertainty has been relatively better acknowledged in stated preference approaches, for instance by requesting respondents to report a range of values rather than a specific value for the change in the provision of an ecosystem service.

13 Technical uncertainty pervades valuation studies especially with regard to the credibility of the estimates of non-use values through stated preference methods and the non-conclusive issue of the large disparity between WTP and WTA value estimates. It has been suggested that combining valuation models and a preference calibration approach may be the way forward to minimize technical uncertainty.

14 The value of the resilience of an ecosystem is related to the expected benefits and costs that occur when the ecosystem shifts to another regime. An analogy can be drawn between the valuation of ecosystem resilience and the valuation of a portfolio of assets in that the value of the asset mix – the ecosystem and its biodiversity – depends on the probability that a shift occurs as well as on the benefits and costs when it does.

15 Current knowledge about biodiversity and ecosystem dynamics at this point is insufficient to implement such portfolio assessment, and monetary analysis will be misleading when ecosystems are near critical thresholds. At the policy level, it is better to address this uncertainty and ignorance by employing a safe minimum standard approach and the precautionary principle.

16 Despite many limitations, valuation exercises can still provide information that is an indispensable component of environmental policy in general. But policy makers should interpret and utilize the valuable information provided by these techniques while acknowledging the limitations of this information.

17 It is likely that new techniques and combinations of different methodological approaches (e.g. monetary, deliberative and multicriteria methods) will be needed in order to properly face future challenges and provide more accurate values that would benefit decision-making processes.

18 A closer collaboration between ecologists and economists may then contribute to develop valuation techniques that are better suited to dealing with the complex relationship between ecosystems and the services they provide to the local and global economies.

19 Future valuation practitioners of biodiversity and ecosystem services should make explicit the procedures and methods used in their studies as well as openly acknowledge any obstacles that they may have encountered.

5 Discounting as an ethical choice

Intertemporal distribution of costs and benefits poses a challenge for the decision makers in justifying resource allocation for a project and policies especially when they have competing demand for the resource available. The challenge becomes more severe if the project entails the impact on ecosystems in the long run. If the impacts of project through its costs and benefits accrue to poor and the rich disproportionately, it further complicates the analysis.

We find that an appropriate rate of discount can guide better choice of strategies and response policies for ecosystem management. We suggest:

1 There is a fundamental difference between the individual-at-a-point-in-time discount rate and the social discount rate.

2   In terms of the discounting equation, estimates of how well-off those in the future will be are the key factor as to how much we should leave the future.

3   A critical factor in discounting is the importance of environmental draw-down (destruction of natural capital) to estimates of the future growth rate of per capita consumption

4   In contrast to the recommendations of conventional economists, a variety of discount rates, including zero and negative rates, should be used depending on the time period involved, the degree of uncertainty, ethical responsibilities to the world's poorest, ethical responsibilities towards future generations, and the scope of project or policy being evaluated.

5   A low discount rate for the entire economy might favour more investment and growth and more environmental destruction. Macroeconomic consequences of a particular discount rate should be considered separately from microeconomic ones.

6   The rich and poor differ greatly in their direct dependence on biodiversity and the services of ecosystems.

7   There are no purely *economic* guidelines for choosing a discount rate. Responsibility to future generations is a matter of ethics, best guesses about the well-being of those in future and preserving life opportunities.

8   In general, a higher discount rate applied to specific cases will lead to the long-term degradation of biodiversity and ecosystems. A four per cent discount rate implies that biodiversity loss 50 years from now will be valued at only one-seventh of the same amount of biodiversity loss today.

9   A critical factor in discounting is the importance of environmental draw-down (destruction of natural capital) to estimates of g (as GDP growth). Is the current generation living on savings that should be passed to their descendants?

6 National policies: Challenges and options

The assessment of evidence on the relationship between ecosystem services and biodiversity helps not only in identifying the policy-relevant insights but also in filling the gaps in understanding the science which is critical for economic analysis. This can further be carried forward for research and must be remembered while designing policies for the national and global decision makers. Some of the emerging questions that are very relevant for economic analysis of change in ecosystems and biodiversity include:

6.1 Links between biodiversity, ecosystems and resilience

i   What are the roles of species interactions and functional diversity for ecosystem resilience?

ii   What are the drivers behind loss of resilience and how do they interact across scales?

iii What are the impacts of climate and related environmental changes on ecosystem functioning through effects on species (re)distribution, numbers and process rates?

6.2 The dynamics of ecosystem services

i   How can we better quantify effects on regulating ecosystem services of an increase in non-sustainable use of provisioning services?

ii What tools can contribute to accurate mapping of land and seascape units in terms of functioning and service provision?

iii What specific tools could contribute to better assessment of spatial and temporal dynamics of service provision, especially in relation to defining who benefits, where and to what extent?

6.3 Understanding the dynamics of governance and management of ecosystems and ecosystem services

i   If all ecosystem services are taken into account, what is the appropriate balance between 'more diverse landscapes generating bundles of ecosystems services' and more intensively managed ecosystems like monocultures for food production?

ii What are the trade-offs and complementarities involved in the provision of bundles of ecosystem services, and how do changes in the configuration of ecosystems affect their value?

iii What are the most effective mechanisms for the governance of non-marketed ecosystem services, and how can these be designed so as to exploit future improvements in our understanding of the relationships between biodiversity, ecosystem functioning and ecosystem services?

6.4 Valuation and benefit transfer method

i   Since marginal values are likely to vary with ecosystem characteristics, socio-economic characteristics of beneficiaries, and ecological context, care needs to be taken to adjust transferred values when there are important differences between study and policy sites.

ii   It should be noted that the market size and rate of distance decay is likely to vary across different ecosystem services from the same ecosystem. It is also important to account for differences in site context in terms of the availability of substitute and complementary ecosystems and services.

iii In cases where a high quality primary valuation study is available for a study site with very similar characteristics to the policy site, the unit transfer method may produce the most precise value estimate. In cases where no value information for a closely similar study site is available, value function or meta-analytic function transfer provide a sound approach for controlling for site-specific characteristics.

iv   Aggregation of transferred unit values across the relevant population or ecosystem area needs to be undertaken carefully to avoid double counting values or misspecifying the market size for an ecosystem service.

v   Future valuation practitioners of biodiversity and ecosystem services should make explicit the procedures and methods used in their studies as well as openly acknowledge any obstacles that they may have encountered.

6.5 Valuations and its context

Social and institutional analyses suggest that valuation is essentially a matter of choosing how to perceive the human being itself, how to perceive human's place in nature and how to perceive nature itself. This is because the way we perceive our natural environment determines the way we value and change it. One way of incorporating a multilayered understanding of human–environment relations, and understanding the value and motivational linkages between the two, is to address the large gap that exists between the language in which the preference of the people for ecosystem services is elicited and the language in which people feel more at home. The languages of research and policy show similar dissonance. The more the discourse moves away from the common lives and real-life concerns to abstruse quantification and reductionism, the more people are likely to give preferences that are fudged and confused as much as these are confusing, merely because the choices we offer are far from adequate (Kumar and Kumar, 2008, p814). Valuation approaches aiming at addressing complex socio-ecological systems require attention to the challenge of understanding problems of credibility, saliency and legitimacy at the intersection of different knowledge systems and access to information at different levels and by different groups (Cash et al, 2006). In this sense, valuation mechanisms should be seen as part of a broader range of diagnostic and assessment tools and political–institutional mechanisms that facilitate the understanding of complex socio-ecological systems (Ostrom, 2009), as well as coproduction, mediation, translation and negotiation of information and knowledge within and across levels (Cash et al, 2006; Brondizio et al, 2009). The main lesson that comes across when one reviews valuation literature is to avoid a 'one size fits all' approach, or as Ostrom (2007) puts it when proposing a framework for the analysis of complex social-ecological systems, 'we need to move beyond panaceas'.

Regulating services provide value through their role in assuring the reliability of service supply over space or time; sometimes expressed in terms of the resilience of the system to environmental shocks. That is, they moderate the variability or uncertainty of the supply of provisioning and cultural services. While an increase in biodiversity may increase production, experimental data indicate that for given environmental conditions this effect is small. The productivity of some biologically diverse communities, for example, has been found to be about 10 per cent higher than the productivity of monocultures, but the effect often saturates at fewer than ten species. If environmental conditions are not constant, however, the effect may increase with the number of species providing that they have different niches and hence different responses to disturbances or changes in environmental conditions. For instance, the regulation of pest and disease outbreaks is affected by food web complexity.

i   Since people care about the reliability (or variability) in the supply of these services (people are generally risk averse), anything that increases reliability (reduces variability) will be valued. The value of regulating services accordingly lies in their impact on the variability in the supply of the provisioning and cultural services. An important factor in this is the diversity of the functional groups responsible for the services involved. The greater the specialization or niche differentiation of the species within a functional group, the wider the range of environmental conditions that group is able to tolerate. In some cases greater diversity with a functional group both increases the mean level and reduces the variability of the services that group supports. Indeed, this portfolio effect turns out to be one of the strongest reasons for maintaining the diversity of functional groups.

ii The general point here is that the value of ecosystem components, including the diversity of the biota, derives from the value of the goods and services they produce. For each of the ecosystem services described in this chapter we have identified its sensitivity to changes in biodiversity. If greater diversity enhances mean yields of valued services it is transparent that diversity will have value. However, it is also true that if greater diversity reduces the variance in the yield of valued services that will also be a source of value. Since people prefer reliability over unreliability, certainty over uncertainty, and stability over variability, they typically choose wider rather than narrower portfolios of assets. Biodiversity can be thought of as a portfolio of biotic resources, the value of which depends on its impact on both mean yields and the variance in yields.

iii It follows that there is a close connection between the value of biodiversity in securing the regulating services, and its value in securing the resilience of ecosystems. Since resilience is a measure of the capacity of ecosystems to function over a range of environmental conditions, a system that is more resilient is also likely to deliver more effective regulating services.

6.6 From micro foundation to macro policy

One of the major criticisms of economic valuation of biodiversity and ecosystem services is that most valuation exercises do not allow for ecosystems and economies to impact each other simultaneously. Also, although not necessarily a criticism, the frame of reference for most economic analysis of ecosystems is at the firm, household or individual industry level. Setting the analysis at the firm, household or industry level masks potential spillovers associated with actions taken in one sector of an economy on other sectors, and the corresponding impacts on macroeconomic variables like gross domestic product (GDP), aggregate savings rates or trade patterns. Similarly, the structural changes accompanying economic growth (sectoral composition), trade and consumption patterns can have far reaching impacts on the health and condition of ecosystems. Two examples of such impacts are: (i) the intensification of agricultural production accompanying economic growth, and its impact on soil salinity and waterlogging, and on genetic diversity; and (ii) regional and national subsidies to fish harvesting and the corresponding impacts on fish stocks and marine biodiversity.

There are other relevant examples where a macroeconomic framework could provide useful insights into how to better manage an ecosystem. One current issue in the economics of coastal ecosystems is the impact of economic growth and the increased conversion of mangrove forests into agricultural or aquacultural uses, and the corresponding impact on the ability of coastal ecosystems to support fish populations. Another issue is the concern with delta ecosystem destruction due to decreased – sometimes non-existent – river flow.

With terrestrial ecosystems, an issue that has received much attention, and will continue to do so in the near future, is carbon sequestration. A simplistic summary of the current discussion is that Southern countries have potential to serve as carbon sinks, but deforestation in these countries provides them with a significant source of GDP. A natural question to ask is, if Northern countries want a Southern country to serve as a carbon sink how much income would that country forgo if it decreased its desired rate of deforestation, or stopped it altogether? The answer to this question probably sets the lower limit on the North's offer price to the Southern country to steward its forest assets differently.

Thus far, the thrust of this TEEB book has been to summarize the dominant conceptual frameworks and related methodologies used to measure the economic costs and benefits of ecosystem management policies. Such policies range from taxes to eliminate externalities in an existing prevailing market (market failures) to policy-induced distortions implemented at regional, national and global levels (e.g. tariffs to protect import-competing sectors or taxes on factors used by sectors that damage ecosystem health). The maintained hypothesis, here, is policy design can be better informed by properly using economic valuation and accounting exercises (with the understanding that policy rankings can be influenced by the discount rate used in the analysis).

The methodologies discussed thus far, however, do not adequately accommodate the interdependencies among different economic subsectors and ecosystem services. The methodologies also are not designed to measure the potential impact of a policy on the entire economy and its underlying ecosystem. The dependence of conventional economic sectors on ecosystems arises not only through the use of tangible factors like timber, water and fish, but also the use of intangible services like waste minimization, climate regulations or the control of vector-borne diseases (MA, 2003, 2005). Each of these services adds value to human well-being, but the ability of ecosystems to provide such services can be influenced by human behaviour.

The economics of tropical mangrove forests illustrate this point. Marine scientists have established a link between mangrove area and the carrying capacity of fish stocks – loosely speaking, the larger the area planted to mangrove forests, the larger the stock of fish the coastal ecosystem can support (see Barbier, 2003, 2009). The simplest economic story embedded in the relationship between mangrove forest area and fish stock is: the smaller the mangrove forest, the more costly it should be to harvest fish. Ignoring the land-conversion process, a natural question to ask is how will net returns to the fishing industry change as mangrove area falls? In answering this question, one might rightfully ignore the rest of the economy – especially if the fishing area contributes little to the overall economy. Alternatively, consider an economy wherein harvested fish are sold to firms who employ capital and labour to process fresh fish, who in turn compete with manufacturing and service sector firms for capital and labour. In this case, a decrease in mangrove area leads to an increase in fish harvesting costs, which in turn decreases the supply of fresh fish to processors. This can lead to higher fresh fish prices, which can place downward pressure on the demand for capital and labour by fish processors. These interactions can have implications for regional wages and rates of return to capital and investment patterns. Empirical examples (non-fishery) in Roe et al (2009) would suggest that the economic impact of a declining mangrove forest on both the fishing fleet and processing sector will depend on how important capital is relative to labour in producing each sector's output.

The two mangrove examples illustrate that some problems in ecosystem economics are well suited to microeconomic analysis, while others are not. Other examples will reveal that some issues can be examined without explicitly accounting for biophysical/ecosystem dynamics, while others should not. Insights into the economics of some issues can be garnered using a simple, single-sector growth model integrated with a biophysical model (e.g. the Dynamic Integrated Climate Economy (DICE) model developed by Nordhaus and Yang, 1996). On the other hand, a careful investigation of the economics of the mangrove-fishery problem in the previous paragraph probably requires integrating fishery dynamics with a dynamic economic model having multiple sectors.

Another issue which must be addressed is the relationship between the relative scale of economic activities and the natural ecosystem to which the economic system is a subset. Accounting for scale effects is critical in understanding how to manage an ecosystem and economy in a sustainable fashion. This management challenge is directly related to the concept of 'the carrying capacity of Nature' (Arrow et al, 1995). Just as the micro units of the economy – e.g. individual households and firms – function as part of a macroeconomic system, the aggregate economy functions as part of a larger system which Daly (1991) refers to as 'the natural ecosystem'.

In response to these omissions, developing a conceptual framework that captures the economics of interactions between large-scale ecosystems and regional or national economies would facilitate the design of regional and national ecosystem and biodiversity policy. Take for example, policy suggested in *The Economics of Ecosystems and Biodiversity in National and International Policy Making* (TEEB in National Policy, 2011), Chapters 2, 4 and 6). The economic theory underlying such policy could benefit by having its roots in dynamic, general equilibrium models. Even more importantly, the model should be empirically implementable. A good starting point for such a model might be found by linking the multi-species, dynamic general equilibrium ecosystem model (GEEM) discussed in Tschirhart (2009), Eichner and Tschirhart (2007) and Finnoff and Tschirhart (2008) with the dynamic, multisector macroeconomic models presented in Roe et al (2009). Such a framework could serve as a nice point of departure for examining the relationship between ecosystem management and (i) economic growth, (ii) structural transformation and (iii) simple trade and balance of payment issues. The Roe et al approach, however, may not be of much value in understanding the relationship between monetary policy and ecosystems.

A multisector, general equilibrium is desirable for two reasons. First, a general equilibrium model provides us with a direct means of understanding the interdependencies among economic subsectors and between these sectors and an ecosystem. Second, we want two or more sectors because policy makers are typically interested in knowing (or having an idea of) the likely impact of a policy on different stakeholder groups, for example manufacturing and agricultural lobbies. The desired framework is dynamic because both ecosystems and economies are dynamic entities, and it is important to understand the short- and long-run impact of a policy on an economy and the ecosystem with which the economy is linked. Furthermore, a long-run view is essential when delving into questions of sustainability. Finally, another desired feature of a model linking economics and the ecosystem would be for the model to accommodate ecosystems defined by two or more natural assets (e.g. the stock of coral reef serving as habitat for a stock of fish). We feel this is important because ecosystems are typically viewed as the result of interplay between two or more species or, more generally, between abiotic factors and biotic organisms.

Several challenges emerge when introducing dynamics into an economics–ecosystem model. For instance, standard approaches to empirical economic dynamic modelling does not typically accommodate hyperbolic or other potentially more complex discounting concepts. In addition, one might need to entertain the possibility of 'shallow-lake' dynamics, which can lead to multiple steady state equilibria (see Mäler et al, 2003; Heijdra and Heijnen, 2009). The model might also need to accommodate transboundary problems, which to address properly in an empirical fashion is quite challenging.

Ecosystem accounting

Two issues linked with natural assets are: (i) the role of natural assets in measuring social welfare and sustainability, and (ii) the role of natural assets in social accounting and input–output tables – often referred to as 'green accounting'. Welfare, its definitions and measurement is the topic of interest to a wide spectrum of disciplines (see Stiglitz et al, 2009). For the past few decades, per capita gross domestic product (GDP) and per capita gross national product (GNP) have been popular indices of welfare. GDP is the total value of all final goods and services produced in a region, and GNP is GDP plus income earned by domestic citizens abroad less income earned by foreign citizens in the region. While GNP is a reasonable measure of economic activity, when measuring welfare in a dynamic setting (e.g. an evolving economy) some economists prefer using wealth or net national product (NNP) as a measure of economic well-being or social welfare. Here, wealth is typically viewed as the real value of stocks, and NNP is equal to GNP less depreciation (see Weitzman, 1976; Dasgupta and Mäler, 2000; Heal and Kriström, 2005; Dasgupta, 2009).

Note, however, that these income and wealth-based measures of welfare have well-known problems. One problem with per capita GDP is that it glosses over issues of distribution, and implicitly assumes the marginal valuation of an additional unit of income is the same for an impoverished person as it is for a rich person. Another problem is that traditional measures of GDP (and NNP) do not account for the depreciation (i.e. degradation) of environmental assets, biodiversity or ecosystems. Creation of the Human Development Index – where GDP is combined with health status and education levels – is an improvement in welfare measurement, but is however silent on natural capital's and ecosystems' contribution to human welfare (Dasgupta, 2009). See Stiglitz et al (2009) for a discussion of economic welfare: definitions, measurement and statistical issues, and data needs. The importance to traditional agriculturalists and subsistence farmers of ecosystem services from forest biomes (e.g. freshwater and soil nutrient cycling, provision of fuelwood and fodder, mitigation of flood and drought damage to crops and property, etc.) has been evaluated by TEEB and found to be a very material component of their household incomes (see *The Economics of Ecosystems and Biodiversity in National and International Policy Making* (TEEB in National Policy, 2011)). Traditional measures of economic performance are also insensitive to such equity and poverty implications of ecosystem services and of their ongoing losses.

The welfare discussion alluded to above is intimately related to the notion of sustainability. Although the issue of sustainability was taken up by Hicks and Lindahl beginning in the 1930s (Heal and Kriström, 2005), and discussed by Solow (1992) the potential long-run impact of environmental damages like global warming and concerns with the future availability of natural resources has more recently resurrected the sustainability discussion. Roughly speaking, an economy is on a sustainable trajectory if real wealth (Dasgupta and Mäler, 2000) or real income (Hicks, 1939), does not fall over time.

The national income account (NIA) is a fundamental macroeconomic indicator which shows the level and performance of economic activities in the economy. The System of National Accounts (SNA) of the United Nations (2003) attempts to provide a benchmarked framework for measuring and summarizing national income data across all activities within an economy and to facilitate comparing such data across countries (UN, 2003). A crucial component of the SNA is the estimation of GDP, where, at given market prices, the gross value of all the goods and services produced within an economy is estimated.

In measuring GDP, the contributions of ecosystem services, such as bioremediation by wetlands, storm and flood protection by mangroves, and the prevention of soil erosion by forests, are ignored. Hence, many ecosystem services which have a welfare-enhancing role do not enter into macroeconomic value calculations. This is due to their relatively low perceived value as these resources and their contributions often fall outside the domain of the market, and hence remain unpriced and undervalued. Ultimately, this means that GDP underestimates the actual level of social welfare because it does not account for contributions from natural resources.

Economists are now in agreement that instead of measuring GDP or income – a flow concept – the more comprehensive measurement of the stock of wealth that includes the value of natural capital is a more meaningful and correct approach (Dasgupta and Mäler, 2000; Arrow et al, 2004; Dasgupta, 2009). The World Bank has attempted to implement the concept of ecosystem accounting, and created two reports in the late 1990s – namely *Monitoring Environmental Progress* (World Bank, 1995) and *Expanding the Measure of Wealth* (World Bank, 1997). These reports are fundamentally based on Pearce and Atkinson's (1993) notion of wealth measurement and savings. Another important milestone in estimating natural wealth occurred in 2006, when the World Bank published *Where Is the Wealth of Nations?* a report that presents 'wealth accounts' of more than 100 countries (World Bank, 2006).

To date, there is a general consensus that natural assets are stocks that should enter a social accounting matrix (SAM) or input–output (IO) table as a factor account, and the provisioning and regulating services, if measurable, should enter as an intermediate input. Green accounts are a crucial ingredient in empirical general equilibrium modelling exercises because the SAM is the link between the macroeconomic theory and its empirical analogue. Although most countries have SAMs for one or more years, very few countries have SAM data that includes natural asset entries (Heal and Kriström, 2003).

Given the myriad of policy issues, it is useful to consider two broad categories of policy. One is related to the economic forces associated with the natural evolution of an economy (e.g. capital deepening and increased labour productivity), and how these forces impact (spill over onto) the exploitation of natural assets and ecosystems. In this category, policy instruments include taxes, subsidies, quotas, licences and property rights that are linked directly to natural assets and ecosystems. Similar instruments linked to other sectors can have indirect impacts on natural assets and ecosystems. The other set of policies are domestic macroeconomic policies (e.g. monetary policy) that cause major fiscal and trade imbalances, which in turn distort domestic product and factor markets. Similarly, foreign policies can have spillover effects on the home country.

Characteristics of a growing economy include capital deepening – here, broadly defined to include human capital – and typically an increase in the service sector's (housing, utilities, transportation, professional, banking and retail services) share of GDP, with most of the service goods not traded in international markets. Also, as economies grow: (i) the share of the workforce in agriculture falls as wages increase, which induces a substitution of capital for labour in production, and (ii) household expenditures on services and entertainment goods increase.

The possible impacts a successful economy can have on ecosystems and biodiversity 'works in reverse' for an unsuccessful, slow-growing economy. Often, poor economic performance is also associated with economic crises and volatility in factor incomes. Invariably, these conditions tend to slow the exodus of labour out of agriculture, slow the rate of capital deepening and dampen a country's incentives and political will to prevent the degradation of natural and environmental resources. Economic crises often result when countries pursue policies that lead to fiscal deficits or external debt that make their economies vulnerable to economic shocks. The needed within-country adjustments – even with the assistance of international agencies and friendly governments – is invariably a decrease in government spending, an increase in transfers from households either directly through taxes and fees, and costs of adjustment as resources are reallocated from the production of home goods to the production of internationally traded goods. Until the imbalances are corrected and debt obligations met, household real disposable income is typically much less than before the shock, with wage income suffering the greatest decline. Ecosystem exploitation (e.g. harvesting timber for cooking and fuel) is exacerbated by an incentive to increase exploitation by those whose wages and employment have fallen, while at the same time, government budgets for the management of these resources is even more constrained.

Finally

Throughout the TEEB series including this book, *The Economics of Ecosystem Biodiversity in National and International Policy Making* (TEEB in National

Policy, 2011) and *The Economics of Ecosystem Biodiversity in Local and Regional Policy and Management* (TEEB in Local Policy, 2011), we follow a tiered approach in analysing problems and suggesting suitable policy responses. We find that at times, it suffices just to *recognize* value – be it intrinsic, spiritual or social – in order to create a cost-effective policy response for conservation or economically sustainable use of biodiversity and ecosystem services. At other times we may need to *demonstrate* economic value in order for policy makers to respond – such as a wetland conserved near Kampala (see TEEB in Local Policy, 2011, Chapter 8) for its waste treatment function instead of reclaiming it for agriculture, or river flats maintained for their many ecosystem services instead of converting them for residential use near New Delhi (TEEB in National Policy, 2011, Chapter 10, Box 10.6).

It is not a 'risk-free' exercise to demonstrate value by deriving and propagating shadow prices. There is always the risk that misguided policy makers or exploitative interests may want to use these prices for the wrong ends. Therefore, our proposition is that the act of valuing the flows and stocks of nature is ethically valid so long as the purpose of that exercise is, first and foremost, to demonstrate value in order to instigate change of behaviour, and to pre-empt damaging trade-offs based on the implicit valuations that are involved in causing the loss of biodiversity and degradation of ecosystems.

TEEB has also focused considerably on changes which *capture* value by rewarding and supporting good conservation through a variety of means – Payments for Environmental Services (PES), IPES, establishing new markets, EHS reforms, etc. (see TEEB in National Policy, 2011, Chapters 5 and 9, and TEEB, 2011b, Chapter 8). These instruments offer a mechanism to translate external, non-market values of ecosystem services into real financial incentives for local actors to provide such services (Ferraro and Kiss, 2002). There is also a need to use existing knowledge and examples of success to develop more effective governance institutions, including property rights regimes and regulatory structures.

Recognizing that biodiversity underpins the foundations of economies, and of human well-being, is one thing. Translating that knowledge into concrete changes that will influence behaviour for the better is another formidable challenge. It is one that must be met if the failures of the recent past are not to be repeated and compounded, with the potential for ever-increasing human and financial costs. This TEEB book and other forthcoming volumes (especially TEEB in National Policy, 2011 and TEEB in Local Policy, 2011) make the case that greater economic and ecological rationality in addressing natural capital is not only necessary but possible, and indeed, that it is amply evident in many instances that deserve more attention, investment and opportunity to replicate and to scale into wider use around the world.

References

Arrow, K. J., Bolin, B., Costanza, R., Dasgupta, P., Folke, C., Holling, C. S., Jansson, B.-O., Levin, S., Mäler, K.-G., Perrings, C. and Pimentel, D. (1995) 'Economic growth, carrying capacity, and the environment', *Science*, vol 268, no 5210, 28 April, pp520–521

Arrow, K. J., Dasgupta, P., Goulder, L., Daily, G., Ehrlich, P. R., Heal, G. M., Levin, S., Mäler, K.-G., Schneider, S., Starrett, D. A. and Walker, B. (2004) 'Are we consuming too much?', *Journal of Economic Perspectives*, vol 18, no 1, pp147–172

Atkinson, G. (2010) 'Valuation and greening the national accounts: Significance, challenges and initial practical steps', Paper for the Environment Department, The World Bank, Washington, DC

Barbier, E. B. (2003) 'Habitat–fisheries linkages and mangrove loss in Thailand', *Contemporary Economic Policy*, vol 21, no 1, pp59–77

Barbier, E. B. (2007) 'Valuing ecosystem services as productive input', *Economic Policy*, vol 22, no 49, pp177–229

Barbier, E. B. (2008) 'Poverty, development, and ecological services', *International Review of Environment and Resource Economics*, vol 2, pp1–27

Barbier, E. B. (2009) 'Ecosystems as natural assets', *Foundations and Trends in Microeconomics*, vol 4, no 8, pp611–681

Bateman, I. J., Mace, G. M., Fezzi, C., Atkinson, G., Barbier, E. B. and Turner, K. (2010) 'Economic analysis for ecosystem service assessments', Draft Paper, National Ecosystem Assessment, Defra, London

Brondizio, E. S., Ostrom, E. and Young, O. (2009) 'Connectivity and the governance of multilevel socio-ecological systems: The role of social capital', *Annual Review of Environment and Resource*, vol 34, pp253–278

Cash, D. W., Adger, W. N., Berkes, F., Garden, P., Lebel, L., Olsson, P., Pritchard, L. and Young, O. (2006) 'Scale and cross-scale dynamics: governance and information in a multilevel world', *Ecology and Society*, vol 11, no 2, p8, www.ecologyandsociety.org/vol11/iss2/art8/

Daily, G. C. (ed) (1997) *Nature's Services: Societal Dependence on Natural Ecosystems*, Island Press, Washington, DC

Daly, H. (1991) 'Towards an environmental macroeconomics', *Land Economics*, vol 67, no 2, pp255–259

Dasgupta, P. (2009) 'The welfare economic theory of green national accounts', *Environment and Resource Economics*, vol 42, pp3–38, DOI 10.1007/s10640-008-9223-y

Dasgupta, P. and Mäler, K.-G. (2000) 'Net national product, wealth, and social well-being', *Environment and Development Economics,* vol 5, pp69–93

Eichner, T. and Tschirhart, J. T. (2007) 'Efficient ecosystem services and naturalness in an ecological/economic model', *Environmental and Resource Economics*, vol 37, no 4, pp733–755

Ferraro, P. J. and Kiss, A. (2002) 'Direct payments for biodiversity conservation', *Science*, vol 298, pp1718–1719

Ferraro, P. J. and Pattanayak, S. K. (2006) 'Money for nothing? A call for empirical evaluation of biodiversity conservation investments', *Plos Biology*, vol 4, pp482–488

Finoff, D. and Tschirhart, J. T. (2008) 'Linking dynamic ecological and economic general equilibrium models', *Resource and Energy Economics*, vol 30, no 2, pp91–114

Freeman, A. M. (2003) *The Measurement of Environmental and Resource Values*, RFF Press, Washington, DC

Hanley, N. and Barbier, E. B. (2009) *Pricing Nature: Cost–Benefit Analysis and Environmental Policy*, Edward Elgar, Cheltenham

Heal, G. and Kriström, B. (2005) 'National Income and the Environment', in Mäler, K.-G. and Vincent, J. R. (eds) *Handbook of Environmental Economics*, Volume 3, Elsevier, Amsterdam

Heal, G. M., Barbier, E. B., Boyle, K. J., Covich, A. P., Gloss, S. P., Hershner, C. H., Hoen, J. P., Pringle, C. M., Polasky, S., Segerson, K. and Shrader-Frechette, K. (2005) *Valuing Ecosystem Services: Towards Better Environmental Decision Making*, The National Academy Press, Washington, DC

Hicks, J. R. (1939) *Value and Capital,* 2nd edn, Oxford University Press, Oxford

Heijdra, B. J. and Heijnen, P. (2009) 'Environmental policy and macroeconomy under the shallow lake dynamics', Working Paper No 2859, CeSIFO, Munich

Kinzig, A. P., Ryan, P., Etienne, M., Allyson, H., Elmqvist, T. and Walker, B. H. (2006) 'Resilience and regime shifts: Assessing cascading effects', *Ecology and Society*, vol 11, no 1, p20

Kumar, M. and Kumar, P. (2008) 'Valuation of ecosystem services: A psycho-cultural perspective', *Ecological Economics*, vol 64, pp808–819

Kumar, P. and Wood, M. D. (2010) *Valuation of Regulating Services of Ecosystems: Methodology and Applications*, Routledge, London

Li, N. and Roe, T. L. (2006) 'Validating dynamic general equilibrium model forecasts', Economic Development Center Working Paper, Dept. of Economics and Dept. of Applied Economics, University of Minnesota, Minneapolis and St. Paul, MN

MA (Millennium Ecosystem Assessment) (2003) *A Conceptual Framework for Assessment*, Island Press, Washington, DC

MA (2005) *Ecosystems and Human Well-being: Summary for Decision Makers*, Island Press, Washington, DC

Mäler, K.-G., Xepapadeas, A. and de Zeeuw, A. (2003) 'The economics of shallow lakes', *Environmental and Resource Economics*, vol 26, pp603–624

Nordhaus, W. and Yang, Z. (1996) 'A regional dynamic general-equilibrium model of alternative climate-change strategies', *American Economic Review*, vol 86, no 4, pp741–765

Ostrom, E. (2007) 'A diagnostic approach for going beyond panaceas', *PNAS*, vol 104, pp15181–15187

Ostrom, E. (2009) 'A general framework for analyzing sustainability of social-ecological systems', *Science*, **vol** 325, pp419–422

Pearce, D. W. and Atkinson, G. (1993) 'Capital theory and measurement of sustainable development', *Ecological Economics*, vol 8, pp103–108

Perrings, C. (2007) 'Going beyond panaceas: Future challenges', *Proceedings of the National Academy of Sciences*, vol 104, pp15179–15180

Perrings, C., Baumgärtner, S., Brock, W. A., Chopra, K., Conte, M., Costello, C., Duraiappah, A., Kinzig, A. P., Pascual, U., Polasky, S., Tschirhart, J. and Xepapadeas, A. (2009) 'The economics of biodiversity and ecosystem services', in Naeem, S., Bunker, D., Hector, A., Loreau, M. and Perrings, C. (eds) *Biodiversity, Ecosystem Functioning, and Human Wellbeing: An Ecological and Economic Perspective*, Oxford University Press, Oxford, pp230–247

Polasky, S. and Segerson, K. (2009) 'Integrating ecology and economics in the study of ecosystem services: Some lessons learned', *Annual Review of Resource Economics*, vol 1, pp409–434

Scheffer, M., Carpenter, S., Foley, J. R., Folke, C. and Walker, B. (2001) 'Catastrophic shifts in ecosystems', *Nature*, vol 413, pp591–596

Solow, R. M. (1992) *An Almost Practical Step Toward Sustainability*, Resources for the Future, Washington, DC

Stiglitz, J., Sen, A. and Fitoussi, J.-P. (2008) *Report of the Commission on the Measurement of Economic and Social Progress, submitted to President Sarkozy*, Paris, France

TEEB (2008) 'The Economics of Ecosystems and Biodiversity: An Interim Report, available at www.teebweb.org, accessed 2 March 2010

TEEB in National Policy (2011) *The Economics of Ecosystems and Biodiversity in National and International Policy Making* (ed Patrick ten Brink), Earthscan, London

TEEB in Local Policy (2011) *The Economics of Ecosystems and Biodiversity in Local and Regional Policy and Management* (eds Heidi Wittmer and Haripriya Gundimeda), Earthscan, London

Tschirhart, J. (2009) 'Models integrating ecology and economics', *Annual Review of Resource Economics*, vol 1, October, pp381–409

United Nations (2003) *Integrated Environmental and Economic Accounting 2003, final draft*, New York, http://unstats.un.org/unsd/envAccounting/seea.htm

Weitzman, M. L. (1976) 'On the welfare significance of national product in a dynamic economy', *Quarterly Journal of Economics*, vol 90, no 1, pp156–162

World Bank (1995) *Monitoring Environmental Progress: A Report on Progress*, Environmental Sustainable Development, Washington, DC

World Bank (1997) *Expanding the Measure of Wealth: Indicators for Sustainable Development*, ESD Studies and Monograph Series No 17, Washington, DC

World Bank (2006) *Where is the Wealth of Nations? Measuring Capital for the 21st Century*, World Bank, Washington, DC

Appendix 1
How the TEEB Framework Can Be Applied: The Amazon Case

Lead authors
Timothy J. Killeen, Rosimeiry Portela

Reviewers
Eduardo Brondízio, Peter H. May

Contents

Introduction   309

1   Services and values at the global scale   310
    1.1   Carbon storage and sequestration   310
    1.2   Habitat service (maintenance of life cycles and gene pool protection)   311
          1.2.1   Existence value   311
          1.2.2   Option value   312

2   Services and values at the continental scale   312
    2.1   Mediation of the regional precipitation regime (through the 'water pump'
          mechanism)   312

3   Services and values at the regional (basin) scale   314
    3.1   Forest growth (for provision of raw materials)   314
    3.2   Erosion prevention   315
    3.3   Water purification   315
    3.4   Nursery service for fish populations   316

4   Services and values at the local scale   317
    4.1   Provide food and other natural resources   317
    4.2   Biological interactions   318
    4.3   Aesthetic beauty   319
    4.4   Cultural heritage   319

5   Limitations and caveats   320

Acknowledgements   321

References   322

Introduction

The Greater Amazon includes not only the Amazon River Basin but also adjacent watersheds with similar climates and ecosystems in Colombia, Venezuela, Bolivia, Peru, Ecuador and the coastal states of Guyana, Suriname and French Guiana. Covering approximately 8 million km², the region has an enormous diversity of landscapes, habitats and ecosystems. The Amazon provides numerous and strikingly clear examples of the value of ecosystem services and biodiversity conservation at four different scales: global, continental, regional and local. Table A1.1 provides a

Table A1.1 Characteristics and values of major ecosystem services of the Amazon at varying scales

	Function	Services	Benefit	Estimated value (US$)
1 Global scale				
1.1	Photosynthesis and maintenance of ecosystem structure	Carbon storage and sequestration	(Global) climate stability Revenues from carbon markets	$1.5–3 trillion (C-stock value) $6.5–13 billion/yr (REDD)
1.2	Evolutionary processes (taxonomic and habitat diversity)	Habitat service (maintenance of life cycles and gene pool protection)	Evolutionary heritage Potential crops and pharmaceuticals	Intangible 73 million/yr (GEF) Unknown
2 Continental scale				
2.1	Convective circulation 'water pump'	Climate regulation (esp. mediation of regional precipitation regime)	Agricultural productivity Hydropower generation	$1–3 billion/yr $75–750 million/yr
3 Regional (Basin) scale				
3.1	Soil formation and nutrient cycling	Forest growth (for provision of raw materials)	Sustainable timber harvest	$4–7 billion/yr
3.2	Ecosystem (vegetation) structure in terrestrial habitats	Erosion prevention	Reduced siltation in hydropower reservoirs	$60–600 million/yr
3.3	Nutrient cycling in wetlands	Water purification	Clean water	Unknown
3.4	Ecosystem structure in freshwater habitats	Nursery service for fish populations	Commercially viable fish populations	100–500 million/yr
4 Local scale				
4.1	Viable wildlife (plant and animal) populations	Provide food and other natural resources	Subsistence life styles Forest products	$500 million – 1 billion/yr
4.2	Food webs, pollination, mycorrhizae	Biological control	Ecological stability, contribute to crop productivity, and disease prevention	Unknown
4.3	Landscape integrity	Aesthetic beauty	Improve quality of life Promote and support tourist industry	$350 million – 1 billion/yr
4.4	Habitat for people	Cultural heritage	Maintain cultural identity and ethical principles	Intangible

Note: Sources and methodological logic for estimated values are provided in the text.

summary of some of these services and an estimate of their economic value derived via 'back of the envelope' methodologies using information in the public domain. The objective of this exercise is not to provide a detailed valuation of Amazon services, but rather to illustrate the application of the TEEB framework and underscore the need for a more comprehensive compilation of the economic significance and the impact on the livelihoods of the people living in the Greater Amazon.

1 Services and values at the global scale

1.1 Carbon storage and sequestration

The Amazon is a vast reservoir of carbon with approximately 76 gigatons (Gt)[1] stored in its above-ground biomass, with perhaps another 30Gt stored in below-ground carbon stocks (Killeen, 2007; Saatchi et al, 2007; Aragão et al, 2009). If released into the atmosphere, this carbon would equal approximately 20 years of fossil fuel consumption and an international markets ($5–10 per ton of CO_2), this would have a value between $1.5 and $3 trillion. This not a realistic valuation, however, because carbon markets do not yet recognize the conservation of standing natural forest as a carbon offset, although the UNFCCC treaty process is developing a policy framework that will compensate countries for reducing emissions from deforestation and forest degradation (REDD). Under this scheme, revenues could be calculated by comparing future levels of deforestation with a baseline, which for many countries might be based on historical rates of deforestation. The deforestation rate in the Amazon during the last two decades is estimated to be ~28,000km²/yr, which translates into approximately 1.3Gt of annual CO_2 emissions (Table A1.2) and the economic value of these emissions can be calculated by estimating their replacement cost in existing markets. For example, approximately $13 billion would purchase an equivalent amount of industrial based emission reductions; if that payment were repeated annually for 30 years, it would equal $388 billion, which when corrected for inflation and expressed in today's currency, would have a net present value of $134 billion.[2]

The ecosystem services provided by the Amazon are not limited to its capacity to store a fixed quantity of carbon or the potential to reduce emissions from deforestation. Recent studies have shown that tropical forest ecosystems are actually net carbon sinks, because the increase in CO_2 concentrations has altered the physiological pathways in plant cells leading to a shift in carbon fluxes from photosynthesis and respiration (Malhi et al, 2008). The net positive difference in the uptake of CO_2, although small when calculated at the scale of a hectare is a large number when extrapolated over the Amazon and is estimated to be roughly equivalent to the emissions from current deforestation. In summary, the Amazon provides ecosystem services for the global economy by storing carbon, but also by sequestering some of the CO_2 that is being released by human-related activities throughout the globe.[3]

Table A1.2 Value of carbon stocks in the Amazon forest based on their replacement value in international markets for energy-based carbon credits

	Forest cover 1990 (×1000ha)	Forest cover 2000 (×1000ha)	Forest cover 2005 (×1000ha)	Annual rate of deforestation (×1000ha/yr)	Carbon emissions @ 125t/ha (×1000t)	CO_2 emissions (×1000t)	Value of emissions @ $10/t CO_2 ($ million)
Bolivia	48,355	46,862	46,070	240	30,001	110,105	1101
Brazil	364,922	348,129	336,873	2250	281,250	1,032,188	10,322
Colombia	59,282	57,839	57,117	144	18,044	66,221	662
Ecuador	12,333	11,953	11,764	38	4748	17,423	174
Peru	72,511	71,727	71,335	78	9800	35,966	360
Venezuela	43,258	42,529	42,164	73	9119	33,466	335
Guyana	15,104	15,104	15,104	—	—	—	—
Suriname	14,776	14,776	14,776	—	—	—	—
French Guiana	13,000	13,000	13,000	—	—	—	—
Total	643,540	621,919	608,202				
Annual rates				2824	352,961	1,295,369	
						Annual total	12,954
						30-year total	388,611
						NPV for 30-year total	134,325

Source: Killeen (2007)

1.2 Habitat service (maintenance of life cycles and gene pool protection)

Biodiversity conservation is the most problematic value to estimate, because of the failure of markets to adequately capture or measure its contribution to the global economy – even though biodiversity has been the foundation for the world's economy since the origin of human civilization. The global significance of biodiversity conservation in the Amazon has two dimensions: (a) maintenance of genetic diversity on Earth (existence value) and (b) maintenance of potential future uses (option value).

1.2.1 Existence value

Individuals across the globe fervently believe conservation of biodiversity to be a moral obligation – to preserve a heritage bequeathed either by a deity or as the end result of millions of years of evolution. In this context, the two most accurate words that describe the value of biodiversity are 'priceless' and 'irreplaceable'. This type of moral valuation is essentially exploited at the global scale by conservation organizations and multilateral organizations and is, in part, the motivation for the Global Environmental Facility (GEF), which since 1991 has invested approximately $438 million that has leveraged an additional $874 million on biodiversity projects in one or more of the eight countries of the Greater Amazon, an average of only $72.8 million/yr (GEF, 2009). A recent manifestation of the recognition of the value of biodiversity and the need to leverage its conservation with more marketable services is the REDD+ initiative, which recognizes that value is added to REDD initiatives if they also contribute to maintaining ecosystem services, biodiversity conservation and improve human livelihoods.

1.2.2 Option value

All food staples are domesticated varieties of wild plants and animals, and most modern pharmaceuticals have been derived from natural products. Thus, one of the most compelling arguments for conserving biodiversity is the potential for new food sources (Heiser, 1990), as well as new medicines and pesticides (Reid et al, 1993; Ortholand and Gane, 2004). Unfortunately, it is difficult to harness markets to support biodiversity conservation in the Amazon, because there are three principal constraints to levying fees for biodiversity conservation:

1 Users are incapable of paying for the goods and services because they have no economic resources and/or the goods and services are part of the 'public commons' in which traditional use makes it difficult to collect fees (i.e. hunting and fishing).
2 It is difficult to place a value on an undiscovered benefit, because we don't know who owns the resource, how much it might be worth, or who might be interested in acquiring that resource (i.e. a potential new crop or drug).
3 It is not plausible to extract fees for knowledge that was acquired in the past and is now in the public domain (i.e. rubber, cassava, quinine and atropine).

As a general rule, the difficulty in generating payment for biodiversity and ecosystem services at the local or regional scale does not mean that these services do not have value, even though that value is intangible to local politicians or landholders who will usually act in their own economic interest. Moreover, efforts to assign economic value on the basis of erroneous assumptions or hopeful scenarios (e.g. bioprospecting) may raise expectations that cannot be met and diminish the validity of other, more convincing arguments.

2 Services and values at the continental scale

2.1 Mediation of the regional precipitation regime (through the 'water pump' mechanism)

The importance of forest cover in maintaining high levels of precipitation in the Amazon has been a basic tenet of ecosystem ecology for decades. The tropical rainforest ecosystem of the Amazon ultimately depends on the humid trade winds that bring water from the Atlantic Ocean – an attribute that provides an enormous element of stability to the Amazon ecosystem. Nonetheless, about 25–50 per cent of the rain that falls on the Amazon is the result of evapotranspiration and precipitation that cycle through the convective systems that form thunderstorms (Salati and Nobre, 1991). Partially deforested landscapes actually experience a slight increase in precipitation as this cyclical process is accelerated by increased evaporation over forest that is associated with increased rain over pastures. However, the volume of water cycled through the convection systems decreases once about 50 per cent of the landscape has been deforested (Kabat et al, 2004) and when a landscape is nearly completely deforested, the amount of water cycled through convective systems decreases by about 10–25 per cent (Nobre et al, 1991).

Large-scale land-use change and the subsequent alteration of the regional precipitation regime within the Amazon may impact other distant regions of the western hemisphere. The meteorological phenomenon known as the Hadley Circulation describes how warm air rises at the equator, moves toward the poles, descends at higher latitudes, and returns toward the equator along the surface of the Earth: rising air promotes precipitation, while descending air suppresses it. This type of long-distance phenomenon is referred to as a 'teleconnection' by climatologists, because it explains how regional manifestations of global warming in different parts of the world are linked and modulated by energy flows (Feddema et al, 2005). There is concern among climatologists that climate change and deforestation may reduce precipitation and increase temperatures within the Amazon (Malhi et al, 2008); climate models also show that these changes may be linked to reduced precipitation in the lower Midwest of the United States (Avissar and Werth, 2005).

A more straightforward example of a teleconnection is the weather system that links the western Amazon with the mid-latitudinal region of the South American continent (Figure A1.1). In this system, a major gyre originates with

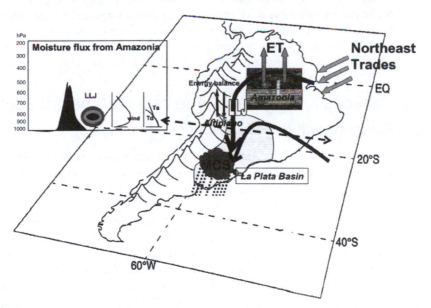

Figure A1.1 *The South American Low-Level Jet (SALLJ) transports water from the central Amazon to the agricultural regions of the Paraguay–Paraná basin*

Note: Deforestation and climate change threaten this important ecosystem service; even a small reduction in precipitation would lead to an annual economic loss in the hundreds of millions to billions of dollars in the Southern Cone and High Andes.

Source: Modified from Marengo et al (2004); © American Meteorological Society

the Atlantic trade winds that pass over the Amazon before curving southwards as it nears the Andes to form the South American Low Level Jet (SALLJ). The impact of the SALLJ is most noticeable during the austral summer when the region of maximum rainfall is displaced to the south and initiates the onset of the South American monsoon, essentially exporting moisture from the Amazon to the seasonally dry regions of subtropical South America (Marengo et al, 2004). A shift in the climate regime of the Amazon would affect this moisture transport system and potentially reduce precipitation in the Paraguay–Paraná River basin, impacting important agricultural areas in eastern Bolivia, southern Brazil, northern Argentina and Paraguay. The agricultural output of this region is estimated to be greater than $100 billion annually[4] and a reduction in precipitation would either reduce yields or cause farmers to change crops or invest in irrigation; a slight reduction in agricultural productivity would have an enormous economic impact (1–3 billion US$/yr). Moreover, Brazil and Paraguay are heavily dependent on hydroelectric energy and a reduction in precipitation would raise the cost of energy for industry and urban centres (Berri et al, 2002).

A similar model can be used to estimate the impact of reduced rainfall on the Itaipú hydropower facility that generates ~94 billion kWh/yr. The replacement value of this existing energy supply would be worth approximately $7.5 billion based on the current regulated tariff for electrical energy in southern Brazil of US$0.08/kWh (IPS, 2009). The 2000 drought associated with the 1999 La Niña event decreased power generation at Itaipú by 15 per cent, representing a loss of income of ~$1.2 billion; similarly, a modified precipitation regime that reduced the water carrying capacity of the SALLJ could impact the generating output of Itaipú, where a 1–10 per cent reduction in electrical power generation would force utility companies to generate energy from an alternative source at an additional cost of between $75 and $750 million annually.

3 Services and values at the regional (basin) scale

3.1 Forest growth (for provision of raw materials)

The productivity of the Amazon forest is a function of radiant energy, water and soil resources, of which the latter plays a key role in determining the growth rate of trees in different parts of the Amazon. Net primary productivity (NPP) in the Amazon varies between 9.3 and 16.0tC/ha/yr and about 15–30 per cent is allocated to stem biomass. One definition of sustainable forestry is that the amount of timber harvested is less than the quantity of wood produced; consequently, a model that assumes 5 per cent of NPP could be harvested annually provides a conservative estimate of the Amazon ecosystem potential as a sustainable source of timber. With an average wood density of 750kg/m³, this would translate into 425–740 million m³ of timber and, assuming that only 25 per cent of this timber had a market value, this would yield between US$4 and 72 billion annually when based on current prices for roundwood of $10–100kg/ m³. This simple calculation provides an estimate of the opportunity cost for 'sustainable' logging between $5 and $89/ha. There are other estimates of the value of timber extracted from the Amazon. For example, the Instituto Brasileiro de Geografia e Estatística (IBGE, 2007) reports timber commerce of approximately

$900 million dollars in 2007; but most of that wood is extracted from a small fraction of the Brazilian Amazon forests via salvage logging operations on the agricultural frontier. A recent report on the opportunity costs of timber in Brazil estimated the value at between US$419 and 615/ha (Verweij et al, 2009) but, as those authors observed, these higher values are not likely to be representative of a forest management model that is truly sustainable.

3.2 Erosion prevention

The value of this ecosystem service can be estimated by evaluating how increased sedimentation decreases the economic utilities of hydropower facilities caused by increased sediment loads from deforestation and intensive land use. As a reservoir fills with sediment, capacity to store water is reduced and electricity generation is curtailed during low water periods. Eventually, the facility will be shut down when the reservoir can no longer store enough water to power the turbines, cover its operating costs, and return a profit (Palmieri et al, 2001). The annual rate of sedimentation can be expressed as the percentage of the storage capacity lost each year due to sedimentation, which varies depending on climate and geology, as well as land-use and watershed management. The lowest reported sedimentation rates are for the United Kingdom with only 0.1 per cent/yr, which implies the average reservoir in the British Isles will last a millennium; however, the world average is about 1 per cent and that translates into an expected lifetime of less than 100 years (Jiahua and Morris, 1992).

The value of forest conservation can be estimated by comparing the lost revenues of a rather small 50MW hydro facility producing 300 million kWh/yr which experiences a sedimentation rate of 0.5 per cent on a forest landscape versus 1 per cent on a deforested landscape (Lawrence et al, 2008). Increased sedimentation would cause the facility to be decommissioned after 65 years with the total lost revenues of ~$300 million from mean lost revenues of ~$6 million/yr. This amount would be greater for very large facilities such as Itaipú, although in that specific example it will take almost three centuries for the siltation process to culminate to the point of decommission.[5] Brazil is expanding investment in the dams and reservoirs within its own country, as well as in neighbouring lands across the region,[6] while funding agencies like the World Bank are increasing their commitments to hydropower as part of their climate change investment strategy (World Bank, 2009). If the lost revenues from the hypothetical 50MW facility described by Lawrence et al (2008) were extrapolated across the region to the ten existing and 89 planned facilities in Brazil (Killeen, 2007), then the annual impact on generating facilities when averaged over their collective lifespan would approximate $600 million/yr, a sum that would be even greater if the similarly untapped potential of the Andean countries was included in the estimation.

3.3 Water purification

Wetlands and other Amazon forest ecosystems have multiple ecosystem functions, such as mediating water flows and acting as sinks for sediments and urban effluents, ensuring that downstream populations enjoy steady clean water supplies. The Amazon has 12.5 per cent of the world's fresh water, while it is one of the most pristine of all the major river basins in the world. The purity of the water in the Amazon and its tributaries is the consequence of the vast natural filter provided by its natural ecosystems for the sediments, nutrients and pollutants that are washed into the rivers by innumerable farms, mines, villages and cities. The relatively pristine state of the waters of the Amazon was recently validated by a systematic effort to study water quality in the rivers of Brazil (Figure A1.2); while these studies demonstrate that most of the watershed remains pristine, there are localized areas that have been impacted by human effluents (Moss and Moss, 2009). The cost of these services are difficult to know due to the 'veracity' of the civil engineer's antiquated paradigm for dealing with pollution (e.g. the solution to pollution is dilution); the vast quantity of the water in the Amazon as yet masks the economic impact of its degradation.

3.4 Nursery service for fish populations

One of the most economically important services of wetlands is providing habitat and a food web that support the basin's strategically important fisheries. Floodplain forests on 'white water' rivers are particularly productive because the sediments washed down from the Andes bring essential chemical nutrients that support a strategically important aquatic ecosystem.[7] Fish migrate locally into the floodplain wetlands during periods of high water to spawn and feed,

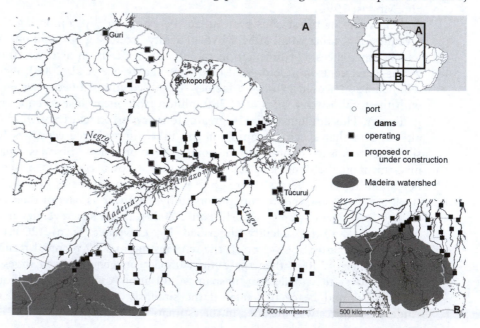

Figure A1.2 *A: Guri, Brokopondo, and Tucuruí are the three largest hydroelectric facilities in the greater Amazon; B: Controversy about the environmental impacts of river dams surrounds projects planned for the Xingu and Madeira rivers*

Note: The Amazon and Tocantins watershed represent 6 per cent of the world's potential hydropower, with 68 per cent of its undeveloped hydropower potential in Brazil.

Source: Killeen (2007)

then return to the river channels during low-water periods. Long-distance migration is a behavioural trait characteristic of many Amazonian fish, including the economically important commercial species such as the *piramutaba* and *dourada*, as well as other species that move within subsectors of the basin, such as the *tambaqui, pacú, jaraqui* and *curimatã* (Barthem and Goulding, 1997).

Fishing is arguably the most important component of the Amazonian economy, providing employment and sustenance to an overwhelming majority of its residents, either directly by subsistence fishing or indirectly by commercial and sport fishing. Large migratory catfish are charismatic species that are the mainstay of the commercial fishing industry and, for that reason, are particularly useful as representatives of the value of ecosystem services at a regional scale. The commercial fishing industry in the Brazilian Amazon generates about $100 million annually and more than 200,000 direct jobs, statistics that do not include related sectors such as boat building, tourism, mechanical shops and other services (Almeida et al, 2001; Ruffino, 2001). The total economic value of fisheries in the Greater Amazon is many times greater than the reported commercial value on the lower Amazon (see Section 4). Our upper estimate of five times the amount documented for the lower Amazon takes into account the upper Amazon and its numerous tributaries, as well as the contribution of sport fishing. In spite of its resiliency, there is concern about the sustainability of current fishing practices, particularly on the main trunk of the Amazon River (Jesús and Kohler, 2004).

4 Services and values at the local scale

4.1 Provide food and other natural resources

Most fishermen in the Amazon are subsistence fisherman and their activities are largely focused at the local scale; fish are the most important source of protein for the approximately 500,000 indigenous and traditional people living in the Amazon, as well as the millions of migrants that have made the region home over the last several decades. Meat from mammals and birds represents an important protein source on all forest landscapes in the Greater Amazon. Restaurants specializing in bush meat are common, particularly along major transportation corridors that transect wilderness areas. Large mammals are subject to overharvesting in areas with moderately dense human populations and are usually the first species to be exterminated in settlement zones. Nonetheless, small mammals and game birds persist in degraded forests and are an important source of protein for many rural families. Because of its informal nature and tendency to be practised in remote places where no data are collected by government agencies, there are no reliable estimates for the economic value of subsistence fishing and hunting.

Somewhat better information is available for the economic value from plant products due to the Brazilian government's efforts to document commerce in a broad category of what are now referred to as non-timber forest products (NTFP) that are traded via some sort of formal market (Table A1.3). The products with the largest trade are all palms, including the açaí (both fruits and hearts), babaçu (oil extracted from seeds) and piaçaba (fibres used for handicraft),

Table A1.3 Trade in non-timber forest products from the Brazilian Amazon

Commodity	Volume (t)	Value (US$)
Latex and rubber	3958	42,000,000
Gums	38	69,000
Waxes	22,463	43,707,000
Fibres	84,141	55,502,000
Tannins	208	53,000
Oils	128,124	71,748,000
Food products	390,192	74,292,000
Cosmetics, dyes etc.	1733	1163
Total	630,857	287,372,163

Source: IBGE (2007)

followed by Brazil nuts, which in Brazil is known as *Castanho do Pará*. The total commerce in these products is a surprising $246 million/yr, but this value excludes other Amazonian countries, such as Bolivia which exports between $50 and 60 million/yr in Brazil nuts and another $4 million in açaí palm hearts annually (CBF, 2005). Many more plant products are not reported, but represent important sources of cash income to supplement subsistence livelihoods; for example, restaurants in all Amazonian cities offer a wide assortment of native fruits, drinks and icecream flavours, while urban residents take pride in having a home barbecue protected by a thatched roof.

4.2 Biological interactions

Many of the other ecosystem services described above are also dependent on this functional attribute of all ecosystems. Food webs are essential for maintaining all wildlife and fish populations, while the productivity of the forest itself is dependent on the ability of invertebrates and fungi to decompose the billions of tons of biomass produced each year. Mycorrhizae and *Rhizobium* symbionts are known to exist for thousands of plants, many of which are economically important timber species or non-timber species. Bees produce honey and play an indispensable role in pollinating coffee and citrus fruits worth hundreds of millions of dollars to the economies of the Amazonian countries.

However, one of the most important economic contributions that forest conservation provides to human economies may be from the avoidance of disease and the costs needed to manage the impacts of disease. Parasitic pathogens such as malaria and leishmaniasis cost governments tens of millions of dollars in health care and lost productivity. New migrants are not adapted either culturally or biologically to a forest ecosystem and thus are more susceptible to these diseases. In the habitats of the agricultural frontier, the traditional host–parasite relationship is often disturbed and the pathogens may find different ways to reproduce or choose alternate hosts, as evidenced by the periodic outbreak of Hanta virus or haemorrhagic fever in the Bolivian Amazon.[8] The cost of an avoided disease is difficult to calculate, because the severity of that disease is unknown, but HIV was once restricted to primates in Central Africa; since it passed to humans it has had a massive impact on the global economy.

4.3 Aesthetic beauty

The scenic landscapes of the Amazon add value to the life of the average citizen, as well as forming a fundamental linchpin to its strategically important tourist industry. Operators in all Amazonian countries offer a diversified assortment of products that includes ecotourism, adventure tourism and cultural tourism for overseas visitors, but also recreational tourism for local and regional inhabitants. It is not just the specialized ecotourism niches that benefit from the natural beauty of the region, however, because all tourists expect to visit areas that are aesthetically pleasing. The revenues from Amazonian tourism are difficult to estimate because most countries have multiple tourist options and do not separate out the portion related to the Amazon. For example, Peru has an approximately $1 billion annual tourist industry, which is dominated by visitors to Cuzco and Machu Picchu, a unique archeological site set in a majestic natural setting (Machu Picchu is part of the Amazon drainage basin on the lower Urubamba). Venezuela's approximately $200 million industry is largely based on the Caribbean, but the Grand Savanna (not Amazonia) is a major domestic tourist destination. Ecuador's $435 million tourist industry is dominated by the Galapagos Islands, but also has important tourist destinations in the Andes that are located within the Amazon watershed. Brazil has a globally important tourist industry that generates about $80 billion revenues per year with between 1 and 2 per cent of that total originating in the Amazon (IBGE, 2007).

Tourism is particularly beneficial because it generates direct benefits at the local level, creating business opportunities for small and medium-sized enterprises, and provides employment for semi-skilled and unskilled labour. When poorly regulated, tourism can cause environmental degradation and cultural homogenization, thus damaging the natural asset that is at the core of its business model. Many of the geographic centres of the tourist industry in the Amazon are situated near or within protected areas. The most important contribution that tourism can make to conservation is job creation at the local level, which generates a vested interest to conserve the forest ecosystem.

4.4 Cultural heritage

The native peoples of the Amazon are proud of their cultural heritage and consider the natural landscape as an essential and irreplaceable component of that cultural heritage. Over the past two decades, the indigenous peoples of the Amazon have demanded and largely obtained control over the natural resources of their traditional landscapes. The legal framework varies from country to country, but in each country some type of formal recognition of these rights is now enshrined in law and followed in practice. The importance of formalizing these rights cannot be quantified by an objective methodology. Similarly, respecting nature is an inherent part of most of the world's great religions, while the major philosophical and scientific frameworks abhor the wasteful depredation of nature.

5 Limitations and caveats

The valuations we provide here loosely follow the proposed TEEB framework for ecosystem services assessment and valuation. It is, however, a preliminary effort and should be interpreted as such. First and foremost, there are problems with the estimate of values from ecosystem services in general and their comparison with estimates made for well-established, traditional economic activities. Although this is not so problematic for provisioning services, such as timber and other marketable goods, they become increasingly difficult as one moves to incipient markets, such as the carbon market, and even more so for markets that are not yet established. This is particularly the case for ecosystem services that are quasi-public goods, such as the mediation of regional precipitation regimes that carry no 'hard' monetary value that might benefit individuals. The current non-market – and hence non-priced – nature of many of these ecosystem services is an impediment to the creation of incentives that would lead land holders in the Amazon to perceive the loss of an ecosystem service as a significant opportunity cost.

Second, valuation relies on many assumptions that are a simplification of extremely complex situations that often depend upon context. For example, the use of estimated monetary value per unit of land (i.e. US$/ha/yr) and extrapolating those values over the entire region disregards the extremely heterogeneous nature of the region (Verweij et al, 2009). This is true in our own use of NPP ranges and average biomass values that we use to estimate the potential economic value of a sustainable timber harvest and climate regulation. Perhaps one of the most challenging aspects of a valuation effort is to account for the fine-scale estimate of value of forest ecosystem services and the opportunity costs of forest conversion. This is mainly the case of values estimated for goods and services in informal markets at the local scale for which there are no available statistics, but which have important implications for assessing the true opportunity costs of avoided deforestation. These values may represent, at aggregate levels, the most compelling argument to protect the forest and services it provides for the communities, many of them poor, who actually live within the Amazon. For example, in the Brazilian Amazon, there are currently at least 10 million rural inhabitants in the region, most of whom are poor settlers in unfamiliar terrain; they lack knowledge of how to best protect and make productive use of these goods and services, and there are still no mechanisms to transmit the global and regionally recognized benefits to stimulate their conservation and wise use.

Despite these and other limitations, it is worthwhile to assess the value of ecosystem services, because this demonstrates their dimension at different scales and the economic impact that would occur due to their loss or, more probably, from a reduction in the quantity and quality of those services. It also underscores the need for a more a detailed assessment and for careful consideration of the costs and benefits of unpriced goods and services; for which the TEEB framework can provide important guidance and a better perspective for integrated assessment.

Finally, this exercise is important for supporting new policies and improving governance at all political levels in the Amazon. By acknowledging the tangible value of these services and their contribution to local and national economies, even a back-of-the-envelope method is sufficiently illuminating to influence most decision makers. This is particularly relevant for the Amazon, which provides a variety of market and non-market goods and services that are extremely important to the individuals who actually live in the Amazon, but also for societies on other continents that indirectly benefit from the existence of the Amazon. The closing of the enormous gap between values and revenues is probably impossible, but a reduction in that gap can be attained by the creation of innovative market mechanisms, while recognizing that non-market measures are essential in order to conserve the goods and services provided by the Amazon ecosystem.

Acknowledgements

Tim Killeen thanks the Tinker Foundation of New York and the James S. Martin 21st Century School and the Environmental Change Institute at the University of Oxford for their support in the preparation of this study.

Notes

1   Gt = 109t, which is equivalent to a Petagram (Pg) = 1015 grams (g); in plain English this would be 76 billion tons. The value of 76Gt is a conservative estimate; if carbon stocks from below-ground biomass and soils were included, this value would be 20–50 per cent greater (Killen, 2007).
2   NPV calculated using discount rate of 10 per cent.
3   This net sequestration will eventually reach a new equilibrium, or flip in the other direction if climate change led to a decrease in precipitation in parts of the Amazon, which would cause a shift in ecosystem function from rainforest to a seasonally dry forest. The resulting increase in emissions from forest degradation could offset attempts to reduce emissions from avoided deforestation.
4   This is a conservative estimate extracted from multiple on-line sources for Argentina, Brazil and Paraguay, including: www.cideiber.com/infopaises/menupaises1.html and www.argentinaahora.com/extranjero/espaniol/bot_ppal/conozca_arg/produccion.asp
5   The current predicted life span of the Itaipú dam is estimated at about 300 years (pers. comm., T. A. Cochrane, July 2009).
6   Two hydroelectric facilities are under construction on the Madeira River, while the Presidents of Peru and Brazil made commitments to jointly invest in six additional hydropower facilities which would generate 7000MW of electricity at an estimated cost of $16 billion. Source: Bank Information Center, see www.bicusa.org/es/Articles.11184.
7   Amazonian rivers are stratified into three broad categories (white, black, clear) based on their chemistry and physical properties; white water floodplain forests, known as *varzea*, are perhaps the most productive freshwater fishery in the world (Barthem and Goulding, 1997).
8   The author is a survivor of a virulent viral pathogen that was diagnosed as either an unknown strain of hanta virus or Bolivian haemorrhagic fever.

References

Almeida, O., McGrath, D. and Ruffino, M. (2001) 'The commercial fisheries of the Lower Amazon: An economic analysis', *Fisheries Management and Ecology*, vol 8, pp15–35

Aragão, L. E. O. C., Malhi, Y., Metcalfe, D. B., Silva-Espejo, J. E., Jiménez, E., Navarrete, D., Almeida, S., Costa, A. C. L., Salinas, N., Phillips, O. L., Anderson, L. O., Baker, T. R., Goncalvez, P. H., Huamán-Ovalle, J., Mamani-Solórzano, M., Meir, P., Monteagudo, A., Peñuela, M. C., Prieto, A., Quesada, C. A., Rozas-Dávila, A., Rudas, A., Silva Junior, J. A. and Vásquez, R. (2009) 'Above- and below-ground net primary productivity across ten Amazonian forests on contrasting soils', *Biogeosciences Discussions*, vol 6, pp2441–2488, available at www.biogeosciences-discuss.net/special_issue34.html

Avissar, R. and Werth, D. (2005) 'Global hydroclimatological teleconnections resulting from tropical deforestation', *Journal of Hydrometeorology*, vol 6, pp134–145

Barthem, R. B. and Goulding, M. (1997) *The Catfish Connection: Ecology, Migration, and Conservation of Amazon Predators*, Columbia University Press, New York

Berri, G. J., Ghietto, M. A. and García, N. O. (2002) 'The influence of ENSO in the flows of the upper Paraná River of South America over the past 100 years', *Journal of Hydrometeorology*, vol 3, pp57–65

CBF (2005) 'Camara Forestal de Bolivia, Estadisticas de exportación', www.cfb.org.bo/CFBInicio/

Feddema, J. J., Oleson, K. W., Bonan, G. B., Mearns, L. O., Buja, L. E., Meehl, G. A. and Washington, W. M. (2005) 'The importance of land-cover change in simulating future climates', *Science*, vol 310, pp1674–1678

GEF (2009) 'The GEF project database', The Global Environment Facility, http://gefonline.org/projects

Heiser, C. B. (1990) 'New perspectives on the origin and evolution of New World domesticated plants: Summary', *Economic Botany*, vol 44 (supplement), pp111–116

IBGE (2007) 'Produção da Extração Vegetal e da Silvicultura – 2007', Instituto Brasileiro de Geografía e Estatística (IBGE), Ministerio de Planajamento, Orcamento e Gestao, www.ibge.gov.br/home/estatistica/economia/pevs/2007/default.shtm

IPS (2009) 'PARAGUAY – BRAZIL: Lugo to seek new terms for Itaipú Dams', 5 September, Inter Press Service, News Agency (see http://ipsnews.net/newsasp?idnews=43812)

Jesús, M. J. and Kohler, C. C. (2004) 'The commercial fishery of the Peruvian Amazon', *Fisheries*, vol 29, pp10–16

Jiahua, F. and Morris, G. (1992) 'Reservoir sedimentation. II: Reservoir desiltation and long-term storage capacity', *Journal of Hydraulic Engineering*, vol 118 (March), pp370–384

Kabat, P., Claussen, M., Dirmeyer, P. A., Gash, J. H. C., Bravo de Guenni, L., Meybeck, M., Pielke, R. A. Sr., Vorosmarty, C. J., Hutjes, R. W. A. and Lutkemeier, S. (eds) (2004) *Vegetation, Water, Humans and the Climate: A New Perspective on an Interactive System*, Springer Verlag, Berlin

Killeen, T. J. (2007) *A Perfect Storm in the Amazon Wilderness: Development and Conservation in the Context of the Initiative for Integration of the Regional Infrastructure of South America (IIRSA): Applications in Applied Biodiversity Science*, Center for Applied Biodiversity Science, Washington, DC

Lawrence, K. S., He Yi, Killeen, T. J. and Emmett, D. (2008) 'Financing conservation through ecosystem services: Implementation in Asia', presented at A Conference on Ecosystem Services (ACES), 'Using Science for Decision Making in Dynamic Systems', 8–11 December, Naples, FL

Malhi, Y., Roberts, J. T., Betts, R. A., Killeen, T. J., Li, W. and Nobre, C. A. (2008) 'Climate change, deforestation and the fate of the Amazon', *Science*, vol 319, pp169–172

Marengo, J., Soares, W., Saulo, C. and Nicolini, M. (2004) 'Climatology of the LLJ east of the Andes as derived from the NCEP reanalyses, characteristics and temporal variability', *Journal of Climate*, vol 17, pp2261–2279

Moss, G. and Moss, M. (2009) 'Brasil das Aguas', www.brasildasaguas.com.br/index.php

Nobre, C. A., Sellers, P. J. and Shukla, J. (1991) 'Amazonian deforestation and regional climate change', *Journal of Climate*, vol 4, pp957–988

Ortholand, J. Y. and Gane, A. (2004) 'Natural products and combinatorial chemistry: Back to the future', *Current Opinion in Chemical Biology*, vol 8, pp271–280

Palmieri, A., Shah, F. and Dinar, A. (2001) 'Economics of reservoir sedimentation and sustainable management of dams', *Journal of Environmental Management*, vol 61, pp149–163

Reid, W. V., Laird, S. A., Gamez, R., Sittenfeld, A., Janzen, D. H., Gollin, M. A. and Juma, C. (1993) 'A New Lease on Life', in Reid, W. V., Laird, S. A., Meyer, C. A., Gamez, R., Sittenfeld, A., Janzen, D. H., Gollin, M. A. and Juma, C. (eds) *Biodiversity Prospecting: Guidelines for Using Genetic and Biochemical Resources Sustainably and Equitably*, World Resources Institute, Washington, DC

Ruffino, M. L. (2001) *Strategies for Managing Biodiversity in Amazonian Fisheries*, The Brazilian Environmental and Renewable Natural Resources Institute (IBAMA), Manaus, Brazil, available at www.unep.org/bpsp/HTML%20files/TS-Fisheries2.html

Saatchi, S. S., Houghton, R. A., dos Santa Alvalá, R. C., Soares, J. V. and Yu, Y. (2007) 'Distribution of aboveground live biomass in the Amazon basin', *Global Change Biology*, vol 13, p816

Salati, E. and Nobre, C. A. (1991) 'Possible climatic impacts of tropical deforestation', *Climate Change*, vol 19, pp177–196

Verweij, P., Schouten, M., van Beukering, P., Triana, J., van der Leeuw, K. and Hess, S. (2009) *Keeping the Amazon Forests Standing: A Matter of Values*, World Wildlife Fund, Gland, Switzerland

World Bank (2009) *Directions in Hydropower*, International Bank for Reconstruction and Development/World Bank, Washington, DC

Appendix 2

Matrix Tables for Wetland and Forest Ecosystems

Coordinating lead authors
Unai Pascual, Roldan Muradian

Lead authors
Luke Brander, Erik Gómez-Baggethun, Berta Martín-López, Madhu Verma

Contributing authors
Paul Armsworth, Michael Christie, Hans Cornelissen, Florian Eppink, Joshua Farley, John Loomis, Leonie Pearson, Charles Perrings, Stephen Polasky

Reviewers
Jeffrey A. McNeely, Richard Norgaard, Rehana Siddiqui, R. David Simpson, R. Kerry Turner

Review editor
R. David Simpson

Table A2.1a Conceptual matrix based on wetland ecosystem services, benefits/value types and valuation approaches

WETLAND SERVICES	Stated preference	Revealed preference	Production based	Cost based	Benefits transfer
PROVISIONING					
Food (e.g. production of fish, wild game/hunting, fruits and grains)	**Choice modelling** Layton et al, 1998; Carlsson et al, 2003; **Contingent ranking** Emerton, 1996; **CVM** Bergstrom et al, 1990; Benessaiah 1998; Hanley and Craig, 1991; **Participatory valuation** Emerton, 2005; **Stakeholder analysis and CVM** Bhatta, 2000		**Factor income/ Production function** Barbier et al, 1991; Barbier, 1993; Costanza et al, 1997; Hodgson and Dixon, 1988; Emerton, 1998; Bann, 1999; Gammage, 1997; Barbier and Strand, 1998; Janssen and Padilla, 1996; Nickerson, 1999; Verma et al, 2003; Khalil, 1999; Emerton, 2005; Stuip et al, 2002; Benessaiah, 1998	**Opportunity cost** Dixon and Sherman, 1990; Hodgson and Dixon, 1988; Kramer et al, 1992, 1995; Emerton, 2005, Ruitenbeek, 1989a, 1989b **Public investments** Powicki, 1998; Emerton, 2005 **Replacement cost** Gren et al, 1994; Abila, 1998 **Restoration cost** Verma et al, 2003	**Benefits transfer** White et al, 2000; Stuip et al, 2002; Costanza et al, 1997
Water (e.g. storage and retention of water for domestic, industrial and agricultural use)		**Public investments** Powicki, 1998; Emerton, 2005	**Factor income** Emerton, 2005	**Opportunity cost** Emerton, 2005 **Replacement cost** Gren et al, 1994 **Restoration cost** Verma et al, 2003; Emerton, 2005	
Raw materials (e.g. fibres, timber, fuelwood, fodder, peat, fertilizer, construction material etc.)	**Contingent ranking** Emerton, 1996 **CVM** Hanley and Craig, 1991 **Participatory valuation** Emerton, 2005	**Public investments** Powicki, 1998; Emerton, 2005	**Factor income** Khalil, 1999; Verma et al, 2003; Emerton, 2005; Stuip et al 2002	**Opportunity cost** Emerton, 2005 **Replacement cost** Gren et al, 1994 **Restoration cost** Emerton, 2005; Verma et al, 2003	

WETLAND SERVICES	Stated preference	Revealed preference	Production based	Cost based	Benefits transfer
Genetic resources (e.g. biochemical production models and test organisms, genes for resistance to plant pathogens)	**Participatory valuation** Emerton, 2005				
Medicinal resources (e.g. extraction of medicines and other materials from biota)	**Participatory valuation** Emerton, 2005			**Avoided cost** Emerton, 2005 **Restoration cost** Emerton, 2005	
Ornamental resources species (e.g. aquarium fish and plants like lotus)	**Participatory valuation** Emerton, 2005				
Human habitat (e.g. forest provide housing to many dwellers)				**Conversion cost** Abila, 1998	
Transport (e.g. wetlands are source of navigation)					
REGULATING					
Air quality regulation (e.g. capturing dust particles)					
Climate regulation (e.g. source of and sink for greenhouse gases; influence local and regional temperature, precipitation, and other climatic processes incl. carbon sequestration)	**Participatory valuation** Emerton, 2005			**Avoided cost** Emerton, 1998, 2003	

WETLAND SERVICES	Stated preference	Revealed preference	Production based	Cost based	Benefits transfer
Moderation of extreme events (e.g storm protection, flood prevention, coastal protection, fire prevention)	**CVM** Hanley and Craig, 1991; Bateman and Turner, 1993 **Participatory valuation** Emerton, 2005			***Avoided cost*** Bann, 1999; Costanza et al, 1997 ***Replacement cost*** Farber and Costanza, 1987	
Regulation of water flows/hydrological regimes (e.g. natural drainage, flood-plain function, storage of water for agriculture or industry, drought prevention groundwater recharge/ discharge)	**Choice modelling** Adamowicz et al, 1994; Birol et al, 2007; Ragkos et al, 2006 **Participatory valuation** Emerton, 2005		***Factor income*** Acharya and Barbier, 2000	***Avoided cost*** Emerton, 2005 ***Replacement cost*** Gren et al, 1994 ***Restoration cost*** Emerton, 2005	
Water purification/ detoxification, and waste treatment/ pollution control (e.g. retention, recovery, and removal of excess nutrients and other pollutants)				***Avoided costs*** Verma et al, 2003 ***Replacement cost*** Emerton, 2005; Gren et al, 1994; Stuip et al, 2002 ***Restoration cost*** Verma et al, 2003	
Erosion prevention (e.g. retention of soils and sediments)	**CVM** Hanley and Craig, 1991; Bateman et al, 1995; Loomis, 2000 **Participatory valuation** Emerton, 2005				
Soil formation/ conservation (e.g. sediment retention and accumulation of organic matter) **Note**: should come under support services	**Choice modelling** Colombo et al, 2006, 2007 **CVM** Loomis, 2000			***Restoration cost*** Emerton, 2005	

WETLAND SERVICES	Stated preference	Revealed preference	Production based	Cost based	Benefits transfer
Pollination *(e.g. habitat for pollinators)*					
Biological control *(e.g. seed dispersal, pest species and disease control)*					
HABITAT/SUPPORT					
Biodiversity and nursery service *(e.g. habitats for resident or transient species)*	*Choice modelling* Brouwer et al, 1999			*Replacement cost* Gren et al, 1994	
Gene pool protection/ endangered species protection				*Replacement cost* Gren et al, 1994	
Nutrient cycling *(e.g. storage, recycling, processing and acquisition of nutrients)*				*Replacement cost* Gren et al, 1994	*Benefits transfer* Andréassen-Gren and Groth, 1995
CULTURAL					
Aesthetic *(e.g. appreciation of natural scenery, other than through deliberate recreational activities)*	*Choice modelling* Bergland, 1997	*Hedonic pricing* Verma et al, 2003			

WETLAND SERVICES	Stated preference	Revealed preference	Production based	Cost based	Benefits transfer
Recreation and tourism/ecotourism, wilderness (remote-non-use) (e.g. opportunities for tourism and recreational activities)	**Choice modelling** Boxall et al, 1996; Carlsson et al, 2003; Hanley et al, 2002; Horne et al, 2004; Boxall and Adamomicz, 2002; Adamowicz et al, 1994, 1998 **CVM** Thibodeau and Ostro, 1981; Murthy and Menkhuas, 1994; Manoharan, 1996; Costanza et al, 1997; Manoharan, 2000; Maharana et al, 2000; Wilson and Carpenter, 1999; Stuip et al, 2002; Bergstrom, 1990; Bell, 1997; Pak and Turker, 2006	**Consumer surplus** Bergstrom et al, 1990 **TCM** Farber and Costanza, 1987; Chopra et al, 1998; Manohoran, 1996; Pak and Turker, 2006; Willis and Garrod, 1991		**Opportunity cost** Loomis et al, 1989 **Replacement and conversion cost** Abila, 1998	**Benefits transfer** Sorg and Loomis, 1984; Loomis et al, 2000; Rosenberger and Loomis, 2000; Andréassen-Gren and Groth, 1995
Educational (e.g. opportunities for formal and informal education and training)					
Spiritual and artistic inspiration (e.g. source of inspiration; many religions attach spiritual, sacred and religious values to aspects of wetland and forest ecosystems)	**CVM** Maharana et al, 2000				
Cultural heritage and identity (e.g. sense of place and belonging)	**Choice modelling** Tuan and Navrud, 2007 **CVM** Shultz et al, 1998; Tuan and Navrud, 2007				
Information for cognitive development					

Table A2.1b Conceptual matrix based on forest ecosystem services, benefits/value types and valuation approaches

FOREST SERVICES	Stated preference	Revealed preference	Production based	Cost based	Benefits transfer
PROVISIONING					
Food (e.g. production of fish, wild game/hunting, fruits and grains)	**Contingent ranking** Lynam et al, 1994 **CVM** Gunawardena et al, 1999; Shaikh et al, 2007; Loomis, 1992	**Hedonic pricing** Livengood, 1983; Loomis, 1992 **Market price** Pattanayak and Kramer, 2001; Chopra and Kadekodi, 1997; Moskowitz and Talberth, 1998; Verma, 2008 **TCM** Barnhill, 1999; Loomis, 1992	**Factor income** Peters et al, 1989; Hodgson and Dixon, 1998; Carret and Loyer, 2003; Anderson, 1987	**Avoided cost** Bann, 1999 **Mitigation cost** **External cost** Emerton, 1999; Madhusudan, 2003 **Opportunity cost** Dixon and Sherman, 1990; Hodgson and Dixon, 1988; Kramer et al, 1992, 1995; Loomis et al, 1989; Ruitenbeek, 1989a, 1989b; Emerton, 1999 **Replacement cost** Rodriguez et al, 2007	**Benefits transfer** Costanza et al, 1997
Water (e.g. storage and retention of water for domestic, industrial and agricultural use)	**CVM** Sutherland and Walsh, 1985	**TCM** Whittington et al, 1990a, 1991	**Factor income** Dunkiel and Sugarman, 1998 **Production function** Aylward and Barbier, 1992; Kumari, 1996; Wilson and Carpenter, 1999	**Avoided cost** Chaturvedi, 1992 **Treatment/mitigation cost** Kumari, 1996	
Raw materials (e.g. fibres, timber, fuelwood, fodder, peat, fertilizer, construction material etc.)	**Contingent ranking** Emerton, 1996 **CVM** Kramer et al, 1992, 1995; Shaikh et al, 2007 **Multi-criteria analysis** Chopra and Kadekodi, 1997	**Market prices** Ammour et al, 2000; Jonish, 1992; Sedjo, 1988; Sedjo and Bowes, 1991; Verissimo et al, 1992; Uhl et al, 1992; Verma, 2000, 2008 **Net price method** Parikh and Haripriya, 1998 **Substitute goods** Adger et al, 1995; Gunatilake et al, 1993; Chopra, 1993; cited in Dixon et al, 1994	**Factor income** Anderson, 1987; Peters et al, 1989; Alcorn, 1989; Godoy and Feaw, 1989; Pearce, 1995; Howard, 1995; Pinedo-Vasquez et al, 1992; Ruitenbeek, 1989a, 1989b; Kumar and Chopra, 2004; Verma, 2008	**Opportunity cost** Chopra et al, 1990; Grieg-Gran, 2006; Kramer et al, 1995; Emerton, 1999; Butry and Pattanayak, 2001; Saastamoinen, 1992 **Replacement cost** Ammour et al, 2000	

FOREST SERVICES	Stated preference	Revealed preference	Production based	Cost based	Benefits transfer
Genetic resources (e.g. biochemical production models and test organisms, genes for resistance to plant pathogens)					
Medicinal resources (e.g. extraction of medicines and other materials from biota)		**Market price** Mendelsohn and Ballick, 1995; Kumar, 2004		**Replacement cost – forest rehabilitation** Cavatassi, 2004	
Ornamental resources species (e.g. aquarium fish and plants like lotus)					
Human habitat (e.g. forests provide housing to many dwellers)					
Transport (e.g wetlands are source of navigation)					
REGULATING					
Air quality regulation (e.g. capturing dust particles)	**Existence + bequest value** Haefele et al, 1992			**Market price/avoided cost** Nowak et al, 2006; Haefele et al, 1992 **Replacement cost** McPherson, 1992; Dwyer et al, 1992	

FOREST SERVICES	Stated preference	Revealed preference	Production based	Cost based	Benefits transfer
Climate regulation (e.g. source of and sink for greenhouse gases; influence local and regional temperature, precipitation, and other climatic processes incl. carbon sequestration)		**Market price** Clinch, 1999; Loomis and Richardson, 2000; Verma, 2008		**Avoided cost** van Kooten and Sohngen, 2007; Dunkiel and Sugarman, 1998; Pearce, 1994; Turner et al, 2003; Kadekodi and Ravindranath, 1997; McPherson, 1992; Dwyer et al, 1992; Pimentel and Wilson, 1997 **Damage cost** Howard, 1995 **Mitigation cost** Van Kooten and Sohngen, 2007 **Replacement cost** Howard, 1995	**Benefits transfer** Dunkiel and Sugarman, 1998; Loomis and Richardson, 2000
Moderation of extreme events (e.g. storm protection, flood prevention, coastal protection, fire prevention)	**CVM** Loomis et al, 2000		**Factor income** Anderson, 1987	**Avoided cost** Pattanayak and Kramer, 2001; Loomis and Gonzalez, 1997; Yaron, 2001; Ruitenbeek, 1992; Paris and Ruzicka, 1991; Myers, 1996 **Replacement cost** Bann, 1998a	
Regulation of water flows/hydrological regimes (e.g natural drainage, floodplain function, water storage for agriculture or industry, drought prevention, groundwater recharge/ discharge)		**Public investments** Ferraro, 2002	**Factor income** Pattanayak and Kramer, 2001	**Damage cost** Yaron, 2001 **Replacement cost** McPherson, 1992; Dwyer et al, 1992	

FOREST SERVICES	Stated preference	Revealed preference	Production based	Cost based	Benefits transfer
Water purification/ detoxification, waste treatment/pollution control (e.g. retention, recovery and removal of excess nutrients and other pollutants)		**TCM** Whittington et al, 1991		**Restoration cost** Adger et al, 1995	
Erosion prevention (e.g. retention of soils and sediments)				**Avoided costs** Bann, 1999; Paris and Ruzicka, 1991 **Replacement costs** Ammour et al, 2000; Kumar, 2005	
Soil formation/ conservation (e.g. sediment retention and accumulation of organic matter) Note: should come under support services	**CVM** Rodriguez et al, 2007			**Avoided cost** Paris and Ruzicka, 1991 **Reduced cost of alternate technology cost** Kadekodi and Ravindranath, 1997 **Replacement cost** Bann, 1998a; Ammour et al, 2000	
Pollination (e.g. habitat for pollinators)			**Factor income** Ricketts et al, 2004; Pattanayak and Kramer, 2001	**Replacement cost** Moskowitz and Talberth, 1998	
Biological control (e.g. seed dispersal, pest species and disease control)	**Option value** Walsh et al, 1984 **Existence + bequest value** Walsh et al, 1984			**Damage cost** Moskowitz and Talberth, 1998; Reid, 1999 **Replacement cost** Rodriguez et al, 2007	

FOREST SERVICES	Stated preference	Revealed preference	Production based	Cost based	Benefits transfer
HABITAT/SUPPORT					
Biodiversity and nursery service (e.g. habitats for resident or transient species)	**Choice modelling** Adamowicz et al, 1998; Hanley et al, 1998 **CVM** Duffield, 1992; Loomis and Ekstrand 1997; Rubin et al, 1991; Loomis et al, 1994; Hagen et al, 1992			**Opportunity cost** Howard, 1997 **Replacement cost** Rodriguez et al, 2007	
Gene pool protection/ endangered species protection		**Public investments** Siikamaki and Layton, 2007; Bruner et al, 2003; Strange et al, 2006; Polasky et al, 2001; Ando et al, 1998			
Nutrient cycling (e.g. storage, recycling, processing, and acquisition of nutrients)					
CULTURAL					
Aesthetic (e.g. appreciation of natural scenery, other than through deliberate recreational activities)		**Hedonic pricing** Garrod and Willis, 1992; Tyrvaninen and Meittinen, 2000; Kramer et al, 2003; Holmes et al, 1998 **TCM** Holmes et al,1998			

FOREST SERVICES	Stated preference	Revealed preference	Production based	Cost based	Benefits transfer
Recreation and tourism/ecotourism wilderness (remote-non-use) *(e.g. opportunities for tourism and recreational activities)*	***Choice modelling*** *Adamowicz et al, 1994; Boxall et al, 1996* ***CVM*** *Adger et al, 1995; Dixon and Sherman, 1990; Hadker et al, 1997; Kumari, 1995; Gunawardena et al, 1999; Flatley and Bennett, 1996; Bateman and Langford, 1997; Willis and Garrod, 1998; Hanley and Ruffell, 1991; Hanley and Ruffell, 1992; Whinteman and Sinclair, 1994; Brown, 1992; Sutherland and Walsh, 1985; Moskowitz and Talberth, 1998; Gilbert et al, 1992; Walsh et al, 1984; Clayton and Mendelsohn, 1993; Walsh and Loomis, 1989; Champ et al, 1997; Loomis and Richardson 2000* ***Participatory method*** *McDaniels and Roessler, 1998* ***Option value*** *Walsh et al, 1984*	***TCM*** *Tobias and Mendelsohn, 1991; Loomis, 1992; Adger et al, 1995; Kramer et al, 1995; Willis and Garrod, 1998; Chopra et al, 1998; Moskowitz and Talberth, 1998; Van Beukering et al, 2003; Manoharan, 1996; Manoharan, 2000; Loomis and Ekstrand, 1998; McDaniels and Roessler, 1998; Brown, 1992; Loomis and Richardson, 2000; Yuan and Christensen, 1992; Barnhill, Power, 1992; Verma, 1999; 2008*	***Production function/ Factor income*** *Hodgson and Dixon, 1988*		***Benefits transfer*** *Walsh and Loomis, 1989*

FOREST SERVICES	Stated preference	Revealed preference	Production based	Cost based	Benefits transfer
Educational *(e.g. opportunities for formal and informal education and training)*		**TCM** *Power, 1992*			
Spiritual and artistic inspiration *(e.g. source of inspiration; many religions attach spiritual, scared and religious values to aspects of wetland and forest ecosystems)*	**Deliberative monetary valuation** *Hanley et al, 2002;* **Contingent ranking** *Garrod and Willis, 1997* **CVM** *Maharana et al, 2000* **CVM/Choice modelling** *Kniivila et al, 2002; McDaniels and Roessler, 1998; Maharana et al, 2000*	**TCM** *Maharana et al, 2000*			
Cultural heritage and identity *(e.g. sense of place and belonging)*					
Information for cognitive development					

Table A2.2a Conceptual matrix based on wetland ecosystem services and valuation approaches

SERVICES	Wetlands				
	Stated preference	Revealed preference	Production based	Cost based	Benefits transfer
PROVISIONING	**Choice modelling** Layton et al, 1998; Carlsson et al, 2003 **Contingent ranking** Emerton, 1996 **CVM** Bergstrom, 1990; Costanza et al, 1997; Benessaiah, 1998; Bhatta, 2000; Hanley and Craig, 1991 **Participatory valuation** Emerton, 2005	**Public investments** Powicki, 1998; Emerton, 2005	**Factor income/** **Production function** Barbier et al, 1991; Barbier, 1993; Costanza et al, 1997; Hodgson and Dixon, 1988; Emerton, 1998, 2005; Bann, 1999; Gammage, 1997; Barbier and Strand, 1998; Janssen and Padilla, 1996; Nickerson, 1999; Verma et al, 2003; Khalil, 1999; Stuip et al, 2002; Benessaiah, 1998	**Avoided cost** Emerton, 2005 **Conversion cost** Abila, 1998 **Public investments** Powicki, 1998; Emerton, 2005 **Opportunity cost** Dixon and Sherman, 1990; Hodgson and Dixon, 1988; Kramer et al, 1992, 1995; Emerton, 2005; Ruitenbeek, 1989a, 1989b **Replacement cost** Gren et al, 1994; Abila, 1998 **Restoration cost** Verma et al, 2003; Emerton, 2005	**Benefits transfer** White et al, 2000; Stuip et al, 2002; Costanza et al, 1997; Schuijt, 2002; Seidl and Moraes, 2000
REGULATING	**Choice modelling** Adamowicz et al, 1994; Birol and Cox, 2007; Ragkos et al, 2006; Colombo et al, 2007; Colombo and Turner, 2006 **CVM** Hanley and Craig, 1991; Bateman and Turner, 1993; Loomis, 2000 **Participatory valuation** Emerton, 2005		**Production function/** **Factor income** Acharya and Barbier, 2000	**Avoided cost** Emerton, 1998, 2003, 2005; Bann, 1999; Verma et al, 2003 **Replacement cost** Farber and Costanza, 1987; Gren et al, 1994; Emerton, 2005; IUCN, 2003; Stuip et al, 2002 **Restoration cost** Emerton, 2005; Verma et al, 2003	**Benefits transfer** Costanza et al, 1997; Seidl and Moraes, 2000

SERVICES	Wetlands				
	Stated preference	Revealed preference	Production based	Cost based	Benefits transfer
HABITAT/SUPPORT	**Choice modelling** Brouwer et al, 1999 **CVM** Ragkos et al, 2006		**Production function/ Factor income** Barbier and Thompson, 1998; Johnston, 2002; Lynne et al, 1981; Ramdial, 1975	**Replacement cost** Gren et al, 1994	**Benefits transfer** Andréassen-Gren and Groth, 1995; White et al, 2000
CULTURAL	**Choice modelling** Bergland, 1997; Tuan and Navrud, 2007; Boxall et al, 1996; Carlsson et al, 2003; Hanley et al, 2002; Horne et al, 2004; Boxall and Adamowicz, 2002; Adamowicz et al, 1994, 1998; Pak and Turker, 2006 **CVM** Thibodeu and Ostro, 1981; Murthy and Menkhuas, 1994; Manoharan, 1996; Costanza et al, 1997; Manoharan, 2000; Maharana et al, 2000; Wilson and Carpenter, 1999; Stuip et al, 2002; Bergstrom et al, 1990; Bell, 1997; Shultz et al, 1998; Tuan et al, 2007	**Consumer surplus** Bergstrom et al, 1990 **Hedonic pricing** Verma et al, 2003 **TCM** Farber and Costanza, 1987; Willis and Garrod, 1991; Chopra et al, 1998; Manoharan, 1996; Pak and Turker, 2006	**Production function/ Factor income** Costanza et al, 1989	**Opportunity cost** Loomis et al, 1989 **Replacement cost** Abila, 1998	**Benefits transfer** Andréassen-Gren and Groth, 1995; Sorg and Loomis, 1984; Loomis et al, 1999; Rosenberger and Loomis, 2000; Seidl and Moraes, 2000; White et al, 2000

Table A2.2b Conceptual matrix based on forest ecosystem services and valuation approaches

SERVICES	Forest				
	Stated preference	Revealed preference	Production based	Cost based	Benefits transfer
PROVISIONING	**Contingent ranking** Lynam et al, 1994; Emerton, 1996 **CVM** Gunawardena et al,1999; Shaikh et al, 2007; Kramer et al, 1992, 1995; Loomis, 1992; Sutherland and Walsh, 1985 **Existence + bequest value** Haefele et al, 1992 **Multi-criteria analysis** Chopra and Kadekodi, 1997	**Hedonic pricing** Livengood, 1983; Loomis, 1992 **Market price** Pattanayak and Kramer, 2001; Ammour et al, 2000; Chopra and Kadekodi, 1997; Moskowitz and Talberth, 1998; Jonish, 1992; Sedjo, 1988; Sedjo and Bowes, 1991; Verissimo et al, 1992; Verma, 2000, 2008; Mendelsohn and Ballick, 1995; Kumar, 2004; Uhl et al, 1992 **Net price method** Parikh and Haripriya, 1998 **Substitute goods** Adger et al, 1995; Gunatilake et al, 1993; Chopra, 1993 **TCM** Whittington et al, 1990a, 1991; Barnhill, 1999; Loomis, 1992	**Factor income** Dunkiel and Sugarman, 1998; Peters et al, 1989; Hodgson and Dixon, 1998; Carret and Loyer, 2003; Anderson, 1987; Alcorn, 1989; Godoy and Feaw, 1989; Howard 1995; Pearce, 1991; Pinedo-Vasquez et al, 1992; Ruitenbeek, 1989a, 1989b; Verma, 2008 **Production function** Aylward and Barbier, 1992; Kumari, 1996; Wilson and Carpenter, 1999; Kumar and Chopra, 2004	**Avoided cost** Bann, 1999; Chaturvedi, 1992 **Mitigation cost** Emerton, 1999; Madhusudan, 2003 **Opportunity cost** Dixon and Sherman, 1990; Hodgson and Dixon, 1988; Kramer et al, 1992, 1995; Loomis et al, 1989; Ruitenbeek, 1989a, 1989b; Emerton, 1999; Chopra et al, 1990; Grieg-Gran, 2006; Butry and Pattanayak, 2001; Saastamoinen, 1992 **Rehabilitation cost** Cavatassi, 2004 **Replacement cost** Ammour et al, 2000; Rodriguez et al, 2007 **Treatment/mitigation cost** Kumari, 1996	**Benefits transfer** Costanza et al, 1997

SERVICES	Forest				
	Stated preference	**Revealed preference**	**Production based**	**Cost based**	**Benefits transfer**
REGULATING	***CVM*** *Loomis et al, 2000; Rodriguez et al, 2007* ***Option value*** *Walsh et al, 1984*	***Market price*** *Clinch, 1999; Loomis and Richardson, 2000; Verma, 2008* ***Public investments*** *Ferraro, 2002* ***TCM*** *Whittington et al, 1990a, 1991*	***Factor income*** *Anderson, 1987; Pattanayak and Kramer, 2001; Ricketts et al, 2004*	***Avoided cost*** *Novak et al, 2006; Haefele et al, 1992; van Kooten and Sohngen, 2007; Dunkiel and Sugarman, 1998; Pearce, 1994; Turner et al, 2003; Kadekodi and Ravindranath, 1997; Bann, 1999; Paris and Ruzicka, 1991; McPherson, 1992; Dwyer et al, 1992; Pimentel et al, 1997; Myers, 1996* ***Damage cost*** *Howard, 1995; Yaron, 2001; Moskowitz and Talberth, 1998; Reid, 1999* ***Mitigation cost*** *Van Kooten and Sohngen, 2007* ***Reduced cost of alternate technology cost*** *Kadekodi and Ravindranath, 1997* ***Restoration cost*** *Adger et al, 1995* ***Replacement cost*** *Howard, 1995; Ammour et al, 2000; Kumar, 2005; Dwyer McPherson 1992; Dwyer et al, 1992; Moskowitz and Talberth, 1998; Rodriguez et al, 2007*	***Benefits transfer*** *Dunkiel and Sugarman, 1998; Loomis and Richardson, 2000*

SERVICES	Forest				
	Stated preference	Revealed preference	Production based	Cost based	Benefits transfer
HABITAT/ SUPPORT	*Choice modelling* Adamowicz et al, 1998; Hanley et al, 1998 **CVM** Duffield, 1992; Loomis and Ekstrand, 1997; Rubin et al, 1991; Loomis et al, 1994; Hagen et al, 1992	*Public investments* Siikamaki and Layton, 2007; Burner et al, 2003; Strange et al, 2006; Polasky et al, 2001; Ando et al, 1998		*Opportunity cost* Howard, 1997 *Replacement cost* Rodriguez et al, 2007	
CULTURAL	*Choice modelling* Kniivila et al, 2002; McDaniels and Roessler, 1998; Maharana et al, 2000 *Contingent ranking* Garrod and Willis, 1997 **CVM** Maharana et al, 2000; Brown, 1992; Sutherland and Walsh, 1985; Moskowitz and Talberth, 1998; Gilbert et al, 1992; Walsh et al, 1984; Clayton and Mendelsohn, 1993; Walsh and Loomis, 1989; Champ et al, 1977; Loomis and Richardson, 2000; Verma, 2008	*Hedonic pricing* Garrod and Willis, 1992; Tyrvaninen and Meittinen, 2000; Kramer et al, 2003 **TCM** Tobias and Mendelsohn, 1991; Loomis, 1992; Adger et al, 1995; Kramer et al, 1995; Willis and Garrod, 1998; Chopra et al, 1998; Moskowitz and Talberth, 1998; Van Beukering et al, 2003; Manoharan, 1996; Manoharan, 2000; Loomis and Ekstrand, 1998;	*Production function/ Factor income* Hodgson and Dixon, 1988		*Benefits transfer* Walsh and Loomis, 1989

SERVICES	Forest				
	Stated preference	Revealed preference	Production based	Cost based	Benefits transfer
	Deliberative monetary valuation Hanley et al, 2002 **Option value** Walsh et al, 1984	McDaniels and Roessler, 1998; Maharana et al, 2000; Holmes et al, 1998; Power, 1992; Brown, 1992; Loomis and Richardson, 2000; Yuan and Christensen, 1992; Power, 1992; Barnhill, 1999			

Table A2.3 Matrix linking specific value types, valuation methods and ecosystem services: Examples from wetland and forest ecosystems

SERVICES	Wetlands				Forests			
	Direct use	Indirect use	Option use	Non-use	Direct use	Indirect use	Option use	Non-use
PROVISIONING								
1 *Food* (e.g. production of fish, wild game/hunting, fruits and grains)	***Stated preference*** **Choice modelling** Layton et al, 1998; Carlsson et al, 2003 **Contingent ranking** Emerton, 1996 **CVM** Bergstrom, 1990; Costanza et al, 1997; Benessaiah, 1998 **Participatory valuation** Emerton, 2005 ***Production based*** **Factor income/ production function** Barbier et al, 1991, 1993; Costanza et al, 1997; Hodgson and Dixon, 1988; Emerton, 1998; Bann, 1999; Gammage, 1997; Barbier and Strand, 1998; Janssen and Padilla, 1996; Nickerson, 1999; Verma, 2001; Khalil, 1999; Emerton, 2005; Stuip et al, 2002; Benessaian, 1998 ***Cost based*** **Replacement cost** Gren et al, 1994; Abila, 1998 ***Benefits transfer*** **Benefits transfer** White et al, 2000; Stuip et al, 2002	*NA*	***Stated preference*** **CVM** Costanza et al, 1997 **Stakeholder analysis and CVM** Bhatta, 2000 ***Cost based*** **Restoration cost** Emerton, 2005	*NA*	***Stated preference*** **Contingent ranking** Lynam et al, 1994 **CVM** Gunawardena et al, 1999; Shaikh et al, 2007; Loomis, 1992 ***Revealed preference*** **Hedonic pricing** Livengood, 1983; Loomis, 1992 **Market price** Pattanayak and Kramer, 2001; Chopra and Kadekodi, 1997; Verma, 2008 **TCM** Barnhill, 1999; Loomis, 1992 ***Production based*** **Factor income** Peters et al, 1989; Hodgson and Dixon, 1998; Carret and Loyer, 2003; Anderson, 1987; Moskowitz and Talberth, 1998; Verma, 2008 ***Cost based*** **Mitigation cost** **External cost** Emerton, 1999; Madhusudan, 2003 **Net revenue** **Avoided cost** Bann, 1999 **Opportunity cost** Dixon and Sherman, 1990; Hodgson and Dixon, 1988; Kramer et al, 1992, 1995; Loomis et al, 1989; Ruitenbeek, 1989a, 1989b; Emerton, 1999 **Replacement cost** Rodriguez et al, 2007	*NA*	*NA*	*NA*

SERVICES	Wetlands				Forests			
	Direct use	Indirect use	Option use	Non-use	Direct use	Indirect use	Option use	Non-use
2 **Water** (e.g. storage and retention of water for domestic, industrial and agricultural use)	**Stated preference** <u>Participatory valuation</u> IUCN-WANI, 2000 **Revealed preference** <u>Public investments</u> Powicki, 1998; Emerton, 2005 **Production based** <u>Factor income</u> Emerton, 2005 **Cost based** <u>Opportunity cost</u> Emerton, 2005 <u>Replacement cost</u> Gren et al, 1994 <u>Restoration cost</u> Verma, 2001	NA	**Cost based** <u>Restoration cost</u> Emerton, 2005	NA	**Revealed preference** <u>TCM</u> Whittington et al, 1990a, 1991 **Production based** <u>Factor income</u> Kumari, 1995; Dunkiel and Sugarman, 1998 **Production function** Aylward and Barbier,1992; Kumari, 1996; Wilson and Carpenter, 1999 **Cost based** <u>Avoided cost</u> Chaturvedi, 1992 **Treatment/Mitigation cost** Kumari, 1996	NA	**Stated preference** <u>CVM</u> Chopra and Kadekodi, 1997	NA
3 **Raw materials** (e.g. fibres, timber, fuelwood, fodder, peat, fertilizer, construction material etc.)	**Stated preference** <u>Contingent ranking</u> Emerton, 1996 <u>CVM</u> Hanley and Craig, 1991 **Participatory valuation** Emerton, 2005 **Production based** <u>Factor income</u> Khalil, 1999; Verma, 2001; Emerton, 2005; Stuip et al, 2002	NA	**Stated preference** **Cost based** <u>Restoration cost</u> Emerton, 2005	NA	**Stated preference** <u>Contingent ranking</u> Emerton, 1996 <u>CVM</u> Kramer et al, 1992, 1995; Shaikh et al, 2007 <u>Multi-criteria analysis</u> Chopra and Kadekodi, 1997 **Revealed preference** <u>Market prices</u> Ammour et al, 2000; Jonish, 1992; Sedjo, 1988; Sedjo and Bowes, 1991; Veríssimo et al, 1992; Verma, 2000, 2008; Uhl et al, 1992	NA	**Stated preference** <u>CVM</u> Ninan and Sathyapalan, 2005 **Cost based** <u>Shadow price</u> Godoy and Feaw, 1989	NA

SERVICES	Wetlands				Forests			
	Direct use	Indirect use	Option use	Non-use	Direct use	Indirect use	Option use	Non-use
	Cost based ***Opportunity cost*** *Dixon and Sherman, 1990; Hodgson and Dixon, 1988; Kramer et al, 1992, 1995; Emerton, 2005; Ruitenbeek, 1989a, 1989b* ***Replacement cost*** *Gren et al, 1994*				***Net price method*** *Parikh and Haripriya, 1998* ***Substitute goods*** *Adger et al, 1995; Gunatilake et al, 1993; Chopra, 1993* ***Production based*** ***Factor income*** *Anderson, 1987; Peters et al, 1989; Alcorn, 1989; Godoy and Feaw, 1989; Howard, 1995; Pearce, 1991; Pinedo-Vasquez et al, 1992; Ruitenbeek, 1989a, 1989b; Kumar and Chopra, 2004; Verma, 2008* ***Cost based*** ***Opportunity cost*** *Chopra et al, 1990; Grieg-Gran, 2006; Kramer et al, 1995; Emerton et al, 1999; Butry and Pattanayak, 2001; Saastamoinen, 1992* ***Replacement cost*** *Ammour et al, 2000*			
4 ***Genetic resources*** *(e.g. biochemical production models and test organisms, genes for resistance to plant pathogens)*	***Stated preference*** *Participatory valuation* *Emerton, 2005*	*NA*				*NA*		*NA*

SERVICES	Wetlands				Forests			
	Direct use	Indirect use	Option use	Non-use	Direct use	Indirect use	Option use	Non-use
5 Medicinal resources (e.g. extraction of medicines and other materials from biota)	Stated preference Participatory valuation Emerton, 2005 Cost based Avoided cost Emerton, 2005	NA	Cost based Restoration cost Emerton, 2005	NA	Revealed preference Market price Mendelsohn and Ballick, 1995; Kumar, 2004 Cost based Replacement cost/forest rehabilitation Cavatassi, 2004	NA		NA
6 Ornamental resources species (e.g. aquarium fish and plants like lotus)	Stated preference Participatory valuation Emerton, 2005	NA		NA		NA		NA
Human habitat (e.g. forest provide housing to many dwellers)		NA		NA		NA		NA
Transport (e.g. wetlands are source of navigation)	Cost based Conversion cost Abila, 1998	NA		NA		NA		NA
REGULATING								
7 Air quality regulation (e.g. capturing dust particles)	NA	NA			NA	Cost based Market price/ Avoided cost Nowak et al, 2006; Haefele et al, 1992 Replacement cost McPherson, 1992; Dwyer et al, 1992		NA Existence + bequest value Haefele et al, 1992

SERVICES	Wetlands				Forests			
	Direct use	Indirect use	Option use	Non-use	Direct use	Indirect use	Option use	Non-use
Climate regulation (e.g. source of and sink for greenhouse gases; influence local and regional temperature, precipitation, and other climatic processes incl. carbon sequestration)	*NA*	***Stated preference*** **Participatory valuation** Emerton, 2005 **<u>Cost based</u>** **Avoided cost** Emerton, 1998, 2003		*NA*	*NA*	***Revealed preference*** **Market price** Clinch, 1999; Loomis and Richardson, 2000; Verma, 2008 **<u>Cost based</u>** **Avoided cost** van Kooten and Sohngen, 2007; Dunkiel and Sugarman, 1998; Pearce, 1994; Turner et al, 2003; Kadekodi and Ravindranath, 1997; McPherson, 1992; Dwyer et al, 1992; Pimentel et al, 1997 **Damage cost** Howard, 1995 **Mitigation cost** van Kooten and Sohngen, 2007 **Replacement cost** Howard, 1995 **<u>Benefits transfer</u>** **Benefits transfer** Dunkiel and Sugarman, 1998; Loomis and Richardson, 2000		*NA*

SERVICES	Wetlands				Forests			
	Direct use	Indirect use	Option use	Non-use	Direct use	Indirect use	Option use	Non-use
9 *Moderation of extreme events* (e.g. storm protection, flood prevention, coastal protection, fire prevention)	*NA*	***Stated preference*** **CVM** *Hanley and Craig, 1991; Bateman and Turner, 1993* **Participatory valuation** *Emerton, 2005* **Cost based** **Avoided cost** *Bann, 1999; Costanza et al, 1997* **Replacement cost** *Farber and Costanza, 1987*		*NA*	*NA*	***Stated preference*** **CVM** *Loomis and Gonzalez, 1997* **Production based** **Factor income** *Anderson, 1987* **Cost based** **Avoided cost** *Pattanayak and Kramer, 2001; Loomis and Gonzalez, 1997; Yaron, 2001; Ruitenbeek, 1992; Paris and Ruzicka, 1991; Myers, 1996* **Replacement cost** *Bann, 1998a*		*NA*

SERVICES	Wetlands				Forests			
	Direct use	Indirect use	Option use	Non-use	Direct use	Indirect use	Option use	Non-use
10 **Regulation of water flows/hydrological regimes** (e.g. natural drainage, floodplain function, storage of water for agriculture or industry, drought prevention, groundwater recharge/discharge)	*NA*	**_Stated preference_** **Choice modelling** *Adamowicz et al, 1994; Birol and Cox, 2007; Ragkos et al, 2006* **Participatory valuation** *Emerton, 2005* **_Production based_** **Factor income** *Acharya and Barbier, 2000* **Cost based** **Avoided cost** *Emerton, 2005* **Replacement cost** *Gren et al, 1994* **Restoration cost** *Emerton, 2005*		*NA*	*NA*	**_Revealed preference_** **Public investments** *Ferraro, 2002* **_Production based_** **Factor income** *Pattanayak and Kramer, 2001*	**PES** *Proano, 2005*	*NA*
11 **Water purification/ detoxification, and waste treatment/ pollution control** (e.g. retention, recovery and removal of excess nutrients and other pollutants)	*NA*	**Cost based** **Avoided costs** *Verma, 2001* **Restoration cost** *Verma, 2001* **Replacement cost** *Emerton, 2005; Gren et al, 1994; IUCN, 2003; Stuip et al, 2002*		*NA*	*NA*	**_Revealed preference_** **TCM** *Whittington et al, 1990a, 1991* **Cost based** **Restoration cost** *Adger et al, 1995*		*NA*

	SERVICES	Wetlands				Forests			
		Direct use	Indirect use	Option use	Non-use	Direct use	Indirect use	Option use	Non-use
12	**Erosion prevention** (e.g. retention of soils and sediments)	*NA*	**Stated preference** *CVM* *Hanley and Craig, 1991; Bateman and Turner, 1993; Loomis, 2000* **Participatory valuation** *Emerton, 2005*		*NA*	*NA*	**Cost based** **Replacement costs/ Avoided costs** *Ammour et al, 2000; Kumar, 2005; Bann, 1999; Paris and Ruzicka, 1991*		*NA*
13	**Soil formation/ conservation** (e.g. sediment retention and accumulation of organic matter) Note: should come under support services	*NA*	**Stated preference** *Choice modelling* *Colombo et al, 2006, 2007* *CVM* *Loomis, 2000* **Cost based** **Restoration cost** *Emerton, 2005*		*NA*	*NA*	**Stated preference** *CVM* *Rodriguez et al, 2007* **Cost based** **Avoided cost** *Paris and Ruzicka, 1991* **Income factor/ Replacement cost** *Bann, 1998a; Ammour et al, 2000* **Reduced cost of alternate technology cost** *Kadekodi, 1997*		*NA*

SERVICES	Wetlands				Forests			
	Direct use	Indirect use	Option use	Non-use	Direct use	Indirect use	Option use	Non-use
14 **Pollination** (e.g. habitat for pollinators)	*NA*			*NA*	*NA*	*Production based* **Factor income** *Ricketts et al, 2004; Patta-nayak and Kramer, 2000* **Cost based** **Replacement cost** *Moskowitz and Talberth, 1998*		*NA*
15 **Biological control** (e.g. seed dispersal, pest species and disease control)	*NA*			*NA*	*NA*	**Cost based** **Damage cost** *Moskowitz and Talberth, 1998; Reid, 1999* **Replacement cost** *Rodriguez et al, 2007*	**Stated preference** **Option value** *Walsh et al, 1984*	*NA* **Existence + Bequest value** *Walsh et al, 1984*
HABITAT/ SUPPORT								
16 **Biodiversity and Nursery service** (e.g. habitats for resident or transient species)	**Stated preference** **Choice modelling** *Brouwer et al, 1999*		**Cost based** **Replacement cost** *Gren et al, 1994*				**Cost based** **Opportunity cost** *Howard, 1997* **Replacement cost** *Rodriguez et al, 2007*	
17 **Gene pool protection/ endangered species protection**			**Stated preference** **Cost based** **Replacement cost** *Gren et al, 1994; Bateman et al, 1995*		**Revealed preference** **Public investments** *Siikamaki and Layton, 2007; Bruner et al, 2003; Strange et al, 2006; Polasky et al, 2001; Ando et al, 1998*		**Cost based** **Opportunity cost** *Chomitz et al, 2005*	**Stated preference** **CVM** *Lehtonen et al, 2003; Mallawaarachi et al, 2001; Garber-Yonts et al, 2004*

SERVICES	Wetlands				Forests			
	Direct use	Indirect use	Option use	Non-use	Direct use	Indirect use	Option use	Non-use
Nutrient cycling *(e.g. storage, recycling, processing and acquisition of nutrients)*		*Stated preference* **Choice modelling** *Carlsson et al, 2003* *Cost based* **Replacement cost** *Gren et al, 1994* *Benefits transfer* **Benefits transfer** *Andréassen Gren and Groth, 1995*						
CULTURAL								
18 **Aesthetic** *(e.g. appreciation of natural scenery, other than through deliberate recreational activities)*	*Stated preference* **Choice modelling** *Bergland, 1997* *Revealed preference* **Hedonic pricing** *Verma, 2000*	NA			*Revealed preference* **Hedonic pricing** *Garrod and Willis, 1992; Tyrvaninen and Meittinen, 2000; Kramer et al, 2003; Holmes et al, 1998* **TCM** *Holmes et al, 1998*	NA		

SERVICES	Wetlands				Forests			
	Direct use	Indirect use	Option use	Non-use	Direct use	Indirect use	Option use	Non-use
19	*Recreation and tourism/Ecotourism, Wilderness (remote-non-use)* (e.g. opportunities for tourism and recreational activities)	*NA*				*NA*	*Stated preference* *Option value* Walsh et al, 1984 *Revealed preference* *Expenditure on wilderness* Balmford et al, 2002	*Stated preference* *Choice Modelling* Hanley et al, 1998 *CVM* Loomis and Richardson, 2000; Kramer et al, 1995; Murthy and Menkhua, 1994; Dixon and Pagiola, 1998; Maharana et al, 2000; Hanley et al, 2002; Garrod and Willis, 1997; Gong, 2003; Dixon and Sherman, 1990; Adger et al, 1995; Walsh et al, 1984; Kramer and Mercer, 1997; Gunawardena et al, 1999; Lockwood et al, 1993
	Stated preference *Choice modelling* Boxall et al, 1996; Carlsson et al, 2003; Hanley et al, 2002; Horne et al, 2004; Boxall and Adamowicz, 2002; Adamowicz et al, 1994, 1998 *CVM* Thibodeu and Ostro, 1981; Murthy and Menkhuas, 1994; Manoharan, 1996; Costanza et al, 1997; Manoharan, 2000; Maharana and Sharma, 2000; Wilson and Carpenter, 1999; Stuip et al, 2002; Bergstrom et al, 1990; Bell, 1997; Pak and Turker, 2006 *Revealed preference* *Consumer surplus* Bergstrom et al, 1990 *TCM* Farber and Costanza, 1987; Chopra et al 1998; Hadker et al, 1997; Manoharan, 1996; Pak and Turker, 2006; Willis and Garrod, 1991 *Cost based* *Opportunity cost* Loomis et al, 1989				*Stated preference* *Choice modelling* Adamowicz et al, 1994; Boxall et al, 1996; *CVM* Adger et al, 1995; Dixon and Sherman, 1990; Hadker et al, 1997; Kumari, 1995; Gunawardena et al, 1999; Flatley and Bennett, 1996; Bateman and Langford, 1997; Willis and Garrod, 1998; Bateman et al, 1995; Hanley and Ruffell, 1991, 1992; Whiteman and Sinclair, 1994; Brown, 1992; Sutherland and Walsh, 1985; Moskowitz and Walsh, 1985; Talberth, 1998; Gilbert et al, 1992; Walsh et al, 1984; Clayton and Mendelsohn, 1993; Walsh and Loomis, 1989; Champ et al, 1997; Loomis and Richardson, 2000 *Participatory method* McDaniels and Roessler, 1998 *Revealed preference* *TCM* Tobias and Mendelsohn, 1991; Loomis, 1992; Adger et al, 1995; Kramer et al, 1995; Willis et al, 1998; Chopra et al, 1998; Moskowitz and Talbert, 1998; Van Beukering and Talbert, 2003; Manoharan, 1996; Manoharan, 2000; Loomis and Ekstrand, 1998; McDaniels and Roessler, 1998; Brown, 1992; Loomis and Richardson, 2000; Yuan and Christensen, 1992; Power, 1992; Barnhill, 1999; Verma, 2008			

SERVICES	Wetlands				Forests			
	Direct use	Indirect use	Option use	Non-use	Direct use	Indirect use	Option use	Non-use
	Replacement and conversion cost Abila, 1998 *Benefits transfer* *Benefits transfer* Sorg and Loomis, 1984; Loomis et al, 1999; Rosenberger and Loomis, 2000; Andréassen-Gren and Groth, 1995				*Production based* *Function/factor income* Hodgson and Dixon, 1988 *Benefits transfer* *Production* *Benefits transfer* Walsh and Loomis, 1989			
20 **Educational** *(e.g. opportunities for formal and informal education and training)*	NA				*Revealed preference* *TCM* Power, 1992	NA		
21 **Spiritual and artistic inspiration** *(e.g. source of inspiration; many religions attach spiritual, sacred and religious values to aspects of wetland and forest ecosystems)*	*Stated preference* *CVM* Maharana and Sharma, 2000				*Revealed preference* *TCM and CVM* Maharana and Sharma, 2000			*Stated preference* **Contingent ranking** Garrod and Willis, 1997 **CVM/Choice modelling** Kniivila et al, 2002; McDaniels and Roessler, 1998; Maharana and Sharma, 2000 **Deliberative monetary valuation** Hanley et al, 2002

SERVICES	Wetlands				Forests			
	Direct use	Indirect use	Option use	Non-use	Direct use	Indirect use	Option use	Non-use
Cultural heritage and identity (e.g. sense of place and belonging)	**Stated preference Choice modelling** *Tuan et al, 2007* **CVM** *Shultz et al, 1998; Tuan et al, 2007*	*NA*				*NA*		
22 **Information for cognitive development** Total economic value	Kirkland, 1988; Thibodeau and Ostro, 1981; Seidl and Moraes, 2000; de Groot, 1992; Emerton and Kekulandala, 2003; Costanza et al, 1997							
Combination of economic values of wetlands/forests	**Benefits transfer** *Costanza et al, 1997; Stuip et al, 2002*	**Benefits transfer** *Stuip et al, 2002, Seidl and Moraes, 2000; de Groot, 1992*	**Benefits transfer** *Costanza et al, 1997; Stuip et al, 2002*	**Benefits transfer** *Costanza et al, 1997; Stuip et al, 2002*	**Benefits transfer** *Costanza et al, 1997; Stuip et al, 2002*	**Benefits transfer** *Costanza et al, 1997; Stuip et al, 2002*	**Benefits transfer** *Costanza et al, 1997; Stuip et al, 2002*	**Benefits transfer** *Costanza et al, 1997; Stuip et al, 2002*

Note: NA = Not applicable – that is, particular combination of value type and use is unlikely (based on TEV+ MA classification amalgamation matrix).

References

Abila, R. (1998) 'Utilization and economic valuation of the Yala Swamp Wetland' University College, Kenya

Acharya, G. and Barbier, E. (2000) 'Valuing ground water recharge through agricultural production in the Hadejia–Nguru wetlands in Northern Nigeria', *Agricultural Economics*, vol 22, pp247–259

Adamowicz, W., Louviere, J. and Williams, M. (1994) 'Combining revealed and stated preference methods for valuing environmental amenities', *Journal of Environmental Economics and Management*, vol 26, no 3, pp271–292

Adamowicz, W., Boxall, P., Williams, M. and Louviere, J. (1998) 'Stated preference approaches for measuring passive use values: Choice experiments and contingent valuation', *American Journal of Agricultural Economics*, vol 80, pp64–75

Adger, W. N., Brown, K., Cerigni, R. and Moran, D. (1995) 'Total economic value of forests in Mexico', *Ambio*, vol 24, no 5, pp286–296

Alcorn, J. (1989) '*An Economic Analysis of Huastec Mayan Forest Management. Fragile Land of Latin America: Strategies for Sustainable Development*, J. Brouwer, Westview Press, Boulder, CO, pp182–206

Aylward, B., Barbier, E.B. (1992) 'Valuing environmental functions in developing countries', *Biodiversity and Conservation*, vol 1, pp34–52

Ammour, T., Windevoxhel, N. and Sencion, G. (2000) *Economic Valuation of Mangrove Ecosystems and Subtropical Forests in Central America: Sustainable Forest Management and Global Climate Change*, Edward Elgar, Cheltenham, pp166–197

Anderson, D. (1987) *The Economics of Afforestation: A Case Study in Africa*, World Bank Occasional Papers, New Series, World Bank, Washington, DC

Andreassen-Gren, M. and Groth, K. H. (1995) 'Economic evaluation of Danube floodplain', WWF International, Gland, Switzerland

Ando, A., Camm, J., Polasky, S. and Solow, A. (1998) 'Species distributions, land values, and efficient conservation', *Science*, vol 279, no 5359, p2126–2128

Balmford A., Bruner, A., Cooper, P., Costanza, R., Farber, S., Green, R. E., Jenkins, M., Jefferiss, P., Jessamy, V., Madden, J., Munro, K., Myers, N., Naeem, S., Paavola, J., Rayment, M., Rosendo, S., Roughgarden, J., Trumper, K. and Turner, R. K. (2002) 'Economic reasons for conserving wild nature', *Science*, vol 297, pp950–953

Bann, C. (1997) *An Economic Analysis of Tropical Forest Land Use Options, Ratanakiri Province, Cambodia*, Economy and Environment Program for Southeast Asia, Ottawa, Canada

Bann, C. (1998a) *The Economic Value of Tropical Forest land Use Options: A Manual for Researchers*, Economy and Environment Program for Southeast Asia, Singapore

Bann, C. (1999) 'A contingent valuation of the mangroves of Benut, Johar State, Malaysia', Report to DANCED, Copenhagen

Barbier, E. and Thompson, J. (1998) 'The value of water: Floodplain versus large-scale irrigation benefits in Northern Nigeria', *Ambio*, vol 27, pp434–440

Barbier, E. B. and Strand, I. (1998) 'Valuing mangrove-fishery linkages', *Environmental and Resource Economics*, vol 12, pp151–166

Barbier, E., Adams, W. and Kimmage, K. (1991) 'Economic valuation of wetland benefits: The Hadejiia-Jama'are floodplain, Nigeria', Paper 91-02, London Environmental Economics Centre, London

Barbier, E. B. (1993) 'Valuing tropical wetland benefits: Economic methodologies and applications', *Geographical Journal*, vol 59, pp22–32

Barbier, E. B., Acreman, M. C. and Knowler, D. (1997) *Economic Valuation of Wetlands: A Guide for Policy Makers and Planners*, Ramsar Convention Bureau, Gland, Switzerland

Barnhill, T. (1999) 'Our green is our gold: The economic benefits of national forests for Southern Appalachian communities', a Forest Link Report, Southern Appalachian Forest Coalition, Asheville, NC

Bateman, I. J. and Turner, R. K. (1993) 'Valuation of the environment, methods and techniques: The contingent valuation method', in Turner, R. K. (ed) *Sustainable Economics and Management: Principles and Practice*, Belhaven Press, London, pp120–191

Bateman, I. J., Langford, I. H. and Graham, A. (1995), 'A survey of non-users' willingness to pay to prevent saline flooding in the Norfolk Broads', CSERGE Working Paper GEC 95-11, Centre for Social and Economic Research on the Global Environment, School of Environmental Sciences, University of East Anglia, Norwich

Bateman, I. and Langford, I. (1997) 'Budget constraint, temporal and ordering effects in contingent valuation studies', *Environment and Planning*, vol 29, no 7, pp215–228

Bell, F. W. (1997) 'The economic value of saltwater marsh supporting marine recreational fishing the Southeastern United States', *Ecological Economics* , vol 21, pp243–254

Benessaiah, N. (1998) 'Merja Zerga. In: Mediterranean wetlands, socio-economic aspects', Ramsar Convention Bureau, Gland, Switzerland, pp65–70

Bergland, O. (1997) 'Valuation of landscape elements using a contingent choice method', Paper to 1997 European Association of Environmental and Resource Economists (EAERE) Conference, Tilburg, June

Bergstrom, J., Stoll, J., Titre, J. and Wright, V. (1990) 'Economic value of wetlands-based recreation', *Ecological Economics*, vol 2, no 2, June, pp129–148

Bhatta, R. (2000) 'Production, accessibility and consumption patterns of aquaculture products in India', Report submitted to ICLARM, Penang, Malaysia

Birol, E. and Cox, V. (2007) 'Using choice experiments to design wetland management programmes: The case of Severn estuary wetland, UK', *Journal of Environmental Planning and Management*, vol 50, no 3, pp363–380

Bolitzer, B. and Netusil, N. R. (2000) 'The impact of open spaces on property values in Portland, Oregon', *Journal of Environmental Management*

Boxall, P. C. and Adamowicz, W. L. (2002) 'Understanding heterogeneous preferences in random utility models: A latent class approach', *Environmental and Resource Economics*, vol 23, pp421–446

Boxall, P., Adamowicz, W., Swait, J., Williams, M. and Louviere, J. (1996) 'A comparison of stated preference methods for environmental valuation', *Ecological Economics*, vol 18, pp243–253

Brander, L. M., Florax, R. J. G. M. and Vermaat, J. E. (2006) 'The empirics of wetland valuation: A comprehensive summary and a meta-analysis of the literature', *Environmental and Resource Economics*, vol 33, pp223–250

Brander, L. M., Ghermandi, A., Kuik, O., Markandya, A., Nunes, P. A. L. D., Schaafsma, M. and Wagtendonk, A. (2008) 'Scaling up ecosystem services values: Methodology, applicability, and a case study', Report to the European Environment Agency, Copenhagen, Denmark

Breaux, A., Faber, S. and Day, J. (1995) 'Using natural coastal wetlands systems for wastewater treatment: An economic benefit analysis', *Journal of Environmental Management*, vol 44, pp285–291

Brouwer, R., Langford, I. H., Bateman, I. J. and Turner R. K. (1999) 'A meta-analysis of wetland contingent valuation studies', *Regional Environmental Change*, vol 1, pp47–57

Brown, G., Reed, P. and Harris, C. C. (2002) 'Testing a place-based theory for environmental evaluation: An Alaska case study', *Applied Geography*, vol 22, no 1, pp49–77

Brown, T. C. (1992) 'Streamflow needs and protection in wilderness areas', in *The Economic Value of Wilderness*, Proceedings of the Conference, pp161–172, General Technical Report SE-78, United States Department of Agriculture, Forest Service, Southeastern Forest Experiment Station, Asheville, NC

Brown, T. C., Harding B. L. and Payton, E. A. (1990) 'Marginal economic value of streamflow: A case study for the Colorado River Basin', *Water Resources Research*, vol 6, pp2845–2859

Bruner, A., Hanks, J. and Hannah, L. (2003) 'How much will effective protected area systems cost?', Presentation to the Vth IUCN World Parks Congress, Durban, South Africa, 8–17 September

Butry, D. T. and Pattanayak, S. K. (2001) 'Economic impacts of tropical forest conservation: The case of logger households around Ruteng Park', Working Paper 01-01, Research Triangle Park, NC

Carpenter, S., Brock W., Hanson, P. (1999) 'Ecological and social dynamics in simple models of ecosystem management', *Conservation Ecology*, vol 3, no 2, p4

Carlsson, F., Frykblom, P. and Liljenstolpe, C. (2003) 'Valuing wetland attributes: An application of choice experiments', *Ecological Economics*, vol 47, pp95–103

Carret, J. C. and Loyer, D. (2003) 'Madagascar protected area network sustainable financing: Economic analysis perspective', Paper contributed to the Vth IUCN World Parks Congress, Durban, South Africa, 8–17 September

Cavatassi, R. (2004) 'Valuation methods for environmental benefits in forestry and watershed investment projects', ESA Working Papers, Agricultural and Development Economics Division, FAO, Rome

Champ, P. A., Bishop, R. C., Brown, T. C. and McCollum D. W. (1997) 'Using donation mechanisms to value nonuse benefits from public goods', *Journal of Environmental Economics and Management*, vol 33, pp151–162

Chapman, P. (1974) 'Energy costs: A review of methods', *Energy Policy*, vol 2, no 2, pp91–103

Chaturvedi, A. N. (1992) 'Environmental value of forest in Almora', in A. Agarwal (ed) *Prices of Forests*, Centre for Science and Environment, New Delhi

Chomitz, K. M., Alger, K. et al (2005) 'Opportunity costs of conservation in a biodiversity hotspot: The case of southern Bahia', *Environment and Development Economics*, vol 10, pp293–312

Chopra, K. (1993) 'The value of non-timber forest products: Estimation for tropical deciduous forests in India', *Economic Botany*, vol 47, no 3, pp251–257

Chopra, K. and Kadekodi, G. K. (1997) 'Natural resource accounting in the Yamuna basin: Accounting of forest resources', Institute of Economic Growth, Delhi

Chopra, K., Kadekodi, G. K. and Murty, M. N. (1988) 'Economic evaluation of people's participation in the management of common property resources', Working Paper no. 3, National Institute of Public Finance and Policy, New Delhi

Chopra, K., Kadekodi, G. K. and Murty, M. N. (1990) *Participatory Development: People and Common Property Resources*, Sage Publications, New Delhi

Clayton, C. and Mendelsohn, R. (1993) 'The value of watchable wildlife: A case study of McNiel River', *Journal of Environmental Management*, vol 39, pp101–106

Clinch, J. P. (1999) *Economics of Irish Forestry: Evaluating the Returns to Economy and Society*, COFORD

Colombo, S., Calatrava-Requena, J. and Hanley, N. (2006) 'Analysing the social benefits of soil conservation measures using stated preference methods', *Ecological Economics*, vol 58, pp850–861

Colombo, S., Calatrava-Requena, J. and Hanley, N. (2007) 'Testing choice experiment for benefit transfer with preference heterogeneity', *American Journal of Agricultural Economics*, vol 89, pp135–151

Contamin, R. and Ellison, A. (2009) 'Indicators of regime shifts in ecological systems: What do we need to know and when do we need to know it?', *Ecological Applications*, vol 19, no 3, pp799–816

Costanza, R. (1980) 'Embodied energy and economic valuation', *Science*, vol 210, pp1219–1024

Costanza, R. (2006) 'Nature: Ecosystems without commodifying them', *Nature*, vol 443, p749

Costanza, R., d'Arge, R., de Groot, R., Farber, S., Grasso, M., Hannon, B., Limburg, K., Naeem, S., O'Neill, R. V., Paruelo, J., Raskin, R. G., Sutoon, P. and van den Belt, M. (1997) 'The value of the world's ecosystem services and natural capital', *Nature*, vol 387, pp253–260

Costanza, R., Farber, S. and Maxwell, J. (1989) 'Valuation and management of wetland ecosystems', *Ecological Economics*, vol 1, pp335–361

Czech, B. and Krausman, P. R. (2001) *The Endangered Species Act: History, Conservation Biology, and Public Policy*, JHU Press, Baltimore, MD

Daly, H. (1996) *Beyond Growth: The Economics of Sustainable Development*, Beacon Press, Boston, MA

Daniels, P. L. and Moore, S. (2002) 'Approaches for quantifying the metabolism of physical economies', *Journal of Industrial Ecology*, vol 5, no 4, pp69–93

de Groot, R. S. (1992) Functions of nature: Evaluation of nature in environmental planning, management and decision-making, Wolters Noordhoff BV, Groningen, the Netherlands, 345pp

Dixon, J. A. and Sherman, P. B. (1990), 'Economics of protected areas: Approaches and applications', East–West Centre, Washington DC, 243pp

Dixon, J. A., Scura, L. F., Carpenter, R. A. and Sherman, P. B. (1994) *Economic Analysis of Environmental Impacts*, Earthscan, London

Dixon, J. and Pagiola, S. (1998) 'Economic analysis and environmental assessment. Environmental Assessment Sourcebook Update', April, Number 23, Environment Department, World Bank, Washington, DC, p14

Duffield, J. W. (1992) 'Total valuation of wildlife and fishery resources: Applications in the northern Rockies', in *The Economic Value of Wilderness*, Proceedings of the Conference, pp97–13, General Technical Report SE-78, United States Department of Agriculture, Forest Service, Southeastern Forest Experiment Station, Asheville, NC

Dunkiel, B. A. S and Sugarman S. (1998), 'Complaint for declaratory, mandatory and injunctive relief', United States District Court for the District of Vermont

Dwyer, J. F., McPherson, E. G., Schroeder, H. W. and Rowntree, R. A. (1992) 'Assessing the benefits and costs of the urban forest', *Journal of Arboriculture*, vol 18, no 5, pp227–234

EEA (2006) 'Land accounts for Europe 1990–2000: Towards integrated land and ecosystem accounting', European Environment Agency Report No 11/2006, Copenhagen, Denmark

Ehrlich, P. and Ehrlich, A. (1981) *Extinction: The Causes and Consequences of the Disappearance of Species*, Random House, New York

Ekins, P., Simon, S., Deutsch, L., Folke, C. and de Groot, R. (2003) 'A framework for the practical application of the concepts of critical natural capital and strong sustainability', *Ecological Economics*, vol 44, pp165–185

Emerton, L. (1996) 'Participatory environmental evaluation: Subsistence forest use around the Aberdares, Kenya', African Wildlife Foundation, Nairobi, Kenya, summarized in Bagri, A., Blockhus, J., Grey, F. and Vorhies, F. (eds) (1998) *Economic Values of Protected Areas: A Guide for Protected Area Managers*, IUCN, Gland

Emerton, L. (1998) 'Balancing the opportunity costs of wildlife conservation for the communities around Lake Mburo National Park, Uganda', Evaluating Eden Discussion Paper No. EE/DP 05, IIED, London

Emerton, L. (1999) *Mount Kenya: The Economics of Community Conservation*, Institute for Development Policy and Management, University of Manchester, Manchester

Emerton L. (2005) 'Values and rewards: Counting and capturing ecosystem water services for sustainable development', IUCN Water, Nature and Economics Technical Paper No. 1, IUCN, Ecosystems and Livelihoods Group Asia

Emerton, L. and Kekulandala, L. D. C. B. (2003) 'Assessment of the economic value of Muthurajawela Wetland, Sri Lanka', Occasional Papers of IUCN, Sri Lanka, No. 4

Farber, S. and Costanza, R. (1987) 'The value of coastal wetlands for protection of property against hurricane wind damage', *Journal of Environmental Economics and Management*, vol 14, pp143–151

Ferraro, P. J. (2002) 'The local costs of establishing protected areas in low-income nations: Ranomafana National Park, Madagascar', *Ecological Economics*, vol 43, nos 2–3, pp261–275

Flatley, G. W. and Bennett, J. W. (1996) 'Using contingent valuation to determine Australian tourists' values for forest conservation in Vanuatu', *Economic Analysis and Policy*, vol 26, no 2, pp111–127

Garber-Yonts, B., J. Kerkvliet et al (2004) 'Public values for biodiversity conservation policies in the Oregon Coast Range', *Forest Science*, vol 50, no 5, pp589–602

Gammage, S. (1997) *Estimating the Returns to Mangrove Conversion: Sustainable Management or Short Term Gain?*, Environmental Economics Discussion Paper No 97-02, International Institute for Environment and Development, London

Garrod, G. D. and Willis, K. G. (1991) 'Estimating the benefits of environmental enhancement: A case study of the River Darent', *Journal of Environmental Planning and Management*, vol 39, pp189–203

Garrod, G. D. and Willis K. G. (1992) 'The environmental economic impact of woodland: A two-stage hedonic price model of the amenity value of forestry in Britain', *Applied Economics*, vol 24, pp715–728

Garrod, G. D. and Willis, K. G. (1997) 'The non-use benefits of enhancing forest biodiversity: A contingent ranking study', *Ecological Economics*, vol 21, no 1, pp45–61

Gilbert, A., Glass, R. and More, T. (1992) 'Valuation of eastern wilderness: Extra market measures of public support', in *The Economic Value of Wilderness*, Proceedings of the Conference, pp57–70, General Technical Report SE-78, United States Department of Agriculture, Forest Service, southeastern Forest Experiment Station, Asheville, NC

Godoy, R. and Feaw, T. (1989) 'The profitability of smallholder rattan cultivation in central Borneo', *Human Ecology*, vol 16, no 4, pp397–420

Gong, Y. (2003) 'Opportunity cost of local people and WTP of off-site residents for biodiversity conservation in Fanjingshan National Nature Reserve in China', CCAP Working Paper 04-E1, 39pp

Gren I. M. (1993) 'Alternative nitrogen reduction policies in the Malar Region, Sweden', *Ecological Economics*, vol 7, pp159–172

Gren, I. (1998) 'The value of investing in wetlands for nitrogen abatement', *European Review of Agricultural Economics*, vol 22, pp157–172

Gren, I.-M., Folke, C., Turner, R. K. and Bateman, I. (1994) 'Primary and secondary values of wetland ecosystems', *Environment and Resource Economics*, vol 4, pp55–74

Grieg-Gran, M. (2006) *The Cost of Avoiding Deforestation*, Report prepared for the Stern Review of the Economics of Climate Change

Gunawardena, M. and Rowan, J. S. (2005) 'Economic valuation of a mangrove ecosystem threatened by shrimp aquaculture in Sri Lanka', *Environmental Management*, vol 36, no 4, pp535–550

Gunawardena, U., Edwards-Jones, G. and McGregor, M. (1999) 'A contingent valuation approach for a tropical rainforest: A case study of Sinharaja rainforest reserve in Sri Lanka', *The Living Forest: The Non-Market Benefits of Forestry*, The Stationery Office, London, pp275–284

Gunatilake, H. M., Senaratne, D. and Abeygunawardena, P. (1993) 'Role of non-timber forest products in the economy of peripheral communities of Knuckles National Wilderness Area of Sri Lanka: A farming systems approach', *Economic Botany*, vol 47, no 3, pp275–281

Haefele, M., Kramer, R. A., and Holmes, T. (1992) 'Estimating the total value of forest quality in high-elevation spruce-fir forests', in *The Economic Value of Wilderness*, General Technical Report SE-78, Southern Forest Experiment Station, Research Triangle Park, NC

Hadker, N., Sharma, S., David. A. and Muraleedharan, T.R. (1997) 'Willingness-to-pay for Borivli National Park: Evidence from a contingent valuation', *Ecological Economics*, vol 21, no 2, pp105–122

Hagen, D., Vincent, J. and Welle, P. (1992) 'Benefits of preserving old-growth forests and the spotted owl', *Contemporary Policy Issues*, vol 10, pp13–25

Hanley, N. and Craig, S. (1991) 'Wilderness development decisions and the Krutilla-Fisher model: The case of Scotland's flow country', *Ecological Economics*, vol 4, no 2, pp45–62

Hanley, N and Ruffell, R. (1991) 'Recreational use values of woodland features', Report to the Forestry Commission, Edinburgh

Hanley, N and Ruffell, R. (1992) 'The valuation of forest characteristics', Working Paper 849, Department of Economics, University of Stirling

Hanley, N., Willis, K., Powe, N. and Anderson, M. (2002) *Valuing the Benefits of Biodiversity in Forests*, Report to the Forestry Commission

Hanley, N., Wright and Adamowicz, W. (1998) 'Using choice experiments to value the environment', *Environmental and Resource Economics*, vol 11, no 3, pp413–428

Hodgson, G. and Dixon, J. A. (1988) *Logging Versus Fisheries and Tourism in Palawan*, Occasional Paper 7, Environment and Policy Institute, East-West Centre, Honolulu, Hawaii

Holmes, T., Alger, K., Zinkhan, C. and Mercer, D. E. (1998) 'The effect of response time on conjoint analysis estimates of rainforest protection values', *Journal of Forest Economics*, vol 4, no 1, pp7–28

Horne, P., Karppinen, H. and Ylinen, E. (2004) 'Citizens' opinions on protecting forest biodiversity' (Kansalaisten mielipiteet metsien monimuotoisuuden turvaamisesta. Metsänomistajien ja kansalaisten näkemykset metsäluonnon monimuotoisuuden turvaamisesta. T. K. Paula Horne, and Ville Ovaskainen, Metsäntutkimuslaitos, Vantaa

Howard, J. L. (1997) 'An estimation of opportunity cost for sustainable ecosystems', Proceedings of the XI World Forestry Congress, Ministry of Forestry, Antalya, Turkey

Howard, P. C. (1995) *The Economics of Protected Areas in Uganda: Costs, Benefits and Policy Issues*, PhD Thesis, University of Edinburgh, Edinburgh

Janssen, R. and Padilla, J. E. (1996) *Valuation and Evaluation of Management Alternatives for the Pagbilao Mangrove Forest*, Environmental Economics Programme, International Institute for Environment and Development (IIED), London

Johnston, R. (2002) 'Valuing estuarine resource services using economic and ecological models: The Peconic estuary system', *Coastal Management*, vol 30, pp47–66

Jonish, J. (1992) 'Sustainable development and employment: Forestry in Malaysia', Working Paper No. 234, International Labour Office, Geneva.

Kadekodi, G. and Ravindranath, N. H. (1997) 'Macroeconomic analysis of forestry options on carbon sequestration in India', *Ecological Economics*, vol 23, pp201–223

Kanazawa, M. (1993) 'Pricing subsidies and economic efficiency: The U.S. Bureau of Reclamation', *Journal of Law and Economics*, vol 36, pp205–234

Khalil, S. (1999) 'Economic valuation of the mangrove ecosystem along the Karachi coastal areas', in Hecht, J. (ed) *The Economic Value of the Environment: Cases from South Asia*, IUCN, Washington DC

King, D. M. and Mazotta, M. (2001) 'Ecosystem valuation', web site, www.ecosystemvaluation.org. Authors affiliated with University of Maryland and University of Rhode Island. Site sponsored by the USDA NRCS and NOAA

Kirkland, W. T. (1998) 'Economic value of Whangantarino wetland, New Zealand', Masters Thesis, Massey University, New Zealand

Kniivilä, M., Ovaskainen, V. and Saastamoinen, O. (2002) 'Costs and benefits of forest conservation: Regional and local comparisons in Eastern Finland', *Journal of Forest Economics*, vol 8, no 2, pp131–150

Kramer, R. A. and Mercer, D. E. (1997) 'Valuing a global environmental good: US residents willingness to pay to protect tropical rainforests', *Land Economics*, vol 73, no 2, pp196–210

Kramer, R. A., Holmes, T. P. and Haefele, M. (2003) 'Contingent valuation of forest ecosystem protection', in Sills, E. O. and Abt, K. L. (eds) *Forests in a Market Economy*, Kluwer Academic Publishers, Dordrect, The Netherlands, pp303–320

Kramer, R., Munasinghe, M., Sharma, N., Mercer, E. and Shyamsundar, P. (1992) 'Valuing a protected tropical forest: A case study in Madagascar', Paper presented at the IVth World Congress on National Parks and Protected Areas, 10–21 February, Caracas, Venezuela

Kramer, R. A., Sharma, N. P. and Munasinghe, M. (1995) *Valuing Tropical Forests: Methodology and Case Study of Madagascar*, World Bank Publications, World Bank, Washington, DC

Krutilla, J. V. and Fisher, A. C. (1975) *The Economics of Natural Environment: Studies in the valuation of Commodity and Amenity Resources*, John Hopkins University Press, Baltimore, MD

Kumar, P. (2004) 'Valuation of medicinal plants for pharmaceutical uses', *Current Science*, vol 86, no 7, pp930–937

Kumar, P. (2005) 'Market for ecosystem services: An overview of experiences and lessons learned', Discussion Paper Series No. 98/2005, Institute of Economic Growth, Delhi

Kumar, P. and Chopra, K. (2004) 'Forest biodiversity and timber extraction: An analysis of the interaction of market and non market mechanism', *Ecological Economics*, vol 49, no 2, pp135–148

Kumari, K. (1995) 'Mainstreaming biodiversity conservation: A Peninsular Malaysian case', Centre for Social and Economic Research on the Global Environment, University of East Anglia, Norwich

Kumari, K. (1996) 'Sustainable forest management: Myth or reality, exploring the prospects for Malaysia', *Ambio*, vol 25, no 7, pp459–467

Layton, J. H, Naeem, S., Thompson, L. J., Hector, A. and Crawley, M. J. (1998) 'Biodiversity and ecosystem function: getting the Ecotron experiment in its correct context', *Functional Ecology*, vol 12, pp848–852

Lehtonen, E., Kuuluvainen, J. et al. (2003) 'Non-market benefits of forest conservation in southern Finland', *Environmental Science and Policy*, vol 6, no 3, pp195–204

Li, C., Kuuluvainen, J., Pouta, E, Rekola, M. and Tahvonen, O. (2004) 'Using choice experiments to value the Natura 2000 nature conservation programs in Finland', *Environmental and Resource Economics*, vol 29, no 3, pp361–374

Lindberg, K., and Aylward, B. (1999) 'Price responsiveness in the developing country nature tourism context: Review and Costa Rica case study', *Journal of Leisure Research*, vol 31, pp282–299

Lindhjem, H. and Navrud, S. (2008) 'How reliable are meta-analyses for international benefit transfer?', *Ecological Economics*, vol 66, pp425–435

Livengood, K. R. (1983) 'Value of big game from markets for hunting leases: The hedonic approach', *Land Economics*, vol 59, no 3, pp287–291

Loomis, J. (1992) 'Importance of joint benefits of wilderness in calculating wilderness recreation benefits in the economic value of wilderness: Proceedings of the conference', General Technical Report SE-78, United States Department of Agriculture, Forest Service, Southeastern Forest Experiment Station, Asheville, NC, pp17–26

Loomis, J. (2000) 'Vertically summing public good demand curves: An empirical comparison of economic versus political jurisdictions', *Land Economics*, vol 76, no 2, pp312–321

Loomis, J. and Ekstrand, E. (1997) 'Economic benefits of critical habitat for the Mexican spotted owl: A scope test using a multiple-bounded contingent valuation survey', *Journal of Agricultural and Resource Economics*, vol 22, no 2, pp356–366

Loomis, J. and Ekstrand, E. (1998) 'Alternative approaches for incorporating respondent uncertainty when estimating willingness to pay: The case of the Mexican spotted owl', *Ecological Economics*, vol 27, no 1, pp29–41

Loomis, J. and Richardson, R. (2000) *Economic Values of Protected Roadless Areas in the United States*, Prepared for the Wilderness Society and Heritage Forests Campaign, Washington, DC, 34pp

Loomis, J. Gonzalez-Caban, A. and Gregory, R. (1994) 'Do reminders of substitutes and budget constraints influence contingent valuation estimates?', *Land Economics*, vol 70, no 4, pp499–506

Loomis, J.B. and A. Gonzalez-Caban (1997) 'Comparing the economic value of reducing fire risk to spotted owl habitat in California and Oregon', *Forest Science*, vol 43, no 4, pp473–482

Loomis, J., González-Cabán, A., Griffin, D. and Wu, E. (2003) 'Linking GIS and recreation demand models to estimate the economic value of using fire to improve deer habitat', USDA Forest Service Proceedings RMRS-P-29

Loomis, J. B., Kent, P., Strange, L., Fausch, K. and Covich, A., (2000) 'Measuring the total economic value of restoring ecosystem services in an impaired river basin: Results from a contingent valuation survey', *Ecological Economics*, vol 33, pp103–117

Loomis, J., Updike, D. and Unkel, W. (1989) 'Consumptive and nonconsumptive values of a game animal: The case of California Deer', *Transactions of the 54th National Association of Wildlife and Natural Resources Conference*, pp640–650

Luckwood, M., Loomis, J. and De Lacy, T. (1993) 'A contingent valuation survey and benefit–cost analysis of forest conservation in East Gippsland, Australia', *Journal of Environmental Management*, vol 38, pp233–243

Lynam, T. J. P, Campbell, B. M. and Vermeulen, S. J. (1994) 'Contingent valuation of multipurpose tree resources in the smallholder farming sector, Zimbabwe', Working Paper series, *Studies in Environmental Economics and Development*, vol 8 (November), Gothenburg University, Gothenburg

Lynne, G. D., Conroy, P. and Prochaska, F. J. (1981) 'Economic value of marsh areas for marine production processes', *Journal of Environmental Economics and Management*, vol 8, pp175–186

MacArthur, R. H. and Wilson, E. O. (2001) *Island Biogeography*, Princeton University Press, Princeton, NJ

MacCauley, D. J. (2006) 'Selling out on nature', *Nature*, vol 443, pp27–28

Madhusudan, M. D. (2003) 'Living amidst large wildlife: Livestock and crop depredation by large mammals in the interior villages of Bhadra Tiger Reserve, South India', *Environmental Management*, vol 31, no 4, pp466–475

Maharana, R. and Sharma, E. (2000) 'Valuing ecotourism in a sacred lake of the Sikkim Himalaya, India', *Environmental Conservation*, vol 27, pp269–277

Mallawaarachchi, T., Blamey, R. K. et al (2001) 'Community values for environmental protection in a cane farming catchment in Northern Australia: A choice modelling study', *Journal of Environmental Management*, vol 62, no 3, pp301–316

Manoharan, T. R. (1996)' Economics of protected areas: A case study of Periyar Tiger Reserve', PhD thesis, Forest Research Institute, Dehra Dun

Manoharan T. R. (2000) ' Natural resource accounting: Economic valuation of intangible benefits of forests', RIS Discussion Paper # 04/2000, Research and Information System for the Non-Aligned and Other Developing Countries, New Delhi

Martín-López, B. (2007) 'Bases socio-ecológicas para la valoración económica de los servicios generados por la biodiversidad: Implicaciones en las políticas de conservación', PhD dissertation, Universidad Autónoma de Madrid, Madrid

McDaniels, T. L. and Roessler, C. (1998) 'Multiattribute elicitation of wilderness preservation benefits: A constructive approach', *Ecological Economics*, vol 27, no 3, pp299–312

McPherson, E. G. (1992) 'Accounting for benefits and costs of urban green space', *Landscape and Urban Planning*, vol 22, pp41–51

Mendelsohn, R. and Ballick, M. J. (1995) 'The value of undiscovered pharmaceutical in tropical forests', *Econ. Bot.*, vol 49, pp223–228

Merlo, M. and Croitoru, L. (2006) *Valuing Mediterranean Forests: Towards Total Economic Value*, CABI publishing, Oxfordshire

Moskowitz, K. and Talberth, J. (1998) *The Economic Case Against Logging Our National Forests*, Forest Guardians, Santa Fe, NM

Murty, M. N and Menkhuas, S. (1994) 'Economic aspects of wildlife protection in the developing countries: A case study of Keiladeo National Park, Bharatpur, India', Institute of Economic Growth, Delhi

Myers, N. (1996) 'Environmental services of biodiversity', *Proceedings of the National Academy of Sciences, USA*, vol 93, pp2764–2769

Naredo, J. M. (2001) 'Quantifying Natural Capital: Beyond Monetary Value', in Munasinghe, M. and Sunkel, O. (eds) *The Sustainability of Long Term Growth: Socioeconomic and Ecological Perspectives*, Edward Elgar, Cheltenham and Northampton, MA

Nepstad, D. C., Stickler, C. M., Soares, B. and Merry, F. (2008) 'Interactions among Amazon land use, forests and climate: Prospects for a near-term forest tipping point', *Philosophical Transactions of the Royal Society B–Biological Sciences*, vol 363, pp1737–1746

Neumayer, E. (2003) *Weak Versus Strong Sustainability: Exploring the Limits of Two Opposing Paradigms*, Edward Elgar, Cheltenham

Nickerson, D. J. (1999) 'Trade-offs of mangrove area development in the Philippines', *Ecological Economics*, vol 28, no 2, pp279–298

Ninan, K. N. and Sathyapalan, J. (2005) 'The economics of biodiversity conservation: A study of a coffee growing region in the Western Ghats of India', *Ecological Economics*, vol 55, no 1, pp61–72

Nowak, D. J., Crane, D. E. and Stevens, J. C. (2006) 'Air pollution removal by urban trees and shrubs in the United States', *Urban Forestry and Urban Greening*, vol 4, nos 3–4, pp115–123

Odum, H. T. (1996) *Environmental Accounting: Emergy and Decision-making*, John Wiley, New York

Pak, M. and Turker, M. F. (2006) 'Estimation of recreational use value of forest resources by using individual travel cost and contingent valuation methods (Kayabasi Forest Recreation Site sample)', *Journal of Applied Science*, vol 6, pp1–5

Parikh, J. and Haripriya, G. S. (1998) 'Environmental accounting in India: Trial estimates for forest resource', IGIDR working paper

Paris, R. and Ruzicka, I. (1991) *Barking Up the Wrong Tree: The Role of Rent Appropriation in Sustainable Tropical Forest Management*, Occasional Paper 1, Asian Development Bank Environment Office, Manila, Philippines

Pattanayak, S. K. and Kramer, R. A. (2001) 'Worth of watersheds: A producer surplus approach for valuing drought mitigation in Eastern Indonesia', *Environment and Development Economics*, vol 6, no 1, pp123–146

Patterson, M. (1998) 'Commensuration and theories of value in ecological economics', *Ecological Economics*, vol 25, no 1, pp105–125

Pearce, D. W. (1991) *Forestry Expansion – A Study of Technical, Economic and Ecological Factors: Assessing the Returns to the Economy and Society for Investments in Forestry*, Occasional Paper No. 47, Forestry Commission, Edinburgh

Pearce, D. W. (1994) *The Economic Value of Biodiversity*, Earthscan, London

Pearce, D. W., Markandya, A. and Barbier, E. (2006) *Blueprint for a Green Economy*, Earthscan, London

Peters, C. M., Gentry, A. H. and Mendelsohn, R. O. (1989) 'Valuation of an Amazonian rainforest', *Nature*, vol 339, no 6227, pp655–656

Philip, L. J. and MacMillan, D. C. (2005) 'Exploring values, context and perceptions in contingent valuation studies: The CV market stall technique and willingness to pay for wildlife conservation', *Journal of Environment Plannning and Management*, vol 48, no 2, pp 257–274

Pimentel, D. and Wilson, C. (1997) 'Economics and environmental benefits of biodiversity', *Bio Science*, vol 47, no 11, pp747–758

Pinedo-Vasquez, M., Zarin, D. and Jipp, P. (1992) 'Economic returns from forest conversion in the Peruvian Amazon', *Ecological Economics*, vol 6, no 2, pp163–173

Polasky, S., Camm, J. D., Garber-Yonts, B. and USDA (2001) 'Selecting biological reserves cost-effectively: An application to terrestrial vertebrate conservation in Oregon', *Land Economics*, vol 77, no 1, pp68–78

Power, T. M. (1992) 'The economics of wildland protection: The view from the local economy', in *The Economic Value of Wilderness*, Proceedings of the Conference, pp175–179, General Technical Report SE-78, United States Department of Agriculture, Forest Service, Southeastern Forest Experiment Station, Asheville, NC

Powicki, C. R. (1998) 'The value of ecological resources', *EPRI Journal*, vol 23, July–August, Palo Alto, CA

Proano, C. E. (2005) 'Payment for water-based environmental services: Ecuador's experiences, lessons learned and ways forward', IUCN, Colombo

Ragkos, A., Psychoudakis, A., Christofi, A. and Theodoridis, A. (2006) 'Using a functional approach to wetland valuation: The case of Zazari-Cheimaditida', *Regional Environmental Change*, vol 6, pp193–200

Ramdial, B. (1975) 'The social and economic importance of the Caroni swamp in Trinidad and Tobago', PhD Thesis, University of Michigan, Ann Arbor, MI

Reid, W. V. (1999) *Capturing the Value of Ecosystem Services to Protect Biodiversity*, World Resources Institute, Washington, DC

Ricketts, T. H., Daily, G. C., Ehrlch, P. R. and Michener, C. D. (2004) 'Economic value of tropical forest to coffee production', *Proceedings of the National Academy of Sciences of the United States of America*, vol 101, no 34, pp12579–12582

Rodriguez, J. P., Balch, J. K. and Rodriguez-Clark, K. M. (2007) 'Assessing extinction risk in the absence of species-level data: quantitative criteria for terrestrial ecosystems', *Biodiversity and Conservation*, vol 16, pp183–209

Rose, N. L. (1990) 'Profitability and product quality: Economic determinants of airline safety performance', *Journal of Political Economy*, vol 98, no 5, pp944–964

Rosenberger, R. S. and Loomis, J. B. (2000) 'Using meta-analysis for benefit transfer: In-sample convergent validity tests of an outdoor recreation database', *Water Resources Research*, vol 36, no 4, pp1097–1107

Rosenberger, R. S. and Phipps, T. T. (2007) 'Correspondence and convergence in benefit transfer accuracy: A meta-analytic review of the literature', in Navrud, S. and Ready, R. (eds) *Environmental Values Transfer: Issues and Methods*, Springer, Dordrecht

Rosenberger, R. S. and Stanley, T. D. (2006) 'Measurement, generalization, and publication: Sources of error in benefit transfers and their management', *Ecological Economics*, vol 60, no 2, pp372–378

Rubin, J., Helfand, G. and Loomis, J. (1991) 'A benefit–cost analysis of the northern spotted owl', *Journal of Forestry*, vol 89, no 12, pp25–30

Ruitenbeek, H. J. (1989a) *Social Cost-Benefit Analysis of the Korup Project, Cameroon*, Prepared for the World Wide Fund for Nature and the Republic of Cameroon

Ruitenbeek, H. J. (1989b) *Economic Analysis of Issues and Projects Relating to the Establishment of the Proposed Cross River National Park (Oban Division) and Support Zone*, Prepared by the World Wide Fund for Nature for Cross River National Parks Project, Nigeria

Ruitenbeek, H. J. (1992) *Mangrove Management: An Economic Analysis of Management Options with a focus on Bintuni Bay, Irian Jaya*, EMDI Environmental Report No. 8, Jakarta and Halifax, NC

Saastamoinen, O. (1992) 'Economic evaluation of biodiversity values of dipterocarp forests in the Philippines', *Second Meeting of the International Society of Ecological Economics (ISEE)*, vol 3, no 6

Salati, E. (1987) 'The Forest and the hydrological cycle', in Dickinson, R. (ed) *The Geophysiology of Amazonia: Vegetation Dasand Climate Interactions*, John Wiley and Sons, New York, pp273–296

Salati, E. and Vose, P. B. (1984) 'Amazon Basin: A system in equilibrium', *Science*, vol 225, pp129–138

Schandl, H., Grünbühel, C. M., Haberl, H. and Weisz, H. (2002) 'Handbook of physical accounting: Measuring bio-physical dimensions of socio-economic activities: MFA – EFA – HANPP', Social Ecology Working Paper 73, Vienna, July 2002

Schuijt, K. (2002) 'Land and water use of wetlands in Africa: Economic values of African wetlands', IIASA Interim Report IR-02-063, International Institute for Applied Systems Analysis, Vienna

Sedjo, R. A. (1988) *The Economics of Natural and Plantation Forests in Indonesia*, FAO, Rome

Sedjo, R. and Bowes, M. (1991) *Managing the Forest for Timber and Ecological Outputs on the Olympic Peninsula*, Resources for the Future, Washington, DC

Seidl, A. and Moraes, A. (2000) 'Global valuation of ecosystem services: Application to the Pantanal da Nhecolandia, Brazil', *Ecological Economics*, vol 33, pp1–6

Seidl, A. and Myrick, E. (2007) *The Economic Valuation of Community Forestry: Analytical Approaches and a Review of the Literature*, Cooperative Extension, Colorado State University, Fort Collins, CO

Shaikh, S. L., Sun, L. and Kooten, G. C. van (2007) 'Treating respondent uncertainty in contingent valuation: A comparison of empirical treatments', *Ecological Economics*, vol 62, no 1, pp115–125

Shultz, S., Pinazzo, J. and Cifuentes, M. (1998) 'Opportunities and limitations of contingent valuation surveys to determine national park entrance fees: Evidence from Costa Rica', *Environment and Development Economics*, vol 3, no 1, pp131–149

Siikamäki, J. and Layton, D. F. (2007) 'Discrete choice survey experiments: A comparison using flexible methods', *Journal of Environmental Economics and Management*, vol 53, no 1, pp122–139

Smith, V. K., van Houtven, G. and Pattanayak, S. K. (2002) 'A benefit transfer via preference calibration: "Prudential algebra" for policy', *Land Economics*, vol 78, pp132–152

Sorg, C. F. and Loomis, J. (1984) *Empirical Estimates of Amenity Forest Values: A Comparative Review*, United States Department of Agriculture, Forest Service, Rocky Mountain Forest and Range Experiment Station, Fort Collins, CO

Spash, C. L. (2002) 'Informing and forming preferences in environmental valuation: Coral reef biodiversity', *Journal of Economic Psychology*, vol 23, pp665–687

Spash, C. L. (2008) 'How much is that ecosystem in the window? The one with the bio-diverse trail', *Environmental Values*, vol 17 (2008), pp259–284

Spash, C. L and Hanley, N. (1995) 'Preferences, information and biodiversity preservation', *Ecological Economics*, vol 12, pp191–208

Strange, N., Rahbek, C. Jepsen, J. K. and Lund, M. P. (2006) 'Using farmland prices to evaluate cost-efficiency of national versus regional reserve selection in Denmark', *Biological Conservation*, vol 128, no 4, pp455–466

Stuip, M. A. M, Baker, C. J. and Oosterberg, W. (2002) 'The socio-economic of wetlands', Wetlands International and RIZA, Wageningen, pp35

Sutherland, R. J. and Walsh, R. G. (1985) 'Effect of distance on the preservation value of water quality', *Land Economics*, vol 61, no 3, pp281–291

Tabarelli, M., Pinto, L. P., Silva, J. M. C., Hirota, M. and Bede, L. (2005) 'Challenges and opportunities for biodiversity conservation in the Brazilian Atlantic Forest', *Conservation Biology*, vol 19, pp695–700

TEEB in National Policy (2011) *The Economics of Ecosystems and Biodiversity in National and International Policy Making* (ed Patrick ten Brink), Earthscan, London

TEEB in Local Policy (2011) *The Economics of Ecosystems and Biodiversity in Local and Regional Policy and Management* (eds Heidi Wittmer and Haripriya Gundineda), Earthscan, London

Thibodeau, F. and Ostro, B. (1981) 'An economic analysis of wetland protection', *Journal of Environmental Management*, vol 12, no 1, January, pp19–30

Tobias, D. and Mendelsohn, R. (1991) 'Valuing ecotourism in a tropical rain-forest reserve' ('Valorando el ecoturismo en una reserva de bosque lluvioso tropical'), *Ambio*, vol 20, no 2, pp91–93

Turner, K. et al (2003) 'Valuing nature: Lessons learned and future research directions', *Ecological Economics*, vol 46, no 3, pp493–510

Tyrvainen, L. and Miettinen, A. (2000) 'Property prices and urban forest amenities', *Journal of Environmental Economics and Management*, vol 39, pp205–223

Tuan, T. H. and Navrud, S. (2007) 'Valuing cultural heritage in developing countries: Comparing and pooling contingent valuation and choice modelling estimates', *Environmental and Resource Economics*, vol 38, pp51–70

Uhl, C., Veríssimo, A., Barreto, P. and Tarifa, R. (1992) 'A evolução da fronteira amazônica: Oportunidades para um desenvolvimento sustentável (The evolution of the Amazonian frontier: Opportunities for sustainable development'), *Pará Desenvolvimento*, IDESP, June (special edition), pp13–31

Van Kooten, G. C. and Sohngen, B. (2007) 'Economics of forest ecosystem carbon sinks: A review', *International Review of Environmental and Resource Economics*, vol 1, no 3, pp237–269

Van Beukering, P. J. H., Cesar, S. J. H. and Janssen M. A. (2003) 'Economic valuation of the Levser National Park on Sumatra, Indonesia', *Ecological Economics*, vol 44, no 1, pp43–62

Veríssimo, A., Barreto, P., Mattos, M., Tarifa, R. and Uhl, C. (1992) 'Logging impacts and prospects for sustainable forest management in an old Amazonian frontier: The case of Paragominas', *Forest Ecology and Management*, vol 55, pp169–199

Verma, M. (2000) *Economic Valuation of Forests of Himachal Pradesh: Himachal Pradesh Forestry Sector Review*, International Institute of Environment and Development (IIED), London, Annex-7

Verma. M. (2001) 'Economic valuation of Bhoj wetland for sustainable use, Report prepared for India: Environmental Management Capacity Building Technical Assistance Project, Indian Institute of Forest Management, Bhopal

Verma, M. (2003) 'Economic valuation of Bhoj wetland', in Parikh, J. and Ram, R. (eds) *Reconciling Environment and Economics: Executive Summaries of EERC*, EERC, IGIDR, Mumbai, pp31–35

Verma, M. (2008) 'Framework for forest resource accounting: Factoring in the intangibles', *International Forestry Review: The Indian Forest Sector – Current Trends and Future Challenges* vol 10, no 2 (special issue), pp362–375

Vermeulen, S. and Koziell, I. (2002) *Integrating Global and Local Values: A Review of Biodiversity Assessment*, Biodiversity and Livelihoods Group, International Institute for Environment and Development, London

Voinov, A. and Farley, J. (2007) 'Reconciling sustainability, systems theory and discounting', *Ecological Economics*, vol 63, pp104–113

Wackernagel, M., Onisto, L., Bello, P., Callejas Linares, A., López Falfán, I. S., Méndez García, J., Suárez Guerrero, A. I. and Suárez Guerrero, M. G. (1999) 'Natural capital accounting with the Ecological Footprint concept', *Ecological Economics*, vol 29, no 3, pp375–390

Walker, B. H., Holling, C. S., Carpenter, S. R. and Kinzig, A. P. (2004) 'Resilience, adaptability, and transformability', *Ecology and Society*, vol 9, no 2, p5, available at www.ecologyandsociety.org/vol9/iss2/art5/

Walker, B. H., Gunderson, L., Kinzig, A. P., Folke, C., Carpenter, S. R. and Schultz, L. (2006) 'A handful of heuristics and some propositions for understanding resilience in social–ecological systems', *Ecology and Society*, vol 11, no 1, p13, available at www.ecologyandsociety.org/vol11/iss1/art13/

Walker, B., Pearson, L., Harris, M., Mäler, K.-G., Li, C.-Z., Biggs, R. and Baynes, T. (2009b) 'Resilience in inclusive wealth: concepts and examples from the Goulburn Broken Catchment', Working Paper, *Environmental and Resource Economics*

Walsh, R. G. and Loomis, J. (1989) 'The non-traditional public valuation (option, bequest, existence) of wilderness', in Freilich, H. R. (comp) *Wilderness Benchmark 1988: Proceedings of the National Wilderness Colloquium*, pp181–192, General Technical Report SE-51, United States Department of Agriclture, Forest Service, Southeastern Forest Experiment Station, Asheville, NC

Walsh, R. G., Loomis, J. B. and Gillman, R. S. (1984) 'Valuing option, existence, and bequest demands for wilderness', *Land Economics*, vol 60, no 1, pp14–29

Wendland, K. J., Honzák, M., Portela, R., Vitale, B., Rubinoff, S. and Randrianarisoa, J. (2010) 'Targeting and implementing payments for ecosystem services: Opportunities for bundling biodiversity conservation with carbon and water services in Madagascar', *Ecological Economics*, in press

White A., Ross, M., Flores, M. (2000) 'Benefits and costs of coral reef and wetland management, Olango Island, Philippines', in Cesar, H. (ed) *Collected Essays on the Economics of Coral Reefs*, CORDIO, pp215–227

Whitten, S. M. and Bennett, J. W. (2002) 'A travel cost study of duck hunting in the upper south east of South Australia', *Australian Geographer*, vol 33, pp207–221

Whittington, D., Briscoe, J., Mu, X., Barron, W. (1990a) 'Estimating the willingness to pay for water services in developing countries: A case study of the use of contingent valuation surveys in Southern Haiti', *Economic Development and Cultural Change*, vol 38, no 2, pp293–311

Whittington, D., Lauria, D. T., Wright, A. M. et al. (1991) 'Willingness to pay for improved sanitation in Kumasi, Ghana: A contingent valuation study in valuing environmental benefits in developing economies', Michigan State University, Special Report No. 29

Whiteman, A. and Sinclair, J. (1994) *The Costs and Benefits of Planting Three Community Forests*, Policy Studies Division, Forestry Commission, Edinburgh

Willis, K. and Garrod, G. (1991) 'Landscape values: A contingent valuation approach and case study of the Yorkshire Dales National Park', Countryside Change working paper 21, University of Newcastle upon Tyne, Newcastle upon Tyne

Willis, K. G. and Garrod, G. D. (1998) 'Biodiversity values for alternative management regimes in remote UK coniferous forests: An iterative bidding polychotomous choice approach', *The Environmentalist*, vol 18, no 3, pp157–166

Wilson, M. A. and Carpenter, S. R. (1999) 'Economic valuation of freshwater ecosystems services in the United States 1971–1997', *Ecological Applications*, vol 9, no 3, pp772–783

Wilson, M. A. and Howarth, R. B. (2002) 'Valuation techniques for achieving social fairness in the distribution of ecosystem services', *Ecological Economics*, vol 41, pp431–443

Yaron, G. (2001) 'Forest, plantation crops or small-scale agriculture: An economic analysis of alternative land use options in the Mount Cameroon area', *Journal of Environmental Planning and Management*, vol 44, no 1, pp85–108

Yuan, M. S. and Christensen, N. A. (1992) 'Wilderness-influenced economic impacts on portal communities: The case of Missoula, Montana', in *The Economic Value of Wilderness*, Proceedings of the Conference, pp191–199, General Technical Report SE-78, United States Department of Agriculture, Forest Service, Southeastern Forest Experiment Station, Asheville, NC

Appendix 3
Estimates of Monetary Values of Ecosystem Services

Coordinating lead authors
Rudolf de Groot and Pushpam Kumar

Lead author on the Database: Sander van der Ploeg, with assistance from Yafei Wang and Tsedekech Weldmichael

Lead authors on the 11 biomes
Salman Hussain (open ocean A3.1), Pieter van Beukering (coral reefs A3.2),
Rosimeiry Portela and Andrea Ghermandi (coastal systems A3.3),
Luke Brander (coastal and inland wetlands A3.4 and A3.5),
Neville Crossman (rivers and lakes A3.6), Mike Christie (tropical forests A3.7),
Florence Bernard (temperate and boreal forests A3.8),
Luis C. Rodriguez (woodlands A3.9), Lars Hein (grasslands A3.10),
David Pitt (polar and high mountain regions A3.11)

Contributing authors
Claire Armstrong, James Benhin, Thomas Binet, James Blignaut, Mahe Charles, Emmanuelle Cohen-Shacham, Jonathan Davies, Lucy Emerton, Pierre Failler,
Naomi Foley, Erik Gomez-Baggethun, Sybille van den Hove, Myles Mander,
Anai Mangos, Simone Maynard, Elisa Oteros-Rozas, Sandra Rajmis, Nalini Rao,
Didier Sauzade, Silvia Silvestri, Rob Tinch

Reviewers
G.K. Kadekodi, Jeffrey A. McNeely, Paulo Nunes

Introduction

This Appendix presents the monetary values found for ecosystem services provided by the main biomes[1] identified in Chapter 1. As has been explained earlier (notably in Chapters 1 and 5), economic values have many shortcomings and limitations, not only in relation to ecosystem services but also to human-made goods and services. They are by definition instrumental, anthropocentric, individual-based, subjective, context-dependent, marginal and state-dependent. For a discussion of these, and other issues, see for example Goulder and Kennedy, 1997; Turner et al, 2003; Baumgärtner et al, 2006; Barbier et al, 2009; EPA, 2009. However, despite these fundamental issues in economic theory and practice, information about the monetary importance of ecosystem services is a powerful and essential tool to make better, more balanced decisions regarding trade-offs involved in land-use options and resource use.

In this Appendix, we present the results of an analysis of 11 main biomes/ecosystem-complexes (i.e. open ocean, coral reefs, coastal systems, coastal wetlands (mangroves and tidal marshes), inland wetlands, rivers and lakes, tropical forests, temperate and boreal forests, woodlands, grasslands and polar and high mountain systems) and collate their monetary values from different socio-economic contexts across the world. For each biome, all 22 ecosystem services identified in Chapter 1 were taken into account in the data collection. With help from the contributing and lead authors, hundreds of publications were screened[2] from which approximately 160 were selected for detailed analysis and data-entry into the 'TEEB database' which was especially designed for this study. Thus far, over 1300 original values (data points) are stored and, based on a number of criteria, slightly over 600 values were used for the analysis presented in this Appendix (details on the database, the selection procedure and original values are available through the TEEB website: www.teebweb.org.)

An important purpose of the TEEB database is the possibility to use the values for scenario-analysis at different scale-levels. To allow for these kind of studies, the database presents the data in one value unit (US$) per ha per year and in a contextual explicit way. For each value, the database includes information on, among others, socio-economic variables, biome type, ecosystem type, ecosystem services and sub-services, valuation method, reference details and the location details of the case study. The web version of the database thus makes it, in principle, possible to analyse the data in relation to the main determining factors of the values, such as influence of income level, population density and proximity of user to the service.

Figures A3.1–A3.3 give an overview of the distribution of the monetary values selected for this Appendix by ecosystem (biome), region and service.

For the purpose of this Appendix, all values were converted into 2007 International Dollar values using the GDP deflators and purchasing power parity converters from the World Bank World Development Indicators 2007 (World Bank, 2007).

To provide a preliminary overview of the range of monetary values found for each ecosystem service, per biome, only the minimum and maximum values are given in this Appendix. Since all values are based on individual case studies

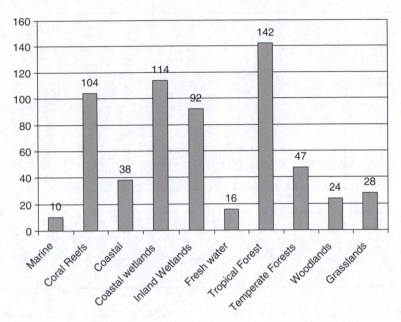

Figure A3.1 *Number of monetary values used for this Appendix per biome*

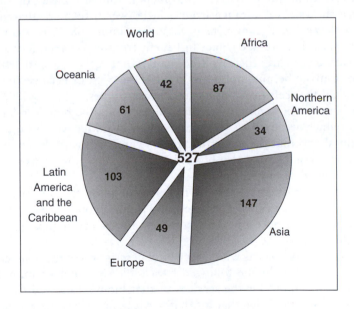

Figure A3.2 *Geographic distribution of the monetary values used in this Appendix*

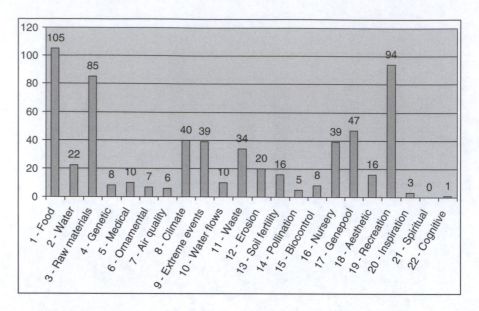

Figure A3.3 *Number of monetary values used in this Appendix for 22 ecosystem services*

this sometimes leads to very wide value ranges. For example, the main economically important service of coral reefs is tourism. Based on 30 studies this service shows a value range from a little over 0 to more than 1 million $/ha/yr (with an average monetary value of almost 68,500 $/ha/yr).[3] This illustrates that using average values in benefit-transfer between locations must be done with great care: there will be many coral reefs that currently have a 0-value for tourism because nobody is going there (yet), or because they are less attractive than the reefs involved in the 30 case studies.

Other issues to be aware of are that values should be based on sustainable use levels (which we tried to verify and when in doubt we chose the lower-bound values) and that the magnitude of the value will vary depending on the socio-economic context (see also Box A3.1 for guidance how to use, or not use, the data presented in this Appendix).

Below, the main results are briefly presented for the 11 main biomes/ecosystems, we distinguished. The desert and tundra biomes are not included in this analysis because too few data points were found on their services and values in this stage of the TEEB study.

Each biome section starts with a very brief description of the main ecosystem types included in that biome followed by a table showing the minimum and maximum values found for the services of that biome, followed by a column with 'single values' (meaning that for that service only one value was found and thus no minimum or maximum could be given). Services that are not applicable to a given biome were left out of the table. A question mark means that that service is applicable to that biome but no (reliable) values were found yet.

Box A3.1 Guidance for use of the data in this book, and link with TEEB in National Policy (2011), TEEB in Local Policy (2011) and TEEB in Business (2011)

An important rationale for developing the TEEB database of value estimates was to provide input to policy appraisal. Specifically, the database was set up so as to provide where possible not only a range of total values for a biome on a per hectare basis but also, where data are available, values *disaggregated on the basis of ecosystem services* (ESSs). This set-up was applied so as to facilitate the application of the Ecosystem Approach. A further benefit of this disaggregation is that it allows policy makers to determine which of the ESSs are pertinent to their particular policy perspective. We presuppose that the objective of the policy maker using this database is to find a monetary value for the benefits of conserving a particular habitat. However the decision as to whether to choose conservation versus the extractive alternative depends on a number of factors, some of which are linked to the nature of individual ESSs. The database user may thus decide to *filter* the values arrived at.

Filtering for appropriate data points

Some of the filters that might be considered are set out below. Once a biome is selected, the total number of available data points/value estimates will be presented. This is important in that filtering only really works if there are sufficient data points for the biome in question.

Locally derived ESSs versus globally derived ESSs

After the user has determined the biome to be considered, the first choice is between (i) ESSs for which benefits are mainly locally derived benefits, (ii) ESSs that are mainly globally derived and finally (iii) ESSs that are both local and global in nature, i.e. all ESSs. The reason for allowing this first stage of filtering is that policy makers might want to focus on ESSs that benefit local people *and local people alone*. This does not imply that these policy makers do not care about global benefits, only that they might look to global donor agencies to fund the positive global externality.

Tourism

There is enormous variability in the value estimates per hectare and one of the reasons for this is that some sites are valued based in part on tourism revenues. Thus the end-user might decide whether values that either (i) include leisure and tourism as an ESS or (ii) exclude it are a better match for the choice the policy maker is seeking valuation estimates for. It would be appropriate to pick (i) if there is the *potential* for tourism activity.

Protected area designation

Many of the data points in the valuation database pertain to protected areas (PAs). Although values derived outside PAs might be useful for analysis within PAs, the end-user might choose to select only these PA data points. Again, it would be appropriate to pick PA if a policy maker is considering the establishment of a PA.

High income/low income

There is evidence from meta-analyses carried out in the environmental economics literature that studies carried out in higher income countries realize a higher value estimate on average.

Appropriate use of the findings

The database of environmental values for biomes and ESSs within these biomes is one of the most extensive (if not *the* most extensive) databases of its kind. All values within the database have been screened with respect to the methodological integrity applied in the primary literature sources. Notwithstanding this, caution must be applied in using the values revealed in searches owing to the inherent limitations of benefits transfer. The results are intended to provide an *indicative* value, not *the* value. Even a primary valuation study cannot offer a precise value for a non-traded ESS, and benefits transfer adds an additional layer of abstraction.

Where the outputs may be particularly useful in the policy debate is in considering the relative value of different ESSs. So even if (say) we do not have a reliable, precise value for 'water purification' we can assess broadly how valuable it is as an ESS relative to others.

For each biome the table is followed by an example of a good case study that has applied the total economic value (TEV) framework, or similar approach, to monetize the total bundle of services provided by that biome/ecosystem, including information on the policy context (purpose) and influence of determining factors (e.g. the socio-economic context).

A3.1 Monetary value of ecosystem services provided by open oceans

The open ocean is the largest area of the marine ecosystem, including deep sea (water and sea floor below 200m). Excluded from this biome section are shelf sea, coral reefs, ocean islands and atolls which are discussed separately in other sections (A3.2–A3.4).

As Table A3.1 shows, based on six data points, the total monetary value of the potential sustainable use of all services of open ocean combined varies between 13 and 84 $/ha/yr. This excludes four services for which only one value was found (which would add 9 $/ha/yr to the total value*).*

Table A3.1 Monetary value of services provided by open oceans

Marine	No. of used estimates	Minimum values ($/ha/yr)	Maximum values ($/ha/yr)	No. of Single estimates	Single values ($/ha/yr)
TOTAL:	6	13	84	4	9
PROVISIONING SERVICES	2	8	22	1	0
1 Food	2	8	22		
3 Raw materials				1	0
4 Genetic resources	?				
5 Medicinal resources	?				
REGULATING SERVICES	4	5	62	1	7
7 Influence on air quality	?				
8 Climate regulation	2	4	55		
11 Waste treatment / water purification	?				
13 Nutrient cycling				1	7
15 Biological control	2	1	7		
HABITAT SERVICES	1	0	0	1	2
16 Lifecycle maintenance (esp. nursery service)					
17 Gene pool protection (conservation)				1	2
CULTURAL SERVICES	1	0	0	1	1
18 Aesthetic information	?				
19 Opportunities for recreation and tourism				1	1
20 Inspiration for culture, art and design	?				
21 Spiritual experience	?				
22 Cognitive information (education and science)	?				

Note: $/ha/yr – 2007 values.

Box A3.2 Example of TEV case study: Benefit–cost assessment of Marine Conservation Zones (MCZs) in UK

Hussain et al (2010) analysed the benefits and costs of the UK Marine and Coastal Access Bill (2009) and specifically the establishment of a network of marine protected areas, termed Marine Conservation Zones (MCZs) in UK legislation. The benefit assessment was commissioned in order to provide an evidence base for this legislation and to meet Impact Assessment guidance.

Two sets of management regimes (with varying degrees of exclusion/reduced anthropogenic impact) were assessed in the context of three network scenarios describing the proposed location of MCZ sites. The main methodological challenges were (i) the lack of appropriate primary valuation studies for BT and (ii) the way that estimates were framed in these studies – namely, in aggregate terms. Aggregate values for different ESSs pertaining to UK temperate marine ecosystems are presented in Beaumont et al (2008), which forms a basis for the values used in Hussain et al (2010).

The methodology developed had to account for the following constraints: (i) the impact of MCZ designation would vary across the different ecosystem services (ESSs); and (ii) within any single ESS, the impacts would vary across different landscape types. The methodology thus scored the impact of designation for each individual ESS/each landscape. This scoring was relative to the benchmark, that is, how much provisioning of the particular ESS/landscape combination would occur without MCZ designation?

Since the only estimates (where available) were for 2007-equivalent provisioning, this had to be used as the benchmark. Two elements were scored: (i) the extent to which MCZs would impact on provisioning, measured as a percentage change relative to 2007 provisioning; and (ii) when this change in provisioning would likely occur – the impact trajectory. The latter meets the requirement for a consistent discount rate to be applied (in this case 3.5 per cent, a HM treasury requirement) for both costs and benefits in Impact Assessment. As well as assigning this score for each ESS/landscape, the methodology had to account for how important one hectare of a particular landscape is relative to other landscapes for that ESS. Marine ecologists determined four categories based on combinations of (i) spatial extent, (ii) proximity to coastline, (iii) average per hectare provisioning.

Once this methodology had been applied, the aggregate benefit estimates for each of the three proposed MCZ networks/two management regimes were calculated. The present value (using the 3.5 per cent discount rate over the 20-year study period) ranged from around £11.0 to £23.5 billion. Applying sensitivity analysis reduced this range from around £6.4 to £15.1 billion. 'Gas and climate regulation' accounted for the bulk of this expected benefit (around 70 per cent) with 'nutrient cycling' and 'leisure and recreation' around 10 per cent each.

The assessment of the costs of the MCZ networks was made by ABPMer (2007). Secondary data and literature were assessed and interviews carried out with affected industries (fisheries, telecommunications, oil and gas extraction etc.); the cost estimate ranged from £0.4 to £1.2 billion, implying a worst-case benefit–cost ratio of five.

The implications of this research are significant: (i) it is possible to apply (to a limited extent) an Ecosystem Approach to the marine biome; (ii) values were found for only seven of the 11 ESSs and yet even these alone derived a significant benefit–cost ratio. The lobbies linked to the exploitation of marine ecosystems are highly organized and well resourced; this kind of research and evidence-based justification for conservation is thus important.

A3.2 Monetary value of ecosystem services provided by coral reefs

The term 'coral reef' generally refers to a marine ecosystem where the main organisms are corals that house algal symbionts within their tissues. These ecosystems require fully marine waters, warm temperatures and ample sunlight. They are therefore restricted to shallow waters of tropical and sub tropical regions. Corals that do not have algal symbionts can also form significant reef communities in deeper, darker and colder waters, but these communities are distinguished as cold-water coral bioherms. Corals are often included in the

Table A3.2 Monetary value of services provided by coral reefs

	Coral reefs	No. of used estimates	Minimum values ($/ha/yr)	Maximum values ($/ha/yr)	No. of single estimates	Single values ($/ha/yr)
	TOTAL:	**101**	**14**	**1,195,478**	**3**	**206,873**
	PROVISIONING SERVICES	**33**	**6**	**20,892**	**1**	**20,078**
1	Food	22	0	3752		
3	Raw materials	6	0	16,792		
4	Genetic resources				1	20,078
5	Medicinal resources	?				
6	Ornamental resources	5	6	348		
	REGULATING SERVICES	**17**	**8**	**33,640**	**2**	**186,795**
7	Influence on air quality	?				
8	Climate regulation				1	627
9	Moderation of extreme events	13	2	33,556		
11	Waste treatment / water purification	2	5	77		
12	Erosion prevention				1	186,168
13	Nutrient cycling	?				
15	Biological control	2	1	7		
	HABITAT SERVICES	**8**	**0**	**56,137**	**0**	**0**
16	Lifecycle maintenance (esp. nursery service)	?				
17	Gene pool protection (conservation)	8	0	56,137		
	CULTURAL SERVICES	**43**	**0**	**1,084,809**	**0**	**0**
18	Aesthetic information	12	0	27,317		
19	Opportunities for recreation and tourism	31	0	1,057,492		
20	Inspiration for culture, art and design	?				
21	Spiritual experience	?				
22	Cognitive information (education and science)	?				

Note: $/ha/yr – 2007 values.

Box A3.3 Example of TEV case study: The total economic value of the coral reefs on Hawaii

Hawaii's coral reef ecosystems provide many goods and services to coastal populations, such as fisheries and tourism. Besides, they form a unique natural ecosystem, with an important biodiversity value as well as scientific and educational value. Also, coral reefs form a natural protection against wave erosion. Without even attempting to measure their intrinsic value, this paper shows that coral reefs, if properly managed, contribute enormously to the welfare of Hawaii through a variety of quantifiable benefits. Net benefits of the State's 166,000 hectares of reef area of the main Hawaiian Islands are estimated at US$360 million a year for Hawaii's economy (Cesar and van Beukering, 2004).

Annual benefits of the Hawaiian coral reef

Types of value	Units	Value
Recreational value	Million$/yr	304
Amenity (real estate) value	Million$/yr	40
Research value	Million$/yr	17
Fishery value	Million$/yr	2.5
Total annual benefits	Million$/yr	363.5

Source: Cesar and van Beukering (2004, p240)

To assess the spatial variation of economic values of the Hawaiian reefs, the overall values are also expressed on a 'per area' basis (Cesar et al, 2002). Three case study sites were considered in particular. The most valuable site in Hawaii, and perhaps even in the world, is Hanauma Bay (Oahu) which had an extremely high intensity of recreational use. Reefs at Hanauma are ecologically average for Hawaiian standards, yet are more than 125 times more valuable (US$92/m^2) than the more ecologically diverse reefs at the Kona Coast (US$0.73/m^2). This demonstrates that economic values can differ dramatically from ecological values or researchers' preferences.

'coastal systems biome' but are dealt with here separately because of their unique and important ecosystem services.

As Table A3.2 shows, based on 101 data points, the total monetary value of the potential sustainable use of all services of coral reefs combined varies between 14 and 1,195,478 $/ha/yr. This excludes three services for which only one value was found (which would add over 200,000 $/ha/yr to the total value, mainly from erosion prevention).

A3.3 Monetary value of ecosystem services provided by coastal systems

The coastal biome includes several distinct ecosystems such as sea-grass fields, shallow seas of continental shelves, rocky shores and beaches, which are found in the terrestrial near-shore as well as the intertidal zones – that is, until the 200m bathymetric line with open oceans (UNEP-WCMC, 2006). Usually, coral reefs and coastal wetlands (mangroves and tidal marshes) are also included in the 'coastal systems-biome' but are dealt with here separately (in A3.2 and A3.4 respectively) because of their unique and important ecosystem services.

Table A3.3 Monetary value of services provided by coastal systems

Coastal systems	No. of used estimates	Minimum value ($/ha/yr)	Maximum value ($/ha/yr)	No. of single estimates	Single values ($/ha/yr)
TOTAL:	32	248	79,580	6	77,907
PROVISIONING SERVICES	19	1	7549	1	1453
1 Food	14	1	7517		
2 (Fresh) water supply				1	1453
3 Raw materials	5	0	32		
4 Genetic resources	?				
5 Medicinal resources	?				
6 Ornamental resources	?				
REGULATING SERVICES	4	170	30,451	2	76,144
7 Influence on air quality	?				
8 Climate regulation	?				
9 Moderation of extreme events				1	76,088
10 Regulation of water flows	?				
11 Waste treatment / water purification	?				
12 Erosion prevention	?				
13 Nutrient cycling / maintenance of soil fertility	4	170	30,451		
14 Pollination	?				
15 Biological control				1	56
HABITAT SERVICES	2	77	164	1	164
16 Lifecycle maintenance (esp. nursery service)	2	77	164		
17 Gene pool protection (conservation)				1	164
CULTURAL SERVICES	7	0	41,416	2	146
18 Aesthetic information				1	110
19 Opportunities for recreation and tourism	7	0	41,416		
20 Inspiration for culture, art and design	?				
21 Spiritual experience	?				
22 Cognitive information (education and science)				1	37

Note: $/ha/yr – 2007 values.

Box A3.4 Example of TEV case study: Valuing the services provided by the Peconic Estuary System, USA

This study looks at the wide range of ecosystem services provided by the Peconic estuary system, NY, USA, with twofold objectives. On the one hand, it aims at informing local coastal policies by assessing the economic impacts of ecological management strategies for the reservation or restoration of the estuary. On the other hand, it discusses various non-market valuation methodologies to identify the most appropriate approaches for different types of services, and highlights the issues arising in the integration of the findings of different methods in a TEV.

The coastal region valued is at the East End of Long Island and comprises a system of bays, islands, watershed lands and coastal communities. It includes a wide range of coastal resources, including fisheries, beaches, parks, open space and wildlife habitat, which are under threat from localized water pollution and loss of coastal habitats due to land conversion by development activities.

The study integrates the results of four economic studies:

A hedonic pricing study examines the value of environmental amenities such as open space and attractive views on the market price of property in the coastal town of Southold. In the 374 investigated parcels of land, the preservation of nearby open space is found to increase property values on average by 12.8 per cent, while dense development and proximity to highways and agricultural land have negative impacts ranging from 13.3 to 16.7 per cent.

A travel-cost study investigates the value of recreational activities such as *swimming, boating, fishing, and bird and wildlife viewing* taking place in the estuary. Based on 1354 completed surveys, the study estimated the consumer surplus that recreationists received, that is, the value above the cost of their recreational trip. Aggregating individual consumer surplus estimates over the whole population of recreationists reveals values equal to 12.1M$/yr for swimming, 18.0M$/yr for boating, 23.7M$/yr for recreational fishing and 27.3M$/yr for bird and wildlife watching.

A productivity function study assesses the value of eelgrass, sand/mud bottoms and inter-tidal salt marshes as a *nursery habitat for fish, shellfish and birds*. The study simulates the biological functions of the ecosystems to assess the marginal per acre value of productivity in terms of gains in commercial value for fish and shellfish, bird-watching and waterfowl hunting. Estimated yearly values per acre are $67 for inter tidal mudflats, $338 for saltmarsh and $1065 for eelgrass.

Finally, a contingent choice study investigates the willingness-to-pay of local residents for the preservation and restoration of key ecosystems in the Peconic estuary. Although the value estimates elicited partly overlap with the results of the other three methods, this study adds the additional dimension of *non-use and existence values* to the picture of the TEV of the estuary. The highest values are found for the preservation of farmland ($6398–9979 acre/yr), eelgrasses ($6003–8186 acre/yr) and wetlands ($4863–6560 acre/yr). Lower values are for undeveloped land ($1203–2080 acre/yr) and shellfish areas ($2724–4555 acre/yr).

Some useful general lessons for the valuation of the TEV of coastal ecosystems can be drawn. First, a single valuation method can hardly capture the complexity of the interactions between different types of land uses and services in coastal areas. Consider the case of farmland in the discussed study. Although hedonic pricing indicates negative *use values* of farmland, the contingent choice experiment shows that the willingness-to-pay of residents for farmland is high, suggesting that *non-use values* may play an important role in determining the total value of such land use.

Second, even when budget and time limitations allow for the implementation of different valuation methodologies, one must consider that integration of their findings is not straightforward. In the present study, simply summing up the values determined with hedonic pricing and the travel cost methods would lead to double-counting of benefits, since property values will likely also reflect the opportunities for recreation available in the neighbourhood. Similarly, the values elicited by the production function will partly reflect the opportunities for bird-watching and waterfowl hunting that high productivity entails.

Source: Johnston et al (2002)

As Table A3.3 shows, based on 32 data points, the total monetary value of the potential sustainable use of all services of coastal systems combined varies between 248 and 79,580 $/ha/yr. This excludes six services for which only one value was found (which would add almost 78,000 $/ha/yr to the total value, mainly from moderation of extreme events).

A3.4 Monetary value of ecosystem services provided by coastal wetlands

The coastal wetlands biome includes two main types of ecosystem – tidal marshes and mangroves (for other coastal systems, see A3.3). The coverage of this section is weighted towards mangrove ecosystems although the available valuation literature on tidal marshes is also presented.

As Table A3.4 shows, based on 112 data points, the total monetary value of the potential sustainable use of all services of coastal wetlands combined varies between 1995 and 215,349 $/ha/yr. This excludes two services for which only one value was found (which would add 960 $/ha/yr to the total value).

Table A3.4 Monetary value of services provided by coastal wetlands

	Coastal wetlands	No. of used estimates	Minimum value ($/ha/yr)	Maximum value ($/ha/yr)	No. of single estimates	Single values ($/ha/yr)
	TOTAL:	**112**	**1995**	**215,349**	**2**	**960**
	PROVISIONING SERVICES	**35**	**44**	**8289**	**0**	**0**
1	Food	12	0	2600		
2	(Fresh) water supply	3	41	4240		
3	Raw materials	18	1	1414		
4	Genetic resources	?				
5	Medicinal resources	2	2	35		
6	Ornamental resources	?				
	REGULATING SERVICES	**26**	**1914**	**135,361**	**2**	**960**
7	Influence on air quality				1	492
8	Climate regulation	6	2	4677		
9	Moderation of extreme events	13	4	9729		
10	Regulation of water flows	?				
11	Waste treatment / water purification	4	1811	120,200		
12	Erosion prevention	3	97	755		
13	Nutrient cycling and maintenance of soil fertility				1	468
14	Pollination	?				
15	Biological control	?				
	HABITAT SERVICES	**38**	**27**	**68,795**	**0**	**0**
16	Lifecycle maintenance (esp. nursery service)	33	2	59,645		
17	Gene pool protection (conservation)	5	25	9150		
	CULTURAL SERVICES	**13**	**10**	**2904**	**0**	**0**
18	Aesthetic information	?				
19	Opportunities for recreation and tourism	13	10	2904		
20	Inspiration for culture, art and design	?				
21	Spiritual experience	?				
22	Cognitive information (education and science)	?				

Note: $/ha/yr – 2007 values.

Box A3.5 Example of TEV case study:
The total economic value of the Muthurajawela
Wetland, Sri Lanka

The Muthurajawela Marsh covers an area of 3068 hectares, and is located near Colombo, the capital of Sri Lanka. It forms a coastal wetland together with the Negombo Lagoon. It is rich in biodiversity and in 1996 part of the wetland was declared a Wetland Sanctuary.

The pressures facing the Muthurajawela wetland are growing. Major threats are urban, residential, recreational, agricultural and industrial developments; over-harvesting of wetland species; and pollution from industrial and domestic wastes. As a result, the wetland has been seriously degraded.

The economic values of ecosystem services and total economic value of the Muthurajawela wetland are presented in the table below. This study used direct market prices to estimate direct use values such as fishing, firewood, agricultural production, recreation and also the support service to downstream fisheries. The replacement cost method was used to value indirect use values including wastewater treatment, freshwater supplies and flood attenuation.

Economic Value of the Muthurajawela Wetland, Sri Lanka

Economic benefit	Economic value per year (converted to 2003 US$)
Flood attenuation	5,033,800
Industrial wastewater treatment	1,682,841
Agricultural production	314,049
Support to downstream fisheries	207,361
Firewood	82,530
Fishing	64,904
Leisure and recreation	54,743
Domestic sewage treatment	44,790
Freshwater supplies for local populations	39,191
Carbon sequestration	8087
TOTAL ECONOMIC VALUE	7,532,297

Source: Emerton and Kekulandala (2003)

A3.5 Monetary value of ecosystem services provided by inland wetlands

This biome-type includes (freshwater) floodplains, swamps/marshes and peat lands. It explicitly does not include coastal wetlands and rivers and lakes, which are addressed in Sections A3.4 and A3.6 respectively.

As Table A3.5 shows, based on 86 data points, the total monetary value of the potential sustainable use of all services of inland wetlands combined varies between 981 and 44,597 $/ha/yr. This excludes six services for which only one value was found (which would add 282 $/ha/yr to the total value).

Table A3.5 Monetary value of services provided by inland wetlands

Inland wetlands	No. of used estimates	Minimum value (US$/ha/yr)	Maximum Value (US$/ha/yr)	No. of single estimates	Single values (US$/ha/yr)
TOTAL:	86	981	44,597	6	282
PROVISIONING SERVICES	34	2	9709	3	167
1 Food	16	0	2090		
2 (Fresh) water supply	6	1	5189		
3 Raw materials	12	1	2430		
4 Genetic resources				1	11
5 Medicinal resources				1	88
6 Ornamental resources				1	68
REGULATING SERVICES	30	321	23,018	3	115
7 Influence on air quality	?				
8 Climate regulation	5	4	351		
9 Moderation of extreme events	7	237	4430		
10 Regulation of water flows	4	14	9369		
11 Waste treatment / water purification	9	40	4280		
12 Erosion prevention				1	84
13 Nutrient cycling and maintenance of soil fertility	5	26	4588		
14 Pollination				1	16
15 Biological control				1	15
HABITAT SERVICES	9	10	3471	0	0
16 Lifecycle maintenance (esp. nursery service)	2	10	917		
17 Gene pool protection (conservation)	7	0	2554		
CULTURAL SERVICES	13	648	8399	0	0
18 Aesthetic information	2	83	3906		
19 Opportunities for recreation and tourism	9	1	3700		
20 Inspiration for culture, art and design	2	564	793		
21 Spiritual experience	?				
22 Cognitive information (education and science)	?				

Note: $/ha/yr – 2007 values.

Box A3.6 Two examples of TEV case studies on inland wetlands

a) Economic value of Whangamarino wetland, North Island, New Zealand (Kirkland, 1988)

Whangamarino wetland is the second largest peat bog and swamp complex on North Island, New Zealand. It is the most important breeding area in New Zealand for *Botaurus poiciloptilus* and a habitat for wintering birds and a diverse invertebrate fauna. The wetland covers an area of 10,320 hectares and supports a commercial fishery, cattle grazing and recreational activities. Estimated use and non-use values for Whangamarino are presented in the table below. These value estimates used the contingent valuation method.

Economic value of Whangamarino wetland, New Zealand

Economic benefit	Economic value per year (converted to 2003 US$)
Non-use preservation	7,247,117
Recreation	2,022,720
Commercial fishing	10,518
Flood control	601,037
TOTAL ECONOMIC VALUE	9,881,392

b) Economic value of the Charles River Basin wetlands, Massachusetts, US (Thibodeau and Ostro, 1981)

The Charles River Basin wetlands in Massachusetts consist of 3455 hectares of freshwater marsh and wooded swamp. This is 75 per cent of all the wetlands in Boston's major watershed. The benefits derived from these wetlands include flood control, amenity values, pollution reduction, water supply and recreational opportunities. Estimates of economic values derived from these wetlands are presented in the table below. Value estimates are obtained using a variety of valuation methods including hedonic pricing, replacement costs and market prices.

Economic value of Charles River Basin wetlands, Massachusetts, US

Economic benefit	Economic value per year (converted to 2003 US$)
Flood damage prevention	39,986,788
Amenity value of living close to the wetland	216,463
Pollution reduction	24,634,150
Recreational value: small game hunting, waterfowl hunting	23,771,954
Recreational value: trout fishing, warm water fishing	6,877,696
TOTAL	95,487,051

A3.6 Monetary value of ecosystem services provided by lakes and rivers

This biome-type includes freshwater rivers and lakes. Saline lakes, and wetlands and floodplains are not included in this biome (see coastal and inland wetlands).

As Table A3.6 shows, based on 12 data points, the total monetary value of the potential sustainable use of all services of rivers and lakes combined varies

Table A3.6 Monetary value of services provided by rivers and lakes

Rivers and lakes	No. of used estimates	Minimum value ($/ha/yr)	Maximum value ($/ha/yr)	No. of single estimates	Single values ($/ha/yr)
TOTAL:	12	1779	13,488	4	812
PROVISIONING SERVICES	5	1169	5776	1	3
1 Food	3	27	196		
2 (Fresh) water supply	2	1141	5580		
3 Raw materials				1	3
4 Genetic resources	?				
5 Medicinal resources	?				
6 Ornamental resources	?				
REGULATING SERVICES	2	305	4978	2	129
7 Influence on air quality	?				
8 Climate regulation				1	126
9 Moderation of extreme events	?				
10 Regulation of water flows	?				
11 Waste treatment / water purification	2	305	4978		
13 Nutrient cycling and maintenance of soil fertility				1	3
15 Biological control	?				
HABITAT SERVICES	0	0	0	1	681
16 Lifecycle maintenance (esp. nursery service)					
17 Gene pool protection (conservation)				1	681
CULTURAL SERVICES	5	305	2733	0	0
18 Aesthetic information	?				
19 Opportunities for recreation and tourism	5	305	2733		
20 Inspiration for culture, art and design	?				
21 Spiritual experience	?				
22 Cognitive information (education and science)	?				

Note: $/ha/yr – 2007 values.

between 1779 and 13,488 $/ha/yr. This excludes four services for which only one value was found (which would add 812 $/ha/yr to the total value).

For other examples of good TEV studies, see Thomas et al (1991).

Box A3.7 Example of TEV case study: TEV of the River Murray, Australia

The 2700km River Murray is Australia's longest freshwater river system and has been heavily modified and developed. Water from the River Murray is used for human consumption, and industrial and agricultural production. The River Murray channel and interconnected wetlands are important habitat for a large diversity of species and many locations along the river are recognized as internationally significant under the Ramsar Convention. The major ecosystem services provided by the river include freshwater for human consumption, recreation and tourism, aesthetics, agricultural production and fishing. Over-development and extraction of water for consumption and production purposes, exacerbated by recent drought, has compromised the ecological health of the river system. In 2007–08, the lack of inflows resulted in near-zero allocations to many irrigators who extract water from the River Murray and its upstream tributaries.

The annual economic values of major ecosystem services provided by the River Murray is listed in the table below. Values are drawn from several sources. Food produced from irrigation water diverted from the River Murray and the tourism and recreation services along the river account for the bulk of economic value. Other smaller but important values are the avoided damages provided by a freshwater system with low salt content, and the maintenance of sufficient environmental flows to maintain riverine species habitat.

TEV of ecosystem services provided by the River Murray, Australia (2007 AU$/Year)

Ecosystem service	Valuation method	Source	Total value ($m)
Recreation and tourism	Market prices	Howard, 2008	2970
Food production	Market prices	Australian Bureau of Statistics, 2008	1600*
Water quantity (environmental flows)	Contingent Valuation	Bennett, 2008	80
Water quality (no salinity)	Avoided cost	Connor, 2008	18
TEV			**4668**

Note: *An estimate for the River Murray water only. Total value of irrigated agriculture in Murray–Darling River Basin is $4600m. Water drawn from the River Murray for irrigation is approximately a third of the total water drawn from the Basin, suggesting the river's water accounts for a third of irrigated agriculture value.

A3.7 Monetary value of ecosystem services provided by tropical forests

The tropical forests biome includes various types of forests, for example moist- or rainforests, deciduous/semi-deciduous broadleaf forest and tropical mountain forests.

Table A3.7 Monetary value of services provided by tropical forests

Tropical forests	No. of used estimates	Minimum value (US$/ha/yr)	Maximum value (US$/ha/yr)	No. of single estimates	Single values (US$/ha/yr)
TOTAL:	**140**	**91**	**23,222**	2	**29**
PROVISIONING SERVICES	**63**	**26**	**9384**	0	**0**
1 Food	24	0	1204		
2 (Fresh) water supply	3	8	875		
3 Raw materials	27	2	3723		
4 Genetic resources	4	14	1799		
5 Medicinal resources	5	1	1782		
6 Ornamental resources	?				
REGULATING SERVICES	**43**	**57**	**7135**	1	**12**
7 Influence on air quality	2	13	957		
8 Climate regulation	10	13	761		
9 Moderation of extreme events	4	8	340		
10 Regulation of water flows	4	2	36		
11 Waste treatment / water purification	6	0	665		
12 Erosion prevention	11	11	3211		
13 Nutrient cycling and maintenance of soil fertility	3	2	1067		
14 Pollination	3	7	99		
15 Biological control				1	12
HABITAT SERVICES	**13**	**6**	**5277**	1	**17**
16 Lifecycle maintenance (esp. nursery service)				1	17
17 Gene pool protection (conservation)	13	6	5277		
CULTURAL SERVICES	**21**	**2**	**1426**	0	**0**
18 Aesthetic information	?				
19 Opportunities for recreation and tourism	21	2	1426		
20 Inspiration for culture, art and design	?				
21 Spiritual experience	?				
22 Cognitive information (education and science)	?				

Note: $/ha/yr – 2007 values.

As Table A3.7 shows, based on 140 data points, the total monetary value of the potential sustainable use of all services of tropical forests combined varies between 91 and 23,222 $/ha/yr. This excludes two services for which only one value was found (which would add 29 $/ha/yr to the total value).

Box A3.8 Example of TEV case study: Economic valuation of the Leuser National Park on Sumatra, Indonesia

One of the best examples of an evaluation of the TEV of tropical forests is the research undertaken by van Beukering et al (2003), which aimed to evaluate the TEV of the ecosystem services associated with the 25,000km² Leuser rainforest and buffer zone, and evaluate the consequences of deforestation on the delivery of these services.

Despite its protected status, about 20 per cent of Leuser National Park has been lost or degraded due to logging, exploitation of non-timber forest products (NTFP), illegal poaching, unsustainable tourism, and conversion to crop plantations. The consequence of this is that there has been a reduction in the forest area (ultimately leading to the development of wastelands), increased soil erosion (reducing agricultural productivity), reduced water retention (leading to increased frequency and intensity of floods and droughts) and reduced pollination and pest control (reducing agricultural productivity). To address these issues, the study examines three possible future scenarios for Leuser: a *deforestation* scenario (i.e. the current trend in logging and exploitation of NTFP continues); a *conservation* scenario (i.e. logging of primary and secondary forest cease, and eco-tourism is developed); and a *selective use* scenario (i.e. logging of primary forest is substantially reduced and logged forests are replanted + some eco-tourism development).

Eleven services were identified as being important for the appraisal of the three scenarios: water supply, fishery, flood and drought prevention, agriculture and plantations, hydro electricity, tourism, biodiversity, carbon sequestration, fire prevention, NTFP and timber. The economic value of the impacts were assessed using a wide range of economic techniques, including production functions, market prices and contingent valuation. The important message here is the fact that no single valuation method is capable of evaluating all the benefits streams; different valuation methods are suited to evaluate different impacts.

Following the approach described above, the authors estimate that the TEV of Leuser National Park (for the period 2000–2030) is US$9538 million for the *conservation* scenario, US$9100 million for the *selective use* scenario and US$6958 million for the *deforestation* scenario.

Finally, it is worth highlighting some key factors that made this an exemplar case study of the value of tropical forests. First, the authors utilized the knowledge and experience of local, regional and national stakeholders at all stages of the research. This is important as it helps to better define the impacts. Second, the use of the 'impact pathway' is important to help identify what the key impacts are. Finally, the research utilized a wide range of valuation methods to assess the impacts.

A3.8 Monetary value of ecosystem services provided by temperate and boreal forests

This biome-type includes temperate and boreal forest, or taiga. Temperate forests can be subdivided into temperate deciduous forest, temperate broadleaf and mixed forest, temperate coniferous forest and temperate rainforest.

Table A3.8 Monetary value of services provided by temperate forests

	Temperate forests	No. of used estimates	Minimum value ($/ha/yr)	Maximum value ($/ha/yr)	No. of single estimates	Single values ($/ha/yr)
	TOTAL:	40	30	4863	7	1281
	PROVISIONING SERVICES	15	25	1736	1	3
1	Food	5	0	1204		
2	(Fresh) water supply	3	0	455		
3	Raw materials	5	2	54		
4	Genetic resources				1	3
5	Medicinal resources	2	23	23		
6	Ornamental resources	?				
	REGULATING SERVICES	14	3	456	5	1277
7	Influence on air quality				1	805
8	Climate regulation	8	3	376		
9	Moderation of extreme events				1	0
10	Regulation of water flows	2	0	3		
11	Waste treatment / water purification	4	0	77		
12	Erosion prevention				1	1
13	Nutrient cycling and maintenance of soil fertility	?				
14	Pollination				1	452
15	Biological control				1	20
	HABITAT SERVICES	7	0	2575	0	0
16	Lifecycle maintenance (esp. nursery service)	?				
17	Gene pool protection (conservation)	7	0	2575		
	CULTURAL SERVICES	4	1	96	1	0
18	Aesthetic information	?				
19	Opportunities for recreation and tourism	4	1	96		
20	Inspiration for culture, art and design				1	0
21	Spiritual experience	?				
22	Cognitive information (education and science)	?				

Note: $/ha/yr – 2007 values.

As Table A3.8 shows, based on 40 data points, the total monetary value of the potential sustainable use of all services of temperate and boreal forests combined varies between 30 and 4863 $/ha/yr. This excludes seven services for which only one value was found (which would add 1281 $/ha/yr to the total value).

Another good TEV study was done on Chilean temperate rainforests by Nahuelhual et al, 2007.

Box A3.9 Example of TEV case study:
Economic valuation of Mediterranean forests

Mediterranean forests provide a wide array of benefits; however, most of them are poorly recognized. This study attempted to value comprehensively all forest benefits in Mediterranean countries. Its objective is to arrive at a rough order of magnitude of total forest value in each country and in the Mediterranean region as a whole, and of the composition of this value, using available data. Forest benefits are identified based on a common framework and valued using a range of methods. The novelty of this study arises from undertaking it on a large scale, within a structured framework that allows for estimates to be aggregated within countries and compared across countries.

The study covered 18 countries, divided into: Southern countries: Morocco, Algeria, Tunisia and Egypt; Eastern countries: Palestine, Israel, Lebanon, Syria, Turkey and Cyprus; Northern countries: Greece, Albania, Croatia, Slovenia, Italy, France, Spain and Portugal.

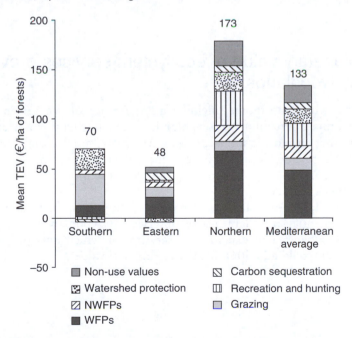

Figure A3.4 *Average estimates of forest benefits at Mediterranean and sub-Mediterranean levels*

The average TEV of Mediterranean forests is about €133/ha. The average TEV in northern countries (about €173/ha) is higher than that in the southern (about €70/ha) and eastern countries (about €48/ha). In per capita terms, forests provide annual benefits of over €50 to the Mediterranean people. Average benefits are higher in northern countries (over €70 per capita) and lower in southern (under €7 per capita) and eastern countries (under €11 per capita). The large difference between the estimates for northern and those for southern and eastern countries is due in part to the much larger extension of forest area relative to population in the north, as well as to their relatively higher quality, thanks to more favourable climatic conditions and lower levels of degradation. To some extent, it is also due to the greater degree of underestimation of benefits in southern and eastern countries (Figure A3.4).

The figure shows the average estimates of forest benefits at Mediterranean and sub-Mediterranean levels.

The study shows that wood forest products (WFPs) such as timber account for only a small portion of total forest benefits. Watershed protection benefits are often much more important. In the southern and eastern Mediterranean, grazing dominates. Recreation is already very important in the northern Mediterranean and its importance is likely to grow throughout the region. This multifunctionality needs to be explicitly recognized and incorporated into forest policy.

Source: Croitoru (2007)

A3.9 Monetary value of ecosystem services provided by woodlands

The 'woodland-biome' includes a large range of vegetation types including savannas, shrublands, scrublands and chaparral interleaved with one another in mosaic landscape patterns distributed along the western coasts of North and South America, and areas around the Mediterranean Sea, South Africa and Australia, jointly representing about 5 per cent of the planet's surface.

As Table A3.9 shows, based on 18 data points, the total monetary value of the potential sustainable use of all services of woodlands varies between 16 and 1950 $/ha/yr. This excludes six services for which only one value was found (which would add 5066 $/ha/yr to the total value).

Table A3.9 Monetary value of services provided by woodlands

Woodlands	No. of used estimates	Minimum value (US$/ha/yr)	Maximum value (US$/ha/yr)	No. of single estimates	Single values (US$/ha/yr)
TOTAL:	18	16	1950	6	5066
PROVISIONING SERVICES	12	7	862	1	25
1 Food	4	0	203		
2 (Fresh) water supply					
3 Raw materials	8	7	659		
4 Genetic resources	?				
5 Medicinal resources	?				
6 Ornamental resources				1	25
REGULATING SERVICES	6	9	1088	2	130
7 Influence on air quality				1	80
8 Climate regulation	2	9	387		
9 Moderation of extreme events	?				
10 Regulation of water flows	?				
11 Waste treatment / water purification	4	0	701		
12 Erosion prevention				1	49
13 Nutrient cycling and maintenance of soil fertility	?				
14 Pollination	?				
15 Biological control	?				
HABITAT SERVICES	0	0	0	2	1005
16 Lifecycle maintenance (esp. nursery service)				1	1003
17 Gene pool protection (conservation)				1	1
CULTURAL SERVICES	0	0	0	1	3907
18 Aesthetic information				1	3907
19 Opportunities for recreation and tourism	?				
20 Inspiration for culture, art and design	?				
21 Spiritual experience	?				
22 Cognitive information (education and science)	?				

Note: $/ha/yr – 2007 values.

Box A3.10 Example of TEV case study: Goods and services from Opuntia scrublands in Ayacucho, Peru

Opuntia scrublands are one of the most important Andean socio-ecosystems in terms of the social and ecological functions that they provide. They perform a major role protecting slopes against erosion, improving the soil properties and providing a variety of products employed in the human diet and in animal feeding, as well as cochineal insects, a highly valued source of dyes.

The ecosystem goods and services provided by Opuntia scrublands are very diverse with regard to the structures and functions involved in their supply, in their level of integration to diverse markets, and with regard to their contribution to human well-being.

Rodriguez et al (2006) contributed to the estimation of the use value of Opuntia scrublands to local communities in Ayacucho by initially exploring the 'cultural domain' of Opuntia in order to identify the ecosystem goods and services recognized by the Andean communities. Then, the local perception of the internal relationships among the goods and services provided by the scrubland was estimated, as well as the relationships between the Opuntia scrublands and other environmental and socio-economic systems existent in the region. The authors presented empirical estimates of the values of the goods and services provided by the Opuntia scrublands and their contribution to household income (see Table below).

Goods and services from Opuntia scrublands in Ayacucho, Peru)

	Average value US$/ha/yr
Provisioning services	**461**
Cochineal production	215.69
Fruit production	100.64
Fodder production	73.62
Fuel production	59.05
Ornamental production	12.41
Habitat service	**497**
Maintaining Cochineal population (for dye production)	496.83
Regulating services	**5**
Erosion control	5
Information function / cultural services	
Not quantified in monetary terms. However, many lyrics of Pumpin music, a traditional genre in Ayacucho are inspired by the Opuntia. Lyrics represent advice, rules and norms for the sustainable use of the goods and services provided by Opuntia scrublands	NA

Note: See section A3.10 for examples of TEV-calculations for fynbos and thicket ecosystems in South Africa.

Source: Rodriguez et al (2006)

A3.10 Monetary value of ecosystem services provided by grasslands

Grasslands occur in a wide variety of environments. They include tropical grasslands (savannas), temperate grasslands (including the European and

Table A3.10 Monetary value of services provided by grasslands

Grasslands	No. of used estimates	Minimum value ($/ha/yr)	Maximum value ($/ha/yr)	No. of single estimates	Single values ($/ha/yr)
TOTAL:	25	297	3091	3	752
PROVISIONING SERVICES	9	237	715	1	0
1 Food	3	4	82		
2 (Fresh) water supply	4	219	602		
3 Raw materials	2	14	31		
4 Genetic resources				1	0
5 Medicinal resources	?				
6 Ornamental resources	?				
REGULATING SERVICES	10	60	2067	2	752
7 Influence on air quality				1	219
8 Climate regulation	5	9	1661		
9 Moderation of extreme events	?				
10 Regulation of water flows	?				
11 Waste treatment / water purification	3	13	358		
12 Erosion prevention	2	38	47		
13 Nutrient cycling and maintenance of soil fertility				1	533
14 Pollination	?				
15 Biological control	?				
HABITAT SERVICES	3	0	298	0	0
16 Lifecycle maintenance (esp. nursery service)	?				
17 Gene pool protection (conservation)	3	0	298		
CULTURAL SERVICES	3	0	11	0	0
18 Aesthetic information	?				
19 Opportunities for recreation and tourism	3	0	11		
20 Inspiration for culture, art and design	?				
21 Spiritual experience	?				
22 Cognitive information (education and science)	?				

Note: $/ha/yr – 2007 values.

Central Asian steppe and North American prairie), boreal grasslands (tundras) and mountainous grasslands (such as the Latin American Paramo highlands). The largest continuous stretch of tropical grassland is the North African Sahel, which stretches from Senegal to the Horn of Africa.

As Table A3.10 shows, based on 25 data points, the total monetary value of the potential sustainable use of all services of grasslands varies between 297 and 3091 $/ha/yr. This excludes three services for which only one value was found (which would add 752 $/ha/yr to the total value).

Box A3.11 Example of TEV case study: The difference in ecosystem services supply before and after restoration in five catchments in dryland areas in South Africa

An example of a best-practice study is an elaborate hydrological–ecological–economic study undertaken to analyse ecosystem rehabilitation options in the Maloti–Drakensberg and Tsitsikamma–Baviaanskloof mountain ranges in South Africa (Blignaut et al, 2010; Mander et al, 2010). These studies targeted a fire-prone grassland ecosystem (the Maloti–Drakensberg sites), and compared it with fynbos and subtropical-thicket sites (the Tsitsikamma–Baviaanskloof), which together form some of South Africa's most strategic sources of fresh water. For example, the Maloti–Drakensberg range occupies less than 5 per cent of South Africa's surface area, yet it produces 25 per cent of the country's runoff through rivers, major dams, and national and international inter-basin transfers.

The specific objective of the studies was to analyse the financial and economic viability of restoration of these catchments, considering the costs of restoration and the benefits of enhanced watershed regulation, carbon sequestration and sediment retention services. Restoration includes the removal of invasive alien woody plant species, the introduction and revegetation of areas that are denuded of any vegetation due to overgrazing with indigenous vegetation, erosion control measures and improved fire management regimes. The results are listed in the table below.

The difference in ecosystem services supply before and after restoration in five catchments in dryland-areas in South Africa[1]

	Unit	Upper-Thukela	Upper-Mzimvubu	Krom	Kouga	Baviaans
		Grasslands biome	Grasslands biome	Fynbos biome	Fynbos biome	Sub-tropical thicket biome
Size of catchment	ha	187,619	397,771	101,798	242,689	160,209
Changes in watershed services						
Change in base-flow	m³/ha/yr	68.6	9.9	196.7	65.4	35.3
Sediment reduction	m³/ha/yr	6.7	12.4	0.9	0.5	0.3
Carbon dioxide sequestration	t//ha/yr	0.7	0.9	1.5	1.2	2.2

Financial and economic analysis of changes in watershed services following restoration

PV of base flow	$/ha/yr	2.82	1.1[2]	7.2	2.4	1.3
PV of carbon	$/ha/yr	10.5	12.6	9.5	7.4	14.0
PV of sediment reduction	$/ha/yr	4.4	8.5	0.3	0.2	0.1
PV of all other services[3]	$/ha/yr	8.7	8.7	1.7	5.5	8.6
PV of total services	$/ha/yr	26.5	31.0	18.7	15.5	24.0
PV of cost of intervention[4]	$/ha/yr	5.1	12.5	7.1	2.9	6.4
NPV of intervention[5]	$/ha/yr	21.5	18.5	11.6	12.6	17.6
Benefit–cost ratio	ratio	5.2	2.5	2.6	5.6	3.7
Average net return per ha: unsust. land use[6]	$/ha/yr	11.3 (±3)	11.3 (±3)	6.7 (±4)	6.7 (±4)	6.7 (±4)

Sources: Blignaut et al (2010); Mander et al (2010)

Notes:
1 Taken over 30 years at a social discount rate of 4 per cent.
2 Taken only for the dry winter months.
3 Value of all other quantifiable services for which a market exists, such as tourism, sustainable agriculture, etc.
4 Intervention implies the cost of restoration and the ensuing annual management action(s) after restoration.
5 Difference between the benefits and the costs.
6 These are the returns before the introduction of restoration and the conversion of the land-use practice to sustainable land management practices. These are therefore the current net financial returns to the landowner/user as a result of current land-use practices that result in increased degradation as a result of, among others, overgrazing and the application of wrong fire-management practices. These values are lower than the net present value (NPV) of restoration, indicating a positive societal benefit and net benefit for the landowner/user if they can be lured into a PES scheme and change their land-use practices.

The study shows that the present value (PV) of the benefits of the examined watershed services ranges from $15.5 to $31/ha/yr over the project period. The PV of the cost (both restoration and management) ranges from $3 to $12.5/ha/yr resulting in an NPV of $11.6 to $21.5/ha/yr. The study concluded that the benefits of introducing improved management practices exceeds cost in low to medium degraded areas, but not in heavily degraded ones. The economic return on the water (baseflow) produced by such a system of improved land-use management, however, far exceeds that of conventional (construction-based) water development programmes and offers meaningful economic and market development opportunities in the study area.

Another interesting study was done by Fernandez-Nunez et al (2007) on an economic evaluation of land-use alternatives between forest, grassland and silvopastoral systems.

A3.11 Monetary value of ecosystem services provided by polar and high mountain systems

The definition of polar and high mountain biomes used here deviates slightly from that used in the Millennium Ecosystem Assessment (MA, 2005). In particular, we define this biome in terms of its cryosphere (Kotlyakov, 2009). Based on this definition, polar regions include all the Arctic seas and much of the Southern Ocean, the tundra/permafrost zone to the tree line, areas where there is long-term snow cover (especially in the Arctic), and submarine zones in the Southern/Arctic oceans. This definition corresponds well with the WWF Arctic ecoregions (www.panda.org), the Udvardy (1975) and Clark and Dingwall (1985) biogeographical provinces for Antarctica.

Similar criteria could be applied to high mountains, extrapolating from the altitudinal maps produced by Messerli and Ives (1997) at the UNU. So, for example, high mountain regions could be defined as those areas higher than the 1000masl mean line.

The MA gives the share of terrestrial space of polar and high mountains as 31 per cent (MA, 2005, Synthesis volume, p31, Table 1.1). Our revised definition would put the cryosphere proportion nearer 50 per cent of terrestrial space (at maximum seasonal extension).

As Christie et al (2005) note, there is currently very little quantification of the monetary value of services provided by polar and high mountain systems. The lack of monetary valuation research, however, should not be interpreted to infer that polar and high mountain areas do not deliver important services. Indeed, it is clear that these cryospheres are of paramount importance in terms of global ecosystem services.

The most important services are briefly discussed below.

1 Fishing

It is estimated that the Southern Ocean contributes around one sixth of the global fish take (Kock, 1992) and that this resource may become increasingly important as other areas are fished out. However, legal protection of these marine resources is fragile (Constable et al, 2000). For example, the Commission for the Conservation of Antarctic Marine Living Resources suggests that 80–90 per cent of the take of the rare Patagonian toothfish was illegal (MA, 2005, p487).

2 Freshwater storage

Approximately 80 per cent of the planet's freshwater is locked up in the ice caps (Pitt, 1995). A significant proportion of the world's population depends on the meltwater of high mountain glaciers. Climate change threatens the existence of these glaciers, which in turn could have significant local and global consequences.

For example, the glaciers in the Himalayas and on the Tibetan plateau sustain the major rivers of India and China, which are used for irrigation of wheat and rice fields. Given that India and China are the world's leading wheat and rice producers, projected melting of the glaciers presents a significant threat to local and global food security (Brown, 2009).

3 Raw materials

Raw materials are very valuable too in the cryosphere (e.g. Orrego-Vicuña, 2009; Emmerson, 2010; Howard, 2010) and becoming a major area for international conflict. The Arctic is said to contain more than a quarter of the world's hydrocarbons (Mikkelsen and Langhelle, 2008) and is widely presumed to be a future flashpoint as nations compete. The Antarctic Treaty System (ATS) currently prohibits exploitation of raw materials and creates the world's largest protected and demilitarized area reserved 'for peace and science': however, the ATS expires in 2041 and its replacement is uncertain. Even now there is conflict over resources. The Australians and New Zealanders are currently taking the Japanese to court over abuses of the whaling moratorium. The British and Argentinians are involving warships as oil drilling is explored in the Falklands/Malvinas, while even old friends like Canada and the USA are at daggers drawn over the NW passage.

4 Climate regulation

Both the Southern Ocean and the Arctic permafrost/tundra are major greenhouse carbon sinks. However, global warming is likely to convert the Arctic permafrost/tundra into a net source of greenhouse gases (including methane) (McGuire et al, 2000). The polar regions also have a significant role in reducing climate change through the albedo effect, that is, they reflect the sun's light back into space (MA, 2005, v1, p859). Prizborski (2010) also suggests that the recent calving of the $2545km^2$ Mertz glacier tongue iceberg may disrupt ocean currents worldwide by blocking the flow of bottom water.

The Pew Report on Arctic melting (Goodstein et al, 2010) estimates that the loss of Arctic snow, ice and permafrost currently costs the world US$61–371 billion annually.

5 Habitat service

The apparently dead and frozen waste of the cryosphere has been called species poor but evidence is accumulating not only of life in the extreme cold (including suspended animation), but also of vibrant hot spots, for example in the polynyas, sea leads, extensive subglacial lakes or on the seamounts, around the volcanic vents and so on. The International Polar Year (IPY) archive will contain faunal census material, though we have some estimates for some species (e.g. Shirihai (2007) for Antarctica, CAFF (2001) and Ervin (2010) in the Arctic), while the international circum-Antarctic census of marine life will be a benchmark in the Southern Ocean. In biomass terms the primary productivity of the Southern

Ocean is enormous: van der Zwaag (1986) estimates that it is more than 50 times that of the North Sea in terms of grams of carbon per m² per annum. The NPP figures in the MA Synthesis Table (MA, 2005) are very low for the polar biome especially and may need revisiting after IPY.

6 Cultural services and tourism

Current there is little information on the aesthetic, recreational, inspirational, spiritual, cognitive etc. values of the cryosphere, and innovative methods such as those highlighted by Christie (2005) will be needed to calculate these types of values. For example, Samson and Pitt (2000) explore the passive use values of the cryosphere including the role it plays in what has been called the noosphere: the realm of ideas which embraces all cultural activities. Pitt (2010) has explored how iconic cryosphere species score in terms of internet hits: penguins top the poll. High mountains contain the most sacred and holy sites of humanity.

The cryosphere is also an important tourism resource. Snyder and Stonehouse (2007) project that in 2010 there will be 1.5 million visitors to the Arctic, 80,000 to the Antarctic, 10 million to the Alps and many more in other high mountains.

Notes

1   Throughout this Appendix we use 'biome' as shorthand for the 11 main types of ecosystem complexes for which we analysed the monetary value of the services they provide. Each biome can be split into several ecosystems, each with its own set of ecosystem services, but for the purpose of this chapter, data on monetary values was presented at the biome-level (for details see www.teebweb.org/Database).

2   In addition to individual publications, the following ecosystem service databases were used: COPI (Ten Brink et al, 2009), EVRI (1997), ENValue (2004), EcoValue (Wilson et al, 2004), Consvalmap (Conservation International, 2006), CaseBase (FSD, 2007), ValueBaseSwe (Sundberg and Söderqvist, 2004), ESD-ARIES (UVM, 2008) and FEEM (Ojea et al, 2009). See www.es-partnership.org for access to most of these databases.

3   Note that often the minimum and maximum values are outliers. When using the information in this Appendix for benefit transfer purposes (which is not recommended since all values are highly context-specific) one should not simply take the average of these minimum and maximum values but consult the original values presented in the Database Matrix on the TEEB website.

4   This Bill is now an Act, see www.defra.gov.uk/environment/marine/legislation/mcaa/index.htm.

References

ABPMer (2007) 'Cost impact of marine biodiversity policies on business – the marine bill', Final Report to Defra

Australian Bureau of Statistics (2008) *Water and the Murray-Darling Basin: A Statistical Profile, 2000–01 to 2005–06*, available at www.abs.gov.au/AUSSTATS/abs@.nsf/mf/4610.0.55.007/

Barbier, E. B., Baumgärtner, S., Chopra, K., Costello, C., Duraiappah, A., Hassan, R., Kinzig, A., Lehman, M., Pascual, U., Polasky, S. and Perrings, C. (2009) 'The Valuation of Ecosystem Services', in Naeem, S., Bunker, D. E., Hector, A., Loreau, M. and Perrings, C. (eds) *Biodiversity, Ecosystem Functioning, and Human Wellbeing: An Ecological and Economic Perspective*, Oxford University Press, Oxford

Baumgärtner, S., Becker, C., Faber, M. and Manstetten, R. (2006) 'Relative and absolute scarcity of nature: Assessing the roles of economics and ecology for biodiversity conservation', *Ecological Economics*, vol 59, no 4, pp487–498

Beaumont, N. J., Austen, M. C., Mangi, S. C. and Townsend, M. (2008) 'Economic valuation for the conservation of marine biodiversity', *Marine Pollution Bulletin*, vol 56, no 3, pp386–396

Bennett, J. (2008) 'Defining and managing environmental flows: Inputs from society', *Economic Papers*, vol 27, no 2, pp167–183

Blignaut, J., Mander, M., Schulze, R., Horan, M., Dickens, C., Pringle, K., Mavundla, K., Mahlangu, I., Wilson, A., McKenzie, M. and McKean, S. (2010) 'Restoring and managing natural capital towards fostering economic development: Evidence from the Drakensberg, South Africa', *Ecological Economics*, vol 69, no 6, pp1313–1323

Brown, L. R. (2009) *Plan B 4.0: Mobilizing to Save Civilization*, W. W. Norton & Company, New York

CAFF (Conservation of Arctic Flora and Fauna) (2001) *Arctic Flora and Fauna: Status and Conservation*, Arctic Council Program for the Conservation of Arctic Flora and Fauna, Helsinki, Finland

Cesar, H. S. J. and van Beukering, P. J. H. (2004) 'Economic valuation of the coral reefs of Hawaii', *Pacific Science*, vol 58, no 2, pp231–242

Cesar, H. S. J., van Beukering, P. J. H. and Pintz, S. (2002) *The Economic Value of Coral Reefs in Hawai'i*, Hawai'i Coral Reef Initiative (HCRI), University of Hawai'i, Honolulu

Christie, P. (2005) 'Is integrated coastal management sustainable?', *Ocean and Coastal Management*, vol 48, pp208–232

Christie, P., Lowry, K., White, A. T., Oracion, E. G., Sievanen, L., Pomeroy, R. S., Pollnac, R. B., Patlis, J. and Eisma, L. (2005) 'Key findings from a multidisciplinary examination of integrated coastal management process sustainability', *Ocean and Coastal Management*, vol 48, pp468–483

Clark, M. and Dingwall, P. (1985) *Conservation of Islands in the Southern Ocean*, prepared with the financial assistance of the World Wildlife Fund, IUCN, Gland, Switzerland and Cambridge, UK

Connor, J. (2008) 'The economics of time delayed salinity impact management in the River Murray', *Water Resources Research*, vol 44, W03401, doi:10.1029/2006WR005745

Conservation International (2006) 'Consvalmap: Conservation International Ecosystem Services Database', available at www.consvalmap.org

Constable, A. J., de la Mare, W. K., Agnew, D. J., Everson, I. and Miller, D. (2000) 'Managing fisheries to conserve the Antarctic marine ecosystem: Practical implementation of the Convention on the Conservation of Antarctic Marine Living Resources (CCAMLR)', *ICES Journal of Marine Science*, vol 57, no 3, pp778–791

Croitoru, L. (2007) 'How much are Mediterranean forests worth?', *Forest Policy and Economics*, vol 9, no 5, pp536–545

Emmerson, C. (2010) *The Future History of the Arctic*, Public Affairs, Perseus Books Group, New York

Emerton, L. and Kekulandala, L. D. C. B. (2003) 'Assessment of the Economic Value of Muthurajawela Wetland', Occasional Papers of IUCN, Sri Lanka No. 4, International Union for Conservation of Nature, Gland, Switzerland

ENVAlue (2004) 'Environmental Valuation Database', developed by the New South Wales Environmental Protection Agency, New Zealand, available at www.environment.nsw.gov.au/envalue/

EPA (2009) *Valuing the Protection of Ecological Systems and Services*, a report of the EPA Science Advisory Committee, EPA-SAB-09-012, May, available at www.epa.gov/sab

Ervin, J. (2010) 'Management and conservation of wildlife in the Arctic', *Encyclopaedia of Earth*, available at www.eoearth.org

EVRI (The Environmental Valuation Reference Inventory) (1997) developed by De Civita, P., Filion, F., Frehs, J. and Jay, M., available at www.evri.ca

Fernandez-Nunez, E., Mosquera-Losada, M. R. and Rigueiro-Rodríguez, A. (2007) 'Economic evaluation of different land use alternatives: Forest, grassland and silvopastoral systems. Permanent and temporary grassland: Plant, environment and economy', *Proceedings of the 14th Symposium of the European Grassland Federation*, Ghent, Belgium, 3–5 September, pp508–511

FSD (2007) *Nature Valuation and Financing CaseBase*, Foundation for Sustainable Development, Wageningen, the Netherlands, available at www.eyes4earth.org/casebase/

Goodstein, E., Huntington, H. and Euskirchen, E. (2010) 'An initial estimate of the cost of lost climate regulation services due to changes in the Arctic cryosphere', Pew Foundation, Philadelphia, PA, and Washington, DC

Goulder, L. H. and Kennedy, J. (1997) 'Valuing Ecosystem Services: Philosophical Bases and Empirical Methods', in Daily, G. C. (ed) *Nature's Services: Societal Dependence on Natural Ecosystems*, Island Press, Washington, DC

Howard, J. L. (2008) 'The future of the Murray River: Amenity re-considered?', *Geographical Research*, vol 46, pp291–302

Howard, R. (2010) *Arctic Gold Rush: The New Race for Tomorrow's Natural Resources*, Continuum, London

Hussain, S. S., Winrow-Giffin, A., Moran, D., Robinson, L. A., Fofana, A., Paramor, O. A. L. and Frid, C. L. J. (2010) 'An ex ante ecological economic assessment of the benefits arising from marine protected areas designation in the UK', Ecological Economics, vol 69, no 4, pp828–838

Johnston, R. J., Grigalunas, T. A., Opaluch, J. J., Mazzotta, M. and Diamantedes, J. (2002) 'Valuing estuarine resource services using economic and ecological models: The Peconic Estuary system', *Coastal Management*, vol 30, no 1, pp47–65

Kirkland, W. T. (1988) 'Preserving the Whangamarino wetland: An application of the contingent valuation method', Masters Thesis, Massey University, New Zealand, in Dumsday, R. G. K., Jakobsson, K. and Ransome, S. (1992) 'State-wide Assessment of Protection of River Segments in Victoria, Australia', Paper presented to a symposium on the management of public resources, Resource Policy Consortium, 21–22 May, Washington, DC

Kock, K.-H. (1992) *Antarctic Fish and Fisheries (Studies in polar research)*, Cambridge University Press, Cambridge

Kotlyakov, V. (2009) 'Cryosphere and climate', *International Polar Year (IPY)*, www.IPY.org

MA (Millennium Ecosystem Assessment) (2005) *Ecosystems and Human Well-being: Synthesis*, Island Press, Washington, DC

Mander, M., Blignaut, J., van Niekerk, M. A., Cowling, R., Horan, M. J. C., Knoesen, D. M., Mills, A., Powell, M. and Schulze, R. E. (2010) 'Baviaanskloof – Tsitsikamma: Payment for ecosystem services: A feasibility assessment', unpublished draft report, SANBI, Pretoria and Cape Town

McGuire, A. D., Clein, J. S., Melillo, J. M., Kicklighter, D. W., Meier, R. A., Vorosmarty, C. J. and Serreze, M. C. (2000) 'Modeling carbon responses of tundra ecosystems to historical and projected climate: Sensitivity of Pan-arctic carbon storage to temporal and spatial variation in climate', *Global Change Biology*, vol 6, supp/1, pp141–159

Messerli, B. and Ives, J. D. (eds) (1997) *Mountains of the World: A Global Priority*, The Parthenon Publishing Group, London and New York

Mikkelsen, A. and Langhelle, O. (eds) (2008) *Arctic Oil and Gas: Sustainability at Risk?*, Routledge Explorations in Environmental Economics, Routledge, Abingdon

Nahuelhual, L., Donoso, P., Lara, A., Núñez, D., Oyarzún, C. and Neira, E. (2007) 'Valuing ecosystem services of Chilean temperate rainforests', *Environment, Development and Sustainability*, vol 9, pp481–499

Ojea, E., Nunes, P. A. L. D. and Loureiro, M. L. (2009) 'Mapping of forest biodiversity values: A plural perspective', Fondazione Eni Enrico Mattei Working Papers, available at www.feem.it/userfiles/attach/Publication/NDL2009/NDL2009-004.pdf

Orrego-Vicuña, F. (ed) (2009) *Antarctic Resources Policy: Scientific, Legal and Political Issues*, Cambridge University Press, Cambridge

Pitt, D. (1995) *Water in a Warmer World: An Open Learning Guide*, Ecotrends 1, Pacific Press, Nampa, ID

Pitt, D. (2010) *Ice Scenarios*, Pacific Press, Nampa

Prizborski, P. (2010) 'Collision calves iceberg from Mertz Glacier Tongue, Antarctica', Earth Observatory NASA, Greenbelt, MD

Rodriguez, L. C., Pascual, U. and Niemeyer, H. M. (2006) 'Local identification and valuation of ecosystem goods and services from Opuntia scrublands of Ayacucho, Peru', *Ecological Economics*, vol 57, pp30–44

Samson, P. R. and Pitt, D. (eds) (2000) *The Biosphere and Noosphere Reader: Global Environment, Society and Change*, Routledge, Abingdon

Shirihai, H. (2007) *A Complete Guide to Antarctic Wildlife: The Birds and Marine Mammals of the Antarctic Continent and the Southern Ocean: The Ultimate Antarctic/Southern Ocean Field Guide*, A & C Black, London

Snyder, J. and Stonehouse, B. (eds) (2007) *Prospects for Polar Tourism*, CABI, Wallingford

Sundberg, S. and Söderqvist, T. (2004) *ValueBaseSWE: A Valuation Study Database for Environmental Change in Sweden*, Beijer International Institute of Ecological Economics, The Royal Swedish Academy of Sciences, Stockholm

TEEB in National Policy (2011) *The Economics of Ecosystems and Biodiversity in National and International Policy Making* (ed Patrick ten Brink), Earthscan, London

TEEB in Local Policy (2011) *The Economics of Ecosystems and Biodiversity in Local and Regional Policy and Management* (eds Heidi Wittmer and Haripriya Gundimeda), Earthscan, London

TEEB in Business (2011) *The Economics of Ecosystems and Biodiversity in Business and Enterprise* (ed Joshua Bishop), Earthscan, London

Ten Brink, P., Bassi, S., Gantioler, S., Kettunen, M., Rayment, M., Foo, V., Bräuer, I., Gerdes, H., Stupak, N., Braat, L., Markandya, A., Chiabai, A., Nunes, P., ten Brink, B. and van Oorschot, M. (2009) *Further Developing Assumptions on Monetary Valuation of Biodiversity Cost Of Policy Inaction (COPI)*, Contract 07.0307/2008/514422/ETU/G1 for DG Environment of the European Commission, Institute for European Environmental Policy (IEEP), London and Brussels

Thibodeau, F. R. and Ostro, B. D. (1981) 'An economic analysis of wetland protection', *Journal of Environmental Management*, vol 12, pp19–30

Thomas, D. H. L., Ayache, F. and Hollis, G. E. (1991) 'Use and non-use values in the conservation of Ichkeul National Park, Tunisia', *Environmental Conservation*, vol 18, pp119–130

Turner, R. K., Paavola, J., Cooper, P., Farber, S., Jessamy, V. and Georgiou, S. (2003) 'Valuing nature: Lessons learned and future research directions', *Ecological Economics*, vol 46, pp493–510

Udvardy, M. (1975) 'A Classification of the Biogeographical Provinces of the World', IUCN Occasional Paper 18, International Union for Conservation of Nature, Morges, Switzerland

UNEP-WCMC (2006) *In the Front Line: Shoreline Protection and Other Ecosystem Services from Mangroves and Coral Reefs*, United Nations Environment Programme (UNEP), World Conservation Monitoring Centre (WCMC), Cambridge, UK

UVM (2008) Ecosystem Service Database (ESD) / ARIES, developed by University of Vermont, USA, available at http://esd.uvm.edu/

Van Beukering, P. J. H., Cesara, H. S. J. and Janssen, M. A. (2003) 'Economic valuation of the Leuser National Park on Sumatra, Indonesia', *Ecological Economics*, vol 44, pp43–62

Van der Zwaag, D. (1986) in: Archer C. and Scrivener, D. (eds) *Northern Waters: Resources and Security Issues*, Routledge, London

Wilson, M. A., Costanza, R. and Troy, A. (2004) *The EcoValue Project*, retrieved from the University of Vermont EcoValue, available at http://ecovalue.uvm.edu

World Bank (2007) *World Development Indicators*, World Bank Publications, Washington, DC

Index

açaí palm fruit   167–168
Adamowicz, W. L.   226
adjusted unit benefit transfer   230
administrators, local   32
aerosols   70
aggregation   29, 232
agricultural landscape   137
agriculture   3, 63, 221–222
agro-ecosystems   56–58
air quality regulation   67–69
albedo   69
altruist values   196
Amazon rainforest   261
amenity services *see* cultural services
appropriation   188
aquaculture   58
Arenas, F.   52
Arrow, K.   171
Ashby, W. R.   172
Atkinson, G.   302
Atlee, T.   173–174
avoided cost method   198
awareness, raising   31

Balmford, A.   56, 119, 137
Balvanera, P.   52
Barbier, E. B.   198–199, 213, 224
Barrios, E.   73
Bateman, J.   235
Beckerman, W.   262
behavioural economics   268–271
Beltratti, A.   269
beneficiary trade-offs   83
benefits   18–19, 27–29, 141–142, 194, 221, 288
benefit transfer (BT)   186, 229–242, 293
    adjusted unit BT   230
    aggregation   232
    equity weighting   236
    meta-analytic function transfer   230
    non-constant marginal values   234–235
    primary estimates   236–237
    resilience   241
    scale   232–233
    scaling up   237–239
    TEV   240
    transfer errors   231–232
    uncertainty   240–241
    unit BT   229–230
    value function transfer   230
    variation in values   233–234

bequest values   196
BII (Biodiversity Intactness Index)   129
biochemical resources   65–66
biodiversity
    change   96, 118
    definition   23
    economics   2–4, 263, 278, 287–289
    ecosystem functions   46–47, 50–53
    ecosystems   44, 273
    ecosystem services   6, 54–56
    Global Biodiversity Assessment   2
    hotspots   78
    importance of   95
    linkages   289–290
    measurement   54–55
    as portfolio of biotic resources   95
    Potsdam Initiative   4
    resilience   219
    theory   45–51
    value of   6, 91
    see also economic valuation; ecosystem services
Biodiversity 2010 Target (CBD)   117, 119
biodiversity change   96, 118
Biodiversity Intactness Index (BII)   129
biofuels   61–62
biological control   75–77
biomass   61, 65
biomes   22–24
biophilia hypothesis   154
biophysical measurements *see* indicators
biophysical structure *see* ecological structure
biophysical valuation   191–192
bioprospecting   160, 196, 224
biotic communities   47–50
birds   66–67
Bird, W.   68
Bowles, S.   161
Bromley, D.   277
Brookshire, D. S.   213
Brundtland report ('Our Common Future')   155
BT *see* benefit transfer
buffering mechanisms   85–86
Bullock, J. M.   52
Bulte, E.   224
business end-users   33

carbon, stores   70
carbon dioxide (CO$_2$)   69–71
carbon sequestration   136–137

CBA (cost-benefit analysis) 30
CBD (Convention on Biological Diversity) 4,
    117, 119, 155–156
Chan, K. M. A. 139
change
    biodiversity 96, 118
    ecosystem services 44, 84–91
    land-cover 130–131
Chichilnisky, G. 269
choice modelling (CM) 200, 202
Christie, M. 202, 204, 227
climate change, economics of 4, 263, 278
climate regulation 69–71, 136
CM (choice modelling) 200, 202
CO$_2$ (carbon dioxide) 69–71
coastal regions 72
coffee 169
co-intelligence 174
commodity chains 166–170, 292
communities of organisms 47–50
condition, indicators of 129–130
connectivity, landscape level 171
conservation 2, 31, 155, 274–276, 291
consumer organizations 33
Contamin, R. 223
contingent valuation method (CV) 200
Convention on Biological Diversity (CBD) 4,
    117, 119, 155–156
coral reefs 220
Costanza, R. 2, 13, 52, 131
cost-based methods 198
cost-benefit analysis (CBA) 30
cost-effectiveness approach 30
critical natural capital 194, 238
Crocker, T. D. 213–214
Cropper, W. 269
cultural services 79–80, 131, 137, 196
CV (contingent valuation method) 200

Daily, G. 2, 13
Damasio, A. 165
Dasgupta, P. 262, 266–267
data enrichment models 217–218
decision making 29–33, 190
definitions
    biodiversity 23
    ecosystem 23
    index (indices) 117
    indicator 116–117
    measure 116
    natural capital 13
    sustainable development 260
    total economic value (TEV) 188
    uncertainty 212
        see also glossary
deforestation 167, 169, 171
de Groot, R. S. 14
de Leo, G. A. 50

deliberative valuation 162–164, 203
demand curves 238
Descola, P. 153, 171
developing countries 227–229, 237, 292–293
direct drivers 1, 32, 130
direct market valuation 197–199
direct use values 194
discounting 259–279
    Amazon 261
    behavioural economics 268–271
    as ethical choice 294–295
    long-term issues 271–279
    overview 260–263, 278–279
    Ramsey discounting equation 264–267
    spatial 235–236
    uncertainty 264, 270
diseases 3
disservices 19, 82
distance decay 235
diversity, indicators of 127
drivers 1, 4, 31–32, 130, 289
dry matter productivity (DMP) 134–136

Earnhart, D. 218
EASAC (European Academies Science
    Advisory Council) 56
ecological benefits and values 28
ecological-economic accounting *see* ecosystem
    accounting
Ecological Footprint 130
ecological production functions 92–93
ecological resilience *see* resilience
ecological restoration 88–89
ecological structure 18
ecology, economics 1, 13–19, 287
economic benefits and values 28–29
economic man 154
economic performance 303
economics
    behavioural 268–271
    biodiversity 2–4, 263, 278, 287–289
    climate change 4, 263, 278
    ecology 1, 13–19, 287
    ecosystems 2–4, 6, 287–289
    environmental 194, 263, 267
    epistemological tradition 154
    intrinsic values 161
    natural capital 187
    psychology 158
    resources 1
    sustainability 260, 266
    see also discounting; economic valuation
*Economics of Climate Change, The: Stern
    Review* 4, 263
Economics of Ecosystems and Biodiversity,
    The *see* TEEB
economic valuation 15–16, 19, 292–294
    challenges of 166–174, 188, 292

complexity   170–171
developing countries   227–229
function   291
global estimate   2
implications   157–160
limitations   156–157, 186, 293
methods   162–164, 171–174, 186
paradigms   191–192
reasons for   190
socio-cultural context   151–152, 155,
     165, 297–298
stakeholders   225–227
uncertainty   186, 212–218, 292–294
see also total economic value; valuation
ecosystem accounting   30, 302–303
ecosystem assessments   11, 288
     see also Millennium Ecosystem Assessment
ecosystem capital *see* natural capital
ecosystem degradation   81
ecosystem engineers   51
ecosystem functions   18, 24–25
     and biodiversity   46–47, 50–53
     process-response model   89–91
ecosystem people (native communities)   27
ecosystem resilience *see* resilience
ecosystems
     biodiversity   44, 273
     definition   23
     economics   2–4, 6, 287–289
     framing   188
     global valuation estimate   2
     interactions   96
     linkages   289–290
     macroeconomic framework   298–301
     people   3, 44, 289
     TEEB classification   38–39
     value of   94
     see also economic valuation; ecosystem
        services
ecosystem services
     benefits   18–19
     biodiversity   6, 54–56
     bundles   81
     cultural and amenity services   79–80
     defining   16–17
     degradation   2–3
     ecological structure   18
     enhancement   3
     evaluation   47
     flow of   291
     functions   18
     habitat services   25, 77–79
     indicators   131–133
     linkages   289–290
     management   84–91
     mapping   139
     markets   6
     Millennium Ecosystem Assessment   12,
        14, 156

multiple   44, 81–84
overview   12–15
provisioning services   56–67
regulating services   67–77
scale   84
TEEB classification   39–40
typology   25–27
value of   6, 91–92
see also economic valuation
EDF (expected damage function)   213
Ehrlich, A. H.   13, 271
Ehrlich, P. R.   13, 271
Eichner, T.   300
Ellen, R. F.   153–154
Ellison, A. M.   223
embedding problem   203
emotions *see* feelings
environment *see* nature
environmental draw-down   279, 295
environmental economics   194, 263, 267
environmental envelope   89
environmentalism   155
Environmental Protection Agency (EPA)   156
environmental regulation services   67–69
environmental shocks   89
environmental valuation *see* economic
     valuation
EPA (Environmental Protection Agency)   156
equity   27
equity premiums   269–270
equity weighting   236
Erickson, J.   158
erosion prevention   72–73
Eshet, T.   231
ethical behaviour   165–166
ethics   264, 295
European Academies Science Advisory Council
     (EASAC)   56
European Environment Agency   30
eutrophication   60, 85–86
existence values   196
expected consumer surplus   224
expected damage function (EDF)   213
expected utility   225
expected values   213
extinction   3, 129, 271–272
extreme events, moderation of   71–72

failures, multiple ecosystem services   81
Farley, J.   238
feelings   165–166
fertilizers   3
fibres   61–62
Figge, F.   221
Finnoff, D.   300
fish   57–58, 66
Fisher, A.   276
fit-for-purpose indicators *see* relevant
     indicators

flooding   71–72
food provision   56–59
forests
    Amazon   261
    climate regulation   70
    deforestation   167, 169, 171
    fuels and fibres   61–62
    resources   169
    timber production   134–136
    valuation methods   204–209, 224–225
    water provision   59, 61
Frame, B.   173
Frederick, S.   265
Freeman, A. M.   212
fuels   61–62
Fuller, R. A.   80
functional diversity   50, 53–54
functional groups   53–54, 94, 298
functions see ecosystem functions

Gadgil, M.   221
GDP (gross domestic product)   301–302
genetic diversity maintenance   78–79
genetic resources   63–65
geographical information systems (GIS)   233
Ghermandi, A.   234
Gintis, H.   161
GIS (geographical information systems)   233
Global Biodiversity Assessment   2
Global Land Cover   130
global valuation estimate   2
glossary   xxix–xxxvii
GNP (gross national product)   301
Görg, C.   171
Gorshkov, V. G.   59
Gotelli, N. J.   52
governance   29–31
Gowdy, J.   154, 158, 161
Grace, J. B.   51
greenhouse gases   69
green space   68, 80
gross domestic product (GDP)   301–302
gross national product (GNP)   301
group valuation   200, 203

habitat services   25, 77–79
Hajjar, R.   74
Hale, C.   159
Hanley, N.   215
HANPP (Human Appropriated Net Primary
    Productivity)   130
Harlan, J. R.   57
Heal, G.   262
hedonic pricing method (HP)   199
Hepburn, C.   262, 270
Heywood, V. H.   57
HGMU (hydrogeomorphic unit)   84
Hicks, J. R.   302

Hill, J.   61
Holling, C. S.   86
Hooper, D. U.   50–51, 53, 57
hotspots   78
HP (hedonic pricing method)   199
Human Appropriated Net Primary
    Productivity (HANPP)   130
Human Development Index   302
human-nature relationship   152–155,
    161–162
humans see people
human well-being
    benefits and values   27–29
    biodiversity   47
    discounting   273
    ecosystem services   18–19, 91–95
    subjective   19, 267
    see also intergenerational welfare
hunger   3
hydrogeomorphic unit (HGMU)   84
hyperbolic discounting   268–269

ignorance   212
inconsistent discounting   269
indicators
    choice of   290–292
    of condition   129–130
    definition   116–117
    of diversity   127
    ecosystem services   131–133
    existing   115, 119–134
    good   117–119
    need for   116–117, 133
    overview   119–126
    of pressures   130–131
    of quantity   127–128
    relevant   115, 134–141, 291
    research and development   115, 133, 291
    TEV   142
indices, definition   117
indigenous groups   153, 159, 170
indirect drivers   1, 4, 31–32, 289
indirect use values   196
individuals see people
information, lack of   116
Inglehart, R.   277
insensitivity to scope   203
instrumental values   189
insurance values   186, 192–194, 218
intergenerational welfare   264–267
    see also human well-being
Interim Report of TEEB   4
intrinsic values   161–162, 189
InVEST model (Natural Capital Project)   134
irrigated agriculture   221–222

Jackson, J.   89, 271
Johansson-Stenman, O.   158

Kahneman, D.   172, 203
Kellert, S. R.   154
Keynes, J. M.   276
keystone species   50–51
Klein, A. M.   74
knowledge gaps   295–301
Kontoleon, A.   200–201, 216
Kremen, C.   54
Krutilla, J.   276–277

Laibson, D.   269
land-cover change   130–131
landraces   57, 63
landscape perception   137
Layke, C.   131
Levin, S. A.   47, 50
Lewin, S.   158
life opportunities   277–278
Living Planet Index   130
local administrators   32
Loomis, J.   235
loss aversion   268
Luck, G. W.   80

MA see Millennium Ecosystem Assessment
Mace, G. M.   118
macroeconomic framework   298–301
Makarieva, A. M.   59
malaria   3
Mäler, K.-G.   266
Mankiw, G.   269
mapping   139, 141–142
    see also indicators; spatial explicitness
Marengo, J. A.   59
marginal valuation   16
marine systems   52, 57–58
    see also oceans
market price-based methods   197–198
markets   6, 187–188, 190, 198
Martinez-Alier, J.   159, 266, 277
mass extinction   271–272
MCA (multi-criteria analysis)   193
McGinnis, M.   172
McGuire, A. D.   136
Mean Species Abundance (MSA) Index
    129–130
measures   115–116, 119–134
    see also indicators
mediated modelling   203
medicinal resources   65–66
Mehra, R.   269
meta-analytic function transfer   230
Miconia calvescens   220
migratory species   77–78
Millennium Development Goals   2
Millennium Ecosystem Assessment (MA)   2–4
    ecosystem services   12, 14, 156
    indicators   117, 119, 131

see also ecosystem assessments
mitigation cost method   198
monetary valuation see economic valuation
Mouritsen, K. N.   50
MSA (Mean Species Abundance) Index   129–130
multi-criteria analysis (MCA)   193
multiple ecosystem services   44, 81–84
Muramatsu, M.   158
Murdiyarso, D.   59

Naidoo, R.   133, 136, 139
national income account (NIA)   302
native communities (ecosystem people)   27
natural capital
    concept developed   14
    critical natural capital   194, 238
    decline in   12
    definition   13
    economics   187
    human well-being   95
Natural Capital Project   134
Natural Environment Research Council
    (NERC)   156
natural hazards see extreme events
nature   152–155, 160–164
Nazarea, N.   159–160
negative drivers   32
Nelson, E.   139
neoclassical economics   20–21
NERC (Natural Environment Research
    Council)   156
neutral drivers   32
Newell, R.   270
NIA (national income account)   302
nitrogen   3, 73
non-constant marginal values   234–235
non-renewable resources   89
non-use values   196, 203
Nordhaus, W.   264
nutrient cycling   73

oceans   271
    see also marine systems
O'Connor, M.   173
'optimist's paradox'   266
option price   224
option values   186, 196, 224
organic farming   57
organisms, communities of   47–50
ornamental resources   66–67
Ostrom, E.   172, 297
'Our Common Future' (Brundtland)   155
output values   192–194
ownership   157–160, 291

Palsson, G.   153
participatory valuation methods   228

part-whole bias   203
Pascual, U.   200–201
passenger pigeons   223
Pauly, D.   89
payments for ecosystem services (PES)   11,
      96, 226
payments for environmental services *see*
      payments for ecosystem services
Pearce, D.   264, 302
peatlands   70
people
      ecosystem people   27
      ecosystems   3, 44, 289
      poor   227, 236, 259, 277–278, 289, 295
      rich   259, 277–278, 289, 295
      TEEB reports   33
      see also human well-being; human-nature
         relationship
Perrings, C.   221
Persson, M.   270
perverse subsidies   31
PES (payments for ecosystem services)   11,
      96, 226
pests   75–76
PF (production function-based methods)
      198–199
pharmaceuticals   65
phosphorus   73
Pizer, W.   270
policy issues   3, 32, 299–301, 303
Polis, G. A.   49
pollination services   74–75
poor people   227, 236, 259, 277–278, 289,
      295
Portney, P.   265
positive drivers   32
positive incentives   31
Potsdam Initiative   4
Potvin, C.   52
Pouta, E.   214
precautionary principle   219, 223, 276, 294
preference-based valuation   191
preference uncertainty   214–215, 240, 293
Prescott, E.   269
pressures, indicators of   130–131
prices   197–198, 224, 270
primary estimates, availability   236–237
process-response model, ecosystem
      functioning   89–91
production function-based methods (PF)
      198–199
productivity   51–53
property   157–160, 291
property rights   160
protected areas   155, 170
provisioning services   56–67
      indicators   131
      timber production   134–136

trade-offs   81
psychology   158
publication selection bias   231
public goods   187

quantity, indicators of   127–128
quasi-option values   196, 224–225

radical uncertainty   212
Ramsey, F.   264
Ramsey discounting equation   264–267
recreation   79–80
Red List Index   129
redundancy   54
regime shifts   86, 220, 223
regulating services   67–77
      carbon sequestration   136–137
      indicators   132
      trade-offs   81
      value of   93, 297–298
Rekola, M.   214
relative prices   270
relevant indicators   115, 134–141, 291
replacement cost method   198
research and development, indicators   115,
      133, 291
resilience   218–225
      biodiversity   219
      definition   86
      factors   89–91
      linkages   290
      TEV framework   194
      transfer benefit   241
      valuing   221–223, 294
resources
      biochemical   65–66
      biodiversity   95
      economics   1
      forests   169
      genetic   63–65
      medicinal   65–66
      non-renewable   89
      ornamental   66–67
response diversity   54
restoration cost method   198
revealed preference methods   199–200
Reyers, B.   139
rice (*Oryza sativa*)   64
Richards, A. J.   74
rich people   259, 277–278, 289, 295
Ricketts, T. H.   139
rights-based approach   277
risk   212, 225
      see also uncertainty
risk aversion   271
risk indexes   214
Rosenberger, R. S.   231
Rubinstein, A.   269

safe minimum standards (SMS) 219, 223, 276, 294
salinization, agriculture 221–222
SAM (social accounting matrix) 303
Sanchirico, J. 221
scale 23, 288
    benefit transfer 232–233
    ecosystem services 84
    stakeholders 226
    sustainability 299
    see also spatial explicitness
scaling up 237–239
scenarios 31, 288–289
scope, insensitivity to 203
Sen, A. K. 152, 158, 171, 264
service-providing unit (SPU) 84
services *see* ecosystem services
service trade-offs 83
Seyoum, A. 169
Shiel, D. 59
shifting baselines 89
Shogren, J. F. 213–214
Shu Yang, F. 80
SMS (safe minimum standards) 219, 223, 276, 294
SNA (System of National Accounts) 302
social accounting matrix (SAM) 303
social appreciation, landscape 137
socio-cultural benefits and values 28
socio-ecological mosaics 23
soils 51, 70, 73–74
Solow, R. 262, 302
spatial discounting 235–236
spatial explicitness 23, 119, 132–133, 139
    see also mapping; scale
spatial interconnectedness, species 47, 49
spatial trade-offs 82–83
species, keystone 50–51
species diversity 51–53
spiritual and aesthetic services 79
SPU (service-providing unit) 84
stabilizing mechanisms 54
stakeholders 11, 118, 186, 225–227, 288
Stanley, T. D. 231
stated preference methods 200–201, 203–204, 240, 293
Stern, N. 4
Sterner, T. 270
Stern Review, The Economics of Climate Change: 4, 263
Stiglitz, J. 302
subsidies, perverse 31
substitutability 13
supply uncertainty 212–214
sustainability 140, 260, 266, 277, 302
sustainable development 260
System of National Accounts (SNA) 302

TC (travel cost method) 199
technical uncertainty 216, 241, 294
TEEB (The Economics of Ecosystems and Biodiversity) 21–33
    biomes 22–24
    drivers 31–32
    ecosystems classification 38–39
    ecosystem services 25–27, 39–40
    focus 29
    governance 29–31
    guidance documents 32–33
    human well-being 27–29
    Interim Report 4
    objectives 4–5, 116–118, 134, 292
    scenarios 31
temporal trade-offs 82
Terrestrial Ecosystem Model (TEM) 136
terrestrial systems 51–52
TEV *see* total economic value
TFP (total factor productivity) 267
The Economics of Ecosystems and Biodiversity *see* TEEB
thresholds
    change 44, 84, 86
    economic valuation 186, 219, 271, 293
    importance of 140–141
    pollination services 75
    resilience 218, 223
    sustainability 140
    see also tipping points
Tilman, D. 1
timber production 134–136
time preference 264
tipping points 44, 75, 80, 90, 219, 290
    see also thresholds
total economic value (TEV)
    benefit transfer 240
    definition 188
    framework 186
    indicators 142
    valuation methods 196–211
    value types 192–196
total factor productivity (TFP) 267
tourism 80
trade-offs 19, 30, 81–83, 160, 174, 288
transfer errors 231–232
travel cost method (TC) 199
Tschirhart, J. T. 300

UN *see* United Nations
uncertainty
    benefit transfer 240–241
    biochemical resources 66
    biological control 77
    climate regulation 70–71
    cultural and amenity services 80
    definition 212

discounting   264, 270
economic valuation   186, 212–218, 292
ecosystem services   18, 288, 293–294
extreme events   72
feelings   166
food provision   59
fuels and fibres   62
genetic resources   65
pollination services   75
soil quality   74
thresholds   219
urban ecosystem services   69
water provision   60–61
UNEP *see* United Nations Environment
   Programme
unit benefit transfer   229–230
United Nations, Brundtland Commission   155
United Nations Environment Programme
   (UNEP)   3, 155
   see also Millennium Ecosystem Assessment
urban environmental regulation
   services   67–69
use values   194, 196
utilitarian perspective   189
utility, expected   225
utility discounting   262–263

valuation
   applying   27
   costs   288
   function   291
   socio-cultural context   151, 156–157,
      297–298
   trade-offs   160, 174
   see also economic valuation
value   19

value aggregation   169
value-articulating institutions   161–163,
   173–174, 290, 291
value function transfer   230
values   27–29, 160–162
Vatn, A.   161, 163
vegetation   67–68
Villéger, S.   50
vulnerability   140

Walker, B. H.   222
Walrasian model   20–21
water provision   59–61
wealth   301
   see also rich people
Weitzman, M.   266, 269, 271
welfare   264–267, 301
well-being *see* human well-being
western perspective, human-nature
   relationship   153–154
Westman, W.   13
wetlands   204–211, 213
Weyant, J.   265
wheat stem rust (*Puccinia graminis*)
   64–65
willingness to accept (WTA)   203, 216, 268
willingness to pay (WTP)   162, 189, 203,
   216–217, 268
Winfree, R.   54
World Bank   302–303
World Resources Institute (WRI)   126
WTA (willingness to accept)   203, 216, 268
WTP (willingness to pay)   162, 189, 203,
   216–217, 268

Zeldes, S.   269